Dedicated to my family, friends, and colleagues
who have supported my life's journey,
to those who have touched my heart and trusted me to touch theirs,
and to those whom I will never meet
but will touch with the words in this book,
and we will be spiritually connected.

Praise for *Soul to Soul Connection and Communication*

Soul to Soul Connection and Communication is a compelling and uplifting piece for now and the ages. The *hand-dome* offers profound insights to not only understand how we each respond to life, but it is especially beneficial to understanding and appreciating individuals from diverse backgrounds.

This book is a comprehensive and enlightening resource for academic leaders and educators who value diversity and inclusive approaches to connecting with and engaging learners. It is written in such eloquent and powerful prose. Thank you for sharing your voice and wisdom with the world.

Sylvia A. Alva, Ph.D.
Provost and Vice President for Academic Affairs

At once, *Soul to Soul Connection and Communication* is a compilation of several, unique self-help techniques and essays on how to create clear-cut communication. Each chapter can be read as a short story. Ruth Forman covers vast and complicated topics such as social injustice in a fresh and personal manner. In this turbulent moment in history, *Soul to Soul Connection and Communication* reveals that it is more important than ever to maintain hope and step into the good that exists. It instructs each of us how to unleash it by first working on ourselves and the words we choose to communicate. We are gently guided toward understanding what it means to be *source-connected*, and how that concept alone can be a simple tool to be used toward creating a sustainable, spiritual life.

Becoming aware of our filters, our personal lenses may provide a solution toward deeper connection and eliminating hatred. Our individual situation and environment don't absolve our responsibility toward becoming better human beings. The author tells us that we have choices about how we decide to consciously engage others while we hold loving space for ourselves. It is a process, but Soul to Soul explains a way through the author's message. The book serves as a practical resource to be read carefully, savoring the words, and sharing them with others out loud for their consideration. It shows us how we are all connected.

Aydin Bengisu, L.Ac., Diplomate O.M.
Acupuncturist and Medical Herbalist

As a physician, I deal with different people every day, and I need to make authentic connections with all types of people. Your book changed my life. The *hand-dome* showed me that all people think differently, and understanding that is the first step to any authentic connection.

Aamer Jamali, MD, FACC, FSCAI

Soul to Soul Connection and Communication is inspirational and motivational as it provides exceptional insight to issues, such as personal development and racism, all affecting society in the modern age. The recollection of the author's personal experiences as well as detailed historic events elevate the relationship of the narrative writing to the reader. I feel spiritually enlightened with a newer perspective of connecting our current events to the importance of our actions and words. This book is a must-read for anyone who is looking to implement personal and spiritual growth, and contribute to positive change in both their social and private life. Love, growth, communication, and positive change is key in creating a united and strong community of self-aware individuals!

Yasmine Sidhu
Religious Studies, B.A, and Business Management, B.S.

Soul to Soul Connection and Communication is a wonderful book and a never-ending source of wisdom and inspiration written by a talented storyteller with an infinite heart.

Linda Reid
Physician and co-author of the award-winning *Sammy Greene Thriller* Series

I was awed by the scope and clarity of your current book *Soul to Soul Connection and Communication*. It's a book that I keep on my side table in our family room so I can refer to it at random whenever I seek inspiration.

Blenda J. Wilson
Retired Higher Education Leader

Ruth Lindeck Forman is a force. Her prime directive is teaching humans to effectively communicate in the name of a better world. She is the person who can make a stranger a friend in a grocery aisle and change their life for the better as a result of their first conversation. Her insight is a gift to humanity. Professional training has focused and polished her lifetime of observation into *Soul to Soul Connection and Communication*. It is a must read.

Colleen Rosenthal
Colleen Rosenthal Photography

I was standing in line behind Ruth to use the restroom at The Soraya, The Performing Arts Center while attending the Soweto Gospel Choir event at California State University, Northridge. Ruth felt my energy and turned around and introduced herself. I discovered that she is a tireless proponent for Civil Rights and her message aligns with my beliefs to have the right to live my dreams. Her ideals uplifted my spirit when I thought it could no longer be uplifted, and gave me the courage to continue when I felt as if my life would never get better.

Nedra Miller
End of Life Doula

Having chosen a lifelong career in education and teacher preparation, I have always admired Ruth Forman's dedication to offering personal insights that can serve to transform lives. Her focus on the unique dual qualities of self-determination and interdependence undergird all of her work—especially as captured in *Soul to Soul Connection and Communication*. The chapter entitled "Personal Lenses" is among my favorite selections from the book, linking personal wellbeing to the choices one makes in identifying negative perspectives and committing to removing these ways of interacting with others and the world.

Michael E. Spagna, Ph.D.
Provost and Vice President for Academic Affairs

Ruth Forman's book is right on in highlighting the issues the United States continues to grapple with: prejudice, racism, and injustice toward people from minority cultures. Her book stuns, awakens, and offers uplifting insights and tools that can help us to work together to resolve the issues at hand and promote justice for all.

Eugene Crayton, Retired Police Officer
Los Angeles Police Department

My life actually began at age eight while living in an iron lung after contracting one of the last pandemics of the polio era. I have lived my life in a wheelchair but have learned to travel and use my mind and imagination to read the great books and ideas of this whole diverse planet. I then traveled into medicine where I worked fighting the great Pandemics like HIV and COVID-19 around the world. While doing this, I have always been involved in civil rights at multiple levels.

Ruth Forman's book is a unique exercise in understanding and improving the inner self to live better with our outer world of diverse human beings. She advocates true communication with each other after recognizing and deleting the negative filters we inherited socially that often inhibits us from the simplicity of the Golden Rule of caring for and helping each other. As a physician who has fought against man's most modern plagues, I have found that we may not always cure or even treat an illness, but we can always at least comfort and care and strive to improve. That is the marvelous part of the many lessons taught through *source-connection* and through the growing self-awareness. Ruth Forman's teachings can lead to better communications for each of us, with each other, and the world we were given to share. Please read her book slowly and thoughtfully, then read it again. We desperately need the ideas and remedies described so well and offers to a world that needs it so much.

Jeffrey E. Galpin MD
Infectious Disease Specialist, Clinical Immunologist, and Internal Medicine
Providence St. Joseph Specialty Medical Group & CMO/Founder of EntellAM LLC

Ruth's *Soul to Soul Connection and Communication* is a feel-good book. Every time I pick it up, I am engulfed, as I reset to a re-grounded happy place and Zen space. This healthy, positive state is essential in dealing with toxic family interactions, as I am dealing with a cancer that is controllable, but not curable.

Francine Golden
Life Friend

This brilliant piece of work by Ruth Forman, once understood and applied, will aid in creating a harmonious work environment that would produce not only excellent work, but also content people and by extension uplift our society.

Desery Ottley Tyson
Assistant Director of Human Resources

This book will benefit all showing us how we view the world and the people who we connect with. Ruth shows us through examples, exercises, and stories how to come from our true self, be kind, and listen deeply. We also become aware of negative filters and perspectives that influence our communication. These facets help create a better world. *Soul to Soul Connection and Communication* is an ageless reference book to help us in our relationships with ourselves, loved ones, co-workers, friends, and strangers.

Leslie Campbell
Artist, Art Teacher, and Kundalini Instructor

Our family is grateful for Ruth and her amazing book, *Soul to Soul Connection and Communication*. My wife, children, and I are immigrants. Even though English is our second language, Ruth's words touch our hearts and expand our minds. To receive the most benefit from the book, a friend comes over at least weekly to translate from English to Farsi to help us better comprehend the pertinent issues and have more meaningful family discussions.

Farham and Farideh Janesar
Scholarly Tailor and Scholarly Chef

Your kind words of affirmation have fueled my passion for fiercely supporting transgender individuals. You are, and continue to be, a truly inspirational storyteller.

Joseph Cayanan, M.S.
Speech and Language Pathologist

Soul to Soul Connection and Communication is a perfect "recipe" for the art of successful human communication in a world of unique, diverse, and cultural systems. Ruth guides you in search of redefining the manner in which you interact on a personal, social, and spiritual level! Personal experience, self-examination tools, humor, research, faith, inspiration, creativity, and a tablespoon or two of good humor will keep you returning to this book just as you would to an old family recipe.

As a swimmer on Team USA's World Transplant Games expeditions for more than sixteen years, interacting with teammates from more than fifty countries; serving as an early childhood special educator; and teaching English to children in Asia, I fully comprehend the relevance of embracing diversity. This is significant when communicating with a myriad of personalities, physical, spiritual, and emotional needs. These along with Ruth's zest for life, a sense of belonging, and quest to promote liberty and peace in self, home, social, and spiritual environments is also beautifully depicted within these pages.

Carol Brown Fitzsimons, M.Ed.VIP KID English Teacher
Early Childhood Education Specialist Team, Ohio/USA Transplant Swimmer

Ruth Forman is a Spiritual Billionaire. She is an amazing force and a terrific vessel to find your path to a spiritual life! Highly recommended her book!

Walter Cox
Private Chauffeur to VIP Clients in Los Angeles

Thank you for encouraging other women to go for their dreams. Your book allows me to crawl up and wrap myself in it. *Soul to Soul Connection and Communication* is powerful, reflective, life-changing. What a gem! Its wisdom is beyond pertinent in today's world, and it will continue to impact generations to come. Forman so eloquently reminds us to breathe in positivity, embrace diversity, and consciously choose love, each and every day. Simultaneously, you'll find yourself using its communication strategies in your home, at school, in business transactions in everyday life. Forman shares her heart and a lifetime of experiences. That alone, is a gift for anyone.

Ashley R. Jackson
Director of Admission, Los Angeles Private School

Ruth's labor of love is a book for the ages! A compelling and heartfelt dialogue is created for the reader in a way that truly reaches the spirit. The lenses, in particular, offer much wisdom for interpreting our external and internal worlds. It is a marvel to have such pertinent information readily at our fingertips in a world desperately longing for genuine connection.

Haley Isman
Substance Abuse Counselor

"Namaste" is an ancient Sanskrit salutation that means "the divine in me greets the divine in you." Ruth describes this state of an encounter from the consciousness of our Divine nature as *"source-connection"* with self and others. This connection affects our everyday transactions and conscious behavior, affecting more peace, joy, and love. Equally important, she shows how to enter into this *source-connected* state through simple, easy, conscious practices. This creates a platform for authentic, genuine connections.

Elizabeth Wu
Retired Regional Coordinator, Clinician-Patient Communication Program
Kaiser Permanente, Southern California

A wonderful book on common sense for living a full and happy life and leading a successful business.

George Simpson
Chairman, NAI Ohio Equities

Your book is such a valuable resource and an invaluable tool for people of all ages. I am an 82-year-old senior, and I see segments of the book that I would love to share with my teenage grandchildren, my siblings, and my friends. It will be a gift to anyone who takes the time to read it.

Carolyn Anderson
Retired Teacher

Ruth Forman's book is like artwork because it is curious, fascinating and enjoyable. Its happiness and feeling allow you to read it with a sense of knowledge and wisdom.

Zooey Richmond, Age 12

A twenty-five year labor of love for all ages and stages of life.

Lee Forman
Your Loving Husband

Praise for Previous Book *Communication Is Connection*

This book has the most honest, down-to-earth information on communication that I have read. It transcends all barriers and encouraged me to walk the talk. This book is a must for everyone!

Gail Henderson-Peter, RN
Director, Medical Group Training
Leading Health Maintenance Organization

This enlightening book is an outstanding training and teaching guide and resource. As a mentor-teacher for the Los Angeles County Office of Education, I use this book for role-playing and group-work activities with teachers, principals, and administrators. They have responded with such enthusiasm that they are adopting it in their language arts, effective education, and multicultural curriculums. It is also a useful tool for conflict resolution especially for at-risk and gang prevention/intervention strategies.

Cedric Anderson
California Teacher of the Year 1996

From a personal and humanistic viewpoint, I loved your book! The insights it offers are easy to grasp and use to achieve the inclusion for all people into our society. I highly recommend this book to everyone who believes in a just democracy.

Blenda J. Wilson
Higher Education Leader

Medical education has many deficiencies. This book is an excellent remedy for one of them, our inability to communicate and educate ourselves and our patients.

Bernie S. Siegel, MD
Author, *Love, Medicine & Miracles*

Like the wave's return to the ocean, Ruth Forman's *Communication Is Connection* shows us that authentic communication takes place when there is connection to one's source and when there is no division between one's thoughts, one's words, and one's actions. This is an excellent book.

Rabbi Stan Levy
B'nai Horin-Children of Freedom

As a medical center Chief of Audiology and Speech Pathology Service for twenty-six years, I am keenly aware of the influence that a positive communication environment has on both personal and professional success. All of us, regardless of our cultural backgrounds, can benefit from guidance in enhancing our inter-actions with others. That is why I find your book so compelling and helpful. Your fine book is technically accurate, spiritually uplifting, and very readable. Successful communication always springs from your own source—your soul. To the extent the individual can enhance and maintain their "*Source-Connection,*" life on this planet will become more worthwhile and fulfilling. Communication is the essence of humanness, and some thoughtful contemplation on how to make it better is welcome.

Wayne R. Hanson, PhD
Chief of Audiology and Speech Pathology Services
Department of Veterans Affairs Medical Center

Your book helps me rediscover myself and provides me with valuable tools to be a more effective communicator.

David Cohan, MBA
Senior Reimbursement Consultant

The message in your book is important, timely, and powerful. Your insights and reflections about why communication can be ineffective are direct and eye-opening. You capably translate the complex mechanics of communication into a language and skill form that anyone who is seriously interested in positive communication can learn and apply in their daily interactions.…The inclusion of a spiritual level in this process, spiritual in the most positive and inclusive sense, is evidence that you speak not just from the mind, but from the heart as well, and therein lies the key to the work-balance.

History has shown us time and again that conflict, unresolved, often ends in violence, which is no resolution. Your book provides a powerful tool toward rectifying the breakdown of communication, and I hardly recommend this book to those in search of solutions on a personal and global level.

Michelle Kendall
Community Relations Manager
National Book Store

Soul to Soul

Connection and Communication

Ruth Lindeck Forman

Soul to Soul Connection and Communication is a work of nonfiction. Some names and identifying details have been changed. Unless identified, any real-life similarities to characters or events are totally coincidental.

Previous editions published by

Third Edition
PAGE PUBLISHING
Conneaut Lake, PA

First originally published by Page Publishing 2022

The title, book cover, and content graphic designs of this work were created by Ruth Lindeck Forman. Graphics for the book cover and book were created by Michael Massoud and Paul Dworsky. Printing by Page Publishing.

Library of Congress Catalog-in-Publication Data, Forman, Ruth Lindeck, *Soul to Soul Connection and Communication*: nonfiction work by Ruth Lindeck Forman, Third edition.

SEL021000 SELF-HELP / Motivational & Inspirational
EDU020000 EDUCATION / Multicultural Education

Purpose: The sole purpose is to enlighten, inspire, and uplift to promote well-being, civility and inclusion. Theme: You have to be aware to care, and if you care you are aware. My fervent hope is to present a totally new twenty-first century communication paradigm to elevate comfort, trust, understanding, and appreciation so more people are willingly to reach out to each other.

ISBN 978-1-64628-861-8 (pbk)
ISBN 978-1-64628-863-2 (hc)
ISBN 978-1-64628-862-5 (digital)

A portion of the proceeds will be donated to support the blind, the environment, education, and justice.

Printed in the United States of America

Contents

Acknowledgment   *i*
Introduction   *v*

Soul to Soul Connection

Source-Connection
    A Spark Within Us   17
    Source-Connection   18
    Define Yourself   19
    Discover Your *Source-Connection*   20
    Create or Strengthen Your *Source-Connection*   24
    Maintain Your *Source-Connection*   26
    Nurture Your *Source-Connection*   27
    Source-Disconnect   32
    Reconnect with Your *Source-Connection*   40
    Source-Voice   43
    Universal Spiritual Connection and Spiritual Internet 45
Hand-Dome
    Why You Feel, Think, Act, Speak, and Write as You Do   47
    The Thumb in the *Hand-Dome* Represents Our Uniqueness   49
    You Are Worthy Just Because You Are   50
    Personal Limitations   50
    Personal Boundaries   52
    Our Breaking Points   56
    First Finger in the *Hand-Dome*: Our Emotions at the Moment   60
    Second Finger in the *Hand-Dome*: Our Past Experiences   61
    Third Finger in the *Hand-Dome*:
        The Values and Communication Style of Our Primary Family   64
    Fourth Finger in the *Hand-Dome*:
        The Values and Communication Style of Our Primary Culture   71
    Different Responses from Each Facet of the *Hand-Dome*   82
    Chart Your Own *Hand-Dome*   86
    Update and Rechart Your *Hand-Dome*   88
    Respect Other People's *Hand-Dome*   91

Personal Lenses

    Personal Lenses   103

    Impact of Our Personal Lenses   107

    Types of Lenses   107

    Internal Lenses   107

    Feel and Fear Lenses   108

    Mistrust/Abandonment Lens   108

    Unworthiness Lens   109

    Not Mattering Lens   110

    Seeking Approval/Wanting to Belong Lens   111

    Insecurity Lens   113

    Lack of Education/Stupidity Lens   113

    Physical Appearance Lens   114

    Failure/Rejection Lens   115

    Financial Insecurity/Not Enough Lens   115

    Health Lens   117

    Bullying Lens   118

    Abuse Lens   120

    Thought and Response Lenses   122

    Control Lens   122

    Defensiveness Lens   123

    Competitiveness Lens   124

    Negativity/Self-Deprecation Lens   124

    Catching Up/Needing to Prove Lens   127

    Questioning What-If Lens   128

    Crying Wolf Lens   128

    Overreacting Lens   128

    Should Be Lens   129

    Rose-Colored Glasses Lens   129

    Expectation/Assumption Lens   130

    Retrospective Regret Lens   131

    Neglected Well-Being/Self-Expectation Lens   133

    Identify, Block, Move, Delete, Replace
        (IBMDR) Technique for Internal Lenses   136

    Preconceived Ideas about People or Situations   138

    External Lenses   143

    Expectations/Assumptions Lens   143

    Culture/Region/Heritage Lens   145

    Socioeconomic/Educational Level Lens   146

    Income Inequality Lens   153

    Religion Lens   156

    Gender Lens   159

Sexual Orientation Lens   174

Age Lens   180

Physical Appearance Lens   187

Handi-abled Lens   189

Overreacting Lens   192

Xenophobia and Islamophobia Lens   193

Prejudice/Racism Lens   200

Reverse Discrimination   232

Organizations for Positive Change   233

Cultural Inequality and Historical Events   241

Identify, Block, Move, Delete, Replace
(IBMDR) Technique for External Lenses   261

Awareness   263

Forman Approach to Identifying Prejudice Within Ourselves   265

Reaching Out to Make Positive Changes   267

Soul to Soul Communication

Communication Is Connection

What Is Communication?   277

Positive Communication Tapestry   278

Difference Between Talk and Communication   279

Communication Between and Among People   279

How We Communicate, What We Say, and How We Act Civilly   282

Respect   284

Labels   286

Communication Is Complex and Challenging   286

Everything Is Relative   289

Find Commonality   290

Communication Comfort Levels   293

Personal, Public, and Professional Facets   294

Private Feelings   296

Presentational Self and Representational Self   296

There Is a Solution   299

You Hear Me, but Are You Listening?

Listening   301

Good Listening Skills   303

Listen in Comfort   304

Become a Better Listener   308

Listen to Your Source-Voice   309

Spiritual Listening   309

Mental Processes for Communication

Effective Communication Is a Two-Way Process and Feedback Loop   313

Basic Concepts of Mental Processes 313
Listening Errors 314
Processing Errors 315
Responding Errors 315

Touch, Sight, or Sound
Neurolinguistic Programming (NLP) 317
Improve Your Weaker Neurolinguistic Programming Channel 324

Take a Look
Nonverbal Communication 327
How We Perceive Face-to-Face Communication 327
First Impression 327
Eyes 331
Mouth 332
Body Language 333
Body Space 335
Touch 336
Gesture 337
Attire 338
Scent 340

It's Not What You Say, but How You Say It
Voice Tone 343
Six Factors of Voice Tone 344
Projection 344
Pitch 346
Rate 349
Volume 349
Intonation 351
Phrasing 352
Tonal 353

Honor Yourself and Choose Your Words Wisely
Verbal Communication 355
Source-Connected Communication 355
Proactive and Reactive Communication 356
Acknowledge Others 358
Direct and Indirect Communication 360
Indirect and Direct Communication 361
Personal Examples 361
Teaching Examples 361
Business Examples 361
Medical Examples 362
Give a Negative Message in a Positive Way 363
The Difference Between Positive and Negative Communication 363

Emotionally Charged Words   364

Evasive   365

I Mode   365

Focus   366

Questions   367

Ask the Questions that Require Answers;
    Make Certain You Get the Necessary Response 369

Sometimes It Is Better to Ask, Even if the Answer Is No   369

Permission by Question   370

You Don't Have to Answer the Question   370

How to Convey Your Message So It Is Understood   371

Why Ideas Stick   372

Say Precisely What You Mean—Be Specific   373

Communicate at the Appropriate Level for the Individual   375

Assumptions   377

Comfort in Saying "No"   378

Small Talk   379

Fillers   380

Don't Complain and Don't Explain   381

Communication Investment   381

Commitment   384

Appreciation   384

One Word Can Make a Significant Difference   385

Soul to Soul Intercultural Communication

Embracing Diversity

Deeply Touched by the Rich Tapestry of Diversity   389

Diversity   391

Intercultural Communication   401

Four A's (AAAA) for Successful Intercultural Communication   401

Why Is It Challenging to Understand People from Other Cultures?   403

Bridging the Communication Gap   405

Two Steps from the Norm   407

Four Roles in an Intercultural Communication Conversation   408

Intercultural Communication Style   411

Intercultural Nonverbal Communication   415

Facial Expression   417

Eye Contact   418

Body Space   419

Touch   420

Gesture   422

Attire   422
Scent   423
Emotions   423
Time   424
Monochronic and Polychronic Time   424
Different Ways to Prioritize Time   425
Different Paces and Concepts of Time   426
Intercultural Voice Tone and Rhythm   427
Projection   429
Pitch   430
Rate   430
Volume   430
Intonation   431
Phrasing   433
Tonal   438
Intercultural Verbal Communication   438
Low Context and High Context   439
Direct and Indirect Communication   442
Power Distance   443
Evasive   443
Asking Questions   444
Face-Saving   445
Saying "No"   445
Small Talk   447
Giggle Response   448
Hissing   449
Response to Prejudice   449
There Are Other Ways   449
Give It a Try   451

Appendix

Positive Solutions to Maintain Harmony   459
Thank You   467
Author's Journey   469
A Time to Pause and Reflect   497
   First Pause on Your *Soul to Soul Connection
   and Communication* Journey
      Source-Connection   497
   Second Pause on Your *Soul to Soul Connection
   and Communication* Journey
      Hand-dome   498

Third Pause on Your *Soul to Soul Connection*
and Communication Journey
    Personal Lenses   499
Fourth Pause on Your *Soul to Soul Connection*
and Communication Journey
    Communication Is Connection   500
Fifth Pause on Your *Soul to Soul Connection*
and Communication Journey
    Listening: You Hear Me, But Are You Listening?   501
Sixth Pause on Your *Soul to Soul Connection*
and Communication Journey
    How You Process Information   502
Seventh Pause on your *Soul to Soul Connection*
and Communication Journey
    Neurolinguistic Programming: Touch, Sight or Sound?   503
Eighth Pause on Your *Soul to Soul Connection*
and Communication Journey
    Nonverbal Communication: Take a Look   504
Ninth Pause on *Soul to Soul Connection and*
Communication Journey
    Voice Tone: It's Not What You Say, But How You Say It   505
Tenth Pause on Your *Soul to Soul Connection*
and Communication Journey
    Verbal Communication: Honor Yourself
    and Choose Your Words Wisely   506
Final Pause on Your *Soul to Soul Connection*
and Communication Journey
    Intercultural Communication: Embracing Diversity   507
Photos Reflecting Selective Narratives   508
Epilogue   511
References   515

List of Figures

Figure 1. *Hand-Dome* Symbol 47
Figure 2. Ten steps to create a *positive communication environment* 277
Figure 3. Positive communication tapestry 278
Figure 4. The difference between talk and communication 279
Figure 5. Two-steps from the norm 407
Figure 6. Factors of your voice tone and rhythm
      that project a positive message 436
Figure 7. Factors of your voice tone and rhythm
      that project a negative message 437

List of Tables

Table 1. *Comparison of Traditional Nonverbal Communication
      Styles of Mainstream U.S. American, Latino, Far East
      Asian, and Middle Eastern Cultures* 416
Table 2. *Comparison of Traditional Vocal Features and Rhythm of
      Mainstream U.S. American, Latino, Far East Asian, Middle
      Eastern, Indian, and Pakistani Languages* 428
Table 3. *Comparison of Traditional Verbal Communication Styles of
      Mainstream U.S. American, Latino, Far East Asian, and Middle
      Eastern Cultures* 438

Acknowledgment

It is with profound gratitude to the universe, I was given a life's path as a messenger to write this book, to which the thoughts flowed from my heart before my mind formed the text. This book was written without expectations other than to promote the best in others, hasten civility into our lives, and advance inclusion. I offer guidance to help bring about change.

My profound appreciation, love, and thanks to my husband, Lee for his enduring love, soft-spoken wisdom, lightheartedness, and companionship, for his outstanding role as a father, and for supporting me during this endeavor, especially during these final years. Special thanks and heartfelt love to my dear children, Gregory Forman, and his wife, Karen Anne Klickstein Forman, my daughter Tamar Schamhart and her husband, Robert Schamhart, and my daughter Gayle Forman and her husband, Nick Tucker, who each in their own special way contributed, supported, and guided me as best they could. Most certainly, my thanks to my grandchildren, who are the icing on the cake: Rebecca and Hannah Forman, Liam and Lucy Schamhart, and Willa and Denbele Tucker for their love, wisdom, and shared frolic. Special thanks also for the sustained love, laughter, and support of my Nevis-island grands, Janella Hanley Paillant and Infatari Hanley, who lived next door and are now adults.

I know that I would not have had the strength to complete this book without the love and support of those loved-ones who are in spiritual form. Deepest admiration and thanks to my parents—my mother, Lotte Richter Lindeck, and my father, Ernst Jacob Levy Lindeck, for their love, integrity, loyalty, and trustworthy promises; their practice of inclusive, just, and outreaching values; and their profound gratitude for life, especially in the United States. Deep affection and respect to my aunts, Anni Biel from New York and Naomi Kudler from Israel. Though they lived far away, I had the fortune and blessing to know them in my youth and much of my adult life. Thanks also to Bertha Hoffman, "Hoffi," who survived the Holocaust and was liberated by Allied forces after she was held at Theresienstadt ghetto-camp. She was a dear friend to my parents, but also took special interest in me and later my family. Last but not least, my parents by marriage, Jess and Corinne Forman, who immediately welcomed and always supported me, and who truly devoted themselves to their children and grandchildren. I write about my grandparents in the "Author's Journey," and fully realize that without them or my ancestors, I would not be who I am.

Special thanks to Margaret Hughes who always championed me, Gail Henderson, who decades ago as a professional colleague supported my works, and then for years as a friend as we supported one another, and to Ralph Mannheimer for his insights that still echo within and are reflected in this book. I could not have gone through the rough patches without Susan Meyer Byer, Dorothy Smith Dempsey, Nancy Phares Cornell, my Ohio childhood friends, and later, in California, Colleen Rosenthal and Jan Burns as we all shared life's laughter and tears.

A heartfelt thanks to my healthcare team of more than twenty-five years who guided me to recovery and promoted my well-being during my numerous surgeries and complex medical challenges. They are Dr. Jeffrey E. Galpin, Dr. Michael Levey, Dr. Hillel Sperling, Pat Rubenstein, Ph.D, Hua Gu, Ph.D, L.Ac, and Joe McSweyn, OMD.

I could never have achieved this milestone without the help of housekeepers Vannessa Williams in Nevis and Lupe Amaya in California. Most special thanks to my dear friend, Kathy Sierra, who first watched over our children when Lee and I traveled abroad in the 1980s, then, stayed in our home while we were in Nevis, and supported me during the time I wrote this book. She came weekly as an angel who quietly did "her thing" to prepare food, take care of the laundry, and assist with small projects. Special thanks also to Rickey Hussain, our outstanding gardener in Nevis, and our former gardeners, especially Ernesto Escalara who maintained the health and beauty of my California garden that beckons and provides a haven.

A most heartfelt appreciation and thanks to the professional colleagues, leaders, staff, and students at California State University, Northridge (CSUN), for their sustained encouragement along the way. Gratitude also to all the individuals over the years who entrusted me with their stories, honored me, and believed my words.

I also want to thank Michael Massoud, who decades ago created then hosted my website; Christopher Cho, my IT consultant, who consistently resolved technical issues; and Nancy Gilpin, my friend and caretaker of odd jobs. Special thanks also to Darrin Cockerill and Paul Dworsky at Calabasas Printing for coming through with flying colors during our twenty-year association and friendship. I want to note the editors who helped translate my initial inherently foreign grammar-syntax-style into your read. In 2014, Colleen Malone-Engel improved the grammar of my first draft. After several rewrites, Jon C. Newman, previously an editor of only smaller works, took on this project and further improved word choice, punctuation, and syntax. Jon is a musician, so his touch added an eloquence. Then, Yasmine Sidhu, who is amazingly wise-beyond-her-years, was so moved and inspired by this read that she endorsed the book months before she committed to add her touch. Judie Schwartz, my seventy-nine-year-old sister-in-heart as she named me, has dementia. Despite that, she still had enough command of the English language to help me choose the exact word when needed. Lastly, the personable and profession Page Publishing Editing team for their lengthy support, expertise, and patience.

My deepest admiration and respect to Douglas King of Corel, who for more than four years has offered his genius, wit, and patience. Finally is Michael E. Spagna Ph.D., former Dean of the Michael D. Eisner College of Education at California State University, Northridge. In 2011, he asked me, "When are you going to rewrite *Communication Is Connection*?" Michael believed in me, encouraged me, and supported my works through the years. Along with those in the spiritual realm, Lee, Douglas King, Paul Dworsky were the pillars who gave me strength to continue when I had very little left, especially during the final intense months. A special thanks to Nevisian Pastor Joseph Liburd's morning lay text messages that were encouraging and often spoke directly to me, They were especially comforting during health-related challenges and time outs.

The acknowledgment is brief—my spiritual leaders Rabbi Stan Levy, Buddhist monk Thich Nhat Hanh, and most dear and wise friend, Eileen Smithen of Zion Village, Nevis, West Indies (who prefers to be called "Blind Eileen" when I write about her), and many other dear ones are further presented in the "Author's Journey" found in the *Appendix*.

Introduction

Greetings

In this lifetime, we are gifted one journey to travel, and our desire is to live most joyfully, passionately, and genuinely as who we are, and who we want—or are meant—to be. Thank you for joining me on my life's journey spanning more than eighty years and sixty years in the field of speech therapy and communication.

My twenty-six-year labor of love *Soul to Soul Connection and Communication* is offered to enhance, inspire, and uplift, to promote well-being, civility. My work presents a positive, universal, relevant, and compelling personal and intercultural communication global paradigm moving forward in the twenty-first century. The reader-friendly journey presents enlightening, mindful, and light-hearted ideas. Your experience includes anecdotes, ideas woven with connections to nature, and socio-political issues such as racism and diversity that are supported by science. These offer insightful, powerful, and practical tools to encourage greater compassion and understanding for the reader and others.

I declare that each person has the sole right to define who they are. This is best defined by what is in a person's heart and soul as a member of the human race. In this ideal, I affirm that each person has the right to live their dreams and they matter. Ruth reminds us how we can always choose to respond positively or negatively and sensitively or insensitively. Likewise, we choose to honor or dishonor ourselves and others. These are our choices, and they are a formative facet of our character and the energy we radiate.

Before we continue, let me ask the following? Can you accept, receive, and trust love from others, and does your love for dear ones flow freely? (Or, are you hesitant and hold back?) Do you listen to and respect what your body tells you? (Or, do you repress what you sense and remain on course?) Do you remain centered and positive when criticism and judgment surround you, and do you easily shrug that off? (Or, do you hold on to and ruminate over such insinuation?) Do you deal well with personal discord or national disarray? (Or, do these overwhelm you?) Are you comfortable with people who have positive views, though different from yours? (Or, do you feel threatened?) Do you easily accept change over which you have no control? (Or is change disruptive?) Do you live calmly in the present moment? (Or, are you often preoccupied by the urgency of now?) Do you come across as easy to deal with and empathetic? (Or are you often told you that you are difficult and unapproachable?) Are you an educator, healthcare provider, or business person, or do you work in the field of communication, law enforcement, government, entertainment, the justice system, or in any occupation that serves a diverse population? If so, do you feel that you possess the current and necessary insights and tools that you need to offer your optimal best practices to ensure just and productive outcomes?

If your response to any of the questions not in parentheses is "no," then trust and join me on a mindful exploration as we gently and thoughtfully reflect upon and embrace our path to truly reveal who we are to help us evolve to the best we can be. We learn to touch, interact, and connect with the best in ourselves, others, and the universe on our *Soul to Soul Connection and Communication* journey.

This book, which combines spirituality, connection, communication, and diversity, is divided into four sections. The first section, *Soul to Soul Connection*, introduces and highlights the *source-connection*. This is our endowed essence and the purest spiritual connection within ourselves. First, we learn to recognize that spiritual connection. Then, we learn how to connect with cherish, and nurture our spirit. Finally, we connect with the essence, the soul of all others before we begin to interact. The mindful breathing technique is also included to help bring us back to the present moment to focus or enjoy.

The *hand-dome* brings an enlightening and a proven awareness that gives meaning to why each person feels, thinks, acts, speaks, and writes as they do at any given moment. This newly acquired *hand-dome* wisdom deeply enhances our understanding of the facets that shape not only ourselves, but also our loved ones, and others. It eloquently offers us the insights to realize another's *hand-dome,* highlighting their uniqueness, attributes, background, limitations, and challenges. These private revelations significantly help us gain a more holistic view and wisdom. This also provides space, insights, and courage to establish our personal boundaries. We learn to apply our *hand-dome's* teachings and then honor and respect those discoveries within ourselves and others. This helps to create a connection of *trust* that also promotes inclusion. The *hand-dome* becomes a trusted friend that we revise as needed and carry throughout our lives.

Lastly in this section, we move to the chapter "*Personal Lenses.*" This lengthy chapter focuses on closing in on and reducing or eliminating the familiar repetitive and negative chatter in our heads that often runs as an endless debilitating loop. This chatter prevents us from feeling and being our very best. Sometimes we are so distraught that volumes of our energy are drained and wasted during our day. Our journey continues to touch on twenty-five *internal lenses* that we may carry about ourselves. Once you have discovered and listed those negative thoughts within, you privately and easily walk through the self-guided *Identify, Block, Move, Delete, Replace (IBMDR) Technique for Internal Lenses* to significantly reduce or erase these thoughts. This advances authenticity, happiness, and fulfillment.

Equally important, we examine ten *external lenses*. We gain in-depth recognition of our preconceived ideas about people, circumstances, and events, and how these misconceptions and false judgments distort how we perceive, process, and then act toward others. Once you have discovered and listed those debilitating and negative thoughts that you carry, you privately and easily walk through the self-guided *Identify, Block, Move, Delete, Replace (IBMDR) Technique for External Lenses.* Then, you reduce or erase the intentional or unintentional destructive harm you caused and replace them with honorable, inclusive, and uplifting views.

Following the presentation of Reverse Discrimination, Organizations for Positive Change, Cultural Inequality and Historical Events, and Awareness, the *Forman Approach to Identify Prejudice Within Ourselves* is introduced. In this process, we continue to deeply look within ourselves to gain an understanding of what we truly believe and feel. Then, through imagery we identify discriminatory and unjustified prejudices degrading others that we may intentionally or unintentionally carry. After all, you have to be aware to care, and if you care you are aware. Reaching Out to Make Positive Changes, and Give it a Try finalize the *Soul to Soul Connection* section.

In the second section, *Soul to Soul Communication,* the first chapter begins with my motto: "Communication is connection. In connection, there is trust. In trust, learning takes place, problems are solved, and needs are met." The chapter follows with a holistic approach to communication that is the essence of our humanity. It highlights the artful dance of listening and true communication and demonstrates the vast difference between communication and mere talk. We learn how to communicate with civility that goes far beyond the politeness of "please" and "thank you." Civility includes awareness, care, gratitude, and mindfulness and they are fundamental in creating and maintaining our *positive communication environment* and aura. Awareness is raised of how we impact others. We gain a broad understanding to make certain that we do not intimidate others, nor allow others to intimidate us. We discover that respect and integrity play a major role in assuring we *source-connect* and don't dishonor or tarnish the dignity of the other person that distorts our conversations.

We gain further insights about how and why people interpret the same experience so differently, and we learn that everything is relative. We discover how to easily find commonality with others. We gain a recognition of the various comfort levels of each individual with a comparison of their comfort levels to the layers of an onion. The difference between *presentational-self,* what we show to others, and *representational-self,* our authentic-self is reviewed. We ask why we hold those differences and identify the disadvantage and dishonor of not being true to ourselves. We also expose the difference between *in-house* personality and *out-house* personality.

A lengthy presentation teaches us the significance of listening not only with our ears, but also with our hearts. We realize that listening in mainstream U.S.A. culture is not as valued as speaking, or as valued in other cultures, especially Asian cultures. Vast insights and skills are presented to become better listeners. The role of the listener and speaker is compared with a tennis game, highlighting techniques to improve listening. We also acquire positive responses when we can't or don't want to listen.

A basic and brief discussion of how we process information most effectively is presented, and we learn not to let others intimidate or rush us. "Neurolinguistic Programming" (NLP) is extremely pertinent, but underestimated and often overlooked. Persons express easily seen visual clues as their preference of touch, sight, or sound. These are presented as: kinesthetic, visual, or verbal modalities. Even the choice of vocabulary offers clues of the preferred modality. Paying attention and integrating these insights facilitates communication, especially in the classrooms, doctor's offices, clinical settings, or when interacting with family members, colleagues, and staff.

To accurately, positively, effectively, and appropriately convey the *meaning* and *intention* of our message, the last three chapters in this section focus on nonverbal communication, voice tone, and verbal communication factors. These chapters present nearly forty topics to provide a comprehensive approach. Subtle changes in our facial expressions, body language, and voice tone positively or negatively affect how we are perceived and constitute 93 percent of face-to-face communication.

Nonverbal communication represents 55 percent of how we perceive face-to-face communication. A captivating discussion on this topic focus on ten factors that when integrated and applied significantly reduces the pitfalls to offer a *positive communication environment*.

Voice tone represents 38 percent of how we perceive face-to-face communication. Of course, when we hear a person's voice over the phone, media, or public announcement system, the voice has greater impact. Just reflect how pivotal the voice is during an emergency. Voice tone is often the catalyst to a calm or panicked response during these events. During our discourse about voice tone, we gain an understanding and learn to optimize the six factors of voice-tone, and how to perfect those so that we precisely convey the *meaning* and *intention* of our needs and goals.

Verbal communication represents only 7 percent of how we perceive face-to-face communication. Yet, when a word is totally off the mark, demeaning, divisive, racist, or slanderous, the impact is far greater. This section gives a fascinating presentation that includes *source-connected* communication and compassion and offers thirteen factors that benefit the creation of your *positive communication environment*. The discussion continues on the topic of questions. Final topics include, Why Ideas Stick, Say Precisely What You Mean—be Specific, Communicate at the Appropriate level for the individual, Assumptions, Comfort in Saying "No," Small Talk, Fillers, Don't Complain and Don't Explain, Communication Investment, Commitment, Appreciation, and One Word Can Make a Significant Difference finalize this section.

In each step of the *Soul to Soul Communication* section, you learn to recognize other person's communication needs and your own. When these are combined, integrated, and applied, they provide a thoughtful and comprehensive understanding and command of communication. Therefore, more people more people are willing to enter your inviting *positive communication environment*.

In the third section, *Soul to Soul Intercultural Communication*, the entire section is devoted to the chapter "Embracing Diversity." Your read begins by declaring that we are deeply touched by the rich tapestry of diversity. We learn to celebrate and embrace diversity in new ways, as migration continues to be an integral factor of the human experience. We are spiritually and personally enriched by the myriad experiences of those who are new to our shores. We are also reminded of the fact that our North American continent was not populated by a single human inhabitant until 14,000 to 20,000 years ago. Consequently, all of our foremothers and forefathers once were immigrants.

This section is packed with nuances, strategies, tables, and tales that help to gain comfort, understanding, and appreciation. Traditions, practices, cuisine, fashion, terms, and lingo that once seemed strange now are integral in our society. Practical and delightful insights and thought-provoking anecdotes from people of countless cultures and walks of life demonstrate the vast similarities we have with each other.

This section and chapter cover more than fifty topics specific to the communication styles of people from various regions, cultures, and experiences. We begin with the significant features of nonverbal communication, voice tone, and verbal communication that were presented in the previous section *Soul to Soul Communication*. However, the information is now expanded to highlight the essential nuances and style for both the speaker whose second language is English, and the person who was born in the U.S.A. and the person who is second generation. Even more challenging is if the other person in the conversation also is a person who speaks English as their second language and whose cultural background is different. In contrast is the individual who was born in this country, has a good command of the English language, and more fully grasps the culture and nuances.

A comprehensive understanding and appreciation of the communication styles and customs that each language and culture bring also are presented. You learn which factors potentially create obstacles for individuals who are learning to speak English, but are not yet familiar nor have not yet mastered the nuanced features of nonverbal or voice tone factors of the U.S.A. culture. This information is equally beneficial for those individuals who misinterpret what the speaker of another language or culture says or does, as they also are not yet enlightened to understand the communication style and finer nuances of other major cultures. The presentation in this chapter gives an in-depth understanding of the challenges faced by those who speak English as their second language, and how to overcome with positive, effective, and appropriate nonverbal and verbal communication.

This section offers ideas and methods that are valuable to create a trusting, comfortable, and enduring bridge to connect and communicate with each other, regardless if the person is *USAan* or *Born-abroad*. These connections enrich all of our lives. For lack of any other term to identify those born in the United States, I coined the term, *USAan*. When we use the word American to define those born in the United States, we insult or exclude those born in South America, Central America, or Canada. If you are uncomfortable with the term *USAan,* let me suggest U.S. American. I also introduce the term *Born-abroad* to replace the emotionally charged words "foreign" or "immigrant."

Next, we explore natural means to reach out and become more comfortable and trusting, so that we may better enjoy the gifts of our family, neighbors, colleagues, educators, staff, service personnel, trades people, healthcare providers, students, workers, clients, or anyone of differing cultural backgrounds, and share our gifts in return.

When the teachings of the three sections, *Soul to Soul Connection, Soul to Soul Communication*, and *Soul to Soul Intercultural Communication* are comfortably applied to precisely give the meaning and intention of the message, communication gaps between and among individuals are substantially reduced and communication bridges are pleasantly more productive. Therefore, more people are willing to reach out to each other.

The fourth section, *Appendix* includes "Positive Solutions to Maintain Harmony," Thank You, and "Author's Journey." This chapter highlights my experiences as a child of respected and wealthy parents who fled Nazi Germany in 1938 and immigrated to Manhattan, New York. There, they were surrounded by comfort and support of my father's siblings and financial aid from extended family. In 1940, I was born. The next year, my family moved to the Midwest, where I spent my early childhood in a blue-collar neighborhood. My mother endured heavy losses of her favorite cousin and other beloved family members who died in the Holocaust, and her mother and sister who lived on separate continents for years. Thus, correspondence provided the only means to share life's experiences. Yet, my mother always remained grateful.

This chapter also spans decades of my life as a mother, wife, colleague, friend, and a deep bond with nature. Although I had undergone a quadruple coronary bypass in my late 40s, a decade later my husband and I hired a local contractor to build our home in a local village in Nevis, West Indies.

The *Appendix* continues with the pivotal *Time to Pause and Reflect* that presents questions for each chapter. This allows you to pause, reflect, and think through what you absorbed. Then, you personalize your responses so that they accurately reflect the *meaning* and *intention* of your message and style. These pauses are pivotal to further enhance your interaction with others.

The *Time to Pause and Reflect Time to Pause and Reflect* also offers the opportunity to create your own *Soul to Soul Connection and Communication* transformative guide. Furthermore, *source-connected*, positive, effective, and appropriate communication create a trusting aura and inviting *positive communication environment* that welcomes others.

The *Appendix* concludes with Photos Reflecting Selective Narratives, Epilogue, and References.

Travel with me and learn about peak life experiences gleaned from my interactions with a multitude of individuals and numerous professions. Discover the story of a homeless illegal immigrant's personal and professional climb to citizenship and eventually up the corporate ladder. Peer into the basic concerns of a vice-president of a leading Asian auto manufacturing company, and gain insights from people who were medical chiefs of staff, laborers, service providers, teachers, nurses, artists, and a collection of others who also sought comfort and acceptance in their new homeland. These experiences complement my tales of off the-beaten-track travels to more than thirty-five countries and a quarter of a century of dealing with medical challenges and special dietary and other needs. Charming, engrossing stories of Nevis folks and fellow global citizens highlight how they triumphed or serenely accepted their challenges.

In addition to communal insights and tools, I offer universal spiritual enlightenment from my Jewish roots and childhood Christian friends. I also learned loving and inclusive values from my professional Catholic colleagues' social justice priorities, '*Born-abroad* clients' spiritual and cultural beliefs, my friends and family who are agnostic, the Rastafarian way of life, Buddhist teachings, and living amidst the Nevisian people.

My hope is that my adventures and inclusive worldviews also will enlighten, inspire, and uplift you to be your genuine best. Moreover, I hope this vision and its fruition champion greater serenity, joy, fulfillment, confidence, and self-actualization, and bring passion, a sense of valuable self-worth, belonging, and community into your life. Finally, I hope to significantly enhance your well-being, and your connection with yourself and others, regardless of culture or background. These will also spread more positive and vital healing energy into our magnificent planet and universe.

Our day-by-day, sometimes moment-by-moment journey reflects our unique star-power and what we alone bring to life and the world. We interact in many roles with different people: family, friends, professional peer, neighbors, strangers, both newly arrived and firmly entrenched immigrants, and those in our community with whom we serve and those who serve us. But most important, is what we learn from our loved ones. After all, we are perceived not so much by what we say, but how we act and what we do.

We also are judged by our silence and our lack of generous deeds. In the end, our actions always speak louder than our words. Perhaps no person on earth—including ourselves—really knows who we truly are. We do not solely determine our life's path, but we are completely in charge of our responses and how we live our lives. In addition, we have to be aware to care, and if we care we are aware. At each moment, we choose to respond positively or negatively and sensitively or insensitively. Likewise, we choose to honor or dishonor ourselves and others. These are our choices, and they are a formative facet of our character and the energy we radiate.

My story (and your read) would not be as profound, inspiring, or uplifting without the various stories from my vast range of experiences with people of different cultures. As each person and their story touched my heart with their trust, they became my teachers as I became theirs. Also included are each person's cultural heritage to enlighten and broaden your perspectives. I firmly believe that if we can discover the commonalities of people of differing backgrounds, these shared similarities will calm suspicion, add comfort and pleasure, and strengthen each connection.

Communication has evolved exponentially from our primal ancestors' initial groans, gestures, and smoke signals. There has been monumental technological advancement in communication forms since the beginning of my professional experience in personal and intercultural communication more than thirty years ago, and since writing the previous editions of this book twenty-three years ago. In recent years, the digital revolution produced the Internet that proved essential during COVID, the first pandemic in a century. Several more platforms evolved to facilitate virtual communication and quarantines. Zoom, WhatsApp video, Instagram, Snapchat, Classmates, LinkedIn, YouTube, as well as texts, tweets, and other social media were part of life. Virtual chats also became more prevalent to share information, discuss ideas, and resolve problems. In addition, digital emoji visually express what we feel or want to relate. An entirely new, abbreviated language form evolved for text messaging. These offspring forever altered the landscape, style and modes by which we search for and receive information, and stay in touch with others. Leaders in education and some from previous generations are concerned by younger people's dwindling ability to connect with others and communicate as comprehensively and effectively in many settings.

Tweet is no longer just a sound; a cloud no longer just floats in the sky; a mouse is no longer just a tiny rodent; and a virus can spread not only from physical germs among us, but rapidly race through cyberspace, crippling our technology and our ability to function as desired or required. Like thieves in the night, keystroke loggers halfway around the world plot to hack and invade our privacy, steal our identify and assets, disable our systems, and influence national and international situations and events—all critically striking our well-being.

Years ago, when the words face and book were usually joined as "a face in a book," one never imagined anything like Facebook, a social platform that instantly connects people around the world. Governments can still invade and conquer sovereign nations and revolutions can still topple governments. But now, without an invading army, changes also are spurred in short periods by the flicks of thousands of text messages, posts, and tweets, Instagram messages, or the latest social app of the current technology. As the global community watches, there is now a refreshing but sometimes terrifying transparency, where horrific words and acts are no longer hidden. Instead, heinous, terrorists' barbaric images and war crimes and their reactions send shock waves that bolt around the world within seconds.

While the many forms of social media (present and future) are and will be incredible and immeasurable tools. But they also have the potential to be extremely addictive, destructive, dishonest, slanderous, and controversial. Their use requires further scrutiny, clarification, and regulation.

Any information, true or false, beneficial or hurtful, praising or slandering can be posted on the Internet. Unless we each take the time to vet, analyze, and reflect, we don't always know facts from fiction or deceit. As the written word is transmitted without a sense of a person's intention, the integrity of communication is lost. In pivotal situations with persons whom you have not met, face-to-face conversation in real time still offers the most accurate perception of seeing, hearing, and sensing another person. Zoom, WhatsApp video, FaceTime, and Skype are a close second.

During the COVID-19 pandemic, in response to safety, health, and climate change, a significant portion of every facet of life became virtual. These insights and tools, especially those promoting diversity and inclusion also serve as a basis for this virtual transformation. This also benefits our loved ones, colleagues, and fellow global humanity. This also reduces costs and helps save our planet.

Together we embarked on our *Soul to Soul Connection and Communication* journey gathering new realizations, acquiring new ideas and tools, finding spiritual enlightenment, and learning practical, time-tested, and easy-to-master skills. These culminated in a completely new, relevant, inclusive, twenty-first century personal and intercultural communication global paradigm. Engaged in this model, we interact with the full spectrum of humanity—our fellow global citizens. We share a pleasant hello, friendship, intimacy, and a connection with those who once appeared so different from us to now enjoy or make critical decisions.

Even though the "Author's Journey" and *Epilogue* are in the final section, I suggest that you read them first. This gives you a perspective of my background that formed the foundation of this book and motivated and inspired me to write this labor of love. Among other informative details and uplifting views, the *Epilogue* notes the book's time parameters.

In my seventies a recent friend stated, "Ruth, this is your calling." It was soon after that I realized this was my destiny. How else can one explain my unusual journey?

At the age of four, one of my granddaughters insightfully remarked, "Every moment is another now." In Nevis, a dear friend often reflects with, "That was then, and this is now." Let me thank you as we begin our journey together to create new "nows" in our lives.

Soul to Soul Connection

Source-Connection

Twinkle, twinkle, little star.
How I wonder what you are.
Up above the world so high.
Like a diamond in the sky.

—Jane Taylor

A Spark Within Us

When a higher power created each of us, a divine spark was gifted within. I named that divine spark *source-connection*. In that sacred purity, the Creator connects with each of us. The ultimate intent is to connect to that sacred place, our *source-connection*—our purest place within—and then to the *source-connection* and that hallowed purity in every other human being. In an ideal world, we would consistently be *source-connected* to a higher power, to ourselves, and to the *source-connection* within all others as we promote well-being, civility, and inclusion. Only through this pure connection with our essence and *source-connection* can we comfortably shine as softly or brightly as we are meant to and genuinely offer the glorious gifts that we each solely bring to the world. An essential commitment to ourselves is to honor and protect the universally bestowed uniqueness and aura that we alone radiate. These are the vital facets that determine who we are and how we present ourselves to others.

Positively interconnecting and integrating our totality—*soul, mind,* and *body*—creates and allows us to be, touch, interact, and achieve our best as we journey through life in gratitude. Our souls inspire our purest, most genuine, and most positive feelings. Our minds receive, process, and store information, then formulate and send signals to our bodies, delivering our messages to others through our nonverbal, verbal, and written communication. While we accept those limitations that we must, a life's endeavor also seeks insights, skills, and trust to improve what we can. It is best to assume responsibility to maintain or turn to positive thoughts and deeds. We neither participate in nor accept attitudes or actions that are worrisome or unpleasant to our or others' spirits.

Too often an individual allows a person, condition, role, leader, institution, or society to identify who they are instead of defining themselves. Each of us defines our one and only self and then determines what we do and how we interact by who we are. We lose touch with the beauty of our souls, our genuine essence—our *source-connection*—so that, at times, we become so disconnected from our *source* that we no longer even know who we are. We cultivate or clutter our minds with books, blogs, classes, gossip, media, posts, texts, tweets, and social media. We recognize and sense the information, attitudes, or behaviors that are toxic to our spiritual well-being, yet we continue to engage in them. We sustain our bodies with nutrition, exercise, and rest. However, far too many of us neglect to nurture our spirits, our *source-connection*, leaving a void and sense of doubt, discontentment, isolation, and nonactualization. For centuries, many civilizations have embraced a belief in the necessity of balancing soul, mind, and body. It is only in recent centuries that technology and science increasingly replaced spirituality in the circle of well-being and its importance in Western civilizations. Indigenous and First Nations people and many other cultures throughout the world never abandoned their spiritual connections, tenets, or rituals, continually cherishing a belief in the sacredness of spirituality and soul. Moreover, Herbert Benson and William Proctor noted in recent publications of Western medicine the necessity of bringing spirituality back into the soul-mind-body loop for personal well-being and healing. A decade and a half later, Dr. Benson still espouses and writes about the spiritual factor of wellness (Benson and Proctor 2010). Other well-recognized physician-authors Andrew Weil, Bernie Siegel, and Larry Dossey also embrace the relationship of spirituality with physical and emotional well-being.

In the 1600s, Baruch Spinoza, a Sephardic Jew in Amsterdam, believed that body and mind are not separate and that God is infinite and encompasses the essence of everything in nature and the universe. Therefore, God is present in all beings (Spinoza 1992). Thich Nhat Hanh, the Zen master Buddhist monk, agrees that the mind, body, and soul are not separate but blended (Thich Nhat Hanh 2009). Even Albert Einstein, the revered scientist of the last century, spoke of spirituality when he stated, "I want to know how God created the world. I am not interested in this or that phenomenon, I want to know his thoughts. The rest are details" (Calaprice 2000).

In the twenty-first century, many possess advanced technology and access to a global plethora of information and instant digital distractions at their fingertips. Some of us, though most definitely unequally, have exponentially amassed more material comforts than ever imagined or obtained access to goals neither fantasized about nor visualized by our ancestors. Yet we realize something is profoundly amiss—a yearning for that sense of belonging, connection, contentment, and serenity that often eludes us.

Source-Connection

After my long search for a term worthy of the profound swirl deep within, the phrase *source-connection* floated into my head and then to my fingers, which keyed in the term. I pondered for a second and then knew the words felt right. I recalled past decades when our family had visited the Dan Springs in Israel, the source of the Jordan River, where I quietly sat bathed by the morning calm, soaking in all the sensations. The coolness of the breeze softly touched my cheeks, the warmth of the sunlight gently permeated my body, and the symphony of bubbling springs lovingly resounded in my ears. The crisp, refreshing scent of the morning dew filled my nostrils, and the swirling movement in shades of green, yellow, and blue danced off the flowing river. I sensed, and was a part of, the source of life that gave birth to this biblical river. The Jordan River gave life to one of the cradles of civilization and provided nourishment and spiritual sustenance to millions. If the springs or source were set in a different environment, the river's course and its contribution to the planet would be different. In the same manner that source gives life to a river, our source provides life and guidance within each of us.

Source-connection begins with the acceptance of a universal spark—a pure power and force greater than ourselves—connecting with that force, and then connecting with one another in that sacred sphere. In that pure, hallowed connection, we first enlighten, inspire, and uplift ourselves and then all others as we receive guidance; we then connect with the *source-connection* and goodness in all others. Although we can achieve greatness and fulfillment without that connection, it is rarely our ultimate, holistic best. We each discover that spiritual place through different paths. We may believe in spirituality in the forms of the Universe, the Creator, a divine energy, a positive force beyond ourselves, our ancestors, nature, or our *source-connection.* In that *source-connection,* we are connected with our soul and our own uniqueness. Tapping into that spring, from which our purest, most authentic, positive, and nurturing energy flows, we find ourselves bathed in pure goodness, strength, courage, comfort, and conviction. This propels us to our finest state. In that pure, undiluted connection, we are never alone; we are harmonious with ourselves and at one with others and the universe.

Our *source-connection* charges our *spiritual energy* and promotes our well-being. We feel whole and at peace. What we perceive and convey reflects our highest selves. We *trust* our instincts, allowing us to make clear and productive decisions that are right for us. These are not decisions responsive to what others expect, demand, or express about who and what we should or should not be or should or should not do. Our decisions are built on our strengths, while we acknowledge our limitations. We are proactive, not reactive, allowing us to fully invest in and fulfill our destiny. Honoring ourselves in calmness, kindness, clarity, passion, honesty, and sincerity, we express our truth as we know it, stating what we can and cannot do and knowing that we do matter. We declare what we feel, desire, and require with comfort, courage, conviction, and confidence. Our heartfelt observations and criticisms are compassionate and constructive, never cruel. When necessary, we know how to tenderly put forth our feelings and concerns without putting down others.

Idealistically, I feel that if everyone truly believes in the *source-connection*—an invisible, universal, spiritual web connecting each of us with one another—hopefully, we will pause, reflect, and be mindful of our *source-connections* before we judge, decide, demean, maim, or kill our global kin.

Define Yourself
Before we continue, we pause to reflect on who and what we are and why people choose to be with us. I know we are all composed of matter, liquid, elements, and spirit and simply are before we are anything else. But we think of ourselves as more than just that. After you have dwelled on that idea, please close your eyes and take some time to gather a sense of who you are. Reflect awhile on everything about you and then complete the following statements by responding with three nouns.

I am a _____, _____, _____.

Then observe the person next to you or a loved one and complete the same question:

You are a _____, _____, _____.

The answers are human being, person, member of the human race, spiritual being in human form, or words akin to these. Too often we also think of ourselves solely in the roles we fulfill and the functions we perform, failing to perceive ourselves as holistic individuals who are separate from what we do. Sometimes we are so lost that we don't even know who we are.

If our response is man, woman, mother, father, daughter, son, teacher, worker, chef, homeless person, police officer, housekeeper, salesperson, nurse, or doctor, then we define who we are by that role instead of defining that role by who we are—the limiting difference is profound! We are far greater than any single role we live; we are life in our totality. When we identify ourselves as a person or human, we are equal to all others. We are neither superior nor inferior to others, nor is another person inferior or superior to us. Yes, certain roles in life such as president, prime minister, premier, king, queen, teacher, physician, or global philanthropist have a notable and broader impact, but they are not more relevant in their humanness than any other individual.

I believe that we each emit an immeasurable energy that is specifically ours and that its intensity and frequency change depending upon our situation and moods. Yes, people are attracted to us by our scent, appearance, personality, carriage, and a long list of other reasons; however, I believe that if the connection is pure—without hidden motive or something to gain—mostly it is the energy we send forth that ultimately determines yay or nay.

Discover Your Source-Connection

During the early decades of my adult life, I knew something was just not right. I sensed that something deep within was profoundly lacking—a far more positive, deeply embedded life force. I didn't know it was possible to change, and I didn't have a clue about how to discover or connect with that internal sacred source. I hadn't tapped into the purest and most powerful force or touched my greatest potential for goodness as a more mindful, positive, and joyful human being. *Source-connection* was the key that unlocked true happiness, gratitude, serenity, and life's meaning for me. And later, it benefitted the multitude of clients and other people with whom I connected and served. It took a long time to feel my soul and become *source-connected*. It took several more decades until I was *source-connected* and had the ability, usually within seconds, to reconnect, engaging mindful breaths, whenever I wanted. When I first felt that *source*, it was a tiny flutter and spark the size of a rice kernel. In time, my *source* grew to the size of a grapefruit and then, at times, a watermelon. Now, my *source-connection* is often a warm, loving, caring, and passionate energy that sometimes engulfs me and emits an inviting aura. At times, I am as calm and peaceful as the water in a tranquil lake with the afterglow of a pastel summer sunset shimmering softly in its reflection. I am so connected with the moment that everything in my universe is harmonious. Then, the joy is so overwhelming that I can feel the tingle of every charged neuron in my body racing to fire its energy as I become one with another person or place. In our homes in Nevis and in Woodland Hills, the birds or geckos serve as barometers, reflecting my emotional and spiritual ease. If I am anxious, frantic, rushed, or upset, they do not come near me or sing in the gardens during my daily morning stretches, yoga, tai chi, qigong routine on the patio in California, or the veranda in Nevis. When I am calm, the geckos and hummingbirds in Nevis, and songbirds and lizards in California, sing or pause to hang out for a while. Sometimes birds at each home fly through the latticed patio or roofed veranda instead of winging above or around. Even some of my grandchildren, in their youth, and our cat, Happy, lingered in that tranquil space.

As parents, most of us would never think to abandon the responsibility of protecting, nourishing, and nurturing our loved ones—children, spouses, partners, parents, friends, pets, or plants—yet we often fail to nurture ourselves. We live in a hectic, demanding, complex, uncertain, diverse, and rapidly changing environment. We are interrupted and intruded upon by disruptive breaking news, invasive updates, technological glitches, hacks, growing demands, monetary fluctuations, economic worries, safety concerns, security threats, national and international terrorist acts, demonstrations, climate change, complicated regulations, privacy loss, and demand for instant responses, yet some yearn for constant gratification in almost every facet of their personal and professional lives.

In the early years of our twenty-first-century reality, we are more diverse than ever, and while this enriches our lives, it also creates challenges. We ask ourselves how we can possibly add anything else to our lives. Well, let me share how you can. If one of your loved ones required twenty minutes of your time each day to improve their physical, mental, emotional, and spiritual well-being, would you have the desire and will to create the time and space to do so? If you can find the time for others, you can certainly create the same for yourself. Would you like to take better care of yourself? If the answer is yes, then come along as we stroll to discover the path that leads to where you wish to go. You are worth it, and you deserve it.

I vividly recall, forty years ago, the first time I heard a stewardess announce the message that is still delivered on every flight before takeoff: "If you are traveling with a child, please place the oxygen mask over yourself first before you put it on the child." The thought popped into my head: How can I best care, nurture, protect, and provide for others if I don't first take care of myself? It took more than thirty years to better implement that valuable lesson, and it continues to be a lifetime process, past my eightieth year, I am almost there.

Once you look deep within and sense that strong need to give to yourself, you will develop the routine that creates, strengthens, nurtures, and nourishes your spirit, creating the connection with your purest *source-connection* to reap those bountiful and everlasting life rewards to achieve your life's destiny. Prioritize your life as only you can to create that space for yourself. Sometimes it necessitates arising twenty minutes earlier each day, going to bed twenty minutes later, or giving up surfing the net, watching Netflix or a TV show, reading, social media, chats, phone calls, or texts. Search out whatever nonessential activity you can either temporarily set aside or permanently eliminate from your life.

We begin by discovering where our *source-connection* resides within us, the place or area in our bodies where we feel the warm sensations of calmness, gratitude, happiness, joy, and acceptance. This may be the spot where we also feel discomfort, frustration, anger, agony, or rejection, but for many, the spot for negative sensations is different. Astronomers endlessly searched for echoes from other heavenly bodies or resonating sounds, probing the universe in search of other life-forms. In a similar way, put your body and brain on search mode until you begin to sense a pleasant, comforting awareness of self in your body, not your head. Most of my clients and lecture participants felt their *source* in the front area of their bodies between the neck and the lower abdomen. Some sense it in the chest, some in the heart, and some in the gut. If the feeling is in your head, it is a thought, not a sensation.

At the beginning of this exercise, many of my clients only heard negative words or repetitive self-chatter in their heads; they were void of any perception of positive sensations in their chest or abdominal area. Sometimes, they only experienced heaviness and negativity before any positive awareness. As they shared their negative feelings, I observed their body language while they searched for clues to the locations of their sensations. When my clients began to describe their feelings, they used gestures indicating where they experienced their *source-connection*. An account analyst gestured by beginning with each hand placed on either side of her chest. As she spoke about her fears and anger, she slowly moved her hands together. Her fingers became more rigid as she interlocked them over her heart. She did not need to say another word; her gestures expressed her despairing feelings. What she conveyed reminded me of a medieval suit of iron armor clamped and bolted shut. Similarly, her negative feelings of inadequacy and fear were locked in her heart. As she spoke, we each felt her burdensome weight robbing her of and draining her energy. Others revealed their negative feelings by clenching fists to convey the locked-in positive feelings. Sometimes it took a few weeks before a person detected the first flicker of any positive feeling, similar to a woman who feels the first flicker of life in the developing fetus inside her womb.

Akin to astronomers who search the universe for signs of life, we trust, search, and open our spirits, tuning in to even the faintest flicker of any positive sensations within. Once we sense that positive sensation within, our awareness will heighten to eventually find the spiritual place deep inside, where we feel either that joy, calm, acceptance, and confidence, or the place we sense the clutches of sadness, fear, doubt, isolation, or rage. Do we feel good when we hug a family member or a friend, stroke a pet, participate in sports, solve an issue, express creativity, commune with nature, hum a melody, sing a song, listen to music, or go deep in introspection, meditation, or prayer? Does the memory of a special person, time, or event evoke loving, uplifting feelings? Usually, there is at least one experience that awakens a warm, pleasant, centered feeling somewhere inside of us. Take particular note when and where that feeling surfaces and try to connect with it. The next time you sense that positive, warm, or calm response, pause to gently focus more intently on its place. Using your breath as the vehicle to imprint the positive sensation, take three slow, deep breaths while closing your eyes, if possible. During each inhalation, connect with the feeling, hold it, and then gently and lovingly embrace it. Pause before releasing each exhalation to savor the sensation. During the exhalation, utter the description of the feeling silently or aloud or visualize the feeling and allow the truth, happiness, and comfort to flow and penetrate deep within.

Once you detect where your soul lives within you, find a private spot in your home that includes a mirror. Stand or sit in front of the mirror and tell yourself what brings you joy, ease, and a sense of belonging. Also, tell yourself what causes pain, sadness, or anger. Observe your body for any subtle change in your facial expression, body language, or tension in your face, hands, or limbs. Often, people unconsciously reach and touch that spot in their body where they feel their *source-connection*. In time, as the sensation intensifies, those vibrations often permeate their entire body.

At age sixty-six, a friend felt passion and his *source-connection* for the first time in his life while holding his first grandchild, the son of his beloved daughter. A producer shared, "My *source-connection* is a feeling of me in my best sense as a special individual with all that is good about me." She added that it felt as warm and fuzzy as a bunny rabbit. To others, it felt like soft rays of light radiating from deep within.

My clients use numerous approaches to become and remain *source-connected*. A physician feels the joy in a golf swing; others listen to music, garden, hike, play sports, create, meditate, pray, or lie under the stars to connect with the universe. Some take soft showers or spend time with family members, friends, loved ones, or pets. Some clients name their *source*; others picture a form, then visualize stroking, watering, or nurturing their *source-connection*. Others verbalize encouragement for growth, inclusion, and embodiment. Some reach to pull in the positive energy from the universe, cupping that energy in their hands, then they place their hands over the spot where they feel their *source*. You will discover your own path to touch and connect with your source to nurture and strengthen your *source-connection*.

Many people ask me, "Do you need to be somewhere special to be *source-connected*?" To me, any place on earth is hallowed ground, as long as that spot helps us feel peaceful, positive, and centered and we feel our *source-connection*. In that connection, we become totally immersed in the present moment. My rabbi, Stan Levy, shared, "True communication is making the other person fully present to you in their 'wholly holy otherness' and your being fully present to them."

Profound spiritual moments occur when I am connected with the Universe, heavenly bodies, a family member, a close friend, or another person, and I engage in an activity in which our synergy totally engulfs me. That fleeting collective energy is sacred, and for that moment, it becomes my Universe. A deeply moving spiritual and enlightening experience occurred in Nevis during the March 2012 planet conjunction. For about a month, the journey of our sister planets utterly captivated me as I watched Jupiter draw closer in its elliptical path to pass its sister Venus. At some point, the full moon was also in the mix. On this evening, a dear local friend and I saw Mars, Jupiter, Venus, and Mercury from our front steps as our eyes gazed upward and westward to the Caribbean Sea. Except for scattered white, puffy, or feathery flowing clouds, we watched the voyage under an unpolluted, unobstructed darkening sky. Connecting with our traveling sibling planets, I deeply sensed the relevance and spiritual interconnectedness with the members of our human race. In losing myself, I always discover and cherish a greater depth of self.

I became aware that though we think we are in the same place, with our feet firmly planted on terra firma, we are actually never in the same place in space. Within our ever-expanding universe, stars are continuously imploding and exploding. Our planet rotates every twenty-four hours while also spinning on its axis, circling the sun every 365 days, except in leap years. We are in a similar elliptical orbit as our sibling planets, though never really in the same place. Shortly after sunset a few nights later, with a backdrop of the bright celestial bodies traveling over the sea until they descended below the horizon, a friend, one of our island grands, my husband, and I shared a lengthy conversation. The ambience of the still night prompted a most profound, open, moving, heartfelt, and enlightening dialogue about the Creator, creation, life, and souls. The question arose, "Who or what created the Creator?" My husband shared that decades ago, his rabbi said, "God is the uncaused cause." This entire phenomenal experience profoundly stirred my soul and became one of the highlights of my lifetime's spiritual experiences. It was a life-changing moment as I gained a far deeper and different perspective about a higher power, life, creation, fellow global citizens, urgency, priority, and necessity than I had previously held.

Create or Strengthen Your Source-Connection

It is rare to experience spontaneous moments that bestow such a profound impact. Fortunately, even with life's multitude of daily stressors, there are a plethora of opportunities to help create, strengthen, and nurture our *source-connection*. There are simple and easily accessible activities that help release stress and allow us to feel our *source-connection*. Find delight and revel in the small gifts of the universe: the first glimpse of hues of light at the birth of a new day, sunlight descending a tree at dawn, the twinkle of a star, the beauty of a rainbow, the unfolding petals of a flower, the chirp of a bird, acts of kindness, being locked into the gaze of a loved one's eyes, or giving or receiving love. Feel the connection with those who passed away, the magnificent and profound universe itself, or find a positive and uplifting thought or activity that works for you.

Another method creates affirmations. Begin by getting in touch with the best part of you, then note what you sense. Initially, it may be difficult to come up with any positive words to describe yourself, especially if you are feeling unworthy, sad, isolated, or depressed. Set aside necessary time to engage in positive activities. Being kind, responsible, trustworthy, loyal, honest, lovable, creative, and caring are characteristics that may take time to evoke. Initially, your affirmations and positive thoughts of self-worth may be intellectual descriptions in your head, not *downloaded, source-connected* feelings that are copied, pasted, and saved until they are planted in your heart and soul.

To make these and any new affirmations permanent, first, you hold a clear vision in your mind of the new, positive beliefs about yourself. Then, you download to *save* and *feel* that belief in your heart and soul, where you feel pleasing sensations. Otherwise, the belief is intellectual and only in the mind and is not heartfelt or embedded in your soul. Only when the new belief is *downloaded* and *saved* in our *hearts* and *souls* do these new, positive ideas, beliefs, feelings, and perceptions become *our new truth*. *Download* is similar to the command that we enter on our computer when we receive pivotal new information and want to save it so it updates or replaces former material that is no longer valid.

Before you continue reading, please note at least three activities that encourage you to feel your endowed uniqueness that has been present since birth. It wasn't something that you had to create; it is a natural trait within you. But at an early age, you may have been unaware of its profound lifelong destiny. Once you discover this trait within yourself that drives your passion, trace how far back you can sense that. Each human being possesses at least one or more special, glorious gifts or traits within that they are meant to give to the world. If you haven't yet found that special gift that drives your passion, be patient and continue this journey.

It was not until I was in my twenties that I realized that one of my strongest attributes was and remains a natural curiosity about life, a deep connection with nature and the Universe, an ability to connect with all types of people, and a keen awareness of biased treatment that has an impact on and harms a person or a group. Before I was five years old, I was already picking up and retaining bits of conversation that dealt with discrimination. It was as though I was endowed with a natural tendency to sense these situations and see what passed over many others.

Name and list your attributes or gifts that you alone imprint with your special style and offer to life, others, and the universe. It may take time until they arise from within and are *downloaded* to become your truth. Do not ask others to help you; these insights and sensations must represent your own genuine desires, feelings, and thoughts, and your awareness of them must spring forth from within. When you gather a sense of yourself, note the description.

Once you feel the spark of your crowning, endowed gifts radiate from your soul, acknowledge your unique attribute or attributes. Begin to note or record your thoughts or create a personal journal. You might begin by saying thus:

> I, (your name), believe that I possess special gifts that I bring to life and our planet.
> My gifts are _____, _____, and _____. I will feel these sensations in my body or thoughts in my mind, then integrate and *download* them into my soul, my *source-connection*, to become my reality and my truth. I will bathe in my *source-connection* despite the countless negative, disparaging, insulting and racist remarks or unpleasant deeds that are thrown at me. These create a toxic situation and a sense of unworthiness and self-doubt, and I feel ugly. When necessary, I will visualize a plastic or plexiglass shield against that negativity, message, or antagonism to protect my self-worth and *source-connection*. I will not tolerate any recurring negativity to permeate me and my spirit I will remain the positive person that I am becoming, want to be, and am meant to be.

This is an affirmation sample. If this does not connect with you, then create your own. Write, text, type, or record it and then read or listen to it daily. As you recognize new, positive attributes about yourself, add them to your affirmations. The reading or recording of your affirmations becomes your life coach, guru, or cheerleader as you listen to or read them aloud or silently to yourself every day. I recommend that you repeat your new mantra or listen to the recording first thing in the morning, through earbuds while carpooling, riding public transportation, walking by yourself, taking your dog for a stroll, after dropping off your children at school or day care, visiting a parent, or later, on your return from lunch.

You can engage in this routine at any time. The best time is your personal daybreak—whatever time begins your day—as the habit helps lay down a positive foundation for your day. This serves as your personal footing as you maneuver through the course ahead.

Maintain Your Source-Connection

Setting a daily time to connect with and nurture your soul creates a pattern to integrate the positive features of your *source-connection* into your life. Commit to a nonnegotiable pact with yourself to partake in pleasant, calming, or inspiring activities that you enjoy and that add positive energy to your well-being. Continue to listen and repeat aloud your own affirmations until your new feelings are *downloaded* and integrated into your heart and soul, to humbly enhance the truth about your unique and special being.

Below are ten sensations or thoughts that help you identify and recognize when you are *source-connected*:

1. You are totally present in the moment, void of any distraction or sense of urgency.
2. You feel a connection with a pure, powerful, positive, and grounded energy within yourself, beyond yourself, and with others.
3. You have a strong sense of who you are, but separate from any role you fulfill.
4. You feel complete, calm, comfortable, and confident and are okay.
5. You feel genuine, possess a strong sense of self-worth, and know that you matter and are relevant.
6. You have a true sense of purpose and direction, and you know that you are on the right track.
7. You feel in control of your life and know that no person or event can overpower you.
8. You are kind, focused, and forgiving.
9. You hold no grudges or any consuming thoughts of loneliness, unworthiness, or self-doubt.
10. You sense your *source-connection* in a noticeable area of your body; that sensation varies along an *intensity spectrum* from barely felt to completely enveloped.

You are fully aware of the tangible sensations of your *source-connection*. Again, each person feels this sensation in a different area of their body—most often in their chest or gut.

Spiritual health cannot be measured in the doctor's office akin to cholesterol levels, nor is it perceived by others such as with weight fluctuations. Spiritual well-being is only experienced by us within ourselves, and it is similarly reflected to others.

Recognizing that it was my responsibility to take care of myself was one of the most painful lessons of my life. I thought that if I took care of others, they would take care of me in a similar way. It wasn't until I was in my sixties that I discovered that each person can only express love, care, comfort, and concern according to their desire and capability at the time. If a person does not have it within, unless they are taught, how can they offer it to others? Their response may or may not mirror our concerns or needs but often reflects their best. A long time ago, a niece remarked, "You can't find flowers in a hardware store." If the aid and ease you desire and seek isn't forthcoming from the person you want, seek prayer, meditation, a friend, or any activity that honorably fulfills that need.

It is solely and totally our responsibility to become and remain spiritually healthy. No other person can do it for us; we must provide that for ourselves. Finding time for spiritual healing and well-being may be quite challenging in our already-hectic, sometimes chaotic, lives as we balance personal, family, career, and social time. *When you truly honor yourself, you will create and honor that space.*

Nurture Your Source-Connection

Before we continue, it is best that we pause to ask ourselves, In which of the following do we most tend to invest? Is it appearance, intelligence, status, prowess, health, or spirit? Except for the soul, which was, is, and forever will be with us, all the other factors vary during our lives.

I strongly believe investing in our *source-connection* requires our utmost dedication. How do you begin your day? In the Jewish tradition, upon awakening to the initial void, one's first thought lays the foundation for the day. In three stages, I created my silent greeting to the gift of each new day. A local friend in Nevis who had Jewish ancestors shared a Jewish prayer: "Thank you, God [or the universe], for the day you have given me. I will be glad and rejoice in it." During my recovery from a parasitic infection and return to California in 2006, a friend from El Salvador suggested that I add the following: "I know you will give me everything that I need for the day." From the time I added the second affirmation, I've always had what I needed for the day. A few years ago, I added, "And I know I will be okay." That belief instantly boosted my resiliency and gave me the strength and belief that I would figure out what I had to do to get through whatever happened that day and that I would be okay.

What do you do to create your positive foundation for each new day? Once you can identify and feel that positive sensation (your *source-connection*), connect with it daily until it is present for you with only the intake and exhalation of three mindful breaths. Nurture your connection until it grows to become an integral part of who you are. Allow it to guide your interaction with others and how you communicate and respond to life. Ideally, I recommend spending twenty minutes daily strengthening your *source-connection*. On travel days, I often wake up as early as 3:30 a.m. to meditate. Find the time that works best for you, a time when you can have complete stillness and are unavailable to anyone or anything except yourself.

At all costs, when and wherever feasible, avoid all toxic situations or relationships. Immediately disengage, walk away, or silently *source-connect* and, with a genuine self-loving smile, breathe in and out and silently say something positive to yourself as you inhale. As you exhale, silently release the anger, frustration, or negativity. I quickly engage the Buddha or Mona Lisa smile. First, slightly close the mouth, then place the tip of the tongue at the upper ridge of the mouth behind the upper front teeth, gently smile, and focus on three mindful breaths. This instantly unites me with my *source-connection*, and I feel its calm and purity. When engaged in this state, I never feel frustrated, overwhelmed, angry, rejected, lonely, or sad. Another paramount factor is partaking in as many enjoyable activities as possible—not to boost your ego, but to create a positive and healing energy that sustains and touches your heart, soul, and life.

Thich Nhat Hanh (Thây) authored several books on inner peace, mindfulness, and interbeing that appreciate the interconnectedness between people and every one of nature's gifts. His readings teach us to find joy in the simplest moments, even in completing tasks we previously perceived as mundane, such as washing dishes, folding laundry, and cleaning. He teaches that when we look deeper into these seemingly thankless, ordinary, time-demanding activities of preparing meals or completing other household chores, we realize the blessings that allowed us to take part in the first place. If there were no home, family, or pet, we would eliminate many chores. However, we would not enjoy the comfort, joy, and connections either. We learn to become thankful for the opportunity to participate in these time-consuming, boring activities.

In addition, as we become mindful of the nourishment, taste, presentation, company, and fulfillment that our mealtime provides, we gain a greater appreciation and understanding that none of our meals would be on our plates or in our cups, bowls, hands, or leaves without the touch of our planet's precious natural gifts: sun, clouds, rain, soil, seeds, plants, and trees. In union with nature's gift is a vast, powerful, and a paramount network of global citizens who provide their lives, time, care, expertise, labor, and separation from loved ones. They dedicate themselves to toil, plant, and harvest, forge steel, build highways, drive trucks, pilot planes, navigate ships, steer trains, construct warehouses, stock shelves, organize stores, and cashier and bag our products. We also must include the soldiers and those thousands of individuals who sacrifice their lives and time and serve to guard or protect us. Together, they keep us safe and provide the resources necessary to produce the food in which we partake. We gather in fellowship with loved ones and friends who nourish our spirits, minds, and bodies. Once we fully embrace that interbeing with every human and element in our planet, we appreciate and, hopefully in *source-connected* mindfulness, live our interconnectedness (Thich Nhat Hanh 2010).

As we begin to look deeper into these tasks, we gain a far greater appreciation for all the others who contributed to our well-being, so we give thanks that we even have the opportunity to enjoy these universe-given edible gifts. A large portion of humanity lacks what we have and would gladly leap at the opportunity to perform the chores that come hand in hand with our bountiful food basket. We become grateful, no longer frustrated, bored, or burdened by chores, as we also offer a deeper gratitude and appreciation for those simple deeds that unknown persons have provided. Before I begin each meal, I now pause and ask those with us to join and take three mindful breaths and gaze into one another's eyes, one person at a time. This act separates us from any thoughts that are unrelated to our time together. Instead, we reflect on the blessings of friendship and nourishment we are about to enjoy, and I thank the Universe for those who sit at our table. This practice also separates the chaos and the multitude of to-do lists of the day and turns our attention to calmer, more reflective moments of gratitude, joy, togetherness, and appreciation of one another's presence, our loved ones, and our meal. Others give their thanks silently or in prayer and often close their eyes. Years ago, our oldest Nevis-island grand added, "God, please provide for those who do not have."

The activities, rituals, and beliefs that nourish our souls are similar to the food, exercise, and rest that nourish our bodies. During moments when we are particularly hurried, menaced, and pressured, or in days when we are constantly pulled offtrack, seemingly in a state of urgency, fragmentation, and feeling like a "chicken with its head cut off," it is even more paramount to pause and feel our *source-connection* as we take three mindful breaths. Slowly inhale soothing energy, exhale stress, and engage the Mona Lisa smile. During those stressful times, at least find a few seconds to recall a memory, create a visualization, glance at nature, and connect with any form of serenity. Inhale its calm, then exhale your stress. These *instant mindful breath-boosters* immediately bolster well-being and improve focus. Another instant boost is to silently or aloud hum a melody or sing a song aloud or to yourself until you feel positive and regain control.

What delights you and puts a smile in your heart or on your face? Whatever it is, include it as part of your day as often as you can. Delight in the sunrise, take an early-morning walk or run, feel the freshness of a new day's dew upon your face as you open the door to sense the outside as you live to experience the gift of another day. I often peer out to see what pastel hues the Creator brushed on the early-morning canvas-sky. As you hug a friend, gaze into a loved one's eyes, stroke a pet, depart from your parents, spouse, partner, relative, or a roommate, or drop off your children or parents, inhale the freshness of the new day. Along the way, pause to smell the fragrance of a flower, feel a snowflake upon your cheek, celebrate the rain, and enjoy the seasons' change. When you walk out the door, drive, commute, or walk to work, take a bus, ride a subway, fly on a plane, or ride a horse or bicycle, remember your three mindful breaths. Gaze out a window, listen to music, meditate or pray to calm yourself down instead of thinking about the responsibilities and demands that lie ahead. There is plenty of time in the long stretch of hours ahead to busy our heads, turn on our digital devices, view our schedules, check for updates, see unpleasant news reports, or think about our challenges and workload. So make a point to take a few moments to engage in three mindful breaths and associate with something special at the beginning of and throughout the day as needed to promote ease and nurture your *source-connection.* In the same way you don't leave home without carrying identification, don't leave home without your *source-connection* tucked into your heart and soul.

For me, meditation is the avenue to create a path or bridge the connection to mindfulness. Mindfulness is being in the present, harmonious within, and at one with the universe. Twice a day for two decades, I have practiced transcendental meditation (TM). This type of meditation is practiced by silently repeating my mantra, two syllables given to me. I sit in a lotus position, on the floor or a pad, legs crossed, hands open, with middle finger and thumb touching, as my arms face upward and rest on my thighs. I can also practice in the car or a waiting room, terminal, or any not-so-quiet spot. Meditation is also practiced in other forms, such as visualizations, focusing on the movement of the breath, engaging in walking meditations, or any approach that quiets the mind and soothes the soul. A favorite mantra was silently uttered during a walking meditation with Thich Nhat Hanh. I learned to slowly inhale as I take a step, utter a phrase, and then pause. Then, I exhale as I slowly take the next step and utter the next phrase of Thây's silent mantra, "*I have arrived. I am home, in the here and the now. I am solid, I am free, in the ultimate I dwell.*" Within seconds, this mantra draws me into a meditative stance.

Meditation also serves as a mental defragmentation that helps delete negative thoughts, quiets my mind, fosters clarity, focus, creativity, and recall, and nurtures my *source-connection.* The practice creates a warm and radiating peaceful internal glow, which I can direct to other places in my body when needed or to those in need. At times the meditation gifts are rare moments of pure ecstasy and consciousness enveloping my being.

While writing this book, I asked myself, How would I describe the meditative experience to others? As I unroll my yoga mat and sit down, I already experience stressful energy begin to flow from my body. While moving inward, I breathe into what feels like a fluid shaft in my chest. I recently discovered that when I visualize the breath entering through my third eye—the wisdom chakra that lies between my eyebrows—and move that visualization down to my heart and soul, I slide into an even more peaceful and nurturing sensation. The deeper the meditation, the calmer I become, and that calmness penetrates my entire body and nurtures my being.

In all my years of meditation, even at rare times when I am overloaded and negative self-chatter is bombarding my head, I consistently emerge more peaceful than when I began. In deep meditation, there is never any awareness of annoyance, anxiety, despair, discomfort, fear, fragmentation, frustration, or urgency.

A fascinating article in *Scientific American,* "Mind of the Mediator," presents an outstanding discussion of what the relationship could be "between Buddhism, an ancient Indian philosophical and spiritual tradition, and modern science" (Ricard, Lutz, and Davidson 2014). That dialogue began when the Fourteenth Dalai Lama, leader of Tibetan Buddhism, addressed the annual meeting of the Society for Neuroscience in 2005. The Dalai Lama himself was trying to find answers about the brain's activity during meditation.

For a decade and a half, more than one hundred monastics who practiced meditation more than ten thousand hours, lay practitioners of Buddhism, and beginners all participated in scientific experiments at the University of Wisconsin at Madison and close to twenty other universities. These studies were coordinated by Matthieu Ricard, a cellular biologist before he became a Buddhist monk, and Antoine Lutz, who is at the forefront of meditation neurobiology studies at both the French National Institute of Health and Medical Research and the University of Wisconsin–Madison, where Richard J. Davidson also introduced the science of brain imaging.

The comparison of the brain scans between those who are seasoned meditation practitioners to those who are beginners or those who did not meditate is beginning to show that people who meditate show great potential for benefits to both their emotional and cognitive states. These benefits can be applied to other fields that promote health, contentment, and knowledge, such as clinical psychology, psychiatry, preventive medicine, and education. The research suggests that "meditation may be effective in treating depression, chronic pain, and cultivating a sense of overall well-being." Studies indicate that even the adult brain "can still be deeply transformed through experience" (Ricard, Lutz, and Davidson 2014).

The article also indicates that teaching meditation may be a tool for anger management, which could be significantly beneficial for relationships and negatively charged situations and for those who live in high-crime neighborhoods. Many other areas are noted in which meditation can make a significant difference in promoting well-being for ourselves and others.

During a conversation about meditation between Oprah Winfrey and David Letterman on *The Late Show*, Letterman said, "You think of it [meditation] as diving into a lake, a pool of water. Doesn't make any difference how deep you go, you're still going to get wet" (Letterman 2013).

In one of his readings, Thây shared, "Our appointment with life is in the present moment" (Thich Nhat Hanh 1991). A woman of Afghan heritage who is a team member of the Thich Nhat Hanh Foundation shared Thây's sentiments: "Anytime you are present in the moment, you are meditating." Some careers are salaried, others billed by the day, job, or time. Life is not always lived in precise increments similar to billable time; life is also freely lived to enjoy.

After my back surgery in 1987, I had to practice physical therapy exercises daily. Over the years, I integrated a forty-minute practice combining yoga, Pilates, qigong, and tai chi movements. This combination did wonders in furthering my emotional and physical well-being. This routine helps me to remain as agile and healthy as possible so that I can enjoy life to the fullest and, foremost, keep the promises I've made to my family. It also allows me to be the most giving and active person that I can be. I gave up countless social activities, time with friends, and entertainment, computer, and pleasure time to maintain this time-consuming and disciplined, yet necessary and beneficial, routine that rewards me far greater than the costs it demands. I know that I am fortunate to be retired, and I am grateful for some help in the house with cooking and cleaning, which allows time, flexibility, and certain freedoms. However, I recall that decades ago, a neighbor who raised three small children and had a career already had the wisdom to create time for daily meditation.

Once we understand, create, nurture, and nourish our *source-connection*, we hopefully recognize that our priority is to *source-connect* with ourselves, our loved ones, and especially our young children, who most require our love, support, and guidance. Years ago, a psychologist told me, "Parents are often so concerned with preparing their children for professions that they fail to encourage them to be themselves." He felt that the worst injustice a parent can do to a child is neglect to honor, nurture, support, and encourage that special spark nestled within them.

One of the people in our local Nevisian village made tremendous sacrifices when her husband died and left her with two teenagers. When it came time for her son and daughter to seek higher education, the mother encouraged and supported her children to take flight wherever they could receive the best education—even if it meant halfway around the world, which it did. The extended family pulled together to financially assist the mother so that each of her children could attain their lofty educational goal without the burden of loans; they helped the children reach their greatest potential and fulfill their destiny.

After our youngest daughter went abroad in high school during her junior year, she returned and graduated from the local high school. She already had a sense of who she was and what she did and did not want to do. She firmly told us, "Save your money and your breath. I'm not going to college right now. What's my hurry through life?" She informed us that she was going back to Europe. She had saved all the money from birthdays, babysitting, and other jobs since she was thirteen and had the funds to travel. She went to Europe and worked as a maid at a backpackers' stop in Amsterdam's red-light district, which I only learned about when I later visited her. When she returned to the United States, she went to college, graduated cum laude, received national honors in her field of study, and became a *New York Times* best-selling author.

Each of us travels through life at a different pace, in different steps, and in different directions. Just as pansies bloom in the spring, marigolds bloom in the summer, mums bloom in the autumn, and primroses bloom in the winter, so does each of us give forth our most profuse blossoms during different seasons of our lives. Most important, and as much as possible, it is best when we journey through life guided by our own life's force and purpose, nurtured by our *source-connection* and on universal time.

Life is a daily growing and learning process. On the day my father passed away, after the nurse had asked him to perform an unfamiliar task, he told me, "Ruth, you learn till the day you die." Years later, when I began to lecture, I added, "And the day you quit learning, you begin to die." Hopefully, as with all journeys, your intent is to move forward. At times, you will backslide, unable to sense your *source-connection* in the same way you can't see or feel the sun hidden by clouds. When that happens, begin mindful breathing, engage your Mona Lisa smile, and ask for more spiritual guidance. Pray, meditate, engage, or reinforce any positive path that heals and strengthens to again propel you forward. When my clients and friends had their patches of self-doubt or despair, each returned to the path that had originally helped them create or strengthen their *source-connection*. In reality, we each have to do what we have to do, to enable us to do what we want to do. The key for reaching our triumphant moments is the belief that it can and will happen, often not on our time, but on universal time.

Remember, our *source-connection* is the soul, heart, and core impetus of our one and only life force, igniting the most positive energy within and inspiring each of us to be and live our absolute, purest, and supreme best. Once you are *source-connected*, you know its connection has been and always will be available; therefore, it is up to each of us to remain connected. Everywhere you go, be sure to carry your connection. Stay as connected as possible wherever you are. Your *source-connection* will always surround you with comfort, courage, conviction, confidence, self-worth, and authenticity.

Source-Disconnect

If we allow it, life itself can be a *source-disconnector.* A disturbing dream, comment, or action; a sad or bad news; discrimination or disrespect, a disappointment, rejection, or argument; morning hassle, traffic, or delay; an illness or inclement weather; or even an upsetting headline could quickly and easily separate us from our *source-connection*. Even if we are *source-connected* most of the time, there will invariably be unexpected moments that disrupt our lives, and we will become disconnected. Decades ago, a human resource director warned, "No matter how spiritually and emotionally healthy we become and how authentic and positive we are, those early experiences in life will always be an integral factor of our baseline. In our darkest and most vulnerable moments, we may often sink back to that most angry, dark, doubtful, and vulnerable baselines." During life, I have learned that when we revert to those former negative thoughts and hurtful feelings, our left brain usually takes over and logically explains, but our right brain takes time to process and believe.

Over my life, there were several times when severe personal storms rocked my core. One of these storms occurred in 2006, when I was medevaced out of Nevis and was told that I would never return. For two months after we returned to California, I was quite depressed at the thought of giving up my life in Nevis. One morning, while lying in bed, I visualized placing one of our colorful plates in Nevis on my stomach and, one by one, portioned on it the feeling of a loved one and something for which I am grateful—at times something as simple as the sound of a breeze or a nearby birdsong. By the time I was finished, my plate was full to the brim and I felt better. During that time, a sensation also developed that I was swimming against a current of water in a long three-foot-wide cement tube under the Malibu pier, but my head was never underwater. It felt as though the ocean's waves kept crashing against me as I was trying to swim out of the tube and into the freedom of the water. The current was so powerful that each wave knocked me back, so I was never moving forward. Two months into my personal storm, I wasn't getting anywhere, so I finally decided not to fight the current but to ask for spiritual help and ride out the storm instead of thrashing against it. As I reflected back on my life, I realized that I consistently emerged stronger and better after facing occasional, most powerful personal storms. I also realized that these storms served to enlighten and strengthen my spirit as well as to help me gain joy, gratitude, and acceptance. They also helped to prepare me for my next life chapter and challenge.

Just as the electrical power unexpectedly cuts out during heavy storms or natural disasters, we may similarly feel cut off from our *source-connection* during personal and professional storms. In our most dire moments—when our reality is shattered—we may find ourselves crashing in a downward spiral. As we reel to recover from that unhinged free fall, we grab our anchor of hope and resilience deep within, which gives us the momentum to take the first breath and step to reconnect with our *source-connection*. Our connection helps us to stabilize ourselves and find our equilibrium, so that in time, we can patiently begin to lift our spirits, heal, and create or accept a new reality.

Due to my previous medical history, when I was present at another's medical emergency, I first felt quite vulnerable. Then, I immediately sent healing energy to the person. A rescuing visualization unfolded within. I imagined pulling on a life cord connected to the Universe, a higher power, ancestors, or loved ones who had passed away. We may be unable to change the circumstances, but if we can grab onto a supportive energy, that alone brings a tremendous boost to our well-being. If these visualizations aren't meaningful or don't appeal to you, create one that provides an urgent response to despair. Draw from the pure power of love and the strength of that visualization to calm your heart, nourish your *source-connection*, provide resilience, and know that eventually you will be okay and that you are still meant to be on this earth at this time. Add these feelings of overcoming adversity to fill your reservoir of resilience, from which you can evoke a flow as needed.

It is best to bear in mind that if we lose a loved one, if our child is lost, runs away, or is abducted, leaves the nest, or tragically dies, we must never lose hope. We also must understand that the more exhausted we are, the more vulnerable we are, and these downward-spiraling events create a greater impact. It also is best to try to hold on and believe that we will not always feel as deeply devastated; that is our only salvation. We may lose the physical connection with our loved one, but we will forever have ourselves, our *source-connection*, and all the positive force within our reservoir to eventually carry on. Just as important, even in our loved one's death, we will know deep in our hearts that we will always carry our *source-connection* with that person. In death, I feel that our loved ones' souls are absolutely pure—now free, unburdened, and untethered of all earthly pain and challenges. The flow from that pure, positive, loving connection also gives us the strength and will to carry on.

At a recent spiritual gathering, a man shared that he had lost his beloved wife. During a later gathering, he said his time with us was so healing that he brought his wife's spirit with him; our hostess asked for her name and graciously welcomed her spirit to join us.

Even as we temporarily lose union with our cores or *source-connection* and we are consumed with stabbing pain or numbness and unable to touch or sense ourselves, others, or our world, hopefully we realize that our *source-connection* remains within us. During these inescapable, turbulent, and distraught times, we understandably feel fragmented, caught in an abyss of confusion, pulled and tossed in many directions, and at times totally lost. We often allow our pain, fears, negative situations, or *lenses* to overwhelm us and the situation. Other times, we allow other people's negative perceptions or behavior to overpower us. Often, when we don't respect our personal boundaries, our situation deteriorates even further.

To a far lesser degree, we may experience similar feelings when we lose our jobs or homes in an economic downturn or by natural disasters: famine, fire, tornado, flood, hurricane, or earthquakes. When these or other monumental events happened to friends, clients, or others, they lost their *source-connection*, and fear or despair immediately rushed in. They experienced knots of tightness in their chests, stomachs, necks, shoulders, or limbs or had the feeling that they were locked in a vise or, even worse, nothingness. They often broke into sweats, felt short of breath, and became disoriented. A program analyst shared, "When I become disconnected, the pleasant, warm feeling leaves my gut and becomes an unpleasantly warm, wet feeling in my armpits." Others felt a fearful free fall, not knowing where they would land or crash and if and how they would survive, let alone overcome.

Sometimes those whom we seek for guidance and healing may intentionally or unintentionally turn us off. Loved ones, parents, friends, physicians, clergy, politicians, counselors, teachers, and law enforcement officers may unknowingly communicate in a demeaning or condescending manner or intentionally take advantage of our vulnerability. Their interaction often comes across as preoccupied, aloof, cold, judgmental, or laced with harsh criticism that burns like rubbing alcohol on an open wound.

Over the years, health-care professionals and teachers have experienced overwhelming urgent demands, costly budget cuts, reimbursement reductions, increasing required documentation, greater accountability, and at times, destabilizing circumstances. These, along with shifting family dynamics and structure and greater time constraints, may add a sense of deeper fragmentation. This diminishes their ability to positively and effectively achieve without taking a massive personal toll. Often, the idealism and hope that drew them into their professions become clouded by disappointment and preoccupation with the fluctuating and increasing priorities and monumental tasks. Some people discover practices to gain strength through adversity and provide even greater compassion, comfort, or care.

Long-term health care is one of the most regulated industries in the state of California. An administrator of a skilled nursing and subacute facility said, "I'm so concerned with all the regulations I often forget that the reason I chose this field was to help the elderly." Physicians face similar changes. There was a time when medical treatment and choices were simpler. The doctors were free to practice medicine without the constraints of complex and sometimes overreaching electronic notations and constant concern for time, cost, and outcomes. Moreover, looming threats of malpractice lawsuits did not hang heavily over their heads. Now physicians not only practice the art of healing but also must keep up with the expanding complexities of evolving treatment plans. This becomes particularly urgent in cases such as the treatment of spreading and possibly mutating filoviruses like Ebola. Practitioners must also stay on top of continually evolving digital documentation protocols, as well as practice defensive medicine to avoid litigation. They also deal with limited time and other restraints, such as increased mandatory guidelines. Yet there are positive changes as well. The focus shifted from reimbursement for tests and procedures ordered to reimbursement rewarding positive outcomes for the patient and a collaborative approach to patient care. There also is more responsibility placed on hospitals to pick up the tab if a patient's readmission is caused by less-than-quality care.

Teachers today are also working under continually evolving paradigms to resolve several paramount challenges. These include raising the performance level and graduation rate of their students, especially for those of lesser-opportunity backgrounds, by significantly improving interest and skill in reading, science, technology, engineering, and math to prepare students— and especially women—to successfully compete in a global economic environment. In addition, teachers train and prepare for the growing concerns of increased gun violence, mass shootings, national and international terrorism, and the most recent pandemic. Another significant challenge is creating a fair and comprehensive tool to evaluate student and teacher performance that complies with local, state, and national standards.

Our student population is also undergoing considerable transformations. This creates complex challenges and demands creative, productive, inclusive solutions for the rapidly evolving demographics. A growing body of information is taught to an expanding and diverse range of students, some of whom bear additional challenges. For example, some work full-time, live in single-parent, extended, or multigenerational families and in crowded conditions, are homeless, live in shelters, are recent immigrants, or were forced to leave their homeland and families behind.

Still, others are the first generation to attend schools of higher learning. Some also live in an environment where English is rarely the preferred or spoken language.

Parents, too, have experienced economic burdens during and following the great recession of 2008, and for some, these burdens continue and will increase. The simultaneous globalization, automation, and transformation of work, the obsolescence of certain manufacturing, sales, and energy sectors, and the rise of service, digital, and health-care industries often require new skills. In some states, 50 percent of the households consist of single parents; in those families with two parents, most often, both work. This places an even greater burden on all with the juggling of home, work, parenting, and personal time. Along with these, there also is an urgency to respond via phone, text messages, or e-mails, and there is often an attachment to social media, which is now common in most people's lives. As a child, how would you feel if a parent didn't take or make the time to listen and acknowledge you with compassion, concern, and encouragement and respond to your needs, questions, or feelings? Or were you actually that child?

Whatever your role in life, without your *source-connection*, I believe that you cannot convey the depths of your love, care, concern, and expertise as compassionately. Parents, teachers, doctors, nurses, colleagues, workers, and people from all walks of life often lose touch with the passion, joy, and vision that attracted them to their respective roles and professions in the first place. If each day they keep alive the inspirations that evoked their initial visions, they won't feel as burdened by the challenges, documentation, regulations, reduced funding, increasing restrictions, stresses, changes, uncertainties, and compounding negative forces they now face.

Personal relationships are similar. As couples journey together through the years, life continuously presents many twists and turns—some by design, others by surprise. In my own experience of a long-lasting relationship—as that is the only one that I can personally measure—there has been a certain level of involvement and energy. Sometimes, as one person backs off, the other moves in so that the balance of energy, not the intensity of involvement, remains the same. When my husband and I celebrated our fiftieth wedding anniversary, many people in Nevis and the United States asked, How did we keep it together? I responded that, during the fifty years of our relationship, we passed over many speed bumps: some slight, some steep, and some that almost cost the marriage. But when we each stopped to take that final look at whether to stay or go, it consistently was the deep love for each other's spirit, the high bar that we had each set for the other's worldview and deeds, and the Krazy Glue that held us together. At the end of the day, attitudes and behaviors can be tweaked, but the core essence remains a given throughout life. Those, along with deep love, shared values, and memories, are the holding forces that draw us together during the most challenging times. A cousin shared it is best to give seventy percent and expect thirty percent.

Both of our homes are built with more glass doors than windows, so we view nature's palette daily from any room. In Nevis, my attention gravitates to the varying scents, sights, and sounds or the sensation of birds, butterflies, flora, dew, rain, and wind. When I make the time, I pause and become lost in the flow and movement of the clouds, planets, constellations, stars, and rising and setting of the moon and sun. I feel blessed to be living almost totally immersed in such a pure, natural paradise part-time for fifteen years and returning to Nevis for twenty-five years. This earthly spot continues to nurture my spirit as I soar there as no other place on this planet.

At times, the sun sends gently soothing rays, other times a penetrating heat, and at times a prolonged, oppressive heat wave that demands escape. I observed that the sun doesn't always shine, the rain doesn't continuously pour, and each sunrise and sunset, day, and season are different. Those omnipresent visual images and temporal changes reflect that each of our personal lives, measured in seconds, moments, days, weeks, years, and chapters, is just as fluid as the weather and the seasons. Consequently, when we expect life to remain the same, we set ourselves up for great disappointment and unrealistic possibilities, and we are unprepared for the unexpected challenges that life presents. Some, even those in their seventies, will argue, "Well, that's how it's always been," or, "That's how I have always done it."

After the 2014 Super Bowl between the Seattle Seahawks and the Denver Broncos—which was the first Super Bowl I watched in its entirety—when we saw the "upset" that most did not predict, I told my husband, "Just because it always was doesn't mean it will always be." Spousal or other kinds of abuse that were once tolerated, swept under the rug, or ignored are no longer tolerated by the public. The public's demand leads the charge for advertisers to pull their sponsorships, forcing the decision makers to hold the accused accountable. As my friend in Nevis constantly reminds me, "That was then, and this is now." Twenty-five hundred years ago, Heraclitus, a Greek philosopher, said, "The only thing constant is change."

Fortunately for couples, there are times that both partners agree on goals, decisions, and solutions. But as the years and decades pass and new chapters unfold, life is not always a smooth ride. When the speed bumps appear, engage in mindful, *source-connected* conversation evoking compassion, kindness, love, respect, support, and encouragement. Compromising actions—but never principles—is often a basic necessity for resolving an issue to both parties' satisfaction. Years ago, the dictum of the times was that marriage is a fifty-fifty proposition. I don't agree, because sometimes it is ninety-ten, and other times ten-ninety. What is required is that the balance and reciprocity throughout life feel fair to each partner. A steadfast Ruthie principle is, "The person who is able does." This edict consistently guided my decisions and framed my disappointments. There are times when one person gives more than their share, and there are times when that is reversed. The problem begins when strong resentment builds up and the other is perceived as not doing their fair share for a prolonged time.

At all times, especially when you are very frustrated or angry, Zen teachings become even more essential and relevant. One of my all-time favorite Zen teachings is this: "When I wonder how to best express myself, I recollect one of my favorite Zen sayings, *'Open mouth, already a big mistake,'* and frisk my planned utterance at three gates before I release it into the world. These three gates are questions: Is it true? Is it necessary? Will it do no harm?" (Johnson 2006). I added three more gates: Is it kind? Is the timing right? And does it add positive energy to the universe? If any of these six gates is no, I visualize a ziplock-type closure and zip my mouth shut. And perhaps it is best if we also question, *Why am I talking?*

In Nevis, it is easy to observe the changing direction and force of the wind patterns in response to the strength and breadth of two competing weather fronts. I feel that relationships are similar. When both people are strong-willed, emotional, and passionate, those attributes and their forces often create more friction and, at times, turbulent patches. Other couples, especially when each partner is evenly keeled or mellow, appear to enjoy a simpler and smoother ride. To most, that is more pleasurable. But I strongly question, Is easier or simpler always better?

Most couples begin with romance, then commitment, then perhaps marriage or a permanent and generally monogamous commitment. Younger couples, who may not be as serious or set in their ways, often expect to make those early career, home, and family decisions together, yet in many cultures, the messages portrayed by movies, television, music, and advertising make it practically impossible to meet the abundant false expectations that people have. In addition, as John Lennon stated, "Life is what happens while you are busy making other plans."

Life's odyssey during all ages and stages brings forth unanticipated frustrations and conflicts, along with emotional, spiritual, physical, or medical challenges. Disappointment, despair, instability, insecurity, hostility, heartbreak, or turmoil may follow. At some time, each of us has to make adjustments and compromises, put dreams or plans on hold, and find realistic and well-managed solutions as we follow life's unfolding paths. What was once a loving, caring relationship may now also include anger, frustration, stress, and uncertainty. Often, we temporarily lose our *source-connection* within ourselves and that beautiful, soul to soul connection that we once deeply shared with each other. Our feelings may become lost in the negative forces that now surround us. This is an uncertain, unnerving, and stressful time.

Revenge, finger-pointing, blame, or name-calling is painful and adds nothing positive to any situation or relationship. Only in a mindful and *source-connected* dialogue that includes compassion and understanding can we hope to truly resolve issues. It is difficult to fully heal a relationship unless we are first *source-connected* within ourselves and with the essence or *source-connection* of the person whom we attracted and bonded with us in the first place. When our spouse or partner unpleasantly and hurtfully disagrees, demeans, or shouts, our natural tendency may be to be reactive and shout back. Whenever we are reactive, in reality, we hand over our integrity and power to that person and permit their attitude or behavior to control and determine who we are and how we respond. By allowing those negative feelings to permeate and fuel our response, we become what we abhor. We are in a *source-disconnected* spiral, caught in a negative and contentious communication environment. During these times, *definitely not our best moments*, our body sends us early warning signs of distress. If the conversation remains negative—both are shouting—the cycle remains nasty, aggressive, or disruptive, maybe even vindictive or combative. Until one disengages, walks away, or infuses the conversation with positive energy, meaningful resolution isn't achieved. Difficult though it is, it is paramount that we not allow the prevailing negative forces to envelop us. When negative feelings of abandonment, anger, betrayal, disappointment, distrust, resentment, retaliation, or unworthiness creep in, look inside to see if they are masking something deeper, because they often are. Pause or stop to analyze your thoughts to discover what is truly behind those negative feelings and to what you initially reacted. Take your time to think through it, uncovering layer by layer until you understand what the basic issue is.

Early in my marriage, my husband held tight reins on the purse strings. I felt that if I paid the bills and was aware of the flow of funds, that would solve the problem. When I began to budget and pay the bills, I soon discovered that wasn't the issue at all; it went far deeper than that.

In writing about Spinoza, Antonio Damasio expresses that a "spiritual life is an intense experience of harmony, to the sense that the organism is functioning with greatest possible perfection, with the desire to act toward others with kindness and generosity." Spinoza also knew that many individuals live in a negative emotional state that is counterproductive to health. As Damasio puts it, Spinoza urges us "to attempt a break between the emotionally competent stimuli that can trigger negative emotions…and substitute emotionally competent stimuli capable of triggering positive and nourishing emotions" (Damasio 2003).

Many Asian people understand the Chinese philosophy that there are opposing energies of yin and yang in one another and the whole. Although yin and yang are interconnected while independent, these folks acknowledge that each requires the other for balance and harmony.

Sometimes, we allow ourselves to get caught up in a negative loop, ruminating on negative thoughts and temporarily unable to escape that contrary and counterproductive cycle. When I feel myself remaining in that negative cycle, I place a thick purple-colored rubber band around my left wrist, pull hard, and let it snap to feel the sting. I repeat that several times. If that doesn't stop my negative thoughts, I remove myself from the situation. I find a quiet spot, close my eyes, and focus on the following visualization until the negative cycle is broken.

Visualize a meadow in front of you with two paths leading off in opposite directions. The path on the left side of the meadow winds through barren trees, with bleak, gray, polluted skies, and is void of color or sound. The path on the right meanders through a meadow that is fully alive, brimming with color, fragrance, soothing sounds, and gentle movements. Happily flitting, singing, and chirping birds are among bountiful shades of flora, bushes, and gently swaying grasses. These are all wrapped under a soft-blue sky with flowing white clouds. Which path do you choose? As we visualize our stroll through the bleak path on the left, snapping ourselves with the rubber band, slowly the negative loop falls away and the truth and positive feelings from our *source* begin to reemerge and reconnect. Integrate the activity with your thoughts and feelings to become positive again. Most of the time, this exercise works, yet at times there are a few enduring, deeply embedded attitudes or behaviors of others that remain fixed and often are difficult to accept despite how hard we try to how positive other aspects of that person are.

Over the years, there continued to be one recurring message or behavior that was deeply troubling and that often reinforced an act in my childhood. It arose from a sense of abandonment and lack of worth carried from childhood. As I matured, I gained greater recognition that I can't change anybody else's attitudes, behavior, or choices; only the other person can do that themselves. I realized that I have the choice and responsibility to change my attitude and responses to those attitudes or behaviors that are demeaning, disappointing, or distasteful. Later, I learned that anger tends to hurt the angered persons most of all.

Throughout most of my adult life, when that situation occurred, I felt helpless and often paralyzed. Even with short periods of psychotherapy throughout those years, I hadn't been able to completely neutralize the misery and didn't possess the tools to respond. Fortunately, I belong to a Buddhist sangha—a gathering—and joined in a chant that Thich Nhat Hanh created. The chant is most beneficial, eclipsing any other previous tool, teaching, or technique. It strengthens my resolve and resilience and helps reconcile what I can't control or change so that I can quickly and positively pivot from a sustained, disturbing attitude.

Before you begin the chant and breathing exercise, take a few mindful breaths to center yourself and follow your breath inward a few times as you inhale and exhale. Then as you slowly inhale, say the word in the first column below, and as you slowly exhale, say the word in the second column. Let the breaths, words, and feelings penetrate deeply as you utter these words silently or aloud.

In	Out
Deep	Slow
Calm	Ease
Smile	*Release*
Present Moment	Wonderful Moment

(Thich Nhat Hanh 1991)

When you reach the word *smile*, pause and reflect on the entire person or situation and smile on that totality. Utter the word *release* as you isolate and release to the universe the negative core attitude or behavior. This frees you from bondage to that inclination or situation that caused deep pain and that you allowed to control you. As you release the suffering with the breath, you discover a warm and liberating feeling as you sense the hurt, pain, or anger dissipate, aware that those feelings are no longer repressed but gone for the present moment. The eventuality of dual feelings about a dear person demonstrates that we often hold two or more very different feelings about an individual. I completely understand that each of us has thorns that adorn our blossoms, and I certainly include myself.

So the next time that painful attitude or event appears, smile to yourself and accept that this is just one of the imperfections of life. For a time, the pain is neutralized until the situation recurs. Then, return to the same exercise; in time, you take charge and begin the process sooner, and eventually immediately.

This breathing technique worked the first time I practiced it. Consistency may require more practice, but trust in the approach and set your mind to make it work. There are some personal challenges that are multipronged and deeply entrenched, which, under certain circumstances, may require more than the breathing technique to release the repressed anger or anguish. In those instances, talk with friends, seek professional help, or reach out to your ancestors, the universe, or a higher power.

Reconnect with Your Source-Connection

Once the ache or anger is finally removed, you feel relieved. Through continued positive breathing and healing, we slowly gain serenity to feel our *source-connection* again. The linking of the calm, cool inhalation with the negative, unproductive chatter in our heads, and then exhaling those useless thoughts, is now a readily available tool that can be used to return to that productive and centered space within. If a physical experience helps to reinforce your reconnection, then return to those activities that initially helped create or nurture your *source-connection*. Remember, you can enjoy exercise, creativity, entertainment, a book, stargazing, prayer, meditation, connection with nature or a loved one, or any honorable activity that evokes and enhances those positive feelings within. Some people who exercise during very stressful periods perform their best at those times as they are totally focused. Be mindful that at every moment, each of us has the capacity, choice, and freedom to reconnect with a visualization or an activity that we enjoy and that elevates our spirits. If you are given a hard time because of discrimination, lack of deserved respect, or any other reasons, push back! Visualize a plastic or plexiglass shield that is impenetrable against that negativity and antagonism to protect yourself-worth and *source-connection*. Do not tolerate any recurring negativity to permeate you and your spirit. Then, remain the positive person that you are becoming, want to be, and are meant to be. Also, simultaneously realize that is most likely the other person's problem, not yours. As they say in Nevis, *don't take it on.*

Compulsive behaviors, such as heavy drinking, narcotic use, binge eating, compulsive shopping, addiction to work or digital devices, ambition, or entertainment to distract us from what is unpleasant within us or our lives, are not healthy responses or lasting solutions. While these unhealthy replacements may offer momentary and temporary gratification, in the long run, there is a negative price for these actions that eventually catch up with us. We often pay a high price for a fleeting high moment. So long as the underlying issue remains unresolved, we continue to schlep the heartbreak, disappointment, or negativity, as we simply kick them down the road. Often, addiction is related to a disease that is very challenging to overcome. A person may desire to become clean, but rehabilitation is often a lengthy process of two steps forward and one step backward. Even when a person is clean, it requires a lifelong commitment and support from others to remain clean.

We cannot always put a resolution deadline on a calendar, but in universal time, we can hopefully succeed and move forward to face the issues and seek and gain resolutions. I have observed within myself and others the tendency to deny or only superficially acknowledge an issue or challenge that hasn't been resolved. I believe that we don't truly face a situation or take it on until we are ready to deal with it. Some abusive patterns are so ingrained that we have normalized them. Until we stop, reflect, and analyze them, we unknowingly continue to abuse others. When we acknowledge our abuse and change our ways, we feel liberated and lighter!

A physician from Korea recalled the loving memory of his ancestors to help him convey his concern to his patients. An engineer from Russia lost her self-doubt when she recalled memories of her supportive and loving grandmother. On her inhalation, she pulled in the warm memory of her grandmother's love; on her exhalation, she cast away any negative feelings of inadequacy, anger, or self-doubt. Another method my clients use is to grab at that negative feeling, thought, situation, or negative self-talk within and throw the energy with a force as far away as they can. One client threw the negative feelings to the tail of a comet, sending it off to the far reaches of the universe. Others visualize placing their negative thoughts in a balloon and letting the wind carry them off. The symbolic act of throwing away reduces and discards old negative patterns and thoughts and supports the removal of negative and destructive beliefs, prejudice, or an unproductive communication style.

As you replace those negative feelings, thoughts, and beliefs with positive ones, inhale and give yourself a smile to reward your accomplishment. Utilizing touch, sight, or sound creates a response to significantly help strengthen and reinforce your new thoughts and ideas. Regarding these senses, if you prefer touch, gently hold or stroke your wrist. If you prefer sight, visualize something pleasant. And if you prefer sound, silently or loudly express meaningful words.

I am Jewish, yet I draw on the spirituality of many other belief systems and religions throughout the world. Decades ago, when I underwent my first coronary bypass surgery, I chose what I believed to be the best team of doctors. They were a diverse team, mostly of Asian and Asian Indian heritage, who practiced at a Catholic hospital. As they wheeled me into the operating room, I surrendered myself to a higher power and put that power in charge. I asked the Creator to guide my surgeon's hands in a precise and swift procedure to safely remove my clogged arteries and replace them in the same precise manner with other arteries and veins from my own body. When they transferred me to my hospital room, I noticed a small statue of Jesus on the cross on the door, and I asked for Jesus's blessings as well. A former colleague, and current friend, of Chinese heritage went to India for a visit and prayed for my recovery at the base of the Himalayas. During my numerous critical health challenges, I requested help from many sources, including the Universe, my deceased ancestors, and my loved ones.

Decades later, living in Nevis, I swam in waters that, unbeknownst to me, had become parasite-polluted after severe and continuous rainstorms, and I became severely infested. Since I served as a Red Cross swim instructor in college, of course I should have known better. I even shouted to my husband, "This smells like sewage water!" But this ill-fated course was a familiar route that I had swum for fifteen years, and I felt safe, so my protective guard wasn't up. If my children or grandchildren had been with me, I would have shouted for everyone to "get out." After weeks of trying to determine the cause of my profuse 24-7 sweats and chills while wearing a down vest, I was finally given a diagnosis. Both my physician in the United States and my cardiologist on St. Kitts, each graduates of the same outstanding Ivy League medical school, agreed on a prescription of a strong dose of antibiotics. I knew the medication was too powerful for my small body and sensitive system, but I was told that it was necessary. Close to the end of the course of medication, I had a severe blood pressure drop that necessitated an emergency medevac transport that evening from Nevis to Puerto Rico, where I was hospitalized for nine days until I passed a treadmill test essential to receive the consent to travel. Rather than having me run on the treadmill, the cardiologist preferred giving an injection to increase my heart rate. But I thought, *No way I am taking any more medication.* Before my treadmill run, I silently called upon the spirits of my deceased relatives and friends and asked for their aid and support. As I began to run on the treadmill, I felt the energy of my loved ones. Within two minutes, the cardiologist had a broad smile on his face; it was my best run to date. During these most challenging times in life, I believe in asking for all the spiritual help that I can receive. Thankfully, it has worked so far. As my friend Blind Eileen, whose story I share throughout the book, regularly reminds me, "Only if it is God's will."

Source-Voice

Do you ever wonder about that voice inside that speaks to you? Some call it conscience. A loved one names it "tummy-voice" and teaches her children to pay attention when it signals. I believe that the inner voice, our *source-voice*, is powered by our *source-connection*, conscience, angels, or those from another realm who perceive what we cannot. We feel guidance or warning in our gut or hear the thought or words in our heads. Even when we can't predict or be aware of what lies ahead, our *source-voice* notes the foresight to see what yet is unknown to us. It is our *source-voice* that warns to protect or urges us to champion our best. Sometimes it resoundingly roars, "Go for it!" Other times, it thunderously warns of impending discomfort or danger or simply says, "Stop," "Don't," or just "Not now, you are about to make a poor choice or decision." So please listen up.

Just as we responsibly attend to warning signs on the road, we must always acknowledge our *source-voice*. If we respond to external advisories, then why not respond to the internal early-warning system that we possess? Do not be afraid of your *source-voice;* it is your friend. Respond positively to its encouragement and heed its warnings.

The *source-voice* warning is analogous to the red of the red-yellow-green universal traffic signal, a red flashing light, or siren. Compare your inner *source-voice* to the indicator lights on the dashboard of your car or the digital devices or voice commands that urge caution. *All serve as warnings that something is amiss.* When passengers are safe and all systems in our car are properly functioning, there is no need for flashes, lights, or commands. The indicator lights on the dashboard or programmed visual solutions or vocal commands only signal or take action as we approach danger or when our car requires attention or correction: gas, oil, water, lights, service, door, seat belt, brakes, or proximity of another vehicle. If you're responsible, you react to the signals. If you are low on gas, you stop and refuel. If your radiator is about to boil over, you stop and add water. If your brakes are bad, you replace them. And if a warning about an approaching crash is sounded, you react.

During all my lectures and consultations over the decades, whenever I asked, "Are the results ever positive when you don't listen to the warnings from your *source-voice?*" the unanimous response was a firm "No." Over time, I have heard people from all walks of life say, "If only I had listened to my gut." The compulsive, unproductive behaviors presented a few pages back may dangerously muffle or block the strength of our *source-voice*, robbing us of guidance and potential serenity.

In 1995, within an hour of departure, my husband prodded me to look at a property in Nevis. So I first stood on the land with a young Nevisian who remains a dear friend. The instant my feet were firmly planted on the soil, a powerful spiritual charge surged from the cauldron of Nevis Peak, charging right through me, and my *source-voice* screamed a resonating "Yes!" A few years later, we built our home on that property. At that time, I had a history of back surgery and quadruple coronary bypass; I knew that my husband would be off-island six to eight weeks in

So with my experiences in mind, and with a more profound understanding of the *source-voice*, I hope you will acknowledge the *source-voice*, heed its warning or follow its encouragement, and save a lot of wish-I-hads or wish-I-hadn'ts. So listen up when that internal spiritual voice bolts "Stop!" or spurs you on to dare to risk to live life more fully.

Universal Spiritual Connection and Spiritual Internet

Once you are truly *source-connected*, you may find that you gained access to a Universal Spiritual Connection (USC) that includes a spiritual internet. The term *spiritual internet* is similar to e-mail, and it is the avenue through which we receive messages from the USC. The USC and the spiritual internet are free, available 24-7, never need to be charged, are never lost, and never crash. We may crash and lose our connection with it, but that connection never disconnects from us. Here is how it works for me. If I need to know about a loved one's well-being, am doubtful, desire information, wish to contact a person, or think about a person I haven't heard from in a long time, I put the energy out to the universe. I think a thought, ask for guidance, or want circumstances to change, and I hold a clear picture in my mind. Then, I spiritually radiate that energy out of my body, akin to a Wi-Fi signal. Sometimes weeks later, occasionally as quickly as the same day, or as instant as instant messaging, I receive the answer. The response comes in the form of a phone call, text message, visualization, e-mail, dream, earthly thought, an unanticipated news report or is found when unexpectedly bumping into the person or while surfing the net. It is a wonderful gift and tool to possess in our vast, complex, demanding, and shifting world. Sometimes when driving on a busy freeway, by sending out an energy field, you can actually clear the path on which you need to travel to get to where you want to be at a certain time when every other major freeway is blocked because of severe weather. This happened when my daughter was in a high school play in the late eighties and Los Angeles was caught in a major downpour. On this special evening, I put the energy out to arrive on time. As I heard on the radio, every other freeway was jammed, but the freeways that I took were clear. This route usually took an hour and a half, but I made it with a few moments to spare.

At a presentation I gave at a university, one of the participants acknowledged that a similar connection had recently worked for her. She had wanted to attend a kundalini yoga workshop but realistically couldn't come up with the $4,000. She put the energy out, and within a week, she was notified that a sponsor would pay her expenses. Afterward, I asked her how she became so spiritual. She shared that while she was growing up in Mexico, her father kept her from other religions and held her close to his indigenous, cultural beliefs.

A friend married early, divorced early, and supported her two sons and herself as a speech therapist. Years later, she met her soul mate and the love of her life. They enjoyed an incredible, short-lived marriage until he was killed in a car accident. She remained single for quite a while and then met a man who was a lot of fun. During courtship, he showed interest and helped repair items in her home. The day after the wedding, he changed and became a totally different person who continued to be fun but quite difficult to live with. As he aged, he developed many complex ailments, and even simple health challenges had complications. When he suddenly died, she felt relief and then shock as she discovered financial uncertainty. After a while, she pulled herself together and moved to create a new, personal space.

When she and I met a few months before she moved, she shared that the one thing that kept her going was teaching a class at SAGE, a program titled "Learning in Retirement" that offers high-quality education on varied topics for retired seniors. There she developed friendships, reflecting her students' fondness, appreciation, and dedication and her ability to make the classes quite enjoyable.

As we walked to the parking lot, with the full moon rising, she shared her concerns and her loneliness. With our arms around each other's waists, looking out at the universe and moon, I commented, "Put it out to the universe." Shortly after, she attended a high school reunion in New York. While commuting, she wished *that she could find somebody who just wanted to hug her.* Upon her return home, a SAGE member called to offer to help her move to a new home. She replied, "Yes, that would be nice to have a man by my side." He showed up and never left her side. He later shared that he had been a widower for five years and had recently thought that it was time to find a companion. He had never acted upon that until the day he helped her. He cares for her and showers her with plenty of hugs. When she shared her story, she declared, "I guess I just put it out to the universe."

While writing this book, I ran into the person who became my Information Technology (IT) consultant at a restaurant when his wife sat catty-corner across from me and recognized me. She asked if I knew the whereabouts of her former colleague Lee, whose face she couldn't see as he sat across from me.

My husband has known me for more than sixty years, and for half those years, he has witnessed what he calls my "mysterious draws to events or things." Without any earthly ability, I gain a sense of the well-being of my family and loved ones even when they are around the world, to find certain items and to receive powerful signs and validation from a realm far beyond our planet. One Mother's Day, after I got off the phone in Nevis with Blind Eileen, I shared with Lee how remarkable our relationship with Eileen has been. I recalled that how we met thirteen years ago seemed to be a fluke and that her magnitude of gratitude, wisdom, and faith is living example of peace of mind and is a gift that she has brought to us. Lee commented, "Life is a series of random events that coalesce into something meaningful." I responded, "I don't think so. I agree with Eileen: *'God had a plan all the time.'*"

By far, the most wonderful gift the *Universal Spiritual Connection* provides is connecting with loved ones who have passed away and the ability to sense that connection in their now spiritual form as though they were fully present, virtually in a pure energy similar to their former persona. In that spiritual form, I easily receive and can readily call upon their love, healing, guidance, and supportive energy.

I hope, in time, if you aren't already familiar with the *Universal Spiritual Connection* or the *spiritual internet*, you will eventually feel a connection with this precious gift. Don't seek it. If you are open to the Universe, that connection will find you. You will sense and hopefully gain trust in it. When you receive it, believe in it. Never abuse its gift or question its purity or intent, for it is a very special connection and gift from our Universe.

Hand-Dome

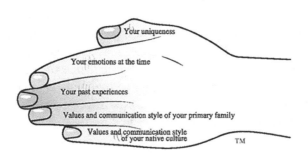

Figure 1. *Hand-Dome* Symbol.

Why You Feel, Think, Act, Speak, and Write as You Do

The *hand-dome* is a concept that eloquently describes why we each feel, think, act, speak, and write as we do at any given moment. It offers us a holistic and enlightened personal inventory to best recognize and appreciate our own uniqueness, attributes, limitations, and the challenges we face. Just as important, the *hand-dome* also offers us the ability to understand and appreciate another person's *hand-dome*, highlighting their uniqueness, attributes, limitations, and challenges. This is especially pertinent during and after major crises when we have to create a realistic and renewed path forward. The *hand-dome* also advances appreciation and inclusion.

When I began to give presentations in the mid-1980s, I used the thumb and four fingers of my hand as an effective analogy to illustrate the facets of the *hand-dome*. As I was writing my previous book, *Communication Is Connection*, I wanted to ennoble the hand to adequately elevate the specialness of each person. One late night while I was at the computer, similar to the term *source-connection*, the term *hand-dome* mystically came through on my *spiritual internet*. I think the word *dome* appeared because Dome of the Rock in Jerusalem, which our family had visited and experienced, is a sacred site for both Muslims and Jews. In addition, Dome Rock is a highly spiritual Native American spot in the California Southern Sierras, where my husband and I often hiked and camped. I accepted the term *hand-dome*. Shortly after, I created the above diagram to further highlight its concept.

The *hand-dome* is a relevant, user-friendly, fluid, and time-tested tool to create self-reflection, and it provides applications that no other personal tool does. These private holistic insights significantly help us attain spiritual, physical, mental, and emotional understanding and well-being. Equally essential, we gain a greater depth of recognition in regard to why our loved ones, students, colleagues, staff, clients, patients, peers, friends, and neighbors feel, think, act, speak, and write as they do. These private insights also significantly help us identify our personal boundaries, spanning from the least hurtful (yet annoying) to more serious and intolerable ones. We learn to identify and clearly determine our boundaries so that when others cross them, if given the choice, we no longer will tolerate their words or deeds. When we each learn to apply our *hand-dome*'s enlightened teachings and honor and respect those facets, not only within ourselves but also in others, we build a more solid, civil, comfortable, compassionate, and *trusted* connection.

The *hand-dome* is a jewel of a friend that we carry forever. As life unfolds, we pass through numerous rites of passage such as graduation, commitment, engagement, marriage, family, and birth. We also cope with health challenges, acute or chronic illness, miscarriage, abortion, abandonment, separation, divorce, and midlife crisis. We may also face relocation, eviction, homelessness, personal or financial losses or gains, and acceptance of loved one's newly revealed sexual identification. Furthermore, we may reckon with climate change causing blistering heat waves or freezing-cold periods, drought, floods, fires, disasters, pandemics, drive-by shootings, gun violence, and national and international terrorism.

In addition, we face disruptive uncertainties and the impact of instant awareness of breaking news regarding national and international cohesiveness and disarray, local and global events, and fluctuating markets. High-level technology that was once reliable now presents constant glitches, updates, and astute hackers who steal or alter the facts. These inconveniences impact us far too frequently, at times daily. Furthermore, disputes over natural resources, shifts of political sands, and other similar situations or events also occur. The rapid evolution of information, automation, regulations, demands, and urgencies also add hustle, burdens, and disharmony within. In life's natural course, we also face aging, decline, and death.

Most of these situations require critical reassessment. All are causes to pause, reflect, and update to rechart our *hand-dome*. This revelation offers the latest insights, awareness, and understanding of our new reality. The *hand-dome* remains an excellent and easy-to-apply resource to grasp our current situation and carve a positive and realistic *source-connected* pathway forward.

In the *hand-dome*, the thumb—which sits separate from the four fingers—represents our special qualities, strengths, attributes, limitations, challenges, and boundaries. The first finger, our pointer or index finger, represents our fluid and fluctuating range of emotions. The second finger, our middle finger, represents the sum of our life's past experiences. The third finger, our ring finger, represents the formative values and communication style of our primary family. The fourth finger, our pinky finger, represents the subtle yet significant values and communication style of our native culture, region, neighborhood, village, clan, or tribe.

Many thoughts from each facet of the *hand-dome* are often factored into forming our responses, but in the end, there is only one factor that prioritizes and determines our thoughts and responses, even if that factor just appeared. We gain two pivotal insights. First, we attain an in-depth comprehension and appreciation of who we are. As we embrace our attributes and hopefully engage them, we also learn to identify, accept, own, and respect, without apology, our limitations and challenges while we fervently seek to improve them. Equally important is defining and establishing our personal boundaries and our response to them.

The second pivotal lesson highlights that every other person's *hand-dome* is and always will be different from ours, so they will inherently respond differently than we do. The *hand-dome* reflects that while our decisions make sense to us most of the time, they may seem totally inept or make no sense to others. So statements such as, "You won't do it like me," "I don't do it your way," "I wouldn't do it your way," "Your brother isn't like that," or "Why can't you do it like your sister?" are mostly meaningless, as we now realize that we usually come from a different place and often respond differently.

When we realize, accept, and feel in our hearts and souls that each minuscule snowflake or grain of sand is created unmatched in the universe, we understand that each person's birthright also is a blending of their unique *hand-dome* facets. This wisdom furthers enlightenment, appreciation, and respect not only for our uniqueness but for the differences in all others as well. That does not suggest that we necessarily accept another's point of view as our own, nor do others have to accept our beliefs, attitude, or behavior. We now recognize and accept that every part and parcel of another person's life path is different from ours. Therefore, they are entitled to respond differently to life than we do, and most often do. Even if people share the same view and express a similar response, their reaction does not necessarily evolve from the exact set of life experiences or circumstances represented by the *hand-dome* facets. This fresh, holistic, and relevant knowledge helps to close gaps and build bridges between people. These bridges overcome obstacles and challenges to create resolutions that once seemed impossible. This leads to greater harmony, trust, and connection with other local, national, or global citizens sharing our earthly visit.

We explore the five spiritual and concrete facets of the *hand-dome*. This offers us a unique experience, which allows us to nonjudgmentally and privately search deeply within to discover new and relevant truths. Combined with courage and a desire to learn and grow, these facets provide a momentous opportunity to enhance our lives. The knowledge gained is not a guessing game. The accuracy and benefits we glean are based on our ability and willingness to be honest with ourselves and others with whom we share life.

Now, take both hands and evenly intertwine your fingers so that the right thumb sits on top of the left thumb. Then, reverse the process so that the left thumb is on top of the right thumb, and also mix up the fingers.

Your *hand-dome* is similar. Each time we respond, there is a complex integration of the five facets of your *hand-dome*. But only one factor plays the *determining role* in how we and others respond at any given moment to any given situation.

The Thumb in the Hand-Dome Represents Our Uniqueness

In our *hand-dome*, the thumb represents our one and only eternal, mystical, special self that we present to the world. Others may bear similar appearances, traits, and styles, but no other person will ever mirror us. Connecting with and integrating these glorious gifts endowed at conception brings clarity, purpose, satisfaction, and serenity into our lives.

To gain a better understanding of our multifaceted, complex selves, we become as clear as possible. Although it may be difficult, we need to be honest and straightforward with ourselves during our internal search. We become aware of our perceived or inherent limitations and then admit and own them. We also must reach within to feel and connect with our precious and celestially bestowed gifts. This allows us *not just to survive but to thrive* as we achieve, enjoy, and excel.

You Are Worthy Just Because You Are

Every life matters. *You are worthy just because you are*, and you are meant to be on this earth at this time. No person is ordinary; every person is special. Remember, we are each endowed with starlike magnificence and talent that we solely bring to life and offer to others and the world. Similar to our individual thumbprints that we leave on all we touch, who we are imprints everything we say and do. Which of the following mostly describe you? Are your special gifts expressed in deep listening, kindness, tenderness, compassion, empathy, patience, generosity, flexibility, strength, agility, or reaching out? Or are creativity, reasoning, perception, logic, and inner and outer beauty your special gifts? Which of the following describe your strongest tendency? Do you shine softly or brightly? Are you grateful and easily satisfied, or is something always missing? Are you critical or in love with love? Do you lead a simple life, appreciate the kindness of strangers, and find bliss in the simplest gifts of the universe? Or do you crave a constant flow of entertainment or activities to distract or satisfy? Do you prefer your own company, or do you seek or require others' companionship and constant attention? Do you express empathy or apathy? And if you are empathetic, do you understand or feel, or do you instinctively reach out to help? Is your self-talk positive and uplifting or negative and destructive? Are you more introverted and reserved, and do you prefer remaining in the background, observing, or are you more extroverted and outgoing, seeking the spotlight and speaking out? Are you vested in comfort or whatever is in your best interest? Are you open to listening to others' views, or are you set in your ideas of being right? Are you flexible or rigid? If you are rigid, is it because your physical and emotional well-being demand a certain disciplined routine to maintain health and harmony?

Do you tend to be simple or complex? Resilient or delicate? Hearty or feeble? Optimistic or cynical? Enthusiastic or lethargic? Leader or follower? Independent or dependent? Curious or uncurious? Progressive or conservative? Laid-back or temperamental? Assured or anxious? Easy or tough? Reconciling or retaliating? Cooperative or contrary? Consistent or inconsistent? Patient or impulsive? Willing or disagreeable? Timely or procrastinating? Enabling or disallowing? Giver or taker? Jealous or satisfied? Are you right-hemisphere or left-hemisphere or both? Are you left-handed, right-handed, or ambidextrous? Do you learn best by touch, sight, or sound? Are you micro or macro, more capable of seeing the forest or the trees? Are you mechanical, creative, or intellectual? Do you choose convenience or expedience? Do you take short cuts or the time to do it right? You imprint these traits in many ways during your life. No other person on the planet has ever or will ever exactly embody you. No matter what, you are worthy simply because you are. Your pure existence makes you matter, and you have a purpose!

Personal Limitations

Taking as unvarnished an inventory as possible of our strengths and limitations grants us a path to connect with those experiences and tasks that create ease, confidence, pleasure, and success. These connections arise from our most primal essence, genes, convictions, and moral compass. This is the first step in recognizing the features of the thumb in the *hand-dome*.

At times, this introspection may be unpleasant, as it is often difficult to acknowledge our limitations. In my decades of personal and, especially, professional experience, I discovered that people who don't acknowledge, accept, or respect their limitations, and sometimes even deny them, continue to stumble over the same challenges and issues year after year. Consequently, they neither recognize their limitations nor seek alternative solutions that are required to achieve more productive and worthwhile outcomes.

Some do not realize that when they repeatedly take an action or continue to make the same decision, the outcome remains the same. If you have not achieved the positive result or met the sought objective, perhaps after the first, or certainly after the second attempt, it is best to alter your approach to achieve better outcomes. Realistically, acknowledging and honoring limitations is critical and offers us the first step to seek desired, sensible, pragmatic, and feasible goals. Some limitations are intrinsic or genetic and may be physical, mental, or emotional. These challenges manifest themselves in response to illness, disorders, disease, strokes, heart attacks, learning disabilities, special needs, addictions, allergies, or lack of emotional or spiritual well-being. Other limitations are extrinsic, accidental, learned, or created by unexpected psychological or socioeconomic events imposed upon us, or simply bad habits picked up from others. Limitations can be fleeting, inconsistent, or persistent; even conditions once considered permanent may be resolved.

As medical, genetic, economic, robotic, technological, and yet unimagined or unknown advances and improvements unfold, what was once thought a permanent condition may find resolution or be eradicated. For example, the Bill & Melinda Gates Foundation is close to eradicating polio from the face of the earth. When I was young, peers who contracted polio were confined to iron lungs. Some emerged with minor challenges, others became paralyzed, and many died. So to follow the pathway to find the cure for polio and to realize the disease will soon be of the past is the miracle of modern medicine. The Giving Pledge was created by billionaires Warren Buffett and Bill and Melinda Gates. It invites the wealthiest people in the world to pledge at least half their wealth to charity during their lives or in their wills. Because of their incredible generosity, all people now have a greater opportunity to achieve plans and dreams that once seemed so out of reach.

When I heard the term *handi-abled*, I immediately embraced it, as it positively expresses what a person ably achieves in spite of their challenges. It doesn't matter how another person achieves; what matters is that it works. More power to all who overcome to make the best of any circumstance and create a more fulfilling life.

Each of us also carries flaws and imperfections. Owning them is not a weakness but a sign of courage, strength, and wisdom that shows our willingness to be honest with ourselves. This allows us to take responsibility so that we can positively change something that caused significant discord within us and others. If we don't acknowledge and take responsibility for a mind-set, habit, or trait, how can we possibly improve? An honest approach also facilitates our relationships with others, as no one has to dance around the "elephant in the room." Our openness, acceptance, and willingness to speak frankly about the issue offers others an avenue to share, discuss, and support us so that we can achieve. This provides a triumphant, win-win solution for all. I haven't found a single person, including myself, who is perfect. Have you?

We also face areas or situations in which, try as we might, we find we truly cannot succeed. Accepting our intrinsic or extrinsic limitations offers the first step to look at where we are and where we need or want to go. This discovery frees us to explore possibilities and find gratitude in what we have and what we can realistically gain.

Personal Boundaries

Personal boundaries are invisible to others. We establish boundaries to honor and protect ourselves from others' unpleasant, destructive, abusive, or abhorrent words, attitudes, and behavior. These corrosive acts and deeds come in the forms of touch, sight, or sound and are expressed in nonverbal, voice tone, verbal, and written communication. All types of abuses cause anguish to our physical, mental, emotional, and spiritual tranquility. In response, we mentally draw a line that we don't want to cross and will not allow others to cross. Boundaries pertain to situations or the manner in which people interact with us. On one side of the boundary, we are at ease and find comfort; on the other, we are guarded and distressed. Each of us identifies those abuses so that we then establish our boundaries to guard, secure, and protect our well-being. In a way, our personal boundaries are similar to putting up walls or fences around our property to keep out those people we don't want to enter or with whom we do not want to interact.

Experiences constantly remind me that situations, gestures, voice tones, or words that are acceptable or pleasant to me may be totally the opposite or have no impact on another person. What is abusive to me may roll off another person's back. What others have strength to conquer, I may not. But how often would we exchange our challenges for those that others face? We are usually not consciously aware of our boundaries and what upsets us. When a person crosses our boundaries, we become upset or respond negatively, yet we are not always attentive to the reasons. It is important to become aware of our sensitivities and set boundaries so that we can honor them while mindfully conveying our feelings and concerns to others. It is only the trust in ourselves, which we can control, that is critical; we cannot reliably expect others to honor our boundaries, as that is something we cannot control. In conclusion, I note that those who are unaware of or have not established their own boundaries tend not to be as aware of nor respect others' boundaries.

A motion picture editor and major family breadwinner separated from her husband. He was very selective and repeatedly turned down employment opportunities. She feared that if she returned to the marriage, she couldn't trust that he would resume earning his portion of the household income. When she *trusted herself* and insisted that her husband bear his fair share in providing income for the family, she returned to the marriage. It is best that we acknowledge and respect our boundaries, yet we must also equally appreciate and respect the boundaries of the people with whom we live, work, and play.

In describing four boundaries, *twig, branch, limb*, and *trunk*, I discuss their impact from least to most severe and compare them to a tree. A *twig boundary* is minor, as a tree twig is easily snapped off by fingers. The *branch boundary* is moderate, as clippers are needed to remove it. A *limb boundary* is difficult and necessitates a saw to remove. The *trunk boundary* is severe, as it requires heavy equipment to remove it. We each establish our self-identified boundaries, reflecting who we are, what we need or want, and what we will not tolerate.

The *twig boundary* is the least rigid and is easily broken, as the consequences are not that significant to us. At times, most of us have splurged on extras in life: a snack, a new article of clothing, a new iTunes song, a toy, tickets to a cultural or sporting event, travel, dining out, gifts to others and ourselves, accessories for our wardrobe, items for our homes, and numerous other expenses. We break our own rules, but if acted upon infrequently, they typically are not significantly consequential to anybody. As circumstances and situations change in life, the enforcement of boundaries and how we honor them fluctuate. When a stuntman went into his own business, he never turned down a job. As demand increased, he established a policy that he would not perform any stunts without a two-day advance notice. What originally had no boundary became a *twig boundary*. Occasionally, an actor with whom he liked to work requested him. When that happened, he ignored his *twig boundary* and he took the gig.

A woman feeling comfortable breaking her budget when she was employed changed her spending habits when she retired and lived on a pension. She watched her expenditures and the spending habits that had once been a *twig boundary* become a *branch boundary* because she was uncomfortable when she didn't maintain a certain balance in her bank account. Her peace of mind was far more meaningful to her than the stress of not having a monetary cushion. Another person may be comfortable and not stressed with a smaller cushion in the same situation.

Crossing a *limb boundary* is more intolerable. Another person might consider occasional annoying behavior a *twig boundary*, which they often overlook. But when others repeat that small annoyance more frequently, intensely, or negatively, what was once a *twig boundary* evolves into first a *branch boundary* and then a *limb boundary*. This may necessitate significant consequences or reprimands, reducing the time spent with that person, severing the relationship, or another response proportionate to our discomfort.

An example of honoring one's *limb boundary* is the story of a widowed accountant who is the sole parent of a young son. He arranged his schedule so that his hours were from 9:00 a.m. to 6:30 p.m., at which time he left, regardless of work deadlines the following day.

The *trunk boundary* symbolizes the most severe boundary and usually calls for removal from the situation or a complete break from the person. Each of us decides which attitudes or behaviors belong to which specific boundary. If a person stole from me without an apparent reason or continually lied to me, I would first speak with them and try to find out why. If they didn't change, I would probably sever the relationship. When our children were younger and they did something wrong or broke something and owned up to it, discussion would follow—especially if they had been warned—but there were no further consequences. When one lied, there were reprimands. Honesty was always held in high esteem in our family.

At a recent presentation at a university, I laid out four scenarios relative to the four types of boundaries. A student who comes to class late once a month may cross a *twig boundary*. If the tardiness increases, the teacher likely talks to the student, inquires about what is going on, and assists the student to help solve the issue. When a student's work is regularly inaccurate, inadequate, or sloppy, the student crosses a *limb boundary.* The teacher may speak out sooner and try to help the student seek a solution. A student who cheats crosses a *branch boundary* and may be placed on probation. And a student who steals something of substance from a professor or leader at the university crosses a *trunk boundary* and most likely will be expelled.

Communication consists of three factors: nonverbal communication, voice tone, and verbal communication. Each factor is expressed positively or negatively and is often misinterpreted because of differing regional or cultural backgrounds, socioeconomic or education level, age, or sexual orientation. A comprehensive and in-depth presentation on communication is presented in the second section of this book, *Soul to Soul Communication*. A further exploration into intercultural communication of and for those *Born-abroad* or who speak English as a Second Language appears in the third section, *Soul to Soul Intercultural Communication*.

The following are examples of crossing boundaries in the three communication facets, beginning with nonverbal communication. A young woman applied for a position as a hostess in a trendy outdoor restaurant. On the first day, a patron flirted with her by affectionately touching her shoulder; she immediately quit her job. Her twin sister readily took the job, stating, "I can deal with that. There are bouncers who will step in if someone becomes really obnoxious." One employee allows her boss to yell at her, while another will not tolerate that voice tone. A spouse or partner allows their mate to shout blistering remarks or text misogynistic insults; another doesn't stand for these verbal violations. A man pats a woman's breast or grabs her behind. What was once quietly accepted as part of the "culture" or "his personality" is no longer being tolerated as it once was. Women around the globe now create and continue to post hashtags when they have been perpetually abused.

Distraught over past reviews in which critiques were harshly doled out, a strong-willed, tenacious social worker told her colleagues, "I'm very sensitive, my feelings easily get hurt. Please be constructive with your criticism." Her colleagues questioned, "Not you?" She replied, "Yes, me." Sometimes people appear very competent, yet emotionally they are quite vulnerable. They don't possess a reservoir of hope or resiliency, which others can't or don't see. Except close family members or friends, others rarely know how deeply sensitive and fragile a person is.

We now have a clearer understanding that abuses come in nonverbal, voice tone, and verbal communication form and are expressed through touch, sight, or sound. Again, these dimensions have an impact on us physically, mentally, emotionally, or spiritually. Please take the necessary time to examine what is abusive to you. If communication with the other person doesn't resolve the issue or you are in a situation that you cannot alter, control, or escape, ask yourself what sort of boundary you need to establish or strengthen. Determine what modification you can realistically make to avoid these abuses and bring more comfort into your life. This becomes paramount because often when we are frustrated, angry, hurt, disappointed, or upset and we don't recognize the underlying cause. If we have not yet consciously defined and communicated our personal boundaries, we cannot be fully aware when someone crosses them.

When we clearly identify and establish boundaries, we gain wisdom to take control, which enables us to communicate mindfully and appropriately with others. In the process, there is less confusion or misunderstanding of events, responses, or words that upset us. But just as important, if not more so, we take the responsibility to protect ourselves and establish a clear response when others cross our boundary. We may choose to say something akin to "Cool it," "Back off," "I see red," or "You are annoying." If necessary, we raise one or both of our hands, with palms facing the person, to motion stop, then voice, "That is not okay." If that doesn't work, we need to take time to think through until we find an honorable means to protect ourselves. Then, we can create an appropriate, meaningful, and proportional response and stand by and honor our decision as best as we can. Another option to try to modify attitudes or behaviors is what Halpern (1976) calls "changing the song and dance." One person sings a song, and in response, the other person dances to the tune. We often can't control or change a person's attitude or behavior through conversation, but if we, the singer, change the tune, we can influence the other, the dancer, to eventually change the step. This approach often leads to positively modifying specific attitudes and behaviors.

When a child continually crosses a boundary and their words or deeds remain abusive to you, a sibling, friend, classmate, parent, or caretaker, it is imperative to respond consistently. Find an appropriate, nonphysical consequence that is proportionate to the misbehavior and significant enough to get the child's attention so they do not repeat their negative attitudes and acts. If their behavior continues, perhaps the parent, caretaker, or teacher needs to seek a different approach, examine if their response is adequate, or question why they do not stick to their plan. When a child proclaims, "This isn't fair," in a *source-connected* tone, explain to them that their attitude or behavior is not fair to others. A Nevisian friend who disciplined his six-year-old child related, "It is far easier to bend a young tree than to train an older one."

As you continue reading this book and throughout life, become aware of your new, existing, or outdated boundaries. Add new boundaries at the bottom of your thumb as you continue to chart your *hand-dome*, an exercise that is introduced later in this chapter. As we become firmer in establishing and enforcing our boundaries and assuring that others respect our needs, those boundaries may become obsolete, as they no longer serve any purpose. We can then remove them from our *hand-dome* chart. As we mature and gain experience, our attitudes and actions will hopefully be more open and accepting of others' positive views and lifestyles, even though they are different from ours, and hopefully, we will also become less judgmental and less rigid.

As we make positive changes, others may not consciously notice these subtleties and continue to interact with us as we once were but no longer are. Family, friends, colleagues, or staff continue to respond to us as if we still act and communicate in our former negative manner, even though our new, positive lifestyle and communication patterns are well established and we walk our talk most of the time. We need to mindfully convey to them that their former perception of us is obsolete and needs to be updated. This is similar to computer programs that over time become obsolete, as they are frequently updated and replaced with several newer versions.

During challenging times, we may temporarily slip back to our former, less desirable ways. It is best to remain diligent and care enough so that when we slide backward, we return to our more recent and productive communication style whenever feasible. Remember, no matter what we say, our actions always speak louder than our words.

It is meaningful to add that children, spouses, and partners often beg that parents or caregivers establish boundaries. A fifteen-year-old daughter of a permissive female executive threw a plate of spaghetti in her mother's face and shouted, "When are you going to put up some rules?" An article by Edward Humes (1996) follows a young child who, at age five, was moved from a decrepit Dodge van—his home—and taken to a youth shelter and then shuffled from one neglectful home to another. No one held the child accountable, forced him to go to school or court, or demanded that he stop perpetrating petty crimes. Before the young man had graduated to adult crime, Humes remembers him saying, "They never gave me a reason to stop, so I didn't." The same quote, "No reason to stop," also applies to any personal or professional negative pattern.

Please allow me to repeat that in my personal and professional experience, I've learned that the more we trust that we will honor and respect our boundaries and communicate our needs to others, the less we have to control our environment.

Our Breaking Points

Each of us has our personal invisible *buttons*, breaking points, and vulnerabilities. It is important to immediately become aware of the impact of agonizing words, ideas, actions, events, or situations and the anxiety, urgency, worry, or disharmony they cause. This prevents our frustration from escalating into irritation, to aggravation, or worse, to aggression. Compare your response with the red-yellow-green lights of traffic signals. Slow down to notice the first sensation of unease. Use caution similar to the attention called for by the yellow light. Observe where and how intensely you sense your distress. If the situation turns out to be nothing, then move on, similar to a green light that signals it's okay to continue. If the distress heightens and strongly signals that the situation is moving in the wrong direction, then stop immediately, similar to approaching a red traffic light. Tune in to your internal signal and follow its command to stop, turn in another direction, or speed away. This mindfulness protects us and allows us to give a positive warning to others so that the interaction halts immediately. Then you can respond in a positive, strong, *source-connected*, self-worthy manner so that the situation does not get worse or out of control. If necessary, don't say a word; turn to the person and, with a strong but neutral facial expression, place your hand closely in front of your face with palm facing the other person to signal *stop*. If the person doesn't stop or you feel uncomfortable, pivot and walk away—or run, if necessary. If you feel the other person quit the badgering, demeaning speech, or behavior and you are okay, cautiously remain and see what happens next. Never remain in a situation in which you feel threatened, bullied, or frightened and your body signals discomfort or danger. If possible, flee as fast as you can. There are some situations or events from which we cannot or do not want to walk away. It is best that we know which individuals, colleagues, family member or members with whom we are unguarded and authentic in most situations. I believe that it is paramount to prioritize our lives to maximize our thoughts, activities, and time with those individuals or which situations bring out the best in us instead of the worst.

When our children were teenagers, my husband told them, "Whenever you are in a situation that is uncomfortable, leave and call us." When our son was a teenager, he rode with a student who was speeding, and our son asked him to slow down. When instead the person drove faster, at the next red traffic light, our son hopped out of the car. When my daughter traveled in Europe with a friend, their first night was spent in a youth hostel. When a few people started mainlining drugs, she and her friend took their valuables and walked the streets till dawn.

A friend was extremely distraught and embroiled in constant confrontation and arguments with her spouse. It wasn't physical violence, but there was plenty of verbal and emotional abuse. One day, she had enough. She drove to an isolated high spot not far from her home and climbed to a high barren plateau, where she reached a fence. She stopped and screamed at the top of her lungs, "HELP ME!" She heard the words echo around her. Although she couldn't cross the barrier, she felt as though she had plowed through. When she looked back, she realized that she had released her anger and fear, and she felt free. As she became more aware of her boundaries, she began to better enforce them to prevent similar situations. If we allow abuse to continue from anyone, those destructive and unacceptable patterns continue to haunt us and wreak havoc throughout our lives; they are more devastating when we are most vulnerable. As we age, we usually become more sensitive, anguish is more intense, and we often find less strength to shrug them off.

Before I leave this section, let me offer some additional insights and clues into self-monitoring when we are heading in an unproductive direction. When we begin to make more mistakes, can't recall information, aren't as sharp as usual, easily become more frustrated or agitated, or drop more things, something is amiss. A close friend shared that when she was a child, if she felt out of sorts, her father taught her to quickly ask herself *if she was tired, hungry, lonely, or angry*. My children often use similar benchmarks to figure out their own children's sudden mood shifts. When our youngest grand was six years old, she coined a new word, *glumsy*, which my daughter thought meant "tired, a bit sad, and off the game." When I heard the term, I thought, *Thank you, granddaughter, for giving me a term to describe how I occasionally feel*. A great-nephew utters *hangry* when he is hungry and feels out of sorts.

My two major stressors are being rushed, which I can control, and extreme heat, which I can't. Even in my younger days, rushing or keeping up with time pressures created stress, and my response to that type of pressure persists. Time in Nevis is respected and spent quite differently than it is in the United States. Completion of tasks and many social events occur on "when it happens" time, not on time measured by a clock or marked on a calendar, and the outcomes are usually successful. The Nevisians are punctual for work in businesses or professional offices, but not for appointments or repairs. They work at each place without dallying until the job is accurately completed but also allow for time for a brief chat. Engaging in casual conversation is a delightful custom of this more-relaxed culture.

Although I am punctual in my professional life, when I have the choice and others aren't waiting, my spirit wants to move in "universal time." This type of time is not ruled by a watch or a calendar.

But tardiness was annoying to my punctual, fast-paced, and often multistop family. So at one point, I decided to avoid the stress for others and myself, plan ahead, and get everything ready to be on time. If their plans were too hectic, or I had to rush too much, I told others to go without me. Since Lee's former accounting profession required punctuality and deadlines, he is often ruled by the clock. Before I recognized that my parents and sibling were also slower-paced and more patient, I thought there was something wrong with me. I used to make up excuses and gave other reasons that I was slower than my family. Once I owned up about which activities I could not comfortably or realistically participate, factoring in pace, time parameters, and stops that they wanted to make, I discovered that I was much better off not joining them. Though probably disappointing, my decision didn't frustrate the family and fostered calm within. I no longer felt guilty or inadequate; it is just who I am and what I can do. A family member told our granddaughter, "Remember the story of the tortoise and the hare. Nana may be the last one out, but she hangs in longer than the rest."

Over the years, the cumulative impact of health issues demands more time and attention. This becomes more critical as tasks also take longer to perform because joints are not as flexible. Unless it is late at night or I am tired, my mind thankfully works sharply enough—most of the time—but my body just doesn't respond as quickly. I no longer rush to answer a call. I have to force myself to allow more time so that I am not under that time pressure. When we travel, I often wake up at 3:30 a.m. to allow plenty of time to peacefully stretch and meditate before we leave. I learned that if I take care of as much as possible the previous night, there is little left to do except get ready in the morning. I am much calmer and less stressed than if I wait until the morning to do the multiple minor tasks, which always seem to require more time than I had planned. After my grandson entered middle school and had to rise half an hour earlier to be on time, I suggested my new routine to him. I explained that feeling rushed in the morning is not a good way to start the day. He later shared that the new routine was helpful. When we honestly take our *personal inventory* and accept our limitations, vulnerabilities, and breaking points, we are far more capable of addressing and creating strategies to minimize their impact.

Most of my life, I was confined to a narrow comfort range between being hot and cold, which was exacerbated when I was infected by a parasite in 2006. Since we cannot accurately predict weather, I often add or remove several layers of clothing a day, which means I tote more than others. You'd be surprised how many people—even strangers—comment on what I carry. Yet I'm the one who easily gets sick if I get chilled or feel faint when overheated. I often wonder why what I schlep is anyone else's concern.

When making dinner reservations, I inform the host or hostess that I am sensitive to drafts and I would greatly appreciate a table that is away from a draft or fan. I also inform my waiter or waitress of my wheat and dairy sensitivities and preference of all beverages without ice. Despite my explanation, my drink is frequently served with ice. Moreover, many folks do not realize that milk, butter, cheese, or cream are dairy products. If the dish contains dairy, my stomach immediately reacts. I learned not to be embarrassed, apologetic, or concerned with others' reactions when I sense the dairy. I politely ask the waiter or waitress to bring an alternative. After all, it is my stomach, not theirs, that reacts in the middle of the night. Yet you'd be surprised how many looks I used to get. As I age and sections of our culture become more tolerant and respectful of sensitivities and differences, chefs are increasingly willing to make modifications, especially as I only select substitutions that are already on the menu. I also always offer to pay extra if necessary.

My husband and I saw entrepreneurial potential in a friend in Nevis when he was a child because he was always personable and capable. He became a successful businessman who owns an upscale restaurant. When I asked him, "What's on the menu that can be prepared dairy-free with ingredients readily available?" He replied, "I remember you are a picky eater." I responded, "No, I have a sensitive stomach," and added, "My comment is best coming from me than a patron who won't return." He hugged and thanked me.

There are stressful workdays when along with a demanding workload, you may also face bad news, heavy traffic, or foul weather and be unable to sense gratitude or anything positive. These situations detract from the warm, happy, and loving atmosphere at home that may await you. Or the day at home with the children or an ailing parent may have been particularly stressful, especially if you also feel overloaded with your workday, and the person arriving is looking forward to a pleasant welcome.

When possible, whether you are the person arriving home or the person awaiting others to arrive, especially on a stressful day, pause and identify your stress. Engage the three mindful breaths, connect with something positive, and then park your negative feelings.

Then later, when the time is right, find quiet to read, relax, chat with a friend or family member, listen to music, watch a program, surf the net, or soak in a tub. If feasible, take a walk, go to the gym, enjoy a movie, connect with social media, join a prayer or meditation group, or engage in any event that makes you feel good. Try to find a solution that is beneficial, healthy, and easily attained.

It is also best for those arriving or awaiting to hold off dumping their complaints, disappointments, or frustrations. Instead of first offering a positive greeting, what sort of message do you send when you focus on the mail or e-mail, check phone or text messages, straighten the house, or engage in other impersonal activities? These are issues that each must take to heart to significantly benefit ourselves and others. If you work in a confined work space, personalize the area with calming or cheerful photos of beloved people and places, mementoes, or something that puts a smile in your heart.

Whenever life becomes hectic, engage the Mona Lisa smile and *instant mindful breath-boosters*. When you can, take a three-minute break to walk to a window, gaze out at the sky, connect with something in nature, or contemplate something that catches your eye. These along with soothing thoughts neutralize fatigue, frustration, or stress. The *instant mindful breath-boosters* and Mona Lisa smile are also calming as you enter a new situation, walk to the car, sit in traffic, wait for a traffic signal to turn, answer the phone, or wait for the computer's timed backup or spinning wheel or hourglass to finish. These breaths return us to the present moment and set the tone for our next meeting, appointment, interaction, or conversation. When under severe stress, we need to take stock and be responsible for quickly and easily shifting to a more positive and productive place. Combined with a sense of gratitude and civility, we then radiate positive energy to our loved ones, colleagues, staff, patients, students, neighbors, service providers, workers, or fellow commuters.

First Finger in the Hand-Dome: Our Emotions at the Moment

In the *hand-dome*, the first finger represents our emotions at the moment. Before we move on, we first identify the spectrum of emotions that we personally feel. Basic emotions include love, optimism, fear, anger, cynicism, sadness, joy, disgust, trust, and surprise. Each of these emotions has a range of feelings within them (Ekman 1990). For instance, apprehension is less intense than fear, and both are less intense than terror. Serenity is less intense than joy, and both are less intense than ecstasy. Universal facial expressions are anger, fear, disgust, happiness, sadness, and surprise (Ekman and Friesen 1975).

Damasio (2003) declares that emotions precede feelings. Neuroscience has not reached the point of measuring emotions, but there are studies of neurons that map feelings. Positive feelings are essential to reach personal homeostasis. He states, "The entire collection of homeostasis process governs life movement by moment in every cell of our bodies." Joy and variations of that promote health and foster creativity and our ability to be kinder and more generous to others. Negative feelings hinder us from being, doing, or acting our best with others.

Emotions are continually shifting, and the resulting fluid feelings flavor the essence of our connection and communication with others. We may wake up in the morning in a terrific mood, then quibble with a loved one, commute through stop-and-go traffic, experience road rage, discover a friend is ill, or learn of a horrific event or disturbing policy or political agenda. It is difficult to maintain the same uplifting sense with life's increasingly unpredictable storms, speed bumps, and curveballs.

The reverse of these situations may occur. We may have an unproductive day that feels as though we spent the time spinning wheels. Then, a captivating sky, soothing song, or pleasant news eases our commute. As we return to a loving home, we feel better. Do the folks awaiting us live in a world of gratitude or "good enough," as do the people in Nevis? Or do we live in a divisive culture that complains, looks for faults, seeks the negative, or constantly looks ahead for what each person wants next instead of appreciating what they already possess? Our expectations and wants are often set so high that we rarely live in gratitude. People have expressed, "Yes, it is easy for you to feel gratitude." Even years ago, when my husband and I lived quite humbly, as I faced my greatest personal and medical challenges, I always felt gratitude. Although my mother was a wealthy woman in pre-Nazi Germany, she and my dad came here with limited financial resources, and yet she was always grateful. Our internal genetic disposition and external environment each play an enormous role in coloring our emotions and responses.

People encounter a variety of emotions, and their intensity, depth, and range are inconsistent. Some folks' mood swings are wide, and others' moods are more consistent. Emotions are expressed through our body language, voice tone, and word choice. A mother noted that her daughter was an emotive child. When upset, the child was overly animated and expressive. It disturbed the mother to see her daughter so often upset. Initially, the mother responded to her in a way that reflected her feelings. After a while, she realized that her child expressed more emotions than she did either because she was more sensitive or that was just her style. The mother learned to tone down what she heard so that she listened with less intensity. In this way, she could more empathetically respond to the child's needs. I learned a similar lesson taking photos of sunsets in Nevis. Digital cameras "see" the sunsets far more vividly than my eye, so I adjusted the camera settings to tone down the hues, more closely reflecting what my eye saw.

I tend to be passionate and emotional, and at times, I may be too intense for some. Others misinterpret my intentions. They receive it with more gusto than intended. With age and wisdom, I am improving reading other people's reactions and know when to turn down the volume for their and my comfort. Mindfulness and monitoring of my responses and those of others are extremely beneficial.

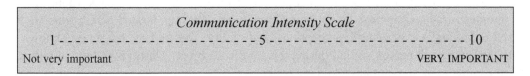

Above is a communication intensity scale from 1 to 10. Number 1 denotes expressing minimal emotion. Number 10 denotes something highly emotional, as when what we express is *very* important. Misunderstandings occur about the urgency or significance of our message when our tone does not accurately reflect what we feel or convey the importance of the point. By not expressing ourselves consistently—meaning one thing but conveying another—our message is often not received as we had hoped. We then face an understanding gap. How do we know when this occurred? The other person's response does not mirror what we expressed; they either overreact or underreact. When this occurs, I stop and politely ask the other person to articulate what they think I meant. I explain, "On a scale of 1 to 10, I intended the message at level 2, and you interpreted it at level 8." Usually, they misunderstood my intention, and by clarifying, I avoid disappointment and further misunderstanding. Yes, they understood the words, but they didn't grasp the intention or the importance that I felt. The intensity level that we use reflects what we feel at the moment, but it may change quickly. Some moods change as rapidly as a moving thunderstorm; other moods fluctuate more consistently and as calmly as a river gently flowing downstream. If a person responds negatively to you, it may have nothing to do with you. It just may be that is what the person feels at the moment or what reflects their general frame of mind.

Second Finger in the Hand-Dome: Our Past Experiences

In the *hand-dome*, the second finger represents all our life's past experiences—from early childhood to those of the previous moments. The *hand-dome* offers us a clearer sense of how these encounters positively or negatively affect us and continue to influence our lives. Nobel Peace Prize laureate Elie Wiesel stated, "We don't live in the past, but the past lives in us"

(Symonds 2007). No matter how we or any other person perceives the situation or experience, each person's reality is based on their own perception and experiences.

Most mornings, I read a passage from a book, *A Time for Peace: Daily Meditations for Twelve-Step Living*, by Mary Ylvisaker Nilsen. In connecting with Mary, I learned that her family was Norwegian with a Lutheran religious background. As an impressionable child, she was convinced by stories from the Bible, also known as the Old Testament, that she was Jewish. When she first heard about the atrocities that the Nazis had perpetrated against Jewish people, she had nightmares of being dragged and separated from her mother, and she experienced duress for months. Mary is no more Jewish than I am Lutheran. Her reality was based on her perception and personalization of the narrative she heard as a child in her Midwestern home.

As young children, a pair of fraternal twins visited a friend's house, and while they played outside, they were exposed to the same event of hearing their father "make a funny noise" not with their mother but with another woman inside the house. One twin carried that memory his entire life; his twin sister couldn't even recollect it. In the 2012 shooting of Trayvon Martin, most people of African cultural heritage, and many from other cultural heritages, believed that Trayvon Martin was murdered, while other persons from differing cultural backgrounds believed the same deed was self-defense by George Zimmerman. These polarized perceptions are based on each individual's experiences, perceptions, and reality. The truth is that no one knows what was going on in each person's mind during the scuffle. Trayvon Martin isn't here to tell us, and George Zimmerman may not have told the truth.

We may respond differently to similar situations that occur at different times. As we encounter different events, gain life experiences, and mature, our recognition and responses may change. A friend from a close-knit family had a brother who died of cancer. During the month prior to his death, he lay in an isolation bubble for leukemia treatment in Washington. Family members from California, New York, and Italy took turns at a round-the-clock bedside vigil. Whenever the brother desired physical contact with a loved one, family members put on gloves and reached into the opening so he could feel their comforting touch. After his tragic death, his sister deeply grieved, often wailing that she wished she also had died. A few years later, her sixteen-year-old son was diagnosed with cancer. He pleaded with her that if he died, she not grieve for him in the same way she had mourned for her brother but instead remember and rejoice in the life they had shared. When he passed away, none of her friends thought she could ever pull herself through her despair to experience joy again. But our friend honored her son's request, and while she privately mourned and thought of him daily, in time she experienced life with laughter and joy. Her devout faith, devotion to others who were grieving, and solid spiritual bond with her deceased son gave her the strength to carry on.

We each have encountered peak moments in our lives that we cherish, and they often become life-changing events. It may be the arrival of a long-desired child, spouse, partner, or family member. For others, it is fulfilling a long-held dream of graduation, entering marriage, having a first child, choosing a first pet, arriving in a new country, moving into a home, completing a major project, or receiving local, national, or global recognition. There are a few "one moment in time" peak experiences that forever alter our perceptions of who we are. Not all peak moments are positive. Sadly, for some, the arrival of another child is initially a burden, as they are already overwhelmed with responsibilities. Despite the initial sense of strain, the event may serve as a catalyst for positive change that eventually brings joy.

Some encounter monumental challenges, often making tremendous sacrifices to achieve desired goals. For others, these achievements were already bestowed on them through similar sacrifices made by previous generations. Some grew up with life handed to them on a silver platter, while others had to grovel, hold two jobs, and work in harsh circumstances simply to get ahead and climb out of poverty. Often, they were reimbursed at a grossly unfair pittance performing tasks at which others sneered.

A young woman whose family had emigrated from Lebanon when she was a child works in a doctor's office. She is insular, but not prejudiced, and she voted for Donald Trump based on one fact. Part of her family remained in Syria and sided with President Assad. When a member of the rebel forces knocked on her relative's door and saw a young man, they ordered him to join their side or they would shoot him. He refused, so they murdered him in front of his father. Due to her stance on terrorism, the woman felt that President Trump would be a strong military leader. Similarly, an elderly health-care professional of spiritual, progressive, and Judaic beliefs was open to a Donald Trump presidency. Her experience decades ago as a nurse caring for children in a refugee camp during the Iraqi-Iranian war shaped her opinion. Another person supported him because of his stance on abortion.

Some experienced devastating, demeaning, horrendous situations or events such as rape, desertion, abandonment, beatings, injustice, war, running for their lives, barely surviving, or escaping death. Others were tricked or coerced into human trafficking or kidnaped at a young age by members of Boko Haram, forced to marry, have sex, and then become pregnant by their captors. When they escaped or were freed, they returned to their villages and met scornful shame instead of relief and compassionate gratitude. Still, others witnessed or were caught in a brutal massacre or heard cries for survival and were heartbroken that they could not help. These left haunting memories and survivor's guilt. Those profound, horrific encounters cannot be easily or quickly shaken off and may never totally leave us. To some degree, they leave an invisible, devastating, and permanent impact. They become major factors in the development of our negative, self-deprecating chatter until we somehow pull ourselves together, make up our minds, and gather help and support from others, the Universe, or the Creator. Hopefully, we realize that although the memory always remains, in time, we will come to accept that "it is what it is." We get a sense that we will somehow eventually triumph, and one day the pain will diminish and we will be okay. Until then, these ordeals and thoughts, and this debilitating self-talk, may spin out of control and profoundly shape our lives and communication. This, along with a range of other negative or unrealistic perceptions, forms negative filters. How we feel, think, act, speak, and write usually stems from childhood, repetitive, or monumental events that we experienced, and they continue to deeply affect us. These filters are discussed in the following chapter, *"Personal Lenses."*

Sometimes a recent happening or wrongdoing alters how we feel and respond. Its emotional impact strongly influences our response. If we are in a good relationship with an individual who says or does something that deeply disappoints, hurts, or angers us, we begin to feel differently toward that person. The feeling may temporarily create a new *lens* or become a more permanent *lens* in the future. The incident may occur only once and not have a lasting impact, or it may be the foundation of a new pattern of how we interact with that person and to life. Unfortunately, we may easily spread our negative attitude to similar situations. What were formerly positive interactions and pleasant feelings between you and the other person—whether personal or professional—often become more uncertain, guarded, negative, or strained, until the issue is addressed through compassionate, forgiving, understanding, and *source-connected* dialogue. If the individual is meaningful in our lives, it is always best to take the time through meditation, guidance, consultation, or discussion with a friend to recognize and resolve the issue. Sometimes, the resolution does not happen on our time because it takes a willingness on both parties to work through it. Until that happens, we must seek goodness and live with the "it is a part of life" circumstances as best as we can until we find the solution.

All our Nevisian friends possess tremendous faith in a higher power and ask for daily guidance and wisdom. Living in Nevis and observing our friends carry on in that faith, I witnessed miracles and impossibilities become realities. In difficult situations, I reach out to the Universe, and I am amazed that the Universe responds. As I aged, gained wisdom, and created spiritual coping responses, I mostly found peace and resolution within a day or so. Yet there were some deeply ingrained challenges that took decades to face and resolve or accept and transcend to achieve the desired worthiness and peace of mind.

Third Finger in the Hand-Dome:
The Values and Communication Style of Our Primary Family

In the *hand-dome*, the third finger represents the values and communication style of our parents, extended family, guardians, or caregivers. The manner in which they interacted with us and one another, as well as their priorities, had a tremendous impact on our values and affects how we communicate as adults in various roles and situations.

What childhood traditions or events do you recall that brought comfort, fun, and a deep sense of belonging and which still put a smile in your heart and on your face? Were those times frequent, occasional, or so rare that they stood out? How were holidays, birthdays, and life cycle events celebrated? Which holidays did you celebrate? What were the fondest memories with your parents, your siblings, or the entire family? Were your childhood years the happiest time in your life, or did you often want to escape? Were family members united as a team, pulling together and supporting one another to face challenges and solve issues calmly, rationally, and democratically? Or were they competitive, divisive, or combative, creating an atmosphere of everyone for themselves, pitting one against the other, or stirring up turmoil? Was the norm a pattern of strife blown out of proportion or bathed in blame, dispute, or repercussions? Did family members feel a connection with the greater community or live with a sense of isolation? From these various childhood observations, we took on our parents' or caregivers' values and learned positive or negative communication styles. All these profoundly affected our early years and laid the foundation of our responses to life.

Emigrating from Nazi Germany only two years before I was born, my mother became a fearful person, which was apparent during my younger years. In addition, my parents moved from New

York City, where family members surrounded them, to Columbus, Ohio, where initially my mother felt isolated, as she didn't know any other person. Later, she enjoyed the support of other German Jewish people who had similarly fled the Nazi regime. Their shared experience created a community and camaraderie among them. Because my father traveled, my mother had to rely on her own ingenuity and resilience. She asked neighbors to aid with laying traps and removing the trapped rodents.

Some of her fears left memorable impressions that I vividly recall to this day. A gal who lived in our flats was Christian. My mother gasped when I mentioned that her phone number, Evergreen 1530, was lower than our Evergreen 8825. After I hung up, I asked my mother why she was so upset. She responded that because Judaism is a much older religion than Christianity, she didn't want me to belittle or insinuate anything about Judaism being older, and perhaps imply wiser. When my mother began driving, every time she heard a siren, she pulled over to the side in angst and trepidation. In my late teens, I was independent, willing to try something different, and often the first to come up with an idea. But as I got older and grasped life's realities, by my twenties, I temporarily became more hesitant and fearful.

While I was growing up, birthdays and holidays were special times in my childhood home. These were set aside for celebration. Delicious aromas wafted from the kitchen as we each chose our menu for the day and usually enjoyed our time with friends and adopted extended family. Even now, birthdays are a "big deal" with our children's families and our grands.

When my husband and I raised our children, we were fortunate that we could decide that after our second child was born, I would remain a stay-at-home mom during their developmental years. My husband is an accountant, so during those precomputer decades, he left the house at 7:00 a.m., returned at 11:00 p.m., and worked a half-day on Saturday. There was no money for babysitters or a night out with the girls, nor was there a possibility to bring in prepared meals or the opportunity to catch a meal at a family member's home or drop off the children.

As the children aged, daily evening meals offered an occasion to share our day's events and often led to lively discussions and debates on human rights, politics, ethics, school events, and life encounters. They were exposed to conventional and alternative ideas and learned not only by what we said but mostly by what we did as well. When the children were old enough to drive, they sometimes stopped by Lee's office at lunchtime; they were always invited to join for lunch and share in conversation with Lee's clients.

When a wealthy client offered a used car to my husband, he asked one of our relatives if she would like to join him in going to Las Vegas to pick up the car; she was delighted to go. The client donated vast portions of his estate to a charitable foundation that distributes annual gifts to worthy charities, educational institutions, and individuals in need. There are numerous streets and buildings that bear his name. As a child, he grew up in an orphanage, and as a teenager, he lost an arm in a farming accident. If you observed his understated style, you might guess that he worked in the kitchen at a hotel. Yet on special occasions and celebrations, he dressed up and looked quite dapper. After Lee picked up the car, all three enjoyed lunch. Later, our relative commented that it was a surprise that they ended up eating at Arby's.

Whenever we had workers or service people in the house, we treated them with respect and equality. During mealtime, they usually joined us or we prepared their lunch and served them when they took their break. Because of these various encounters, our children became comfortable with people from different walks of life and cultural backgrounds. As early as junior high, our children asked questions that clued me in that they were already solidifying their own foundations. They certainly did not agree with everything, so they continued some of their childhood ideas, attitudes, interactions, or priorities and discarded others. Understandably, as they matured, they forged their own journeys and experienced new adventures. They passed through several rites of passage—graduation, marriage, and then childbirth. They retained values that had been cherished from childhood, combined them with those they had more recently acquired, and wove them with those of their spouses, and later their children. These created new yet at times similar values, lifestyles, and priorities.

What values did you glean from your primary family? Which of the following were most important: you and your siblings, relatives, and friends, or others in the community? Were caring, commitment, and respect for self and others, especially children, women, elders, and the most vulnerable, paramount?

Did your parents or caregivers cherish and believe in your worth? Was there a parent, grandparent, caregiver, teacher, clergy member, or neighbor who saw that unique, sparking star potential within you? Did they spur you on with unwavering encouragement to achieve what you never thought probable? Did parents or caregivers participate in school functions, meetings, and parent-teacher conferences? If not, was there anyone supporting you during your academic years? Did your parents live together, marry, or divorce? If they separated or divorced, did they positively pull together for your benefit, or did they constantly criticize the absent parent or attempt to tear you away from them? Or did you grow up living with a single parent, both parents, or in an extended family in a multigenerational setting? Were men role models, or were fathers present, absent, incarcerated, killed, or deceased? Were your parents straight or gay, young or old, and of different or the same religion and cultural heritage?

Were your parents mostly present, quick to respond when you needed it, and always looking out for your best interest? Or were they self-absorbed, off hanging out with friends, or absentee? Was your family mostly stable or unstable, and were there times when you were frightened because you didn't know who was going to take care of you? Was there a sense of cooperation, competition, or divisiveness among family members? Were any of your caregivers or siblings physically, mentally, or emotionally ill, addicted to opiates, alcohol, or narcotics, or have any other dependencies? Were they abusive to you, a sibling, or one another? Did you have a family member who had a genetic disability or debilitating sickness or was repeatedly undergoing cancer treatments, recovering from a terrible accident, war injury, posttraumatic stress syndrome (PTS), or traumatic brain injury (TBI)? Did those require extra care and patience, and did that seem to drain most of or all the energy of your family's primary caregiver? Or were you enlisted to be the main provider and be responsible for their physical, mental, and emotional needs?

Was your home a single- or multiple-unit dwelling in the inner city, barrio, hood, metropolis, or suburbs? Did you live on a farm with nearby neighbors? Did you live in a remote rural village surrounded by a loving family? Did your family use what was available, plan ahead, and become self-reliant and independent? Did you live on a reservation with extended family and honor the land? Was engaging in hard work and taking responsibility for one's own actions and attitudes meaningful, or were family members always looking for a handout from others or the government? Did they accept responsibility or point fingers and blame others when plans didn't work out as they thought? Did they have a sense of gratitude and make do with what was available? Or did they complain that there was never enough or look around to see and compare what others had? Were you surrounded by fear, famine, gun violence, terrorism, war, uncertainty, or oppression? Were power, status, wealth, possessions, acquisitions, tenacity, or resilience valued? Did they hoard or give generously? Were deeds genuine, superficial, or intended to self-promote?

Was there a sense of cooperation, competition, or divisiveness among family members? Did your family value conformity or individualism? Was your family always looking beyond to see what others had or were doing and then conforming to that, or did they remain true to their ideals? Were you often compared with others and asked or told, "Why can't you be like that person?" Were attitudes rigid either one way or the other, or were gray zones of moderation and flexibility the norm?

Did you get what you wanted when you wanted it, or did you have to wait until a later time or a special occasion? Did you pitch in to pay for a desired item or event? Was instant gratification encouraged, or were you directed to find other paths for happiness? Did you sense a basic structure, or was it chaotic? What type of discipline did you receive? Was it justifiable? If adults spanked you, was it to express their concern with the intention to lead you to a more productive path? Or did you feel the beatings were to release their frustration or anger?

Were health, diet, exercise, sports, culture, community service, and entertainment a part of your life? Were sports and games always played competitively, or were they also played for fun? Were you taught manners and an awareness of others? If food wasn't plentiful, were you taught to share? And if it was plentiful, did adults contribute to or work at food shelters or in some way donate so others didn't go hungry? Did you experience stoicism, survival, courage, honesty, pride, and modesty or shame, deceit, and guilt? Did your family praise kindness, intelligence, education, arts, reading, creativity, and travel or focus on status and possessions?

Were family meals usually eaten together? Did you wait for others, or did everyone help themselves or eat when they found the time? Were eating utensils chopsticks, skewers, tongs, toothpicks, cutlery, fingers, or a type of soft bread, and was food served on a plate, in a cup, on a leaf, or a stone? Was a woman or a man the main breadwinner, or were they both or equal contributors? Were chores and responsibilities shared fairly, performed by the one who had the time and was most capable, or based solely on gender or age? Was free time usually spent alone or together, engaged in enjoyable activities? Were the caregivers in your family punctual, mostly rushing to be on time, or perpetually late? Did they save money and put a portion away for a rainy day, or did they live from paycheck to paycheck and constantly have to catch up? Or did they have a choice to put some money away but still spent it all? Were cleanliness, outward appearances, or face-saving important? What were the political and religious beliefs in your home?

Our perception of the values of attitudes and actions of our primary family helped mold our value system. Yet as young parents, we often lack maturity and gain a steadfast desire to forge our own path. We may not think through or are unable to foresee the results of our actions or decisions. As we matured and our personality continued to evolve, we embraced or rejected certain values. Sometimes in our desire to run from our negative childhood memories, we focus on singular acts or negate entire experiences, yet we fail to isolate the positive values that we gleaned from what we perceived as a completely negative experience. If we want to create a standard for our children to be kind, charitable, appreciative, responsible, accountable, or exhibit other positive attitudes or deeds, we also have to reflect back on how our parents or caregivers instilled those or other highly regarded traits in us.

Yet we also learned negative values. In these problematic instances, we may have difficulty because those characteristics also became an integral part of us. Old, entrenched bad habits are often hard to break; the longer we bear them, the more challenging it is to alter or discard them. Years ago, even when I knew that I wanted to change an attitude or behavior to something more positive, it was challenging and required commitment and hard work. During that time, a friend shared that we find comfort in the familiar, even if it is negative. The negative behavior is a known—similar to a bad friend. We often hesitate to try something new because we don't know what the "new friend" will be like. It takes trust, courage, strength, and a willingness to risk and change direction, similar to walking on a frozen lake and not knowing where the thin ice begins. Hopefully, when the time feels right, we will take that leap of faith and hasten forward to encourage our best.

Our primary families also shaped the positive and negative communication patterns that we learned and carried into adulthood. Was communication in your home relaxed, guarded, bossy, argumentative, mostly withheld, or silent? Did anyone in your primary, extended, or multigenerational family listen to and comfort you? Did they communicate strength and understanding, or were they fearful and aggressive? Did they bully one another? Did they acknowledge your feelings, values, and attributes, or did they dismiss, discount, or sugarcoat them? Or did they cut you off, change topics, or put you down? Did you feel cherished, worthy, loved and that you mattered for just being you, and how did they express that? Did they make you feel you were the most important person in the world when they were with you? Or did they express love only when you made them proud, excelled in academics, sports, or music, or responded to their demands and needs?

Were you honored and supported to create your own path in reaching your fullest potential, or were you deftly persuaded to live under a pretense of making choices and decisions while living up to the path that mirrored their role in the community? How spontaneously was love conveyed? Was it part of the tradition with formal "Good morning" and "Good night" greetings, and were you, the child, the one who they expected to initiate the endearing message? Was it assumed that providing necessities were the only means of expressing love? Were parents or caregivers affectionate with you and one another in expressing their love and endearments, both nonverbally with hugs, kisses, gifts, or tokens of appreciation and verbally with "I love you" or similar expressions? Were compliments given to add to your feelings of self-worth and self-esteem? Or did they leave you with an emptiness by neglecting to convey that they cared? Did they patiently explain when you didn't understand and try to take steps to help you seek solutions, or did they use words to imply you were lazy, stupid, or disgusting? Did they take responsibility, or did they yell at you, beat you, blame you or others, or find excuses when things went wrong? Did anyone question, "Why me?" or "What did I do?" How did family members react in these situations? Did they share feelings with you, or did they withhold them and keep them to themselves? Did you get a warm sense of connection and belonging, or did you feel abandoned, isolated, lonely, and rejected, often on the outside longingly looking to be let in? Some of these formative occurrences that you faced as a child may continue to daunt or boost your self-worth, attitudes, and communication patterns as an adult.

Were adults open to others' views, rigid, or highly invested in being right? Was there an adult who insisted on having their own way, doing what they wanted when they wanted? If so, were they frustrated or angry when their plans were interrupted? Were issues fairly resolved in respectful discussions during regular family meetings? Was each member, young and old, allowed an equal say and encouraged to question or suggest? Or was one adult the self-proclaimed ruler—the *benevolent dictator*? Were consequences consistently and fairly doled out? Did each member praise those who deserved it and rally around those who needed the extra boost? Or were there some who withheld their support?

When our children were growing up, there was lots of love for all three of them. Unfortunately, there also was tension and arguing. As with many marriages, both husband and wife had observed and learned disagreeable communication patterns and rigid gender roles from their parents' interaction with each other. Young couples often lack maturity, insights, skills, or the courage to change. These changes require compassionate and supportive dialogue with willing family members, spouses, or partners. However, in some families, meaningful conversations are rare. Some family members speak only about the necessities and keep their feelings to themselves. Other families spend lots of time sharing and discussing everything in minute detail, revealing their days' events. For others, comfort is somewhere between.

Often, a strong competitive streak exists among children of small or large families. Mealtime is not only a time to carve and eat food but also a time to carve out a place to be heard. Mouths are often as busy spitting out words as they are hastily swallowing food. Each child has to speak rapidly or interrupt their siblings' talk time to get a word in. These children rarely learn to be good listeners. As adults, they are more interested in getting their point across than listening to others. Immediately after posing a question, before the other person completes the answer, they bring up a new topic or add that something they are doing is bigger, better, or more expensive. Sometimes, it is totally opposite in large or small families, as members listen and express care and concern with siblings. Because there was no one to listen or respond to the feelings of, some kept their thoughts, feelings, desires, or needs to themselves. As adults, they maintain privacy, keep their own council, and fear intimacy, as it may be difficult to gain trust that someone will always be there to listen, care, or acknowledge their feelings, ideas, and concerns.

In some families, parents resent the responsibility of raising children, so they mostly "do their own thing." They may use video games to occupy their children's minds. Others react by playing the martyr role, pouting when outcomes don't go their way, degrading others, or holding their anger. Some people shout and blame others when they are under duress. This only creates discomfort and adds to the stress, which ultimately affects the family in various forms. When a person is upset, they may use the "silent treatment" and not speak to their spouse, partner, or child. Not having the maturity or wisdom to comprehend the situation, a person, especially a child, may feel confused or unnecessarily blame themselves.

In each instance, inappropriate, harmful, hurtful communication patterns reflect negative or inadequate feelings. Consequently, children do not pick up positive and effective communication patterns that are essential to resolve life's challenges or fulfill personal needs.

In some ways, we give our children what we yearned for but never received, thinking that is what they desire or require. In doing so, we often fail to look at what is necessary, meaningful, and wished by each child. Our giving may also reflect the experiences, possessions, or care we felt were lacking in our childhoods. We may overreach in indulgence or involvement, sincerely believing that they benefit our children. Although that overreach fills a void within us, our children often want something entirely different. The sad truth is that the cycle often perpetuates itself from generation to generation.

A person felt her mother was not involved in her activities as a child and postponed a career path until her children were older so she could participate in many activities with them. Another person's immigrant parents deeply supported her as a person, but although she excelled academically, they expressed very little interest in her studies. Later, with the support of her husband, she chose a career path and became quite successful. When her children grew up, she took extreme interest and supported their every step and success with pride. To her surprise, shortly after graduation, her daughter exclaimed, "You are always hovering."

Another person, who grew up in poverty, worked hard and excelled in his career, providing the family with financial comfort, but not with much personal time to participate in family activities. His son grew up feeling neglected, so as an adult he carved out a lifestyle that provided financial comfort but also allowed ample time to participate in many weekly activities with his family. Another person who felt homely as a child often told her daughter that she was beautiful. At one point, her daughter told her, "You say it so often it becomes meaningless."

I will share my own communication stories. Half my lifetime ago, through psychoanalysis, introspection, reading, prayer, teaching, and learning from my husband, children, students, clients, and friends, I took my first steps toward communicating more positively in personal situations than I had as a younger, less mature adult and parent. In my midforties, as a speech and communication consultant, I had the transformative experience of working with people from all walks of life and forty different cultures in the field of personal and intercultural communication. Many of them trusted me with their deepest and often long-held thoughts as they learned to communicate more positively, effectively, and comfortably in their new personal and professional surroundings and U.S. homeland. These experiences deeply enriched my understanding of their family's and community's acceptable styles for communicating positively, effectively, and appropriately and expressing differing worldviews of various cultures and situations.

During one of my first lectures to a group of physicians from Korean and Russian cultures, I presented the insights and tools to communicate positively and lovingly with their families. A male physician from Russia who was Jewish asked, "Ruth, do you always talk as nicely with your family as you speak with us?" I responded honestly, "No, but from now on I will try even harder." Although I don't always hit the mark, I know when I've missed. There are countless times when I can respond negatively but I hold my remarks.

Before we move to the next finger in the *hand-dome*, let me share this final loving story. Over recent years, we have enjoyed spending time with friends and their young twin boys, now nine years old. Their father teaches them that they each are the most vital person in each other's lives. He asks them daily, "Who loves you the most? Who is always there for you? Whom can you turn to all the time? Whom will you always be there for?" And each time one twin shouts the other twin's or his own name. The father began teaching his sons before they were four years old. If he continues, this twin connection serves to lay a lifelong trust.

Fourth Finger in the Hand-Dome:
The Values and Communication Style of Our Primary Culture

In the *hand-dome*, the fourth finger represents the values and communication style of our primary culture, region, or neighborhood—often called the hood or village—where we grew up. Some values and experiences that I present may be totally foreign and hard to fathom. They are included to offer new insights to help you gain broader awareness of the values and the experiences your family, friends, neighbors, students, patients, clients, colleagues, or staff may have encountered. This is pivotal as we continue to evolve into a more diverse and global society. In the near future of the United States, the combined minorities will be the majority.

Let's begin the inquiry and insights about your background. On which continent were you born, and what is your cultural heritage? Was it in the Northern or Southern Hemisphere, a large or small country, or part of an archipelago? Did you live in a city, on a farm or reservation, in the mountains, or in a desert, or by a body of water? Were the changes in the seasons subtle or extreme? Was the air you inhaled fresh and invigorating or polluted and oppressive? Did you live in an impoverished country, struggling out of severe poverty and experiencing the effects of colonialism, communism, or economic downturn? Or was it progressing toward or thriving in prosperity? Did your country emerge through nonviolent means to gain its freedom from a colonial power to become the largest democracy in the world? Was your country governed by royalty, dictators, terrorists, theocrats, oligarchists or seized in a coup, or were there leaders who evoked decency, integrity, morality, and leadership skills declared in honest, fair, and free elections?

Were elections manipulated to purposely create obstacles for minorities and limit their lawful participation in the process? Were election processes corrupted, enabling foreign governments to hack information, which was modified and disseminated to influence the electorate? Could any citizen aspire to become a leader, or only males of certain status? Could every citizen participate and easily vote—regardless of gender, socioeconomic or education level, religion, caste, or skin tone? Was the polling place easily accessible? Were polls open long enough to ensure that everyone had the time and opportunity to vote before or after work and on weekends so they were not penalized for missing work? Was voting day declared a holiday to make it easier for every citizen to exercise their rights? Was it necessary to present documentation such as a birth certificate, driver's license, or wedding certificate of seventy years ago, and was this a hardship for those elderly citizens who never drove or couldn't locate their papers? Was transportation readily available for elderly and *handi-abled* individuals to help them reach their polling place? Or was voter suppression or disenfranchisement in play? Did your state or district accept firearm registration but reject student university registration? Were health care, education, protection, and basic needs equally provided to everyone by your country? Was education free, easily accessed, or just for the privileged? Did you feel that you were treated equally?

Did people believe in a higher power, prayer, karma, the universe, nature, or self to help heal? Were healers doctors, acupuncturists, shamans, tribal elders, homeopaths, or naturopaths? Did families use home remedies, plants, herbs, massage, or laying on of hands to get well? Or was Western medicine and pharmaceuticals the preferred intervention? Were walk-in health-care community clinics nearby, and were they staffed by warm, comforting, competent health-care providers readily available around the clock or only during set hours? And were consultations, medicine, and treatment affordable or free? Did the staff offer comfort and converse with you in an understanding and accepting manner? Did they make you feel relevant? Or were they condescending, adding to your sense of unworthiness? Were members of the medical team easily understood, and did they respect your culture, style, and lingo? Were nurses and teachers highly respected?

What were the living situations of your early childhood? Did you live in a primitive, remote village in a well-structured hut? Did you sleep in a tepee or tent under the stars, or did you live a nomadic life in the desert, often experiencing thirst or fear of starvation? Did you live in a First Nation culture, where tribal members respected the natural resources gifted by the Universe? Had they lived there for centuries and now faced extinction or pollution? Were these conditions in response to laws and deeds of governing bodies other than your tribal elders? Did you live among the high mountain peaks at the rooftops of our planet and walk the icy mountain roads? Was your home a circular igloo handcrafted of ice blocks in the winter, similar to the insulation of kiln-baked bricks in warmer climates? Did you live in a hermitage amid serenity? Did you reside in a shanty town, a crack house, a homeless shelter by railroad tracks, or under a bridge? Did you live in a crowded, filthy, run-down, rat-infested tenement owned by a slumlord, or in a sea of devastation? Did you live in the jungle under a thatched roof? Was shelter created from natural resources nearby? Were your shelters constructed with cloth, hide, clay, straw, used corrugated boxes, or metal scraps?

Did you live in an archipelago, on the bayou, where your Acadian ancestors developed a special and deep sense of community, or the Carolina Sea Islands, where your African ancestors created a proud, robust Mullah culture? Did you live in a community that rebuffed all modern electrical influences, drove carriages rather than cars, and didn't allow computers in their homes?

Was your neighborhood lined with rows of cement blocks, or bricks in well-maintained projects that were spruced up with a few colorful plants? Were walls of concrete enhanced by street art or mural landscapes that were either free-form or colorfully depicted the positive or negative aspects of the local culture? Or did others deface buildings and walls with obscene graffiti to mark their territory? Did you have fun running through city sprinklers in the summer heat? Were public swimming pools nearby?

Was your home a house, condominium, an apartment complex, or high-rise that was well-constructed and complied with current safety codes? Was that located on a farm, in a town, in an inner city, a metropolis, or a suburb lined with sidewalks, trees, and flora? Did you reside in a modest home that was pleasant, tidy, and comfortable in a blue-collar neighborhood squeezed together on small lots? Did children play outside or inside at one another's homes or yards? Did you live in a moderate-size home with large-enough lots for gardens, swimming pools, or spas? Did children play outside and with one another, or were they rarely visible? Did you live in a home crowded with extended family where all pitched in? Did you reside in a gated community, in a large, spacious home with heat, air-conditioning, running water, power, and clubhouse that served as a gathering place for the elite? Or did you live on an estate in a mansion equipped with state-of-the-art gadgets that digitally monitored functions for your comfort? Was it lavishly furnished with amenities, and did it provide ample grounds for swimming pools, tennis courts, guest homes, stables, putting greens, or golf courses? In any of these above locations, did people tend to keep to themselves or join in the community, and did folks greet strangers? Did you experience our national shame of homeless individuals nearby or as you exited the freeway? Did neighbors attend to their pets' droppings? Did folks stop and urinate on the curb?

Did you live among people of similar privileged socioeconomic backgrounds? Did many people suffer from "affluenza," or did they play by the rules, appreciate their wealth, and help others? Were there safe, well-maintained parks equipped with kept-up playground equipment, swimming pools, and clean restrooms with functioning toilets within walking distance from your home? Did parents, caregivers, friends, and children gather after school and on weekends to enjoy one another? Did children spontaneously play in yards or streets or have playdates that were always supervised, or did young siblings take care of one another?

Was food in your neighborhood, region, or country abundant, or was it rationed or scarce? Could you purchase a variety of healthy, fresh foods that were familiar and used in preparing the meals that you enjoyed at similar costs to those in neighboring communities and surrounding suburbs? Did people on your reservation, farm, neighborhood, or village go to bed satisfied, or hungry and cold? Was looking out for your siblings the bedrock value, or was it each child for themselves? Were you affected by famine, natural disasters, pollution, epidemics, pandemics, or nuclear accidents? Were tribes, clans, or religious sects always vying for power and fighting with one another, or did they cooperate and encourage reciprocity and equal benefits?

Did you encounter civil war, or were you victimized by aggression, gun violence, terrorism, or war from other groups or countries? Did your country initiate wars or readily come to the aid of others when help was required, or both? Did it get involved, remain neutral, participate in, or turn a blind eye to a lack of human rights and injustice? Were the returning soldiers who had gone to war to protect and fight for you and your country embraced? When they returned home, did they receive the help, care, support, and education they deserved from the community and country? Or except for family members or comrades, were they abandoned or left pretty much to fend for themselves after the welcome-home fanfare faded away? Were the mind-sets in your neighborhood mostly individualistic, inclusive, tribal, or terroristic? Did the people of your culture tend to be punctual, rushing to be on time, or perpetually late? Did you sense civility, awareness, and concern for others at school, medical settings, gathering places, or houses of worship?

Did people typically save their money and put a portion away for a rainy day, or did they live from paycheck to paycheck or fall deeply in debt to keep up with others? Or did they have a choice to put some money away but still spent it all? When a natural disaster, tragedy, or local, national, or international crisis occurred, did they turn their backs, or did they open their hearts, homes, and wallets or donate time and energy to aid others? Were immigration policies fair and just?

Did families work together and help raise one another's children, pitch in to build homes, plant and harvest crops, live in the same yard, and serve from the same pot? Or was it mostly each person and family for themselves, or somewhere between, including backyard greetings and help when needed? Did you sense respect for one another, elders, youth, or everyone? Did you belong to a service organization, youth, leadership, or religious group, or gang or terrorist group? Were sports, music, art, drama, or after-school enrichment offered in your schools? Were you limited by your place in society or offered the opportunity to improve the quality of your life? Did equality exist between girls and boys, or did the males receive preferential treatment and perform fewer chores?

Was family, work, education, cleanliness, diet, power, status, strength, individualism, conformity, bravery, courage, survival, or punctuality important? Were honesty, kindness, tolerance, beauty, intelligence, religion, sports, travel, community service, or personal time ideas and values that you learned? Did you primarily gain values from your elders, peers, school, church, synagogue, mosque, sangha, on the streets, or in the great outdoors? Did you pick up information from newspapers, radio, television, social media, smartphones, computer, or chats or gossip? Was gender equality practiced, or were women viewed as inferior? Was womanizing a way of life? Were parents in monogamous relationships totally committed to each other, with or without the formality of marriage? Were marriages arranged, or could you choose your spouse or partner? Was polygamy practiced in your community? After also holding part-time or full-time jobs, did women remain home at night, performing all the household chores and child-rearing responsibilities, while the men met at the local square, plaza, pub, or bar to socialize and have fun?

Were people fearful of gangs, civil unrest, gun violence, authority, government, or terrorism? Did you live in an area where drive-by shootings were so prevalent that your family was grateful at the end of every day that everyone was home safe? Was a family member or friend wrongfully murdered or unfairly incarcerated? Were you or was anyone you knew sexually harassed, abducted, raped, or sodomized? Were you or was anyone you knew held for ransom, a subject of human trafficking, sold to serve as a maid or wife, or forced to provide sexual pleasures to others? Were you or was anyone you knew sexually harassed or violated by a family member? Was there a parent, caregiver, clergy member, or public servant that you felt you could turn to for help, justice, and healing? Or were you wrongfully shamed or made to feel guilty and bear the burden silently within, squarely on your own fragile shoulders?

Did family members or friends help you, and did your community enjoy a tightly knit sisterhood or brotherhood that helped and supported one another during times of crisis or need? Or did you navigate your hardships alone or with help of a higher power or other force beyond? Was it more prestigious to go to jail than college? Was having your own baby in your teens—without marriage—meaningful to you and your friends? Were you expected to drop out of school to help support the family? Did people in your community have numerous children, anticipating that some children would not have the basics to survive past infancy or early childhood? Was face-saving critical? Did people misread your kindness for weakness? Were you perceived as a fool for not being strong or allowing people to take advantage of you? What were the predominant political and religious beliefs in your neighborhood?

Did family members or loved ones have to travel great distances for long periods to find jobs offering a decent wage to maintain a middle-class standard of living or help lift the family out of poverty? Were working conditions crowded, harsh, unsafe, polluted, or endured for long hours with limited benefits? Or did people work in buildings meeting strict safety codes under the strictest human rights conditions, working shifts within a reasonable length of time and taking mandated breaks during the day? Were they protected by health care, workers' compensation, or labor unions and provided time off for breaks or restorative vacations? Did you live in a village where you saw miners, who earned a pittance at a great peril, descend deeply to underground caverns to extract stones that became expensive baubles to adorn the rich? Were the streets or boulevards in your neighborhood lined with sidewalks, green trees, and scents of fragrant flowers that changed color with the seasons? Or were the streets in your neighborhood dangerous, drab, potholed, lined with gray concrete, abundant with dead rodents, and reeking of rotting garbage and decay?

Did you see yaks climb in very high altitudes, llamas with their long necks and warm, cuddly coats, or camels chew their cud as they caravanned across the desert? Or did you live in a town similar to Cateura, Paraguay, which was established to collect trash but became famous? There, Fazio Chavez, one of Cateura's citizens who was an ecological environmentalist, had an epiphany. So he decided to create musical instruments from the trash and teach the children to play the instruments. This eventually gave birth to the now-renowned Recycled Orchestra.

Was the air quiet, or did you hear balmy breezes blowing through the trees, howling wind across a plain, or voracious tornadoes barreling down? Or did you enjoy sounds of children's laughter, adults' chatter, music playing, birds singing, roosters crowing, donkeys braying, sheep baaing, or buffalo stampeding? Did the din include droning traffic, honking horns, screeching brakes, thundering trucks, or terrifying and random but familiar gunshots, rockets, bombs, or explosions? Did sirens pierce the noisy night with accompanying screams of terror and agony in response to attacks? Did you or family members feel that law enforcement was friend or foe? Did you, your family members, or your neighbors carry a registered or unregistered weapon, either openly or concealed, to feel safe?

If you grew up in the inner city or a war-torn country lined with rubble, acting tough and having "street smarts" may have played a monumental role in keeping you safe or even alive. In the inner city, toughness takes on a special meaning. A student once told me, "If I didn't have 'attitude' on the streets, I would have had the 'shit beaten out of me.'" A classmate added, "If I didn't act tough, my sister wouldn't be alive today." When I asked these youths, "What is special and good about you?" the response was often, "I'm alive, not dead." At that time, I never heard nor thought I would hear similar comments from children in other parts of our country.

Your neighborhood influenced your values and communication style as much as the country and region in which you lived. Did you feel you belonged to those people who shared the hills, rivers, mountains, woods, streets, parks, sidewalks, cul-de-sacs, or garbage with you, or did you look at your neighbors and ask yourself, "Do I really belong here, and do I matter here?" Did you ask yourself, "Am I worthy or adequate?" Or did you question, "Is this neighborhood worthy of me?" Was your family the first or among the first of your cultural heritage, religious background, sexual orientation, or political leaning to live in your neighborhood? If so, were you treated with kindness and respect and asked to join in, or did you sit on the sidelines and feel isolated or excluded? Did you feel any nuanced or blatant stereotyping, discrimination, or racism from neighbors, health-care providers, merchants, or teachers due to your socioeconomic or cultural heritage or accent or attire? Did you have access to the same healthy and organic food as those living in communities near your home?

Were day care centers in your neighborhood staffed with caring, knowledgeable, loving people who not only took care of basic hygiene and physical demands but also provided nutritional, well-balanced, and tasty meals? Was the environment a place where learning was fun and youngsters attained the essential skills necessary to give them a solid foundation and fair chance in life? Were those centers easily affordable or provided by the government, or did people make tremendous sacrifices so that their children could attend? Did you attend school in a one-room schoolhouse where they taught all grades, or in a drab, older, graffiti-ridden building in the inner city? Or was your school located on spacious, green, manicured grounds lined with lots of shade trees?

Were your teachers dedicated, inspiring, passionate, and supportive? Did they make learning fun, desirable, and interesting, or did they begrudgingly drag themselves into the classroom, bringing a sense of despair, exhaustion, frustration? Did your teacher need to provide basic school supplies, or did the system provide you with adequate, current, and necessary school supplies and learning materials? Did you enjoy state-of-the-art computer equipment, auditoriums, gymnasiums, performing arts centers, and science labs? Were positive and educational programs offered free for additional after-school enrichment and participation?

Did your parents or others in the neighborhood mostly work at home, did they commute long hours to reach their place of employment, or was their construction site, factory, hospital, office, or school an easy jaunt? Did they cycle, carpool, or walk, or were they chauffeured? Was rapid public transportation readily available, or did their commute require wasted hours bogged down on freeways—often in bumper-to-bumper traffic? Did your parents or others in the neighborhood take a ferry, paddle a boat, walk through the woods, or ride a horse or in a donkey-drawn cart?

Or did they commute by bus, subway, train, trolley, helicopter, or commercial or private plane? Again, these and various other factors left an indelible imprint that later influenced and motivated you to accept, alter, or reject those familiar lifestyle patterns and values. When the values of the culture, region, and neighborhood were similar to those of your primary family, there is an overlap. In these instances, the values are usually even more firmly ingrained and more challenging to overcome.

Our primary culture also shaped the positive and negative communication patterns that we learned and carried into adulthood. In small towns scattered across United States, especially in the South, the pace is often slower than in metropolises throughout the country. In slower-paced U.S. communities, you stroll instead of rush at a feverish pace. In small towns, people take time to pause, greet, and chat with one another. Small talk usually begins the conversation before a person takes care of business. This type of communication is also more personal, as people are often more familiar with one another and families have often known one another for generations. Even in a rapid metropolis such as New York, or a commuter city such as Los Angeles, you can always make the time to chat with the merchants whose shops you frequent and begin to build relationships and a sense of community.

Did you grow up in a culture where people didn't ask questions, never said no, or dismissed or discounted the youth? Did you have your place in society, and were you usually identified by your family, role, or station in life? Did people acknowledge your feelings and allow you to positively express yourself, or did they teach you to be strong, silent, and stoic? Was affection expressed nonverbally with hugs, kisses, tokens, or gifts, or verbally, with a form of "I love you," or not expressed at all? Were compliments an embarrassment, appreciated, or considered haughty? Were questions answered patiently, or was it assumed you would find answers yourself? Did people speak loudly or in a confrontational manner, or were they civil, quiet, or reserved? Did you live in fear of shaming your loved ones or your community?

Decades ago, my husband had been listening to the news following the uprising in Los Angeles. A high school student who lives thirty miles away in the inner city of Los Angeles spoke with a reporter. My husband said, "It's hard to believe that the student and I live in the same city. In reality, we live in vastly different worlds." Just the fact that "uprising" is called *riot* in some parts of town and *disturbance* or *civil disobedience* in another is culturally significant and again demonstrates vastly different perceptions of the same incident. That deeply divided disconnect between one community and another within the same city or town persists. This was loudly expressed in response to a grand jury's decision pertaining to the death of Michael Brown in Ferguson, Missouri, in 2014. That divisiveness again "reared its ugly head" in response to the tragic, wrongful-choke-hold death of Eric Garner in Staten Island. The deep, polarized division also loudly manifested itself in the political arena of the 2016 presidential election cycle.

Some of these events were deeply embedded and became enduring memories that can replay vividly in your mind. Values and communication patterns that you learned, adopted, and integrated may still appear in the manner you express yourself. As you matured and your own personality developed, you further embraced, altered, or rejected those values or communication patterns. Even when you want to reject what you learned, it may be difficult because those values have become such an integral part of you. These feelings and values that you learned from your childhood community and country also became a part of your sense of self and influence how you perceive others. They informed the way in which you created your value system.

During my personal and professional life's path and adventuresome travels, many people, strangers, teachers, patients, clients, and friends from all walks of life and from countless differing cultures and experiences continue to share their life's stories. To enlighten you, here are some events and experiences that profoundly struck me.

A physician from Vietnam shared memories of her marriage. When they notified her at the hospital that she had two hours to board the plane and leave Vietnam, she left with only the possessions she had with her; the photo album of her marriage remained behind. Many others lost far more, often a temporary or permanent connection with their families and loved ones. A physician who arrived from Africa had to work as a janitor at McDonald's because no one believed that he was a physician until his papers arrived. He couldn't even get a menial job in a drugstore. A friend from Central America said her children had to adjust to the quiet, yet safer, night sounds of traffic without the sirens and explosions that had been their norms. They often asked, "Where are the guns?"

As an attorney became more aware of his *hand-dome*, he noted his special traits were sensitivity and concern for others and that he valued feeling carefree and having fun. At a deeper level, he also realized that he despised confrontation. His retention of spoken words was poor, so he lacked a major skill necessary in litigation. In addition, he recognized that to feel more masculine, he had completely suppressed his sensitivity. He finally understood why he felt numb most of the time and had difficulty communicating with others. He had nullified his most dear and special quality—sensitivity. When we began to work together, he communicated in a stiff, formal, and apathetic manner. At thirty-seven, he resembled a sullen man in his sixties. His facial expression, limp appearance, and flat voice tone expressed no concern or enthusiasm, suggesting he lived a harsh life. One day, he proclaimed, "I'm existing, not living."

In his spare time, he found little enjoyment by spending hours watching television. Without additional cost, he took down his bike from the ceiling hooks and began cycling, walking, and spending more time with his wife. He had fun riding his bike with her, and she thoroughly enjoyed the additional time, attention, and activity with him. He embraced his sensitivity, made significant positive changes, and spent more leisure time enjoying activities he thoroughly liked. Living more closely to his core values and attributes, he gained confidence, became more genuine, and communicated in a self-confident, relaxed manner that reflected the facial expressions of an assured and comfortable thirty-seven-year-old person.

An embarrassed human resources director of a major insurance company sought help for a very competent, computer-literate employee from Honduras. While sitting at his computer, he responded to the regional vice president's question, "I am not going to show you what I do. Your breath stinks. Go do something about it." While consulting with him, I learned that from the time he was eight years old until he illegally entered the United States, he grew up on the streets in Honduras with other youths his age. When they picked up strong body odors from their peers because they lacked the opportunity to bathe or wash their clothing, they used condescending language to convey that they cared. I taught him that language that was appropriate on the inner-city streets in Central America was definitely not appropriate in corporate U.S.A. with a regional vice president—or anyone else. My client quickly asked me, "Do you want me to lie?" I said, "Of course not. Just learn to say what is necessary, learn how to say it positively, and keep other thoughts to yourself."

When I visited a classroom of students from low-opportunity areas, the teacher conveyed that she suspected that the new students had defaced the building. This was quite disturbing, as the classroom was held in a well-kept mini mall. She said, "Once the students buy into our alternative school program, they take ownership and assume responsibility. With pride, the students begin to take interest in keeping the classroom and property clean. But until they are invested, they often deface the building, desks, and room." I explained the insights of the last finger in the *hand-dome* and asked, "If the students' homes and neighborhoods are defaced, dirty, or littered without explanation, how would they understand that the rules of the new school in a new neighborhood are different from what they are accustomed to?" As similar situations arose, she explained the different standards to the students. They responded positively, making it more pleasant for everyone.

Years ago, a documentary on PBS presented the point that in some areas, it isn't "cool" to carry books home or do well in school. This created a perception that you wanted to be better than your peers. There also was a fear of losing the identity of your African or Latino heritage. Then, in some neighborhoods, it was more prestigious to go to a notable prison than a community college, state university, Ivy League, or top ten university. A physical therapist shared that she had grown up in a neighborhood where kids made fun of her and called her a teacher's pet because she was a good student. I asked, "How did you overcome the taunting?" She said, "With my mother, there was no choice—you just did well in school. My brother and I are the first and only college graduates of our generation in our family, even among our cousins."

Twenty-five years later, we continue to grapple with similar perceptions and results, though they may not be quite as profound. With continued concern and a broader coalition of and inspiration from leaders and celebrities, there are rapidly evolving innovative methods to reach and teach. A plethora of new emerging paradigms, programs, and ideas is at the core of improving our exponentially growing diversity and educational demands. These include focus on standards, accountability, and uplifting youth of minority or *lesser-opportunity* backgrounds. Distant learning, stronger demand, and compulsory student and parent cooperation play a significant role in helping students reach their given potential. An example of such a program is the Hidden Genius Project. More information may be found at http://hiddengenius.org.

A continuing challenge is a fair assessment and evaluation of students' and teachers' performance. Bill Gates has put his time and expertise to find a viable system for teacher evaluation, student performance, and fairly measuring improvement. In 2013, Gates stated that while we (the

US) spend more money on education than any other country, our results are "poor" (Gates 2013). He added that certain features, such as making good use of time in the classroom, making learning interesting, and addressing the needs of those students who are behind and who are ahead, serve as good indicators of effective teaching.

A program on PBS called *Science Genius* highlights teaching students in the inner cities and lesser-opportunity neighborhoods to create a rap or hip-hop song pairing science terms with music. One student sat with his arms crossed, resting on his desk, as his head peered out from his hoodie. He clearly expressed the disconnect and boredom he felt in his New York science class. Once the teacher explained pairing hip-hop and rap with the science terms to create one's own song, he emerged so energized that he couldn't wait to get home after school. He created his own music, utilizing the scientific vocabulary in a way that he could grasp and explain it. He grew so confident that he exuberantly explained his desire to attend college and become a scientist (https://genius.com/artists/science-genius). This experience resonated with memories of the 1960s, when teachers in inner-city schools watched students' math scores rise as they connected the logic and angles of geometry with playing pool.

What remains deeply disturbing, however, is the stark contrast between the progress of academically elevating our students and the increasing proliferation of the doubly unjust profitable "school to prison pipeline system."

In our early years living in Nevis, Lee often spent four to six weeks in the United States while I remained in Nevis. During that time, I never felt alone. In those years, which were shortly after my second coronary bypass, one of our neighbors tended a small goat herd along with his full-time construction job. Before our friend left for work in the morning, he led the goats to pasture. If the bedroom shutters were still shut, he knocked on the living room door to see if I was all right. Years later, when the lights in our office were on late at night, his wife called to see if everything was okay. And on the other side of our home, if Lee and I were up late or the shutters were not open by 8:00 a.m., our other neighboring friends would call or knock on the door and ask, "Is everything okay?"

There was always a neighbor looking out for me or ready to chat. As I walked around the village, people whom I hadn't yet met greeted me in their delightful, melodic voices and engaged in conversation. To this date, people don't walk around using their cell phones but do use them in restaurants. It also was considered extremely rude not to greet a person or respond.

Years ago, that level of friendliness and concern was missing in our suburban Southern California neighborhood. Back then, while we walked the neighborhood or as we sat on our front porch, watching neighbors pass by, when we greeted "Good morning," "Good afternoon," "Good night," or "Hello," they often responded with a perplexed expression or silence. With the culture changing, younger generations moving in, and the teaching of civility in the classroom on the rise, that communication has thankfully improved, as now almost everyone either nods, responds, or initiates the greeting.

Consulting for thirty years in the field of personal and intercultural communication and during world travels, folks often asked me about the values and attitudes of people from other cultures. I respond by briefly explaining the *hand-dome*. Many people don't realize that each person from any given culture or religion, even an individual who is an identical twin, possesses their own special gifts and style that they alone offer to the world. Furthermore, each carries past experiences, values, and communication patterns from their primary family, neighborhood, and country, which affect each person differently. People often think that everyone from a specific group or culture is the same. They often ask, "What are the Chinese, Mexicans, Iranians, or Russians like?" I respond that each individual is different. Though they often share similar values and communication styles, each person has their own unique perception, approach, and response to life's events. Each individual from a specific culture or background is different from every other person, who also is of the same culture or background. Each person, rendered with singular qualities, walks their own path on their own time as they travel through life. Even when people try to mimic a style or manner, it is never identical. Each individual subtly or boldly imprints who they are with their one-of-a-kind declaration.

Each individual who belongs to the same group or religion either holds similar belief systems, remains different from one another, or is mysterious. Those who do not associate with organized religion but believe in a higher power remain singular. Therefore, they are different from others of the same belief. For as many people who believe in Christianity, there are that many different Christians. For as many people who believe in Catholicism, there are that many different Catholics; some adhere to certain dictates, but others do not. Some Catholics privately use artificial means of birth control, but others consider it sinful. For as many people who believe in Judaism, there are that many different Jews. Some Jews strictly adhere to keeping kosher, but others do not. Some folks of various followings touch those of opposite genders in public, but others do not. For as many people who believe in Islam, there are that many different Muslims. Some Muslims partake of alcohol, but others do not. Some Muslim women wear head scarves, and some do not. Some men wear head coverings in solidarity with their wives, who wear hijabs, but others do not. For as many people who believe in Sikhism, there are that many different Sikhs. Some wear turbans, but others do not. For as many people who believe in Buddhism, there are that many different Buddhists. Some live Spartan lives, rejecting unnecessary material possessions; others adhere to Buddhist philosophy yet enjoy material goods—most live somewhere between. For as many people who believe in Hinduism, there are that many different Hindus. Some people choose to display a shrine of many Gods in their homes, but others do not. For as many people who are atheists and do not believe, there are that many different Non-believers.

Some who are firm believers in their religion are peaceful and accepting of others; some are militant, intolerant of others' beliefs, and even willing to die or engage in mass murder or genocide for their convictions. Some are mindful of their own attitudes or behaviors and respond to life with compassionate recognition. Some focus more or solely on others' attitudes and behavior but are still compassionate. Some clearly see flaws in others but aren't mindful enough or lack courage to stop and look within to see if they also possess similar flaws. As within any group, some are righteous and caring people, concerned with others' welfare, while others primarily benefit themselves and their loved ones, failing to look out for anyone else—and the rest are somewhere between. As my grandmother often reminded me, "Every person makes up their own religion."

Different Responses from Each Facet of the Hand-Dome

As I previously mentioned, each time you respond, there is a complex integration of the five factors of your *hand-dome*. But only one factor plays the determining role in how you—and others—respond at the moment. Let's look at two persons' responses during a day. A man of Latino heritage wakes up in his usual pleasant mood. Early in the day, he speaks out at a staff meeting, while others are afraid to say what is on their minds. His unique pleasant and forthright style are represented in the thumb of his *hand-dome*. In the afternoon, he feels sad after learning of an illness in the family. His emotion, at the time, are represented in the first finger of his *hand-dome*. At a dinner meeting, he sits quietly and somberly as he listens to the dismal numbers report on raising money for a charitable organization. He recalls a previous successful outcome when he served as chairman of a charity fundraiser, so he volunteers again. His positive response reflects a previous fruitful experience. His past experiences are represented in the second finger of his *hand-dome*. In the evening, at home before bedtime, he warmly hugs and kisses his child goodnight, which reflects a nonverbal communication tradition that he learned from his father. The values and communication style of his primary family are represented in the third finger of his *hand-dome*. His father spoke respectfully to his mother, yet this man often puts down his wife. This macho response was common among his peers in his childhood neighborhood. The values and communication style of his primary culture are represented in the fourth finger of his *hand-dome*.

In another case, a very bright, assertive, and usually even-tempered woman of Chinese heritage becomes an aggressive, daring, and a darting driver as she accesses the freeway. At work, she is a powerhouse, leading her team in a strong and decisive manner. She is well-liked and respected by her peers and often socializes with them. Her confident responses and capable style are represented in her uniqueness in the thumb of her *hand-dome*. Publicly, she displays a narrow range of emotions; yet internally, she encounters a broad range of deeply-felt emotions, which she doesn't feel she can express. In her role as a mother, she is usually very patient as she helps her children with their homework. But if she has had a stressful work day and is also dealing with extenuating taxing circumstances, she may abruptly scream at the family. Her emotions, at the time, are represented in the first finger of her *hand-dome*. When she returns home, she is respectful, often voices her opinion, and is somewhat subdued—though hardly as quiet and withholding as her mother was. During dinner, she responds to her husband of Asian heritage. Her somewhat submissive response mirrors the manner in which her mother spoke to her father. The values and communication style of her primary family are represented in the third finger of her *hand-dome*. She feels a strong obligation to help her invalid mother as she sends packages and transfers funds monthly to her aging family in China. Taking care of elders and family is an esteemed value she experienced as a child. The values and communication style of her primary culture are represented in the fourth finger of her *hand-dome*.

My husband and I had business with a former policeman, the son of a preacher, who had received three thousand letters of appreciation during his twenty-nine years of service on the police force. Conversing with him, I was struck that his communication style was quite different from many law enforcement officers with whom I had spoken. This officer was very spiritual and soft-spoken, and he exhibited none of the body language or condescending manner that I had occasionally heard from some other officers. He was clearly *source-connected*. I said, "I feel you are much more of the preacher's son than a former police officer." He replied that he always physically and spiritually consoled critically injured victims. While he tended to their pain and fear, he also suggested that if they believed in a higher power, they should begin to pray for help. The values and communication style that he learned from his primary family continued to be the predominating force in how he lived his life.

Two physical therapists who were equally competent reacted differently to their patients' needs. One therapist, born in the United States, lacked the patience to review treatment plans with patients' older family members. Contrarily, the other therapist was from the Philippines and enjoyed interaction with elders and spent as much time as necessary with them. When an irritated doctor called three times to speak to the physical therapist from the Philippines, she never returned his calls. When supervisors asked the physical therapist why she behaved that way, she responded that as a child she was taught to be respectful and somewhat fearful of doctors. She remained afraid, so she avoided returning the calls. Possibly, culture played a role in how both therapists responded in different situations. A caring nurse from Asia respectfully conversed with a patient. However, she didn't smile or maintain eye contact, and she mumbled. She did not ask a question when she was uncertain of a procedure. These responses are examples of the communication styles that reflect native culture represented by the fourth finger of the *hand-dome*.

Several people shared that they were surprised to discover that their ancestors were Jewish, as they had never been told. When an elderly woman learned that her mother was Jewish, she was quite upset that the information was withheld. She recalled that *telling the truth* was paramount in her childhood home. I suggested that she view the situation through the eyes of a seventy-year-old with wisdom and maturity and try to understand. While she felt her mother betrayed her, her mother was actually trying to protect her from any harm similar to atrocities that Jewish and other people had been subjected to during the Holocaust. A woman from Cuba shared that she thought her family was converso Jews who were expelled from Spain, possibly during the Spanish Inquisition. Her family had kept their Judaism very private when they immigrated to Cuba. As she embraced Judaism, she recalled certain familiar foodstuff and customs—void of religion or prayer—that she had witnessed as a child in her grandparents' home in Cuba.

A director of an intercultural consulting organization asked me, "Why did a person who supported affirmative action change his mind?" I said, "One factor in his *hand-dome* became more relevant than it previously was. Perhaps he was politically motivated, felt it was no longer relevant, or now thinks that affirmative action did more harm than good. You won't know unless you ask him. Even then, he may not be aware of the real reason or may not want to tell you what it is. The only thing you know for certain is that something has changed."

Some factors in your *hand-dome* are temporary, some permanent; others fluctuate or alter during your life. Your past experiences, values and the communication style of your primary family, native culture, and the community in which you grew up remain the same. But as you mature, evolve, and gain wisdom, you may view your past experiences through different eyes. It is similar to rereading the same book over the years. While the words are familiar, every read touches you differently, often offering new and enlightening perceptions. Life's attained enlightenment, perception, and encounters all affect you and are catalysts for change in your perception and response to life.

As you continue your journey and mature, you create greater autonomy for yourself, experience new situations and events, and join with new people, such as a roommate, friend, spouse, or partner. Chances are, you also relocate to new neighborhoods, states, or countries or change jobs. These positive or negative events alter your *hand-dome* and the way you feel, think, act, speak, and write. You may discover new attributes, abilities, and resilience that you never knew you possessed. Or you may face unexpected and unprepared-for limitations due to health, economic, personal, or professional changes, advances, or upheavals. These transitions can be for the better—or for the worse—if you let them. Remember, at each moment, we choose to respond positively or negatively and sensitively or insensitively. Likewise, we choose to honor or dishonor ourselves and others. These are our choices, and they are a formative facet of our character and aura. Even in the direst moments, you can choose to find gratitude and maintain self-respect.

Before we leave this section of the *hand-dome*, let me pause and share some more pertinent happenings that highlight the *hand-dome*'s teachings. During our years in Nevis, my husband and I invited numerous Nevisian friends to share Sabbath dinner. We also held annual Passover Seders and invited different people. Though a few friends often attended, one of our closest friends joined every Seder.

Lee and I thoroughly delighted in broadening our understanding while also sharing our stories. None of our Nevisian friends had ever attended a Passover Seder. At some level, our Jewish history parallels that of our Nevisian friends, whose descendants also endured harsh slavery. As the evening went on, we enjoyed the most lively, profound, enlightening, and lighthearted Seder discourses. Our friends' hope, resilience, positive attitude, and belief that they will always be okay continue to inspire me.

At a later Seder, our friend from Michigan, who had shared that she discovered later in life that her mother had been Jewish, related that her ancestors had changed their name to Carvalho when they left Spain in the late 1400s. Her husband came from Alsace-Lorraine, an area between Germany and France that was alternately governed by each country. His family name didn't change, but they did not know which spelling or pronunciation to use. My husband told the story that his great-grandfather, who had lived in Russia during the pogroms, was sent to Germany with stern warnings never to return to Russia. In Germany, a man who was named Fuhrman employed him, and he became the foreman of the man's business.

When Lee's ancestors arrived in America, similar to many Jewish immigrants, they changed their surname to Forman to sound less Jewish and more acceptable. He never discovered the family's original name. My family emigrated from Germany during the Nazi period. Before departing for America, they contemplated what new name to use when they arrived in the country. A family member noticed a linden tree at the corner (*ecke* in German), so they combined the two and created the name Lindeck to replace the Jewish-sounding surname Levy, and Lindeck became my maiden name. Many Jewish immigrants followed suit. One devout religious immigrant who had a Polish-Jewish-sounding name did not know what name to choose, so the immigration officer gave him the Irish name Kelly.

Many of our Nevisian friends also continued to share newly discovered details about their ancestral history. All our Nevisian friends carry the surname of their ancestors' plantation owners—not the names of their African lineage. Many younger Nevisians give their children African names. During slavery and colonial times, Nevis was the first point of entry in the Caribbean to drop off slaves from Africa. Even so, the ancestors of most of our friends came from other neighboring islands. One of our friends explained that after the end of slavery and the termination of the sugar plantations and rum manufacture, most of the Nevisian ancestors went to other Caribbean islands, England, or Canada in search of employment. His ancestors ended up in Trinidad, Panama, and Jamaica. Some of our Nevisian friends also had Jewish ancestors: some from Ethiopia, and others dating from colonial times, when Jews were primarily merchants and comprised 25 percent of the European population in Charlestown, the capital of Nevis.

Alexander Hamilton was born in Nevis, where he received his early formal education at the "Jew's School" (Ezratty 2002). After moving to St. Croix, he then left for New Jersey and then to New York to further his studies. Later, he became a member of the Continental Congress prior to becoming one of the Founding Fathers of the United States. Hamilton served as the first U.S. secretary of the treasury and established the national banking system. His picture is on the U.S. ten-dollar bill. Centuries later, in the Broadway musical *Hamilton*, he received much-deserved recognition for his lasting contributions.

If you really want to discover your deep, primal roots and research your journey forward from the African Eve, who was the mother of all *Homo sapiens* around 180,000 years ago, then go to National Geographic's website at https://genographic.nationalgeographic.com. The evidence states that every woman carries the same mitochondrial gene as every other woman—even the Maoris in New Zealand, who belong to an ancient South Pacific culture and formerly one of the most remote cultures in the world. This research brings you forward to about ten thousand years ago. Its findings led us to discover that the ancestors of one of our closest Nevisian friends (the same person who has shared each Seder with us) and my husband's ancestors traveled together in the same clan in Africa for twenty to thirty thousand years, in a journey that began sixty thousand years ago.

Alex Haley is the creator of the miniseries *Roots*. He said, "In all of us there is a hunger, marrow-deep, to know our heritage, to know who we are and where we have come from. Without this enriching knowledge, there is a hollow yearning. No matter what our attainments in life, there is still a vacuum, an emptiness, and the most disquieting loneliness" (Haley, n.d.). For more information on genealogy, let me also suggest www.ancestry.com and www.MySlaveAncestors.com. Besides genealogy, 23andme.com offers a more holistic approach, including health-related facts.

We have completed an understanding of how the five facets of your *hand-dome*, when integrated and applied, contribute to how you think, feel, act, speak, and write. The following charting of your *hand-dome* offers a unique, private, and personal inventory with a holistic summary, as no other tool provides. Shortly, you will have the opportunity to chart your own *hand-dome* diagram to give you a broader and more enriched appreciation of yourself and others.

Chart Your Own Hand-Dome

To achieve the most meaningful result from charting your own *hand-dome*, I created a specific and most beneficial path that provides the greatest insights and gains. As with anything worthwhile, the *personal inventory* takes time, forethought, and afterthought as you think through each facet and write down your thoughts in the thumb or appropriate finger. Before you actually begin to chart your *hand-dome*, you will first create your own inventory—similar to a blueprint. So please get a few sheets of eight-and-a-half-by-eleven-inch paper and title *Personal Inventory for My hand-dome* at the top of the first sheet. Please list the following five headings under the title: your thumb, first, second, third, and fourth fingers. Under each heading, please take your time and honestly reflect on the information. Then, place in the appropriate subheading. You are not providing information to or for anyone but offering yourself an honest reflection of who you are, so please suspend all judgment. The more honest you are with yourself, the more significant the gains from the realizations of your *hand-dome*. This leads to the best possible personal path forward for a more joyous, comfortable, productive, passionate, self-actualizing, and genuine self.

After you ponder each facet, you chart your *hand-dome* in an organized, pleasing fashion. The first heading of your personal inventory is your thumb that represents your uniqueness, limitations, challenges, and boundaries. The second heading is your first finger that represents your emotions. The third heading is your second finger that represents your past experiences. The fourth heading is your third finger that represents the values and communication style of your primary family. The final and fifth heading is your fourth finger that represents the values and communication style of your culture and the neighborhood in which you grew up. You also will separate the positive and negative aspects of each, then prioritize the frequency and impact where appropriate.

At each heading, pause and reflect for a while. When you are ready, write down your insights and thoughts and keep this list until you have completed it. Then, begin to create your own *hand-dome* diagram. For now, you are simply building your *personal inventory*.

Under the first heading, your *thumb* represents your uniqueness, boundaries, challenges, and limitations. Please think about the qualities that you inherently possess and that personify who you are—your gifts, talents, and passions. If there is nothing that excites you or creates passion at this time, do not fret about it. Sooner or later, you will find it, or it will find you—as Nevis found me—on universal time, as it was meant to be. Bring to mind your most positive special attributes, what brings you the greatest joy, and what is the dream that lights up your life to be fully engaged. This state promotes your self-worth, regardless if others find it useless or unworthy. Likewise, think about the negative thoughts that run through your mind—your repetitive *negative chatter* or any qualities or limitations that you feel adversely affect your interaction with others or your ability to achieve your potential. Ponder until you are ready, then note your positive gifts, talents, and passions. Also, note the limiting and negative features and the reasons they hold you back. Finally, note the positive aspects on top and the limiting ones below them.

Next, we move to the second heading, your first finger that represents your emotions. Take your time to consider and gather the full range of emotions that you experience. Are your feelings mostly positive, bright, sunny, and uplifting, and do your feelings advocate your well-being? Or are the feelings gloomy, sad, dark, or angry, and do they drag you down, detracting from your sense of well-being, self-worth, and serenity? Ponder until you are ready, then note the positive and negative emotions that you experience and place them in order. First, write the positive feelings on top and the negative feelings below them. Then, again reflect about each group and rate their frequency, most to least. After the reflection, place the most positive and most frequent emotions on top and the most negative and least frequent ones below them.

Then, we move to the third heading, your second finger that represents your past experiences. Think of all the monumental and life-changing events that left a huge mark on you. How did they alter, influence, or hinder you when forging a different or opposite approach or response in the future? Ponder until you are ready, then jot down the positive and negative events and place them in order. First, write the positive experiences on top, and then negative below them. Again, think through them and first place each positive, then negative experience based on their impact, top to bottom.

Continue with the fourth heading, your third finger that represents the values and communication style of your primary family. Which values were important, and how did you and others interact with one another? What was your role within your family, and how did you feel about your role and yourself? How did your family interact with other families in your neighborhood and community? Ponder until you are ready, then note first the values and then the communication style of your primary family and place them in order, the positive values and communication style on the top and then the negative ones on the bottom. Think through them and place the positive and negative values and communication style based on their impact, top to bottom.

Last is the fifth heading, your fourth finger that represents the values and communication style of your primary culture, neighborhood, village, clan, or tribe. What was considered imperative, and how did individuals and groups interact with one another? What was your role within your community? How did you feel as a member of your community, and how were you perceived? Ponder until you are ready, then jot down first the values and then the communication style of your primary culture, neighborhood, village, clan, or tribe and place them in order, positive on top and then negative on the bottom. After noting the values and communication style, reflect and place the positive values and communication style based on their impact, top to bottom.

Once you gain a clear understanding of the insights in your *personal inventory*, you begin to chart your own *hand-dome*. Throughout life, you continue to discover further significant insights about yourself and others of which you were totally unaware. Charting your *hand-dome* serves as a compelling, enlightening personal guide. The information presents a clearer, holistic view and greater understanding of why you feel, think, act, speak, and write as you do. Embrace your *hand-dome*; it reflects you.

Please refer to the illustration of the *hand-dome* diagram at the beginning of this chapter presented in a horizontal plane from left to right. As you begin to trace your hand for your personal *hand-dome* diagram on a new sheet of paper, place your hand in a vertical position, fingers at the top and wrist at the bottom. Spread your thumb and fingers as far apart as possible and include your wrist and as much of your arm as will fit. Then, copy in pencil the insights from your *personal inventory*, placing the information in the appropriate corresponding thumb or finger in the *hand-dome* diagram. Enjoy and embrace the process; it is fun, enlightening, and solely yours.

Years ago, when clients started to trace their own hand, some uttered something akin to "I haven't done this in a long time" or "This reminds me of kindergarten." Yet when they completed the information, many were wowed by the *hand-dome*.

As you place the words top to bottom inside the thumb and each finger of your *hand-dome* diagram, it is perfectly okay to write past the lines. If you run out of space, you can also continue to write past your wrist or at the side; this is your *hand-dome*, and no one will judge it. Once you have read the entire book and gained greater awareness after each chapter, jot the new awareness in your *hand-dome* so it is current for the moment. These contemplations continue to reflect new information and changes as our fluid lives continually emerge, at times soaring as high as birds in the sky or at other times sinking and shifting as grains of sand. As we age and monumental life events unfold, the *hand-dome* continues to be a comforting and reliable friend to help update our perception and reality as we form new responses to people and situations. As new realizations pop into your head, add them to your *hand-dome* diagram.

The *hand-dome* is a powerful tool for helping committed young couples gain a greater recognition of each other at the beginning of their journey. They glean how each perceives, prioritizes, and responds to the simple and complex—the desires, dreams, joys, needs, challenges, and demands that life presents. These insights elevate greater understanding of the value each places on themselves, the other, children, friends, extended family, work, leisure, community, religion, and social life. These further highlight how and where we spend time, resources, and funds, plus our physical, mental, emotional, and spiritual energy.

Update and Rechart Your Hand-Dome

As you begin to grasp the enormous benefits of these new discoveries that the *hand-dome* provides, you gain *trust* in its wisdom. It highlights the values and responses that you and others hold and informs you of those values and responses that are best to modify, replace, or discard, as they no longer serve you well. Perhaps in the past you were not fully aware of your negative communication patterns and their detrimental impact on others. You may also have lacked a method to create a personal, holistic, and candid inventory. Or possibly you were in denial or lacked the courage and will to kindly reflect and honestly look within yourself. But now you possess a new jewel of a tool to engage.

Our personal values and moral compass are always at the core of our essence. Some values we hold dear reveal who we are now, and they are an integral part of our core, our essence. Some values—honesty, kindness, empathy, sharing, community, and giving—are those we will always embrace and hold close to our hearts. Yet other values that we observed at an earlier age have always been uncomfortable and disingenuous. These principles, which we adopted during childhood or the not-so-distant past, now strongly conflict with what is authentic, meaningful, and true to who we want to be. Often, we remain unaware of this struggle until we have encountered life more independently, removed from the intense daily influences of our primary family or neighborhood. We may have tried to alter, avoid, or discard those values or ways to interact. Perhaps it was most often impossible to face in such a precise environment or situation. We either had to wait for or create the opportunity for positive personal change.

Besides examining our values, we need to look at how we interact with others and they with us. We need to include the facets of our nonverbal, voice tone, and verbal communication. Are the traits positive or negative, promoting or degrading, uplifting or demeaning? Are there distasteful patterns from early childhood, or did we pick up some obnoxious communication patterns to show off, act tough, play cool, express power, or push away?

If our facets of nonverbal, voice tone, and verbal communication come across negatively, our first impression will always be poor and not represent our worthy best. This certainly keeps us from reaching our highest potential and achieving our greatest happiness, fulfillment, and success in life. One of our most significant communication challenges is to change what is most debilitating to us and improve our communication style to project our *source-connected* best.

The second major communication challenge is the abusive impressions we leave when we disrespect, demean, or harshly express judgmental, misogynist, prejudiced, racial, sexist thoughts or slurs about and toward others. This is deeply disturbing and causes significant discomfort for them. These negative thoughts also create negativity within ourselves, which is also not conducive to our well-being. In either case, we bear the immense and impeding burden of our communication issues.

Negative communication patterns, along with physical, mental, emotional, or spiritual abuse, whether learned in the home or on the street, persist and are often perpetuated from generation to generation. Nothing changes until we become aware of and own these attitudes, behaviors, and habits. Once we are aware, care, and possess the courage and will, we decide, observe, and analyze. Then, one by one, we modify, replace, or discard these inferior or abusive patterns to make productive changes.

If you did not like the attitudes or interactions within your primary family, or with people in your native culture or community in which you grew up, please take inventory to see if you continued to mirror and follow some of those same destructive patterns. If you did not like the attitudes or manners in which people interacted with you or with one another and you continue to carry those same thoughts and use those same patterns, others may be offended by you. Again, as you mature and travel through life, you have the choice to own responsibility and change or remain as you are until you are ready to take that leap of faith and move forward. Let me remind you that even if we want to change, we are often reluctant and have reservations about the unknown. There is comfort in familiarity, even if it is negative and counterproductive to our best interest.

Since none of us human beings are always perfect, try as we might, we never *get it right all the time*. As our lives continue, there are events or people who will challenge our thoughts and values. When we come to that fork in the road, we are offered an opportunity to re-evaluate and decide whether we want to continue to hold those values or communication styles or whether the time is right to revisit, reconsider, modify, or release them. If so, we *erase* and *replace* the negative and embrace a thought, idea, or communication facet that positively serves self-worth and provides comfort and trust with others. (The *Identify, Block, Move, Delete, Replace (IBMDR) Technique* is presented in the following the chapter, "*Personal Lenses*.")

How we honor ourselves, treat our loved ones, view our religious beliefs, spend money, prioritize time, and engage in activities that we treasure is based on values that are important to us. For example, at a presentation, a high-ranking university educator shared a thought. "If you are unhappy with where you are headed, rather than continue a counterproductive path, pause and reflect on 'what got you here, isn't going to get you where you want to go.'" She was inspired by the book *What Got You Here Won't Get You There* (Goldsmith and Reiter 2007).

Without our *source-connection*, self-searching, or a demanded about-face, change in ourselves and others may be too painful, challenging, demeaning, or frightening. Often, the catalyst for change is an "aha" moment, the "hundredth monkey," or the "straw that broke the camel's back." In addition, a life-threatening event, critical medical challenge or recovery, a rite of passage, an ultimatum thrust upon us, or a multitude of other major incentives is a cause for change. I have observed that we keep at bay what is uncomfortable until we are ready to face head-on any personal transformation or demand change from self and others. Only when we are ready do we begin to honestly and realistically deal with our personal transformation or demand transformation from others. In our own time, desire, and will, or perhaps in response to a strong urgency, we finally begin to look inward to deal, modify, tackle, or eliminate the adverse habit, behavior, or attitude within us. A comprehensive, mindful, effective, and uplifting communication style is presented in the second section, *Soul to Soul Communication*.

Charting our *hand-dome* is a wonderful exercise for family members and colleagues to map privately or together to enrich their relationships with greater respect and compassion. This blueprint leads the way to strengthen bonds, collaborations, and participation in understanding and compromising to find resolution, which furthers commonality and cohesiveness. These promote positive and win-win solutions and aid in overcoming gaps that were once too wide to cross in our exponentially evolving, further intertwined, and diverse global community.

The *hand-dome* also serves as a dear friend throughout life's journey as personal and professional situations and relationships subtly or drastically change. The *hand-dome* is a jewel of a tool for anyone who encountered an unpredicted circumstance and for those who are unprepared for illness, accidents, economic downturn, divorce, terrorism, loss of a loved one, or any event that alters their life, ability, or outlook. Since no one has the foresight to anticipate every unexpected twist, these sudden events often catch us by surprise and place even greater physical, mental, or emotional burdens upon us, robbing us of that desired spiritual serenity.

Holding the *hand-dome* as a reminder, we can always emphasize that although we no longer have some relationships or abilities that we once possessed or held dear, our core essence, which ultimately defines us, remains intact and pure. Each new situation requires that we trust our ability to honestly and realistically create the vision and belief in our ability to reasonably achieve what we can. Simultaneously, it is best that we strongly reject focusing on where we once were, what we have accomplished, or what others expect. Again, let me share what one of my granddaughters, at the age of four, announced: "Every moment is another now." In appreciation for the moment, also maintain an eye on the future and create and hold on to a positive and realistic vision of what is achievable. Always cherish your special essence. Place your worthy and beautiful essence at the center of your path and cultivate a sense of gratitude for even the smallest of life's gifts. A motherlike life mentor and dear friend claimed this as her theme song: "For I have learned, in whatsoever state I am, therewith to be content" (Phil. 4:11, AV).

Respect Other People's Hand-Dome

As we acquire further realizations, appreciation, and respect for ourselves as represented by the *hand-dome*, we gain a core belief and recognize that we are the one and only person in the world who perceives and responds to life exactly as we do. Simultaneously, we come to recognize that every other human being on the planet has the same birthright and therefore views and responds to life as only the individual can. When I asked a young salesman in a hardware store to explain how something functions, he demonstrated and then confidently added, "That's real easy." I responded, "What is really easy for you in your early twenties may not be really easy for me in my early seventies." He smiled. Therefore, responses such as "I can, why can't you?" "Why can't they do it like I do?" or "Your brother was my student, I expect you…" forever lose all validity.

When a former gardener laid a new drip irrigation hose, I asked him if he also could also remove the clumpy, claylike dirt and replace it with planter mix. He said, "You know, this is a waste of time and energy." I walked away, and when I returned a few moments later, I said, "We each prioritize differently how we spend our time, energy, and money." Then I walked away. When I returned, I noticed that he had replaced the dirt.

While some are egalitarian, others may have difficulty in accepting directions or instructions from those of the opposite sex. In these cases, it is best to frame your request so that the person thinks it is their idea. Sometimes, I inquire, "What do you think about this idea?" Often, they think it is worthy and you don't have to go further to achieve your objective. Other times, it is not quite so easy and so you kindly and firmly state, "This is what I would like you to do." As best as we can—not through our own eyes, standards, experiences, or worldviews—look at others and try to step into their shoes. Our goal no longer seeks constant agreement but instead shifts to compassionate and thoughtful compromise that results in win-win solutions.

No person is invisible; neither is any person subservient or inferior to another, and they all build an ensuing consensus on mutual respect. At first, this may be an intellectual exercise, but hopefully this mutual regard will flow from our hearts, confirming that we truly respect each person's individuality and the perspective to which they are entitled. Although others' world-views may be quite different from ours, conversations must be stated in a positive, neutral, or nonthreatening manner. As issues arise that require resolution, we immediately bring to mind the *hand-dome* and what it represents, not only for us, but for the other person as well. If you do not know the other person well enough to understand their *hand-dome*, it is best to at least inquire, in a polite, not interrogative or degrading manner what it would take to resolve the issue. Then listen from your *source-connected* heart and be void of any judgment or any thoughts of "I am better," "I am smarter," "I am right," or "I am the boss."

This certainly does not imply that we will always agree on more than what we previously agreed, but it offers a pleasant, new paradigm on how to move forward. In differences that seem insurmountable, assume a positive and nonconfrontational approach, using body language and voice tone that express and build trust and comfort. Then ask the other person to state their objection or sticking point. As you listen, monitor yourself and check to see if you listen with your heart, as well as your ears, and that you are in an open-minded, attentive position. If you recognize any negativity, set aside those prejudged thoughts or biases. Listen attentively, then verbally confirm to the person what you heard, so that you can validate the *meaning* and *intention*. This indicates that you desire a clear and mutual comprehension of the situation, event, dilemma, choice, or roadblock to seek a mutually agreeable solution.

At times, situations are downright difficult and goals are simply unattainable. It seems that regardless of how positively we try to communicate, some people just won't meet halfway or show any interest in budging from their position. Silently ask yourself what it is that the other person does not recognize and why they do not cooperate. Ask the other person what it takes to achieve the goal. Perhaps a firmly held value or an unenlightened belief, lack of courage, stubbornness, or pure obstinacy keeps the other person unwilling or unable to listen, connect, communicate, or move forward to seek mutual solutions.

If you can, try to find that soul to soul connection. If further discussion or resolution remains unattainable, seek other avenues with other people to return to the discussion. Departing the conversation on a positive note leaves the door open for future possibilities to create a positive environment where trust and comfort pervade and where you can hopefully find a mutual resolution.

If this solution does not work, back off temporarily or permanently. Despite our efforts, there are some mutual goals in life that cannot be met when desired. Eventually, it will happen; it may take decades, centuries, or millennia, but with time, the resolution is found. Wars end, diseases are eradicated, justice prevails, treaties are signed, and deals are made. Lofty goals often evade us but are met on universal time, not on desired personal, professional, or calendar time, and perhaps not in our lifetime.

No one is truly a winner when we force our way or opinion so that the other person feels subjugated. We don't accomplish what we set out to do when we win and the other person loses. We claim victory but leave the other deflated, defeated, and resentful, which only fosters a feeling of ill will, creating an entirely new set of issues. It is best if everyone wins something.

With new insights and communication skills that you acquire and continue to attain, you gain a volume of ideas and tools to communicate more positively and effectively to solve challenges. The objective that always remains is to create a win-win situation in which at least one significant positive value of each person is honored.

Senator John McCain, a Republican from Arizona, is a shining example of a person with an honorable trait in his *hand-dome*. The civil, decent, and highly respected war hero and maverick always puts country ahead of party as he seeks bipartisan resolutions.

Members of the 113th U.S. Congress tried to resolve issues on health care, climate change, gun control, access to education, the growing income gap, immigration reform, and alternative energy. The body's vast divisiveness was clearly evident, and most issues faced insurmountable obstruction. Part of the issue was that each side was firmly entrenched in their belief system. The opposition party clearly refused the other party any victory. Individuals also lacked moral character and courage to go against party doctrine or stand up to racism to vote for policies of the common good for the people in the country.

When there is a mutual desire to find a solution, the obvious goal is to seek a common kernel within each view and use that as a starting point to build on for positive and collective resolutions. Neither side is going to achieve everything they want, nor should either side compromise their core values. A compassionate and respectful compromise is always the path to resolution. The same principles apply in any personal or professional relationship and encounter.

Before we move on, I want to emphasize that I believe there is always a reason to explain that each person feels, thinks, acts, speaks, and writes as they do. We don't always have the time, inclination, choice, ability, or a person's trust to discover when we observe something is amiss. At times, we may also place the onus on ourselves when that clearly is not the case.

Unable to walk in another's shoes, we can never exactly know but can only guess why a person makes the choices they make. Some decisions make no sense to us and often seem counterproductive. Although at times we assume we know, quite often, we draw the wrong conclusions. If a person with whom you interact personally or professionally gives you a hard time, is unresponsive, argumentative, downright mean, or is just unwilling to move ahead or accommodate, try to recognize that the person is probably doing the best that they can at the moment. However, they may also be extremely stubborn, refrain from trying to find a solution, or simply block any resolution that benefits you or anybody else. Nonetheless, if we could get inside that person and walk in their shoes even for a little while, we could see views from their perspective. Then we might discover a lack of enlightenment or a positive or negative, honorable or dishonorable trait represented in their *hand-dome* that prevents them from cooperating and doing their best or what is right at the time.

It is best to never try to force another person to change their lifestyle or harmful habits. But if they remain unacceptable or intolerable, we can alter our response to them or walk away. This often motivates enough to lead another person to modify, remove, and replace their harmful lifestyle ideas or habits with more positive ones. Only a person's own desire and will determine, without resentment, when and how change occurs. Even when a person tries to change, the change may be too little, too late, or not enough to make a difference.

When a stranger is giving me a hard time, under most circumstances, I try to cut a lot of slack when I don't understand a situation or a response and give the person the benefit of the doubt. Again, I firmly believe that being enlightened and unwedded to our ideas contributes to doing the best we can with what we have at the time.

I will now relate some of the most relevant stories entrusted to me that will hopefully inspire you. With the exception of one person, I received permission from each of these people to share their story. The following anecdotes highlight the benefits of understanding the insights provided by the *hand-dome* and are among my most poignant personal and professional experiences; they rocked me to my core.

Years ago, I heard a radio broadcast featuring Rosewood Community Education Center in Southern California, led by Sandy Osborn and Cedric Anderson, California Teacher of the Year 1994. The center's program offered an uplifting and realistic approach to give youth another chance to walk a positive, crime-free road and avoid juvenile detention camps. The youngsters, who were less than fourteen years of age, were on their way to becoming hardcore juvenile criminals as they had all been involved in crime and had carried a weapon. I was so impressed by the story of youths who were attempting to replace their former bad deeds with new, positive ones that I called Cedric. I asked him if I could visit his classroom and connect with the students; he kindly invited me to come.

On my first visit with what I later named *turn-around* students (a term that I preferred rather than the negative *at-risk*), I met Cedric and Sandy. There were no behavioral issues in this class, where students called their teachers by their first names, Sandy and Cedric. The students sensed how deeply their teachers cared about them. When they presented ideas on communication with their students, they were attentive and responsive. Sandy and Cedric's example reminded me that respect doesn't come from *sir* or *ma'am* but rather from how we treat one another. Cedric later remarked, "You never know what lies in the heart, mind, body, and soul of any individual until that person is given an opportunity to have a positive and meaningful experience with someone or something."

I believe that the students also felt that my message was sent from my heart to theirs with the sole intention to help. I didn't see any youth as a former gang member or juvenile delinquent but connected with each individual as a human being. I recognized and sensed that in their few years of life, they had already experienced tremendous adversity and were trying with all their might to overcome and turn around their former negative existence to experience more positive and productive "nows" in their lives.

Before I began my short talk, I asked each student to give me their names. Then, I told them that when we communicate face-to-face, the impression we give is received 55 percent though our nonverbal communication, 38 percent through our voice tone, and only 7 percent through our actual words. So I demonstrated different forms of body language that expressed toughness, obnoxiousness, and boredom, as well as acceptance and friendliness. I also introduced the *source-connection*. As my eyes wandered among the students, I noticed a small-for-his-age youth who stared at me with "attitude" that glaringly projected, "Don't look at me, don't talk to me, and don't you dare mess with me."

When I returned for further visits, I heard him tell Sandy, "You don't know how hard it is for me to talk nicely. Every person in my family, my mother, auntie, and grandmother, always hollered at me. No one ever spoke nicely to me—they just yelled. Even if I wanted to help with dinner, my mom shouted, 'What are you doing?' Then I go outside and I have to be tough or the kids will beat me up."

I asked him if I could put my hand on his shoulder and explain why it was so difficult for him to be nice. He said I could, so I gently laid my hand on his shoulder and showed him an illustration of the *hand-dome*. I said, "Look at the thumb. That represents who you are. You are spirited by nature, but so am I. If that energy is channeled in a positive way, you can bring passion to something positive that you believe in. Now, let's look at your second finger. Most of your experiences were frightening and negative. Next, let's look at your primary family's communication style— lots of yelling, little encouragement. Lastly, look at your native culture and the neighborhood you grew up in. It was tough, with lots of violence and gangs. You had to act tough and speak tough to survive. You have a lot to overcome, far more than most of your teachers and counselors—who ask you to change—ever had to." I told him, "Hang in there and believe in yourself." I also told him that I believed in him and that he could change. He responded, "I want to give up." With my heart aching and tears in my eyes, I looked at him and said, "You can't. You have too much to offer. You can become a leader because you know from experience and can teach youth with similar experiences to overcome similar obstacles that you've conquered." I felt that beneath that hard exterior shell was a very bright, perceptive young man. He was later mainstreamed back to a regular high school, and all the negative labels were removed from his record. Then he moved to Lancaster. My husband and I saw him a couple of times with his mother. We gave him a used computer. Then, I learned from his former teacher that he fell on hard times and unfortunately ended up in jail. He called a few times from jail, and I expressed support and belief in him. He contacted me again when he was released from jail, and we kept in touch even after we moved to Nevis. Then at one point, I lost touch with him and contacted his former teacher, but he also had lost touch with him.

When I attended a gathering with people from different cultural backgrounds, a fascinating exchange unfolded. One guest asked, "If there was a fire and an infant was lying on the side of the step, blocking our escape path, would we halt to grab that infant, knowing those few seconds could hinder our safety and result in our death?" Another dear and trusted guest responded, "If you are escaping a fire and your shoes are slowing down your escape, you kick off your shoes." I knew that her birth mother had died when she was young, and perhaps she had felt so unprotected as a child that preservation of her own life was paramount. Nevertheless, I was taken aback by her remark.

Knowing my friend quite well, I stopped by to chat. I wanted to confirm if my observation was accurate. She said *that it definitely was not*. She continued that even though she had lost her birth mom at a young age, Mamma, one of the women in her village, embraced and bathed her in unconditional love as naturally as her birth mom would have.

She further shared that she had watched recent scenes on television where roofs collapsed and people stampeded like herds of cattle, responding as *human beings*, not *humane beings*. She added, "How do I know how I will respond in a real-life situation? I would rather portray myself as not so righteous and prove myself wrong than the other way around." She believed that no one can know for certain how they will actually respond in those critical moments. She hoped she would be different, but she didn't know. I admired her honesty and self-reflection.

I also strongly sense that as long as we are sitting in a safe and comfortable place, none of us can predict how we would react in any grave, life-threatening, or unjust situation. We may think and say we would respond in a certain way, yet in reality we may react in just the opposite way of what we had predicted. I also added that it is not for us to judge what another person would do in any situation. However, we have the right and necessity to observe and make decisions in response to intolerable situations thrust upon us or others and take whatever moral and honorable action is deemed necessary to preserve our and others' well-being.

A guest also paraphrased Bruno Bettelheim. She stated, "*When we cross our own definition of humanity, we can never return to the same place of purity we had before we crossed it.*" I believe no matter how much forgiveness and redemption we seek or receive for past deeds, there will always be a deep scar within us from whenever we inflicted significant pain on another person.

When a woman received an anniversary gift from her husband, she was disappointed because it wasn't what she wanted. She couldn't grasp why he gave her that specific gift; she thought the gift he gave didn't reflect his caring for her. I explained that one facet in his *hand-dome* reflected his vision of beauty, though not necessarily hers. "Perhaps he just chose that ring because he thought you would like it, he liked it, or he had seen a similar ring that he thought was beautiful."

When chatting with a person who was in her third year of containment of a rare type of cancer, I was describing a person with a type A personality. After I uttered "Type A," she immediately interrupted me and questioned, "Do you mean blood type?" Her months in the hospital, weeks in isolation, and the painstaking measures to ensure that any blood transfusion exactly matched her blood type framed her response.

Decades ago, when my husband and I first visited Nevis, adjacent to the recently opened Four Seasons Resort was a small BBQ grill that served guests, locals, and construction workers. In a very short time, the engaging owner's bar and grill blossomed into a legendary, renowned spot that later was written up in the top tourist magazines and newspapers in the United States and Europe. The three of us each overcame challenges and shared numerous conversations and celebrations. At an earlier time, when I hadn't yet totally absorbed some of the humble Nevisian nonmaterialistic views, I asked him through my *USAan success lens*, "How does it feel not to be poor anymore?" He quickly and succinctly replied, "I was never poor. I always had values, mon!" His profound response was an enlightening moment that forever reinforced my divorce of success with money.

When I needed an arborist to plant a tree, I received an estimate from a person who was employed by a nearby company. His facial expression, which showed discomfort when we talked about prejudice toward minorities did not sit well with me. The following morning, approaching my home was a young man wearing a baseball hat and clothes similar to those worn by people who come to our house to solicit, proselytize, or drop off information. When I peered out from the window, I saw a beautiful spirit shine through the young man's dark-brown eyes. So I asked him, "What are you selling, or which religion do you represent?" He smiled and said, "Neither." He stated his name and said that he was a licensed member of the International Society of Arborists. I invited him in and explained that we needed to have a tree planted and another tree pruned. Then, I suggested that he sit in the family room and give me an estimate. I commented that there was something about his spirit that had touched me and we would use him. While he and his young crew worked, I learned about his personal and professional background. I also noticed that his crew was very patient as I explained that I wanted the trees trimmed to ensure safety and shade, perhaps not as aesthetically balanced as others usually prefer. When I mentioned the team's patience, the owner of the start-up business shared that the person tethered high in the tree and the person who pruned followed their fathers' footsteps. He told me that his crew was the first generation born in the United States.

He commented that many of the older generation who had emigrated from Mexico regularly hustled and bustled and followed the adage that "time is money," so they didn't take the time to build relationships with their clients. He said that his peers had a different philosophy—time is life. So he and many of their generation decided that if they went into business, they would take more time with each client to build relationships. It was exhausting to constantly hustle and push, though they would be as professional as their fathers. I asked him if he knew why that might possibly be. He said, "No, I don't." I explained, "I can't be sure, but most often people who had immigrated to the United States came to overcome poverty, oppression, or other harsh circumstances. Since life in their native culture wasn't easy, they often came to build a more prosperous, safer, and secure life. They usually arrived with very little money, and so they felt they had to hustle more." I guessed that he had it better off as a child than his father had; he agreed. I explained the facets of the *hand-dome* to enlighten him, and he smiled. Eventually, he compromised and adopted some of his father's ways to provide income for his extended family.

When my brother-in-law had a stroke following brain surgery, it took him longer to recover than expected, and his speech remained impaired throughout life. In despair, he felt that he had totally lost himself. Although his soul and core values remained unchanged, people reacted differently to him. I shared that although he spoke and acted differently, his soul remained the same. His innate caring, loving, gentle, warm, compassionate, and attentive persona remained intact. In time, he felt revitalized and began to focus on those positive feelings. Later, in his mideighties, using a walker, he took a bus to buy a few ingredients for a baker at his assisted-living facility. If a person looked perplexed or didn't understand him, he said, "If you don't understand me, I will say it again and speak slower." He loved his independence and felt good that he still could help others.

When returning from Nevis to California, my husband and I often stopped on the East Coast to visit our son and family. When the head of housekeeping came to refresh our room, she noticed the luggage piled in a corner of the room and asked, "Why do you have so many pieces of luggage?" I told her that we were returning from a small Caribbean island where we live half the year. Then she asked, "What do you do there?" I told her that we live in a village, totally immersed in local life, and shared some of our experiences. Each day when she came to our room, we chatted, then we became and remained friends. On the last day, she trusted me enough to share her profoundly moving experience. She said that her mother, who had tremendous faith in God, was an incredible woman who always led by good examples. She added that her mother had taken in a young woman who had been on drugs and provided food, shelter, and clothing. For some unknown reason, the woman who had taken refuge in her mother's home turned against and killed her mother.

She continued that she had visited the woman in jail and forgave the woman who murdered her mother. When I questioned how she could forgive, she said it was a testament to her mother. "The only way I can truly honor my mother is to follow her example and live the way she lived." My mind ran to the second or middle finger of the *hand-dome*. This finger represents past experiences, and the third finger of the *hand-dome*, which represents the values and communication style of the primary family. But I also knew there was a very special, forgiving, and honorable attribute within this unbelievably devout and inspirational woman, which the thumb of her *hand-dome* represents.

Another time, I stopped briefly to chat with a woman who works the front desk at a doctor's office. I have known her for a long time, and we became friends. She recently shared that my life story and writings inspire her. Knowing a little bit about her life and that she was raising three children without any support from their father, I responded, "I inspire you and you inspire and motivate me to continue writing…so there you go."

When I noticed that her appearance had changed over the last year and I finally asked her, "What is going on?" she shared that she had taken on the herculean task of raising seven children—her twin daughters and son and her sister's kids, two girls and two boys, whom she took in when her mom got sick. She shared that she also took in her mom, whom she had nursed for over a year before she passed away from leukemia.

I was so taken aback that I called her at home to ask her where she got her strength. She asked me, "Did you know that I was a recovering addict and my twins were born in prison? My last brush with the law was when I visited a friend in prison and was caught with the last bit of a joint. It was the best thing that happened to me to get my life together. It wasn't an easy road, but I am so grateful. I had wonderful kids who worked with me. I am blessed more than most." She also shared that her father had deserted the family when she was young and he died when she was eighteen. She continued, "During the entire time I went through rehabilitation, my mom never gave up on me. Both me and my siblings were addicts and my sister and I didn't really get along. When I was twelve years old, my mom had heart surgery, so I became the caregiver of my brothers and sisters, and I set the rules. When my mom got better and came home, I had to give up the role as head of the household. Now I had to follow the rules instead of setting them; it wasn't easy."

I asked about her mom. She said, "My mom always had a huge heart. After my sister died of heart disease and her husband was killed in a car accident two years later, my mom took in my sister's kids. When my mom became ill with leukemia, I took her and my two nieces and two nephews in." After her mom passed away, my friend took care of seven children for more than a year. Even her doctors recently told her she should give up the boys, saying, "It's too much for you." She asked me, "How can you give up on your family? What am I going to do, kick them out or put them in a foster home?" She said that her own daughters were doing very well in school and she saw potential in her niece and nephews. Hopefully, they will all get scholarships for college. A nephew may end up living with her for a while. He went through a lot when he was twelve years old. Although he is nearly eighteen years old now, he just isn't that emotionally mature.

I asked her, "What's your heritage, who set the example, how did you become so strong, and do you have any help?" She replied that her cultural heritage was Irish, Scottish, and German, and I responded, "Those are strong cultures." She further shared that coming through rehabilitation and overcoming drugs gave her great strength, along with her mother's example of always opening her big heart to help others. She feels blessed that she lives in her mother's home, which is paid for, though she continues to maintain the house and pay taxes. And I can vouch that she works in one of the most healing doctors' offices that I visit. Just sitting in the waiting room, I feel a wonderful, calm, caring, and healing energy. Before I got off the phone, I told her, "You are my hero for the year."

Our roles as professionals often influence how we respond to life. I recall that when I was a speech pathologist serving patients in acute facilities, an elderly patient required a common outpatient surgery. One child who was an administrator at what was then named convalescent home wanted the parent to experience absolutely no pain and was okay with using narcotics as long as necessary so that the parent suffered no misery whatsoever. The other child was a teacher and wanted the parent to have as little narcotics as necessary to maintain at the most a minimal discomfort so that the parent's mental faculties could function as well as possible.

Since I continue to be plagued by the depth of hatred and racism and the pain it has caused my dear ones, I decided to ask several of them from various cultures, how does racism personally impact them. I chose each of the following individuals, as they are leaders in one of their life's roles. Diverting from former more familiar responses, I share the following that are quite different and reflect each person's *hand-dome.*

A longtime friend was born in the Caribbean, but lived many of her earlier adult years in a European country heavily ingrained in institutionalized racism. The person told me that when she was a young child, her mother had told that people are going to give her a hard time or be mean to her because of her skin color. The mother who was a very religious woman said, "Don't worry, God will take care of it." So, no matter when or if she senses discrimination or put downs, she stated, "She doesn't pay any attention to it and goes on with her life." She discovered after she responded to a racist term with a racist term that she once was a racist herself and immediately stopped. Since then, she prays for those persons who discriminate or are racists to heal their ways. Her response reflects the third finger of her *hand-dome*, the values and communication style and of our primary family.

A recent friend of African heritage used to constantly promote herself on Facebook. So, I asked her why does she do that. I observed from her posts that she is a very intelligent woman who succinctly and passionately expresses her ideas and keeps her FB friends up to date relating to family and persons of African heritage, especially during Black History Month. She also does a lot of good in the world, goes out of her way to help others, and is naturally attractive. She shared that she was overcome with racism and feeling ugly and inadequate into her late-forties. When I asked her, what caused this, she replied, "I grew up in the middle of the country in a state that is a hotbed of racism. So, for years I was surrounded by the message that I am ugly and worthless." Her response represents the fourth finger of her *hand-dome*, the values and communication style and of our primary culture.

Another person who is renown in his field of expertise is from India and is an observant Muslim. He stated that because of his skin tone and the fact that he wears a beard, he is identified as a Muslim. He is also a kind human being, loving family man, and is quite protective of his family. His family and friends have been harassed and some have been threatened with their lives. So, he feels he has to be quite vigilant for potential danger.

He also shared that this continues to cause numerous missed personal and professional opportunities. Because he is professionally recognized, he has been invited to speak or join in discussions, but declines if the state is in a certain section of the country, as he fears for his life. He has learned to accept that it is what it is and he got over being sad or angry. He recalls his mother's message when he was a young child, "Don't use your soap to clean another person's laundry." So, he knows discrimination is the other person's problem, even though he is the recipient. Most recently, he picked up information on social media including that a man who resembles persons born in India also wore a beard, and was mistaken as a Muslim. Without any provocation, he was instantly shot dead. My friend's response represents primarily the second finger of his *hand-dome*, his past experience, and the fourth finger that represents the values and communication style and of our primary culture.

Another person is a man who recalls an incident as a young child living in an All-American Midwestern city where there were no fences in neighborhood yards. When a ball landed in a neighbor's back yard, he walked over and picked it up. Often, the woman in the house yelled at him, "Dirty Jew, don't come into my yard." He got tired of hearing that so one day he told the woman, "If you call me that again, I'll punch you in the mouth." She never uttered those words again. Even though he was a skinny little kid, he also beat up some brothers in his neighborhood who had been cruel to him. After he beat them up, they never touched him again. When I asked him, who taught him to respond like that, he replied, "Nobody, I just had enough." His response represents his thumb in the *hand-dome* that is just who he is.

Lastly is the story of a woman who has several siblings. Her father was a sergeant in the military so the family was often transferred to another location. Her father did not believe in spankings, but her mother did. However, she was very kind and taught her children to always be kind and not hold grudges. With the exception of one sister, they mostly stood up for themselves. One day this very small child of African heritage was grabbed by three students who pushed her under a school stairwell and beat her up. When she told her mother, her mother said, "Find those girls and one at a time beat them up and tell them, "If you ever touch me again, the next time you will have to face my sisters and me." After she had beat up each of the students, they never bothered her again. Again, this reflects the third finger in the *hand-dome*.

And most lighthearted and surprising of all occurred when my hairstylist visited our home and saw a close-up photo of five bright lime-green mounds of moss of different widths growing on a large branch. She immediately responded, "I see five heads of hair waiting to be styled and cut." The texture prompted her surprising remark.

Before we leave this chapter, reflect again to embrace and celebrate the beauty, significance, and uniqueness of who you are. You will always be one of a kind, because after you and every other individual are created, each mold is thrown away. So delight in your glorious worth and who you are and be who you want, or were meant, or dream to be. Without apology, accept and honor your limitations, but at the same time, do your best to adapt or improve as much as you can. Respect your boundaries, adopt a "zero tolerance policy" of any form of abuse from others, advocate for your well-being, and take the best possible care of yourself. Whenever possible, do not allow yourself to remain stuck and frozen in unproductive habits or antagonistic situations.

Now that you've grasped the concept of your *hand-dome*, you've not only acquired a more profound understanding of yourself but also gained greater compassion and a broader respect for and appreciation of why others feel, think, act, and express themselves as they do. Along with that, remember that your *source-connection* is the purest, most essential and inspiring force within you. So please include that entrusted connection in every aspect of your life. Bring to life your glorious endowed qualities and talents in all your relationships, and remember to passionately and regularly participate in meaningful, joyful, fun, and uplifting activities as you live life more wholly.

Personal Lenses

A lens marred with distortions
Can't capture the beauty true.
Similarly, your personal lenses
Block the best in others and you.

Personal Lenses

More than anything, our *personal lenses* pollute the purity that flows from our souls and hinder the unique radiance, glow, and beauty that softly or brightly shines from our *source-connections*. Being raised Jewish, I believe that a person's soul is pure at birth and remains present within each of us—yes, even within those who have spoken the cruelest words or committed humanity's most heinous atrocities. To varying degrees, *personal lenses* are boosted into creation by an intentional or unintentional, recognized or unrecognized, or conscious or unconscious trampling on the spirit. Consequently, life's garbage heaped upon us often buries our spirits, causing us to become unrecognizable to ourselves and others. I do believe that somewhere beneath that foul rubbish lies the pure life-force spark endowed at the moment of, or sometime after, conception. And that remains pure until the moment of death, when that divine spark leaves our bodies to return to the Universe, from where it came. I believe that throughout our lives, while our souls remain pure, our attitudes and behaviors can, do, and often must change to reflect our goodness in response to life's constantly evolving desired or undesired events. I definitely cannot explain a Manson or know what the basal element was that motivated and radicalized a Hitler, Stalin, al-Zarqawi, or bin Laden or other individuals or terrorist groups to spew such virulent hatred and commit such vehemently barbaric and abhorrent acts. Nevertheless, I deeply believe that the trampling of the spirit, experiencing war, or witnessing a horrendous event or something horrifically abominable to the spirit can lead to a significant mutation and perhaps even a colossal corruption of one's moral sense of right or wrong. Our fellow human beings represent the best and worst of humanity. Daily, around the world, there are those who take lofty risks to help others, often at great peril and sacrifice to themselves—sometimes even at the cost of giving their lives.

Personal Lenses are perceptions and feelings that we carry based on our past experiences, values, attitudes, and emotions. Although some *lenses* are positive, many *lenses* tend to be negative. Similar to software viruses that corrupt the integrity of the computer's operations, our negative *lenses* block us from allowing our essence to spring forth with all its glory. *Negative lenses* are toxic and distort our perception and response to the world. Please let me share again the sentiments expressed by the renowned Nobel Peace Prize laureate Elie Wiesel: "We don't live in the past, but the past lives in us."

Negative lenses are based on feelings, fears, or experiences that once felt valid but are no longer productive or relevant. A *lens* may have evolved in our childhoods as a form of protection, created as a defensive wall against unfriendly words and isolated or recurring troublesome actions thrust upon us. The *lens* probably developed in response to a demeaning isolated or recurring incident or experience, combative language, or negative reactions we perceived or received. As children, we had not yet developed the tools to isolate the fear or negativity from those certain situations. Consequently, we clung to the negative incident in its entirety, including our response, and created a negative *lens* that we applied to many similar events in our life.

Because we did not possess the rational mental ability, maturity, or wisdom to isolate the *one* negative factor from the incident or situation, the perception of the total experience from that moment hurt or crippled us in the long run. Eventually, we added this new adversarial *negative lens* to our perception and, in varying degrees, applied those undermining thoughts to all similar situations. In 1998, I wrote, "You may have formed these feelings when your mind was not developed enough to have the words or thoughts for understanding the events." Later, I discovered that Daniel Goleman, in *Emotional Intelligence*, stated something akin to my observation. He wrote, "One reason we can be so baffled by our emotional outbursts is that they often date from a time early in our lives when situations and events were bewildering and we did not yet possess the ability to make sense of it. We may have the chaotic feelings, but not the words for the memories that formed them." Goleman calls these responses "out-of-date neural alarms" (Goleman 1995).

To better comprehend the concept of *lenses*, imagine that you are wearing several pairs of eyeglasses of different prescriptions, each representing a person, situation, or event in your life. One pair of glasses represents the values you learned from your primary parent or caregiver. That person cherished you, thought you could do no wrong, and satisfied almost your every need. The next pair of glasses represents a former fifth-grade student who publicly humiliated you. Another pair belongs to a neighbor or teacher who always put you down and implied that you "would never amount to anything," "were up to no good," or "stupid," especially when you didn't know an answer, or declared that you were "bad," "naughty," or "disgusting" when you acted up. Yet another pair of glasses represents a community leader who espoused suspicion and hatred of people of differing cultures, religions, or regions. One pair represents the newscaster from whom you received local, national, and international news. Still, another pair represents your learning a new academic skill at which you initially struggled. The last pair is a more recent prescription, formed in response to bullying or social media. Even if you only wore one pair of these glasses, that one pair would impair your vision, and therefore your perception. Imagine if you wore all these eyeglasses at the same time; they would significantly distort your perception and how you personally view and respond to others and life.

Some of your peak or repetitive positive and negative life's experiences, and the memory of those perceptions, developed into either an *internal lens* or *external lens*. Another approach to look at a *lens* is to picture a hoop. Imagine passing through several hoops to reach your *source-connected* truth as each hoop adds another distorted layer, blocking you from your purest essence. The more *lenses* you bear, or the more hoops you pass through, the greater your perception is distorted, and the impact of their cumulative effect on you and others becomes more debilitating. The *lenses* presented are similar to those outdated, distorted, and negative attitudes, experiences, or views from our past that we still carry. The memories of those experiences often shape any thought or response to life. As humans, we perceive an experience, image, or information, then process it. Then, we store it as memory until we call upon that memory to respond to life through our nonverbal, voice-tone, verbal, or written communication. If that information is distorted from the get-go, we must realize that to some degree our *lenses* work against us.

Do not confuse *personal lenses* with what Michael A. Singer (2007) calls the "uninvited roommate," that barrage of random, spontaneous, undesired, or unrelated thoughts that constantly drone on in the background, akin to the ticker tape news feed on the bottom of a TV screen. *personal lenses* are different. They are the familiar, repetitive, and often demeaning "chatter" in our heads often imposed upon us by others. They create negative feelings, fear, or self-doubt. Is there an internal mantra that reverberates "You're no good," "Not good enough," "You should," "What if," "You'll fail," "Catch up," "No one wants you," or "Shame on you?"

Do you carry a sense of unworthiness that you don't matter or are "less than" simply because of your appearance, condition, specific feature, mental or physical ability, age, gender, sexual orientation, neighborhood, socioeconomic or educational level, cultural heritage, religion, or *handi-abled*? These negative feelings and thoughts are responses to your *personal lenses* and are "mind fields" that you placed in your mental path, erupting under your feet as you trod on through life. These mental "mind fields" cripple our ability to shine as softly or brightly as we were meant to live. They interfere with our enjoyment of a self-actualizing, fulfilling, and productive life. This prevents us from reaching our destiny and the pinnacle from which we can offer our glorious gifts and discover our life's purpose. It is the degree to which these *lenses* negatively interfere with our well-being, thought processes, positive outlook, and the manner in which we communicate that creates the hindrance.

Unfortunately, we may be unaware of some of our *negative lenses* and not realize how destructive they are. For years, we probably carried some *lenses* that we once felt were necessary, essentially dragging a garbage bag around with us every day. These *lenses* are such an integral part of our being that we continue to carry them to the present, where they remain unnecessary, unproductive, and often considerably burdensome. This robs us of satisfaction and success in our lives. Deepak Chopra says, "Just realizing that you place an interpretation on everything is a major step in freeing yourself from the past" (Chopra 2010).

Remember that the second finger in your *hand-dome* represents your past experiences and includes your *personal lenses*. As you become aware of your own *lenses*, you add them to your *hand-dome*. The *Identify, Block, Move, Delete, Replace (IBMDR) Technique* for both *internal* and *external lenses* teaches you how to minimize or eliminate your *lenses*. This technique is presented for both *internal* and *external lenses* later in this chapter.

Most of my clients, along with many other people who had difficulty communicating positively with others, were *source-disconnected*. Aside from that, they were unaware of the *lenses* they carried and, at times, the monumental debilitating impact these *lenses* had on them. When *lenses* are brought to light, individuals clearly recognize that the heavy weight of their negative effects significantly reduces their focus and drain their energy. A young professional in a managerial position routinely heard, "I need to catch up" or "What will they think?" When asked a question, she hesitated, questioning herself before responding. Others overrespond to prove their point, *driving* their ideas rather than *giving* them, as they feel others often reject their ideas or decisions.

Many *lenses* that are presented—and the ones that you still carry—began in childhood and are perpetuated, remaining quite sabotaging. Other, more recent monumental experiences that often create new *lenses* and cause internal unrest, a sense of turmoil, or lack of ability are responses to personal loss. The *lenses* are due to abuse, bullying, addiction, sexual harassment, separation, or death, fighting or surviving war, failing health, or financial decline. If the person doesn't deal with them positively, the recently formed *lens* will become permanent until we engage the *Identify, Block, Move, Delete, Replace Technique*. These past or recent *lenses* negatively alter our feelings, thoughts, and numerous responses to life and are expressed through our nonverbal, voice-tone, verbal, and written communication. This chapter presents a discussion on various situations that my clients, family, friends, and I experienced and *lenses* that we duly created.

Because of my own early childhood "outsider" experiences and perception that I didn't belong, the *seeking approval/wanting to belong lens* was one of my strongest and most painful *internal lenses*. While I never compromised my principles or values, for years I spent—and wasted—too much emotional, physical, mental, and spiritual energy striving for acceptance, seeking validation, and at times mentally beating myself up.

As a young adult, I willingly and lovingly gave the best of my imperfect self to my husband and children, yet with others, I pushed beyond my limits in hopes that they would accept me. Though I knew it was not in my best interest, I would occasionally jeopardize my health, as I took on many activities and responsibilities to prove myself. Often, I was not my best advocate and, perhaps at times, was my worst enemy. Sometimes, we have to get out of our own way.

Now, finally, in my eightieth year and following the lead of my dear friend Blind Eileen, I say, "Yes, if my body tells me." I recently shared with another senior, "You can only do what you can do. It doesn't matter what others expect, state what you 'should do,' or what you once were able to do. It only matters what you can comfortably do now." We also do what we have to do to enable us to do what we want to do. Sometimes others may not comprehend, but in many ways, we know ourselves best. Blind Eileen taught me to embrace what we still can do instead of "grieving" for what once was. Although it is definitely not easy, this principle is valid for any age, condition, or change in our lives—whether it is losing a loved one from separation or death, returning from surviving a war, living with an injury, posttraumatic stress syndrome, or traumatic brain injury, battling with or recovering from cancer, having less financial means, or missing any other circumstance or ability that you once had and no longer possess. As a Nevisian friend reminds me, "That was then, and this is now."

Impact of Our Personal Lenses

A twenty-three-year-old man shared that he had feared failure since he was six years old. While consulting with me, he discovered the devastating impact that his *lenses* had on him. He was a sensitive child who had adored his father. In the first grade, he flunked a test. When he reported his grade at home, his father yelled and beat him. His feelings toward his father changed instantly from adoration to fear, and these feelings remained throughout his life. From that time until he entered junior college to get a degree in law enforcement, he felt he had failed. During the entirety of his school years, whenever he thought that he couldn't do well on an exam, he stopped trying. Even though intelligence tests noted that he was at a genius level, he barely made good-enough grades to pass each year. Starting in junior high school, he gained weight, smoked, chewed his nails, and became involved in petty crime. Finally, he recalled a loving grandfather who had been a law enforcement officer. At nineteen, with the memory of his grandfather in mind, he began to turn his life around. He quit biting his nails, quit smoking, lost weight, and excelled in college, even making the dean's list. Still, he said that he had a very difficult time studying. No matter how pleasant he found his tasks and activities, he was always anxious about the future. When he began to fill the second finger in his *hand-dome*, representing his past experiences, he wrote that he was a failure. He noted that his fear of failing consumed him 80 percent of the time. It was no surprise as to why he had such a difficult time focusing on anything.

I then reminded him of his successes: quitting smoking, losing weight, ceasing criminal activity, and achieving better grades. When I asked him to visualize the word *success* etched on his open palm and place it in front of him, he placed the image eight inches away from of his face, implying a lack of associating himself with success. When I requested that he imagine an image of the words *fear of failure* etched on his open palm in front of him, he placed his palm almost touching his face, indicating a constant obstacle. The gap was so tiny that I could barely slip a piece of paper between his palm and face.

Types of Lenses

The *lenses* presented in this chapter fall into two main categories: *internal lenses* and *external lenses*. *Internal lenses* affect our attention inward, focusing on ourselves. *External lenses* affect our attention outward, focusing on others. Although people develop similar *lenses*, they evolve from different experiences. What negatively impacts one person may not even faze another. We create each *lens* at various times in response to different interactions or events of varying degrees of impact. Some *lenses* are temporary, and others remain permanent. Both types of *lenses* block us from the purity of our *source-connection* and create those negative thoughts in our head that corrupt the integrity of our perceptions, processes, and responses.

Internal Lenses

Internal lenses fall into two subcategories, *feel and fear lenses* and *thought and response lenses*. Some *internal lenses* are felt more, and some are feared more. When there is an overlap of *feel* and *fear lenses*, the *lens* may be even more ingrained and, consequently, have greater consequences. The *thought and response lenses* are also created in response to our life's experiences.

Feel and Fear Lenses

The *internal lenses* presented in the *feel and fear* category are *mistrust/abandonment, unworthiness, not mattering, seeking approval/wanting to belong, insecurity, lack of education/stupidity, physical appearance, failure/rejection, financial insecurity/not enough, health, bullying, abuse,* or any other personal negative thoughts we carry.

The *internal lenses* presented in the *thought and response* category are *control, defensiveness, competitiveness, negativity/self-deprecation, catch up/need to prove, questioning "what if," crying wolf, overreacting, "should be," "rose-colored glasses," expectations/assumptions, retrospective regret, neglected well-being/self-expectation,* or any other personal negative chatter that often "speaks silently."

Mistrust/Abandonment Lens

Again, some *lenses* are temporary, but others are permanent, and some fall between. The following is an example of a *temporary lens*. When I called to confirm a speaking engagement, the woman replied, "I thought you were canceling, because the other speaker just called to cancel." Whenever *lenses* develop, they affect our thoughts and feelings from that point forward until we stop, note, analyze, gain clarity, and delete them. Distrust often follows when others betray, disappoint, hurt, or repeatedly lie to us. In response, we develop a *mistrust lens* that we then apply to similar situations.

After months of dating, a woman's boyfriend suddenly broke up with her. When she began to date again, she was unable to commit to any man she dated for fear of his leaving her as her former boyfriend had done. It was a long time before she again trusted another person enough to commit to marriage. When a man was laid off during one of the downsizing economic cycles, he became fearful of losing his position again and remained on edge for years even though he was never again laid off.

When fathers, mothers, or partners abandon their children, or when wives, husbands, or partners abandon their spouses or partners, these physical or emotional breaks often create a lifelong impact of varying degrees that is felt at various times. During my lifelong personal and professional experiences, I've observed that even adults in their fifties and sixties continue to have issues with abandonment. Some of their mothers and fathers went off to other places to seek work and support their family back home. Some people left and sent funds home but never returned. Still, others left but were never heard from again. The child was left behind to be raised lovingly, or not so lovingly, by family members or others who took them in. Some never even met nor ever knew the parent who deserted them. They never asked, were never told, or didn't always recognize the relationship of either their biological mother or their biological father who disappeared. The parents often built the union that created the child on false hopes and illusive promises. Men promised women marriage that they never fulfilled. Even as these women became pregnant, the men often vowed to care for the child or commit to marriage, even if it meant leaving their current wives, but that rarely happened.

Children who grow up with mothers and fathers who live under the same roof may also feel less worthy if their parents prioritize serving their professional or volunteer roles in the community more than their children's needs. While these adults may be caring people, their primary focus and time are dedicated to caring for those outside the home and not foremost attending to the physical or emotional needs of those in the home, especially their children. Former U.S. First Lady Jacqueline Kennedy often expressed that her role as a mother was the most relevant role in her life. Now, because both parents or caretakers usually work to provide income for today's lifestyle, finding the time to serve everyone's well-being, including their own, is a delicate balancing act. It is best when each partner or family member is flexible and assumes as much responsibility as they can, when they can. Let me again share, "The person who is able does."

Those who felt abandoned often share characteristics of striving to prove their self-worth as they exhaust themselves by overly indulging their children. Consciously or unconsciously, they expect others to fill the void left by abandonment, or they live with a sense of unworthiness. Some question whether there was something wrong with them that drove away their absent parent, or worse yet, some even blame themselves. Sometimes, the parent was physically present but emotionally detached and never supported the child. Even some children who are adopted and cherished by the most loving families are ambiguous about their situation. As adults, those who felt abandoned often continue to look back at the circumstances from their childhood perspective.

Often, over the years, I heard or witnessed a situation in which the parents of a young or preteen child separated. The parent with whom the child remained created new relationships, wedded, and had a child with the new spouse. Unless the parent makes a concerted effort to make the child feel as loved and welcomed as before, the youth feels abandoned. This sense of double abandonment, without a loving person reaching out or a belief in a higher power, is often the turning point for a child who had previously rarely been in trouble. The youth begins to feel so lonely and desperate that they turn to drugs, opioids, gangs, or terrorist groups. These organizations' members prey on the most vulnerable, waiting with open arms to accept them into their "new family." This situation arises especially in war zones, where parents, extended family, and caregivers are sometimes all killed. Some of these abandoned youth and older folks live on the streets and create their own homeless community with those who share similar experiences. No one can measure how deep the scar that a father's, mother's, or caregiver's abandonment leaves on a child at any age, even if it happens before the child is born. These *trust and mistrust lenses* related to relationships and career continue to ebb and flow throughout our lives' cycles. Some of these experiences barely leave scars, while others leave deeply penetrating wounds that take decades to heal or may never heal entirely. Yet the scars remain invisible to others.

Unworthiness Lens

Feeling unworthy affects our feelings, thoughts, decisions, and communication. Most of my clients who carried this *lens* since their childhood perceived that their achievements were rarely good enough. The mantras they heard as children were "You'll never amount to anything," "No one will want to marry you," "You're stupid," "You're not good enough," "Second place doesn't count," "Why can't you be like Nancy?" or "You can do better." Others' achievements were models of what others expected of them, and if they couldn't achieve this artificial standard, they felt unworthy and that they did not matter. Often, others blamed my clients, family, and friends when things went wrong, even when it wasn't their fault.

As a result, individuals who carry an *unworthiness lens* often live and communicate in fear. The saddest part is that they don't demand respect or stand up for themselves. They accept many forms of abuse because they feel they deserve it or don't know anything different. They take on emotional guilt for most of the failures that happen in their personal relationships and professional situations, even when they aren't responsible, always thinking, "Now, what did I do wrong?" They usually do not feel or realize the full impact of the successes they achieve.

One client recalled a natural disaster that gutted his family's home when he was a young child. At four years of age, he was sent by his parents to live with his grandmother during the rebuilding of his home, while his younger brother remained with his parents. His sense of unworthiness began early when they sent him away. He could not grasp why his baby brother could stay home with Mom and Dad. To add salt to the wound, during his high school years and beyond, his mother constantly told him, "This isn't good enough" or "You can do better." Early in his banking career, he showed great promise, but instead of continuing on this career path, he continued to hear his mother's voice, "This isn't good enough, you can do better." So he left banking. Next, he tried a career outside his area of expertise; he failed. For more than twenty years, he continued to sabotage himself as he took positions for which he was unqualified and minimized any successes he achieved. What looked like a promising future instead became a series of failures. If you reviewed his credentials, you would notice that he had passed state-accredited examinations in record time and held numerous notable positions. Nevertheless, he never celebrated, cherished, or embraced those achievements. When he spoke, he definitely did not convey his professionalism and knowledge. His communication was flat, hesitant, and apologetic, so he appeared uncertain. Naturally, he had difficulty persuading others of his abilities.

Others are afraid to ask for help when they require it because they feel they are undeserving and will be rejected. They are often stymied when numerous caring individuals rush in to help, as they never felt their own self-worth. In my experience, a lack of self-worth or feeling that you don't matter are among the most crippling and difficult obstacles to overcome.

Not Mattering Lens

There are many people, especially male youth living in the "hoods" of Baltimore, Chicago, Philadelphia, and other major cities, who learned early on that while their lives are cherished by their loved ones, they do not matter to the greater society: not on the streets, in their cars, at their schools, or in the courts. Though I never personally interacted with individuals of African heritage from those neighborhoods, I have read books and certainly have seen their stories and images on the news and social media. I am all too familiar with the statistics regarding those whose lives were cut short or those instances in which such a person's actions prematurely cost their own, the police, or others' lives. From the inception of the United States to now, approaching four centuries later, mainstream U.S. society has given most of the youth of African heritage a very raw and often inhumane deal.

Individuals of African heritage and their family members continue to live in constant humiliation and fear that someone might mutilate or murder their sons, husbands, lovers, fathers, uncles, or cousins for no other reason than the darker skin tone of their African heritage. This is a real and present danger that daily grips and worries these people and their loved ones. At a very young age, they learned they were not entitled to the same privilege, protection, access, or consequences as those of European and other heritages. Until recently, they were not portrayed positively, justly, or equally in advertisements, commercials, movies, or theaters. This left the impression that their lives did not matter as much as those of European heritage, whom they saw on TV living in the suburbs and surrounded by white picket fences.

Different but still horrendous treatment applies to the Native Americans living in the United States as well. Initially, pioneers and other folks of European heritage in positions of power slaughtered their ancestors, overran or confiscated their homeland, and placed their culture under siege. They were forcefully relegated to "reservations," a place where they had to make monumental adjustments, no longer enjoying and being immersed in their daily and sacred traditions. Instead, they had to adapt to a new lifestyle, often far removed from places where, for thousands of centuries, their ancestors had practiced their customs and spiritual rituals, living life in accord with their values, honoring Mother Earth.

Although there were others of minority cultures or religious beliefs who similarly did not matter to the majority of greater society, few experienced the centuries-long inhumane brutality as those of African or Native American culture endured.

Seeking Approval/Wanting to Belong Lens

Others feel their self-worth but know that they just haven't connected with like-minded or like-spirited people. Therefore, they sense that they don't belong or that something remains amiss, and some sense a deep void. Even if they like who they are, they may put the onus on themselves, thinking "I am weird" or "Something is wrong with me."

Wanting approval can be so intense that some become disingenuous, lose touch with their truth, or dishonor themselves. In business, people may distort the truth to get a project approved. Others may say a task is complete just to meet deadlines when they are fully aware that the task is not properly completed. They lack the courage to inform their colleagues or superiors that they are behind schedule. Perhaps they do not want to disappoint others, or they fear they will lose their job.

People who carry this *lens* may also attempt to sustain a personal bond by showering others with material or monetary gifts far beyond their means. A gift purely given from the heart brings joy to the recipient that is an unexpected reward for the giver. In the twelfth century, the Jewish philosopher Maimonides stated that the most honorable gift is to give without the recipient's knowledge of the donor.

People who carry a *wanting approval lens* may also exaggerate to gain acceptance. If there is opposition to their views on a controversial topic, they may try to appease or remain quiet. Others may compromise their values, ending with very little representing who they truly are. In their hearts, they wish they had the courage and conviction to say and do what they feel, but they can't. Wanting approval and acceptance is far more important to them. People who carry a *wanting approval lens* often vacillate or are indecisive, so they frequently change their minds. They are conflicted between doing what they know is in their best interest and trying to please others. Unbeknownst to others, an individual who seeks approval makes decisions that conform to another's desires or dictates; therefore, they forfeit and dishonor what is right for them. In that mind-set, when anticipated outcomes are not as planned, they may blame the person whom they were trying to please, shouting, "It's all your fault!" No one understands how they arrived at that conclusion, Yet in their mind their decisions were based on the other person's needs, desires, or demands, so why should they take the responsibility? In personal relationships, they often suppress their feelings because they want to avoid strife at all costs. They also possess a greater longing for approval, especially from their parents, peers, spouses, partners, or children.

Those who seek the approval of others often do not fully appreciate the great cost to themselves. When the aim of their response is primarily reactive to another person's request, demand, or oppression rather than taking care of their own needs, they eventually pay a price. A respected businessman in our community suffered from hypertension and shared that his medications barely reduced his blood pressure. When he constantly rushed to please his clients' demands and commit to meet unrealistic and sometimes impossible deadlines, he paid a price. He said, "When I am under pressure, my head feels as if it is rapidly shaking from side to side, which is very disturbing." As he was unaware that the constant barrage of rushing, stressful, and negative thoughts played a role in his heightened blood pressure, it became apparent that he didn't realize the connection between mental stress and physical health and well-being.

In another instance, a client who feared her husband's wrath and dominant male chauvinistic patterns suppressed her feelings until she no longer had a sense of who she was. If friends asked her how she liked a movie, she responded according to how her husband liked it. At age thirty-five, she began psychotherapy and told the therapist she didn't know where she ended and her husband began. She expressed her feelings by touching her thumb with her index finger to make a circle and then entwining the other thumb with the index finger to make two circles, reminiscent of childhood paper chains. One circle represented her, and the other her spouse. She was so lost that she felt she was drowning.

In a desire to overcome feelings of inadequacy, rejection, ugliness, stupidity, or lack of financial means, those of any age, but especially teenagers, engage in sexual activity even when they don't want to, in hopes of keeping their partner in the relationship or reaching an eventual marriage, or at times in an effort to raise their socioeconomic status. Others indulge in harmful activities, such as binge-eating, excessive alcohol consumption, drugs, or crime, often surrendering to peer pressure, when deep down they know that their choices are not in their best interest. They may feel compelled to conform to the "trend." They often feel they are stuck or that there are no other options, especially when they continue to seek peer approval, do not benefit from adult support, or lack the will to overcome challenges or cling to something greater than themselves. Often, they aren't even aware that there is a different path to alter their response to those who oppress, discount, or demean them, so they continue to partake in self-destructive behavior. People with a solid core, or those who believe their body is a temple, simply walk away. But there are multitudes who feel loved ones did not treasure them enough or give the unconditional love necessary to develop that solid foundation of self-worth.

A young woman attended a party where almost everyone was snorting cocaine. When a guy drew a line of coke on her hand, she immediately blew the powder in his face. Angrily, he said, "Hey, you just wasted one hundred dollars!" She snapped back, "What word didn't you get when I told you *I don't do coke*?" She was certainly not a "goody-goody" but had unyielding convictions. These are some reasons that people extend themselves far beyond what they know is right, and their responses often seem totally out of place. There are times during any age or stage of our lives when we also chip away so much of who we are in hopes of pleasing a person who is special to us. In the end, we are lost, and we ponder what the future might bring, as we no longer recognize or may not even like ourselves.

There are some pillars in our community whom we admire or idolize and others who become disingenuous to gain recognition. At some point, we discover they were fooling most others, including their closest loved ones, but mostly themselves. Sometimes, sadly and shockingly, they take their own lives. If we look deep into our hearts and are completely honest with ourselves, we give ourselves permission to solely define who we are. If we don't fall into the trap of envy, allow others to determine our necessities, or talk ourselves into thinking we can accomplish something even though we know the price is too high, then hopefully we will be okay. Just be aware that as we look up to those great achievers, we are clueless about the possible negative thoughts that drum in their heads or are unaware of whom they've shoved aside to achieve their status or by what deceitful, unethical, or immoral methods they reached such heights.

Insecurity Lens

Feelings of insecurity manifest themselves in many actions. Folks who frequently ridicule, distort, discount, or bully others or their ideas or behavior often act like this to promote themselves. When you confront them with your own concern, their response may be, "You don't know what you are talking about," "That's ridiculous," or "I never heard of anything so stupid." By putting others down, they try to elevate themselves, making themselves feel better and smarter or that they matter more. This type of communication typically stems from a *feeling insecure* or *inadequate lens*. When you want to feel important or have an urge to belong, you may interrupt others' conversations and add a personal anecdote on the same topic. Sometimes, people use this approach because they think it adds interest or enlightening information to the conversation; others do it to gain a sense of belonging. One may brag, exaggerate, or indicate that their accomplishments are greater than others' in hopes that they will be held in higher esteem. Then again, those who vacillate back and forth, appear wishy-washy, are indecisive, or take what seems to be an extremely long time to make a simple choice do so because they fear failure. They prefer to commit to nothing rather than fail at something.

Lack of Education/Stupidity Lens

A female attorney recalled that she gave a speech when she was in the sixth grade. Her classmates had jeered and ridiculed her, calling her "stupid." She remembered that incident her entire life. Thirty years later, as an attorney, she found herself in a virtual verbal paralysis when recalling her past humiliation and fears. She froze or tripped over her words due to past sneering. I asked her to list her accomplishments since then. She had received excellent grades in law school, wrote concise and articulate briefs, and was personable with clients. When she analyzed her former thoughts—being made fun of when she was twelve—and put them into the current context of a forty-year-old accomplished attorney, she had a different perspective. She used an earlier version of the *Identify, Block, Move, Delete, Replace Technique* to overcome her previous fears until she could no longer recall them.

An astute businesswoman was the middle child in a family that stressed the importance of academic achievement. Her parents did not acknowledge her other significant personal attributes and abilities. Though the woman was very perceptive, capable, and thoughtful and excelled in many areas, academics were not her strength. She was also sandwiched between siblings who were high achievers. As an adult, she continued to rate herself as "less than," and whenever a person questioned her, she replied, "You must think I'm stupid." Her thoughts and negative voice reflected the inferiority she still felt.

An Ivy League graduate who had gone through public schools while many of his classmates had attended private schools felt inferior when he compared himself with them. He put himself under so much pressure, believing that he had to know everything, that he was often rude to people, especially to his staff. While we may admire others and adopt their prized style, comparison to them is harmful. The only productive comparison we can make in our own best interest is comparing where we were, where we are, and where we realistically hope to go. Yet even that comparison is not always in our best interest.

Physical Appearance Lens

I would guess that at some point in everyone's lives, most of us have felt unattractive. If we don't feel pretty on the inside, we certainly are not going to feel pretty on the outside. The media also plays a significant role in creating an unrealistic standard. Folks can be considerably cruel with looks or comments like, "You look ugly," "Your hair is sticking out," "Your outfit doesn't match," "Your skin is too dark," "You are too skinny," "You put on weight," "Your ears lie too flat," "Your nose is too big," or "What's up with your complexion?" There are innumerable ways to get a message that you are unattractive. It is hard enough coming from peers and friends but profoundly more damaging when an unsolicited message comes from a loved one, especially your parents, spouse, partner, or child. However, sincere compliments are kind and often appreciated. When I told my then four-year-old grand that I didn't like my hair, she said, "Nana, your hair is beautiful. You should love it."

An accomplished professional shared that although her husband and children told her *she was beautiful*, she didn't feel it as a younger woman. As she matured and gained broad respect and success, she felt more worthy. Then, when she looked at old photos, she realized that she actually was attractive, though she never felt or saw it before.

An attorney who was close to retirement came from a large family with lots of brothers. When I saw his family photo, it reflected that he was always quite handsome. He said that his mother didn't want his good looks to go to his head, so she constantly told him, "You are ugly." The man shared that his mother's words had quite an impact. It wasn't until he was twenty-five years old and had taken psychotherapy that he felt good about himself. His mother could have instead kindly stated, "You are very handsome, but don't ever let it go to your head." Seemingly, harmful words about appearance or any attribute, even spoken in jest, often create a long-lasting, debilitating impact.

Despite outward appearance, whether you are wearing a miniskirt, suit, dress, pants, wig, extensions, yarmulke, hijab, burka, turban or show visible roots, it is best to never allow anyone to label who you are by how you look; to put it simply, do not judge the contents of a book by its cover.

Failure/Rejection Lens

The *failure lens* often develops when parents are extremely critical and do not balance that criticism with praise. When a child makes a mistake or fails and parents harshly reprimand or use corporal punishment, the effects are harmful and, at times, devastating. Instead, it is best for parents to take the time to chat positively with the child and focus on the child's esteemed attributes by appreciating and complimenting them when the child expresses them. Gaining recognition of the child's challenges and trying to find solutions leaves a more positive impact than responding with demeaning language, which lies heavily on a child. Some can easily brush off these negative put-downs, but others find this type of reaction belittling. As with other *lenses*, people with a *fear of failure lens* don't make decisions easily or may continually vacillate in their opinions. Most everyone requires time to make major decisions, but some people contemplate much longer. They are so fearful of making the wrong decision or a mistake that they do not state their position until they feel that they are forced to do so. For them, making no decision is far better than taking a chance and making the wrong choice. If you know a family member or colleague who appears to possess all the necessary information yet repeatedly fails to decide or vacillates back and forth, a *fear of failure lens* is a feasible reason.

Fear of rejection also holds people back from reaching out to others, and they often wait for others to reach out to them. They may want to inquire about the welfare of an extended family member or old friend but back off for fear that they are imposing or will be rejected. Excuses they use are, "They might be busy," or "This might not be a good time."

Financial Insecurity/Not Enough Lens

The *financial insecurity lens* occurs when you previously felt financially or materially deprived, lost your job, depleted your savings, or saw your wealth vanish into thin air. Although you now possess more financial security than you ever dreamed, the sense or fear of not having enough money remains throughout life. If you rationally examine your financial portfolio, you realize that you have enough funds. But the feeling that you once were impoverished, deprived, and insecure still drives you. Usually, the first thought that crosses your mind is the cost of an item or event—even if you could afford the expense to attend tens or hundreds of times over. Even as you age, hanging onto your money often remains more important than providing additional comfort or pleasure.

As a young woman, an acquaintance struggled and counted her pennies. In retirement, she admitted that though she had more money than she could ever want or spend, the cost of anything remained a primary concern. When her daughter was engaged, she said the reason she did not attend a wedding shower was that she did not want to spend money on another gift. People with *financial insecurity lenses* may often talk about the cost of things—not to brag, but to express concern about how much they've spent or saved. People who appear to possess an abundance of wealth often don't feel they have enough. At a gathering, a woman who had donated $100,000 to an organization and who lives in a spacious home with an enormous garden filled with hundreds of flowers told the hostess that she was leaving and asked if she could take home the floral centerpiece. The hostess said it was too early in the evening to remove the flowers. When the hostess left the room, the woman looked around to see if anyone was watching her. She then took most of the flowers out of the floral arrangement and left the party.

Many parents who felt financially impoverished as children will give in to their own child's every desire without requiring any accountability in attitude, behavior, or responsibility for taking care of possessions. The child may damage a new bike, lose several cell phones, or be involved in a few car accidents, but each time, their possessions are repaired or replaced. These parents recall how deprived they felt as youngsters, with fewer toys, clothes, cars, or experiences than their peers. They often work long hours, sacrificing time for themselves and with their families, to provide an excess of material goods and experiences for their children. They do not question the child's preference for material presents over their parents' presence. They also do not fully realize how receiving everything they want when they want it can negatively affect the child's life. The child may miss the opportunity to earn money or learn to take responsibility for their possessions. This pattern establishes false and unrealistic expectations of free lunches and sets an unhealthy precedent in later personal relationships and career success.

Children who were indulged in this way often do not realize why they have to work to succeed in relationships or at the workplace. They are overindulged and perceive that everything should be coming to them without accountability, effort, or responsibility if they break or lose something. However, at other times, showering a child with love language expressed by attending events, including them in an abundance of experiences, and giving them material possessions fosters appreciation and gratitude. This can promote generosity to others, especially when children felt a giving spirit in their parents and were involved in visits to the elderly, less fortunate, ill, *handi-abled*, or veterans. Their family may have volunteered at schools, hospitals, and food banks, dropped off holiday baskets, mentored young professionals, assisted those from other cultures, or performed other kind and charitable deeds.

A kindhearted, brilliant, and an outstanding neurosurgeon grew up in humble beginnings. His family had survived the atrocities in Europe. That incident, compounded by the monetary impact of managed health care, consumed him and put him under tremendous pressure to constantly achieve more and strive to make more money. His expertise and skill in the operating room never failed, but the *financial insecurity lens* that burned within expressed itself in the curt manner with which he communicated with colleagues and staff.

Health Lens

The *health lens* is undue concern expressed by a person who is often ill or had a serious disease or lost a spouse, partner, child, or parent to illness. I am not suggesting that a person who battled cancer and is in remission frightens too easily when something feels unusual or their body feels as it did prior to the cancer diagnosis. It often takes years before a person no longer freezes in fear when a faint possibility of the disease reappears. After I underwent my first coronary bypass procedure, whenever I felt a certain unease, I became very anxious. I ended up in the emergency room a few times. Since I had always been asymptomatic except for shortness of breath, every unusual pang in my chest caused concern. In those early years, I had difficulty differentiating between heart attack symptoms and anything else. I explained to one of my physicians that it is similar to a gardener who spots a tiny green speck sprout up from the soil. Initially, you can't decipher whether the sprout erupted from a seed that you sowed or a volunteer weed; it takes a while to identify which it is.

When one is having a heart attack, symptoms associated with a heart attack, or a very unusual, sometimes internally sinking or closing down feeling, it is never prudent to wait or ignore the symptoms. In fact, my symptoms weren't associated with heart attacks—just a strong sense that something was wrong. One of my physicians gave me a guideline: wait about five minutes and monitor yourself. If nothing changes, wait ten minutes more, and if you don't think it is a heart attack, take a pill he recommended. If the situation hasn't changed in forty-five minutes, head for the hospital. Occasionally, I went through this routine. Then, my husband would ask, "Do you need to go to the hospital?" And I usually said, "No." A few years ago in California, as I awoke, I immediately felt something "off" in my body. After forty-five minutes, I said, "We need to head to the hospital." By the time we arrived, my blood pressure and heart rate had dropped significantly. After many tests, the doctor recommended reducing two-thirds of my cardiovascular medication. Living a calmer and more simplified lifestyle in Nevis and adhering to Thich Nhat Hanh's teachings, especially his calming mindful breaths, combined to positively affect my health.

People who carry a *health lens* often worry unduly about their health or the health of others. These concerns dominate their conversation as they constantly talk about who is ill, fret over others' outcomes, dwell on their own and other people's health challenges, and note what new remedies are available. Even when no one is seriously ill, they often agonize over every minor ailment that they or others have. Sometimes physicians can find the cause of their illness or discomfort; sometimes they can't. When the doctors can't discover anything wrong, family members, and sometimes physicians, begin to perceive these patients as hypochondriacs. Unfortunately, when these people become gravely ill, family members do not take them seriously, so they may wait too long before seeking medical attention, and at times it is too late to begin treatment.

A fine line exists between overreacting and not speaking out loudly enough when you are concerned. The sister of a dear childhood friend was a chain smoker and had been a heavy drinker. In her early seventies, she became ill, and doctors diagnosed a urinary tract infection. Over the next two months, she lost weight and developed symptoms that resembled dementia and Alzheimer's disease. Many thought her symptoms were related to her past history, but her eldest daughter kept demanding, "At least give her another urine test." The doctors ignored the request. Two days before she died, she became very confused and could hardly function. Her daughter took her to the hospital, where she underwent comprehensive testing. The doctor ruled out lung cancer and pneumonia and noted that she had septicemia. The diagnosis was confirmed as the cause of her demise on the death certificate. During the previous summer, my friend's sister had received her paralegal certificate from The Ohio State University and was passionately looking forward to implementing her new legal skills to help those with addictions. Her daughter regretted that she had not "*demanded more* from anyone who would listen." She felt that if she had, her mother would still be alive.

While resting one afternoon, my daughter Gayle developed symptoms that she thought might be related to her heart. Her experience and my history of heart disease inspired Gayle to write the book *Leave Me*. She began to question what she would do if she required surgery. Gayle's book is the story of a mother who suddenly requires coronary bypass surgery.

In the book, the stress of being the primary caregiver and carrying the responsibility of career and family all falls on the main character. After surgery, she decides to flee home to heal and find herself. During an interview with Robin Young on WOSU/*NPR* about *Leave Me*, Gayle admonished the audience, "Don't ignore the symptoms" (Free 2016). While driving to work at a local university campus, a professor was listening to the interview while she was stuck in bumper-to-bumper traffic. She was not feeling well but kept telling herself that she had to get to campus to teach her classes. As her symptoms continued and intensified, she broke out in a sweat. At the end of Gayle's interview, she firmly repeated, "Don't ignore the symptoms!" So the listener turned off at the next exit, drove to the hospital, and found that indeed she was in the midst of a heart attack that required an emergency procedure to open a clogged artery.

There is a huge difference between anguishing about something and engaging proactively. A friend in her late thirties had two daughters. She had lost her mother when she was twenty-five years old. The woman discovered she had inherited the mutated BRCA gene, which greatly increases the risk of developing breast or ovarian cancer. Years before the procedure was in the public eye, she decided to take the most prudent measures available to give her the optimal outcome so that her children wouldn't have to face her premature death. She traveled to a distant medical center to undergo a series of complex medical procedures and incurred a significant debt that took her more than a decade to pay off.

Bullying Lens

Bullying, in any form, is perpetrated by individuals or groups who are unenlightened and insecure and who dislike or even detest others. Their remarks or actions have nothing to do with the recipient but reflect the person who speaks the words or inflicts the acts. Bullying is a repetitive and aggressive mode of communication and behavior that manifests in physical and verbal forms and significantly affects the recipient's well-being. Physical bullying may be expressed by shoving, hitting, punching, kicking, lunging, tripping, and hair-pulling. Acts also include damaging, hiding, or stealing belongings, as well as making lewd gestures. Bullying also persuades others who would not have otherwise initiated these acts to join in because they are cowardly, feel less worthy, or haven't been taught better by parents or caretakers. There is a sadistic nature to bullying, as one of the goals is to make the other person feel powerless or inferior. This creates a sense of superiority in the perpetrator's mind and provides an unrighteous and mean-spirited sense of power. Verbal bullying spews words that taunt and demean and includes name-calling, racial or gender slurs, or spreading false rumors about a person. The intent of verbal bullying is to poke fun, embarrass, or humiliate. This is even more despicable when boys or men attack girls or women.

All these actions bear one thing in common—the desire to harm a person, cause anguish, or make them feel frightened, uncomfortable, and less worthy. When any of these acts are repeated in a single session, or over a prolonged period, that's bullying. A person specializing in family law states, "If you repeat something more than twice, that's bullying."

There are four roles in the bullying process: the person who bullies (the perpetrator), the person who is bullied (the victim), the person who is the bystander, and the person who is the upstander. The person who is the victim may not have the choice, strength, or courage to walk away or just peacefully continue what they were doing. The person who bullies and the person who stands by are cowards. The person who is an upstander is courageous, righteous, and willing to put themselves at risk by choosing to support the victim. None of these roles are fixed, and there are many examples of persons who once bullied and then evolved to become upstanders. These individuals often enlighten and encourage others to change their ways, giving themselves and others an advantage in the process and in their new roles.

There are many situations that feed bullying. The home environment is often the first place in which a child witnesses bullying between parents or caretakers. Or they may experience the beginning of bullying by either bullying others or being the recipient of bullying. At times, this bullying pattern creates a sense of unworthiness within the victim; they may then permit this crippling behavior to continue in select situations throughout most—if not all—of their lives. From the moment of birth, it is best that the child instantly feels comfort, love, and acceptance. It is also in the newborn's best interest if parents and caregivers believe in their hearts and souls that the child is worthy just because they are. These endearing feelings and energy affect their child's fragile spirit and humanness to help create a foundation of self-worth and belonging. Without that support, certain conditions contribute to low self-esteem and a sense of unworthiness. This often leaves a child more vulnerable to become a bully or a victim. Similar to a ball that needs air to bounce, we must not allow others to deflate us. Those who bully seem to instinctively know whom to bully, as they hone in and prey on the weakest and most vulnerable. Parents, teachers, and caretakers are also guilty, as they deny or fail to dole out or enforce consequences that are commensurate with the bully's tormenting comments or behaviors. At times, when principals or teachers reprimand a student's bullying behavior, parents and caretakers admonish the educators. Other parents profusely apologize and clearly indicate by their words and deeds that they do not in any form support this type of behavior. In the end, as in many situations, the child has a mind of their own.

The bullied child is the recipient of cruelty. When the child is not honored and cherished just for who they are, they are often ridiculed, demeaned, or labeled "disappointing," "a failure," or "disgusting." At times, they are made to feel that not even their very best is good enough. Often, another child's achievements are held as the benchmark that the child is expected to reach. It is worthwhile to recognize others' abilities and praise others' honorable standards and suggest that the child emulate those ideals, but we cannot demand that our child have the capacity or will to mirror those traits. By doing so, we place a heavy burden on young shoulders. We teach best by example and providing support and tools to help the child reach their fullest potential, especially actualizing their endowed abilities and passions.

Many people whom I met were bullied because of appearance, culture, religion, sexual orientation, lack of skills, lack of love, or a swath of other reasons. Again, only the victim and bystanders who witness the cruelty realize the impact of these experiences and how profoundly the emotional or spiritual scars remain.

Bullying probably began at the beginning of time and has often reared its ugly head throughout the history of human civilization. With the advent of global media, a more laid-back society, family separations, economic stress, global uncertainty, and violence-laced entertainment, violence became more pervasive. During the US 2016 political arena, a leading presidential candidate exhibited and encouraged bullying, divisive, and demeaning rhetoric. These words and actions unleashed permission to incite danger, divisiveness, and hatred. This leads to an unpleasant atmosphere that, in some instances, is transferred from person to person. Worse yet, this contentious energy field often creates a harmful and unpleasant national and international atmosphere.

Abuse Lens

When a person has experienced physical, mental, verbal, or emotional abuse, or bullying, sexual harassment, abduction, rape, sodomy, or human trafficking, these violating and heinous experiences and events leave profound and humiliating memories. In varying degrees, these affect a person's spirit, attitudes, or behaviors throughout their lives. This may manifest in a combative style. These feelings and thoughts can lie dormant or erupt, similar to a volcano spewing forth steam or lava, scalding the spirit. In varying degrees and at different times, these memories are reflected in how a person feels, thinks, acts, or speaks. Sometimes, these memories catch us off guard, similar to a wave that throws us off-balance; other times, words uttered by others are so powerful that it feels like a huge wave flipping us upside down.

A very attractive physician was often molested by male passengers as she survived the local war by escaping from Vietnam with the boat people. Twenty years later, whenever a male patient or a father of a young patient complimented her physical beauty, even her hands, or reached to touch her hand or shoulder in a gesture of appreciation, she recoiled. Her facial expressions and body language immediately took on a repulsed or defensive pose. That response sent quite a negative, confusing, and insulting message to the patient or parent, who were only showing appreciation.

A woman recalled that as a child, she was made fun of by her classmates and blathered behind her back about her achievements. As an adult, she was suspicious of colleagues gathered at the water cooler, imagining that they were gossiping about her. A high school teacher shared that a student who was sexually molested often talked about Peeping Toms and the need to install alarms in her house. Other people might think that these responses are examples of paranoia or that people are overreacting, but these responses often reflect a person's previous abusive experiences.

Verbal abuse, especially later in life, is troubling when it appears unexpectedly from an adult child, sibling, or a partner or spouse whose abusive tendencies had never surfaced before. This is particularly challenging when the person had previously maintained the ability to resolve issues in a mindful manner.

During a bout of physical therapy, a man who knew of me but I didn't yet know opened up and shared his story while we were walking side by side on the treadmill twice a week for couple weeks. When he was a young child, his mother's boyfriend sodomized him. He carried that pain and shame for years. In high school, he tried to drown his sorrow in alcohol. His mother yelled, "Why can't you just put it behind you?" He told me, "Her words were almost as painful as the attack itself." At that time in his life, he hadn't discovered the path out of his dismal despair. I ran into him again at physical therapy, and he related that he enjoyed his new job and seemed to be in a better place.

A woman from a remote, mountainous area came from a dysfunctional family. Her mother was a kind, intelligent woman who suffered from alcoholism, and her father deserted the family. As a child, she often had to fend for herself, participate in some questionable activities, and adopt a tough attitude to survive. She loved to visit a neighbor who daily read the Bible aloud to her grandchildren. As she listened, she learned values from Scriptures. Fortunately, she was a bright child and good student. She went on to graduate and developed a respected career path. She gained the respect of the community and helped her family as well as those in need. And yet decades later, she often cried out in her sleep, "I don't want to go to hell." No one except her immediate family would ever know how deeply the scars of her youth still affected her.

I have only met a very few soldiers returning from the Iraq or Afghanistan wars, but I am well aware of and am empathetic to the sacrifices and horrors that many of our armed forces encountered and endured. The ensuing posttraumatic stress disorder or traumatic brain injuries leave daily physical, psychological, and emotional struggles and challenges, and unspoken nightmares often remain. I applaud as I witness how they triumph to achieve different forms of greatness. I have known several individuals who survived severe brutality, homelessness, imprisonment, fires, or the Holocaust yet had the strength and will to overcome and be caring, loving, engaging, contributing, and often very financially successful individuals. Each person's response to similar situations depends on their basic nature, their resilience, the love and support they receive, their faith in a power beyond themselves, and the facets of their *hand-dome*.

Many people, including family members, other dear ones, or fellow global citizens, experienced or witnessed torture, rape, incest, sexual harassment, abduction, major accidents, natural disasters, war, terrorism, atrocities, infernos, or holocausts. Those memories continue to haunt a person forever. We can never completely comprehend how profoundly widespread these abuses are or always know whether any person endured or witnessed such an event. Only individuals who experienced such atrocities possess the endowed right to truly grasp their sense of lingering physical, mental, emotional, and psychological anguish or spiritual disease. At times, those who most intimately share life with them may get a glimpse into their anguish, as memories of horror or fear appear in distraught facial expressions when they think no one is looking or they softly whisper when they think no one is listening. Nevertheless, the memories of each person or event are never permanently eradicated.

So when we look at other people and think they have it all, or when we don't understand their motivation or response, we remind ourselves that we haven't witnessed and don't know their innermost nagging memories, concerns, or life experiences. The scars of these horrific and agonizing events are not often as visibly apparent as are scars on our skin. Nevertheless, the memories remain imprinted to some degree in the dark corners of a person's mind and the inner sanctum of their heart.

Thought and Response Lenses

The *lenses* presented in this section are *control, defensiveness, competitiveness, negativity/ self-deprecation, catching up/needing to prove, questioning "what if," crying wolf, overreacting, "should be," "rose-colored glasses," expectations/assumptions, retrospective regret*, and *neglected well-being/self-expectation*.

Control Lens

The need to control our or others' physical environment stems in part from a basic insecurity. This sense of unworthiness prevents us from standing up and stating our needs and preferences or demanding the respect we deserve from others. The need to hold the upper hand occurs if there was a strong controlling adult in our childhood or later on in our lives. As adults, we continue to feel controlled, although that may not be another's intention.

A friend whose mother was very controlling felt that any suggestion that his wife made was a means to control him. As he aged, he usually did not perceive the potential dangers that lay ahead when participating in sports or maneuvering through unfamiliar surroundings. He often bruised and hurt himself. Whenever his wife offered suggestions, he turned and walked away after the first few words were uttered. Even though her recommendations were similar to others' or physicians', he constantly felt badgered. When family members urged him to see a doctor about symptoms of a potentially serious medical issue that were visible to them but unapparent to him, he remained reluctant. Similarly, a physical therapist was upset when her forty-year-old husband required unavoidable knee surgery. She had often tried to teach him good posture and appropriate bending, reaching, and lifting methods for the heavy appliances that he serviced, but he refused to pay attention.

A physician from Korea had exceptionally good rapport with his patients and support staff *until* a patient, their family, or staff doubted or questioned his "authority." In his childhood, he had memories of his father, a physician, whom the patients in his village obeyed and respected. In other words, they did exactly what he told them—no questions asked. Forty years later, when patients or nurses questioned the physician's "recommendations," he recalled his childhood memory of his father's obedient patients. The doctor strongly resented his patients and staff when they did not comply with his recommendations or orders. He became livid; he could feel the anger begin to foment in his body. His facial expressions and voice tone immediately reflected this anger, much to the detriment of his professional relationships.

To help him replace his negative attitude with a positive approach, I explained that physicians from all cultures—including U.S. physicians—are challenged with our population's increasing diversity. What is appropriate in one culture is not necessarily acceptable in another. Furthermore, our twenty-first-century global media offers a wealth of credible and false online information for any symptom, illness, diagnosis, or treatment plan. Although the physician remains the expert who gives the diagnoses and makes the recommendations, the patient or family ultimately decide whether to accept them.

To help him overcome the *authority lens* and the need to "control" his patients, my first request was that he write the word *authority* in capital letters, AUTHORITY. Then I told him to mark a large X through AUTHORITY and replace the word with *expertise*. It was not enough to recognize the difference; he had to feel it as well. By the end of the session, he felt that he had overcome an enduring negative feeling and had the insight to embark on a new, more positive and effective approach with his patients.

I observed that as people stand up and gain more confidence in themselves, they are clearer in asserting their needs. In time, they realize that they no longer need to control their environment, as others now positively and respectfully respond to their needs or requests.

Defensiveness Lens

If you were constantly compared with others and received the brunt of harsh criticism or cruel prejudice during childhood or later, you may have protected yourself by developing a *defensiveness lens*, which is expressed with a defensive attitude. You rarely accept responsibility in a situation that has not gone well and are quick to blame another or something else. You may completely deflect the conversation back to the other person or manipulate the information so that you are always right, similar to a falling cat that twists as it positions itself and lands on all four paws.

People who carry a *defensiveness lens* often do not want to hear a word about any of their shortcomings, questionable actions, or negative communication patterns. They believe that any unfavorable message or constructive criticism implies "you're wrong." The communication of those who carry a *defensiveness lens* reflects a negative attitude tainted with negative communication: nonverbal, voice tone, or verbal. Their predictable responses may be "Not me," "I'm not wrong," "It wasn't my fault," "I wasn't supposed to do it," "Another person was using the equipment," or "The information was hard to find." A person who carries a *defensiveness lens* will instantaneously deflect critique and respond by turning the issue back onto the person who brought it up. If you ask, "Why isn't the report finished?" a deflecting response is, "Well, your reports aren't always finished on time either." Deflecting responses create a verbal pattern similar to the visual image of a volleyball player who instinctively volleys the ball away in any direction instead of controlling the ball to pass it to a teammate. A person created this *defensiveness lens* to repel any negative comment. They do not listen to the information, process it, or take it on in any way.

To further bolster their stance, they may process positive and negative information quite differently. They quickly process and retain many negative events or conversations but discard or fail to process many positive events with similar regularity or intensity. Consequently, their gloomy perception becomes their reality but often does not reflect truth. This selective process is not limited to those with a *defensive lens* but can apply to others.

Competitiveness Lens

A person with a *competitiveness lens* likes to have the upper hand and lets you know that their experience is always greater, more significant, or better than yours. Instead of listening to you and then sharing, they interrupt and quickly comment. One client came from a large competitive family of humble beginnings. Her father felt that by constantly comparing and pitting one child against the other, each child would be motivated to try harder to succeed and become accomplished, financially successful adults. In some way, the father's design worked because each child excelled in their field, yet many remain quite competitive. They are cohesive and fun at family gatherings, but that attitude betrays their lack of indication to reach out to help family members during life's storms. My client shared that when she was asked a question, before she completed her response, her siblings interrupted to state something similar, implying that their ideas, purchases, or experiences had greater value, impact, and significance. My client also mentioned that when a sibling asked her, "What did you get when you went shopping?" before she could finish answering, her sister interrupted, noting that she had bought something more expensive or attractive.

People who are competitive express these characteristics not only in verbal responses but also in their actions. In professional settings, sports, and different aspects of life, a person who competes to achieve their best is understandable, but this competitive force also drives their personal lives as they try to outdo others in every aspect. If a family member does something special or thoughtful, they will try to one-up them. Again, these patterns are not exclusive to large families; they can apply to anyone.

Negativity/Self-Deprecation Lens

When we carry a *negativity lens* or *self-deprecation lens*, we unconsciously display defensive body language to reveal distaste or frustration. Those negative thoughts and feelings influence what we say and how we say it. Do people react negatively to you? Do you arch your eyebrows, scrunch up your face, curl your lips, or roll your eyes? Do you sigh or raise your voice? Are you abrupt, rude, or arrogant? Do you seethe with anger, feel livid, or want to scream? Do you see yourself as inferior to others or minimize your experiences or status?

A physician's patients thought he was rude, arrogant, and intimidating. While consulting with him, I discovered that he carried a *negativity lens*. In his childhood, his parents used negatively charged language, conveying words that were both pessimistic and harsh. Word choices such as *scalding* instead of *hot* and *never* or *always* instead of *sometimes* are negatively slanted responses. As an adult, he perceived the world and conveyed his responses more negatively and severely than necessary. When a patient asked about eating red meat marbled with excessive fat, the physician warned, "That will give you a heart attack, and you could die." A more appropriate, less frightening, yet still significant response is, "Eating red meat will raise your cholesterol levels, which puts you at greater risk for heart disease." Another example of giving a negative cast is saying "It wasn't negative," or "It wasn't bad," instead of "It was positive," or "It was okay." State the possibility, not the improbability. The physician's *negativity lens* developed in response to vocabulary and communication style that he had heard and learned from his father as a child.

People who communicate negatively describe situations more severely than necessary, and they use a preponderance of naysaying words, such as *never, no,* or *nothing.* They focus heavily on anticipating the worst. Please note: just because you're incapable of a certain undertaking or have failed, don't let that prevent you from achieving what you can. When I was quite young, I commented to an adult, "Can't can't do anything."

Some people inherently perceive and feel experiences more negatively than others and describe these in negative terms. Others perceive and communicate more negatively to protect themselves. If they feel and express themselves more pessimistically, it helps them prepare for the worst-case scenario.

A producer of television commercials learned that she was detail-oriented yet she couldn't see the big picture. She admitted she was more oriented toward "micro" than "macro." Instead of apologizing by saying, "I'm sorry, I'm not good at seeing the complete concept," she learned to respond positively, "That's a great idea. How do you see it?" After the directors gained the more holistic information, she filled in the necessary details. Walking into a clinic where patients received physical therapy, a woman exclaimed, "This looks like a disaster area." One patient who diligently strived to walk again retorted, "No, this is the recovery zone."

Physicians who diagnose lumps as malignant before receiving lab results give a premature and more concerning diagnosis, which may be inaccurate or unnecessary. When a patient asks, "What do you think the results will be?" I recommend replying, "Let's wait until the test results are back." I know too many people who spent weekends or days waiting in anguish, suspecting the worst because their physicians said, "It's probably cancer," when it wasn't. A dermatologist told a friend, "It looks like melanoma," only to discover it was a basal cell cancer, which is far less invasive and not life-threatening. If the physician had waited for the test results before giving an inaccurate diagnosis, my friend would have been spared hours of uncertainty. When offering treatment options to a patient, I recommend that physicians start with the least severe protocol and move to the most severe.

Years ago, when I began the procedures to determine the cause of my angina, I had problems on the first treadmill run. When I asked my internist, "Now what?" he calmly replied, "First, a thallium treadmill, then an angiogram, then angioplasty or bypass surgery, if necessary." Eventually, I underwent quadruple coronary bypass surgery. A more frightening initial response would be, "You will need bypass surgery." I will always be grateful for that gentle easing into the options and eventual process. Except in life-threatening emergencies, when urgency is required, that gradual, realistic approach is more comforting. Also, remember to focus on what is possible as far as preventive care, or a proactive choice, such as palliative care.

Another way people who carry a *negativity lens* respond to life is to first look at the negative side of a situation. My husband is the opposite. He avoids being in a "negative space" at any cost and rarely focuses on the downside of any situation until it happens. He doesn't project into the future to foresee what hardships or inconveniences a surgery, professional move, or lifestyle change will bring. Decades ago, he merged his accounting practice with a larger firm. Shortly after the merger, he told me, "I didn't realize it would require this kind of an adjustment." When he underwent knee surgery, he said, "I didn't realize the recovery would be this slow or take this long." Whenever there is a health challenge with a family member, my husband always says, "Let's cross that bridge when we get to it." He refuses to spend time solving issues until he actually is faced with the issue and needs to make a decision. An interesting aspect of our sixty years of marriage is that the less I worry about certain matters, the more concerned he becomes.

Others who carry the *negativity lens* begin their conversation with the negative information rather than save it for the end. When I asked a client why she does that, she responded, "I want to get the negative information out of the way so that I can move forward and end on a positive note." Yet others often did not see it that way and thought she always complained.

The *negativity lens* pertains not only to the words and language we use but also to our non-verbal facial expressions and body language. During past lectures, while participants stated their dislike of others' use of negatively tainted words, their facial expressions and body language did not remain neutral. With them being unaware of the incongruity, their negative nods and facial expressions were just as detracting. Even deliberate sighs or raised eyebrows send a message.

Self-deprecation is also a form of negative communication. This leads to the listener's sense that the person demeans themselves or does not appreciate what they possess, which possibly makes others uncomfortable. When we use the adjective *starter*, as in *starter house*, *starter car*, *starter job*, *starter wardrobe*, or *starter husband*, we belittle what we have. Have you ever visited a person who recently moved into a new home and shortly after they welcome you they immediately note everything they want to replace instead of appreciating what they already have? I recall this type of response quite often, with one exception since childhood. It is an attitude in the United States that I've never experienced in my fifteen years living in Nevis. Some people also have a difficult time accepting compliments and minimize the other's kind words. When I experience this, I wonder why they apologize, and ask myself, "Why do they have to downplay?" Perhaps it's a form of humility or embarrassment.

An owner of a gift shop always underrated himself by mentioning the experiences he didn't have instead of acknowledging those that gave him pleasure. If he was planning a trip abroad, he shared his plans and then stated, "I haven't traveled to as many places as you." If a colleague commented about his nice attire, he responded, "I found this at a thrift shop. I can't afford department stores." When he had an open house for his staff, a guest commented about the cool travel memorabilia on display. He belittled his artisans' handcrafted collection and said, "I don't own expensive items. These are just local knickknacks." Regardless of how often others complimented him, he always felt compelled to tell the other person what he didn't have, hadn't done, or couldn't do. Whatever the reason, his responses made others uncomfortable. It felt as if he was always putting himself beneath others. Otherwise, he was a kind and supportive boss.

Catching Up/Needing to Prove Lens

More than twenty-five years ago, a friend who was director of human resources at a medical facility shared that she always had to strive harder to catch up because she was a woman and a person of African heritage. Decades later, I was chatting with another woman of African heritage, a human resource director in the travel industry, and a woman of Latino heritage who was a leader in higher education. Both were frustrated with "always catching up," as both were women from minority cultures. Living among the Nevisian people, I often felt that perhaps people of European ancestry should *catch up* with many of them. Nevisian culture values wisdom, friendly manners, dedication to education (as exemplified with a 98 percent literacy rate), and mostly remaining positive and always grateful. There are many other types of *catch up lenses.* One is realistically trying to catch up to attain desired skill sets or access; that is positive. In 2014, President Obama announced his intention to empower and help young men of color improve their skills. He assured that he would remain involved his entire life (Jarrett and Johnson 2014).

Catching up materialistically, such as "keeping up with the Joneses" or some other superficial standard, can be dangerous. By emulating a lifestyle that is beyond our means, we put ourselves and our families under tremendous stress to keep up with another's standard. But why would we give others, the media, or advertisers the power to determine our standard of living or let them tell us what we should possess or how we can best prioritize our money? In that mind-set, we may never be satisfied with each new purchase or accomplishment, as we always focus on the "next" item or plan. In the end, the issue is not about what you possess but what possesses *you* that matters. The happiest people don't have the best of everything, but they make the best of everything.

We could be the youngest child, from another culture, recovering from an accident, illness, or downturned economy, or an injured soldier returning from war. By holding on to hope, we increase the potential for reaching a specific goal or a desired state of mind. Trying to catch up from either where we once were or soon hope to be also has its downside and is somewhat unrealistic. The past is lost; the future is gained. Living in either of these planes dishonors where we are at the moment. Judaism, Buddhism, Christianity, and other religions and beliefs negate living anywhere except fully in the present and only moment we have, the *I-am-here moment*, and finding joy and gratitude therein. Even as a young man, Pavel Friedman found solace in the present moment in a concentration camp during the Holocaust when a dandelion called out to him (Friedman 1942). My husband's mantra is, "Learn from the past, live in the present, and look forward to the future."

There are many more *catch up lenses* in life, but they only drain our daily dose of positive physical, mental, emotional, and spiritual energy that is bestowed upon us each day. Although it seems tough at times, the more we live in the present and appreciate life, the better off we are.

Living in the present gifts us more energy and focus. Enjoy each step as you reach a goal while reminding yourself that the journey is always far more important than the goal itself. Once that is reached, that moment vanishes in an instant and is frozen in time. The ongoing journey remains the richness of life that leads us to those precious and fleeting moments.

Moving toward the best version of ourselves is not always achieved by a desired time or date, but it is often achieved—or perhaps preordained—in universal time.

Questioning What-If Lens

What if was my mantra during my early twenties, as I was often waiting for another shoe to drop. People who respond to life thinking or stating *what if* have not developed or are out of touch with their own coping skills. When unpredictable or uncontrollable events or situations arise, they feel caught off guard, as they didn't have a plan in place. At some point in their lives, they learned to or were forced to repress their needs and responses to please or take care of others; therefore, they never developed their personal "first aid" coping mechanism. Because it was always more urgent to be responsible for a parent's, sibling's, or another's needs, they rarely had the opportunity to create their own guide to life. As situations arose, they often first thought of and responded to others' wants, demands, or expectations. However, they did not have a clue about how to take care of their own physical, emotional, or spiritual needs. They were often taken aback when considering how to respond to unpredictable or uncontrollable situations. People with the *what-if lens* may create scenarios in their minds of means to respond in a multitude of situations. Often, they hesitate before they react because they are mentally running through these responses or are debating between responding to their needs or those required or demanded by others.

Crying Wolf Lens

If you usually complain or cry wolf, those who are familiar with you are most likely aware of your nuanced *crying wolf lens*. If you worry about financial hardships when realistically there is no logical reason, others may not take you seriously when money falls short. If you continually complain about trivial health issues that were dealt with and unduly angst about your or others' health, others will not pay attention when your body is in distress. When you become ill, doctors and family members may not take you seriously until it becomes too late. They often respond, "You know Mom. She is always complaining about something." Yes, Mom complained her entire life about one ache or another—only this time it may be legitimate and urgent. With a prevalence of false alarms, it is understandable that doctors and family members may be slow to react in a real emergency. So when an acute event occurs, people may discount your concerns; consequently, they may not respond to the reality, no matter what the situation. They read it as one of your complaints.

Overreacting Lens

I believe that most of us embellish at some time in our lives. It is the extent to which we exaggerate that causes us to lose credibility or favor with others. When we want to make a point or seek another's approval or validation, we often overstate our point by repeating it too frequently and using more intense *nonverbal*, *voice-tone*, and *verbal* responses than required.

Some people, especially younger people on a new path, desperately seek the approval and support of their family. When these are not forthcoming, their frustration or sense of rejection desperately manifests itself by causing them to dig even deeper into their newfound values, mind-set, or change in their lives' trajectory. They don't realize that the more they drive home their point, the more they alienate those whose support they sought hard to earn.

Years ago, when I had newfound ideas and shared them, or added another facet to my life, I was very excited. Since I spoke passionately about what was new in my life, some family members or friends thought I was deftly trying to persuade them to accept my beliefs as their own. I wasn't; I was excited and wanted to be heard and validated. Other forms of overreacting are presented later in the *External Lenses* section of this chapter.

Should Be Lens

There are two types of *should be lenses*: one that emanates from within, from our own sense of values and responsibilities, and the other *should be* that is imposed upon us. There are times that I don't want to do something but my *source-voice* prompts me forward. Then my "Don't want to" voluntarily shifts to "Yes, I will," and lately, "I get to." A man shared that he visits the sick and the elderly because it is his "duty." I was aware of the situation and the fondness and compassion the person feels. So I added, you fulfill it because it is your "duty from the heart." Sometimes, other people impose their own views of the situation and express, badger, or try to "shame" or "guilt" you into *you should*.

Pay attention to the negative self-chatter echoing "You should" in your head. Monitor to see whose *should* it is. Is this your own thought, or does it reflect another person's past or present suggestion or demand? If you are uncertain as to how to respond, just think through it until the response is right for you. When you frequently follow another's "you should" dictum, feelings of resentment eventually creep in. Then, to some degree, these reflect in your actions, voice tone, expressions, or words, especially if you end up doing many tasks you don't want to do for an extended period. Think of the *shoulds* you performed in your life in response to another person's requests or demands, while under duress, or out of a sense of guilt or responsibility—but not from your heart. Did you end up resenting the task, or did you pleasantly and willingly take it on? If people continue to lay the *should* on you, when you begin to resent their remarks, respond kindly at the appropriate time with *source-connected* communication akin to "If I thought I should, I would." If that does not feel right, create your own response, remain quiet, or simply walk away. Shortly after we were married, my husband taught me that *if it doesn't come from your heart, don't do it*. It was a wonderful lesson, as I've learned that when I respond from my heart, there is never any expectation or resentment and my emotional energy remains intact.

Rose-Colored Glasses Lens

You've probably heard the expression "She sees the world through rose-colored glasses." If you recall the beginning of the presentation on *lenses*, I stated that *lenses* are only an issue if they interfere with living our life in the most productive and realistic manner possible. If we only see the goodness yet remain realistic and make sound choices and decisions, then the *rose-colored glasses lens* is not an issue. It often boosts us to greater heights—and that is good. However, this *lens* can also create a misleading perception that our abilities are greater than reality.

When we are unrealistic about our lives, we are unable to anticipate or prepare for unexpected situations. We tend to take on unnecessary financial burdens, overcommit, and put our physical and emotional health on the line *in the hope that* something will pan out. We leave ourselves vulnerable for disappointment and failure. These factors are burdensome, and that stress affects those around us. In these situations, we lose the precious balance that promotes holistic well-being. We are far better off waiting until time, funds, physical stamina, mental clarity, and emotional energy are available.

A suggested guideline is to perceive positively, process realistically, and act wisely. While I've always budgeted funds well, I usually think I'll have more time than I realistically do, and that is quite stressful. I also have a tendency to over commit. I recall that as a dear cousin aged, he responded to invitations, "We'll play it by ear." I have reached that stage in life when I can't predict the circumstances ahead and no longer have the will or the energy to force my body to push through as strongly as it once could. Occasionally, I will use the phrase "I'll make a note, and if I can, I'll be there" instead of confirming way ahead. For social get-togethers, people in Nevis often tell me, "Check back with me a few days before." Years ago, a close Nevisian friend asked me, "How can I say yes when I have no idea how I will feel that day or what I will have to do?" No wonder our friends in Nevis are cooler, calmer, and more collected.

Expectation/Assumption Lens

The *expectation/assumption lens* falls in both *internal* and *external lens* categories. The *internal expectation lens* represents the expectations we put on ourselves. This *lens* begins early in life, and though the thoughts may change, whatever our age, we still hold assumptions based on expectations. Early in life, we already expect a routine in response to events in our very limited environment. An infant cries and is fed. When the infant cries and is not fed as promptly as it is used to, it cries louder. And if it still is not fed, the baby wails, thrashing its tiny limbs. Yet as the infant develops, the toddler becomes aware that in its expanding life, nothing remains quite the same. Mothers or fathers have fluctuating and increasing time demands, caregivers change, foods taste different, weather changes, moods swing, and comfort varies. Later, change comes with the birth of a sibling, a move to a new home, the disappearance of a pet, the abandonment by a loved one, divorce, the death of a parent, the arrival of a new stepparent, or a multitude of other situations. Whatever caused the change, expectations based on former experiences have an impact and often lead to disappointment and emotional disease. What had always been constant no longer is.

From the most positive side to the most negative side of life's spectrum, expectations and assumptions have an effect. Managed and realistic expectations and assumptions for positive outcomes enhance, inspire, and uplift. Expectations and assumptions with negative results leave us disappointed or shattered. Living a life that seems "too perfect" can also lead to issues. Even youths who were raised in the most positive and supportive homes and excelled in the classroom, on the field, in the arts, at extracurricular activities, and socially with their peers are often stunned when they don't make the team, are not accepted into the college or university of their choice, experience a breakup, don't get the job, or suffer any disappointment or rejection. It is even more difficult when we set ourselves up believing we are the most qualified and then another person achieves what we thought was ours. Until that first disappointment, we often expect and assume that what happened in the past will continue in the future. At the other end of the spectrum are those who had lived an impoverished life, experienced great personal loss, or felt they didn't matter yet they pulled themselves up by the bootstraps or were suddenly given a golden opportunity. They may begin to excel in practically everything they touch, and life remains positive in most situations. Due to their former harsh reality, they often expect the other shoe to drop.

Because of our previous successes, we may incorrectly expect success to continue and assume that we will always achieve our goals. If we become complacent or unappreciative of what we have and what we need to do to keep a relationship or maintain a certain standard, we are vulnerable to disappointment. Sometimes, people who were successful in one area incorrectly assume their qualifications will automatically transfer with them and that they will be equally valued in another environment. This perception could pertain to a relationship, a job, a college, or a move to an urban, suburban, rural, or overseas location, or to a smaller or larger home. When we do not actualize our vision, reach our goal, or are not chosen or accepted because the competition is steeper or because different standards are required, we are disappointed. Unrealistic and unmanaged expectations and assumptions often lead to great disappointment. I chatted with the adult daughter of parents who had emigrated from the Middle East. I commented about the remarkable achievements of her highly educated first-generation parents and all they overcame. I said, "You must be so proud of your parents." She responded, "I am, and I have huge shoes to fill." I replied, "The only shoes that you have to fill are the ones that you wear each day."

Years ago, my son told me, "Mom, you always expected the best but accepted the best I could do." I have always felt the only expectation we can truly have is an honest, managed, and realistic expectation of ourselves in the present moment and a vision of how we evolve as human beings. We can certainly set goals that we hope to reach and maintain standards that reflect our moral compass and hope that our loved ones also support them. In healthy and agenda-free relationships, we choose friends who are like-minded, embracing similar values, standards, and interests while providing good company, fun, and comfort.

And please let me remind you, whatever the circumstances—with health, finances, personal responsibilities, aging, or other aspects—you can only do what you can do with what you have and are capable of at the time.

Retrospective Regret Lens

The *retrospective regret lens* refers to a previous deed, experience, or interaction where we wish we could go back in time to act or respond differently to another person or situation. For whatever reasons, our environment, lack of maturity, knowledge, or experience, our self-centeredness, different priorities, or other obstacles, we chose the wrong path and now wish we had done it differently. Sometimes we have an opportunity to make amends, apologize, enlighten, and reconnect with a more positive response to reflect who we now are.

A former client, a physician from an Asian country, felt extremely sad and guilty and continued to be tormented because she was unable to attend her father's funeral. She did not know where her father was buried, so she couldn't visit his grave site. I shared my devout belief in a spiritual connection with those who passed away; we can reach out to their souls in the Universe on a plane that we don't yet know. I suggested she find a quiet place that provides serenity to feel and connect with her father's spirit and share what is in her heart.

If you are uncomfortable with this way to connect or cannot find other means to resolve what burdens your heart and send negative chatter to your head, then another option is to release the feelings and thoughts to the universe and hope the ones we lost receive the messages. Carrying those negative thoughts forward is not beneficial for anybody and does not honor our deceased loved ones or ourselves.

A friend often shared that he dreads one recurring thought and nightmare of a past event and wishes that he could change what happened. I responded, "While we can be accountable, we can never change the past. We can only move forward in the future." I suggested that he try to get in touch with the other person involved. If you are in this situation, first reintroduce yourself and offer friendly conversation, then state the purpose of your call and try to get together. Be open, frank, and speak from the heart as you share how you would approach or respond differently than you did in the past. I suggest that you express how sorry you are about your previous thoughts, words, or behavior. Don't be upset if the other person doesn't instantly forgive you or even acknowledge your attempt to make amends. Their change of heart may come later or not at all. At least you know that you tried to make it right.

While I deeply recognize that many suffer from guilt, guilt is not a tenet in the Jewish religion, although guilt is a prevalent factor in the Jewish and many other cultures. I do not feel guilt, but that certainly does not imply that I don't deeply regret certain attitudes, acts, words, or take responsibility for wrongdoings that I committed in the past. As I continued to mature, gained the insights and courage to face my imperfections, and acknowledged the impact and pain that I had caused, I shared my discoveries with those individuals I had hurt.

The memory of the pain we caused others is never erased from our being, but if we correct our major grievances and never repeat them, it is best that we don't carry forward that emotional burden.

When I hear others tell me, "They make me feel guilty," I respond, "No one can make you feel guilty. You have to allow it." Mindful breathing and meditation help create the ability to block those *guilt trips* (or traps) that others try to lay on us. They can only stick if we allow it. Only each person determines what we can and cannot do to please others, with what we currently possess.

When I checked with Rabbi Stan Levy to confirm that my thoughts were consistent with Jewish tenets, he eloquently replied, "To be guilty of something is not the same as having guilt.

Guilt paralyzes us, but responsibility motivates us to action. It is about taking responsibility for a wrong that we have committed when we hurt another person or ourselves, and we take whatever steps necessary to make amends, including being truly sorry for what we have done."

I am guessing that everyone has acted in a way they wish they hadn't. A young woman spent time in jail for smuggling marijuana. Others committed deeds that shamed or embarrassed them. I always remind them, if they truly changed their attitudes and behavior and don't revert to those patterns, that certainly is a closed chapter of their personal experiences. Shaka Senghor shares that we must first acknowledge, then apologize, and then atone (Senghor 2014). Even if others define you by such a deed, make sure you don't let that determine who you are. We are far greater than any single attitude, behavior, role, or event. In the end, we are the sum of all we are and how we live our lives.

Neglected Well-Being/Self-Expectation Lens

This is one of the most universal *lenses*. Whose *well-being* most often first comes to mind in personal and family situations? I will never forget one of those life-changing moments that happened decades ago. When I joined a gathering, the hostess spotted me and exclaimed, "Five of my favorite people are here." I looked around and saw her husband, two children, and myself and silently counted four people. I pondered for a minute and then asked myself, "Who is the fifth person?" It later dawned on me that she had included herself. Hillel, a Jewish elder born in 110 BC, is renowned for his profound statement, "If I am not for myself, who will be? And if I'm only for myself, then what am I? If not now, when?"

Decades ago, when Rosie and Alexander visited us from Romania, Rosie shared another profound insight. One afternoon, she divulged, "Ruth, there is always one person in your life whom you love or look out for the most. It could be your spouse or partner, mother, father, sister, brother, husband, or child." I often reflect on her eye-opening wisdom. Also, reflect with which family member or members are you mostly comfortable and authentic?

We each fulfill many roles, and there are times when one person requires the most attention, concern, and love at that moment or for a while. That surely is the case when a child is born and during their infancy and younger years. The priority of time is also paramount when a soldier returns from war or a family member or beloved friend is recovering from an accident, addiction, surgery, fighting cancer, or a tragic disaster that occurred or when a loved one or aging parent is nearing the final stage of life.

Sometimes when a new sibling arrives, if they are not immediately or shortly thereafter included, an older sibling may feel something is amiss and perhaps feel displaced because they are not getting the same amount of attention to which they were accustomed. Later, the parent may spend more time and appear to be more physically engaged with one child, although another child's emotional needs may be considered most often. It takes an instant for this situation to cross the person's mind with the *neglected well-being lens*. They immediately sense the slight by acutely sensing the pause, sideways glance, or unspoken words or seeing when another person's needs are taken into greater consideration than their own. These thoughts transpire instantaneously, and others may be totally unaware of what happened between the two individuals. This also applies to any caregiver who has to prioritize their time and energy to care for another person. If we usually first think of the needs of a particular child or individual, we must become aware of this priority, as the other child, siblings, or family members certainly sense it already. Once we are mindful of others' feelings, we can adjust our priorities and attention so there is a more equal distribution of our time and care. Moreover, we can try to help others understand the situation and, perhaps our sense of that individual's vulnerability or specific needs.

Again, I ask, during most of your days and life, whose back and *well-being* do you prioritize most frequently? I believe that in this scenario, each of us needs to be aware. Do you mostly put the same person first, or do you shift from person to person? Do you mostly give out energy or receive others' energy, or is the flow pretty even? Where do you put yourself? Do you always take care of yourself first, last, never, or somewhere between? Also, who loves you the most, and who do you love the most? Who brings out your worst, who brings out your best, and who has your back? In addition, ask yourself, do you draw strength from within, a deity, the Universe, or loved ones, or do you give your strength to your loved ones? Finally, ask yourself if you are a good mommie or good daddy to your inner child?

For those who don't put themselves in the equation at all, it's about time that you do so. We may spend much time visibly taking physical care of ourselves, but it is the invisible, emotional, and spiritual care that best promotes our *well-being*.

From my personal experience and lifelong observations, I feel that most children have genetic similarities to each parent. As we raise a child, there are certain traits and processes that we inherently share and intuitively sense. It is our deep love for our children that allows us to gain a sense about them and strengthen our bonds and connections, whether they came from under our hearts or in our hearts, do not share our genetic similarities as solidly or at all, or were adopted.

When I was a speech therapist in my late twenties, I helped individuals recover from strokes and accidents. My patients taught me an incredible lesson. Those who had always lived pleasing others were far more distraught and resentful than those who had followed their passion and dreams. I observed that those who had most thought of others and had not included themselves also had more difficulty accepting and adjusting to their new physical, mental, emotional, and spiritual challenges. Those people who had self-actualized and had honored their own emotional needs and well-being from time to time were far more accepting of their new reality. This acceptance is not limited to people who have had strokes or were in accidents but is experienced in many realms.

I have known people who became more bitter as they grew older because they had spent their lives giving too much of themselves to others. They felt their giving was expected, or a *should*, and so they neglected themselves. As they aged, those women who lived prior to women's lib or weren't strong enough to buck the system were angry that they had given away so much of themselves. They resented the fact that there was no reciprocity, and they harbored their disappointment. Consequently, these people, both women and men, were often unpleasant to be around. Therefore, others stayed away, which created more loneliness and annoyance. I also knew many who lived into their nineties or reached one hundred who had led fulfilling, though at times extremely harsh, lives. Yet they always carried a deep sense of gratitude until their death. Their positive attitude drew others to drink from their rich life's well and experience their serenity, wisdom, and wit.

Often those who most love us are not our flesh and blood. We don't need to feel guilty of loving or caring for one person the most; it is what it is. What matters is that the other family members whom we love and who depend on us—especially, but not solely, when they are young—feel that they receive their just due and are treated fairly. It is best that we never continually comment in the presence of other family members how special or favored one person is or singularly name that child in an endearing term. We only privately share that special bond. Otherwise, these sentiments add salt to the wound of the person or persons who already feel they are somewhat slighted, never good enough, are rarely thought of first, or are not wanted or cherished as deeply.

Before we leave the *neglected well-being and self-expectation lens*, I want to address the incredible stress that we place on ourselves by setting false or self-imposed deadlines, overcommitting, or placing unrealistic or unmanaged expectations or intentions on ourselves based on what we could previously accomplish, especially in situations where we can't control the time or events. These unrealistic self-expectations severely rob us of our well-being and serenity, especially as we age and decline.

I know that I could not possibly cover everyone's *lenses*. Please add and include other *lenses* in your list. Whatever *internal lens* about yourself appears on your internal "home page," use the *Identify, Block, Move, Delete, Replace Technique* to minimize or delete those negative, debilitating thoughts that you either carried for a long time or just recently acquired. The *IBMDR Technique* follows shortly.

Now that you have gained a far clearer recognition of your *internal lenses*, you realize *lenses* are obstructive. It is not only our *lenses* that distort how we perceive and process information and respond to others, but other people's *lenses* distort their perception of us as well. Even worse, these negative *lenses* are very detrimental to our well-being, adding a dose of toxicity to our perception and expression.

At each instant, we are what we feel and experience. Others may perceive us with our former *lenses*, even when they are obsolete and no longer a part of our perception or responses. Kindhearted people with good intentions who converse negatively obscure their true value. They have strong *lenses* or may not pick up social cues. Do people react negatively to you even when you think you're conversing or acting positively?

When a friend from Nevis visited, she met with a half sister whom she hadn't seen in thirty years. It was obvious to everyone that they closely resembled each other and their father. Within a few moments after the half sister arrived, while they were still greeting each other in our front hall, she shared that she was a Marine sergeant who had served two tours of duty in the Iraq war and she was honorably discharged. Her eldest daughter, who was six years old, immediately announced that *her mom was almost killed four times*.

After we had chatted for a couple of hours, I gathered that this woman, now in her midthirties, was quite together and grounded, so I asked her how she reached this state. She told us that she was born in Nevis to Nevisian parents and the family moved to the United States when she was four years old. She spent much of her youth in the toughest areas of the Bronx. When she was in her early twenties, she knew there was something inside of her that she didn't like, so at her young age, she had the wisdom and courage to ask several friends and family members to "describe her in as many words as they can." The words that poured out were *loving*, *caring*, and *giving*, but also *angry*. She knew she had to address the anger to get on with life and to live it in the positive way that she wanted, so she joined the military. It took a couple of years for her to work through her anger. She no longer carries one iota of that negativity. Her manner, style, confidence, grace, and sense of purpose reminded my husband and me of the Nevisian women we know.

Difficult as it may be, move gently inside yourself and try to identify the situation and isolate the feeling of each *internal lens*. Where does that negative feeling come from? How far back into your childhood can you trace the negative feeling and the related incident? You need to recall the following: the *feeling*, the *fear*, the *thought*, your *response* to the specific incident, and the time in your life when that event first occurred. Now, isolate the feeling and the situation and move them into your present life, much as you would block and move a paragraph from an outdated word document into a current one. The intense feeling and memory of the incident remain the same, but you realize that your response changes because your reaction then was based on who you then were. You had not yet acquired all the accomplishments, coping skills, insights, and tools that you gained as you matured during the years between then and now. While the memories of those detrimental experiences from your childhood stay put, you now possess a broader personal inventory that you didn't have then to approach and resolve current similar situations. Naturally, you gain even more experiences as your life's journey continues. To your great relief, you will note that those negative feelings and *lenses* that you created are no longer relevant. Still, you have carried those negative, burdensome *feel and fear* and *thought and response lenses* throughout your life to where you are now. Imagine an actor or actress in a drama repeating the lines from a specific scene of the past, although the lines and settings are now of a different era. Obviously, some lines are no longer fitting. Similarly, the negative, obsolete *internal lenses* that are burdensome also are no longer relevant.

Let me remind you that each of us, created by the same Creator or force in our individual glorious perfections and not-so-glorious imperfections, is an equal member of the one and only human race inhabiting planet Earth, now and always. Steadfastly hold deep in your hearts that if you were created and given the gift of life, then just as monumentally as those invisible molecules of breath that you inhale and exhale exist, so is your existence just as monumental. Yet you are visible, you do matter, and there is a purpose to your life. We now move to reduce or eliminate those *internal lenses* that are detrimental to us.

Identify, Block, Move, Delete, Replace (IBMDR) Technique for Internal Lenses

The *IBMDR Technique* significantly helps *erase* and *replace* your *internal lenses*. Once you truly comprehend how harmful and irrelevant these *internal lenses* are, you begin the process.

After you identified all the *internal lenses*, while also noting the impact of the unworthy and demeaning thoughts that you have carried about yourself, make a list of those *lenses*. First, list the *feel* and *fear lenses*, then the *thought and response lenses*.

Think through each *lens* and step. Then take your time to gain a clear understanding of the event, situation, or experience that created those negative thoughts, your *internal lenses*. Was that *lens* created in response to a personal experience, close family member's or friend's experience, in your home, or in your primary village, tribe, clan, hood, or community? Or were you influenced by peers, teachers, clergy, community leaders, or an event, the mass media, or social media? To enlighten your awareness, prioritize your *internal lenses* by placing the *lens* that affects you most at the top of your list. Then, one by one, recall, reflect, and *identify* the situation, conversation, or event that initially created that *internal lens*. Once you truly recognize how destructive and irrelevant those thoughts are, ask yourself several questions. Do you want to exchange your former harmful *internal lenses* that create the ongoing harmful, negative, abusive *self-chatter* in your head? If so, do you want to *replace* them with enlightening, present, self-loving, trusting, and confident thoughts and feelings? These new thoughts and feelings are abundant with a positive sense of *source-connected* acceptance, self-worth, and well-being. To *erase* and *replace* each former *internal lens* and *embrace* a new, positive, and productive truth, please proceed.

Choose the first *internal lens* to eliminate. Now, *block* that specific *internal lens*—similar to *blocking* text in a document. Visualize placing the thought of that *internal lens* at shoulder height behind you, indicating that it is an experience of the past. Then, use your right or left arm to comfortably reach behind you as far as you can. Next, with your open hand, grab and bring the *blocked* memory of that negative *feeling and fear* or *thought and response* forward in your hand. Then, *move* the negative thought and experience into the present moment, directly in front of your open or closed eyes, until you feel an intense sense of it. When you have a strong sense of the demeaning impact of your *internal lens*, temporarily *move* to the side the memory of the past harmful experience.

Now, list all the positive accomplishments, coping skills, education, experiences, street smarts, and wisdom that you have acquired and now possess since the *internal lens* was initially formed. These new assets help to overcome or minimize the impact of those previous, undermining *internal lenses*. Pause and deeply reflect on your current holistic self. Ask yourself, Are you as vulnerable now as you were when that event occurred? What is the likelihood that this exact situation will repeat itself? Pause again to focus sharply on your new inventory of skills, accomplishments, and experiences.

Next, one by one, bring each of the former *feel and fear* or *thought and response internal lenses* that you had temporarily set aside. Again, place that former negative *internal lens* in front of your open or closed eyes. Keep in mind that these *lenses*, which are now irrelevant, rob us and keep us from our best—our purest, most genuine *source-connection*—by creating harmful, depleting, unworthy energy within. To *replace* each former *internal lens*, repeat the process. Continue to *delete*, one by one, each former negative *internal lens*. Visualize tapping the Delete key on a keyboard while focusing on *deleting* the former debilitating *internal lens*.

Now, one by one, *replace* and *embrace* each of your former *internal lenses* with the positive, updated, confident, uplifting, and worthy version of yourself. It is likely that you previously did not give yourself full credit for your gained assets and accomplishments. Since you now possess an awareness of your *internal lenses*, as those former debilitating *internal lenses* continue to pop into your head, continue to repeat the *IBMDR Technique* until your former *internal lenses* rarely or no longer affect you or are so slight that they don't bother you. Be patient; this will take time, but it works.

Let me remind you of the meaning of the term *download* in this context. To make these new insights and ideas permanent, you first create a clear vision in your mind and heart of the newly discovered positive and genuine truth about yourself. Then, most compelling, you *download* to *save* and *feel* that belief, not in your head, but *below in your heart and soul*. Only when we have *downloaded* and *saved* the new belief in our *hearts* and *souls* do these new, positive beliefs, feelings, ideas, and perceptions become our *new truth*. This is similar to downloading a document that you received and want to save on a digital device. Reviewing the information is not enough. You must also engage the *save* command to access the ideas and feelings in the future.

Once these *internal lenses* no longer constantly and adversely affect you, you will be amazed at how energized, focused, and liberated you are and feel. You will feel lighter and celebrate your newly gained sense of self-worth. We now move to those thoughts, ideas, and biases we have about others.

Preconceived Ideas about People or Situations

Before we advance to *external lenses*, we need to recognize that we also carry preconceived ideas about individuals or situations that immediately distort our observation and consequently tarnish our responses. These negative perceptions and ideas interfere with positive responses to others and taint all forms of our nonverbal, voice-tone, verbal, and written communication. This causes significant emotional disease and isolation for others as it twists the truth about them.

Most people journey through life with preconceived ideas about people, events, situations, relationships, marriage, life, death, and eternity. Each feels their perception is right. It is their reality, but not necessarily anyone else's. What is truth? Some place all their faith in scientific data, only to discover that there is now a "new truth." Centuries ago, the earth was considered flat; now we know better. With accelerating and more complex technology, our ability to view and comprehend our universe exponentially increased. New discoveries increasingly support or dispute previous concepts. Until recently, Pluto was considered a planet, then it wasn't, then it was again. However we categorize Pluto, it is what it is.

Religions are similar to astronomy. For eons, certain beliefs held true. But in time, artifacts were discovered and new doctrines reinforced or replaced what we once thought was the truth. Through my clients' and my own broad experiences, I have known and experienced human beings of several beliefs and faiths: Baha'is, Buddhists, Christians, Ethical Culturists, Evangelicals, Hindus, Muslims, Jews, Spiritual Renewalists, Sikhs, Rastafarians, and as well as Atheists, Agnostics, and Non-believers.

The sun rises in the east and sets in the west. Seasons unfold in a preordained order. Waves lap upon the shore, then recede in a continuing cycle. Specific constellations appear in the sky every season, and planets orbit along their own complementary trajectory. Though viewed differently from each hemisphere, to the lay observer, their journey is predictable. For me, our planet, the Universe, and the Creator are my truth, because they are consistent. So where do you put your faith and trust, and who's to say who is right?

When you receive a gift, you don't know whether you will like it or not until you open it. What if you did not open the present because you didn't like the wrapping? Perhaps you missed a precious opportunity. Now, picture another precious gift—a special, fun-loving, caring, talented human being—inside the box. The box is wrapped in various shades representing the full spectrum of our multihued fellow human beings or with symbols from various faiths, cultures, political parties, socioeconomic levels, or with pictures of people who are *handi-abled*, obese, anorexic, straight, gay, young, or old. If your biased views prevented you from opening the package, you might never have peeked inside. Perhaps you missed the opportunity to meet one of the most special, loving, and compatible human beings.

Thây teaches a poignant tale. A father thought his son had died. Later, there was a knock on the door. The man answered the door and saw a boy standing outside who exclaimed, "Hello, Father, I am your son." The father was so stuck in his belief that he responded, "My son is dead. You cannot be him." And then he closed the door (Thich Nhat Hanh 2005). We lose a lot when we are so invested in our belief that we are not open to listening to another's positively stated viewpoint. This applies to any belief relevant to family, religion, politics, science, or any other topic.

When I ran into a friend whose profession is in law enforcement, I learned a valuable lesson. Our social concerns and moral codes are in sync, but politically, we are opposites. During our conversation, he shared a protocol that is engaged when he pulls over a driver, especially on a busy highway or freeway. Once the car has stopped, he immediately turns on a video camera before approaching the driver. He then directs the driver to get out of the car and walk to the passenger's side that is not visible to others. If he and the driver remain on the driver's side next to the flowing traffic, there is a greater chance of an accident or injury to the officer, as he is closest to speeding cars. In my friend's professional lingo, they call this narrow area between the traffic and stopped car the no-leg zone. He further explained that defense attorneys and liberal groups have accused the department of directing the driver out of view to those passing by, or perhaps not always in the camera's eye, so the pulled-over driver is more vulnerable to potential abuse. I thanked him for opening my eyes to be more open-minded, as without his insight, I would usually have supported the driver under question. I highly respect my friend, whom I have known for a decade. He is a fair person and is driven by his moral compass. I also told him, "I sincerely believe that not all law enforcement officers hold your high standards. If they did, you and I wouldn't be having our conversation."

For decades, I have known or heard of people of African heritage, including top-ranking sports figures, television anchors, and Pulitzer Prize winners—the full gamut of high-level, admired professionals—who personally relate their encounters with law officers. They note that they were unjustifiably pulled over, frisked, falsely accused, or abused.

How often do you avoid a situation because of a preconceived idea, only to discover you were wrong? You didn't ask for something because you didn't think you would get it, only to discover that you easily could have had it. You think a woman is incapable of completing a project, only to discover that she masterminded the concept. Or you award a project to a colleague with prestigious letters following their surname, assuming that the person will be more capable of the task, only to discover that they were unable to master the challenge and incapable of completing the project in a timely manner.

How often do you meet a man bulging with muscles and think that he isn't smart or sensitive or think a person is an emotionally detached nerd, only to discover that they are empathetic, tender, and a thoughtful person? Do you think all kind but ambitious men are sensitive to your needs? Do you think all people who are overweight are lazy? Do you think all attractive blond women are dumb? Or that all women are bossy? Years ago, I struggled with my stereotype about people who are overweight. Looking at them, I questioned why they carried that extra weight. I tried hard to change my thoughts; I can still recall when I finally did. I was standing in line, waiting to make a phone call, and in front of me stood a woman who must have weighed more than 250 pounds. I wondered why she was so "fat." Then, I caught myself for the last time, as I stopped. I realized my question was none of my business and finally focused on the belief that underneath the fullness was a fellow human being. The person's outward appearance has nothing to do with the wonder of the human spirit inside.

We often recall the celebration of special traditions within our primary family, holidays, birthdays, vacations, anniversaries, rites of passage, and other milestones, and the sadness or sense of isolation when we did not have them. Often, as adults living with a friend, spouse, or partner, when occasions arise, we have preconceived expectations of how we would like the other person to respond, mirroring the wonderful memory of our childhood experience. Sometimes, we are in for a rude awakening if we do not express our specific desires to the other person. If you want to celebrate an event in a certain style with treasured traditions, save yourself disappointment and avoid disharmony. Share your wish list with the other person. Be mindful of the *hand-dome* and that the other person may have a vastly different concept of celebration time or not want to celebrate at all. This leads to compromise, or perhaps even finding that the other's tradition is so welcoming that it becomes a tradition in your own family or relationship.

On a fireman's first birthday as a married man, his wife forgot his birthday and didn't throw him a party; he was furious. He had fond memories of his mother throwing a lavish annual birthday bash for his father, with all his friends and relatives. Festivities included balloons, flowers, gifts, and cake. On the flip side, we may also recoil as we recall the memories of significant days in our childhood that we dreaded or during which we felt isolated. We need to share that information with our loved ones so that they don't repeat any of those traditions. A husband whose mother often feigned illness so that she could rest and pass on the parenting and household responsibilities had no empathy when his wife became ill. To make matters worse, the wife recalled that her father was compassionate and attentive when her mother was sick. Her dad prepared special meals, placed them on a tray with a small vase of flowers, and carried the lovingly prepared food upstairs to the bedroom. When the man's wife required bed rest, she was stunned when he flung dry toast at her.

Preconceived ideas also raise the notion that a person is worthy when they are not. When a professional colleague was in graduate school, she was a straight-A student. In her last semester, family members were ill and she was unable to devote the usual time to a project. She felt that she clearly had turned in an inferior paper. Because of the *halo effect* of her previous papers, she received an undeserved A. She felt that her academic reputation, rather than the project's value, determined the grade.

A woman whose company *downsized* concluded that they demoted her friend because she wasn't capable in the position she had held. Later, when she and I spoke, I asked her about her new position. She shared, "I know it appears that they gave me a less prestigious position because I used to work in a private office with a window and I now work in a cubicle in a room with several other people, but I actually requested the change. Although I took a pay cut and another position, I'm in a department where I will eventually experience more growth and find the work more enjoyable."

How many times in life has our observation been right on but our conclusion totally wrong? This premise is the foundation of misunderstandings in almost every situation imaginable, in all walks of life, cultures, and families. I know from personal experience that friends, colleagues, and family members accurately observed me, but at times, some drew conclusions that were 180 degrees from the truth. When the erring conclusion occurs in small matters, it is best to let it slide and save the conversation for misconceptions that matter more. It is only through mindful, heart-to-heart, and *source-connected* communication that we overcome these misunderstandings to again travel a more comfortable, loving, and respectful path.

Unless you absolutely know the facts "from the horse's mouth," it is best that you keep your thoughts to yourself and don't respond. It is very difficult for human beings to accurately observe *every* situation purely devoid of any preconceived ideas. Knowing that, it behooves us to become far more vigilant of our preconceptions, assumptions, or biases. When our prejudices and biases color our thoughts, we need to stop and analyze from where these thoughts arose. Are they realistic? When rare prejudiced thoughts used to pop into my head, I immediately took time to examine what influenced them. I realized the prejudiced stereotypes that insidiously permeate much of our media had influenced my thoughts and they were not based on any fact or personal experience.

Former clients shared their initial desires when first arriving in the United States. One client from India loved "American-made movies," especially since movies are a prized form of entertainment produced in India's highly acclaimed Bollywood region. He humorously shared that upon his first arrival to Los Angeles, he instructed his driver to go to Hollywood and Vine in hopes of "witnessing" a robbery in action.

When our daughters entered their teenage years, the fad of wearing torn and faded jeans was the trend. My husband and I were okay with the fad until neighbors started questioning our judgment. When I shared this with my father-in-law, who had raised seven hip and successful children, he replied, "Ruth, as long as they're good kids and their clothing is clean, what does it matter? Are they harming anyone?"

Thirty years ago, when tattoos became popular among my children's peers, I learned to accept the personal statement expressed with a few tattoos on a person's body. But entire limbs and backs of the body—then rare—made me uncomfortable because my Jewish faith does not embrace tattoos and, for the most part, I appreciate the body in its unaltered form. In addition, during my youth, none of my schoolmates had tattoos. Back then, tattoos were associated with youths who lived a promiscuous or gang-affiliated lifestyle.

As National Geographic and travel magazines began to publish more photos of people throughout our planet wearing colorful face and body paint, covered in various shades of mud, iconic tattoos, and multiple nose, lip, tongue, and navel piercing adornments, I understood and appreciated their cultural value and stories. I also grew accustomed to and accepting of tattoos, piercings, and ornaments and all the fun shades of hair color, which are mostly flattering. I recognize and feel in my heart that those details have no place in a *source-connection* with one another.

Recently, a family member said, "I don't believe you don't discriminate at some point." I responded, "I don't think I do." Let me share what I do experience. For years, I supported gay rights. When I visited New York, I saw a middle-aged gay couple with a young child, each from a different cultural heritage. It took me by surprise, and so I checked it out. I knew and validated in my heart that I continually supported gay rights and adoption, whatever the age or culture of the parent, yet when I experienced it personally for the first time, I was taken aback. In seconds, I smiled as I instantly updated the recent reality and was happy that both the loving parents and child had found one another. When I recently stopped at a restaurant and saw a man who was middle-aged and covered with tattoos, again, I was caught off guard. I had to stop and mentally update my former perception and my *source-connected* acceptance.

Whenever we judge a person by their abilities (or lack thereof), differences, attire, diet, accent, or communication style and then link those judgments to a culture, religion, group, region, or age group as *abnormal*, that attachment reflects a bias and leads to discrimination. Decades ago, I questioned, whose norm is *normal?* Whenever information or categories are requested, but not mandated, and the information serves to positively inform or elevate, it is best to comply. There are also periods when society seems to place individuals in a category. When given the choice, I prefer to describe the person's abilities, attitudes, behavior, or special traits rather than use a categorizing label.

When you don't like or are uncomfortable with another person's communication style, their delivery expressed through body language, gestures, facial expressions, voice tone, or words that are offensive to you, recall that behind all that negative barrage, each one is first a fellow human being. We don't know, nor do we need to, the reason for the person's style, attitudes, or actions.

The discomfort or dislike is based on a one-to-one interaction, reflecting attitudes and behaviors that are unpleasant and not linked in any way with any region, religion, culture, or other group. That is very different from discrimination.

While sitting in a waiting room, a woman sat close by and chewed on something that made the noisy sound of frequently clacking dentures. I found the sound irritating and blocked out the thought. After we had been waiting for more than an hour, she began talking about a double cervical fusion she underwent two years ago following an accident with a flatbed truck loaded with a car. I immediately thought of the *hand-dome*, which again taught me that we just don't always know—or need to know—the cause of what we find annoying. I was even more grateful that I had driven out the negative thought so that I could then empathize with the woman.

External Lenses

External lenses affect our attention outward, focusing on others. The *external lenses* presented are *expectations/assumptions, culture/region/heritage, socioeconomic/educational level, income inequality, religion, gender, sexual orientation, age, physical appearance, handi-abled, overreacting, xenophobia/Islamophobia, prejudice/racism,* and *reverse discrimination.* The anecdotes highlighting *external lenses* are based on my experiences with people with whom I have professionally engaged, connected during travels, and encountered in checkout lines, as well as personal conversations with workers, service people, family, friends, and neighbors.

Reflecting on my more than seventy-five years, I realized that I carried preconceived ideas and some *external lenses* based on appearance, gender, or political fringe party beliefs. In steps, I halted the last remnants of those thought processes a while ago. It is an ongoing, worthwhile, and liberating process. Still, obsolete misconceptions occasionally pop into my thoughts like undesired, unblocked pop-ups on a computer screen.

Expectations/Assumptions Lens

At the end of the *internal lenses* section, we concluded our discussion on self-expectations. We now continue the chapter by looking at our *external lenses*, beginning with *our expectations* of life and others. How often were we disappointed because a person, institution, event, or period in our life didn't meet our hopes and expectations? How can we hold realistic expectations of others, their lives, or the situations that we can't control? We assume that others will exactly know our desires and how and when to meet them. We are incapable of precisely knowing that. The specific point is that our needs are taken care of in a way that works, though not necessarily mirroring our way of accomplishing it.

Often, our expectations are based on what we know, our standards, and what seems probable. As I previously mentioned, realistically, each person can only give what they are capable and desirous of at the moment. Often, we expect reciprocity that mirrors our attitudes and deeds. I was often disappointed, as it took me decades to recognize that the return never exactly matches what I give because no one is identical to me. Once I understood that idea, I became far more accepting of what others gave me. Nevertheless, on rare occasions, I still find this challenging.

Much of what a person gives reflects the information highlighted in their *hand-dome* or signals that they are not yet enlightened.

A longtime friend shared, "Just because somebody needs something or expects something from you doesn't mean it is your need. You don't have to consent. If you do, it also doesn't always have to be on the other person's time." I learned that when I rely on my husband to fulfill what he is capable of, he comes through as a shining star, but when I rely on something he does not do well, I fail for asking.

Assumptions are dangerous and a setup for disappointment or failure. We all hold certain standards by which we try to live, and even then, our attitudes or actions often disappoint us. When we assume something is going to be the same as it invariably was, we often fail. At seventy, I had to take another written exam to renew my driver's license. In a casual conversation with a friend who is a highway patrol officer, he stated that the terms used in rules about measuring distance had recently changed to "seconds" and "feet." I assumed that was professional lingo. I never realized until I took the test that the guideline of measuring distance between cars and signaling to other drivers is now in seconds and feet, not the familiar car lengths that I had known. Assumptions can get us into trouble. A friend often says, when things haven't turned out as I expected "but I assumed," I would guess a significant number of disappointments, unmet project completions, countless other plans, and unfortunate automobile accidents occur when we are caught in the web of assumptions, guesstimates, and unmanaged or unrealistic expectations.

Each of our lives' foundations is based on patterns that we experienced with regularity, and they are the cornerstones of our rock-solid stability and comfort. Yet there are increasingly more times when the old rules, patterns, paradigms, or traditions no longer apply. There is often one incident that alters the situation, and perhaps the former lifelong routine never again returns. We remain mindful that the "truths" throughout our lives change as life's circumstances change, such as by aging, recent relationships, different communities, current leaders, and climate. We cannot assume that the past will automatically slide into the present. The more we are aware that the only constant in life is change, the fewer assumptions and worries we carry.

People often ask me how to deal with communication gaps when each assumes the other person will take the necessary responsibility or has the same information that they have. I recommend that they confirm and validate that each person is on the same page and each has identical information, as well as ensuring that each is crystal clear on the task, process, and goal from the beginning of the job or project until its successful completion.

We often expect others' standards to mirror our own, which they rarely do, because others are uniquely different and have differing standards, methods, or styles to achieve the same goal or just live life. Decades ago, while my father visited me, we ran errands. He noted that I continually preferred to take the slower roads through the curvy and hilly streets adorned with trees and flowers. My route included a few stop signs. My dad was curious about why I didn't use a shorter, quicker, more direct route on streets that had more lanes and were lined with billboards and numerous signs and were potentially more congested. I shared that I enjoyed soothing nature more than busy streets.

A friend who is usually quite upbeat and enjoys a large extended family stopped to chat before the winter holidays. It quickly became clear that she was quite distraught. Decades ago, she lost a son to cancer. Her other son, a pilot, lives in the Midwest. His flying schedule is unpredictable, so it is difficult to plan a visit. When she looked at a recent family photo, in which our family had gathered from other states to celebrate a family event, she began to cry. She shared that she always pictured that when she was old, a large family would surround her.

Life happens when we have other plans. Assumptions about how life's events will unfold aren't necessarily borne out; some are deeply disappointing, while others are more fruitful than we ever imagined. We can hope, wish, and pray, but that does not mean all our dreams will ever become a reality. Placing our hopes and dreams on assumptions and expectations of how life unfolds, over which we absolutely have no control, often leads to great disappointment. During those times, gratitude for the basic and simple things in life and reflecting on wonderful memories offer a soothing antidote.

Before we begin to further explore the *external lenses*, I will illustrate my point with an image. Just imagine that instead of dragging your thirty- to fifty-pound bag of *internal lenses* luggage only from curbside to check in, you schlep that "heavyweight baggage" all the way through life. Yes, there are times—of shorter or longer duration—when you park your "baggage" in the corner, but at some point, you again grab the handle and drag your self-doubting, demeaning, or downgrading thoughts through life until you finally stop and decide *enough is enough*.

This time, the difference is that the *external lenses* baggage not only harms others but also menaces you. Since scientists can now measure emotions, they are beginning to prove that it is harmful for your health to experience negative emotions, such as hate and anger. Moreover, you reflect these negative emotions upon others. When doing so, it is hard to imagine the sorrow, deceit, disgrace, and disservice you bring to another human being's spirit when you dishonor and demean them, especially when fueled by prejudice and racism. These are expressed through your words, deeds, expressions, and the negative energy that you emit.

This lifetime unease—this rattling of the human spirit that individuals and society create—also is manifested in a questioning glance, dirty look, road-blocking obstruction, or the theft of basic human and civil rights, or life. This oppression forces the recipients to go through life's obstacle course with a bolting thundercloud hanging overhead, forcing them to constantly be on the lookout, to dodge and skirt the negative *lenses'* impact and hateful baggage that are hurled or dumped on them. I ask you, Is that fair, and would you ever choose a similar path through lifelong "mind-fields" for any of your loved ones or yourself?

Culture/Region/Heritage Lens

As we continue to become a more global, complex, and diverse society, we need to be aware of our biases toward people with differing views, from other neighborhoods, cultural heritages, geographic regions, nationalities, or archipelagos. What we read, heard, or experienced with another person from the same region occasionally taints our perception. There may be similarities in customs, dress, diet, style, or values, but that does not imply that one person from the same area will think and act alike.

Years ago, shortly after affirmative action became law, I overheard a familiar elderly man comment about a person of African heritage, saying, "They should thank their lucky stars that they were born in America." I asked, "Why? Do you think slavery was a fortunate experience?" I later asked him if he thought he was prejudiced, and he replied, "No." Maybe he wasn't, but he certainly wasn't aware of, or hadn't focused on, the historical unjust hardships suffered by those of African heritage.

During a flight, my husband sat next to a professional of European heritage from the Deep South. He told my husband that when he travels to the North, East, or West Coast, he is discriminated against because of his Southern drawl and is presumed to be a "dumb redneck," as he put it. *Redneck* is also a negative, discriminating term associated with people who hold narrower social views.

Occasionally, I am in a situation in which a person shares a negative experience with a person of another culture. These experiences pertain to shopping at a sale, building a house, teaching a child, reviewing a bid, or another unfavorable circumstance, and the other person states, "Well, you know how they are." Something similar occurs when people interact with others of a minority culture and a person says, "You're different from the others." These types of phrases send strong signals to others that these comments toward the specified group of people carry an unquestionably discriminating bias.

Socioeconomic/Educational Level Lens

Since the founding of our nation, the search for a freer, safer, more secure, and more prosperous life with the possibility of upward mobility to live the American dream has been the major draw for immigrants. In current times, the American dream is far more difficult to attain, as the income-inequality gap has never been greater between the social classes and the haves and have-nots. There are numerous reasons, including greater demand for evolving renewable energy industries, increased globalization, outsourcing, robotics, obsolescence, digitalization, and stagnant wages due to political policies. However, the greatest injustice is the indecency and pure greed among some of the top one percent of the population. Under current policy, even two people working forty-hour weeks would still fall into the poverty level.

While economics and income are invariably an issue during presidential election cycles, the 2016 cycle proposed solutions that were more divisive than ever before. Focus on jobs had a significant impact on the 2016 election, as the country became more polarized. One view declared that we are stronger together and enriched by the diversity and skills of those from other cultures and social strata, and advocated for significantly and fairly raising minimum wages, promoting technical training, creating tuition-free public community colleges and universities, and instituting a living wage. The other view was simply to bring jobs home, maintain a minimum wage at the current level, become a more insular country, reduce environmental and financial regulations, and keep certain minorities from entering or advancing in the United States.

J. D. Vance (2016) authored an outstanding, graphic, and historical memoir, *Hillbilly Elegy*, about his Kentucky roots. The book provides a rich bird's-eye view into the culture, traditions, temperament, communication style, poverty, and attitudes toward how justice is served in his hillbilly culture. He speaks fondly of his tight connection with his grandmother, a stern, enlightened, and somewhat-crazy woman, who guided him to value education and never dishonor the family. Although his surroundings and family history screamed poverty, Vance was fortunate that his grandparents had the foresight to relocate from the coal-mining area of eastern Kentucky to the productive steel mills in southern Ohio. Vance, who served in the Marines, where he acquired skills and a better temperament, later graduated from The Ohio State University and Yale Law School to emerge as a person of privilege.

We learn that those culturally akin to hillbilly folks, who also migrated from Kentucky, primarily are of Protestant faith, of Irish and Scottish heritage, and carry shared values and traditions. Vance recalls that they were hard workers, held similar jobs, experienced a tradition of intergenerational violence, and assumed a certain mean toughness. Loyalty to family, telling it like it is, and refusal to call in police or government officials was the law. They frowned upon those who violated that rule, as they only believed in their "hillbilly justice" and that they alone should deal with the problem. Choices didn't matter, as there was a sense of hopelessness, and it was not up to outsiders or government to fix it.

Though those of hillbilly background are now spread out in rural New York, northern Alabama, and other Rust Belt areas and states, Vance concludes that they are "relatively culturally homogenous" and they expect their children to live the upward-mobility dream. Many of his generation witnessed their manufacturing jobs go overseas. They experience firsthand the impact of globalization, digitalization, and declining need for their skills. These, along with other reasons, are key to why they slipped back into the poverty that their families had experienced for the last two hundred years. In an interview with Vance on *Fareed Zakaria GPS*, on the topic "Understanding Trump's Working-class Support," host Fareed Zakaria summed up the message of the book: "In a sense, your family is a symbol for these vast swaths of the white working class, who used to work in…the Southern slave economy, in steel mills, in coal mines, stable jobs, but not particularly upwardly mobile" (Zakaria 2016b).

In hillbilly culture, they take constructive criticism as a personal insult, and apologies are not forthcoming. Yet Vance acknowledges that ensuing positive dialogues is necessary to resolve issues. Political correctness is the opposite of conversations heard around traditional dining room or kitchen tables, at church, or during other gatherings. As previously mentioned, the income gap between the highly wealthy and those in poverty is greater than ever. These reasons explain why people of the hillbilly culture gravitated to the unconventional presidential candidate Donald Trump, whose motto is "Make America Great Again." He also focused heavily on creating more jobs and bringing jobs home while epitomizing a familiar and comfortable style.

With that background and the current 2016 divisive political environment, Zakaria suggests that they are "suspicious of cities and cosmopolitan elites and people with a lot of education" (2016b). So they are naturally more comfortable listening to and identifying with the style and "off the cuff," "politically incorrect," and crass remarks of the Republican presidential nominee, Donald Trump. I also believe that they were turned off by the educated, coolheaded, and measured manners of President Obama, or the wonkish policy proposal contents and uncertainties of the Democratic presidential nominee, Hillary Clinton, or her surrogates. To some, these are elitist attitudes that further added distrust of Clinton and government.

Vance states that while you want a leader who uses good judgment and delivers "policy rooted in evidence," you remain more comfortable with someone with whom you have an emotional and gut-level connection. Vance further explains that those people who hold political power do not usually live in the same neighborhoods with those who are struggling in the new and current economy; this disconnect furthers alienation.

Vance conveys his message to his own community as "a compassionate and sympathetic message to the heart." He hopes his message will serve to improve the lives of the kids of his community, which he loves and claims as his own. His heartfelt and well-intended message is not always positively perceived by his hillbilly folks.

We cannot dismiss the legitimate concerns or angst of those who feel a sense of cultural displacement as they witness many of their norms and jobs slip away. They realize that the lifestyles and careers they once held are simply not returning or, if they are, not in the same way.

My professional experiences as a consultant and lecturer taught me that while education is valued the world over, too many people who hold high positions requiring advanced degrees often look down on, dismiss, or demean honest, hardworking people who lack high school or postsecondary education. Growing up in a blue-collar neighborhood in Columbus, Ohio, I learned early in my life that every person has a story to tell and every person has something valuable to offer. Close family ties, hard-work ethics, a basic sense of decency and civility, and unconditional love and support were paramount in most of my early childhood friends' families.

Over the years, I gained a magnitude of basic wisdom, loving insights, savvy street smarts, and valuable gems from people of more than fifty cultures. Many hold a wide range of jobs and professions, including housekeepers, gardeners, seamstresses, beauticians, aestheticians, massage therapists, delivery persons, and service people, while others are educators, doctors, chiefs of staff, CEOs, nurses, staff, accountants, directors, and lawyers. Some of these people, who led harsh, burdensome lives, also lacked family, community, or government support and were certainly not handed life on a silver platter. Instead, they experienced hardship or poverty. Their life stories taught more about coping skills, abilities to adapt, and overcoming hardships than have many of my peers who could not even imagine or fully grasp the reality of such experiences. Some had to make basic choices about whether to put food on the table, pay utilities, budget for fuel, or buy necessary medication or clothing. They did not have the option of dining at fancy restaurants, dressing in designer fashions, or driving a cool car. Regardless, these people have as much, if not more, depth, insight, joy, strength, resilience, character, and ability to have fun and enjoy the simplest thoughts, which often provoke joyous laughter.

The saying "Don't judge a book by its cover" has passed the test of time, reflecting its truth. The sharing with and trust from a wide range of individuals contributes as much to my knowledge as the books I've read, lectures I've attended, or classes I've taken during my university studies. Drawing conclusions about a person based solely on their educational or socioeconomic level leaves you empty-handed. When I spoke with a highly intelligent parent about his terrific children, he replied, "Yes, they are smart." I reminded him that very smart people plan and execute the most insidious acts and added, "Smart is not enough. What is far more important is what is in a person's heart."

Although there are immeasurable outstanding global philanthropic, government, religious, or business organizations that foster microeconomics, I only mention one. John Hatch pioneered the concept of village banking when he worked with lesser-opportunity and low-income farmers in Bolivia in 1984. His plan aided these farmers to obtain loans through a collective guarantee. A year later, Hatch established the Foundation for International Community Assistance (FINCA). FINCA's subsidiaries now reach twenty-three countries in Africa, Eurasia, the Middle East, South Asia, and Latin America, and the funds support hundreds of organizations. FINCA is the most diverse of any microfinance provider, serving 1.5 million people. The individual recipients or small businesses also learn to create their own solutions. Moreover, in 2005, Former United Nations Secretary General Kofi Annan stated, "Microfinance is an idea whose time has come." In 2011, FINCA achieved $1 billion in small-loan distribution, and in 2013, FINCA reached one million clients (http://www.finca.org).

Hatch says, "FINCA is not a typical charity. Although we are a nonprofit, we operate using sound business principles and an entrepreneurial spirit. We have developed a very innovative organizational structure that set a new standard for the microfinance industry that allows us to mobilize private and commercial capital while keeping true to our mission." This serves as a hand-up instead of a handout model and is a tremendous boost to family income, nutrition, employment, and well-being for those who had no hope to borrow, as they did not qualify for traditional bank loans. These loans have uplifted families and communities alike, reducing global poverty by creating employment.

When I read a sign that succinctly stated, "Saw it, wanted it, threw a fit, got it," to me, that was the epitome of why an entitlement mind-set causes desperation and rage throughout the world. Sasheer Zamata, a noted comedian on *Saturday Night Live* who aced her impersonation of First Lady Michelle Obama, expanded the privilege notion through her role as an activist and an ACLU ambassador. She created a video and wrote a column highlighting "privilege and how it shields people from being aware of challenges other people might face." In my own experience, most people associated privilege with "white folk" and those of the upper socioeconomic class. But in ACLU's *STAND* magazine, Zamata enlightens the reader that "everyone has privilege: a privilege is an advantage that you might have over another person." Some advantages that she lists are "gender, race, sexuality, income, physical ability and so on" (Zamata 2016).

A copyeditor realized a long time ago that he had privilege as a male. One example is that they do not pay women and those of minority heritages wages equal to those of white men hold-ing the same positions, and they are far from equal in elected government positions. He also realized that if he were Christian, he would have a privilege that many of his Jewish faith and those of other faiths do not enjoy.

It also is hard to recognize some of our attributes as privilege because they are innate. Others, such as social class, were either gained or not in our control. Zamata states, "It is easier to point out our disadvantages and reasons why we don't occupy social standing than acknowledge why we are where we are" (Zamata 2016). I acknowledge that idea to some degree; we are aware of our traits and disadvantages because we live with them. I am aware that others and society also point out those facts.

But many givens, which we have taken for granted, are pointed out by Zamata as she exposes privilege and leads us to examine the following. *We might be privileged* if the only "gang activity" we ever saw was in a movie, or we live in a neighborhood where we can easily order fresh vegetables at a drive-through, or we alone determine what we can do with our bodies, or we can enter a restroom whose image doesn't reflect who we are without being stopped or questioned, or no one disapproves of our hairstyles or head gear, or we were never pulled over by a cop because of our outward appearance. She goes on to declare that we *might be privileged* if we "have health insurance [or] went to a school where having books, computers, sports facilities, and a good amount of teachers was the norm." She also notes that we *might be privileged* "if we become defensive when others mention that we are privileged" (Zamata 2016).

Zamata also offers her own privileges that include: "writing part of this essay from a resort in St. Lucia… have time and money to take a vacation…[don't have to check each time if there are enough funds to cover writing a check, [have] the ability to give voice to be heard by many people." She concludes that "acknowledging privilege shouldn't be about making anyone feel guilty"] (Zamata 2016). By pointing out possible privileges, she has enabled many to appreciate the privileges that we have yet previously may not perceived as such. Zamata certainly raised our awareness so that we can help others.

Hopefully, with a new recognition of additional privileges within ourselves, these notions will bolster a sense of *self-worth* and, just as relevant, further support and aid those individuals who do not enjoy as much privilege.

"Learn today. Earn tomorrow" is the slogan of our village's St. Thomas Primary School in Nevis. As emphasized, the literacy rate in Nevis is 98 percent (in a population of twelve thousand). When I asked how they achieved this, the principal confirmed, "Parents and teachers highly value and understand the importance of education. Teachers volunteer their time from mid-March until exam time in July to remain after school a few days a week and come in a couple of hours on Saturday mornings to help their students reach their highest level and score well on tests."

Over the years, I worked with the popular principal of the major secondary school in Nevis. He always has a warm smile on his face, and the students feel comfortable approaching him with a concern, question, or just to chat. I mostly admire him because he is equally dedicated to the brightest and the most challenged students. He is guided by the principle "that we all have a purpose here on earth and each student possesses the innate ability to achieve greatness. Different pathways will take each one there. But ultimately, each student is capable of making their positive contribution to our universe."

When Lee and I offered tickets for a premiere performance at our Nevis Performing Arts Centre to a cook's daughter from Guyana who was first in her secondary-school class, she replied, "Thank you, but I can't. It is exam time." During those "study months," the most diligent students participate in, practice, and attend sporting events, school functions, and church, and they study. There is no TV or text time, just "study time."

A gentleman who dedicates his life to fund-raising at a university to help students with high potential, especially for those who are first-generation U.S. Americans with low income, shared his enlightening story. His mother, who grew up in Guatemala, a third world country, was a bright woman who dreamed of attending college to become a doctor or an attorney. When she shared her hopes and vision with her parents, her father laughed and told her she should focus on finding a good husband and having a family. When this intelligent and clever young woman turned eighteen, she asked her parents for permission to visit the United States and stay with her mother's close friend for a couple of weeks; her parents agreed. That two-week vacation turned into fifteen years before she returned to Guatemala. She had understood that her goal of a better quality of life for herself as a woman could not happen in Guatemala. She realized that she would have to leave her own homeland and, most importantly, her family. In the United States, she married, had a son, and then divorced.

A single parent, she now raised that son. He was also intellectually gifted and loved going to school. In his youth, as an only child, he knew that he could hang out with his friends at school. His mother had to work long hours to provide food, shelter, and clothing. Unfortunately, and understandably, during those lengthy hours and days, the young man was left alone too much. He was easily bored and "very easily" spent much time hanging out on the streets. Then, there were no after-school enrichment programs offered at his local junior high school. "Besides," he said, "I'm not sure I would have attended, because it wasn't cool." Growing up with peers from similar low-income neighborhoods, these children were left alone to their own devices and did what they wanted whenever they wanted. Being young, unwise, and without any parental supervision or guidance, many in that situation got in a lot of trouble. Although he claims he usually seemed to find himself in minor trouble, he always excelled in school.

Fortunately for him, a friend's older sister recognized his potential, as she handed him a list of courses that he should request that his school counselor schedule. The courses included higher math and a second language. His counselor had different plans. It was then that he realized that there was a two-track course path, one road to simply graduate and the other to prepare for college. As he matured, he recognized that college preparatory courses had far more demanding yet appropriate coursework.

Close to the end of his senior year in high school, his mother kept asking, "What do you want to do with the rest of your life?" As he told me, "She firmly stated that if I want to go to college, work full-time, or live in her home, I needed to make a decision soon, or I could get the hell out of her house." The young man didn't make the decision his mother liked, so she kicked him out. He landed on the streets for a couple of weeks until he decided he needed to make better choices for his future.

He was admitted into a leading university with one of the most outstanding records of raising students' income levels from the time of admission up to their first job after graduation. They also accepted the young man into the Educational Opportunity Program (EOP), which served fellow students with high potential who came from similar first-generation and low-income or lesser-opportunity backgrounds. They provided these students with a team of mentors and support services to help navigate the path to graduation and fulfillment of their visions and dreams of a better life. They also had to embrace a determination and vision to do something for themselves, become a productive member of society, and more imperative, give back to their communities.

He later became a captivating, passionate, and motivating fund-raiser. When he led an event to raise funds for the EOP, an attendee commented that she thought programs similar to EOP were a waste of money. This person claimed that she never asked anyone for help, that she pulled herself up by her own bootstraps and did everything herself. So the gentleman asked her a simple question, "What kind of car do you drive?" She responded, "I drive a Lexus." Then he asked her, "Does your Lexus have a Global Positioning System (GPS) navigation setup in it?" She replied, "Yes, it does." Then he asked, "Do you use it?" She answered, "Yes, I do." Then he requested that she turn off her GPS, pick a favorite restaurant in town, and find the restaurant. She responded that she was sure she could find her way by asking people or using a Thomas Guide, as people had done prior to GPS.

She then asked what his point was. He replied, "You have a GPS in your car that is literally at your fingertips, which you can easily access anytime you want while you are driving to find a specific location." He pressed on with his next points. "Did your parents ever talk to you about college? Did family members, neighbors, or friends go to college?" She answered yes to all the questions. He then continued, "Well, imagine that your car didn't have a GPS. It might cause a small inconvenience for you. Now, imagine a young person who grew up in a family that never had a family member or any close friend attend college and who might not have had the fortune of involvement of both parents." The woman repeated, "What's your point?" He eloquently and convincingly responded, "You might have done everything yourself, but you had access to people that could provide you direction, offer you advice, tips, and suggestions about living a better quality of life. In other words, you grew up with a more valuable road map—a better human GPS—about life than did many others." Most people don't have a close relative or friend who offered advice and directed them on college and career choices, investing, traveling, and leading healthy, productive lifestyles. This charismatic gentleman's life's journey and his most succinct and potent linkage of a GPS to a human being's life's journey struck a chord within her.

A friend and neighbor's grandfather was a banker in Iran who became extremely wealthy. During his lifetime, he had acquired an extensive, exquisite, and exceptional collection of art and artifacts worth thousands of dollars, which he enjoyed in his home. After her grandfather's home was looted—as were many of the Jewish homes in his town—my friend's father was unable to complete his education. He urged his children to each acquire a college education so that wherever they went, they would be able to work. And he added, "No one can ever rob you of your knowledge." Before she retired, for decades, my friend served as a nurse on the medical and surgical floor at UCLA, and her siblings also are health-care professionals.

As an Emmy winner and three-time Academy Award nominee, Viola Davis has an incredible story of how she lived through abject poverty with few choices and then rose to fame that is uplifting. Then, she and her family lived rent-free in Rhode Island at 128 Washington Street, in a rat-infested building slated to be demolished. To her, hunger was worse than the vermin or sounds where they lived. She dreaded when the welfare check ran out and the pangs of physical and psychological hunger kicked in. In hopes of getting food, she resorted to honorably befriending others, ravaging through dumpsters to find edible scraps, and even joining summer programs only to get snacks. She was constantly conscious of being hungry, especially at school. She said, "I was always so hungry and ashamed I couldn't tap into my potential. I couldn't get into the business of being me." Over the years, she and her sister experienced nightmares about their childhood, which they titled "128 Washington Street."

At eight years old, Davis won her first acting prize at a local school. Her innate talent and passion shone brightly enough for her to earn a scholarship, first at a Rhode Island college, and later at the Juilliard School in New York. Early in her acting career, she already received Broadway's coveted Tony Award.

Her incredible badge of personal comfort and courage was displayed during an episode of *How to Get Away with Murder*. "Davis removes her makeup, eyelashes, and a wig, physically and figuratively stripping herself vulnerable before she confronts her husband about his infidelity. She wanted to show a woman so powerful, so put together in the outside world taking off her mask [that she could say], 'I'm finally comfortable with my story'" (Hayasaki 2015). A suggestion from theologist Joseph Campbell's thoughts resonated within Davis as she connected with his words, "The privilege of a lifetime is being who you are."

Davis has raised more than $4.5 million to fight hunger with a new campaign with the Safeway Foundation and the Entertainment Industry Foundation. Davis says, "This is the richest country in the world. There's no reason kids should be going to school hungry. Food is something that everyone should have. It just is" (Hunger Is, n.d.).

Income Inequality Lens

Thanks to a suggestion from Marion Wright, who was then director of the National Association for the Advancement of Colored People's Legal Defense and Education Fund, even Dr. King became more aware of the need to focus on the issue of economic security for everyone. So in 1967, Dr. King, along with the Southern Christian Leadership Conference (SCLC), planned nonviolent gatherings of two thousand poor people in Washington, DC, and also in states and cities in the South and the North. The intent was to create the Poor People's Campaign, in which he would meet with government officials and "demand jobs, unemployment insurance, a fair minimum wage, and education for poor adults and children designed to improve their self-image and self-esteem" (King Encyclopedia, n.d.).

King understood—as we now more broadly realize—that income inequality creates poverty. At that time, a collaborative and determined group of leaders of Native American, Puerto Rican, Mexican, and poor white (European heritage) communities pledged to join the campaign. After Dr. King's assassination in 1968, efforts continued briefly but eventually dwindled, the results being a mere few hundred counties qualifying "for free surplus food distribution, and securing promises from several federal agencies to hire poor people to help run programs for the poor," as stated by the King Encyclopedia.

In the 2016 presidential election season, the topic of income inequality finally became front and center instead of hung up in the closet. Two antiestablishment candidates could not be more diametrically opposed in rhetoric or style. One points to expulsion and exclusion for many; the other champions inclusion of all. But they have a few ideas in common. Both vehemently oppose the current international trade deals. However, one candidate addresses the unemployment rate primarily focused on those in the Rust Belt; the other addresses the unemployment issue across the board, with additional focus on minorities. One speaks solely of trade to increase job growth; the other proposes free education for all as a path toward prosperity.

There is a significant link between access to excellent education and reaching its critical graduation goal and the comfort level of success and the degree one can achieve. The achievement of a high school diploma, a basic certificate in any field, or an associate or bachelor's degree is a major factor in determining the socioeconomic level and whether life is a constant struggle or is financially stable. Those who do not graduate high school are left behind with a monumental disadvantage.

The Bureau of Labor Statistics posted a chart on March 15, 2016, comparing median usual weekly earnings and unemployment rates for persons aged twenty-five and older. The figures are based on earning full-time and salaried wages. A person with less than a high school diploma earned $493 per week, and their unemployment rate was 8 percent. Those with a high school diploma earned $678 per week, and their unemployment rate was 5.4 percent. Those with some college but no degree earned $738 per week, and their unemployment rate was 3.8 percent. Those with an associate's degree earned $798 per week, and their unemployment rate was 3.8 percent. Those with a bachelor's degree earned $1,137, and their unemployment rate was 2.8 percent; those with a master's degree earned $1,341 per week, and their unemployment rate was 2.4 percent; those with a professional degree earned $1,730 per week, and their unemployment rate was 1.5 percent; and lastly, those with a doctoral degree earned $1,623 per week, and their unemployment was 1.7 percent. According to the chart, "The report does not take into account completion of training programs in the form of apprenticeships and other on-the-job training, which may also influence earnings and unemployment rates" (USDL, n.d.).

According to the Education Writer's Association (EWA) report, "nearly two-thirds of low-income Hispanics ages 3–5 attend some form of early education, nearly on par with those of

European heritage" (Gross 2016). It appears that contrary to public opinion, preschool children of Latino heritage do not remain at home with family but are enrolled in pre-K programs such as Head Start, or in community or church-based programs, at rates comparable to children of other heritages. Evidence points to a positive impact for preschoolers of low-income Latino heritage who significantly benefit from local, state, and federal investments to help fund these preschool programs. Furthermore, Professor Gigliana Melzi reported to EWA that various research shows that children who attend pre-K programs have a higher probability of graduating high school and, on average, even earn a higher income in midlife than those who do not benefit from early education.

The University of Illinois at Chicago found that both in Los Angeles and New York City, about 30 percent of people of African heritage between the ages of twenty to twenty-four were out of work or out of school. In Chicago, the statistic was even more shocking, as nearly half the men of African heritage in the same age group were not working or in school. When you add the number of men of African heritage who are incarcerated (some for mere possession of marijuana), this figure goes up from 42 to more than 50 percent, depending on whose figures you use (Cordova and Wilson 2016).

The crisis of permanent joblessness, in Chicago and elsewhere, is concentrated in minority neighborhoods. This is an outrageous fact in a culture where a CEO's income can be up to nearly two thousand times a median worker's pay (Chamberlain 2015). These facts certainly engender a person's sense of abandonment by their community and country and leads to a vulnerable sense of hopelessness. It is no wonder that these issues fuel street violence, social corrosion, and drug dealing, along with an underlying lack of well-being that fosters a culture of despair. It also is no small wonder that intense anger persists in this age group. In part, that hostility stems from a person's inability to secure meaningful work. Understandably, they do not gain a sense of dignity. These feelings may be expressed nonviolently or violently. Although I never condone violence, I can certainly recognize the underlying sense of disenfranchisement and resignation that festers when they repress feelings of joblessness and unworthiness for long periods.

Under the Recovery Act of 2009, following the Great Recession of 2008, a program began that created 260,000 temporary jobs. In 2013, the Economic Mobility Corporation, a nonprofit organization, released a study showing that 37 percent of the workers performed well enough that they were permanently hired. This successful program occurred in Florida, California, Mississippi, and Wisconsin and was key in increasing job training and securing meaningful employment to keep workers afloat during challenging times. This type of program was a potent tool in increasing employment for those of minority cultures. Unfortunately, after the 2010 elections, Congress no longer funded these types of programs.

Following the Great Depression, many subsidized worker programs were public jobs, but those offered during the Obama administration following the Great Recession in the 2009 program were primarily placed in the private sector. In a program with great potential, some private businesses partnered with community colleges to train unemployed workers for permanent, higher-paying jobs.

There are many factors that lead to the sense of despair, discontent, and disenfranchisement that many people feel, especially those of minority cultures and particularly those of African heritage. This is especially pertinent as they often experience only the "highway into poverty and barely a sidewalk out" (Smiley 2016). Poverty, racism, and militarism are certainly issues that fuel these underlying factors. But as indicated earlier, the levels of education and one's lifetime income certainly correlate and play a major role in a person's sense of stability and satisfaction.

But there is great hope. And that hope lies in Chancellor Timothy P. White's declaration of a "race to the moon," reminiscent of the U.S. 1960 race to the moon. The chancellor leads the California State University (CSU) system, the largest higher education system in the world. In early 2016, the chancellor announced his intention: "Our goal, 'our moon,' must be a quality bachelor's degree for every Californian willing and able to earn it—with an achievement gap of zero." He further stated, "That means the same opportunity to succeed for every student. This is how we empower the disenfranchised" (Zonkel 2016).

A few days after his "moon race" proclamation, Chancellor White was the guest of honor at a reception at California State University, Northridge, where I had the pleasure of meeting and briefly conversing with him. I gained a strong sense of his deep passion, empathy, and dedication to the advancement of CSU students, his desire to uplift them and our country, and to potentially create a model for improving the world.

I continue to have great faith in Chancellor White and CSU system. In just a few years, Chancellor White demonstrated his commitment and achieved success; there was a significant increase in CSU first-time freshmen graduating in four years. I firmly believe these noble goals allowed students to feel deep pride as they enter the workforce earning substantial salaries. This increases productivity and adds millions of dollars to the economy.

Religion Lens

Each of the prominent religions and beliefs teaches values of inclusion and looking out for one another and sets a moral code for right and wrong. Yet human history has proved that many wars were fought in the name of religion, which clearly contradicts the religious doctrines. The actions of those waging war often abhorrently rejected their own declarations. Not only were wars fought against people of other persuasions, but deep discord and division also exist among the sects within many beliefs. While the authentic doctrines seek to enlighten, inspire, and uplift, the words and actions of some who claim to adhere to the precepts significantly perverted their religious intent. Their blasphemous rhetoric and murderous deeds are mortifying and barbaric.

Many who are observant and faithful to their ideals are very adept at judging and clearly stating when they see others do wrong. However, they themselves avoid the necessary introspection to see that they often possess the same negative attitude and engage in the same deplorable responses or behaviors that they judge. Many spend too much time judging how others practice their faith instead of looking inward to monitor their own words and deeds. Because they are busy looking outward, they do not possess the courage, mindfulness, or will to look inward into their humanity to see what is in their heart.

In conversations with people who question which day to pray, how often to pray, where or to whom to pray, my response is, "If there is a Creator and if there is a heaven, how do you think we will be judged? Is it by the way we chose to live our lives, true to self, kind, understanding, and respectfully helping others? Or do you think we will be judged by what we wore or when, where, how, and with whom we practiced the traditions of our religion?" To me, a good person is a good person. Their belief system is not relevant, as long as they are mindful, honest, kind, respectful, and generous of spirit. Decades ago, when I attended a conference of health-care professionals, the person sitting beside me asked, "Which religion do you think is closer to God?" I looked up at an ornate chandelier that hung above our table and commented, "Do you see the chandelier hanging above? Do you notice that the same electric current passing through the same wire equally lights hundreds of light bulbs? I believe that whoever or whatever force created us gave light and vision to the various religious doctrines of the world." I also shared, "If you were born into a Jewish family and I were born into a Christian family, we may each be practicing each other's religion, or a different one altogether." If asked the same question today, I would add, "Or another way of life, belief, or no religion at all."

I recollect watching Israeli Prime Minister Yitzhak Rabin's funeral decades ago and being distressed by the word *they* when the commentator referred to people who were Jews or Arabs. Whether a person is peace-loving or hate-filled, usually each responds in their own way that is somewhat different from that of any other person. One person may have wanted to see the 1995 peace mission in the Middle East fail due to fear of losing the land on which they live, and another person may have hoped for failure because of Arab or Israeli mistrust, or another may have responded to an ill-perceived divine mandate. Peace uplifts; hatred disheartens. Each person comes to that "place" from their own journey. It is a journey of individuals, a collection of "she," "he," "we," and "they," but not "them."

Many vigorously voiced that the Religious Freedom Restoration Act signed by Indiana Governor Mike Pence was highly discriminatory. (Further presentation of this topic follows in "*Sexual Orientation Lens*.") As my husband and I discussed the law, my husband succinctly stated, "Everyone has the right to freedom of religion. What they don't have is the right to interfere in my secular life."

In September 2015 in Irving, Texas, Ahmed Mohamed, a fourteen-year-old boy of the Muslim faith who thoroughly enjoyed tinkering and repairing at home, took a homemade alarm clock to show an engineering teacher. When it later began to beep in another class, suspicions were raised that his clock was an explosive device, so they sent him to the principal's office. If a bomb were really suspected, wouldn't the principal have made an immediate, urgent public announcement for everyone to evacuate the school? If the child were really a threat, wouldn't the person they summoned have been from the bomb squad, rather than the police? I know that in today's uncertain environment, caution remains prudent. But we must question again, If the child had resembled a child of European heritage, would the same procedures have applied?

When they asked the Irving Chief of Police the same question, he replied that he would have followed the same procedure. Thankfully, then-President Obama reached out and invited talented

Ahmed to bring his device to the White House. Farhana Khera, President and Executive Director of Muslim Advocates, asked the Department of Justice to investigate the Irving High School and the Irving Police Department (Fernandez and Hauser 2015).

There are many tenets to each religion and numerous interpretations of the principles. As previously shared, my grandmother said, "Every person makes up their own religion." Each person decides how strictly they adhere to each command and ideal, which ones they will faithfully observe, which ones they will compromise, and which ones they will ignore. Their faith-based values are more paramount than the appropriateness of cultural attitudes.

Ibtihaj Muhammad is a woman of athletic prowess and a devout Muslim. She is a tenacious, speedy, and mighty athlete. Most sports require gear that did not conform to Muslim customs. When she discovered fencing, she finally found a sport in which she could wear a hijab and remain true to herself. As one of the world's finest fencers, she became an Olympian with the U.S. team at the 2016 Summer Olympic Games in Rio de Janeiro. Prior to the Olympic Games, Congressman Keith Ellison noted in "The 100 Most Influential People" for 2016 in *Time* magazine, "That's not just the story of Ibtihaj Muhammad. That's the story of America" (Ellison 2016).

There are Jewish and Muslim individuals who will not shake hands with people of the opposite sex and will not touch or shake hands in any personal or professional setting. As with other principles, the observance of this practice fluctuates. The medical profession is an exception, among others. A doctor has to touch their patients during diagnosis and treatment. A woman from India who was Muslim had an extremely difficult time shaking hands with male clients. As a customer relations supervisor, she had to shake hands with clients. When the clients extended their hands, she pulled her hands behind her back. Withdrawing her hands was a form of nonverbal communication, indicating that she did not want any contact. Her clients misunderstood her withdrawal, occasionally took it personally, and were often offended. When my client learned the meaning behind her nonverbal communication, she sincerely desired to seek a solution. She and I tried several alternatives that were appropriate for the professional setting and acceptable to her. The win-win solution that we found was washing her hands after meeting her clients and shaking their hands and before she moved on to her next task or client. The compromise worked for her, and her refusal to shake hands no longer offended her clients.

At a recent business open house, when a female guest offered a handshake to an orthodox Jewish man, he rudely told the woman, "I can't shake your hand. I'm orthodox." Some people later commented, "How ridiculous." He handled the situation correctly, taking responsibility for his beliefs and actions and offering an explanation. But his curt voice tone detracted from his message and left a negative impression. His comment would have been more acceptable if he had conveyed his beliefs in a thoughtful and courteous manner. Without communication, a person's refusal to shake another's hand may be misconstrued as discomfort or dislike. I recommend that you communicate from your *source-connection* and state, "My personal beliefs [or my religious beliefs] prohibit me from shaking hands with you. I hope that you won't take it personally," or in a pleasant, *source-connected* voice, simply own it and state, "I'm orthodox. I can't shake your hand." To me, this is no different than when a person offers a dessert that contains dairy (I am lactose intolerant) and I politely inform them, "No, thank you. I am sensitive to dairy products."

At the Church of the Epiphany, an Episcopal congregation, it became routine for members of both the Christian and Muslim faith to pray under the same roof at different times. This tradition began eight years ago, when Reverend Elizabeth Gardner invited "the Muslim faithful, who were looking for a place to worship, to share the same space." Reverend Gardner extended the invitation and said, "It is our job to be the hands and feet of peace in the world...by loving one another" (Werner 2016). When Muslim coordinator Farooq Syed organized services eight years ago, fifty members joined, and now their congregation has grown to three hundred, making the Muslim parish the largest part of the church's congregation (Zaimov 2016).

Member Sayeed Bond, who is homeless, joined the Muslim faith twenty years ago. By chance, he attended his first service three years ago. He now helps roll out the prayer rugs on Friday nights, beneath stained glass windows depicting Jesus and amid the peal of ringing church bells. Syed shared that it is amazing to witness and further stated, "It is a moment of reflection for people who think we are different. We are all the same." CBS commentator Anne-Marie Green concluded that she saw "Muslims and Christians in a church bearing witness to an epiphany together" (Green 2016).

I still recall hearing the news in 1964 that Cassius Clay was the youngest boxer to win the world heavyweight championship. Who could have predicted that the champ, who was last in his high school graduating class, would later receive an honorary degree from Princeton? Early on, Clay chose to embrace Islam and change his name to Muhammad Ali. Along with his protest against discrimination, his faith guided him to oppose the Vietnam War. When they drafted him into the military, he refused to serve and consequently was stripped of his heavyweight championship title. Even though they offered him the choice to participate in the military as an inspiring entertainer, he stood firm in his convictions and refused, as it was still the same war that he devoutly opposed. Over the years, Ali donated millions of dollars to numerous charities, but his commitment to his faith, which he held supreme, was his most inspiring facet. It defined a man of great integrity and principles; it was a decision that solely affected him.

Gender Lens

Perhaps the time will come when there are no set biases between men and women, and we will perceive the person for who they are without immediately attaching any gender-related preconceptions of their thoughts or actions. When we carry a *gender lens* that generalizes that *all* men or *all* women are _____, we discriminate based on gender.

My eighty-nine-year-old sister-in-heart shared that when she was a child attending religious school, she drew a picture of a woman wearing a robe and a crown and showed the image to the rabbi. He asked her if that was a picture of a queen. When she replied, "It is God," the rabbi said, "That's a woman, and God is a man." My sister-in-heart quickly challenged, "How do you know?" Then she recalled hearing the word *impertinent* but did not know what that meant.

Universally, in most areas, women and girls have not achieved equality with men and boys in access, wages, power, human rights, and protection under the law. In most areas around the globe, society views and treats women as significantly inferior to men. Most unwillingly, women continue to experience sexual harassment and are subjects of heinous forms of abuse, rape, abduction, and human trafficking. Terrorist groups, such as Boko Haram, also hold them in bondage to serve a man's pleasure or sell them for marriage or servitude. The ritual of female genital cutting or circumcision, Female Genital Mutilation (FGM), is prevalent in some cultures. A quarterly report produced by *Medecins Sans Frontieres / Doctors Without Borders* states that "3.6 million girls were cut in 2013, a number that will rise to 6.6 million by 2050 at current rates" (Nicolai 2015).

Most people cannot possibly fathom and are utterly repulsed by the thought of the heinous acts of abduction, rape, sex trafficking, torture, and murder committed around the globe against women and especially young girls. Until recently, most remained silent on these issues. Fortunately, global citizens around the world no longer remain silent or stand still, as women begin to speak out and are gaining equal rights and the same protection.

On the positive side, statistics show that in many countries, including the United States, more women now attend and graduate from colleges and universities than men. Female pilots, astronauts, and combat soldiers are also more common in the US armed forces, and women now reach higher ranks. Over the years, gender equality has been steadily rising. However, there is still a long way to go to attain equal pay, access, health-care and pharmaceutical benefits, advancement in women's health research, and most crucially, attaining a woman's right to make choices over her own body. Women also advanced in the financial, educational, and global political worlds as heads of financial systems and educational institutions and as CEOs of major organizations, including Fortune 500 companies. In the political arena, there are more female heads of state and women in high governmental positions than ever before. However, in the United States, at the local, state, and national government levels, in high-level financial institutions, medical organizations, and digital technology or spectator sports industries, women still lag far behind in numbers, rank, and pay despite female demographics. It clearly remains visible that when women are deeply involved at higher levels, more compromises take place.

In many parts of the world, they teach girls that they can excel in any field they want, regardless of their gender. But more often, they tell girls how to act, speak, and think, when to drive, whom to marry, what studies, roles, and careers to seek, and who they "should" be. I suggest that when a girl is confident enough and ready, she then defines to others who she is and wants to be. With confidence and female pride, she responds, "That's because I am a girl, I'm proud of it, and that won't hold me back from anything I want to do." For eons, women have buckled under male suppression. In matriarchal societies, women stand taller.

Harry Belafonte sings a song, "Man Smart (Woman Smarter)." The lyrics, which ring, "But I say that the woman of today is smarter than man in every way," personify what I observe in many facets of Nevisian life. This is proved by the fact that fourteen out of fifteen primary and secondary schools in Nevis are headed by women.

I am fortunate that I came from a strong, independent line of women who are my role models, and I am aware that I carry their DNA in my genes. (See "Author's Journey" in the *Appendix* of the book.) My mother, who was an assertive woman, often said, "Women have the children because they are stronger." Yet as a wife, there were times that I caved and didn't hold my rightful ground. However, I always felt intellectually equal to men. Men may have more physical prowess, but that alone does not determine strength or grit. Now, past seventy-five, I believe that the woman is stronger, and under that macho male bravado often lies a very tenderhearted and gentle soul.

It is best to let each person, male or female, stand on their own merits and prove their capabilities instead of prejudging based on gender. Some cultures rejoice in the birth of a son more than a daughter. A gift from the Creator, regardless of gender, is a treasure to cherish. In 2010, Sheryl Sandberg, Facebook COO, appeared on *TED Talks*, making the point that women hold themselves back. Viewers around the world identified with her message and began to share their stories and struggles. The resounding response inspired her to write the book *Lean In: Women, Work and the Will to Lead*. Her initial message explored the question of why women had not caught up with men in leadership roles and stressed that women should focus on what they can do instead of what they cannot do. *Lean In* philosophy serves as a piece of the global conversation, empowering women with fresh, positive, and proactive ideas pertinent to early twenty-first-century life. Her follow-up book, *Lean in for Graduates*, offers concrete, meaningful thoughts and sayings to guide women as they redetermine who they are and carve out new roles to successfully achieve their goals. Sandberg stresses the importance of finding a willing partner to share parenting and household responsibilities (Sandberg 2014). Please allow me to stress again, whenever we allow another person or society to label us in any way, we fail. The only person who has the right to define us is our one and only self.

Strong women have existed long before the women's liberation movement of the 1960s and 1970s. Dr. Mary McLeod Bethune is testimony to that statement. How many first ladies can you name? Did you include Mary McLeod Bethune, "who ultimately became a revered educator, activist, humanitarian, stateswoman, and leader whom they knew in her day as 'the first lady of the Negro race'" (Marech 2015)? Bethune came from very humble beginnings and became quite an astonishing woman. She was the second youngest of seventeen brothers and sisters, who were all born to former slaves. She was raised on a farm in South Carolina, where at age five, she started working in the fields. One day, Mary was with her working mother when a little white girl suddenly took her book away, claiming that Mary couldn't read. At that moment, Mary's life changed and "her will to learn was ignited." Of all her siblings, she was the only child to receive an education, and she did not mind the eight-mile walk to school each day.

In 1904, "Bethune went on to found a girl's school [the Daytona Literary and Industrial Training School for Negro Girls] in Daytona Beach, Florida. She started the school with $1.50 and just six students, including her son Albert, from a short-lived marriage." In 1923, the school began to merge with Cookman Institute of Jacksonville, Florida (founded in 1872), remained coed, and affiliated with the prestigious United Methodist Church. Finally, two years later, the merger to become the Daytona-Cookman Collegiate Institute was completed. In 1931, the college became accredited as a junior college, and the school's name was officially changed to Bethune-Cookman College to reflect the leadership of Dr. Mary McLeod Bethune. The university motto was "Enter to learn, depart to serve," and the school included a farm, high school, and nursing school. Later in her career, Bethune worked for four presidents and was friends with Eleanor Roosevelt, "who appointed her head of the Negro Division of the National Youth Administration, making her the highest-ranking African-American woman in the federal government" (BCU, n.d.). She also served in the Black Cabinet and unofficially advised prominent leaders of African heritage (Marech 2015).

"Bethune founded the National Council of Negro Women (NCNW) in 1935 and became the first president of the organization. From 1935 to her death in 1955, she was the single most important African-American woman who people saw functioning at the national level." She had purchased a rowhouse with the aid of Marshall Field's charity fund, and a fire later damaged the NCNW headquarters. It turns out that Bethune was quite the historian as well. Years after she had passed away, a "treasure trove of historic materials on African-American women" was found in a dilapidated carriage house. They had gathered the information in hopes that one day it would be "central to the study of [US] American history." The U.S. National Park Services moved the massive collection, and discussion continues about the future of this treasure. The U.S. National Park Service also restored the rowhouse in 1994, where copies of Bethune's last will and testament reside with the words "I leave you love, I leave you hope…leave you racial dignity…I leave you finally, a responsibility to our young people" (Marech 2015). Her wisdom is available for all visitors to experience.

This gender section focuses more on women than on men because men have forever dominated U.S. and global cultures. Even every time we handle U.S. currency, we see a man's portrait. Therefore, it is historically monumental that Harriet Tubman, an African American abolitionist and a Union spy during the American Civil War, will replace former President Andrew Jackson on the $20 bill. Inspirational Tubman was fearless and continues to profoundly inspire generations of individuals. Against all odds and guided solely by God's voice, Tubman relentlessly persevered rescuing more than 700 slaves. As a Conductor in the Underground Railroad, without fail she led each person to freedom through treacherous terrain. Since she also freed her people from slavery, she is called "Moses of Her People." She is also regarded as more heroic than slaveholder Jackson.

In April 2016, Treasury Secretary Jack Lew announced the decision to put Harriet Tubman on the $20 bill. Coincidently, $20 reflects the amount of the monthly pension that she received as a widow and for her service as a nurse, cook, and spy during the Civil War. Lew also stated that Women's Suffragist Lucretia Mott will appear on the back of the $10 bill. Mott followed the Quaker's beliefs (also known as Friends) and helped initiate the women's rights movement by organizing the Seneca Falls Convention to advance the cause of voting rights for women (USDT, n.d.).

Additionally, Lew announced that the back of the new $5 bill will honor those with a significant connection to the Lincoln Memorial. These include former First Lady Eleanor Roosevelt, world-renowned opera singer Marian Anderson, and iconic civil rights leader Dr. Martin Luther King Jr. First Lady Roosevelt is being honored for her lifelong humanitarian and civil rights efforts, including supporting a performance in 1939 by Marion Anderson at the Memorial when concert halls in the United States remained segregated. Dr. Martin Luther King Jr. delivered his historic "I Have a Dream" speech in front of hundreds of thousands at the Lincoln Memorial. King peerlessly led the civil rights movement for those of African heritage as no other person had since President Lincoln. He was also the youngest person of African heritage to receive the Nobel Peace Prize. He gave his life for his deep, nonviolent, and stalwart beliefs to achieve racial justice (USDT, n.d.). These images will remind us daily that each person advanced the cause of civil rights and freedom in an especially illuminating way.

During World War II, Caroline Kennedy's father, John F. Kennedy, was captain of PT-109 (a Patrol Torpedo boat). A Japanese destroyer struck and ripped the boat apart, tossing the crew into the water. In 1960, John Kennedy was elected the thirty-fifth president of the United States. In 2015, Ambassador Caroline Kennedy began her service in Japan, one of the U.S.A.'s strongest Asian allies. Although their economy stagnated for a while, Japan has the third largest global economy. Japan also has the most educated women in the world. Ambassador Kennedy is working closely with conservative Japanese Prime Minister Shinzo Abe, who created Abenomics in 2012 to boost the Gross Domestic Product (GDP). "A feature of Abenomics is the concept of womanomics with goals to add more women into the workforce, increase women's senior managerial roles by 30 percent by 2020, urge companies to place at least one woman on each board, and add 400,000 nursery schools by 2018" (O'Donnell 2015).

Ruth Bader Ginsburg, a Brooklyn gal, in her youth demonstrated tremendous intellect and creativity as she excelled in every role. Her mother taught her to be independent and a lady; she prematurely died the day prior to Ruth's high school graduation. Ruth Bader and Marty Ginsburg married and equally decided to attended Harvard Law School. Duly challenged with being pregnant with her first child and attending law school, she was told by her father-in-law, "Ruth, if you really don't want to start law school, you have a good reason to resist the undertaking.… But if you really want to study law, you will stop worrying and find a way to manage child and school." Ginsburg also relies on a "routine of hard work, discipline and little sleep to 'carry her along.'" (Ginsburg, Hartnett, and Williams 2016). When her husband took a job in New York, she transferred to Columbia Law School. Although she made *Harvard Law Review*, *Columbia Law Review*, and tied for first place in her graduating class, many professions and law firms discriminated against hiring women. So she served as a professor of law at Columbia University, lectured at Rutgers School of Law, and later became general council of the American Civil Liberties Union.

Ginsburg renewed interest in the early-1970s moot case of Air Force Captain Susan Struck, who is Catholic and a nurse and became pregnant. Then, pregnancy mandated a discharge from military service. So the choice was to have an abortion or carry the baby and then give it up for adoption. Ginsburg wished a ruling had occurred to permanently establish a woman's right to choose (Ginsburg, Hartnett, and Williams 2016).

In 1993, after serving as justice on several lower courts, Ginsburg was nominated by President Bill Clinton as the second woman to serve as a justice on the Supreme Court. Although Ginsburg often takes a more centrist and pragmatic position, she excels as the most steadfast, progressive, and powerful advocate for all human rights, and especially women's and voting rights. President Obama also appointed Sonia Sotomayer and Elena Kagan to the court. However, the meme "You can't spell *truth* without Ruth," tells it all.

Ginsburg reached out to those of totally opposing political views. Mutual respect for written words, understanding the Constitution, and their love of opera forged her lifelong friendship with fellow Justice Antonin Scalia. She is also a devoted historian. Ginsburg triumphed over pancreatic cancer. She exudes the aura of a woman of tremendous heart and is a valiant warrior of indomitable strength who expresses the courage of her convictions. While her physical stature is tiny, her accomplishments are mighty.

Early on, a law professor told her, "Women feel, men think." Her mother-in-law also told her, "In every good marriage, it helps sometimes to be a little deaf" (Ginsburg, Hartnett, and Williams 2016). Although she stayed out of the limelight for most of her life, Ginsburg became an iconic pop culture figure in her early eighties, so much so that nail art, tattoos, and coloring books were created in her name. Kate McKinnon also portrayed her on *Saturday Night Live*, and she appeared in an operatic piece "Justice at the Opera" (Midgette 2016). She was given the moniker, Notorious RBG.

Besides serving as an impeccable first lady, Michelle Obama is a lawyer and author who graduated from Princeton University and Harvard Law School. She grew up in a loving, stable, middle-class home on the South Side of Chicago, Illinois. Her father, Fraser Robinson III, worked for the city water department and had multiple sclerosis. Her mother, Marion Shields Robinson, moved into the White House while Michelle was first lady.

Michelle is an exemplary human being, both as a person and as mom in chief. She and her mother are keen on what is key, so they dedicated themselves to raising two exemplary, intelligent, and beautiful girls, Malia and Sasha. As the caretaker in chief, the first lady also devoted her energy and passion to many worthy causes. With obesity affecting one out of three children born today, Michelle focused on bringing awareness of healthy nutrition by planting her first White House Kitchen Garden in 2008. "Her baby" became an annual tradition, with young students joining in the planting, caring, and harvesting of leafy green vegetables, berries, and other healthy foods. These were often unfamiliar and certainly not favorite pickings for them. Along with the garden, Michelle launched *Let's Move!* to encourage the youth to exercise. In her hip, upbeat, and iconic style, she showed students fun ways to enjoy numerous activities. Studies show that children who exercise are more focused and perform, learn, and feel better about themselves (http://www.letsmoveschools.org).

Reach Higher is another initiative launched by Michelle, and it inspires all students to take charge of their lives and chart a course beyond high school. The goal is to attain relevant skills and expertise at a community college, university, or trade school and earn either a certificate or a diploma. The program's ambitious but pertinent "'North Star' goal is for the U.S.A. to again attain the highest proportion of college graduates in the world by 2020" (http://whitehouse.gov/reach-higher).

Michelle also joined Dr. Jill Biden in creating *Joining Forces*, an organization that benefits not only those who served in our armed forces but also their families. In that role, she elevated awareness of the challenges some of our veterans face. She also created programs and built bridges with organizations to promote and educate the public on how to assist and offer additional support to returning vets. These programs also created incentives to those who hire returning vets. Veterans tend to have outstanding skills and a genuine concern for their team members. I have employed veterans; they invariably set a high standard, making sure their work is complete and does not disturb other systems. Much to my relief, they get the job done the first time so that a follow-up service call is not required.

Because she sees herself and her daughters as American girls, Michelle "simply cannot walk away from" their less fortunate sisters (https://letgirlslearn.gov). Michelle also led *Let Girls Learn*, a US government initiative connected to the Peace Corps, and served as a spokesperson for the sixty-three million girls around the world who need an education. Educating them is a multipronged challenge combined with cultural, financial, age, and safety issues. When girls are more productive, they are more confident, and society as a whole benefits. Since every community presents a "different set of circumstances," there is no one set formula. Michelle stated that members of the Peace Corps provide exactly what is needed—awareness and engagement. Their usual two-year commitment fosters trust and continuity. In the fall of 2016, Michelle, along with Stephen Colbert, put on a show for the spouses or partners of the leaders attending the United Nations General Assembly to partner with several organizations and leaders. She raised more than one billion dollars for programs to support and educate girls. These programs are now implemented in several countries on at least three continents.

In a documentary called *Let Girls Rise*, Michelle relates her experiences to a group of students and tells them, "You should be valued. You are unique. You want to be different, you want to be special. The fact that you have been able to overcome…that made me feel smarter that made me feel better…because I have had to overcome situations which other people never had to overcome." When asked if she and the president planned to remain involved after they left the White House, she responded, "Of course, my husband and I will continue to work to make change" (Colbert 2016).

In 2012, I had the fortune and pleasure of attending a small donor luncheon for Michelle Obama and had a few minutes to converse with her. Two of her remarks still resonate intensely within. Speaking for President Obama and herself, she said, "When they go low, we go high." She also said something akin to thus: when some become successful, they close the door behind them; we reach back and lift up others.

In a heartfelt, revealing, and intimate interview of Michelle by Oprah in *First Lady, Michelle Obama, Says Farewell to the White House*, Michelle highlighted many of her experiences as the first lady over their eight years in office. For me, her most touching piece was her poignant response to the ugly labels and comments that were thrust upon her by individuals and cable news during the 2008 presidential election. At first, she was blown back, but then she thought, "Dang, you don't know me." She then realized that it wasn't about her but about those who spoke or wrote about her. She also realized, "We're so afraid of each other." She further pointed out that who we are has nothing to do with color or wealth. She added, "It's about the values…and how we live our lives." Then Michelle decided, "Okay. Let me live my life *out loud* so that people can then see and then judge for themselves.…Don't dial it back, don't dilute it, don't apologize for it. It speaks for itself" (Winfrey 2016). Michelle served the nation with grace, dignity, and heart and made the United States of America and the world proud.

Hillary Rodham Clinton grew up in a middle- and working-class neighborhood with a some-what-abusive father and a very positive, deeply loving, and religious mother. Her mother instilled her deep faith into young Hillary and taught her to serve others. When the taunts of another child sent tearful Hillary running home for safety, her mother immediately sent her back outside, instructing her to learn to deal with jeers. Men made fun of Hillary when she and only one other woman in her class entered Yale Law School. After that tearful childhood experience, she decided to keep her feelings to herself and rarely displayed her emotions in public.

Upon graduating from law school, she joined Marian Wright Edelman at the Children's Defense League, where she began her devotion to serve disadvantaged and lower-income youth, minorities, and those with disabilities. Hillary Rodham Clinton began her political tenure as the first lady of Arkansas, promoting literacy for young children. As first lady at the White House, and later as a senator from New York, she continued to promote children's and women's issues. Years ago in China, she declared the courage of her convictions, "Women's rights are human rights and human rights are women's rights."

Decades later, she accepted the invitation from her former presidential candidate rival, President Barack Obama, to serve as U.S. secretary of state. Clinton logged more miles in that capacity than any other secretary of state, and she was instrumental in many significant deals and decisions of the president. When she ran for president in 2016 as a Democrat, she was clearly the most qualified person in history to run. During that time, the standards of her appearance, whether she smiled, and her personal character were all set much higher than those set for her Republican male opponent. While she put cracks in the ceiling as the first female presidential nominee of a major party, she did not shatter that formidable glass ceiling. Though her campaign misstepped and was fraught with hacked leaks and Russian intervention, she was also subject to a great deal of fake news, lies, and misconceptions. She and the majority of the Democratic Party (including myself) did not heed the outcry of the hurting working-class men of primarily European heritage in their forties and fifties living in rural areas and specific urban areas, holding values and jobs similar to those of the Rust Belt. But there was also another significant factor that others could not measure, and that was the implied *gender bias*. We will never know to what extent this *gender bias* was responsible for her inability to at last shatter that glass ceiling and become the first woman president of the United States.

As we enter a new and unprecedented era in 2017 U.S. history, who would have guessed that women's rights to decide what is best for their bodies would again be in doubt? Our politicians, majority of whom are male, religious, and of European heritage, are now primarily responsible for deciding on rulings to defund advocacy for women's issues, which would mandate limiting women's ability to choose. The Constitution clearly states that there is "separation of church and state," yet the incoming conservative administration, both the president and vice president, feel that abortion is criminal. Their doctrine is based on personal and religious beliefs; allowing these beliefs to influence secular policy defies the Constitution.

On MAKERS, Melinda Gates, who is the cochair and trustee of the Bill and Melinda Gates Foundation, identifies a leader as a person who uses her voice to speak for others. She shared that she gained tremendous confidence and learned to use her voice as a student at an all-girls high school. As she applied for leading universities as a computer science major, she strived to be the valedictorian of her high school class to help achieve her goals. She was chosen, and a requirement was writing the commencement speech. She was nervous about writing and giving her speech. Her mother suggested that she go to her drama teacher, who had believed in her and rehearsed with her. When her teacher was moved to tears, Melinda thought, *I think I have it.* She then shared the following from her speech. "If you are successful, it is because somewhere, sometime, someone gave you a life or an idea that started you in the right direction." She continued, "Remember you are also indebted in life until you help some less fortunate person just as you were helped" (Gates, n.d.).

She met her husband, Bill Gates, while working at Microsoft. She experienced the company's passion that fueled her own excitement about the changes that computer software could make. She said that during the couple's first trip to Africa, she and Bill easily decided that the vast majority of their resources would return to help elevate others.

Often during her life, Melinda questioned whether she was setting a good role model for her children, especially for her eldest daughter. She knew that as a leader, she had to use her voice to speak up for women's issues, and she constantly questioned how she could improve the lives of women. While focusing on the common beliefs shared with her Catholic faith, she rebuked Vatican policy by choosing to provide contraceptives for women in low-income countries. These women pleaded for help in preventing more pregnancies because they wanted to adequately provide for the children they had. Joining with British prime minister David Cameron and the United Nations, they would provide contraceptives to more than 120 million women in developing countries by the beginning of the next decade (Bill & Melinda Gates Foundation, n.d.). Her voice gave volumes to the message that when we uplift a woman, we uplift the family, which uplifts a community. She felt that it is a "moral imperative" to do just that.

Melinda also noted significant improvements for women in poorer countries. Although they are educating more women, there are not enough women acquiring meaningful secondary education. She places the responsibility for the disparity on many factors, including government, financial institutions, business policies, media, and family structure. In organizations, there are men who mentor women, but they neither help them reach higher levels nor freeze the employee pool until the number of women equals the men. Another concern is which family member becomes the primary caregiver when both spouses or partners work. Melinda also feels there is no value given to those who take care of the young and the old. Our government is also accountable for not offering maternity leave or helping small businesses reach that goal.

While more women graduate from medical and law school these days, most remain reluctant to enter the computer science field. Melinda stated that when she went to college in the mid-1980s, 37 percent of the students in that field were women. Now, thirty years later, the number has dropped to 18 percent. Melinda notes that women are not comfortable or welcomed in the tech industry. The media is another outlet that relies on women experts or analysts only 25 percent of the time. A major disparity persists between men and women CEOs of leading companies and institutions.

During the 2015 Year of the Woman, Melinda reiterated her message about economic inequality between women and men. In an interview with Stephanie Ruhle on Bloomberg television, she responded passionately and frankly on the "No Ceiling Report: Women Not There Yet, We Have a Long Way to Go." She emphasized that women are left behind throughout the world and added, "When you empower women, all over the world, societies thrive." She highlighted some factors holding women back, including the pay gap, the lower number of women employed, and the lack of property rights and access to financial services compared with men in low-income countries.

When Stephanie Ruhle questioned Melinda on some data of the "No Ceiling Report," she responded that each country must create its own solutions. There is no "one size fits all" answer. She continued that "the 'magic bullet' is to invest in education. Significant progress has been made to help girls achieve primary education equal to boys, but girls haven't reached the same quality secondary education gains and that would help a lot." Ruhle also noted that women around the world are safer and then asked Melinda to give her opinion on the greatest gains and challenges. She replied, "There has been a significant improvement in infant mortality, which has been reduced by 50 percent. The greatest challenge still remains lack of access to drought resistant seeds for women in Third World countries who primarily are farmers" (Ruhle 2015).

The brilliant, kindhearted, and generous Oprah Winfrey remains among the foremost loved, recognized, and respected icons. One of her greatest strengths is finding common ground between people who were previously so opposed to one another's views. She then uses that kernel to create a bridge between them to seek the resolution that previously escaped them. During and after her twenty-five years of hosting *The Oprah Winfrey Show*, she continues to use her powerful voice to promote justice and goodwill as she inspires and uplifts women. Although she is a celebrity, she is first a most genuine human being with a big heart, who openly shares her personal experiences, heartbreaks, challenges, and triumphs. She also highlights women's challenges, fears, pain, doubts of self-worth and convinces them to be their best and cheers their victories.

Since education is a primary concern, she encourages literacy and interest through Oprah's Book Club. She continues to champion women's well-being by touching on topics of health, diet, exercise, sex, beauty, meditation, books, and fashion in her monthly *Oprah* magazine. Her personal touch has connected with millions of individuals from all backgrounds, and she remains close to some of her guests; she often posts their triumphs. She generously gives much of her fortune to help people, especially women and girls.

As a woman of African heritage, she founded and became the benefactor of the Oprah Winfrey Leadership Academy for Girls in South Africa in 2007. She joyfully feels that she is "mom" to every girl. In her opening remarks at the world-class school, she said, "Through exemplary service to their communities, they have demonstrated their potential to effect positive and enduring change. The Academy will nurture this potential, and raise the next generation of transformative South African leaders" (http://www.oprah.com). I recall at one point years ago, she expressed, "What matters most is what is in your heart."

I would also like to note a few of her most recent milestone accomplishments. In 2011, Oprah launched the OWN television network. In 2016, she served as an executive producer of *Queen Sugar*, a U.S. American documentary drama series. The series, which aired on OWN, was created, directed, and executively produced by acclaimed Ava DuVernay, and the production boasted all-female directors. The series is based on the book of the same title written by Natalie Baszile and presented the story of a family of African heritage living in the rural South. The narrative weaves their uplifting story of coming together and bonding to fulfill their deceased father's dream. The series highlights the struggles of betrayal, institutional racism, an unjust legal system, incarceration and its lingering impact upon re-entry into society, and each person's triumph despite their daunting obstacles.

Early in her career, it was suggested that Oprah change her name to Susie so people could better relate with her, but she remained true to herself. With innumerable other qualities and awards, as well as becoming the pinnacle and first Black female billionaire, she was honored foremost for her ability to help us discover the best in ourselves. For these outstanding qualities, President Obama awarded Oprah the Medal of Freedom.

When the Super Bowl celebrated its fiftieth anniversary, Beyoncé was featured at the prized halftime performance. During the dazzling extravaganza, the stellar performers Coldplay and Bruno Mars also sang, but Beyoncé took the headlines. She capitalized on the power of her presence, talent, and appeal to deliver a powerful message about injustices against people of African heritage to the world on the global stage. At that instant, she transformed herself from a performer to also become a powerful force on the political stage. Some cheered and some booed the transformation. It was reminiscent of Bob Dylan, Nobel laureate for literature; Bob Marley; Pete Seeger; Joan Baez; Bono; and Bruce Springsteen, who not only used their celebrated, endowed talents to entertain but also chose to passionately enlighten the world about injustices and issues close to their hearts. I applaud them for their courage and convictions. Beyoncé's lyrics and songs will render a powerful voice to heighten awareness of racism and vast injustices, especially in the legal system. This accelerates Martin Luther King Jr.'s words: "The arc of the moral universe is long, but it bends toward justice."

In graphics in a video called "Transformation," released the prior day, were raw and made reference to Huey Newton, the leader of the Black Panther movement. Newton declared, "Violence is as American as apple pie." Statistics prove that there is more violence in the United States now, and the current mass killings are U.S. American phenomena unmatched in the Western world. "This is an unprecedented moment in popular music culture," said Daphne Brooks, professor in the Department of African American Studies at Yale University. "Never before have we seen a pop icon, especially an African American woman, use her platform as a musician, as a celebrity, to make some of the boldest, most ferocious, most inspiring political statements about the Black Freedom struggle" (Rose, King, and O'Donnell 2016).

While starring in *Desperate Housewives*, the number one television show in the world, Eva Longoria also made time to take nightly classes to receive her master's degree in Chicano / a studies at California State University, Northridge (CSUN). The title of her thesis was "Success STEMS from Diversity: The Value of Latinas in STEM Careers," where STEM stands for science, technology, engineering, and math (Maresca 2013).

As Longoria read *Occupied Immigrants* by Dr. Rodolfo Acuna, she began to question the lack of civil rights for those of Latino heritage. The severe hardships endured by farmworkers initially sparked her interest. She had so many questions that she called the author and told him, "I would love to sit with you one day and pick your brain. This book changed my life" (Martin 2016). Dr. Acuna invited her to meet him at CSUN, and he told her that one cannot understand the path forward if one does not understand the history. That, along with her lack of knowledge when she heard discussions about Latinos, ignited her desire to increase her awareness and learn more about immigrants. Her experiences and dialogue with professors and classmates evolved into activism. "What I mostly learned—and how it contributed to my political activism—was making sure others knew we're not a monolithic community. We're a diverse community [in the United States], even under the umbrella of Mexican-American or Latino or Hispanic. There are so many origins…Puerto Rican, Cuban, Nuyorican, or Texican, as I call myself." She stated that where a person lives has an impact on their perception of their country and their place in it (Martin 2016).

Longoria is a ninth-generation Latina and comes from an entwined and rich, multicultural heritage. Her seventh great-grandfather received almost four thousand acres (6.25 square miles) of land along the Rio Grande in a grant from the king of Spain, and her family has retained that acreage for more than a century. Longoria continues to excel in numerous other areas: writing, directing, producing, and an entrepreneurial business with a fashion line that arrived in the fall of 2016. But her most significant role is that of an activist. In 2009, the *Hollywood Reporter* named her Philanthropist of the Year (Baum 2015). Longoria offers a crucial voice to the Latino community. She encourages the younger generation that education and voting are the primary means to lift themselves up to a more prosperous life.

Zainab Salbi was born in Baghdad, Iraq. Her father served as personal pilot for Iraqi dictator Saddam Hussein. In response to psychological abuse from Hussein, Salbi chose to dedicate her life to women around the world. In the early 1990s, as newlyweds, Zainab and her husband, Amjad Atallah, a Palestinian American, were deeply moved by the plight of the women of the former Yugoslavia. Many women were forced into the now-infamous "ethnic cleansing" camps, where they were subject to rape and murder. A survivor of the camps who lost her husband and children cried, "I thought the world had forgotten us" (Wikipedia Contributors 2015).

When Salbi moved to the United States, she wrote and spoke out on rape and the other plights of women during war. She was a frequent guest on *The Oprah Winfrey Show*, and President Bill Clinton honored her. She attended leading universities in London, majoring in economics, sociology, and women's studies. As noted on their website, "In 1993, Salbi and Atallah founded Women for Women International in support of women survivors of war in Bosnia and Herzegovina, Rwanda, Kosovo, Nigeria, Colombia, Afghanistan, Iraq, the Democratic Republic of Congo and Sudan. Under Salbi's tenure as CEO of Women for Women International, the organization reached more than 400,000 women in eight conflict areas, distributed more than $100 million in direct aid and microcredit loans, trained thousands of women in rights awareness, and helped thousands more to start their own small businesses" (http://www.womenforwomeninternational.com).

Nearly twenty-five years later, Salbi is an unbeatable force in promoting women around the world. She stated that "when we give out of fullness, we give [fully]. When we give out of scarcity, we do not give fully." She shared with Oprah that the great Sufi poet Rumi inspires her and she randomly chooses his words to guide her through the day. She sees beauty in everything, and the photo of her on the website reflects the profound joy with which she lives life (OWN, n.d.).

Nadia Murad is remarkable for her ability to maintain her spirit while witnessing the worst atrocities. At nineteen, Murad lost all but herself; she lost her home and her Yezidi culture, the ISIS murdered her mother, and she witnessed the massacre of male members of her family. If that were not enough to cripple one's spirit, she also "was kidnaped, sold and endlessly raped by members of ISIS" (OWN, n.d.).

When she was twenty-three years old, she transformed her inconceivably horrific experiences into a powerful, enlightening, and inspiring force. According to Eve Ensler in *Time* magazine, "She stands in a long, invisible history of fierce, indomitable women who rise from the scorched earth of rape during war, to break the odious silence and demand justice and freedom for their sisters." This courageous and unique young woman now is "a beacon of light and truth," as she travels the globe "speaking out about the genocide of her people and demanding the release of 3,000 women still held in bondage" (OWN, n.d.). In 2015, she presented her story to the first UN Security Council meeting on human trafficking in New York City. With Greece closing its borders and the United States no longer accepting refugees from terrorism-stricken areas, Nadia reminds everyone that the United States invaded Iraq and left its arms behind in the war zones, allowing ISIS to seize the very weapons that the terrorist group now brutally wields. She further proclaims that the United States waited too long to intervene to stop the heinous brutality against her Yezidi people. Ensler closes by stating, "At 23, Nadia Murad is risking everything to awaken us. I hope we are listening, because we too are responsible" (Ensler 2016).

You don't have to be Melinda Gates, Oprah Winfrey, Eva Longoria, Zainab Salbi, or Nadia Murad to be a change agent. Wilda Spalding is such a change agent, working tirelessly "in the field of human rights at the United Nations in Geneva for more than forty years." Her work with nongovernmental organizations (NGOs) began when Wilda was part of the core team creating the 1979 International Year of the Child for the United Nations. Using hand jive, she passionately led delegates in the song "Rise and Shine and Give God the Glory, Glory," touching their hearts, dedicating herself to helping implement that wondrous milestone. The public U.S. Congressional Record states, "Mr. Speaker, I rise today to pay tribute to World Wins Corporation and its president, Wilda Spalding. I'm convinced that if there were more people like Wilda Spalding, then such lofty ideals as world peace would not seem nearly so elusive."

After attending an event at Geneva's Grand Casino years ago, Wilda hosted and produced a night of blues for diplomats and the general public. A sign language interpreter for the deaf and hard of hearing was present. A few days later, when the United Nations voted on the Convention on the Human Rights of Persons with Disabilities at the United Nations Palais, the power of deaf communication at the concert so deeply impressed the Greek ambassador that he changed his mind and voted to help. Over the years, Wilda has continued to seek solutions by touching people's hearts through art, dance, music, culture, couture, and eclectic country picnics.

Wilda also advocated for the marginalized—indigenous people, children, those at risk, the unvoiced, and particularly, the disabled. On their behalf, she brought her favorite recipes of the homemade cookies to the staff serving members of both Houses of Congress. Her gesture served to highlight the importance of a pending vote and hopefully influence staff to talk to their "bosses" to find a compromise. After a back-and-forth between the House of Representatives and Senate, a Senate member (whose staff enjoyed Wilda's "Cookie Lady" cookies) finally modified wording that led to the passage of the 1990 Americans with Disabilities Act, a federal civil rights law that prohibits discrimination against the *handi-abled*.

Later, as part of another NGO delegation to Geneva, Wilda brought youth designers of the "coolest" packaging art for condoms to promote usage by young girls and women around the world. Another year, at one of her "Fete d'Excellence" concerts held prior to a key United Nations vote, she wore an indigenous designer's haute couture dress to draw attention to that culture's rich heritage rather than focus on the atrocities they continually face. She subtly raised awareness of the sensitive subject.

Although Wilda is in her seventies, has undergone several serious injuries (some resulting from a car accident), and relentlessly continues to face numerous physical challenges, she continues to devote her life to touching others' hearts by listening as she champions people who only have occasional voices advocating on their behalf.

During the Baltimore riots in April 2015 that followed the killing of Freddie Gray, most of the demonstrators were peaceful protesters. However, some were local youth who threw bricks and stones at police officers, looted, and vandalized Baltimore, causing tremendous destruction to the city. During one of these events, when Toya Graham made eye contact with her son wearing a mask, she lost it. "I was shocked, I was angry, because you never want to see your child out there doing that." She was also concerned because she did not want her child to become another victim, similar to Freddie Gray or numerous other youth and older men of African heritage. So she ran after her son, punched him, and pulled him out of that situation. Graham is a no-nonsense mom who taught her son right from wrong and often keeps him from leaving the house because she dreads the thought of him "lost to the streets." The video of Graham went viral and even caught the eye of Baltimore Police commissioner Anthony Batts, who commented, "I wish I had more parents who took charge of their kids tonight." Others chanted, "Bring on the moms!" Many national newspapers' front-page banners proclaimed her as Mom of the Year (O'Donnell 2015).

Graham is a devoted mother who runs a tight ship, goes to work, worships on Sundays, and spends the rest of her time with her family of six children. She had recently lost her job, so she seized the opportunity to check on her son's whereabouts that day and speak out to other mothers. She stated, "We don't know where those mothers are at, a lot of mothers have to provide for their children.…You can talk until you're blue in the face to your children, but at the end of the day they gonna make their own decisions. As parents, we just have to follow through to make sure that's where they are supposed to be at" (O'Donnell 2015).

Decades ago, the phrase "*Men are from Mars and women are from Venus*" was abuzz following the release of the book of the same title by John Gray in 1992. Now twenty-five years later, following the 2016 presidential election, questions arose about the negative implications and bias in branding US presidential candidate Hillary Clinton simply as "woman" instead of considering her positions on issues. Chloë Grace Moretz, an actress in her late teens and a self-proclaimed millennial, asked Stephen Colbert, "Why can't we just be gender neutral?" (Colbert 2016). This increasingly popular movement, gender neutrality, "describes the idea that policies, language, and other social institutions should avoid distinguishing roles according to people's sex or gender, to avoid discrimination arising from the impression that there are social roles for which one gender is more suited than another" (Wikipedia Contributors 2016). The Lilly Ledbetter Fair Pay Act guaranteed equal pay for women and men throughout the US government. Although it was the first bill signed into law by President Obama in 2009, gross pay gaps between women and men, along with a multitude of other inequalities, continue to permeate life in the United States and around the world.

The story of the U.S. national women's soccer team suing for equal pay quickly grabbed my attention because my granddaughter, who lives in Seattle, Washington, plays soccer. She was thrilled to have attended the soccer game in which the US women became the World Cup champions in nearby Vancouver, Canada, in the fall of 2015.

Alex Morgan, Carli Lloyd, Becky Sauerbrunn, Megan Rapinoe, and Hope Solo are members of the World Cup and Olympic championship teams who "are all demanding treatment and equal pay." They claimed that the men received almost four times more than the amount they received and "are not only demanding equal pay, but equal treatment, travel accommodations, and field conditions" (Axelrod 2016).

Each team member received a $75,000 bonus for winning the championship, while the men would have received $390,000 for the same feat. The women filed a complaint with the Equal

Opportunity Employment Commission, stating "that they earned $2 million for winning the world cup, while the men earned $9 million for losing in the round by 16" (Axelrod 2016).

On a previous *CBS This Morning* program, Hope Solo said, "This is the time to push for equality and what is right, and people are paying attention" (Axelrod 2016).

Women are disrespected and undervalued in almost every global arena, and this fact is again perpetuated in women's sports. Besides more wins than the men on the field, the women's soccer team has noticeably increased the popularity of the sport both in the stadium and on international TV networks. It appears that women's soccer is financially subsidizing men's soccer. Furthermore, the U.S. men's soccer team failed to qualify for the 2016 Olympics.

Many women who reach the pinnacle in institutions, organizations, politics, and almost every other environment continually face a forceful pushback from the implied bias of the "the gender issue." If a man is congenial, intelligent, organized, assertive, and direct, people view him as a good leader. Yet if a woman leads with the same qualities, she is often viewed as pushy, unfeminine, or manipulative. If she does not have a pleasant personality, people and the media may frame her as incapable.

One woman who comes from a diverse background and is a leader at a university shared that a woman of minority heritage experiences double scrutiny, opposition, and criticism. Individuals in those positions have to process through two *lenses* every time they respond in the professional arena.

Another woman who is of Asian heritage shared that earlier in her career she had prepared all the material for an important project but her supervisor did not allow her to present the information or give her a promotion because she was not perceived as an "executive." Yet she was so capable that she eventually advanced to a significant leadership role in the training of physician-patient communication for the Southern California region of the major health maintenance organization (HMO).

Sexual Orientation Lens

During my early teens in the 1950s, I became keenly aware that some people loved others of the same gender, not as friends, but affectionately, similarly to the way my parents loved each other. From those early moments, I thought it was different, but never strange. At an intimate party for a circle of friends, it was hard to miss the boisterous conversation about the happenings in the group, including those who were gay. Once, I overheard a few who mimicked the gay sibling of one of guests; I found that quite disturbing. If a family member, friend, or business associate was gay or lesbian, my parents mentioned it as a description but never in a taunting or derogatory tone.

In the late 1970s, an organized open struggle for equality among the gay community began with the protests at a speech on human rights by Vice President Walter Mondale in Golden Gate

Park, San Francisco. A year later, Harvey Milk was the first openly gay man elected to public office in the United States. Milk pleaded for others to come out of the closet. The formerly closeted community has expanded over the almost forty years since to include individuals who are lesbian, gay, bisexual, transgender, or self-identify as queer (LGBTQ). In 1984, Zeke Zeidler, a student at California State University, Northridge, announced that he was gay. He was the first openly gay person in California to be elected student body president.

Fortunately, a decade ago, barriers pertaining to sexual orientation began to fall as people in the United States and in many other countries became enlightened and laws advanced to uphold everyone's civil rights. During that time, Pride Centers began to appear on colleges and universities with an initial focus on "national benchmarking tools…to create safer more inclusive campus communities…and improve the academic experience and quality of campus life" (https://www.campusprideindex.org). Gradually, more campuses became involved, and what began as policies and programs for the LGBTQ communities progressed to include an open-door approach embracing everyone. Support during that period increased with lightning speed. Initially, the United States lifted its ban on homosexuals serving openly in the military. Support for same-sex marriage continued to grow as more states ratified same-sex marriage laws. Even Pope Francis softened his views on homosexuality, stating, "If someone is gay and he searches for the Lord and has good will, who am I to judge?" (Donadio 2013).

At the other end of the spectrum, sustained support continued for defining marriage only between a man and a woman. Then suddenly everything rapidly changed, culminating on June 27, 2015, when the U.S. Supreme Court announced its decision in *Obergefell v. Hodges*. This ruling established the right of same-sex marriage throughout the country. Sexual orientation remained a seismic topic, as evidenced by the split that spilled over into the 2016 presidential election arena and divided families, politicians, and groups.

But the majority of the people in the United States, especially the youth, firmly believe that everyone makes their own choices. Some regard lesbian and gay rights as the last civil rights issue. Progress continues as many laws support equal rights for people of different sexual orientations. Legality is one thing; the implementation of laws and changing hearts and minds is always another issue, as it creates the greatest challenge against any form of discrimination. When we overcome that challenge, outstanding progress will prevail, as we will no longer allow public discrimination against the LGBTQ community.

In January 2017, *National Geographic* magazine devoted an entire edition to the "gender revolution," redefining gender and listing the following terms: *agender, androgynous, cisgender, gender binary, gender conformity, gender dysphoria, gender expression, gender fluid, gender identity, gender marker, gender nonconforming, gender queer, intersex, LGBTQ, nonbinary, pronouns, puberty suppression, queer, sexual orientation, transgender, transsexual* (Green and Maurer 2017). Some choose to avoid labeling their sexual preferences and may choose to simply say, "We are two women who are in love." Others choose not to label their sexual identity and may prefer the pronoun *they*. Each person has the sole right to identify which gender they are and how and when they express that to others. Fortunately, we now more widely accept all types of sexual identities and orientations.

Many people whose religions condemn people of different sexual orientations were taught that homosexuality is a sin. Some people were persuaded that different sexual orientations were wrong, abnormal, or shameful. Still, others had negative experiences of those of the same sex "coming on" to them. Due to these factors, some continue to hold negative or condemning thoughts about the sexual preferences of others. I join the majority who believe that what transpires privately between two consenting adults is their own choice. When we *source-connect* with one another and believe that the same Creator gave life to each of us, we respect the dignity and equality that we morally accord to each person.

As mentioned in the *"Religion Lens"* section, Indiana Governor Mike Pence signed Senate Bill 101, the Religious Freedom Restoration Act, behind closed doors in March 2015. The bill prohibited any form of state or local government from substantially "burdening" a person's ability to exercise their religion. The law, citing religious beliefs, gives a person the right to refuse service to any customer. So if the customer is gay, lesbian, bisexual, transgender, or queer, the person may not be entitled to the services offered by a business. This discriminatory and marginalizing act sets the significant gay rights gains back decades.

Many notable companies and organizations, including Apple, Angie's List, Salesforce, and the National Basketball Association, immediately condemned this law. Apple chief executive, Tim Cook, spoke quickly and forcefully about the dangers of the new legislation passed in other states, including Indiana. He stated, "I have great reverence for religious freedom. As a child, I was baptized in a Baptist church, and faith has always been an important part of my life. I was never taught, nor do I believe, that religion should be used as an excuse to discriminate. This isn't a political issue. It isn't a religious issue. This is about how we treat each other as human beings. Opposing discrimination takes courage. With the lives and dignity of so many people at stake, it's time for all of us to be courageous" (Cook 2015).

Angie's List CEO, Bill Oesterle, said his company halted plans for a $40 million expansion of its Indianapolis headquarters because of its opposition to the religious freedom law. Charles Barkley, a former NBA player, loudly protested the law, voicing his opinion, "As long as anti-gay legislation exists in any state, I strongly believe big events such as the Final Four and Super Bowl should not be held in those states' cities" (Bowerman 2015).

Even as Governor Pence firmly stated they would not change the law and requested legislative amendments to qualify equality, Indiana continued to face backlash. Almost two weeks later, organizations continued to cancel or show concern about upcoming events and conventions in the state. "Chris Gahl, vice president of Visit Indy, the lead promoter for Indianapolis, said he has been in 'full crisis mode' since the furor erupted," and Traci Bratton, owner of the Hoosier Candle Company, stated, "Hoosier hospitality has been thrown out the window" (Schroeder 2015). Growing up in the neighboring state of Ohio, I have observed that Indianapolis has never had a glowing reputation but it developed into a vibrant city that hosted a Super Bowl and many major conventions.

Controversies facing transgender people continue to exist in the U.S. The most recent issue is the choice of restrooms for those who are transgender. Despite facing persistent opposition, members of the transgender community continue to gain a greater voice as they seek understanding, acceptance, and equal protection under the law. Sharply divided responses relating to bathroom choices were voiced in many places across the country, yet people who are transgender want to reflect and honor who they really are rather than being defined by their body at birth.

Shortly after New York announced transgender people's freedom to use the restroom of their choice, other states continued to grapple with the issue. Some states passed state laws decreeing that they require a person to use the bathroom that coincides with the sex on their birth certificate. This practice supersedes municipality rulings that allow those who are transgender to make their own restroom choice.

In the United States, the Constitution is the law of the land, and it affirms separation of church and state. Civil rights laws also prohibit discrimination against a person based on sex or race. Therefore, the law supersedes religious beliefs.

In 2015, California State University, Northridge was the first university in the country to provide the Oasis, a place to "relax, revive, and succeed." This marvelous accomplishment is the first wellness center of its type on any college or university campus in the nation. It brings several departments on campus together to collaborate and provide services to its students. The Oasis is devoted to "the mind-body-spirit connection and offers nutrition counseling, meditation, massages, acupuncture, nap pods, workshops [and yoga] focused on wellness and managing stress—all intended to promote student academic success" (http://www.csun.edu/oasis). An adjacent outdoor labyrinth walk amidst the flora, bushes, and trees offers a deep connection with nature that further benefits serenity and well-being.

The Oasis is designed with a gender-inclusive restroom that displays the symbols of a toilet and wheelchair and the words ALL-GENDER RESTROOM in print and braille on the entrance door. Upon entering the restroom, one would notice to the left a row of sinks on each side of the small area and another door that leads to several stalls, each with a floor-to-ceiling door and a toilet.

A recent addition to the ideas resolving the restroom challenge begins with a new entry door that has four symbols on it. They are a male symbol, a female symbol, a left-sided female and right-sided male symbol (identifying transgender), and a wheelchair symbol.

Norah O'Donnell (2016) reported that newspapers across the country tell of the divided response to bathroom choice across the country. Headlines stated, "Divided Iowa Senate Votes to Protect Transgender People from Hate Crimes," "Tennessee Lawmakers to Consider Transgender Bathroom Bill," and "Battle Brewing over Transgender Bathroom Laws in State Capitals," among others. O'Donnell's colleague John Blackstone highlights a new book, *Raising Ryland*, by Hillary Whittington. The book helps raise awareness about transgender people.

When Jeff and Hillary Whittington were raising a child they thought was a girl, at an early age, their "daughter" began announcing in many ways that *she* was a *he*. In a video when *she* was three years old while taking a bath with *her* baby sister, *she* said, "This is my sister Brynley and I'm her brother Ryland" (Blackstone and O'Donnell 2016).

She was born deaf and had already had a cochlear implant. Understandably, both parents, especially her father, avoided the fact that their *daughter* related and expressed *herself* as a boy. Eventually, key markers made it quite evident that Ryland was not a girl. Even as concerned, loving, and open-minded parents, they did not comprehend what it meant to be transgender. "After much research, counseling, and soul-searching, the parents came to the inescapable conclusion that Ryland's gender identity did not match the sex on *her* birth certificate" (Blackstone and O'Donnell 2016).

With the support of his parents, by the time Ryland was five years old, he began living as a boy. When John Blackstone asked Ryland *how he felt looking back at pictures of himself as a girl*, he replied, "Kind of…a little weird." When Blackstone further questioned *what made the child so strong and so determined*, Ryland paused and then said, "I just had a weird feeling that I wanted to be a boy" (Blackstone and O'Donnell 2016). Ryland also shared that his refusal to wear girls' clothing was his way of showing his parents that he was a boy.

Dr. Stephen Rosenthal, who researches the long-term outcomes of medical treatment for transgender youth, as funded by the National Institutes of Health, said that "this is just as likely to be hardwired, as sexual orientation is not a choice."

Rosenthal stated that "treatment is crucial because an alarming 41% of transgender people attempt suicide." Research in the *Journal of Pediatrics* shows that "children who have socially transitioned to the gender which they identified experience developmentally normative levels of depression and anxiety." Rosenthal further shared that by enabling the child to become who they really are, "everything turns around." Ryland's parents were unwilling to live with the alarming suicide rate, so they concluded that they would rather have a living son than a dead daughter. They strongly affirmed that after Ryland lived as a boy, "he was so proud and happy and comfortable" (Blackstone and O'Donnell 2016).

In March 2016, Governor Nathan Deal of Georgia vetoed a bill that allows faith-based organizations and businesses to deny services and jobs to people of the LGBTQ community. The controversy ensued between religious freedom and civil rights. Deal, who was not up for re-election, stated that he did not refuse to sign the bill because many businesses signaled relocation to Georgia, while others warned they would go elsewhere. Rather, the governor said that his decision was "about the character of our state and the character of our people." He further stated, "Georgia is a welcoming state. It is full of loving, kind, and generous people…I intend to do my part to keep it that way" (CNN Wire Service 2016).

In March 2016, North Carolina Governor Pat McCrory signed HB 2, a far-reaching law that bars transgender people from using bathrooms that do not reflect the gender on their birth certificates and supersedes any more progressive laws within the state that allow individuals to use the restroom of their choice. Shortly thereafter, many voices began to oppose the ruling. As of May 2016, seventy-five businesses relocated, boycotts were declared, and events were canceled. Among performers who canceled events in North Carolina were former Beatle Ringo Starr, Itzhak Perlman, and Bruce Springsteen. The Boss called his announcement "the strongest means [he has] for raising [his] voice in opposition to those who continue to push [them] backwards instead of forwards" (Allen 2016).

Jimmy Buffett honored his scheduled events, but further events will depend on future laws. LGBTQ supporter Cyndi Lauper decided to stage her event but plans "a day to build public support to repeal HB 2." Michael Moore held the release of his new film *Where to Invade Next* until North Carolina changes its law. Dow Chemical, a major employer in the state, called the bill an "attempt to undermine equality" (Philipps 2016). Therefore, some companies who were inconsistent when dealing with countries who violate citizens' civil liberties and engage in unfair practices began speaking up on this issue. These include Deutsche Bank, PayPal, Pepsi, Hyatt, Levi Strauss & Co., xHamster, Hewlett Packard, Whole Foods, and Lionsgate (Miller 2016).

In North Carolina, there are no legal protections for gays and lesbians at this time. This denotes that a private business in any city within the state can refuse to serve a person who is gay. A bakery can refuse to make a cake for a wedding of a gay couple (Harrison 2016).

In May 2016, Attorney General Loretta E. Lynch announced that "the Justice Department had filed a complaint against the state of North Carolina, the University of North Carolina (UNC) and the North Carolina Department of Public Safety (DPS) alleging that they are discriminating against transgender individuals violating federal law because of the state's compliance with and implementation of House Bill 2. This bill requires public agencies to treat transgender individuals, whose gender identity does not match the sex they were assigned at birth differently from similarly situated non-transgender individuals." The North Carolina HB 2 bill violates federal laws, including Title IX of the Education Amendments of 1972 and the Violence Against Women Reauthorization Act of 2013 (VARA) (USDJ 2016).

Lynch continued, "These laws are violating the founding principles of the US American Constitution that require equal protection for all." She further proclaimed that her actions echo far more than just bathrooms. Although practices in the United States did not always follow the founding principles, she stated, "This is not a time to act out of fear. This is a time to summon our national virtues of inclusivity, diversity, compassion, and open-mindedness. What we must not do—what we must never do—is turn on our neighbors, our family members, our fellow Americans, for something they cannot control, and deny what makes them human" (USDJ 2016).

Lastly is the amazing gift of Ellen DeGeneres. In her authenticity, generosity, kindness, and humor, Ellen is an amazing human being. She is a humanist, animal activist, and the most prominent spokesperson for the LGBT community.

Ellen learned early, when her mother was heartbroken by her divorce, that her iconic humor could easily bring laughter about ordinary things into her mother's life. She realized that comedy makes a difference in people's moods. Shortly after, she began her career as a stand-up comedian. In the early 1980s, she was named "The Funniest Person in America" (Melendez 2012). She also recognized that music and dance are universal and positively change people's lives.

During her childhood and teenage years, Ellen's life was marked with struggles of loss, sexual abuse, and tragedy. Ellen continually searched within for reasons and answers to create a new path for herself. She became a success playing straight roles, but the dishonesty was a heavy burden. When she had the courage and candor to risk it all, she announced, "I am gay," on a live TV show to Oprah, who played a psychiatrist. After that, when many shunned her, advertisers dropped her show, so she forged a path that included voice-overs, which further endeared her to the public.

Eventually, the country's attitude toward and acceptance of various sexual orientations turned around, and she became the moderator of *The Ellen DeGeneres Show*, a most awarded TV production. Ellen was honored to host countless TV shows, including the *Annual Emmy Awards* shortly after the September 11 terrorist attacks in 2001. In 2007, she hosted the *Academy Awards* shortly after the national Katrina tragedy. She said, "I am honored, because it's times like this that we really need laughter" (Melendez 2012). Now more than ever, she deeply comprehends the global divisive atmosphere. Her timely comedy is cool, funny, smart, inclusive, down-to-earth, and most of all, an uplifting antidote. She ends each show by reminding the audience to "be kind to one another."

Ellen is not only generous in spirit and deeds but she also has raised millions of dollars for countless causes and individuals in need. She constantly surprises people around the country and those in her audience with wondrous gifts.

To honor Ellen for all she contributes to make the world a better place, President Obama presented Ellen with the coveted Presidential Medal of Freedom in 2016.

Ellen and her wife, Portia de Rossi, were married in 2008. They continue to be deeply in love and appreciate the specialness about each other. Ellen states the greatest gift that Portia gives her is that she understands her.

Age Lens

From the time we are born, age is a discriminating factor. Even in the first couple days, weeks, and months of a child's life, we have unrealistic and inaccurate expectations and draw incorrect conclusions based on what we see. Often, based on a predetermined norm to evaluate our child, we wrongfully compare one infant to another. One child who never crawled but scooted on her behind to get around didn't stand until she was sixteen months old. Physicians informed her parents that reading would probably be challenging for her because she had not developed a crawling pattern. At sixteen, she read Dostoevsky and Vonnegut, and as an adult, she became a highly respected and popular young adult author.

We also draw conclusions about the young and presume that they are incapable when they are capable or that they do not understand when they do. We do not readily accept their opinions or advice because we think they do not have the necessary realization or knowledge when they may. Many cream-of-the-crop entrepreneurs already showed creativity and vision in their youth, late teens, or early twenties, yet because they had not reached an expected calendar-dictated maturity level, we often overlooked or discounted them. Look at the great pioneers and innovators of our digital age technology who began inventing in a garage or basement while in their late teens or early twenties. These precocious youths led the world into the digital era of enlightenment: global messaging, never-before-imagined technology, and instantly accessible information on computers, smartphones, tablets, and whatever else will be available in the future. These lifesaving tools can solve issues, monitor patients, adjust medication, coordinate evacuations, or perform robotic surgery from the next room, down the hall, or halfway around the world.

Even during youthful innocence, enlightened with on-the-mark perception and insightful wisdom, each of my three children was already teaching me to be a better person and a better mom. It is best to experience, perceive, and form an opinion about a person based on their perceptions, words, deeds, and accomplishments, not by the higher or lower number of birthdays marked by a calendar or a person's wrinkles, pace, or gait.

Youth has regularly been at the forefront of social change, as they are neither bound by the rules and traditions of their elders nor restricted by multiple responsibilities to family. Youth all over the world, on our farms, in our communities, villages, mountains, desserts, disaster areas, and diaspora are shining examples of the human spirit's triumph and deserve our highest respect. But seldom does youth beacon as brightly as Malala Yousafzai, whose speech in 2008, titled "How Dare the Taliban Take Away My Basic Right to Education?" angered and defied the Taliban of Swat Valley in Pakistan. Malala took that courageous stand for girls' education as she attended a school founded by her father, Ziauddin Yousafzai. In 2011, she received Pakistan's first National Youth Peace Prize and was nominated by Archbishop Desmond Tutu for the International Children's Peace Prize.

In 2012, Malala was shot in the head by a Taliban gunman who tried to silence her. With the world looking on and offering prayers and positive energy, Malala's courageous and tenacious will to triumph elevated her prominence to broadcast her attitude, message, style, and remarkable achievements. Her progress was reported as she was airlifted from nation to nation, facing overwhelming odds to undergo a series of complex surgeries and procedure. Not only did she survive but she also garnered a champion's role. As she recovered, she again led the fight for universal education for women with fortitude, grace, dignity, and humor. In 2014, Malala became the first Pakistani and the youngest recipient (at age seventeen) of the coveted Nobel Peace Prize, along with corecipient Kailash Satyarthi, an Asian Indian child rights campaigner. "She accepted the prize on behalf of the world's children and she will continue to work for education until every child can go to school" (Malala Fund, n.d.).

In her acceptance speech in Norway, with dignitaries and her parents proudly looking on, she first thanked her supporters around the world for their encouraging words, which "strengthened and inspired" her. She then thanked her father, "for not clipping my wings, for letting me fly," and her mother, "for inspiring me to be patient, and always speak the truth." She also praised Kailash Satyarthi for his work and reminded the world "that an Indian and Pakistani can work together." Her courage and conviction exemplify a leader, as she extolled Islamic teachings.

Malala, in her wise-beyond-her-years style, expressing concern, confidence, humility, and humor, continues to succinctly articulate and bring forth her passionate ideals of peace, education, and equality for all. She created the hashtag #BooksNotBullets, met with world leaders, and challenged them with the fact that "if the whole world stopped spending money on the military for just eight days, we could have the $39 billion still needed to provide twelve years of free, quality education to every child on the planet." A movie about her story, titled *He Named Me Malala*, first aired on *National Geographic* (Biography, n.d.).

Xiuthezcatl Martinez is a talented and committed sixteen-year-old who is an "indigenous change agent, environmentalist, public speaker, eco, and hip-hop artist, and he serves as Youth Director of Earth Guardians" (http://www.earthguardians.org). He is a member of the Aztec tribe, whose warriors' practices and cultural values of taking care of the earth were passed down through the generations. In 2013, Martinez received the U.S. Community Service Award from President Obama and was the youngest change maker to serve on the President's Youth Council. He travels around the world to ignite and inspire youth to become voices of change and challenges them to remain true to their values and culture and resist adopting the ways of a materialistic world.

Martinez has given three speeches at the United Nations on the topic of the environment and climate change. When he appeared on *Real Time with Bill Maher*, Maher commented that he was probably the youngest person to appear on the show. Maher lauded Martinez, stating, "You're a warrior for the environment which is a great cause" (Maher 2016).

Martinez, along with twenty other youths, sued the government with the organization Earth Guardians. The suit claims that the government is "directly in violation of our public trust and of our Constitutional right to a healthy atmosphere." Maher questioned, "And you think breathing is part of your rights?" The Constitution guarantees life, liberty, and property, and how can we have life if we can't breathe? Martinez responded, "Climate change is the defining issue of our time." Maher replied, "Yes, that is the issue and if you don't solve those issues there are no other issues" (Maher 2016).

As Martinez travels around the word, he senses that people are disconnected from others and the planet and that the youth are "systematically disempowered from the time we're born." With the overpowering impact of technology and crises everywhere, there's no way for our voice to be heard. So this young generation is prepared to globally engage their passion, art, and music and join together to make a difference. "It's our world," their passion, art, and music, and join together to make a difference (Maher 2016).

When further questioned by Maher on how to reach those in his generation who rely on social media for their news, Martinez noted that mainstream media doesn't treat his generation as leaders. He also stated that the youth grasp humanity's potential and create incredible solutions, such as an amazing future of living more simply with less "stuff." He continued with the belief that the youth must take that message to their elders. Maher confirmed the power of joining the idealism of the youth with the wisdom of the elders.

During the past several decades, the youth have dominated fashion, ideas, and culture. With a shift in demographics, 20 percent of the population in the United States soon will be senior citizens. Naturally, this entails a gradual shift to greater awareness of and focus on the needs, styles, and desires of the elderly. That change will thrust us toward seeking new methods and inventions driven by these emerging factors.

Ageism against seniors is quite prevalent, as people tend to associate certain negative characteristics with aging and then lump all people of a certain age together, creating an unfair stereotype. A forty-year-old with young children moved into a neighborhood with many peers her age. She loved to garden, as it was her form of meditation. Her friends questioned, "Why do you garden? That's for old people." David Letterman poignantly reminded us of aging as he announced his retirement from CBS's *The Late Show*. "You can't help but think about the passage of time.... It happens to all of us; it's the way of life" (Lloyd 2015). And while age certainly carries a diminishing factor, we can't relegate all those in certain age groups into one norm.

When I was a freshman in college in 1958, my dorm counselor often warned, "Don't make fun of old age. Just hope to reach it." There are numerous cultures throughout the world in which tradition, values, and religious doctrines consistently hold elders in great esteem, valuing their experience and wisdom. I recently spoke with a youth in Nevis, now in his late teens, and shared that a person his age whom he knew helped my husband and later surprised him and paid for dinner. He replied, "You took care of us, now we take care of you." When a granddaughter visited us in California, we called Nevis and she spoke at length to Blind Eileen, displaying tremendous maturity for her young age.

When I told her that my granddaughter was only eleven years old, Eileen exclaimed, "What?" My granddaughter was also amazed that Eileen still took the time to exercise daily in her bed. She had also explained her routine and practices of profound wisdom to my granddaughter. Eileen's parting words to her were, "Don't let a man rule you." After the call, my granddaughter and I talked about age. I said, "This is a perfect example of how we shouldn't judge people by their age. Look, Eileen thought you were much older, and who would suspect that a ninety-eight-year-old woman still had such clarity?" Eileen later shared, "No two people age alike." I reflected that some people age like fine wine; others become less endearing.

It was a delightful treat to meet a colleague's ninety-seven-year-old and very engaged father, E. G. Stassinopoulos, who likes to be called Stass. He currently serves as Emeritus Physicist with a specialty in Radiation Physics at NASA's Goddard Space Flight Center in Maryland. Stass used to be head of the NASA / GSFC Radiation Physics Office, which no longer exists. He goes to NASA about two days a week and still conducts research and writes papers that are accepted for publication.

Stass shared many harsh situations, such as assaults by Hitler Youth in the 1930s in Germany, escaping death while working for the resistance during the Nazi occupation in Greece, escaping death during World War II, and later, making heart-wrenching decisions. I asked him if he ever lets things get him down, and he replied, "I tell myself to be happy. There is always somebody worse off than you, so I can always find happiness."

During his life, Stassinopoulos received numerous awards for his contributions to space travel safety. These include the IEEE Radiation Effects Award (2000), the APOLLO-XI Achievement Award, a Faculte des Sciences medal from the Academie de Montpellier in France, the NASA Exceptional Service Medal in 1992, and the GSFC Award of Merit in 1999 (Wikipedia Contributors 2017).

He recently penned an essay on the *Huffington Post* blog titled "There You Are, Stephen Hawking." In this essay, he offers a rebuttal to Hawking's statements about surviving the probability that, within the next millennium, humans will have contributed to their own demise and mass extinction as mankind "will continue to devour the planet's resources at unusual rates" (Chassiakos 2016). Hawking believes the only way that civilization can survive is to colonize and populate other planets. Stassinopoulos states that our current technology makes it impossible to travel to the more-distant universe. Even if we could, he believes that the traits, policies, and priorities that are rendering our planet uninhabitable will only continue and we will destroy any new environment as well. Stassinopoulos also shares a poem, "H Polis," by the Greek poet P. C. Cavafy, whose words express the "intrinsic bane of the human condition," which suggests the futility of adventuring to look for a better life elsewhere. Stassinopoulos promotes that we "live long and prosper here on our beautiful planet earth."

A friend whom I have known since we were nine years old has been blessed with seventy-three years of life without any major health issues. After college, he became a buyer for Federated Department Stores but gave it up and moved to Asheville, North Carolina. There, he became a massage therapist and married the love of his life, who died ten years later. For most of his life, he was extremely active and enjoyed the arts, walking, and gardening. He also participated in ballroom dancing several times a week, where he developed numerous friendships.

After his wife died, he maintained a healthy diet, continued his active life, was surrounded by friends, and forever remained grateful and elated. When he reached seventy-three, he required back surgery to ease severe pain, which it did. But it left him with limiting pain when he walked. Even after trying various new exercises, techniques, and treatments, he had no luck in eliminating his misery. He had to modify his entire lifestyle, as he could only stand for two to three hours a day. He also had to choose whether to give one massage, enjoy the arts, or run errands. Finally, he decided that although he did his part to remain healthy, his body parts were given a seventy-three-year warranty, and that was it. I reminded him that he did receive an extended warranty and that no one gets it all.

A friend of Chinese heritage and I share a twenty-five-year relationship that began with us as professional colleagues. She turned seventy right after retiring. As she shared her concerns about aging and her mental acuity framed by her cultural tradition, I reminded her that age is only a state of mind. We have the choice of framing that stage of life as we want, dictated by health and desire and not influenced by any expected norm. Some weeks later, she shared a wonderful story about her eighty-seven-year-old mother, who had always fulfilled each role of her life as was expected, ruled by her cultural traditions.

Recently, her mother decided to turn her entire lifestyle upside down and began living as she wanted for the remaining years ahead. She no longer conformed to the rigid traditional norms but finally felt free from any expectations dictated by culture or others. She made major changes that surprised everyone. Shortly thereafter, she announced to her daughter, "At last, I feel liberated." Bob Dylan had a similar thought when he sang, "He not busy being born is busy dying."

Harriette Thompson of Charlotte, North Carolina, is a ninety-two-year-old who ran the Rock 'n' Roll Marathon in San Diego, California, in May 2015. She is a two-time cancer survivor, and although she is an inspiration for many, she "doesn't feel she deserves the interest but is enjoying it" (Janes 2015). She ran the year's race for her son, who also runs and was diagnosed with cancer. Harriette has raised $100,000 for the Leukemia and Lymphoma Society. When asked, "What made it possible?" she replied, "I've done it before. So I thought if I did it before, maybe I can do it again." Likewise, in my California office, there is a former wooden grape-drying tray imprinted with an image of two birds flying, one above the other. The inscription reads, "They can because they think they can."

I have known ninety-year-olds whose outlook uplifts as some in their fifties, and fifty-year-olds whose outlook drags down as some in their nineties. A dear friend approaching seventy, recognizing that her memory has started to fade, often comments, "My flashlight is not working so well today," which keeps the situation lighthearted.

A favorite piece, "*Desiderata*," or "Go Placidly," advises, "Take kindly the counsel of the years, gracefully surrendering the things of youth" (Ehrmann 1948). More than anyone I know, Blind Eileen exemplifies that as she gracefully embraces old age, accepts its surrender, and continues to share her most personal challenges, triumphs, and new insights. As she approaches one hundred years of age, she still lives alone, keeps me posted on which senses are still "alert," and delights in activities in which she can still partake. She listens daily to national and international news to keep her mind sharp, stretches in bed to keep her body limber, and continues to have her wit. As one of my trips to Nevis was approaching, she warned that if the weather was bad, I shouldn't fly, as "there are no cobwebs up there to hold on to."

In recent years, the Buddhist monk and teacher Thich Nhat Hanh, aged eighty-seven, was silenced by a stroke. With round-the-clock health-care providers, support team, and global prayers, he engages in nonverbal communication to direct his needs and desires to carry on. He travels internationally and serves as he can. Both Thây and Eileen share a deep connection with nature, and each cherishes deeply held beliefs. For Thây, that belief is Buddha, and for Eileen that is an unequivocal connection with God and Jesus. Each of their beliefs serves as anchors that provide strength and omnipotent serenity. They are among my wisest spiritual teachers.

In a segment called "Young at Heart" on *PBS NewsHour*, a beautiful story was narrated of an intergenerational connection between children from infancy to five years old and seniors up to almost one hundred years old. It portrayed the sensitivity, fondness, and fun that those who are very young and those who are very old can truly enjoy with one another.

This heartwarming scene takes place at Providence Mount Saint Vincent nursing home in Seattle, which houses the Intergenerational Learning Center (ILC), an "award-winning child care program within a skilled nursing home and assisted living center" (Providence, n.d.). There, seniors enjoy their young friends three times weekly, and the youngsters enjoy their elderly friends. During visits, five hundred residents experience 125 children as they high-five, play peekaboo, listen to stories, paint together, and clap their hands in rhythm to music while the children jump, dance, and frolic.

In 1991, this admirable facility was established with the idea of an intergenerational program. Administrator Charlene Boyd stated, "We wanted to create a place where people come to live rather than die....They have fun [and] feel happiness instead of boredom and isolation." The purpose also included the creation of a positive learning experience and the "magic formula" for both generations. Many seniors love children, but their families live far away, so this interaction provides the opportunity to enjoy the children's laughter, innocence, and joy. The children also sense the appreciation and happiness they bring to the seniors. "Everyone is getting something positive at the moment," expressed a resident's daughter (Providence, n.d.).

Children quickly adjust and adapt to the needs of the individual seniors, and they intuitively know to whom they have to speak louder, which they just accept as *it is what it is*. When they pair seniors with early signs of dementia with five-year-olds, there is a similarity in the way their brains function, so they are almost parallel in some behaviors, such as communication, painting, or preparing and wrapping sandwiches for the homeless. Their abilities and conversations smoothly flow between them.

A teacher shared, "When the seniors hear the sound of the toddlers, it is as though sunlight just came through the window." In the hall, there is a grab bar for seniors to pull themselves up so that they can look through the window and experience the joy. When a ninety-five-year-old was asked what it feels like, she responded, "Happiness. It sure beats television and it makes me feel silly."

When a senior friend dies and a child inquires about that person, "they are directed to sharing the fun memories [of] that person. The teacher also explained that "at that age they are too young to conceptualize death" (Wise 2016).

According to the National Alliance for Caregiving, there are more than nine million individuals in the "sandwich generation" who are responsible for both their children and their parents. Balancing the care of both generations, along with additional responsibilities, is a delicate and at times exhausting act. There are many other challenges for this group. Fortunately, there are support groups and blogs. Communities and government organizations also offer services. One essential task is teaching their children respect for their elders and teaching their elders an understanding of the youth. I recollect a conversation years ago when a friend of a younger generation brought her toddler to visit. The toddler dropped her apple on the floor and put it back in her mouth. I quickly responded, "Should she eat that dirty piece of food?" I was taught not to let my children eat food from the floor. My friend kindly but firmly stated, "Ruth, we have different standards."

During Blind Eileen's hundredth year, she shared that she prayed to God, "Do not forsake me when I grow old." She then added, "Nobody knows what old age is until you reach it, and everyone feels it different." Kindness, understanding, patience, and aid are required with the elderly. Do not admonish them when they don't get the fine nuances of social media or can't perform a task. It may also be challenging to understand instructions, questionnaires, or what looms ahead.

When parents don't acknowledge the insights of their children, or when teachers and employers do not accept the recommendations of younger people, they allow the label "young" to block them from hearing common sense or wisdom uttered by youth. When younger people do not hear the common sense or wisdom of the older generation and seniors because they are "too old and out of touch," they, too, miss out because of the attached label "old." My Rabbi Stan Levy shared the following from the Talmud, a collection of Jewish law and tradition collected in Babylonia and Palestine centuries ago: "Blessed is the generation in which the old listen to the young. And doubly blessed is the generation in which the young listen to the old." A four-year-old who was infirmed since birth tenderly comforted the loved ones around him as he prepared them for his death.

Age and generation are becoming so relevant that a serviceman shared that his company trained each employee about the features of each generation from the Greatest Generation, Silent Generation, Baby Boomers, Generation X, Generation Y, also known as the Millennials, Generation Z. But he quickly added, "You know, not every person that you meet of that generation is going to exactly fit the mold. Some really blow me away."

Physical Appearance Lens

How often have we seen a person or an image of a person and instantly formed a positive or negative opinion? I used to be guilty of this. We observe and classify their carriage, attire, style, hair, weight, and expression. Posture was always something I immediately noticed, especially when a person carried themselves with a confident bearing. We look at thin, coarse, or frizzy hair, which often carries negative descriptions, such as "bald," "thinning," "nappy," or "bushy." We may also think that another person's skin is "too pale," "too fair," "too clear," "too dark," "too blotchy," "too wrinkled," "too pimpled," "too scarred," or "too freckled." We form an opinion of whether their fashion is in style, too revealing, too plain, or age-appropriate. Decades ago, we even used to look at hemline levels to see if they were too high or low enough. Often, when I was told that what I was wearing was out of style, I responded, "But what if I like it, the outfit looks good, feels good, and fits? Should I let my own standards guide me or be dictated by others, the media, or the fashion industry?" Friends have shared that they even hesitate to attend their respective houses of worship because their clothing isn't pretty or stylish enough. They also don't want to be the brunt of judgmental glances or watch others flaunt their fancy outfits.

People are also categorized by short or tall height. Men have shared that others assumed they played basketball because they are tall. There is a term, *Napoleon complex*, describing short males who feel inadequate and at times present an exaggerated bravado to compensate. Young and tall women have expressed their height woes to me, and I've responded, "Look at how First Lady Michelle Obama, Princess Diana, Nicole Kidman, Julia Roberts, and many other tall and composed women carry themselves." At the shorter end of the height spectrum, the complimentary adage "From a tiny spark bursts a mighty flame" often holds true.

Friends have also shared that their intelligent, bright, caring, and talented teenage sons are concerned about being short. I grew up seeing shorter men marry taller women, as my father was shorter than my mother. I laud the woman who values her man for his intangible qualities rather than how many inches tall he stands.

In an "On the Road" segment on *CBS Nightly News*, Steve Hartman presented a heartwarming story about Adam Reid at American Heritage High School in Plantation, Florida. "He is the one student who stands above the others and is the one student who stands below them." Adam has a medical condition and is four feet, five inches tall, yet he chose the running back position on the football team. He works harder than most others, although he can't achieve what the larger and taller players can. When Steve asked him, "What made you think you could do it?" he replied, "Nothing ever told me I couldn't." With a few seconds remaining and the team in the lead, the coach put Adam in the game and told him to duck before he got tackled. He didn't listen and ran with the ball, moving it forward five yards. Afterward, Adam told Steve, "I don't feel like I am out of the ordinary, just part of the team, and that's how everyone should feel." He added, "Be careful what you do, and love what you do, and the outcome will be remarkable." Hartman's closing comment: "You don't need altitude when you have attitude" (Hartman 2015).

Comments are often made about a person's weight fluctuation, either too much or not enough. There is a difference between being overweight and obese. Overweight occurs from extra muscle, bone, water, and excess body fat, but obesity is a medical condition characterized by a pathological accumulation of body fat, mostly from overeating, and this can lead to illness or premature death. Currently in the United States, an alarmingly high obesity rate persists, and for many, that appearance is a turnoff. Yet in other cultures, a plump woman is desirable. In the 1960s, rapt attention was paid to the waifish British model and actress Twiggy, and the mainstream public's desire was to be pencil-thin. Growing up, I never saw fashionable clothing designed for extralarge sizes. Fortunately, the stigma against full-bodied women is not as pronounced as it once was, and clothing that is fashionably flowing or formfitting, in soft or bold colors, simple or patterned, are finally available in extra- to extra-extra-large sizes.

When we recognize that a person who is anorexic or obese has a medical condition, whether self-induced or not, mindful, *source-connected* concern and empathy are more compassionate responses than stares, comments, or judgments. To me, the beauty of a person radiates from their soul, not their appearance.

Handi-abled Lens

I had a lengthy conversation with a highly respected physician in his field of expertise, infectious disease. As a child, he contracted polio and spent time in an iron lung. As we chatted, he spoke about years ago when he was "crippled," and before he finished the sentence, he stopped. He said, "Today the word *crippled* is politically incorrect." He then continued, "We've gone from *crippled* to *handicapped* to *differently abled*." At that point, I introduced him to the term *handi-abled*, which I had recently heard on the news. He smiled and then remarked, "It doesn't matter what you call it. The person's situation remains the same." I reflected that unfortunately, a lack of respect and compassion also remain the same in a myriad of places throughout the world.

Noelia Garella, thirty-one, is the first teacher in Argentina with Down syndrome. Her story went viral as she shared that a nursery school teacher had called her "monster" (Manner 2016). Garella's warmth and positive attitude contribute to her ability to handle her group as she teaches rudimentary reading steps to her preschool students.

A teenage neighbor shared that when she taught children with special needs, each child had a skill to offer. Even one child with an IQ as low as 60 could help sort things.

The doctor with whom I spoke also recalled a time when seeing people in wheelchairs wasn't as commonplace as it now is. As a young child, I watched others turn away as a person approached in a wheelchair, although I always wondered why. As I matured, I stopped to smile and engage with the child or adult in the wheelchair and their caregiver.

It is uplifting to witness the new generation of prostheses, which are customized hands, feet, limbs, and blades in varying shapes and forms. These increase the person's self-esteem, mobility, and flexibility and encourage them to fulfill their specific desire and meet their goals and needs. The prostheses can be accessorized with fashionable stockings and footwear.

Television ads for charities such as *Wounded Warrior* spare nothing in showing a veteran's valiant endurance and also the impact on and support of the extended family. These images highlight a veteran's fortitude and resilience to overcome enormous obstacles through arduous and grueling treatment therapies, endured for months or years.

Both *Time* magazine (Vick and Waxman 2014) and *CBS Evening News* (Pelley 2014) relate the uplifting story of Cedric King, an Iraqi veteran whose legs were both amputated at different levels of his thighs. Through excruciating pain and significant challenges, he endured months of vigorous rehabilitation, learning to first walk on prosthetic legs, then to run on prosthetic blades. He then inspired others as he achieved a run in the 2014 Boston Marathon. He called his condition "a gift because it gave [him] life purpose." He feels "there is no other reason [he is] alive other than to show people the impossible really isn't impossible" (Vick and Waxman 2014; Pelley 2014).

The Invictus Games is an international Paralympic-style multisport event created by Britain's Prince Harry in honor of his beloved mother, Princess Diana, who was killed in an automobile accident in 1997 (Wikipedia Contributors 2014b).

Participants in these events are the military men and women who were wounded or became ill during their service to their country. These heroic veterans compete in sports including archery, indoor rowing, powerlifting, road cycling, sitting volleyball, swimming, track and field, wheelchair basketball, wheelchair rugby, and wheelchair tennis. The second Invictus Games were held in Orlando, Florida, in May 2016, with five hundred athletes participating from fifteen countries. These individuals emulate the spirit of serving in the armed forces, an arena that most values the trust that each has one another's back. In that *I-have-your-back* spirit, each offers "camaraderie, encouragement, and support for their brothers- and sisters-in-arms. These military competitors use the power of sport for healing through their recovery, rehabilitation, and reintegration into their communities" (Wikipedia Contributors 2014b). The term *Invictus* means unconquered, unsubdued, and invincible, and these games serve to highlight the incredible triumph of the armed force's members to showcase their stellar accomplishments. Minus limbs and fit with custom prosthetic blades, legs, and arms, they let their gallant physical, mental, emotional, and spiritual victories highlight their heroic endurance, tenacious competitiveness, and ingenious methods to develop and succeed in personalized *handi-able* style. It was thrilling to watch sports played in innovative forms and inspiring to marvel at the triumphant spirit that overcomes and creates champions displaying prowess and perseverance.

One of the most profound and deeply stirring events that I have witnessed is Muhammad Ali, "The Greatest." During the prime of his career, he delivered an agile, powerful, and rapid punch in the ring. Decades later in the grips of Parkinson's disease that altered his speech and movements, with gracious resolve, he raised his arm to light the torch at the opening of the 1996 Olympics. Again, his presence showed the world that he was a man of conviction and spirit who would not let his condition detract from who he was and what he was about. He will forever reign as the most inspirational global champ.

Before we leave this section, even though dyslexia is not an illness, and I am not an expert in the field, I feel compelled to mention this topic. Estimates vary, but about 10 percent of the U.S. population has dyslexia, and not all individuals are receiving special training. Dyslexia is not an illness. It is a learning disorder that remains incurable, but with special training can successfully be managed. Dyslexia impacts people from all walks of life and cultural backgrounds. Dyslexia is not tied to intelligence. Dyslexia is the most common neurological cause of reading, writing, and spelling errors, as letters in words are mixed up. If dyslexia is not treated, it is understandable that these students may drop out of school at higher rates. Therefore, they often face discrimination in the workplace and don't get the job. So, lacking a productive activity to occupy their time, these students are at greater risk to end up in trouble, and possibly incarcerated. I firmly believe that not enough is being done nationally to provide help for these students. One well-respected official declared that he prioritizes screening students who have learning problems or get into trouble. If diagnosed with dyslexia, then specific training will be provided for these students.

Recently, I was again reminded of the wide reach of dyslexia. Even accomplished individuals are burdened with dyslexia. So, the simple task of writing emails is challenging. As with every other aspect in life, each person responds slightly differently. Part of their response reflects the support they received in their homes, schools, and from friends. Some were often bullied and others were privately challenged. Some constantly feared "messing up," or being made fun of. Others, including those in the medical and comparable fields, and even those who are highly respected, are especially diligent in their notations or oral arguments to make sure that they are accurate. So in a way, dyslexia is always on or in the back of their minds.

A significant aspect of the dyslexia training is creating personal strategies. Once these are established, they require committed practice until the best practices eventually are spontaneous. This reduces stress and provides comfort and fulfillment. And of course, as with everyone, when we remain overwhelmed, we do not do our best.

As I aged and wore hearing aids, whenever I virtually connected with a member of a technical support team, after the introduction, I immediately stated, "I am a senior, wearing heading aids, so please talk slower and louder." It often took one or two gentle reminders, especially with individuals who spoke more rapidly in their primary language. Eventually, they all kindly accommodated my needs and issues were resolved. Therefore, I strongly encourage those who have dyslexia to own that trait. I leave to their discretion that when necessary, they speak up not as a victim, but solely to inform.

Finally before we leave this section, I also feel compelled to comment on the following. Currently, mental illness does not receive the same compassion, respect, or funding as physical ailments. This disparity severely impedes individuals and their families who are affected by mental illness. This situation hinders an open dialogue and hampers the ability to seek and receive advice to make informed decisions that lead to personal and necessary treatment. In the past decade, mental illness became extremely apparent with increasingly deadly shootings at schools, churches, malls, open spaces, and other places. The rise in drug use also is significantly alarming, as exponentially increasing opiate addictions and deaths are striking youth and adults of every socioeconomic level in the nation. And just as disturbing is the high suicide rate among the youth and returning veterans.

By not acknowledging the vast and complex mental health issues, raising national consciousness, or significantly updating the woefully inadequate funding and treatment of our health care, our nation sends a clear message to our citizens—and the world—that individuals with mental health issues are just not that worthy. The stigma associated with mental illness must be removed, and the wellness must be advanced by our entire nation.

Until we accept that all people matter and that mental illness is a malady as significant as heart disease, polio, or cancer, little will change. Except for lifestyle, diet, heredity, or environment, these illnesses are neither a choice nor a curse. As a nation, it is imperative that we pay attention, prioritize, and develop a compassionate attitude and create appropriate and stellar policies that support essential funding to provide excellent treatment and counseling for all. The powerful and greedy pharmaceutical industry and immoral physicians must also be held accountable and pay the consequences when they fail to help patients, purposely create disorder or harm, and overcharge for or overprescribe medications. This is paramount for those who promote addiction. Otherwise, significant losses continue to strike those who are innocent, naive, or vulnerable at alarming rates. Instead of being recipients of goodwill and kindness, we continue to leave the patients and their families out on a limb, stigmatized and often feeling shame and guilt, or that they don't matter.

Our woefully archaic and inadequate mental health paradigm depreciates a person's sense of self-worth even though the person and their family make every effort to achieve their best. I often heard, "Why can't they do better?" I've also heard, "You better stay away from that person. You don't know how they will react."

When we, on a community and national scale, reach out to uplift, stand strong, and vote for policies that hasten a person's ability to become as independent, productive, and self-actualized as possible, then being *handi-abled* or having any type of physical, mental, or emotional challenge will have achieved its deserved due and just respect. With these in mind, we hope that those who are *handi-abled* or mentally ill will no longer suffer additional costly and burdensome neglect and discrimination.

Overreacting Lens

During my life, I met many parents, spouses, or partners who could not deal with their children's, spouse's, or partner's intense emotional responses. Sometimes these responses were over-the-top, but other times, they simply realistically and sincerely reflected how the child or adult felt and responded to life.

Just imagine that you feel things quite deeply and you express your thoughts and feelings to those who either do not feel or discipline themselves not to feel so deeply. They may feel threatened, uncomfortable, or unable to take responsibility for their role in the child's or adult's needs, discomfort, or lack of fulfillment. The parent, spouse, or partner may not comprehend or be skilled enough to change the events or circumstances that created the emotional response. As caretakers, they may also be unwilling to accept their own imperfections and responsibility, or they may feel guilt.

Rolling one's eyes or using emotionally charged words may release one's frustration with the child, but it certainly does nothing to boost the youth's wounded self-esteem, foster the child's well-being, or improve their feelings about their condition or themselves.

While writing this book, I met a lovely, soft-spoken gentleman, now in his early fifties, who shared his experience with major depression as a youngster, teenager, and young adult. During his early years of experiencing severe depression, science had not yet discovered the role that a chemical imbalance played in this form of mental illness, and at times, life was extremely challenging and difficult. The pain was so piercing and profound that he often thought of suicide.

Yet the only response from his parents was, "Just get out in the sunshine. Why can't you get over this?"

When science and medical knowledge finally advanced to recognize that depression is a mental illness caused by chemical imbalance, it was the beginning of a managing process of trial and error until he found the medications that allowed him to feel lighter and enjoy life more fully. Writing music was a positive, creative outlet for him, where he could channel his creative energy and focus on something promising in hopes of becoming a rock star. When the reality set in that he was not going to be a famous rock star, he found a way to create music, become involved in the music industry by editing information that promoted and marketed music, and simply just enjoyed music. He even created a CD.

On our first meeting, he also spontaneously volunteered his experience with severe bouts with depression. He shared that it was like a "white-knuckle, roller-coaster ride," not knowing when or how the pain was going to end. Years later, he has comfort knowing that when these episodes occur, he is not as bowled over or hit as hard by deep despair because he knows he will prevail and will eventually come out of it.

In speaking with him several times over the next couple of months, I observed that he appears to have his life together and tries to follow a routine that he knows will bring him ease and lightness. He routinely takes his dog for a walk, attends social functions, meets with supportive friends, and enjoys a lovely lady in his life. I personally know people who suffer from depression, and I have read articles and stories that depict their deep pain, anxiety, and fear. I would never ask a person who experiences depression what it feels like, because I would not want to be responsible for leading them to that dark place. So it was a privilege to have his trust and for him to share the information. Later, when I asked if he would be willing to share his experience in this book to hopefully enlighten others, he immediately agreed. The worst thing we can do to anyone who has mental illness is to ignore, doubt, demean, or question, "Why can't you just get over this and move on?"

Xenophobia and Islamophobia Lens

People from near and far-flung corners of the planet arrived to play a role in the narrative and lay down the foundation of the United States. They flock to our shores and haphazardly tread in search of a better life for themselves, their families, and future generations. Each wave of immigrants brings its own strengths, traits, values, and customs to join those who made an earlier trek. This is the legend of the continuation to enrich the expanding fabric of this democracy called the United States of America. Since all of humanity originated in Africa, none of us are, or ever were, indigenous to this continent. Sadly, most new arrivals do not—or did not—receive a warm, open-armed welcome. The most famous reminder of the U.S. American dream was—and hopefully forever will be—the gift from France, our majestic Statue of Liberty. She arises on Liberty Island in the New York Harbor and offers Emma Lazarus's welcome, "Give me your tired, your poor, your huddled masses yearning to breathe free, the wretched refuse of your teeming shore. Send these, the homeless, tempest-tossed to me, I lift my lamp beside the golden door."

When I hear the vitriolic rhetoric against those of the Muslim faith or those from Syria, I recall the 1939 story of the ship *St. Louis*, which was loaded with 900 Jewish passengers who were escaping the atrocities of Nazi Germany and searching for freedom and life in the United States. They were close enough to Florida to see the approaching lights but were turned away. President Roosevelt noted that even a decade after the Great Depression, an overwhelming majority of the country rejected the policy of accepting immigrants. The *St. Louis* continued to Cuba, but it was embroiled in its own domestic affairs, so the ship returned to Europe. There, Great Britain took in 288 refugees, while France, Belgium, and the Netherlands took in the other 620 before they fell to the Nazis. Of those, only 87 could emigrate, 254 died in the Holocaust, and only 287, almost one-third of the fleeing refugees, survived.

"There but for the grace of God, go I." My great-uncle, who had emigrated from Germany to the United States in the 1880s, sponsored my grandmother, my parents, and at least ten members of my extended family. One aunt became a physical therapist and eventually headed the department of physical therapy at the Hospital of Joint Diseases in New York. Another aunt became a pediatric nurse. Their children, my four cousins, were a generation older than me. My great-uncle provided many of them with an education at outstanding schools, including the Ethical Culture Fieldston College and the Wharton School of Business in Philadelphia. My cousin who graduated from Wharton became the manager of one of the first hotels on the Las Vegas strip. Others became x-ray technicians and entrepreneurs, and one cousin even served with the Allied forces in Europe in World War II. They captured him, and he became a prisoner of war. After the war, with the support of his GI bill, he attended a university in the South, eventually earned his PhD in geology, and was employed by a major oil company. In his nineties, he still hikes in the Rockies and he continues to live an independent life. Each relative contributed to enrich our diverse national tapestry.

In the summer of 1942, the SS *Drottningholm* left Sweden for New York City carrying hundreds of Jewish refugees escaping the Third Reich. One of the passengers was not a refugee but a Nazi spy who was sent by the Gestapo to secure information about American industries. At that time, even President Franklin D. Roosevelt joined the chorus claiming that "Jewish immigration threatened national security." In her book *Beyond Belief*, Deborah Lipstadt, a historian for *The New Republic*, points out that paranoia and fear shaped attitudes and only a handful of immigrants turned out to be spies. If we look at the Manzanar and other internment camps in California, the Heart Mountain camp in Wyoming, and the seven other internment camps in the country that held almost one hundred thousand Americans of Japanese heritage, we will realize that those policies that were established during a state of panic and fearmongering did not work in the past. They will not work in the present or future either because these acts are a stark betrayal of the founding principles that we hold dear and for which our treasured soldiers sacrificed their lives.

Before we move on, let me briefly share my experience with the treasure trove of folks whose services I've sought over the decades and who also remain friends. As I like to wear hand-crafted clothing for special occasions and buy shoes that support my back, I keep them for decades, so as they have required repair or alteration, I have sought talented individuals. These women and men are of Ethiopian, Korean, Armenian, and Mexican heritages. Since I avoid invasive facial procedures, I have had the pleasure of chatting with aestheticians of Brazilian, Nevisian, and Russian heritages who provided facials and products. In addition, men and women from Native American, Irish, and Turkish heritages in the U.S. and in other countries such as Romania, Nevis, and many others along my life's travels have complemented my well-being with herbs, massage, and wisdom.

I have lived through former waves of immigration, but never in my lifetime have I experienced anything as undemocratic and vulgar as the virulent, rabble-rousing anti-American rhetoric espoused by the man who became the forty-fifth president of the United States of America in 2016 and his followers. He declared during the presidential race that he wanted to block all Muslims from entering the country—even Muslims who are U.S. citizens returning home. There was also a sharp voice echoing, "Keep out Syrian refugees."

Religious and antidefamation organizations and clergy stepped up to the plate and vigilantly spoke out against holding one group or members of a religion as solely responsible for terrorism. Pastor T. D. Jakes, bishop of the Potter's House Church, shared that as Christians, it is natural to hold dear to our beliefs, but we must simultaneously be tolerant and recognize that others have their own belief systems. We also realize that "in the context of any religious group there are always extreme views who use their religiosity for their own purposes.…We can't judge the whole by the few.…It is detrimental to discriminate and focus on one group of people when information shows us that terrorists come in all colors, kinds, and classes" (Jakes 2015).

Nancy Baron-Baer, Regional Director of The Anti-Defamation League (ADL), sent a letter to Governor Jack Markell of Delaware thanking him "for your compassionate and strong statement regarding the welcoming of Syrian refugees to Delaware, and your refusal to join the growing number of governors who will not welcome Syrian refugees in their states in the wake of the [November 2015] Paris terror attacks."

Let me briefly share how those of Syrian heritage have enriched my life. I often leaf through the book *The Home Planet*. When I was writing this book, Muhammad Ahmad Faris's words particularly stood out. They read, "From space I saw Earth—indescribably beautiful with the scars of national boundaries gone" (Kelley 1988). Faris was the first person of Syrian heritage and the second Arab in space. A Sangha sister from Syria enlightens with a charming and sweet innocence and brings an open and honest voice about life to our Buddhist gatherings. She put me in touch with one of my editors, a person who touched my soul, understood the spirit of my message, and helped create form and give elegance to some of my ideas when I was stuck.

The next person richly uplifted me in recent years, particularly when I most needed it. She is an exotic, beautiful woman whose expertise as a talented massage therapist was posted about on the internet. With the restrictive challenges that I faced while writing this book, her intuitive sense of my spirit's and body's needs continuously amazes me. She sensed the knots in my body, had the touch and skills to knead them out, and knew exactly how much or little pressure to apply, and where my body most demanded attention. Her treatments always left me refreshed and invigorated. I also loved the stories of her rich, fun-loving, and diverse heritage. Her maternal grandmother was from Syria, and her maternal grandfather from Cuba. We delighted in the rich adventures that her family, and especially her mother, had experienced. We also giggled at similar events, as on rare occasions each of us had both shown up at appointments or events hours or days early.

A former hairstylist recommended a superior hair dye brand that uniformly covers and holds the color. During conversations, she shared that she was born in Afghanistan. She is very open-minded and accepting of those with differing religions and cultures. Most of all, she enlightened me with her insights and perspective of the recent history of Afghanistan and the surrounding region. Her husband attended Harvard University to earn his MBA. She is of Muslim belief and had posted on Facebook, "Have you ever touched a Muslim?"

A couple who are both friends and neighbors are of Muslim faith, very progressive, and friendly. The wife is a very attractive, upbeat, astute, and successful real estate broker at an exclusive firm. She is a cool, stylish woman who always remains very humble. Her husband is a soft-spoken accountant.

We chat at each other's homes and attend each other's special family events. We are always welcome to knock on each other's door, and when I drop in for a cup of tea, we continue our like-minded conversations. When we see each other outside in the mornings, I cross the street to chat about life, family, health, politics, travel plans, or what's blooming in our gardens. When she hasn't seen me for a while, especially while I was writing this book, she knocks on my door to give me a hug, often on days when I most need it.

When her eldest daughter was pregnant, every evening after work, my friend prepared and packed a warm, healthy dinner for her daughter and husband. Her eldest daughter married a man of the same cultural and religious background, her middle daughter married a man of Mexican heritage, and her youngest daughter married a nurse of African, Portuguese, and Jewish heritage. Hospitality is one of the most treasured values of those who practice Islam, and she and her husband exemplify that tradition.

During the 2016 presidential campaign cycle, New York City's police commissioner, Bill Bratton, sharply rebuked comments by presidential candidate Ted Cruz. Following the March 2016 terrorist attack in Brussels, Cruz called for police to "patrol and secure Muslim communities before they become radicalized."

Bratton stated that after 9/11, the "Muslim community…felt [the NYPD] were spying on them…were trying to intimidate them…[and] were not concerned with their concerns." Bratton and the NYPD had worked hard to rectify their preconceptions and sought ways to improve relations with the Muslim community. He further corrected Cruz, "We already patrol and secure Muslim neighborhoods, the same way we patrol and secure other neighborhoods" (Sit 2016). In addition, the commissioner wrote an op-ed piece in the *New York Daily News* declaring, "No, we do not single out any populace, Black, white, yellow or brown for selective enforcement." Bratton continued, "When people call the police, we rush to help them. When people break the law, we move to arrest them....We do not 'patrol and secure' neighborhoods based on selective enforcement because of race or religion, nor will we use the police and an occupying force to intimidate a populace or a religion to appease the provocative chatter of politicians seeking to exploit fear." Earlier, Bratton had slammed Cruz for his "barbs" against New York Mayor Bill de Blasio by proclaiming simply, "He doesn't know what the hell he's talking about" (Bratton 2016). President Barack Obama, Democratic presidential candidate Hillary Clinton, and the Council on American-Islamic Relations also condemned Cruz's proposal.

A letter written by Sofia Ali-Khan, who is of Muslim faith and U.S. culture, appeared in *Tricycle*, a Buddhist magazine. The letter read thus:

> Dear Non-Muslim Allies, I am writing to you because it has gotten just that bad. I have found myself telling too many people about the advice given to me years ago by the late composer Herbert Brun, a German Jew who fled Germany at the age of fifteen: "Be sure that your passport is in order." It's not enough to laugh at Donald Trump [and some other Republican 2016 presidential candidates] anymore. The rhetoric about Muslims has gotten so nasty, and is everywhere, on every channel, every newsfeed. It clearly fuels daily events of targeted violence, vandalism, vigilante harassment, discrimination. I want you to know that it has gotten bad enough that my family and I talk about what to keep on hand if we need to leave quickly, and where we should go, maybe if the election goes the wrong way, or if folks get stirred up enough to be dangerous before the election. When things seem less scary, we talk about a five- or a ten-year plan to go somewhere that cops don't carry guns and hate speech isn't allowed on network television. And if you don't already know this about me, I want you to know that I was born in this country. I have lived my whole life in this country. I have spent my entire adult life working to help the poor, the disabled, and the dispossessed access to the legal system in this country....Call out hate speech when you hear it—if it incites hatred or violence against a specified group, call it out in your living room, at work, with friends, and in public. (Ali-Khan 2016)

During the pivotal 2016 Jewish High Holiday services, my Rabbi, Stan Levy, pointed out that a single word separates the difference between a profound teaching in the Torah, the text of the Jewish faith, and a profound teaching in the Quran, the text of the Islamic faith. The Torah tells us, "He who saves a life saves the *world*," and the Quran tells us, "He who saves a life saves *humankind*."

Amani Al-Khatahtbeh is a remarkable, brilliant, exceptional, and accomplished young woman not because she is Muslim but because of who she is as a person. Through introspection, awareness, an in-depth search and commitment to her Islamic ideals, she dedicated herself to make the world a better place. She created a path and a powerful voice and received deserved respect, fortifying shoulders on which other Muslim girls can stand. In her book *Muslim Girl: A Coming of Age*, she speaks her truth in a compelling, passionate, raw, and riveting read. The audio version broadens our experience as we listen more fully to sense and appreciate her experiences, logic, passion, and command of the English language, not as a Muslim or a woman, but as an author. The reader may initially disagree with her perspectives, but it behooves us all to give her ideas an opportunity to significantly enlighten us, which it does. Amani Al-Khatahtbeh begins by citing Prophet Muhammad, "Forgive him who wrongs you; join him who cuts you off; do good to him who does evil to you; and speak the truth even if is against you" (Al-Khatahtbeh 2016).

As a nine-year-old child of Muslim heritage in New Jersey, she witnessed the unfathomable 9/11 bombing of the twin towers not through the media but from her home. She could not make sense of it. In a flash, the event shattered her young world, as a new, heightened Islamophobic era set in. Her father immediately warned, "They're going to blame us." Following the event, her family was constantly bullied as requests mounted for evictions of Muslims. Tires were slashed at her father's shop, eggs were hurled into her home, and accusations arose that her father "wanted to bomb a toy store." It all became intolerable. Al-Khatahtbeh felt that the entire world hated her, and "that was a heavy feeling for a child" (Al-Khatahtbeh 2016). Life became so unbearable that her father decided to return to their homeland, Jordan. There, she bonded with her cousin and heard the narrative of Muslims and Arabs in their "own voices." She was unfamiliar with many customs, such as eating certain foods with fingers, and she did not recognize a picture of the very popular King Abdullah II.

Al-Khatahtbeh was so inspired by the heroic and upright responses of Muslims of past generations that she decided to embrace and cherish her heritage more and began to wear a hijab. When Al-Khatahtbeh's mother became ill, her father decided to return to New Jersey for medical care. During this time, she felt isolated, fragmented, and vulnerable. She didn't fit in anywhere, nor could she connect with her peers but stood aside. A teacher told her that her large size intimated classmates, and another teacher told her to "smile more and be more bouncy." Until a teacher finally asked if she wanted to be "first" in her class, and then supported that goal, Al-Khatahtbeh never envisioned being anything but "second." Later, she noticed that her father also had "internalized disqualification" (Al-Khatahtbeh 2016).

As a strong, "Yes We Can"–chanting supporter of the 2008 presidential candidate Barack Obama, she was very disappointed when then President-elect Obama remained silent as Operation Cast Lead began prior to his inauguration. This was the first Israeli military invasion of Occupied Palestine that she was old enough to grasp. It was the first time she felt "utterly powerless" and that events were completely out of her control. She felt the Israeli response was neither balanced nor proportional and that the U.S. media's persistent biased portrayal of 1.6 billion Muslims in the world was presented in a negative and inferior light.

Shortly before graduation, she began to think about the Muslim girl. Like many of her millennia peers who felt isolated, she turned to the internet to find her "community." After searching many sites and blogs, she realized that few sites addressed her specific desire from the perspective of a female Muslim. She stumbled across the discussion of a Muslim female wearing nail polish while remaining true to their rituals "prior to and during actual prayer." After she analyzed the different angles, it suddenly began to make sense. "It was so liberating to see a regular Muslim woman exercise her right to logically interpret her religion for herself in a way that accommodated her gendered lifestyle. I began to create a larger picture of spirituality and worship that contextualized my womanhood" (Al-Khatahtbeh 2016). Furthermore, she felt "that to derive these logical conclusions about my religion," she had to examine the fundamental Islamic principles from her perspective. These were "justice, social equality, racial equality, and most important of all, gender equality."

The search for a broader understanding and application of "Islamic feminism" became her lifelong goal to deal with both racism and sexism, issues similar to those facing women of different heritages. She also points out that when "white" individuals commit horrendous mass shootings, they are said to be "mentally disturbed," yet when folks of darker skin tones commit similar acts, they are labeled "terrorist." She sincerely believes that no other group undergoes the same scrutiny as do Muslims and shares her mental defenses, such as not standing too close to the edge of the subway platform for fear of somebody pushing her over onto the train tracks.

Al-Khatahtbeh presents numerous instances in which she felt demeaned or dehumanized. She highlights the changes she had to undertake to become physically attractive enough to advance her ideas without abandoning her principles. In doing so, before she was twenty-five years old, she met many dignitaries, reputable individuals, and Hollywood stars. She learned to "play the game to change the game" (Al-Khatahtbeh 2016). She sat next to former president Bill Clinton and was afforded the opportunity to express her views to benefit those in her broader world. As a contributing spokesperson in this era who appeared on the cover of *Teen Vogue* wearing a hijab, she is a leader in bringing forth many female and sexist issues in the years leading up to and into the Trump era. In response to the times, nationally and internationally, many people—mostly women—marched to demonstrate against sexism, racism, and sexual and other abuses; they also focused on inequality in every sector of life. The protesters demanded the right to make choices over their own bodies, equal access to opportunity, and parity in education, medical research, medications, income, leadership roles, government positions, and scientific and technology arenas. During this period, these topics frequently became front and center in the national dialogue.

Al-Khatahtbeh pleads that we not perceive every woman or Muslim person through her eyes but view them as singular individuals, which is the only truth. More information can be found at www.muslimgirl.com.

Hopefully, her enlightenment will pique our interest so that when the desire is genuine, we also reach out, greet, and converse in *source-connection* with women who wear head scarves as we fully realize that they are members of the same, one and only human race that we are.

I share Sofia Ali-Khan's piece, Amani Al-Khatahtbeh's story, my experiences, and the Torah's and Quran's words to help dispel the undeserved, unjustified, paranoid monolithic fear of the vast majority of those who practice Islam or are of the Syrian culture. I also highlight the unjustified discrimination and deep anxiety many of these individuals face daily. There are some bad apples in every religion, sect, culture, political group, and organization, but they do not represent everyone who practices these beliefs. They also do not represent the ideals of a specific country, certain groups, or organizations. We must never condemn all those who are Muslim or

Syrian. Targeted profiling and outright prejudice are diametrically opposed to the spirit and laws of the US Constitution.

I once chose Uber to take me to an appointment, but I was unable to reach them for my return home, as my smartphone's keypad locked; I didn't have a way home. I called a local cab service but was informed that there was a thirty- to forty-minute wait. Because I wanted to be home before out-of-town family arrived, that wait was too long.

In desperation, I waved down the next car leaving the parking lot. The driver, who had a friendly face, looked as if he were in his thirties and from the Middle East. He drove a car that was older and had some dents. I asked if I could pay him to take me home, about fifteen minutes away. He said, "Sure," so I hopped in the car. Always interested in cultural backgrounds, I asked him about his cultural background, and he replied, "I am from Libya." I then introduced myself, "Hi, I'm Ruth," and he responded, "Hi, I'm Shalom." Surprised, I commented, "That sounds like a Jewish name," and he replied, "It is." We had a nice chat, and as he dropped me off, I asked, "Is there anything that I can give you?" and he promptly replied, "Pay it forward."

Prejudice/Racism Lens

When I was seven years old, while riding a bus to swim lessons at the YWCA in Columbus, Ohio, I recall reading a banner above the window across the aisle. The banner read, "*Ecidujerp—Prejudice. Either way it makes no sense.*" I believed it then; I believe it now. Looking back at that moment nearly seventy years ago, I realize those words created the foundation of my lifelong awareness of prejudice. I later heard a clarion call that drove me to use my words to enlighten others and to fight against any form of injustice. Perhaps at that time, the seed was also planted for this book's tagline, "You have to be aware to care, and if you care, you are aware." We are hard-pressed to find a person who doesn't carry prejudice against another person, or at least something that might simply manifest itself as a lack of awareness.

Prejudice is a complex, irrational, negative attitude toward individual members of a group or an entire group based on a person's perceived similar or different characteristics or affiliation. A person who is prejudiced or racist perceives another person as a member of a group, not as an individual, and certainly not as a *source-connected* human being or fellow global citizen. These adversely biased thoughts and feelings are associated with differing cultural or regional heritage, socioeconomic or educational level, religion, gender, sexual orientation, age, appearance, ability, profession, government, political party, or other groups. Any assumption or association we link to a person taints our perception and response. Our perception misrepresents who they are and immediately dishonors the person. We lose the purity of our *source-connected* interaction with those individuals. This distorts the foundation of our connection and contaminates our synergy, which would have otherwise had the potential to further a positive and trusting connection.

We usually identify racism solely by what is in one's heart and consequently conveyed and acted upon. People who carry a *prejudiced* or *racist lens* often use derogatory words to label a group. Their communication may be more subtle. They may refer to a person of a minority, different cultural heritage, or any group as "they," "them," or worse. Some people who use these collective terms to refer to any person of a differing or a minority group are often unaware that they are prejudiced. Unfortunately, if you bring it to their attention, they still may not perceive or acknowledge their prejudice. They may shrug it off, spouting, "I didn't mean it," or "It was just a joke," or a "Slip of the tongue." My mother had a saying in German that when translated in English stated, "In jest said, in earnest meant."

In early 2016, Governor Paul LePage of Maine discussed Maine's rising heroin and other opiate crises. At a town hall meeting, he blurted out racially charged comments: "These are guys with the name of 'D-Money,' 'Smoothie,' 'Shifty', these types of guys. They come from Connecticut and New York; they come up here, they sell their heroin, and they go back home. Incidentally, half the time they impregnate a young, white girl before they leave, which is a real sad thing because then we have another issue that we've got to deal with down the road" (Reilly 2016).

Later, when they questioned him to find out if he thought these names were "Black," he said, "I don't know that there [sic] white, Black, Asian, I don't know." When some implied that his comments were racist, LePage indicated that the media was just after him. He paraphrased the Rocky movies: "Yous [sic] don't like me, and I don't like you....I sincerely mean that" (Reilly 2016).

The most painful takeaway of his comments is the realization that he is similar to millions of others who express racism publicly or behind closed doors. He and other, like-minded individuals are either totally unaware or in denial of their racist feelings. Almost a year earlier, during the twentieth anniversary of the Los Angeles Times Festival of Books, Karen Grigsby Bates moderated a panel called "Speaking Out: Human Rights and Social Justice." A conversation ensued on the continued struggle for equality among minority groups, including especially Blacks and gays, whose persecution seems never-ending. Journalist Erin Aubry Kaplan noted "that it's remarkable that we're still at this point" (Foxhall 2015). Later, a woman shared that she felt the Creator created one design with billions of patterns.

I believe that people who carry racist feelings can gain further insight into what it is like to be Black in America by reading the raw and compelling truth in the outstanding book *Between the World and Me*, by Ta-Nehisi Coates. His passionate dialogue with his son provokes heartbreak within, and it monumentally heightened my understanding of what it feels like to be looking from the inside out on what I can only experience from the outside looking in.

Almost every individual I know from a wide range of cultures and various professions, and many clients I served who are of African, Asian, Latino, or Middle Eastern heritages or former Communist countries have experienced discrimination. History proves that the depth and breadth of bigotry are unprecedented compared to what individuals of African heritage experience almost every day in the U.S. It is hard to put a figure on it, but I would guesstimate (without any scientific data) that between 30 and 50 percent of the population has preconceived notions about people of differing cultural backgrounds, although there are some who do not realize or publicly express it.

Fifty years ago, when I was a Girl Scout counselor at a sleepover camp, I recall feeling somewhat shocked when the granddaughter of a renowned neurosurgeon at the leading university questioned the Jewish star around my neck. When I gently replied, "I am Jewish," she quickly remarked, "I thought all Jews had horns on their head."

An astute supervisor of a utility company came to our home to inspect dead tree branches that could potentially fall on overhead electric wires. When we pointed out the situation, he not only understood the challenge but was also quite knowledgeable about the tree's origin, species, and subspecies.

During our conversation, he inquired about my husband's and my professions. When I told him I was writing a book about personal and intercultural communication, he shared an experience from his first day at work. Even though he didn't resemble a person of Latino heritage, both his first name and surname are unquestionably Latino. When he introduced himself to one of his coworkers, the person's response was, "Oh, another Mexican, just what we need." The man, who was not yet a supervisor, felt humiliated, kept his mouth shut, and turned away. But the memory of that moment still stings. I suggested that in the future, if he felt comfortable, when a person makes the same or similar remark to him, he sincerely smile from the heart and, with pride and humility, respond, "Yes, I am, and I'm proud of my heritage." Another option is, "I'm a fellow human being of Latino heritage, and I'm proud of it." He could then extend his hand and say, "Hello, my name is Carlos. What is your name?"

A person who assists us with home maintenance also shared a heartwarming story about his childhood. Although he was too young to recall his parents' divorce, he vividly remembers when he started walking to school in kindergarten. Every morning, his dad arrived early and parked his car just outside the schoolyard, waiting to give him and his brothers breakfast and a thermos of hot chocolate. His exuberantly illuminating eyes that sprung from such a deep well of love are testimony to that memory and bond.

He commented that he had diametrically opposed experiences because his mother is of European heritage and his father is of Latino heritage. With him growing up in the Midwest, people mostly reacted to his Latino heritage and often called him "wetback." Now that he resides in Southern California, people usually perceive him to be of European heritage and treat him with respect. Those who are confused skeptically glance at him.

An attractive, classy woman who was born in Central America grew up in a tightly knit middle-class Latino community in California. Her entire family became citizens. When she received a scholarship to a prestigious university, students immediately labeled her an immigrant. The remark stunned her, as no person had ever framed her that way. I suggested that in the future, if she is comfortable, she kindly respond, "I am a person, just like you. I think all of us or our ancestors are immigrants. Some are just more recent arrivals than others." Another friend was a teacher in Mexico, where they respectfully called her Miss Esmerelda. When she immigrated to California, she was named "this one." If she had allowed it, she would have lost her personal identity and been reduced to the object *this*.

Please allow me to repeat for emphasis: I do not think that those who are recipients of any type of discrimination must quietly accept the humiliation, be stoic, stand silent, or "suck it up." In a *source-connected* manner, if you feel safe and are comfortable, take the lead and communicate with pride and humility the richness of your family values and cultural heritage. At some point, we decide that we will no longer tolerate any person, situation, or institution to label who we are. As I previously stated and will repeat, each of us is the only one who has the right to define ourselves.

Perhaps it is best if that definition is also guided by what is in our hearts and souls, along with our bestowed attributes that we alone bring to the world. These deeply imprint our one and only style.

A man of Mexican heritage spoke fluent English that indicated that he had lived in this country for a while. He never shared where he lived, but he often spoke of his children, who each excelled in school. While working on a project at our home, he didn't show up one day. There was a previous time when he didn't show up but came a few days later and explained that his child was ill. So the next time he didn't come, I thought that there was probably another plausible reason. When he didn't return the entire week and his voice mail no longer picked up, I became concerned and called the friend who had referred him. She said he didn't return her call either. Since his cell phone number was the only contact we had, there was no other way to inquire about his disappearance. We assumed he was deported, as we never heard from him again.

In the book *In the Country We Love*, actress Diane Guerrero vividly, painfully, piercingly portrays what she experienced growing up with her parents, who had arrived illegally from Colombia to create a better life for themselves and their family. Her early homelife was filled with love, frolic, music, dance, and traditions. But at a young age, she already felt the looming threat of deportation. She regularly joined her "Papi" as he went to a "swindling" lawyer to make payments toward securing a green card.

When a stranger began staking out their home, she racked her brain, wondering *whether she might have brought on God's wrath*. Her "Mami" was arrested and deported but again returned illegally. Then, the family moved to a new location, where her mother was arrested and deported again. She and her depressed dad moved to a small apartment. At nights, she could hear the rats scurrying and climbing in the walls. Then, at age fourteen, Diane arrived home to find that her father had been arrested and was later deported. There wasn't any government or other agency who was aware of her situation. Out of kindness, family and friends took her in until she finished high school. During middle school, her voice, talents, and pleasant appearance were already noted. With many people supporting her, she auditioned and was accepted into the theater department at the Boston Arts Academy.

The absolutely amazing inner strength that Guerrero carried is that she never revealed any of her weighty tribulations to her teachers, classmates, or most of her friends. Yet even though she had been given many opportunities that included studying in England and achieving successes and enduring failures, and despite her caring boyfriend, self-mutilation and attempts at committing suicide were desperate responses to her life's journey.

I highly recommend this book. I have tremendous respect for Guerrero's fortitude to have borne her travesties for years and, more so, for her courage to come forth and share the horrific plight of thousands of innocent children who are also purposefully separated from their parents. Guerrero's book validates that a lack of a comprehensive immigration policy and shameful, unjust immigration procedures leave immeasurable scars on thousands of families caught up in the morass. At times, our broken and often deplorable immigration policies round up and deport undeserving human beings. This action devastates individuals, rips apart the family fabric, and places a terrible stain on our nation's soul.

A recognized, highly-respected, and now wealthy health-care practitioner earned his medical degree and practiced as a trauma surgeon in China. He also received his master's degree and PhD in the field of integrated Oriental and alternative medicines. He is the first medical doctor with a PhD trained in China to practice acupuncture in the United States. Decades later, he and his wife continue to get stares. His wife was discriminated against as she tried to purchase pricey makeup and the saleswoman asked, "Would you like me to show you some makeup that you can afford?"

During the first wave of the COVID-19 pandemic, discrimination, harm, and murders significantly spiked against individuals of Asian, and particularly Chinese and Pacific Islander heritages. This was partially in response to the fact that the Virus originated in China, and top officials and others frequently referred to it as the "Chinese virus." But equally pertinent, top officials and others in the media frequently referred to it as the "Chinese Virus."

The manager of housekeeping at an upscale major hotel chain who was of Mexican heritage wore her everyday casual attire on the weekends. As she approached her fairly new Mercedes and unlocked the car, a person asked her, "How can you afford that car?" She was deeply offended but didn't respond. I suggested in the future, if she is comfortable, that she respond, "I work hard and save my money." My husband suggested that she also state, "I hope one day that you can afford one too."

At tremendous sacrifice, an eighteen-year-old woman heavyheartedly left her family behind in Taiwan to come to the United States to pursue her education. Her mother was hard of hearing at birth and had been continually discriminated against her entire life. This hardship inspired the young woman's greatest passion, and it drove her to help support her mother and help others overcome similar challenges.

When she arrived in the Midwest to live with family, she experienced years of prejudice, beginning with a male student who was also learning English. He kept calling her "cheena." She said, "I didn't know what it meant at first, but from the way he looked at me, I felt he was acting like he was superior to me, and he thought that I didn't understand him, so he could say anything he wanted to me." Later, while she attended community college, one of her female classmates broadcasted an insinuation that she wasn't very smart. She now recognizes that she spoke with a noticeable accent and that she understood English better than she spoke it.

When this lovely, bright, attractive, and poised woman transferred to CSUN, she enrolled in the Communication Disorders and Sciences Department. She was fortunate to have met a very supportive lady who told her, "It's silly to treat people who do not speak English that well as if they are *stupid* or any less, because we never know what these individuals experienced in their lives." She added, "I always admire individuals who have courage and are working hard toward their goals in a different country, speaking a different language." These encouraging words were meaningful to my friend.

After fifteen arduous years of excelling as a student and putting herself through school, she received her master's degree. She was admired, respected, and supported by her peers and teachers so much that she earned many awards.

A woman from El Salvador who cashiers at a gas station in an upscale neighborhood was asked by a client to come out and look at something in his car. When she replied, "It is against the owner's policy to leave the cash register unattended, and since there's no one else here right now, I won't be able to help you," the man turned to her and said, "Why don't you go back to where you came from and get an education?" Let me suggest the following: With the exception of that type of question posed to a person who appears to be a descendant of the African Diaspora, that you respond from your heart and reply, "I came to America for similar reasons that your family did."

A young saleswoman from Samoa shared the story of her baby sister, who, a decade ago, had a rare anomaly and almost died. The younger sibling, with strong and steady support from all family members, became a sports figure in her field. As the saleswoman spoke, her pride was evident. We chatted on numerous topics. When I asked her if she had been discriminated against, she said, "No, but social media is full of discrimination." Prevalent comments like "Join our kind" are the most offensive to her. Later, I realized that as a global citizen of the human race, she is already a member of the "our kind" club.

Our society does not honor the spirituality and contributions of Native Americans, whose ancestors dwelled in North America longer than any other group. Instead, they continue to be exploited and annihilated by those of European heritage throughout the centuries. The most recent event occurred in 2016, when the plight of the Native American Standing Rock Sioux tribe became front-page news as the Dakota Access Pipeline (DAPL) confrontation began. I would be considerably remiss if I did not raise awareness of the continual struggle and almost-complete genocide of their people and culture by European settlers. But before I continue down that shameful road, I will briefly highlight the beauty of many Native American cultures, which celebrate a deep spiritual connection with the Universe, offer profound wisdom, extol appreciation and respect for our planet and the value of sharing its tremendous offerings, even though many are dwindling, endangered, or extinct. These reflect the purest tenets of their beliefs. Although the term *Native American* is a colonial term, in the United States, some Native Americans prefer the term *indigenous people* or their individual tribe names. In Canada, the preferred term is First Nations people. For the sake of clarity, I will apply the terms commonly used in the United States.

Native American and Alaska Native peoples usually call their deities Great Spirits, although they are considerably different for each tribe. Members observe their natural surroundings to seek a spiritual connection, gain understanding of creation, and create their own creed. The geographic features and species inhabiting their environment take on spiritual prominence. Navajo tribes live in the mountainous area of the Four Corners, where modern-day Arizona, Utah, Colorado, and New Mexico connect, and they embrace a different outlook than members of the Sioux, Cheyenne, Comanche, or Blackfoot (a colonial term) tribes. These tribes live on the plains, away from the forests and amid plentiful wildlife, especially buffalo. The Pueblo tribes, whose name is Spanish, sustain a long history of farming. They build their dwellings of stone, adobe, and wood; their structures are characterized by a flat roof.

For decades, scientific consensus maintained that the first migration to the American continents began with the arrival of First Nations people (a term created by the indigenous people of Canada), who crossed the Bering Straits from Asia between fourteen thousand and sixteen thousand years ago (https://genographic.nationalgeographic.com/land-bridge). Historically, Native Americans denied that fact. As they explored the continent, they were awestruck by the ever-changing beauty unfolding before their eyes. A friend of Cheyenne heritage recounted that "they felt there was such an abundance within the 'sea to sea' that they had to share."

In many Native American cultures, the circle, which represents unity, symbolizes the essence of their beliefs. They point to the round sun, moon, and planets and the fact that even a stone dropped into a pool of water sends out rings (Mani 1958). Native Americans also look to the sky and cosmos to gain better understanding of who they are and to help organize their lives. The sun and moon are their daily timepieces; the movements of the celestial bodies also guide their time to hunt, fish, and plant.

Native American tribes were awed by and relied on those creatures that lived nearby, flew above, or flashed below in the water. Their members tuned into the seasonal migrations as they looked forward to each season for the return of familiar species that were their lifelines to food, shelter, and clothing. They connected with the tranquil flow of the stream, the gentle lap of the lake, and the rapid movement of a river or the robust waves of the ocean. Mountain peaks had spiritual meaning. They visited those sites for traditional ceremonial days of thanksgiving. They celebrated the summer and winter solstice and monthly arrival of the sliver of a new moon to honor what the planet and seasons had provided. With profound respect for creation, the Native Americans grasped the spirit and honored the rich abundance that each living gift offered.

They did not believe in property ownership as those of other cultures do but that the land belonged to the great spirits that inspired their spirituality. They had great respect for maintaining the land's purity and preserving Mother Earth as they found it. They were and remain the original environmentalists.

A fascinating, comprehensive, and beautifully illustrated book, *Native Universe...Voices of Indian America*, offers an outstanding and enlightening saga of our Native American brothers and sisters. Native Americans did not chronicle their traditions, values, and spiritual beliefs in a canonical text such as the Bible, Quran, other religious books, or secular wisdom. Their history, customs, laws, literature, religion, and philosophy were collected, conveyed, passed down, and preserved by the elders from generation to generation through their oral folklore, art, poetry, dance, and ceremonies. I believe that although their method of sharing wisdom was different from traditional religious texts, the Native Americans' rituals were and remain as timeless and valuable as any. Traditionally, they created artifacts from what they found nearby, to which they artistically gave meaning. Some Native American tribes created masks out of parts of the animals, birds, or fish, which were an integral part of their lives. Each conveys its own rich story of their heritage. These masks were often worn during ceremonial events to express the significance of that species.

Various Native American tribes gave thanks and prayers through medicine bundles formed with parts of plants, feathers, sticks, and even tobacco, which they gathered from their surroundings. Native Americans who remain true to their beliefs profoundly respect the earth and practice many rituals to offer gratitude to the great spirits. Their ceremonies provide a way to give thanks, request help, and reconnect with the spiritual or physical realm of the past or present. Seneca author John Mohawk "invites a new day with the Dawn Song of his people." They pass down many unique ceremonial songs, dances, and sacred rites to be continued through physical movement to make the world "whole and right" (McMaster and Trafzer 2008). The totem pole, which is not a religious symbol, is prevalent in the Pacific Northwest. Its carved and colorful symbols represent significant cultural aspects, chronicling genealogy, historical events, and tribal life.

Since the Native American people are spiritually and physically deeply attuned to their environment, they named geographic sites and places with the sense they received from their surroundings. Mount Shasta, or "mountain of great gifts," in Northern California exemplifies that. The local tribe believes that the mountain and its surroundings offer an abundance of great gifts. And they are right. The mountain offered these gifts long before future generations of people from folks around the world started visiting to rejuvenate spiritually and enjoy its abundance of recreational activities.

My first experiences with Native American culture were trips to the "Indian Mounds" in Newark, Ohio. During that time, people frolicked on the novel terrain in the pristine countryside. Since then, the Indian Mounds, now also referred to as the Newark Earthworks—Great Circle, are given the designated signage of respect they deserve, PREHISTORIC EARTHWORKS—PLEASE STAY OFF. Reflecting on my childhood experience, I was appalled at the lack of awareness and respect for this sacred burial site. This site is unofficially considered one of the great wonders of the world. It sits on four acres that scholars believe to be more than 2,000 years old. They are considered the world's largest geometric earthworks with walls twelve-feet-high. These are a "complex of earthworks aligned so precisely with the rise and set of the moon that modern surveying equipment could not do better" (ICTMN 2013).

As a spiritual person, seasoned hiker, and environmentalist, I continue to be moved when hiking amid former Native American grounds or sacred places. These inspirational experiences reinforced my tremendous respect for Native Americans' spiritual values and, above all, their profound appreciation, respect, and gratitude for all that our planet provides. They fully recognize and purposefully promote the dire need for humanity's commitment to strategize another race-to-the-moon type of urgent, ambitious, and herculean effort to halt and reverse climate change and save our Mother Earth for future generations.

Many local trailheads begin within fifteen minutes of my home. All were former Chumash Indian sites within the Santa Monica Mountains or along the Southern California coast. Sierra Club leaders who were quite knowledgeable about the customs, wisdom, and medicinal plants of the Chumash people led most of the hikes that I participated in. From these leaders, I learned that the coastal sage plant was not only a culinary and medicinal herb but also served as a deodorant. Often, some harmful plants, such as poison oak, and its antidote, mugwort, grow close together. The Chumash Indians were also quite entrepreneurial, as they used their handcrafted canoes to ferry twenty-two miles to (Santa) Catalina Island and returned with goods unavailable on the "mainland."

When our family toured the pyramids in Tulum, on the Yucatan Peninsula in Mexico, the guide described how the alignment of a small hole in the temple casts a stardust when the sun rises on the summer and winter solstices. This suggests that the Maya's knowledge and application of higher math were comparable to the Egyptians' knowledge at the time they built their pyramids.

When my husband and I traveled along the Sunshine Coast of British Columbia, we stopped at the museum of the First Nations people of the Salish tribe, where we purchased the book *Chief Dan George*. He became quite well-known as an actor, writer, singer, and speaker. He received many awards and honors, including a Doctor of Law degree from Simon Frazer University, a National Society of Film Critics Award, and an Oscar nomination. George attended a Catholic school to learn the "ways of the white man," but those years were difficult for him and many other Native American children in similar situations, as they "were distant from their family, culture, language, and custom" (George 2004). George always championed his people and is known for his "Lament for Confederation" speech that he delivered on Canada's Centennial. He expresses sadness for his people and grieves for the loss of his forests and the "flashing and dancing fish" in his rivers, now replaced with "canned fish." His lamentations denounce the strange customs that he did not comprehend but were "pressed down on him so he could no longer breathe." He laments the use of the scathing term *savage* when he fought to protect his land, and *lazy* when he did not welcome the "white man's customs," and bemoans that they robbed him of his dignity and stripped him of his role as chief. But he also predicted that his people, the young braves and chiefs, would learn the Canadian customs and education and eventually sit in the houses of government and "shatter the barriers of isolation" (George 2014).

Perhaps one of the greatest injustices of all was those the early European settlers perpetrated against the indigenous people, who, for previous centuries, had inhabited the land. Their four-hundred-year-long massacres significantly destroyed much of the native population, originally estimated by some historians at around 65 million throughout the American continents and the Caribbean. Much of the information is speculative, as there was no accurate method to attain a census. Of those 65 million, 5 million were estimated to live on land that is now the United States.

In 2010, the US Census reported that 5.2 million people in the United States identified themselves as American Indian and Alaska Native. This count is a combination of 2.9 million people who identify themselves as simply being Native American or Alaska Native and the other 2.3 million individuals identifying as both Native American and another cultural heritage. However, Native Americans of singular heritage have shown significant population growth, increasing 18 percent compared to the overall population growth of all Americans at 9.7 percent (USCB 2012).

A recent piece written by Matthew Gindin (2017) reports the estimated Native American population before Christopher Columbus's arrival was as high as 18 million in North America and 112 million in the Western Hemisphere. In his piece, he cites historian-expert Roxanne Dunbar-Oritz, who states, "Genocide was the inherent overall policy of the United States from its founding." She validates her statement by citing the United Nations definition of *genocide*:

> Any of the following acts committed with intent to destroy, in whole or in part, a national, ethnical, racial or religious group, such as killing members of the group; causing serious bodily or mental harm to members of the group; deliberately inflicting on the group conditions of life calculated to bring about its physical destruction in whole or in part; imposing measures intended to prevent births within the group; and forcibly transferring children of the group to another group.

While many tribes in the United States were considerably peaceful in nature, others were more aggressive, yet even the peaceful tribes became aggressive and warlike as they fought against those who confiscated their land, destroyed their culture, or annihilated their people. As within any culture, religion, or tribe, there invariably are those who pervert initially pure, generous, and inclusive beliefs to advocate some of the worst internecine acts toward members of their greater family. Comparison to the warring groups' killings overshadows the deaths inflicted by those of European heritage. Their most significant cause of death stemmed from malnutrition, which was the result of relocation and the spread of many diseases, but some purposely transmitted by the European settlers. (Gindin 2017).

Major assaults began in 1814, when Major General Andrew Jackson led an expedition with Indian allies against the Creek Indians, climaxing in the Battle of Horseshoe Bend (what is now Alabama, near the Georgia border). There, Jackson's force soundly defeated the Creeks and destroyed their military power. Following, Jackson negotiated several treaties in exchange for their own land farther west. He then forced a treaty upon the Native Americans whereby they surrendered to the United States more than twenty million acres of their traditional land—about one-half of current Alabama and one-fifth of Georgia. Over the next decade, Jackson led the way in the Indian removal campaign, helping to negotiate nine of the eleven major treaties to remove indigenous people (McMaster and Trafzer 2008).

According to PBS, "In 1823, the Supreme Court handed down a decision that allowed Native Americans to live on the land but not hold title to it." The Supreme Court's view stated, "Their right of occupancy was subordinate to the United States right of discovery." In response, the

Native Americans instituted polices that restricted sale of land to the government to secure the land on which they still lived. Other nonviolent attempts included collective farming with other tribes, but this only made the European settlers "jealous and resentful" (PBS, n.d.).

Andrew Jackson was elected president in 1828 with the promise "to open vast tracts of land in the west to white settlement" (Busiek 2015). He enacted the Indian Removal Act on May 28, 1830. This act established a process whereby the president could grant land west of the Mississippi River to tribes who agreed to give up their homelands. As incentives, the law promised Native Americans financial and material assistance to reach their new locations and begin new lives and guaranteed that the tribes would always live on their new property under the US government's protection. With the act in place, Jackson and his followers were free to persuade, bribe, and threaten tribes into signing removal treaties and leaving the Southeast. A few tribes went peacefully, but many resisted the relocation policy (The Library of Congress 2017).

The Cherokee Nation resisted the act in court by asserting that the Georgia law restricted their freedoms on tribal lands. In his 1831 ruling on *Cherokee Nation v. the State of Georgia*, Chief Justice John Marshall declared that "the Indian territory is admitted to compose a part of the United States" and affirmed that the tribes were "domestic dependent nations" and "their relation to the United States resembles that of a ward to his guardian." However, in the following year, the Supreme Court reversed itself and ruled that Indian tribes were indeed sovereign and immune from Georgia laws. Nevertheless, in 1835, President Jackson refused to heed the court's decision. Against the wishes of a majority of sixteen thousand Cherokees, Major Ridge, leader of the rogue Cherokee faction, met with a federal delegation and signed the treaty, establishing a two-year deadline before the beginning of their relocation. In 1835, Congress ratified the Treaty of New Echota against the protests of Daniel Webster and Henry Clay. Principal Cherokee Chief John Ross attempted a desperate hold on their land. This attempt faltered in 1838, when, under the guns of federal troops and Georgia State militia, the Cherokee tribe was forced to walk the dry plains across Mississippi.

When they left on their coerced and heartbreaking march over land and water, they "covered more than two thousand treacherous miles, through portions of nine states; their crippling journey is known as the 'Trail of Tears'" (http://www.cinprograms.org). Evidence indicates that between three thousand and four thousand of the fifteen thousand to sixteen thousand Cherokees died en route from the brutal conditions (New World Encyclopedia 2015).

During the decade of the 1830s, Andrew Jackson's federal government Indian removal campaign forced the relocation of five Native American tribes from their homelands in the southeastern part of the United States. The Indian Territory west of the Mississippi River was established with the following precedent: In 1831, the people of the Choctaw Nation; in 1832, the people of the Seminole Nation; in 1834, the people of the Creek Nation; and the people of the Chickasaw nation in 1837. In the spring of 1838, the Cherokee Nation tilled their fields and planted rows of corn and beans in the fertile Appalachian valleys as they had done for generations. When the deadline passed, the US army charged through the Cherokee's homelands, rounding them up and holding them in stockades, sometimes for months, covered with only the clothes on their backs and anything they could grab.

Jackson's government almost succeeded with what they had set out to accomplish. By the end of his presidency, he had signed almost seventy removal treaties into law, which resulted in relocating nearly fifty thousand eastern Indians to Indian Territory. They defined this area as the region belonging to the United States west of the Mississippi River but excluded the states of Missouri and Iowa, plus the Territory of Arkansas. This act opened millions of acres of rich land east of the Mississippi to white settlers. Despite the vastness of the Indian Territory, the government intended that they would constrict the Indians' destination to a more limited area that later became eastern Oklahoma.

Except for a few Seminoles resisting removal in Florida and within the area from the Atlantic to the Mississippi River, no Native American tribes resided in the South by the 1840s. Through a combination of coerced treaties and the contravention of treaties and judicial determination, the U.S. government succeeded in paving the way for the westward expansion and the incorporation of new territories as part of the United States.

Since the Native Americans did not believe in land ownership, they could not grasp the idea of treaties, which related strongly to others' concepts of specified boundaries. McMaster and Trafzer claim that "in cases where this failed, the government sometimes violated both treaties and Supreme Court rulings to facilitate the spread of European Americans westward across the continent." Although the numbers vary, by the time the relocations were complete, between forty-six thousand and one hundred thousand Native Americans had perished due to extreme weather, starvation, and disease (Gindin 2017). This relocation opened twenty-five million acres for white (European heritage) settlers.

In 1924, the US Congress passed the Indian Citizenship Act, which gave Native Americans a "dual citizenship." The Act signified that they are citizens of both their sovereign native land and the United States.

Sam Morningstar is a Native American who served in the US military and has a master's degree in tribal policy discipline. When questioned by Quora, "Are Native Americans treated badly in the US?" Morningstar responded, "No, not at all." He goes on to say thus:

> Look, reality is I am not mistreated in my daily life. Nothing keeps me down. I have no major dysfunction in my immediate family. We are not alcoholics. Some of us even have college degrees. Things have changed for the better over the last century or so. We still have to advocate for self-determination and sovereignty, but that will never change—that is an ongoing thing. But, we are not passive or conquered people either. Most Americans that I meet actually are really fascinated with tribal culture and are not rude to me or my family. (Nicola 2015)

Unfortunately, statistics show that Native Americans are not excelling in school. "Instead, graduation rates for Native American students are sliding backwards, according to 'Diplomas Count 2013,' an annual report June 7, 2013, by Education Week. Roughly 51 percent of Native

American students in the class of 2010 earned a high school diploma. That's down from 54 percent in 2008, when graduation rates for the group reached its peak" (Sheehy 2013). However, there are more resources, grants, and scholarships available to Native Americans. A few helpful websites about scholarships include http:// www.collegescholarships.org/grants/native-american. htm and http://www.collegefund.org/ content/about_us.

Recently, Native Americans found monumental success through the 1990 Supreme Court case *Salazar v. Ramah Navajo Chapter*, which dealt with a breach of contract lawsuit. The Supreme Court ruled, "The United States government, when it enters into a contract with a Native American (Indian) tribe for services, must pay contracts in full so long as funds are available, regardless of whether sufficient funds are available to pay all such contracts." It was an arduous process that took twenty-two years to conclude. "Immediately after the decision was reached in the Supreme Court, tribes began to press the United States for payments. The Principal Chief of the Cherokee Nation, Bill John Baker, met with President Obama on July 20, 2012, to discuss the issue. After several years of negotiations, the federal government agreed to pay $940 million to settle the remaining claims in the lawsuit" (Wikipedia Contributors 2013).

In 2002, John Bennett Herrington, an enrolled member of the Chickasaw tribe, was the first Native American astronaut. He honored his native heritage by carrying the Chickasaw Nation flag, a small Hopi pot signifying corn from Herrington's surroundings, and eagle feathers symbolizing prayer (McMaster and Trafzer 2008).

Centuries later, Thanksgiving celebrations leave some Native Americans in an uncertain frame of mind. Michael Reifel of the Apache tribe recalls his parents' ambiguous feelings toward the Thanksgiving celebration. These ambiguities were expressed through the hunt and feast on "deer instead of turkey and wild turnips rather than sweet potatoes.…Thanksgiving has long carried a distinct resonance for Native Americans, who see the holiday as more than an embellished story of Pilgrims and Indians looking past their differences to break bread. For some, it is a 'national day of mourning'" (Parvini 2015).

Native Americans also hold a different perspective of Columbus Day. This U.S. federal holiday is a day of mourning for many Native Americans throughout our nation. "The tribes have renamed Columbus Day Indigenous People's Day. They don't believe Columbus discovered them. They believe they discovered Columbus trespassing" (L. O'Donnell 2016).

Similar to most of the US treaties with Native Americans, the government initially gave North Dakota land to the Sioux people, but over the years, parcel by parcel, it was eventually confiscated from them. "We have stood side by side in peaceful prayer and will continue to do so as we fight to permanently protect that which is sacred to all of us" (Indianz 2016).

Initially, a Dakota Excess oil pipeline was routed north through Bismarck, North Dakota, but the town's citizens (92.4 percent of which are of European descent) cried out against the route as they felt it threatened their water supply. In 2014, the proposed pipeline under the

Missouri River was then rerouted adjacent to the Standing Rock Sioux Tribe Reservation (Lim 2016). In April 2016, the tribe began to protest the construction of the Dakota Access Pipeline (DAPL), as it passed through and disrupted their ancient burial grounds and posed potential severe threats to their water and food supply. The Standing Rock Sioux Tribe name themselves "water protectors."

LaDonna Allard stated, "We've never had a voice, but we've always been protecting our resources and standing up for our water. Nothing changes" (Lim 2016). Protesters were arrested a day after a federal appeals court in Washington, DC, issued an order that allowed construction of the controversial pipeline to continue. The tribe called the ruling a disappointment but reiterated the peaceful nature of the resistance movement. They continued to ask supporters to join in peaceful prayer, while noting that any violence is unwelcome and harmful to the cause. The tribal members believe that "ultimately, the right decision—the moral decision—is made to protect our people, our sacred places, our land and our resources" (Stand with Standing Rock 2016).

Eventually, thousands of people from the Standing Rock Sioux Tribe, other Native American tribes across the nation, First Nations in Canada, and non-Native supporters in the United States and around the world joined the protest. They traveled from distant places to stand in solidarity against the harmful and destructive proposed Dakota Access Pipeline. Celebrities also joined the protest as it grew into the largest Native American protest in U.S. history. The Oceti Sakowin camp was established to house the thousands of "water protectors." As the camp grew in size and scope, the Standing Rock Sioux Tribe also requested that those joining their peaceful protest honor and maintain their standard of an alcohol- and drug-free zone and negate any pursuit of violent acts. The camp was kept up in orderly fashion, with everyone participating in tasks to ensure a well-organized, clean, safe, and peaceful environment.

Tactics by the Army Corps of Engineers to remove the protesters initially included the use of rubber bullets and cold water sprayed upon the protesters. As winter arrived, cannons of water doused the demonstrators, causing more serious injuries and critical hypothermia. Following the incidents, the governor of North Dakota ordered the removal of all protesters by December 5, 2016. As the deadline loomed, hundreds more flocked to join the protests, including two thousand US Veterans, who stood with their fellow human beings. With other national and election news then history, public networks joined cable news, congressional members, and the buzz on twitter using the hashtag #NoDAPL to broadcast these events. The opposition grew so powerful that enough petitions were signed to halt the removal of the protesters. Nearing the end of his presidency, President Obama finally reversed the order for the Army Corps of Engineers to remove the protesters.

In the fall of 2016, as the movement grew during the cold, bitter winter, a new president was elected. His proposed policies did not honor Native American tradition and were not environmentally friendly, as he declared his intention to expand oil production. Following the presidential election and a couple of days before the proposed removal of the protesters, David Archambault II, Chairman of the Standing Rock Sioux Tribe, pointed out the significance of having the veterans standing with them. He proclaimed, "Their presence is symbolic. It's representing the men and women who fought for this nation's freedom. They're coming here, not to start a war, but to let the nation [and world] know that it's not right to treat indigenous peoples, to treat tribes in this way.…We have to start listening to tribes" (Brangham 2016).

When government officials questioned the "safety concerns" for protesters remaining on the freezing plains, Archambault stated, "It's not safe for law enforcement to spray water on water protectors in sub-zero, sub-freezing temperatures" (Brangham 2016). Besides, if anyone knows how to prepare, live, and remain safe in freezing weather, it is the Native American people. They lived in teepees for centuries and kept warm with coats and hoods fashioned from buffalo hides.

Protesters settled in, even with a temporary halt of DAPL, while facing colder and more severe weather. They occasionally took refuge in local Native American casinos. Protesters continued to arrive, and they traveled from distant places, as they were quite uncertain of what the future might bring with the new president. During the election cycle, these protests also proved that while other progressive views lost, the victories of the No DAPL movement were significant. At least for a short time, the lack of Native Americans' civil rights finally gained national attention. Hopefully, the focus and support will continue as the national struggle for civil rights marches on.

On a positive note, California's groundbreaking carbon market and the Nature Conservancy's cutting-edge forest carbon cap-and-trade program benefitted the environment and the Yurok Native American tribe. The conservation and rehabilitation of the Yurok's ancestral forest lands along the Klammath River in California are an essential part of that program. The reforestation provided the Yuroks eight hundred thousand carbon offset units, providing substantial monetary "carbon cache" resources to the tribe. Susan Masten, a Yurok tribal leader, states, "Reacquiring our land is imperative to us, and it's mandated by our Constitution" (Strand 2016).

So it is a win-win situation, as the reforestation reduces the carbon footprint and advances the Yurok's ability to reclaim much of their pristine ancestral land. The funds empowered the Yuroks to restore the health of their river that serves as both a highway and a provider. They take pleasure in restoring the eel and salmon population and reintroducing wildlife after their prolonged absence. The slopes of the river provide trees with acorns that sustain a substantial food source. The cache also encourages the reclamation and use of earlier cultural artifacts. These breathe new life into their native Yurok culture, food sources, and lifestyle. Masten is proud of the reclaimed artifacts and intricate baskets and states, "It's as if you could hear them saying, 'Take me home, take me home'" (Strand 2016). The benefit of the carbon offset goes far beyond the financial gains by renewing interest in medicinal plants, traditional diet, and traditional basket weaving.

At one point, the Yurok tribe inhabited fifty villages on a fifty-eight-thousand-acre reservation. Due to deadly disease, conflicts, and tribal displacements, the reservation dwindled to three thousand acres. Without anyone to tend the land, the acreage became "unsuitable for farming" and was sold to loggers, who stripped the forest (Strand 2016). However, it is promising to witness the highly respected, stalwart environmental organization Nature Conservancies collaborating with the Native American people to carve a mutually beneficial path to restore the lifestyle and traditions of their ancestors. Furthermore, future acquisitions of Indigenous Peoples' lands is essential in establishing equitable national land back acts.

Other good news shines light on the gains that Native Americans and other Native people are achieving in restoring their ancestral languages. People do not understand that language extinction is as monumental as plant or species extinction. Bob Holman states, "By the end of this century, half the world's languages will have vanished....The death of a language robs humanity of ideas, belief systems and knowledge of the natural word" (Haworth 2017). Those who can speak their native language possess a rich gift.

Ofelia Zepeda is a poet who was dedicated to restoring her tribal O'odham language. She was also an activist who was instrumental in advancing the Native American Languages Act in 1990. A few years later, Congress passed the Esther Martinez Native American Language Preservation Act in 2006. The act provides support for language immersion and restoration programs. In 2015, a Native American Indian Summit met to celebrate the twenty-fifth anniversary of the Native American Language Act.

Zepeda recalls the words of her childhood and oral folklore spoken by family and tribal ancestors. These words, especially about nature, help create her poetry and the vocabulary essential to restoring O'odham. She is fluent in both English and her native language, and her poetry reflects that. In recognition of her life's contributions, she received a Distinguished Service Award from the Modern Language Association. She is at the "intersection of history and contemporary life of traditions and modernity, and of the influence of the deep past and the present" (Haworth 2017).

To further explore the Native American road to fairness and justice, please let me pique interest to the National Museum of the American Indian (NMAI), a component of the Smithsonian Institute. The NMAI has the most extensive collection of Native American artifacts, representing ten thousand years from more than one thousand indigenous cultures. Additionally, the National Congress of American Indians (NCAI) was founded in 1994. This is the oldest, largest, and most representative of American Indian and Alaska Native organizations serving the broad interests of tribal governments and communities.

I recall an attractive middle-aged saleswoman of Armenian heritage. When she was a child, her parents had immigrated to Syria with the hope to live in a more peaceful and productive environment. She was taught to be open to and trusting of people of differing cultures to broaden her experiences and worldview. She also shared that in Syria, she knew and enjoyed people of African heritage. She personally never experienced or heard about discrimination against those of African heritage until she moved to the United States.

For decades, I frequented shops or used services of those of Armenian heritage. Recently, two people of Armenian culture each shared a fascinating story. The first person, in his early forties, owns a local jewelry and repair shop. He and I discussed discrimination for almost two decades. Photos of diverse friends that he displays prove that he is not prejudiced. When I shared my concern about prejudice against people of African heritage, he shared that when he grew up in Armenia, he was curious about people from other cultures and wanted to celebrate their "special good stuff" with them. He shared that in his circle, they held people of African heritage in high esteem because they were cool, expressive, and people with whom he could easily chat. Though men of African heritage had robbed him several times in California, his attitude never changed. He realized that the U.S. American culture plays a major role in the reason some people of African heritage resort to crime.

Shortly after a college friend with mutual Midwest roots moved to California, she began to date a man of African heritage. Whenever her boyfriend visited her, he had to pass through the upscale neighborhoods along Wilshire Boulevard, and almost every time, police stopped and questioned him. Another friend of African heritage was deeply hurt and angry when he got into an elevator where the only other passenger was a woman of European heritage. She immediately clutched her purse closer to her, sending the message that she was uncomfortable and suspicious that the man might rob her. He was rightfully offended. I suggested that the next time a similar incident occurs, if comfortable, he speak from his heart in a *source-connected* voice and offer, "I'm a human being just like you are. I'm not going to rob you any more than you're going to rob me." A woman had immigrated with her family as an innocent young child as she had never experienced discrimination. Yet upon arrival, her brother immediately made fun of her because of her accent. Decades later, in the national arena, as an accomplished and respected adult, she shared that she was and continues to be discriminated against so much that it feels like a multitude of daily bee stings. Over the years, President Barack Obama and Oprah Winfrey, along with renowned Pulitzer Prize journalists and television moderators of African heritage, shared their tales of safety concerns. They worried for themselves, their children, and others' children, especially the males in their families, anxiously wondering whether these dear ones would return home accused, distraught, maimed, or even alive at the end of the day.

I personally became privy to an experience that exposes the depth and prevalence of prejudice and racism in our country. A PhD graduate of Stanford University became a professor at a progressive university in a conservative state. She is of African heritage; her husband is of European heritage. Their children resemble their mother except for their skin tone and hair texture and color, which resemble their father's. When her young son was learning to walk, they went for a stroll and she let him walk couple of steps in front of her. Suddenly, the toddler headed for the street. Naturally, she darted after him to prevent him from running into danger. Some people of European heritage chased after her to question what she was doing. She was completely astonished. She was a protective mother running after her child in case he ran into the street. What would you do if your toddler (or any toddler) was running ahead toward danger? Since that incident, she feels compelled to carry copies of her children's birth certificates with her. How many of us feel we have to carry our children's birth certificates to prove that we are the legitimate parent?

A major league baseball player of African heritage was warned at an early age by his loving, grounded, and protective mother. She advised him to follow instructions, behave, and show manners and respect whenever he might be pulled over or questioned by anyone in law enforcement. She admonished him, "Whatever you do, don't run, because if you do, you're as good as dead."

While visiting a loved one at a Veterans Administration Medical Center in California, the then-retired National League player and his six-year-old nephew (who could *pass* as white) went to the restroom. When a man entered the restroom and first saw the youngster, and then the two of them together, he commented, "I don't mean to sound like I'm discriminating, but what's going on here?" The uncle firmly replied, "You are discriminating, and you better back off. Blacks come in all colors." As the uncle and his nephew walked back to their loved one's room, the wise six-year-old turned to his uncle and said, "He doesn't know my mother is Black."

Even when discriminatory words aren't uttered, nonverbal subconscious messages are delivered. A friend shared her own story about her multicultural grandchildren. To many, the children don't look like siblings, as one resembles the mother and the other looks like the father. She recently had an experience in Southern California where she, her husband, and her grandchildren vacationed at a trendy hotel. The pool was enclosed, and the Jacuzzi was outside. The children naturally played between the two. At one point, my friend asked her grandchildren if they could play in the pool for a while and then go out to the spa so she wouldn't have to run back and forth to watch them. The children agreed. As she walked out to the spa with her two grandchildren, she saw a woman who, up until that moment, had been busy reading. When one grandchild called out "Nana," the woman stopped and peered up from her iPad over her glasses with a questioning glance. My friend felt quite offended and shared that it seemed the woman was fine as long as the person thought my friend was the "nanny" but couldn't figure out how they could call her "Nana" or didn't like it when she did.

I suggested that when people stare at her with questioning eyes, if she feels safe and comfortable, she *ask* in a *source-connected* and enlightened way, "Is there anything I can help you with?" As I previously said, I firmly believe that people who are the recipients of prejudiced looks, stares, or remarks should not have to sit back, swallow the abuse, and do nothing about it. I suggest that if you are comfortable and feel safe, a positive first step is to address the demeaning situation in a *source-connected* manner. If the person appears approachable, you may want to find commonality and add a lighthearted comment, such as, "We are lucky with the weather," "It is lovely to enjoy the pool," or a similar pertinent, pleasant comment.

As I mentioned before and again, I firmly believe that whenever we allow another person, institution, society, or our condition to describe who we are, we fail as we hand over that power to others. There is only one person who has the right to truly define us, and that is our one and only self. As a child, a colleague of African heritage told his mother, "The kids at school call me names." His mother replied, "It doesn't matter what they call you. What matters is how you respond."

In 1996, a discrimination suit was brought against the leaders at Texaco, who thought keeping discriminatory words out of the workplace was enough to prevent hostilities. Decades ago, I was stunned to silence when I heard the comment of a leader with a PhD at a diversified university. The woman and I frequently spoke of the 1960s racial uprisings; both of us had been involved in different groups of people from diverse backgrounds. Their goals were to collectively dialogue with folks in the ravaged communities to discuss breaking down the fear, animosity, and prejudice that existed between people. The woman mentioned that she knew a woman who had married a Black man who grew up in the inner city. She shared that this man was refined, was well educated, had a career in a respectable profession, and dressed well. Then the educator added, "The man was 'normal' except that he was 'Black.'" I was shocked. To many people, the word *normal* implies typical or standard. So if a person isn't normal, is there something wrong with them? And if so, by whose standard? After I gathered my senses, I called the woman and shared what I had heard. She remembered and acknowledged what she had said and responded that she didn't think normal was a good choice of words. She added, "I should've used another word."

I shared that guarding our speech or using another word does not resolve the issue; the only enduring solution is changing the underlying concept—our attitudes and behaviors. Simultaneously, we adopt the belief that we are all equal members of the same human race. The woman thanked me for bringing "normal" to her attention and added, "Most of us are racists. How could we not be? Since early childhood, we have been bombarded with racism in the books we read in school, the media, and the stereotypes we learned." Many would agree that unfortunately, similar ideas and comments continue today, decades later, in a new century, even when we've had a president of African heritage. At least with the prevalence of social media, the hatred and division are now exposed. This further engages more people and ideas, which ultimately leads to productive dialogue to further elevate understanding and inclusion.

Many of us hold our personal standards and beliefs as the norms that should be applied to everyone. We often do not consider that there are many "norms," not just our own cultural standards or beliefs. "Normal" within a financial realm spans the spectrum from severe poverty to struggling, to modest, to comfortable, to wealthy, and at the very top, the 1 percent of the unfathomably wealthy. The principles of Christianity, Judaism, Islam, Buddhism, Hinduism, Sikhism, and Rastafarianism, or those of the Non-believers, are all norms to their specific belief systems. However, we do not have the right to impose our standards on others or try to coerce or manipulate them to accept "ours" as their norm. Each person has their own heterogeneous and homogenous views of normal behaviors and values. There are those incapable of stepping out of their comfort zones, who observe or judge others. Then, they make suggestions based solely on what they would do. Still, they believe that people should adopt their specific personal beliefs, norms, or mind-set.

We need to broaden our horizons to recognize and accept that there are many norms, not just our own. As long as the individual's norms are not abusive, disrespectful, or threatening to our or others' beliefs or existence, we must respect that the person is entitled to their view. However, if an individual espouses or acts upon deeds that foster domestic or international terrorism or harming or killing others, then by all means, we reject those ideas. If you are comfortable, you might want to ask such a person why they hold those beliefs, then try to shed a more positive view. If they are not interested, then in a sincere demeanor, simply say, "I can't accept that," and then politely walk away.

Decades ago, while a police officer of European heritage was fighting for his life, he learned that two officers of African heritage had volunteered to donate their blood to save his life. Because the officer lost half of his blood, it was critical that he undergo an immediate artery-to-artery (direct donor) blood transfusion. Following the transfusion, the police officer, who had been close to death, pictured his lighter arm receiving a gift of life—the same colored-red blood—from the darker arm of his fellow officer and reflected, "How can I remain a bigot when a Black person's blood saved my life?" Hopefully, those who have not yet reached this point do not have to experience a life-threatening event to realize that those who appear "so different" or are "others" are actually fellow members of the same human race.

At an enriching multispiritual retreat, a chief of an African tribe taught us how to drum, and dancers of a Native American tribe presented a sacred rain dance that had never been presented off the reservation. People from a wide range of beliefs and cultures attended. Each person came in a spirit of peace with the desire to learn more about one another. Our mutual intent was to return to our respective communities, connect more positively with one another, and appreciate the vast richness of our cultures' differences.

It was astounding to listen to folks interact with one another. At times, they included rancor from past experiences, as though it was a part of what was happening among them right now. When a woman of African heritage spoke with a woman of European heritage, she communicated as though the other person was personally responsible for the inhumanity and abuse perpetuated against her ancestors during slavery. When a Jewish man spoke with a Christian woman, he spoke to her as if she were also responsible for the atrocities and genocide perpetrated against his deceased family during the Holocaust. Often during the weekend, I heard the echo of these horrendous histories enter a conversation. Those heinous events of the past had nothing to do with the present human-human dialogue or sense of peace and inclusion that was the purpose of our gathering.

Eradicating prejudice and racism often feels like "two steps forward, one step backward." I believe the 2014 Super Bowl monumentally raised the bar with two outstanding commercials that perhaps were the catalysts for others to express their desire for inclusion. My favorite was a Cheerios commercial portraying a family of mixed heritages. The first ad showed a father placing three Cheerios then adding a fourth on the tablecloth to tell his cute, multiheritage young daughter that she was going to have a new baby brother. The child pondered a second, then smiled and added another Cheerio and stated, "And a puppy." The second ad, a Chevrolet commercial, highlighted a diverse family riding in their car. This was groundbreaking, similar to the gay couple getting married on a Rose Bowl Parade float just a month before.

Following the Super Bowl ads, there was an increase of diverse people in TV ads. People of minorities stood in the forefront and portrayed leadership roles, such as boss, decision maker, or problem solver. Television commercials and programming became so blended and inclusive that I almost take it for granted. Some networks that I viewed became progressive and presented shows that included almost every minority group. Some had moderators of minority heritages, while other networks regressed and replaced them with those of European heritage. The integration seen in many magazine ads also caught up. Eventually, this issue will not exist as the minority becomes the majority and their voice, power, and influence will change the face of our country, which will significantly affect advertising. Hopefully soon, readers will scratch their heads and wonder what I was writing about.

Five years ago, who would have guessed that *12 Years a Slave* would be made into a movie, let alone receive the Academy Award for Best Picture in 2014, and that Lupita Nyong'o would win the Oscar for Best Supporting Actress? Yet the following year, not a single person of a minority culture was nominated by the Academy for a leading or supporting role for Best Actor or Actress, or for Best Picture or Best Director. Many were stunned that the film *Selma* was totally overlooked, even with David Oyelowo's outstanding performance as Martin Luther King Jr. Also passed by was Ava DuVernay, the female director who highlighted the prominence of women's roles in the civil rights movement. While the United States continues to make vast strides in certain areas toward awareness and equality, it lacks progress when it pertains to minorities. In 2015, there was a discouraging and discounting repeat in the lack of diversity among the Academy's nominees. Although there were many opportunities to include the increasing number of outstanding movies and casts, not one actor, actress, or director of a minority culture was nominated. The powerful Academy decision makers appear to be among the biggest laggers in correcting injustice. For some, this severely tarnished the cachet and respect that they once held. With all the incredible artistic talent of members in minority communities, at some point, the Academy's nominating committee will recognize them, and some will be winners. Finally in spring of 2020, Ava DuVernay was asked to join the Board of Governors for the Academy to promote diversity.

Although many are afraid to use labels laced with discrimination, too many U.S. elected officials, and other prominent figures, act as though they are above suspicion and continue to "misspeak" and use ethnic and racial slurs when they think the microphones are off, that no one can hear or is listening, or that they can get away with such a comment. They do not expect a video to go viral, or they just don't care. In 2014, billionaire Donald Sterling, owner of the National Basketball Association's (NBA) Los Angeles Clippers, was recorded spewing venomous, rude, and racist remarks. In the past, such comments were swept under the rug and the response would hardly bear consequences. This time, the overwhelming and unbelievable national outcry surprised many.

The NBA delivered a bold, swift, decisive, and just response that terminated Sterling's involvement in any activity associated with NBA basketball. In addition, Sterling was fined $2.5 million. President Obama commented, "I think that we just have to be clear and steady in denouncing it, teaching our children differently, but also remaining hopeful that part of why statements like this stand out so much is because there has been this shift in how we view ourselves" (Pace 2014).

Following the scandalous news of Donald Sterling's revelations, former NBA player Kareem Abdul-Jabbar pointed out that Mr. Sterling had a history of discrimination toward not just Black but also Hispanic people. He explained that nothing had been done in response. His exhortation to all members of society was, "Let's use this tawdry incident to remind ourselves of the old saying: 'Eternal vigilance is the price of freedom.' Instead of being content to punish Sterling and go back to sleep, we need to be inspired to vigilantly seek out, expose, and eliminate racism at its first signs" (Abdul-Jabbar 2014). On the *Daily Show*, Jon Stewart succinctly remarked, "Here's the thing about racism in this country. The reaction to Sterling…the overwhelming condemnation makes it clear that we have made enormous progress in teaching everyone that racism is bad. Where we seem to have dropped the ball is in teaching people what racism actually is, which allows people to say these incredible racist things while insisting they would never" (Stewart 2014).

Although racism persists in our society, the media coverage of the Sterling scandal highlighted its influence on our perspectives on prejudice. While we witnessed rapid and positive changes in media advertisement within a couple years, these swift changes were not paralleled in the publishing industry. Until recently, many illustrations of individuals of different cultural heritage were not favorably represented or were completely absent in most publications, including fashion magazines. Those of African heritage wore sweaters, while others wore suits. They also sat or stood at the sidelines or were placed in the back of the group. These images reminded me of Rosa Parks sitting in the back of the bus. They were also reminiscent of my childhood, when the media only portrayed minorities as cooks, maids, or in other service positions and never as leaders. The one exception was sports coverage, where they included or represented many of African or Latino heritage.

I recall that once when I was leafing through the pages of an unsolicited catalog offering upscale fashion, I noticed that the models were only women of European heritage. I called the company and asked if any people of African, Asian, or Latino heritage bought their merchandise. The person replied that she thought they did. I asked her, if she were a member of a minority group, how she would feel looking through a catalog and not finding a similar person with whom to identify. Is there an implication that people of minority groups cannot afford your merchandise? For a while, the catalog's models were more diverse, but then this company and another one in the industry reverted to featuring only models of European heritage for their spring travel catalog. Upon seeing that, I called back and told them that I was upset that they had regressed and, if I didn't see a change, I would discontinue shopping at their fashion chain. The next catalog again was filled with more models of diversity, and the catalog after that displayed a woman of African heritage on the cover. I don't know if I was the "hundredth monkey" or if my words made an impact, but changes occurred. Unfortunately, too many companies continue to engage only those of European heritage. In early 2016, I was disheartened to see that some of our national professional journals or magazines serving children continued to discriminate against minorities by highlighting them in inferior roles. Moreover, they did not include the children's stories or photos except in their advertisement.

My husband also became more aware. When he ran through one of the leading running magazines, he found the same discrimination. When he called the magazine, he shared that the lack of diversity surprised him, especially because many outstanding runners, and often marathon winners, are of African heritage. The person thanked my husband, and the centerfold of the next issue displayed an ad featuring a man of African heritage and a woman of European heritage running. In the following issues of *Runner's World*, the inclusive trend continued, and within months, the magazine featured a person of African heritage on the front cover. Sometimes, all a person needs is the gift of a gentle nudge from the heart toward awareness, as they truly want to do the right thing and become a part of the new, inclusive paradigm.

The documentary *Waiting for Superman* discussed the failures of public education, and it highlighted the story of visionary educator Geoffrey Canada, who turned one hundred blocks of what were once Harlem's slums into a beacon of learning. A panel discussion followed the presentation, moderated by a prominent dean. I was unable to attend, but I was very interested in the audience's perception and response to the film, so I contacted the dean. The dean replied *that some saw value and others did not.* He was aware of my professional background and my decades of experience in personal and intercultural communication. He also knew that my husband and I lived part-time in a local village and are fully immersed in local life in Nevis.

I commented to the dean how strange I found it that some inner-city students of African heritage fail in school in the United States although they share the same genetic pools as our friends in Nevis, which has a 98 percent literacy rate. I related the journey of some youngsters from our local village who achieved great success. Two brothers in the US Navy often attained the highest test scores and rankings among their peers. Others lived with relatives to seek a higher education in Canada or study law at universities in England. At age fifteen, one of our friends fixed a computer issue, in just half an hour, that neither the manufacturers of my computer nor of my camera could resolve. Our friend later received a four-year scholarship to a university in Taiwan to receive a Bachelor's of Computer Science. The first academic year was spent in a total language-immersion program. Upon graduation, he continued to earn his master's degree, and then, at significant sacrifice and absence from home, he continued to attain his doctorate degree in computer science, specializing in biomedicine.

Another dear friend whom we have known for more than half his life is now in his midforties. He entered a rigorous university in Canada with aggressive academic scheduling and completed his junior and senior years in one year, attained a perfect 4.0 grade point average, and received chancellor honors. He later earned his PhD in public and international affairs from a US American university. He now resides in South Carolina with his wife, who earned her PhD in social work, and their two daughters, who are enrolled in high-achieving classes. His eldest daughter was accepted at Yale, Princeton, Harvard, Duke, and eight other top universities in the country.

I have expressed how deeply I believe that the disparity between the more successful outcomes of mainstream U.S. companies and less successful outcomes of underserved socioeconomic communities has nothing to do with genetics but arises from unjust national social attitudes, priorities, and policies. In addition, our justice system routinely and unfairly hands down unequal judgments between those who smoke crack and reside in the inner cities and those who snort cocaine and live in wealthier socioeconomic communities. Those of the inner cities are often further disadvantaged, as they are neither as privileged nor as well connected as wealthier people. Consequently, they do not benefit from equal access to high-quality legal representation. Accordingly, they are disproportionally incarcerated while others go free. Moreover, they lack the same opportunities to have their records expunged. In 2014, Senator Cory Booker, a

Democrat from New Jersey, teamed with Senator Rand Paul, a Republican from Kentucky, to cosponsor the Redeem Act, which includes a process to seal or expunge records relating to non-violent or juvenile offenses. It has failed to pass because every factor in the penal system requires significant review and modification or elimination. The resolution and reduction of the financial costs of incarceration are significant, but far more consequential is the toll on human life. The lost years, indignity of incarceration, and uncalled-for lengthy prison sentences—especially for a wrongly incarcerated person who ultimately is found to be innocent—are beyond extremely unjust. These human costs can never be recovered.

Increased attention to for-profit prisons was brought to light in the fall of 2016. "According to the Bureau of Justice Statistic, 7 percent of state prisoners, 18 percent of federal prisoners in 2016, and inmates in local jails in Texas, Louisiana, and a handful of other states are held in for-profit systems. U.S. Immigration and Customs Enforcement reported that in 2016, private prisons held nearly three-quarters of federal immigration detainees." In Colorado, one in four prisoners is in an outsourced, for-profit prison (ACLU, n.d.).

During the final months of the Obama administration, after the ACLU gathered 250,000 signatures for a petition to cease outsourcing federal prisoners to private prisons, the Department of Justice ordered the Bureau of Prisons to begin phasing out the use of private prisons. Private prisons are inhumane profit machines where the bottom line is often more important than people's lives (ACLU, n.d.).

The inequities of either government-run or private, for-profit prison policies continue to create an environment of stark disadvantages. The absence of positive male role models, burdens placed on single-parent families, and reduced household income for economically disadvantaged populations easily stunt family opportunities and individual well-being. I predict that historians will revisit this street-to-prison pipeline and condemn these policies, similar to the condemnation of the Japanese internment camps.

Statistics and incidents about systemic racism are very revealing. In 2015, a majority of "Black people" in the United States—more than three out of five—said they or a family member personally experienced being treated unfairly by the police and their race was the reason. Half of African American respondents, including six in ten Black men, said they had been personally treated unfairly by police because of their race, compared with 3 percent of whites. Another 15 percent said they knew of a family member who had been treated unfairly by the police because of their race. This information, from a survey conducted by the Associated Press–NORC Center for Public Affairs Research, came as the Michael Brown shooting in Ferguson, Missouri, approached its first anniversary. The nation continues to grapple with police-related deaths of those of African heritage (Holland 2015).

In February 2016, the *Los Angeles Times* Sunday front-page edition ran a powerful graphic in which two thousand Black dots appeared, representing two thousand police shootings in six counties in Southern California since 2014. A lone red dot starkly stood out; it represented the only officer whom they prosecuted and later acquitted (Dolan 2016).

John Legend's acceptance speech upon receiving the Oscar for Best Song, "Glory," from the movie *Selma*, passionately reminded us that Selma is happening now. Voting rights, painfully gained by those who sacrificed and gave their lives a half-century ago, are now stripped away in many areas of our country. Legend commented starkly in his conclusion, "There are more Black people under correctional control than there were slaves in 1850" (Pearce 2015). That statistic was shocking. During the 2016 presidential primary season, a main theme of candidate Senator Bernie Sanders's platform focused on statistics regarding the disparity between those of minorities, especially between those of African American and European heritage.

Bryan Stevenson (2014) reports that currently, few people are aware that United States, with a population of around 319 million, has the highest incarceration rate in the world—even higher than China's, with its population of 1.35 billion. Additionally, there are nearly six million people in the United States on probation or parole. "One in every fifteen people born in the United States in 2001 is expected to go to jail or prison; one in every three Black babies born in this century is expected to be incarcerated." He further states, "Only a handful of countries permitted the death penalty for children, and the United States was one of them." Many of his Alabama clients "were on death row for crimes they were accused of committing when they were sixteen- or seventeen-year-old children." He also notes that "many states had changed their laws to make it easier to prosecute children as adults" (Stevenson 2014).

Senator Bernie Sanders (2016) stated that youth of African heritage are four times more likely to be arrested for smoking pot than those of European heritage, though both cultures have the same percentage of pot smokers.

As responsible adults, we break down those stereotypes within ourselves. The president of an international communication consulting firm commented, "Every form of humanity comes in every shape, color, and ethnic group." He added, "I'm a recovering bigot," although this man was of African heritage. Prejudice, as well as the deep desire to right existing bigotry, occurs in every cultural, racial, religious, or regional divide across the entire country and the world.

Discriminatory events continue to occur too frequently, but most are now met with lightning-speed consequences. In March 2015, a video of the Greek fraternity at the University of Oklahoma (OU) surfaced on social media and immediately went viral. Members were seen chanting racial slurs and singing about lynchings. University President David Boren swiftly responded on his Twitter, "If the video is indeed of OU students, this behavior will not be tolerated and is contrary to all of our values. We are investigating."

The National President of the fraternity weighed in quickly on Twitter as well: "The chapter has immediately been placed on a cease and desist. No place for racism. They will be dealt with. I know I speak for all when I say I'm disgusted and shocked by the video involving our SAE chapter at OU. They will be dealt with" (Murphy 2015). As soon as the fraternity members accepted responsibility, they were ordered out of the fraternity house. After the evidence was confirmed, the twenty-five members received punishment of community service and diversity training, and two leaders were expelled. Isaac Hill, president of the university's Black Student Association, joined with students and athletes from an African heritage fraternity to meet with some student leaders of the decommissioned SAE chapter. After listening to the members' apology, Hill was satisfied and commented, "I believe the students were very sincere in their apologies, and we are all glad for that" (Murphy 2015.) Students dressed in black gathered at the OU campus to protest racist slurs. I recall that I saw a response from a student of African heritage who said something akin to *"Whoever thought we would have white people protesting on our behalf?"*

On the April 2, 2015, edition of *Hardball*, MSNBC aired a segment titled "Racism on Campus," in which moderator Chris Matthews led an outstanding and affirming discourse with the decisive and fair-minded university President Boren. The president shared his fervent view that racial slurs were moral issues and nothing less. He stated, "The culture has to change dramatically not just on college campuses but all across the country. We have to join together and have zero tolerance [and] stop the epidemic of racism across the country." He also said that he hoped that OU was doing its part and added that "each of us [has] to do our part in every situation. If we hear any type of racial slur or ethnic joke, each must immediately respond, turn to the person, and from the heart let that person know that that's not who we are and not what we're about. It is the only way we are going to put a stop to what I call a severe cancer within our democracy." Boren said that the students at OU immediately began to gather and join in one voice, proclaiming, "This is our community, this is our family, this is not who we are" (Murphy 2015).

President Boren set a high bar for morality and righteousness. Again, it behooves each of us to stand up, stand strong, and have the moral strength and courage to instantly speak against even the slightest injustices and innuendoes. In a mindful manner, it is also important that we inform the other person that these types of remarks, slurs, or jokes do not belong in a democracy and that we certainly do not want that toxicity in our presence or our homes.

In his eloquent, soft-spoken, and seasoned style, Bob Schieffer, moderator of *Face the Nation*, responded to the current rash of stories about bad cops. He shared that the early days of his training as a cop included working the beat to witness the news through his *own* eyes. He learned that every story is someone's "worst moment." He added, "You don't read about all the cops who deal day in and out with the worst dregs, schemers, or murderers whom the police deal with humanely as they should" (Schieffer 2015b).

Schieffer continued emphasizing the officer's challenge to maintain a humane response as he recalled an event when a child beater tried to justify his behavior by conveying *that the kid had kept him awake*. He stated, "It wasn't easy to remain passive, it took a lot of professional training and strong character not to respond in anger." He knows because he recalls, "Sometimes, I wanted to hit them myself. I didn't, but it helped me understand how hard it is to do a cop's job right. As hard as it is, the great majority of our cops still do just that" (Schieffer 2015a).

The timeline of recent wrongful deaths of young and old men and women of African heritage are profound travesties against the U.S. democracy. The 2012 fatal shooting of seventeen-year-old Trayvon Martin by George Zimmerman began a rash of incidents of continued violence, resulting in the unjustified deaths of many men of African heritage. Zimmerman was a coordinator of a neighborhood watch that was not registered with the National Neighborhood Watch Program. When they tried him, the jury ruled that Zimmerman acted in self-defense. I often asked, "If Trayvon Martin had been of European heritage and resembled the outward features of George Zimmerman, and George Zimmerman had been of African heritage and resembled the outward features of Trayvon Martin, do you think the jury's decision would have been the same?"

The subsequent murders, committed mostly by those of European heritage, clearly exemplify the deep divide and disconnect between our communities in the modern age. The next major outcry occurred in response to a grand jury's decision not to charge Police Officer Darren Wilson, who shot Michael Brown in Ferguson, Missouri. Brown, a heavyset unarmed eighteen-year-old, was walking in the middle of the street with a friend who had just robbed a store for a pack of cigarillos. Officer Wilson was unaware of the robbery before he shot Brown. Following the official autopsy, Brown's family arranged an independent autopsy with Dr. Michael M. Baden, who was eighty years old, retired, a renowned New York–based medical examiner, and one of approximately four hundred board-certified forensic pathologists in the nation. Baden stated that Brown had sustained six gunshot wounds and added, "In my capacity as the forensic examiner for the New York State Police, I would say, 'You're not supposed to shoot so many times'" (Bosman and Goldstein 2014). After his death, Michael Brown's body lay in the heat for four hours before any medical personnel arrived. I would guess this visual image did nothing to encourage calm among those who were so heartbroken, who felt cheated and undeserving of yet another wrongful death.

In January 2015, they discovered that the Ferguson grand jury who failed to indict Police Officer Darren Wilson for shooting Michael Brown was misdirected on a key point of the "use of force law" (Collins 2015). Grievously and shockingly, the error was compounded by the prosecutor's failure to correct the misdirection on this crucial point of law until the final day of the three-month-long hearing. Furthermore, the jury was instructed to take into consideration a law that a police officer can use deadly force when someone flees. But that Missouri statute, under which officers were permitted to use deadly force on a fleeing suspect even if the felony was not of a violent nature, was ruled unconstitutional thirty-eight years prior. In 1977, the U.S. Supreme Court struck down the statute as "an arbitrary imposition of death. In fact an officer must believe there to be a threat of imminent harm before he or she is justified in opening fire" (Collins 2015).

In July 2014, another overreach culminated with Eric Garner's pleading utterance, "I can't breathe," repeated eleven times before his tragic choke hold death in Staten Island, New York. There, "officers approached Garner on suspicion of selling single cigarettes from packs without tax stamps" (Wikipedia Contributors 2014a). He suffered from chronic bronchial asthma and obesity and was dead within an hour. This is another horrific example of police brutality.

Then, in November of the same year, twelve-year-old Tamir Rice was tragically shot by a police officer whose former evaluation implied he was unfit to be a policeman. The initial report to the police stated that a child was waving a gun that did not have a coded cap to indicate that it was a toy. The 911 dispatcher did not inform the responding police officer that the gun was "probably fake" and that the person waving it was "probably a juvenile" (Williams and Smith 2015).

One of the most repulsive scenes that I saw during this period was the abhorrent murder of Walter Scott by Police Officer Michael Slager in North Charleston, South Carolina, on April 8, 2015. As I watched, riveted in sheer horror, disgust, and disbelief, the video showed a defenseless, unarmed middle-aged man of African heritage fleeing to escape the eight bullets fired, five of which riddled his back until he dropped and died. I could not believe what I saw. The scene looked unreal. To Slager, Walter Scott did not matter, and in his mind, there was no relevance to Scott's life. The police officer, filled with an unrealistic and exaggerated fear, rage, or hatred, had absolutely no regard for Scott's humanity as he blatantly continued to aim and fire, emptying his weapon. Officer Slager knew he was wrong, as he immediately handcuffed Scott, who lay shot on the ground, and then quickly picked up the dropped Taser that lay several feet away to underhandedly place it close to the fallen man. Shamefully, a fellow officer of African heritage also participated in this heinous police brutality act and deceit.

Fortunately for the community, nation, and world, this heinous act was caught on video by an innocent and responsible bystander. The only redeeming moment of this entire horrific act was the swift and just response of Mayor Keith Summey, who immediately called for Officer Michael Slager's arrest and charged him with murder. "When you're wrong, you're wrong...and if you make a bad decision, [I] don't care if you're behind the shield or just a citizen on the street, you have to live by that decision" (Schmidt and Apuzzo 2015).

In 1985, the Supreme Court ruled in *Tennessee v. Garner* that an officer may use deadly force against a fleeing suspect only when there is probable cause that the suspect "poses a significant threat of death or serious physical injury to the officer or others" (Schmidt and Apuzzo 2015). Walter Scott was unarmed, and while fleeing, he did not pose a single threat.

Following the Walter Scott death in South Carolina, a very solemn congressman, James Clyburn, Congressional House member from North Charleston, was interviewed by Chris Matthews on *Hardball*. Representative Clyburn began the interview by expressing, "I have been blessed growing up in South Carolina." Clyburn commented that these were his people, that they were good people like the leaders, governor, chief of police, and mayor, who acted quickly and appropriately. He went on to state thus:

> A climate has been created in this country that has caused these changes to occur all over....This so called American Legislative Exchange Council (ALEC) [has] been drawing up these pieces of legislation like 'stand your ground,' and that legislation gives people a license to be vigilantes. [Also there are these] so-called photo ID laws and unfair redistricting plans. These people are a cancer on the innards of our society, and it's time for our elected officials to start speaking out about this because this climate that is being created is not a good climate...and that is why you have these rogue police officers feeling they have license to do what they want, and there will be no consequences for it, and I believe that is the mind-set of this police officer. (Matthews 2015a).

Another bizarre and tragic case of a deadly law enforcement encounter with a man of African heritage is that of Freddie Gray in Baltimore in April 2015. Apparently, after a police officer made eye contact, Gray, who had not committed a crime but did carry a switchblade, immediately began to run, causing officers to give chase. Gray, aged twenty-six, did not resist arrest, nor was he shot by police officers. Gray had a history of asthma and requested an inhaler that officers denied. They dragged him to the police car, placed him inside but did not buckle him up, and proceeded to the police station. When they arrived, 80 percent of his spinal cord was severed. Although he lived in a high-crime area and previously had scrapes with the law, the only questionable factor in this case was the switchblade in his pocket. Baltimore mayor Stephanie Rawlings-Blake said, "We know that having a knife is not necessarily a crime" (Graham 2015).

Later, thousands of frustrated people gathered to demonstrate peacefully regarding their unanswered questions about yet another police overreach. It was peaceful for the most part, except a few "outsiders" who began looting and damaging police cars. Mayor Rawlings-Blake and Congressman Elijah Cummings called for peace and asked others to text those protesting to keep it peaceful. Some marchers told outsiders, "This is our house; we will protect our house" (Schieffer 2015b).

Cummings told *Face the Nation* moderator Bob Schieffer, "This whole police-community race relation is the civil rights cause of this generation, no doubt about it." He also stressed the importance of using smartphones and body cameras to capture police-citizen interactions. When Schieffer asked Cummings if he thought the elected officials in his district in Baltimore were fair, Cummings replied, "Yes." He added that he was happy that the Federal Department of Justice was also stepping in to investigate the civil rights issues and to thoroughly evaluate the entire system. Cummings concluded, "We have to take this heart to heart and figure out what is right and what is wrong. This is a significant moment. If we don't correct this now, it will only get worse" (Schieffer 2015b).

A few days later, on April 29, 2015, Mayor Rawlings-Blake stated, "If with the nation watching, three Black women at three different levels can't get justice and healing for this community, you tell me where we're gonna get it in our country" (Sabia 2015). She was speaking about herself, Baltimore prosecutor and Maryland's state attorney Marilyn Mosby, and Loretta Lynch, the recently appointed U.S. attorney general. By May 1, 2015, Prosecutor Marilyn Mosby stated, "What happened to Freddie Gray was illegal, and what happened to him in custody was murder." They charged and later indicted all six police officers. The most serious charge was of second-degree murder for the driver. Other charges ranged from involuntary manslaughter to assault and false imprisonment. The Gray family stated that this was the first step in seeking justice. Again, they dropped all charges against all the police officers.

In September 2016, another police shooting under questionable circumstances occurred involving a man of African heritage, Keith Lamont Scott. Early in the Charlotte, North Carolina, investigation, and before they announced anything affirmative, riots occurred in response to the act, causing property damage and injury to individuals. The Scott family did not support any of these incidents, but they do support individuals' right to peacefully voice their frustration and anger. When they released the police video to the public, it was inconclusive.

Attorney Justin Bamberg, who, along with Eduardo Curry and Charles Monnett, represented the Scott family, eloquently, succinctly, and with deep forethought asked that we step back and look at why these outcries occur. "We do have a problem. Many citizens in this country feel that minorities, when encountered with police, feel they are guilty until proven innocent, they are a threat until they prove they are not a threat, and quite frankly, many feel they are inhuman until they prove to be human. That is an underlying problem." In the book *Born a Crime*, Trevor Noah shares how his family, especially his mother, devised strategies and games to avoid unwanted attention or stopped holding his hand in certain public situations. When he was a child in South Africa, before the downfall of apartheid, it was against the law for individuals of European heritage to marry those of African heritage. But here in the United States of America, there is no such law! Yet as Bamberg expressed, many of African heritage feel that some folks think that they are guilty of breaking a law even though they haven't been formally accused, arrested, or found guilty (Noah 2016).

Bamberg strongly supported the right to calmly voice opposition to injustice in the right way and declared, "We don't want you to destroy the very community you live in. The [Scott] family doesn't want that either." Bamberg also reminded us to be mindful that we are becoming desensitized to all this wrongful brutality and killing because we have seen these videos over and over. Curry voiced his desire for due process, and Monnett added, "All we want is the truth" (Snow 2016).

I acknowledge that justice and policing are complex, finely tuned, and delicate and require split-second decisions on which lives hinge. Nevertheless, it remains unfathomable that we do not possess the national will to create a nonlethal response, other than a Taser, for those who appear more erratic than pose danger.

Within a few months, in the historic and charming city of Charleston, South Carolina, the founding Mother Emanuel African Methodist Episcopal (AME) Church, which has stood since 1816 as an upright and majestic house of worship on Calhoun Street, was the scene of an abhorrent and tragic event. Because of its longtime tradition and deep roots of love and forgiveness, it is one of the most respected churches in America. The AME church had been burned to the ground twice before and both times was rebuilt stronger than ever. The first minister was hanged. Later, within its walls, many greats, including Nobel Peace Prize laureate Dr. Martin Luther King Jr., led prayers of deep faith, love, and forgiveness.

In June 2015, during a Bible study class in the basement of the AME church, a cunning murderer who had been welcomed to join the class committed a dastardly act that he had meticulously planned, killing the peace-loving, forgiving, deeply religious, and welcoming group. The individuals attending the prayer study ranged from young to old—seventeen to eighty-seven—and included six women, two men, and the highly respected and beloved Pastor Clementa Pinckney. As the news broke, the name of the street address and city hit me hard, as the church sits four blocks from where my son and his family reside. Over the years and on my most recent trip, I had often passed the house of worship. I began to pray for whoever the people were—the congregation, the community, and our nation.

As the names and faces appeared, I felt that those were my sisters and brothers who could easily have been my friends or colleagues. Many reminded me of my friends and loved ones in the United States and in Nevis. As the media revealed each new bit of information, collective heartbreak and sadness penetrated deeper and deeper. Yet in stark contrast, the families and friends of the AME community offered and taught us love and forgiveness.

There is something horribly wrong within our national fabric when such decent, loving, and forgiving people—who open-heartedly and kindly welcomed a stranger into their midst—cannot peacefully gather in a sanctuary to innocently study and pray with a rightful expectation of returning home safely. We are supposedly the greatest country in the world, spending more of our human treasure and financial resources than any other country to protect and defend our people while fighting terrorism around the world. Yet we fail to protect our people at home and ensure their safety. Somehow, the people in the United States and our elected national government representatives lack the conviction to protect their sisters and brothers. Instead of a sad chasm, it would be best if a comprehensive approach were already in place rather than just more discourse or removing symbols.

Remarks by leaders and intellectuals of African heritage offered incredible insight. At the time of the wicked act at the Mother Emanuel AME Church, the first president of African heritage led the United States. They asked President Obama to deliver the eulogy for the beloved, righteous, and respected moral voice of the South Carolina State Senate, Pastor Clementa Pinckney, along with the other eight members of the "Emanuel 9" who lost their lives. President Barack Obama soulfully orated the most poignant, forthright, raw, and honest facts, often unknown to mainstream U.S. America. Much of this information is not presented in our history books and, consequently, not discussed in our classrooms.

The president laid out his thought-provoking and brutally honest message as a fellow human being of African heritage. Now more than ever before, he conveyed his hope that this time there would be a tectonic shift to peacefully move forward not just policing and justice but also equal voting rights, access, infrastructure, nutrition, housing, education, and opportunity, not only for the "Johnny" but for the "Jamali" as well. He articulated that he knew these are also the hopes and dreams of many Americans of all types of backgrounds, heritage, age, and strata. The president exuded the amazing grace that a higher power solely bestows. He spontaneously led the singing of the hymn "*Amazing Grace*," the lyrics of which were written centuries ago by a man who had captained a ship bringing slaves to our shores. Through his stark imagery, the president reminded us all, including himself, that we were blind but now we see. He passionately charged that the time to seize opportunity is now for each of us who envisions a more *United* States of equality for all. With this motivation and will, we can peacefully propel a united and just movement that will finally make more than a dent. It will create a monumental shift to uplift all people.

Many of these events and their divided reactions demonstrate a deep continued disconnect between communities within the same city or town. As witnessed in response to Michael Brown's death in Ferguson, Missouri, these communal divisions prominently exist across our nation. They met the grand jury's failure to indict with a far more vigorous roar, following the razor-sharp three-way divide reflecting those agreeing or disagreeing with the judgment. There also were divisions within those who fiercely disagreed with the decision.

With every new incident, I sensed a grassroots awakening, even if the process was "two steps forward and one step backward." Even in Ferguson, citizens of differing cultural heritage had pressed together for reconciliation as they fostered a deep yearning to mobilize and create connection, communication, collaboration, and cooperation. The outpouring of a broad spectrum of humanity hopes to forge and champion new ideas of mutual respect, inclusion, transparency, and justice for individuals, community, and country. Most often, enlightening, inspiring, and uplifting peaceful paths emerge from the ashes of horror. Those of African and other heritages who peacefully and passionately fought this fight hoped that by this time, we would finally eliminate one of the United States' greatest travesties, the cruel injustice of our legal system.

Some members of the human race no longer stand silent while others are abused, oppressed, or murdered. Those are united, are aware, and do care. Yet at times, grassroots people, not agitators, may feel so crushed and hopeless that they believe they have no other option but to resort to riot. Martin Luther King Jr. understood this when he stated, "Riot is the language of the unheard" (King 1968). These responses that continue to occur in rapid, cohesive, and appropriate protest of the heinous discriminatory, racist, and marginalizing events gave others and me a pause of deep hope that the inclusive outcry is not just momentary. It may be the beginning of a new, far-reaching, forward-moving civil rights movement.

Members of the Mother Emanuel AME church, and the people and community of Charleston, South Carolina, did not go to the streets to protest, riot, or loot. Instead, they united a diverse community to pay their respects and offer forgiveness to the killer. Out of deep sorrow and pain, a message from one of the oldest and most respected churches in America was brought forth: love and forgiveness remain the only answer. We often claim that we need a "model" to lead, but now we look no further.

Along with the national investigations and dialogue, this hopefully will be the final critical chapter of the civil rights movement for those of African heritage. The burning of their churches, the predominance of innocent males' blatant wrongful killings by "peace officers," and the unjust and unparalleled incarcerations will be exposed, and this will lead to positive and just resolutions.

Due to stereotypes, fear, suspicion, and hatred, we limit the opportunity to get to know others. Hoping to improve the situation, we change labels from "crippled" to "handicapped" to "disabled" to "differently abled" to "people with disabilities" to "*handi-abled.*" Another transformation evolved from terms "colored" to the "N-word" to "Negro" to "Black" to "African American," then back to "Black" or "African heritage." We may want to be "politically correct," but the real issue is, Do we strive to be *humanely correct*?

Changing labels is akin to a Band-Aid that covers the wound. What really drives positive transformations are heartfelt, inclusive, and uplifting paradigm shifts in the way we perceive and interact with one another. Do we look at the outward shell, or do we *source-connect* to sense the other person's spirit and energy?

Reverse Discrimination

Reverse discrimination also exists; it is prejudice by a person of a minority toward a person of the majority. Any person of any culture, religion, gender, socioeconomic level, sexual orientation, or minority must be mindful of this factor. Although the responsibility clearly lies within ourselves, it is usually easier to blame others or find other reasons when we fail or feel offended. When an acquaintance's son didn't get into the college of his choice, she blamed the students of minority cultures instead of realizing that her son's qualifications were not good enough. When a student of African heritage approached a recently graduated, idealistic teacher of European heritage and uttered her first comment, "You think I'm invisible," the young teacher was taken aback. He grew up in a family that had chosen to live in a neighborhood side by side with people of African heritage. His father was a respected physician in the community.

My husband and I spent an afternoon at a deserted beach on an isolated side of a Caribbean island. As we drove down a rural road to the main road, two young local guys hailed a ride. We picked them up and chatted with them a few minutes. As we approached the drop-off spot, one man remarked, "You're not racist like the other white tourists." My husband replied, "No, we're not, but don't accuse everyone of European heritage as racist. That's also discrimination."

A law enforcement officer of European heritage on a late-night freeway patrol with his partner of African heritage saw a car drive by at ninety miles an hour. Of course, the officer turned on the siren and chased the car to give the driver a ticket. When the traffic penalty came under review, they questioned the officer, "Did you see what color the driver was? Was the driver wearing anything unusual that would identify him with a gang? Was the driver young or old?" The officer replied, "No. He was speeding at ninety miles an hour, and so I gave him a ticket for a speeding violation."

There is often a fine line between reverse discrimination and actual discrimination. A person of a minority culture or religion who constantly experiences discrimination and a person who has not faced cultural or religious discrimination often observe or hear an identical event with contrasting views. When a highly competent, pleasant, outspoken saleswoman (of African heritage) achieved the highest sales numbers in her department, she was offered a very slight pay increase. The miffed saleswoman responded, "Oh no, that doesn't seem enough." She then inquired about her colleague's raise. When she discovered that her colleague, who was one step behind her in sales and of European heritage, had been awarded a far greater increase than they had offered her, she said, "It makes no sense. I don't understand why if I brought in more money, I didn't receive at least as great a salary increase, if not more." She further requested that they *please check with the supervisor and get back to me with an answer*. When she checked back, the saleswoman was informed that there was a new policy in the department. "We no longer go by the amount of sales—as we did in the past—but evaluate by the level of education." She further stated that her colleague had a bachelor's degree and she did not. The saleswoman replied, "When I began here years ago, I had not earned a college degree, but I received my bachelor's degree many years ago, and that is on my record." After the supervisor checked her records and confirmed that she had indeed received her bachelor's degree, the saleswoman finally received fair compensation that was commensurate with her achievement and education level. She always questioned if discrimination or the mistaken information about her education level was the main factor in her initial lower pay increase.

Questions of reverse discrimination continue to persist in the U.S. culture and in the courts. The first case, which the Supreme Court heard in 1970, involved a student of European heritage who had good grades and accused a California medical school of twice denying him entrance because he was white. Over the decades, there have often been people of European heritage who feel they are slighted, neglected, or shut out because people of minorities have to catch up. Until justice and equality catch up for those who are of minority heritages as opposed to those of European heritage, these questions will continue.

Organizations for Positive Change

Organizations are paramount to achieving positive change. However, it remains "we the people" who physically, mentally, emotionally, and spiritually give from our hearts—not egos or condescending attitudes—who are change agents. It remains "we the people" who seek to reach out to those left behind, bring them into the circle, and strive to uplift them. And there are those who became or remain politically active, peacefully demonstrate, or in other mindful ways brazenly proclaim and vigorously work to tear down demeaning and divisive walls of hatred and exclusivity. It is good-hearted individuals who fill the roles in pertinent community outreach programs, philanthropic groups, universities, and religious and way-of-life communities.

A plethora of outstanding organizations has and continues to diligently empower, enlighten, and overcome challenges. I list a few that promote equality and inclusion, especially for those of African, Latino, Asian, Native American, and Middle Eastern heritage. Additionally, there are organizations that further the causes of or address the needs of those human beings of different sexual orientations and religions who are targets of increasing repulsive and xenophobic rhetoric in the United States.

The Southern Poverty Law Center (SPLC) was founded in 1971 by two civil rights lawyers, Morris Dees, the son of a sharecropper, and Joseph Levin Jr., who is Jewish. Since then, the organization has grown in scope and international stature and is often sought by respected media outlets to provide facts pertaining to increasingly alarming hate crimes. Its dedicated focus is to help those who are most vulnerable; its leaders are dedicated to fighting hate and bigotry. The organization litigates to reduce the impact of hateful radical extremists, educates to advance understanding and equality, and advocates for equal justice.

In 2014, a presentation by the outreach director of the Southern Poverty Law Center (SPLC) titled "*Hate, Bigotry and Anti-Semitism: SPLC Responds*" was offered at a local Orthodox Jewish synagogue. During the dialogue, the moderator focused on anti-Semitism and discrimination against those of African heritage. She shared that although much progress was achieved in fighting discrimination against all minorities, hate groups in the United States increased 50 percent from

2000 to 2014, with a significant increase in neo-Nazi groups. Hate groups exist in every state except in Hawaii. The *Teaching Tolerance Program*, which "provides free resources to help children reject hate, embrace diversity, and respect differences," is one of the SPLC's outstanding programs. In the hope of reducing discrimination, an annual "Mix It Up at Lunch Day" provides time for students to move out of their usual social comfort zone and eat lunch with a student with whom they usually do not interact. This experience helps reduce hurtful discrimination during students' most vulnerable period of the school day. Each school creates its own innovative way to celebrate the day, helping students feel more comfortable with one another and accepting of their differences.

In March 2015, the SPLC proved the broadness of their reach in fighting all forms of discrimination. They reached a settlement with Mississippi's Moss Point School District on behalf of a young female student who was subjected to pervasive anti-LGBT bullying and harassment from persons of all levels within the school, including administrators. "As part of the settlement, the school district agreed to adopt and implement new anti-bullying and discrimination policies and procedures, as well as equal educational opportunity policies. These prohibited bullying and harassment based on sexual orientation and gender identity or expression" (SPLC 2015).

"Although the Ku Klux Klan has diminished in number, the national undercurrent of racism may be far more pervasive" (Woodruff 2016). On *PBS NewsHour*, special correspondent Charlayne Hunter-Gault questioned Heidi Beirch, the leader of the Intelligence Project at SPLC, on their methods of combating white supremacy hate crimes. Beirch responded that in 1981, SPLC began filing civil lawsuits to bankrupt the Ku Klux Klan, which eventually reached the Imperial Klans of America. Without funds, dismantled hate groups lose the means to attack. This pattern of lawsuits and bankruptcies has been successful. When questioned about the cause of the significant rise of white supremacy hate groups in the twenty-first century, Beirch responded that their increase began when the 2000 census report predicted that in 2042, current minorities would be the majority in the United States. These facts fueled the rising number of hate groups.

A sharp rise in hate groups also occurred following the election of Barack Hussein Obama II, the first U.S. president of African heritage. Hatred of Black people is a driving force, but hate crimes expand to include Latinos and immigrants. Perpetrators also target LGBT communities and are currently merging with other types of hate groups to viciously target Muslims (Hunter-Gault 2016).

Hunter-Gault also questioned the role of the "lone wolf." Beirch responded that therein lies the greatest threat, as there is no way of knowing whether a person who visits a hate or terrorist group website becomes so radicalized that they will go on a mass shooting spree, as did Dylann Roof. When further questioned about any solutions, Beirch offered that the Department of Justice restored a domestic terrorist unit to vigorously gather intelligence about white supremacist hate groups. (The unit was disbanded after the 9/11 investigation was completed.) Southern Poverty Law Center publishes information through their *Intelligence Reports*, which they offer at no charge to law enforcement agencies.

When further questioned as to whether education was a key for building tolerance within those who hate, Beirch responded that education was the most significant factor. Most people learn discrimination and hatred in the home, and without anything positive to counter it, how will a person become more tolerant and accepting of others? Exposing the corruption of white supremacist leaders to their followers is a good tool. Education can also be experiential. Beirch shared one of her favorite stories about a woman who went to prison for her involvement with a skinhead group. There, while attending a community activity, for the first time she met a woman of a different color and Jamaican heritage, and they became friends. The experience changed her life so much that she now runs an organization called Life After Hate.

Former right-wing white supremacists who had transformed their lives formed the organization. Based on their personal experiences, they now stand up to educate young people to abandon or turn against joining that type of movement. They claim, "We serve to inspire, educate, guide and counsel" (Life After Hate, n.d.).

Another organization fighting hatred is the Anti-Defamation League (ADL), founded in 1913 to "stop the defamation of the Jewish people and to secure justice and fair treatment for all." Their motto is, "Imagine a World Without Hate." Over the century, the ADL has grown significantly and now promotes enlightenment and fights not only anti-Semitism but all civil rights issues. They also "educate and train pre-K through universities, community groups, corporations, civic associations, religious organizations, and law enforcement agencies. This organization also offers free online newsletters on numerous current topics."

Muslim Advocates is another national legal advocacy and educational organization "that functions on the front lines of civil rights to guarantee freedom and justice for Americans of all faiths" (Anti-Defamation League, n.d.).

This organization offers a calm, inclusive, and thoughtful voice to address the concerns of those who observe Islam and to ensure that justice is served on their behalf. The staff has sound experience in the courts and strong connections with Congress and the Obama administration. Religious and other groups outside the government join them to fight against injustice toward Muslims. The organization also counters anti-Muslim bigotry and hate crimes by educating people about their rights.

Cesar Chavez was a farmworker of Mexican heritage who became an iconic figure leading the charge to improve civil rights, especially for Latino farmworkers. Living in Southern California during his time, I was fully aware of their plight. On many family excursions, we often saw men and women bent over, picking produce in fertile fields in scotching heat for hours. Chavez's nonviolent approach was aggressive and passionate as he led the struggle to gain farmworkers' rights. To support his mission, our family boycotted iceberg lettuce and grapes for years. "By the late 1970s, his tactics had forced growers to recognize the United Farm Workers as the bargaining agent for 50,000 field workers in California and Florida." After Chavez's death, his birthday (March 31) became a celebrated state holiday in California, Colorado, and Texas. Many streets, schools, and parks now bear his name.

In response to the lack of a national Latino civil rights organization in the early 1960s, the National Council of La Raza (NCLR), the largest national Hispanic civil rights and advocacy organization in the United States, was founded in 1968. The organization now has a network of nearly three hundred affiliated community-based organizations and reaches millions of Hispanics. To achieve its mission, NCLR conducts "applied research and policy analysis," offers advocacy, and provides a Latino perspective in six key areas—assets and/or investments, civil rights and immigration, education, employment, economic status, and health. The organization is a leader in encouraging the Latino community to get out and vote during elections. NCLR also reports about the positive impact of DACA for individuals on local and national scales and supports the policy (NCLR, n.d.).

A good friend of Mexican heritage is an attorney specializing in family law. For decades, he also aided migrant workers from Coachella Valley in California. He believes that the Mexican American Legal Defense and Education Fund (MALDEF) is the nation's leading Latino legal civil rights organization. "Often described as the 'law firm of the Latino community,' MALDEF promotes social change through advocacy, communications, community education, and litigation in the areas of education, employment, immigrant rights, and political access" (http://www.maldef.org). These programs provide several positive pathways for people in Latino communities to attain greater prosperity and inclusion in mainstream U.S.A. society.

During the COVID-19 pandemic, the unemployment rate for those of Latino heritage significantly exceeded any other group. They held the majority of jobs in the travel and food service industries that were hit exceptionally hard.

In addition, either because of their voluminous numbers as healthcare providers or pre-consisting conditions, the mortality rate of this Latino group far exceeds any other group.

The National Association for the Advancement of Colored People (NAACP) was founded more than one hundred years ago in 1909, partially in response to continued lynchings and a race riot in 1908 in Springfield, Illinois. The initial group included Mary White Ovington and Osward Garrison, both descendants of abolitionists, and Villard William English Walling and Dr. Henry Moscowitz. When they called for a meeting to discuss racial justice, sixty people attended. At that time, W. E. B. Dubois, Ida B. Wells-Barnett, and Mary Church Terrell came on board. These individuals were of various heritages, cultures, and religions (NAACP, n.d.).

Rosa Parks was an active member in the Montgomery chapter of the NAACP. In 1955, she refused to move from her seat in the front of a bus to a seat in the "colored" section in the back. During that time, Dr. Martin Luther King Jr. was on the executive board of the NAACP and was chosen to lead boycotts against the bus system. Eventually, the US district court ruled in *Broader v. Gayle* that racial segregation on public buses was unconstitutional, citing the Fourteenth Amendment.

Dr. Martin Luther King Jr. later joined other civil rights activists to establish the Southern Christian Leadership Conference. Inspired by the nonviolent ideals of India's Mahatma Gandhi, Dr. King led sit-ins and marches to end segregation and disenfranchisement of voters with African heritage. He was a preacher, a passionate visionary, and a world-class orator, endowed with tremendous grit and courage, who was often incarcerated for his beliefs. On August 28, 1963, at the Lincoln Memorial in Washington, DC, Dr. King delivered his most famous speech, which called for an end to racism in America. Close to the end of the speech, gospel singer Mahalia Jackson cried out, "Tell them about the dream, Martin." And so, without notes, he delivered the final section of his speech, declaring, "I have a dream that one day this nation will rise up and live out the true meaning of its creed: 'We hold these truths to be self-evident, that all men are created equal.'…I have a dream that my four little children will one day live in a nation where they will not be judged by the color of the skin but by the content of their character." According to a 1999 poll by the University of Wisconsin–Madison, this became the top-ranked speech of the twentieth century (http://www.news.wisc.edu).

In June 1964, the Civil Rights Act became law, and in September of that year, Dr. King received the Nobel Peace Prize "for his dynamic leadership of the civil rights movement and steadfast commitment to achieving racial justice through nonviolent action" (CRDL, n.d.). In 1965, in protests to the killing of activist deacon Jimmie Lee Jackson, Dr. King led the march from Selma to Montgomery, Alabama. The first attempt, known as Bloody Sunday, failed as the marchers were met by brutal force and gassed after they crossed the Edmund Pettus Bridge. Rabbi Abraham Joshua Heschel, Greek Orthodox Archbishop Iakovos, and civil rights activist John Lewis, who was injured, participated in that Bloody Sunday march. This event was so appalling that it aired nationally as breaking news on CBS.

The movie *Selma* portrayed Dr. King as a passionate, committed, and a courageous leader who never betrayed his nonviolent values. He was a thoughtful leader of unbroken determination who led President Lyndon Johnson to call for the Voting Rights Act, which Congress enacted in 1965. Let me add that I strongly support the renaming of the Edmund Pettus Bridge to the John Lewis Bridge.

The NAACP now has more than half a million members from the United States and around the world. It is the premier organization for championing civil rights and equal opportunity, as well as registering voters. During the 2008 and 2012 elections, the NAACP played a major role at the community level in helping those of African heritage register to vote and assisting them to the polls. They also peacefully demonstrated to bring attention to injustice. On August 1, 2015, a broad coalition of civil rights and religious leaders embarked on the one-thousand-mile trek America's Journey for Justice from Selma, Alabama, to Washington, DC. This marked the commemoration of the fiftieth anniversary of the Voting Rights Act. It also brought attention to social justice concerns, including voting rights, racial profiling, the high rate of incarceration of Black men and women, and the disproportionately high rate of school suspensions and discipline for minority children (NAACP 2015).

Any organization that champions educating and uplifting a diverse population of underserved, high-potential, and most vulnerable people in our society looms big in my heart. The Harlem Children's Zone Inc. (HCZ) is one of those organizations. Geoffrey Canada understood that knowledge is power when he took over a school that served Harlem, a community in Manhattan that was once considered a slum. In recent years, the area has transformed and now is quite upscale. HCZ was established in 1970 initially as the city's first truancy-prevention program; in its early years, it served one city block. It now encompasses more than one hundred blocks and serves ten thousand minority students and adults who often outscore students of European heritage in math (http://www.hcz.org).

A most worthy organization, Equal Justice Initiative (EJI), is committed to raising awareness of the overwhelming injustices against basic human rights for the most vulnerable individuals in U.S. society (https://eji.org). Highlights of Bryan Stevenson, Founder and Executive Director of EJI, are presented later in this chapter.

Another very positive organization, the Dream Corps, was founded in 2014 by Van Jones, who has been a civil rights leader for more than twenty years. He vigorously fought for social, economic, racial, and environmental justice. Dream Corps "sits at the intersection of technology, entrepreneurship, ecology, and social justice" (http://www.thedreamcorps.org). Its lofty mission were publicly declared in 2015, and among others, they include uplifting those who are the most vulnerable, reducing prison terms, and training one hundred thousand people in computer skills. Former Princeton University Emeritus Professor Cornel West, now Professor at the Union Theological Seminary, and New Jersey Senator Cory Booker also support this organization and are finding avenues to work with former opponents. Former Congressman Newt Gingrich, Wisconsin Governor Scott Walker, and the Koch brothers are also joining the cause to reach these lofty goals.

Shortly after Dream Corps' rollout, the *Sacramento Bee*, a California newspaper, published Jones's plans, and the newspaper claimed, "Finally, a movement to roll back the prison industry" (Jones 2015). The article lauds their efforts toward reversing the "lock 'em up" mentality and highlights the disproportionate numbers of those from minority groups behind bars for nonviolent or drug-related crimes.

In 2016, as a response to hateful and divisive rhetoric, Van Jones initiated the *Love Army* within the Dream Corps. *Love Army*'s goal is to form a community of love and inclusion and to reach out especially to those who, for a variety of reasons, voted for Trump but do not espouse his hateful rhetoric. This positive message serves as an alternative to—and I believe helps to minimize and perhaps even neutralize—the hatred and divisiveness of some of Trump's supporters.

The People's Institute for Survival and Beyond (PISAB) is one of the foremost organizations in the country that offers antiracism training and organizing. These workshops are designed for hospitals, prisons, churches, and local and regional governments. Nationally and internationally, more than five hundred thousand people have benefitted from these workshops. Reverend David Billings now directs the institute, which was founded thirty years ago by Ronald Chisholm and Dr. Jim Dunn. The PISAB principles are thus: "Undoing Racism®, Learning from History, Sharing Culture, Developing Leadership, Maintaining Accountability, Networking, Analyzing Power, Gatekeeping, and Undoing Internalized Racial Oppression" (http://www.pisab.org).

Within hours after the jury acquitted George Zimmerman of any crime following the shooting of Trayvon Martin in July 2013, the phrase "Black Lives Matter" (BLM) came to the minds of three accomplished women, Patrisse Cullors, Alicia Garza, and Opal Tometi. The phrase quickly raced through social media and cyberspace to become the number one new term in 2014. There are many movements, but I firmly believe that BLM will become the most relevant international organization promoting justice and inclusion for all. I sensed that its positive credo and actions would serve as a far-reaching, inclusive model for demanding equal justice. The organization was founded on the principles of identifying and eradicating the dehumanization and persecution of their Black brothers and sisters, along with LGBT people and the *handi-abled*. Nonviolent principles guide the organization's acts of rightful civil disobedience, which are promoted by love, cohesion, and generosity of spirit. In the spring of 2016, there were already thirty-six chapters, including one in Toronto and one in Ghana. If the organization remains true to its founding core principles and is not highjacked or corrupted, I believe the movement will span the globe.

Black Lives Matter will be the leading force to fight this national cancer of systemic racism in the twenty-first century. The organization is led by people learning to unconditionally celebrate their essence. They are spiritually free with the knowledge that they, too, can stand on the shoulders of President Barack Obama and one day become the president of the United States and leader of the free world, or anything they desire. In honor of Beyoncé's rollout of the Transformation Tour video, her husband Jay-Z pledged 1.5 million dollars to Black Lives Matter.

In 2016, the organization brought forth a Palestinian manifesto that supports Palestinians. Some of their wording against Israel is inaccurate, as there is no evidence of genocide. Israel has not initiated a program to exterminate all Palestinians. As a Jewish person, I can support both Israel and a two-state solution between Palestine and Israel. Being pro-one aspect does not necessitate being anti-another aspect of the equation. Supporting a two-state solution is not "anti-Israel." I am hopeful that people who are Jewish and all others recognize this difference so that anti-Semitism does not follow and a mutually viable two-state solution is found. An e-mail from the Southern Poverty Law Center declared that "Black Lives Matter is not a hate group" (SPLC 2016).

Besides the organizations listed, the following are also worthy of your consideration. They are United Nations, Urban National League, Jewish World Watch (JWW), and Rock the Vote. Though I mention a few throughout my book that are close to my heart, they are only a minuscule fraction of the existing outstanding national and global organizations; please find one that connects with your heart, ideals, and passion.

Before concluding this section, I would like to mention my experience of attending the Poverty Tour: A Call to Conscience, led by PBS commentator Tavis Smiley and Dr. Cornel West, at the tour's final presentation at the Wilshire Boulevard Temple, Los Angeles, in 2011. It was the first such event that I had attended in years. Dr. West delivered a powerful message about the inexcusable inequality in our country. The words resonated deeply, stroked my passion, and motivated me to become even more involved and outspoken. The evident love and decades-long bond between Tavis Smiley and Rabbi Steve Leader was quite moving, featuring an honest and raw insider's view.

A few of the books that profoundly deepened my understanding of those of African heritage are *Slavery by Another Name*, which aired as a PBS special and was written by Daniel Blackman;

Between the World and Me by Ta-Nehisi Coates; *Dream a World Anew: The African American Experience and the Shaping of America*, edited by Kinshasha Holman Conwill; *Behind God's Back: Gullah Memories* by Herb Frazier; *Right to Ride: Streetcar Boycotts and African American Citizenship in the Era of Plessy v. Ferguson* by Blair L. M. Kelley; *My Journey with Maya* by Tavis Smiley and David Ritz; *The Covenant with Black America: Ten Years Later* by Tavis Smiley; *Just Mercy: A Story of Justice and Redemption* by Bryan Stevenson; *Rebuild the Dream* by Van Jones; and *The Warmth of Other Suns* by Pulitzer Prize winner Isabel Wilkerson. I also highly recommend the piece "Decline to State" by Susanna Barkataki, which appeared in Thich Nhat Hanh's book *Together We Are One*.

Let me also add a select few outstanding contributors in the arts and communicative fields: Whoopi Goldberg, Gwen Ifill, and Spike Lee. Goldberg must have had a strong sense of her spirit when she changed her name to Whoopi, as she is the epitome of the word. Though she began her career portraying a mistreated woman in *The Color Purple*, Whoopi has evolved into a highly respected comedian, moderator, powerful outspoken satirist, civil and human rights advocate.

Of all the occasions on television and movies that I saw Whoopi, her role as the psychic in *Ghost* was my favorite. I still have an old CD with Whoopi, Billy Crystal, and Robin Williams in 1986 in their first four-hour fund raiser *Comic Relief* that raised $2.5 million dollars to help individuals who are homeless to provide assistance and healthcare.

Whoopi is beloved and one of only ten people to have won an Oscar, Grammy, Emmy, Tony, as well as a Daytime Emmy Award (10-facts-about.com). In spring 2020, she was asked to serve on the Board of Governors for the Academy Awards Board. This honor is most essential and appropriate to promote diversity.

Gwen Ifill was born the daughter of preacher. In touch with her inherent gifts and love of people, civility, and fair and honest discourse, she became a journalist. She articulated with agency, asked tough questions, and framed them in her singular style. She is greatly respected for the questions she posed that others had given little or no thought.

In 1999, Ifill became the first woman of African heritage to fill the role of moderator and managing editor of the weekly political show *Washington Week.* Later, on *PBS Nightly News,* she and Judy Woodruff became the first all-female anchors. She received the prestigious George Foster Peabody Award for her political news coverage. She reached the highest level writing for the *Washington Post* and a best-selling author of *The Breakthrough: Politics and Race in the Age of Obama.*

Ifill had a sincere, sunny, and upright style that occasionally included her body moving to music. She reminds me of one of my Nevisian friends, as Ifill also lived by the creed of *faith, family, and friends.*

Spike Lee is an unparalleled and masterful film producer, director, film editor, professor, and outspoken and passionate civil and human rights advocate. His voice either leads the chorus or joins the chorus to sharply call out abuses and their responses that are lacking, too weak, or too strong. His first movie, *Do the Right Thing,* combining comedy and drama, was controversial to some, but others thought he had a gift of foretelling the possibilities. He has a very creative, potpourri style which adds to the captivation of his audience. I recall how taken I was by his brilliant portrayal of this enlightening and inclusive Malcolm X film. In 2019, the timely movie *BlacKkKlansman* was partially fact based that exposed the virulent hatred ideology and acts of white supremacy at the highest level in the country. The Academy awarded Lee his first win, but there were many other categories that the film could have received this coveted statue.

In a brilliant piece by Dr. Cornel West, "Firebrand: Fifty Years Later, the Prophetic Voice of Malcolm X Still Speaks Truth to Power," West laments the thefts of the lives of Malcolm X and Dr. Martin Luther King Jr. (West 2015). West then evokes a stirring portrayal of a hypothetical current, civil, and robust exchange of words between Malcolm, the ultimately nonviolent Sunni Muslim, and Dr. King, the nonviolent Christian.

West further states, "Malcolm had a revolutionary fire and Martin had a moral fire," but in the end, they evolve to a blended message. West believes in the Black youth. I most certainly do not, in any way, equate myself to West's brilliance, passion, commitment, or stature, but with what I witnessed, read, and heard, my hopes and beliefs lie not only in our national youth of all cultures but also in the youth of our global society. I fervently hope that this young generation have enough fire in their bellies to galvanize into a unified, inclusive, nonviolent, determined, and focused front. Then, they can channel and lead with that passion to forever reverse this national centuries-long curse. This scourge of vast wasted human potential and dignity continues to affect far too many. As West concludes, "It is a beautiful thing to be on fire for justice" (West 2015).

In response to an essay about the tragic death of the Emanuel 9 in Charleston, which I previously presented in this chapter, a female student of Asian Indian heritage recalled Mahatma Gandhi when she shared, "The one thing I am learning and realizing is that we, especially the youth, need to stand up and make a change. The media focuses more on the negative than the positive. The same media spreads certain labels for each ethnic group, and it's the same media that the youth uses to make a point about racism, inequality, and freedom of choice. We should not reiterate the media's words. It's time to use our own words 'to make the change we want to see.'"

Cultural Inequality and Historical Events

For most of my life, I have felt that society has stacked the cards against the people of African heritage on every front. This despicable mind-set began with the assistance of their own people. Fellow human beings in Africa were captured, shackled, and forced to lie in their own excrement as they heard their loved ones' raging screams fighting off violating rape while crossing the Middle Passage to their "new home" in North America and the West Indies. If that were not horrific enough to dehumanize and demoralize their spirit, when they finally reached the destination, those who had survived were separated from one another. These individuals were not even given the comfort of connecting, communicating, or commiserating with familiar faces or touching their loved ones' hearts or bodies. Similar to other people of subjugated communities throughout the world, one of the slaves' survival reactions was to create their own *dialect* to communicate with one another so that their tormenting oppressors could not comprehend what they felt or expressed. Developing this unfamiliar language with its own grammatical structure empowered those who were slaves and served as a form to communicate, gain control and dignity, seek limited freedom, develop camaraderie, find comfort, and plot to escape as they were subjected to treatment not even befitting an animal.

I often reflect that from the conception of our nation's original sin of slavery until our present moment, despairingly, there has never been liberty and justice for all. No other cultural groups of immigrants or U.S. citizens ever suffered the same pervasive, abusive history as those of African heritage. Every other person from every other culture, even those who came as "indentured servants" to work a period of time to pay off their transportation costs, entered our nation of their own free will. Certainly, some came at great risk, many experienced enduring hardships, and others died along the way. The newly arrived immigrants were often paid a pittance of what was fair, but each made the choice to arrive here.

In both the 2008 and 2012 elections, President Barack Obama was victorious. He became the first person of African heritage to serve in the role of president of the United States. Even in victory, some immediately questioned the legitimacy of his U.S. American citizenship. Although his father is Kenyan, his mother was born in the U.S.A. The president's birth certificate confirmed that he was born in Hawaii. Still, rants continued from the sidelines throughout his presidency that he wasn't a "real American." That was one of many sentiments expressed blocking him from fulfilling his duty—as stated in the US Constitution—to nominate a Supreme Court justice to fill the vacancy when a justice died.

During the 2016 presidential election cycle, voter disenfranchisement continued and grew in too many states. This resulted in reducing or eliminating available polling hours, days, and sites and included hidden forms of poll taxes. Furthermore, requirements to produce legal documents were especially challenging for seniors who did not drive or could not locate their birth or marriage certificates. In some states, gun registration was valid identification but student identification (ID) was not. Voter disenfranchisement punishes those of African heritage more than any other group of people. We have come a long way as a nation, but we still have a long way to go to achieve equality for this basic democratic right.

Though progress has been achieved, there are still far too many instances where legislators of European heritage purposely established and maintained an order of discrimination and disparity, particularly by gerrymandering congressional districts. This manipulation disadvantages those of certain groups or socioeconomic classes of people. These processes continue to disproportionately affect many of our citizens and severely disenfranchise far too many people, particularly those of African heritage.

Finally, front and center in the 2016 presidential primary cycle, Bernie Sanders, a candidate of European heritage, claimed to be a socialist revolutionary. Even so, he amassed a nonviolent following and proclaimed a cohesive message, broadcasting it loud and clear for the country and world to hear of how prejudiced we are as a nation. He declared, "My father was born in Poland,

and nobody is asking me for my birth certificate like they did President Obama.... That is because my skin is white" (LoBianco 2016).

Most people are unaware of when racism first appeared on U.S. soil. We are not exposed to early seventeenth-century laws that were purposely passed to ensure that those of African heritage never gained the power to achieve stature or a voice for their lives' destiny in America. By the early 1600s, plantation systems were established in Virginia and "whites" who were convicts, homeless, vagabonds, or very poor—especially the Irish—were forced to work and were also treated as slaves.

In 1619, when Black Americans first came to the United States as part of the workforce, "Blacks and whites worked side by side, married each other freely, ran away from their masters together," indicating their trust with each other. Together with guns drawn, they "even rose up against the rich. Initially, Blacks had the same freedoms, rights, and social status as whites... American society was mainly divided by class, not race" (Abagond 2014).

Slowly and systematically, from 1640 to 1723, laws were established primarily throughout the Southern colonies in America and the Caribbean to make sure that those of African heritage did not attain power, grow stronger, or unite to overthrow the plantation owners of European descent. Laws denying them the civil right "to vote, bear arms, marry whites, hold property, get an education, testify in court," or publicly congregate in groups of more than three people were established and enforced (Abagond 2014). These laws, which were intended to be enacted in perpetuity for those of African heritage, were for the most part eventually overturned. Yet the spirit of some of these laws still culturally exists in the hearts of some people.

Charlayne Hunter-Gault interviewed Reverend Billings of PISAB in the "Race Matters Series" on the *PBS NewsHour*. Billings maintains that those of African heritage never had the same chance "to achieve or maintain the same success or attain the power and wealth of those of European heritage...that his own power stems from being a white man in a nation that he says was designed to benefit him above others" (Hunter-Gault 2016).

Whichever cultural segment we examine, we find disparity. Whether we evaluate fairness and justice under the law, similar access to and opportunity for excellent education systems, or schools consistently staffed with outstanding teachers and support personnel, disparity persists. We must also observe whether educators' salaries are commensurate with those in nearby communities. Moreover, we must consider if an area is physically safe and devoid of mold or other hazardous materials. We also question if governments sufficiently fund schools with essentials such as books, papers, and copy machines so that teachers don't have to pay for these basics.

Furthermore, we ask, Are lunchrooms, bathrooms, and playgrounds kept up? Are classrooms comfortable, warm, or cool enough, pleasant, well equipped, and maintained? Do students have access to computers, science labs, Wi-Fi, and the internet? Are music, drama, and art offered? Are there sports activities, cultural centers, or after-school enrichment programs? Are these backed by parents and community involvement? In minority communities, these basic standards are rarely equal to those of schools in surrounding middle-class or upper-class neighborhoods. Economic justice and security are required.

Inequities in health care also continue to be pervasive in these minority communities. Many individuals lack outstanding community health-care delivery provided by caring and dedicated doctors, nurses, and support staff who understand the culture, lingo, and needs of the patients they serve. Medical equipment is not always available, reliable, or current.

This absence of standard health care reaffirms a sense of unworthiness and the idea that the patients' lives don't matter as much. Lack of local business opportunities, entertainment centers, or the ability to create wealth through real estate investment also contributes to this injustice.

Disparities also persist in neighborhoods in regard to the availability of a variety of culturally savored, healthy, fresh food and produce and basic household goods at a fair and reasonable price. *Food desert* is a term for a geographic area where residents without cars must travel farther than one mile to reach a large grocery store or supermarket that sells produce. Some are in rural areas, but 80 percent of these *food deserts* are in cities and in low-opportunity and low-socioeconomic-level areas, where people are usually minorities (http://www.foodispower.org).

In a report by the Economic Research Service of the U.S. Department of Agriculture, limited food choices in close proximity negatively affect about 2.3 million people (or 2.2 percent of all U.S. households). Access to healthy foods and produce often requires several buses or train trips. The types of food found in delis, liquor stores, and convenience stores are often fatty, processed foods and sodas. This poor diet increases incidences of type 2 diabetes and heart disease and typically contributes to an unhealthy lifestyle.

In a segment entitled "Food Desert" on *The Nightly Show with Larry Wilmore*, contributor Jordan Carlos visited a major city and shopped at a "food desert" shop. There, he found items filled with sugar (often disguised as high-fructose corn syrup), sodium, cholesterol, trans fats, sodium nitrates, preservatives, artificial flavors, sodium aluminum, phosphates, or other unhealthy substances. After walking another seven-tenths of a mile, Carlos found another shop that filled their shelves with Jell-O, snack packs, cake mix, icing, and liquid sugar (Wilmore 2016). To expand the scope of this unjust issue, a few years later food security, especially for minorities and the homeless gained broad support.

With few exceptions, a huge disparity exists in public transportation. This story broke in early 2015 when *Daily Mail* published an article about James Robertson, a factory worker from Detroit earning $10.55 an hour, who walked more than twenty miles daily from his home to his job since his last car broke down. If the lack of efficient and modern public transportation, living-wage jobs, and healthy work environments in nearby neighborhoods that serve minority groups don't bring additional light to the despairing disparity and double standards inherent in our system, I don't know what does. In every aspect of U.S. culture, attitudes and policies are purposely rigged so that the playing field is never level. This is one aspect of what systemic racism looks like.

Another instance of systemic racism is the alarming disparity that is amplified and reverberates during natural disasters, epidemics, and pandemics. This significant agonizing increase in mortality rates is apparent among the folks of African heritage, especially in the homeless population and persons in prison systems throughout the country. This disparity tragically also bears down on individuals of Latino heritage as they provide the overwhelming personnel who serve as healthcare providers. What becomes crystal clear during these times is the overwhelming lack of nearby and affordable clinics and hospitals, and the inhumane and grossly unfair practices in prisons that have always existed.

It was shocking to discover the significant increase of incarceration during the last few decades of women of color and individuals of Indigenous People either for drug use or property offense. Pregnant women are even shackled during health related appointments and labor. The majority of women had a child under the age of eighteen.

Equally cruel is that many U.S. states continue to maintain inhumane and tortuous ways pertaining to lengthy periods of solitary confinement without any outdoor activities, family visits or contact with loved ones. In addition, sensory deprivation or overload in dark or constantly lit cells, or any interaction with another human being for more than twenty-two hours occur. Often individuals as young as teens and those fifty-five years and older, or persons dealing with mental and physical issues are held for months, years, or decades, in this tortuous confinement. Individuals held in these cruel conditions are not offered any restorative programs. In several states, the minimum solitary confinement's principles of the United Nation's Nelson Mandela Rules are not being adhered to.

Again, these tortuous restrictions impact minorities at higher rates, especially individuals of African heritage. It is hard to believe that this is happening in the nation that is supposed to the beacon on the hill that espouses human rights.

During the first wave of COVID-19, further injustices in law enforcement, inequality of healthcare, basic needs such as food and housing security, increased homelessness, the wealth gap, and lack of equal access to opportunities that create wealth occurred, Additional acts of wrongful killings continued against human beings of African heritage. Some acts recurred assuming impunity. The souls are Breonna Taylor, Ahmaud Arbery, George Floyd, Rayshard Brooks, Elijah McClain, Jacob Blake, Jr., and Daniel I. Prude that was revealed months later. With a heavy heart, I know these individuals' tragedies are not the end of these sorrowful killings.

Even during social-distancing and mandated masks, human beings from every spectrum felt so compelled to respond to these deliberate acts that they chose social justice over social distancing. Millions of people joined peaceful Black Lives Matter and other protests in a multitude of major cities and small towns throughout the country and the world. In each instance of wrongful deaths, BLM protests immediately popped up.

It is as though individuals of this targeted group of human beings first are thrown under the bus, and then continually mortally driven over. Similarly, a large kettle filled with grief and tears always sits nearby ready to be poured with breaking news of the next assault.

The 2016 lead-poisoned water calamity in Flint, Michigan, also disproportionately affected citizens of African heritage and those living in poverty. It began with an attempt by the state's governor to save money. Because of government officials' apathy, denial, and neglect, a wide-spread disaster occurred pertaining to water contaminated with high levels of lead. The toxic lead predominantly affected young children, as their age group is at greater risk because "their bodies absorb lead at a higher rate" (WebMD 2017).

Lead poisoning affects all the body's organs but does the greatest damage to the brain. It severely stunts or reverses development and debilitates a child's behavior, affecting their speech and hearing. Their ability to focus, learn, retain, and use other cognitive skills is also at risk. Even with years of rehabilitation and therapy, the damage may be irreversible. Again, please ask yourself if you honestly believe that if the same lead-filled, contaminated water flowed through pipes to homes in Newport Beach, California; Powell, Ohio; Salt Lake City, Utah; Durham, North Carolina; or Houston, Texas, would the same "ignore, deny, or do-nothing" policy be tolerated?

Before the majority of voters in California deemed affirmative action to be illegal in 1997, many civil rights laws prohibiting prejudice were in place, yet prejudice and discrimination remain rampant. Laws cannot mandate an eradication of prejudice and bigotry from people's hearts; laws can only mandate that justice be equally served. Recognizing and observing the laws are merely exercises of the mind. These ideals will not become our personal or national response until new, more positive, inclusive, *soul to soul* paradigms are fused into our mainstream and are *downloaded* and integrated into our hearts and souls.

Now, we backtrack to early 2015. Attorney General Eric Holder was the longest-serving attorney general so far and the first of African heritage. Shortly before he retired, Melissa Harris-Perry interviewed him. She posed the question, "Are you optimistic about the possibility of perfecting the union?" Holder replied, "Yes, I am. That's the beauty of this country....With fits and starts, we take two steps forward and one step backward always focused on progress....Through slavery and segregation, we have made remarkable progress. But progress is not enough, it is simply an indication of how you're doing. There are goals we ultimately have to meet. But I am optimistic that our kids will live in an America that is more just and equal than I am now" (Holder 2015).

A few months later, President Obama's comments again uplifted the nation with his forceful, passionate commemoration of the heroes of Bloody Sunday fifty years ago in Selma, Alabama. The president reminded us of the perseverance and dedication of earlier heroes. He stated, "We gather here to celebrate them. We gather here to honor the courage of ordinary Americans willing to endure billy clubs, chastising rods, tear gas, and the trampling hoof; men and women who despite the gush of blood and splintered bone would stay true to their North Star and keep marching toward justice" (Obama 2015).

During this era, I was heartened by and grateful for the vast advances we have achieved in the hard fight to gain voting rights for women and those of African heritage, fair practices for laborers, advances for those with disabilities, and leadership roles for women and those of diverse backgrounds. In addition, comfort and pride have been gained by those of different sexual orientations and those individuals from historically disadvantaged groups who moved up or reached the highest rung on the professional and corporate ladder. But we must remain mindful that we maintain what has been achieved and simultaneously remain vigilant that we still have much more to accomplish.

We may pause, applaud, and appreciate what has been achieved, but our march is far from over. The president urged us to shed our complacency and cynicism, to join together, to scrutinize and fully acknowledge the injustices that remain woven into our American fabric. He urgently prompted us to restore the Voting Rights Act as originally enacted in 1965, now encumbered by burdensome constraints specifically targeting minority groups. The act should ensure that every registered voter has the freedom to voice their choice for president, vice president, and members of Congress who enact decisions that affect their lives, positively or negatively.

He prodded us to join together to collectively ensure that our criminal system justly serves all and not just some, that policing equally protects all citizens, and that we seek an end to unfair sentences and overcrowded prisons.

Obama looked to the youth, who regularly lead the charge that moves our country forward and upward, step by step, challenge by challenge, into a more perfect union. Our Founding Fathers envisioned this foremost ideal of our democracy. Again, the president reminded us of the hope and goodwill of Americans of all backgrounds and cultures who achieved excellence and exceptionalism during our more than 250 years of democracy.

We continue as we follow along with the scene in the United States during the 2016 political season. The movement to put diversity front and center and to address the drastic income inequality between the upper 1 percent of the population and the remaining 99 percent was led by presidential candidate Bernie Sanders. The significant income gap, virulent, divisive, and racist rhetoric expressed by a candidate of a different party, and the lack of inclusion were major forces in the anger expressed nonviolently and violently during the 2016 presidential nomination cycle.

During the heated political season, two additional wrongful murders by police officers occurred against exceptional youth, Philando Castle of Minnesota and Alton Sterling of Baton Rouge, who were admired for their generous spirits. Following the murders, a Black Lives Matter protest was held. Prior to the protest, the BLM organizers had consulted with the Dallas Police Department. The protest was initially so peaceful that the Dallas PD even posted photos on their Twitter feed of two of their own officers, one Black and one white, smiling at a man with a sign that read, "No justice, no peace." During the peaceful march, police officers were also present in the streets, ready to assist if something went awry, which it did—due to one severely deranged individual. The sniper fired a fusillade of bullets, and the unthinkable occurred. As the demonstration turned unruly, Black Lives Matter protesters assisted the police in directing people to safety.

The sniper continued, and five exceptional police officers, Lorne Arens, Michael Krol, Michael Smith, Patrick Zamarripa, and Brent Thompson, were ruthlessly shot down by a person who had served in the U.S. military. These five officers were exemplary, both in their service and as human beings. As the days unfolded prior to the Memorial Service for Fallen Dallas Police Officers, it became clear that Dallas has its own exceptionalism. Mayor Mike Rawlings described Chief of Police David Brown as "his rock," and they are true brothers and partners. Though they are of differing heritages, together they diligently strived to implement one of the best practiced, progressive, and respected police departments in the nation.

At the time of the event, President Obama was attending a conference in Europe and expressed his sincere condolences; he often reiterated that "America is not as divided as it appears." Vice President Biden delivered an official heartfelt message of condolences to the families and hope to the nation. Attorney General Loretta Lynch spoke from the Department of Justice (DOJ), and she was the first to acknowledge the right of individuals to gather in peaceful protest to express their anger at yet another unjust killing of a man of African heritage. Lynch declared, "This has been a week of profound grief and heartbreaking loss....The peaceful protest that was planned in Dallas last night was organized in response to the tragic deaths of Alton Sterling in Louisiana and Philando Castile in Minnesota." She acknowledged the pain and a justified "sense of helplessness, of uncertainty and of fear" that individuals feel and strongly reminded us that violence is never the response. The attorney general continued with a call for "calm, peaceful, collaborative and determined action" and reminded us of the ease of acquiring deadly guns. She further stated thus:

> We must reflect on the kind of country we want to build and the kind of society we want to pass on to our children. We must reject the easy impulses of bitterness and rancor and embrace the difficult work of finding a path forward together. Above all, we must remind ourselves that we are all Americans— and that, as Americans, we share not just a common land, but a common life. Those we have lost this week have come from different neighborhoods and backgrounds—but today, they are mourned by officers and residents, by family and friends—by men and women and children who loved them, who needed them and who forever will miss them. They are mourned by all of us.

She acknowledged "our brothers and sisters who wear the badge" and the "daily difficult and dangerous work that they do to keep our streets safe and nation secure" (Lynch 2016).

I then heard her declare support for those who are leading the way to further the outcry against injustice and unfairness: "To those who seek to improve our country through peaceful protest and protected speech: I want you to know that your voice is important. Do not be discouraged by those who use your lawful actions as cover for their heinous violence. We will continue to safeguard your constitutional rights and to work with you in the difficult mission of building a better nation and a brighter future." She completed her deeply felt, timely message to turn to one another to help heal, reminding us that "we are one nation and that we stand together and asked that God bless us all with everlasting grace and the United States of America" (Lynch 2016).

Chief Charles H. Ramsey, former Philadelphia Police Commissioner and Co-chairman of the President's Task Force of 21st Century Policing, also spoke at the service. Ramsey stated that there are bad apples in most professions and also acknowledged that the major cities have advanced rapidly to more mindful policing, though there is still much to accomplish (President's Task Force on 21st Century Policing 2015).

Shortly after, Secretary of Homeland Security Jeh Johnson and New York Police Commissioner Bill Bratton appeared on *Meet the Press* and offered insights and recommendations for a growing sense of hopelessness and division in the country fueled by "region, income, culture, and racism" (Todd 2016). Johnson reminded us that neither "the shooter is reflective of the broader movement to bring about change in police practices," [nor is] "any police officer who engages in excessive force…representative of the larger law enforcement community."

At the Memorial Service for Fallen Dallas Police Officers, former President Bush, who, with his wife, Laura, call Dallas their home, eloquently spoke from the heart and conveyed his grief and heartbreak as well as his gratitude that every officer accepted a calling that sets them apart. President Bush reminded us that being a police officer also requires self-control. He poignantly expressed that forces seem to be pulling us apart more than holding us together. He also stated that "argument turns too easily into animosity. Disagreement escalates too quickly into dehumanization" and that we see the worst in other groups while only seeing the best in ourselves. "We have never been held together by blood or background. We are bound by things of the spirit, by shared commitments to common ideals" (Bush 2016). President Bush also reminded us that our common ground of unity is at the core of our democratic values and that we are "brothers and sisters" to one another. He called upon us to build the values of a just, humane country of our best dreams and highest purpose, reflecting how those fallen Dallas officers had lived.

At the memorial service, President Obama's heartfelt, brilliant, and precisely chosen words highlighted that these fallen heroes and those throughout the country were bonded by a "commitment to something larger than themselves." Police officers don't expect thanks, and their salaries are not meant to provide excess wealth, but their greatest reward is their awareness that they help others, often those most in need. They are driven and dedicated "in knowing that our entire way of life in America depends on the rule of law; that the maintenance of that law is a hard and daily labor; that in this country, we don't have soldiers in the streets or militias setting the rules" (Obama 2016). An officer of European heritage helped Shetamia Taylor, a woman of African heritage, as she was shot trying to shield her four sons, whom she brought along to protest the incidents of Black men being killed. She told the Dallas PD, "Thank you for being heroes." Today, her twelve-year-old son wants to be a cop when he grows up. President Obama noted that he saw people who mourned both for the fallen officers and the Sterling and Castile families.

During the president's speech, he gracefully began a delicate balancing act, shifting between the heroism of the fallen officers and his belief in the goodness of the American people. His dialogue punctuated the injustices experienced by Castile and Sterling, two more wrongful deaths of two more young Black men. The president's brilliant, soulful words lifted the national conversation of previously avoided topics of fear, racism, and injustice in mainstream society. While such conversations had been hushed in public, these topics certainly are addressed in the comfort and safety of the homes, churches, and workplaces within the greater African heritage communities (Obama 2016).

President Obama further stated that "the phrase Black Lives Matter simply refers to the specific notion there is a specific vulnerability for African Americans that needs to be addressed." Based on history and personal experience, he believes that "there is a greater presumption in the dangerousness that arises from the social and cultural perception that has been fed to folks for a long time. It's not as bad as it used to be, but it has a history. Black Lives Matter is not meant to suggest that other lives don't matter. It's to suggest that other folks aren't experiencing this particular vulnerability" (Obama 2016).

The president explained that for some, asking for fair treatment automatically means an anti–law enforcement attitude or looking out exclusively for Black lives rather than looking out for everyone. The president emphasized that the police cannot entirely shoulder responsibility but called for parents to be more involved by stressing to their children the importance of police protection and having "the talk" with their children, which no other ethnic group has to discuss. It is also the responsibility of the people in our nation, especially community, civic, and religious leaders, to foster concern and engage in productive, inclusive, and respectful dialogue among all in the community before crises happen.

The president wondered if an African American community that feels unfairly targeted by police and police departments, who are unfairly maligned for doing their jobs, can ever comprehend the other's experiences to bridge the racial divide. Often, through "perseverance, character, and hope" we can find that center of shared American values that hold us together (Obama 2016).

President Obama continued, "We also know that centuries of racial discrimination—of slavery, and subjugation, and Jim Crow—they didn't simply vanish with the end of lawful segregation. They didn't just stop when Dr. King made a speech, or the Voting Rights Act and the Civil Rights Act was enacted. Race relations have improved dramatically in my lifetime. Those who deny it are dishonoring the struggles that helped us achieve that progress" (Obama 2016).

The president also acknowledged that those of Latino, Native American, or Middle Eastern cultures also experience bigotry and are affected by an unwillingness in our nation to adequately invest in decent schools and programs to lift them out of poverty, fund drug treatment, or properly treat mental health issues.

Listening to these speeches, I gained a profound respect and admiration for those officers of good heart who put their lives on the line each day and rarely flinch or run from danger. I hope that this national dialogue, which was set into motion by the pinnacle of our democracy, continues among our like-minded citizenry. It is imperative that we calmly, mindfully, and in a *source-connected* way examine our biases, discomforts, and suspicions and begin to join together to seek positive solutions that work for all people. Then, I believe we will again advance equality as Martin Luther King Jr. described when he said, "The arc of the moral universe is long, but it bends toward justice."

The following week, David Muir held the *President and People: A National Conversation* town hall meeting, which aired on ABC and other worldwide networks, raising the national conversation on race relations even higher. The president spoke with Cameron, the fifteen-year-old son of Alton Sterling, whose sobbing image a week earlier was very sad to watch. But the young man had gallantly and courageously pulled himself together. With a poised, kind, and humble presence, he requested of President Obama, "You keep all these families and my family safe and the people and the rest of the good police officers safe from bad people and bad police officers. I want to ask for your help to unite all the races of this world" (Muir 2016). The ensuing dialogue and these types of courageous and heartfelt pleas for respect toward and acceptance of one another gave hope not only to the president but also to others and me. And so at last, a national conversation about racism had begun as no other in the past. This dialogue must continue with candor and commitment despite whatever political climate exists and persists.

The recent slew of murders by officers of the law against those of African heritage continues. These applications of excessive force or blatant murder are now caught more frequently on police video cameras or cell phone recordings. Yet to date, not a single police officer has been convicted of a crime. The Dallas Police shootings may not have occurred if these types of incidences or racially motivated killings had only manifested as isolated incidents in the past few years instead of being woven into our national fabric from the earliest periods of our nation, or if life, liberty, and the pursuit of happiness were equally attainable, or if the political rhetoric of the 2016 election weren't as heated and divisive, or if the threat of terrorism were not so prevalent. "An eye for an eye" never resolves anything and only leads to more blindness and destruction. I do understand the pent-up and festering frustration, rage, and feelings of unworthiness and dehumanization that can result in senseless and drastic events that leave a deep scar on an individual, on our democracy, and on our nation's heart.

In my heart, retaliation is never justified. I never condone violence, wrongful killings, or murder, but I realize how they can occur. Early in my life, I saw and felt the institutional racism and inequality that permeate our nation. A reaction to these underlying issues manifested itself in a vicious, heinous act of murder by a man in Dallas who had served in the U.S. military. He must have felt such profound despair and rage that murder, an act so abhorrent to him, was the only means to express his vehement anger and hatred.

I heard the word *unfair* expressed about the tragedy, but those in blue who take an oath to dedicate their lives to serve and protect are fully aware of the heroism expected from them and the risks they face each day. But what is fair about the innocent youth, especially males of African heritage, who are fully aware that each day they or their loved ones are at risk of being frisked, arrested, maimed, or killed—sometimes even in the safety and comfort of their own homes— just because of the color of their skin? They did not take an oath to protect anyone, but they are assured equal protection under the Equal Protection Clause of the Fourteenth Amendment to the Constitution, which was established within the first century of our nation. Now, more than ever, we each have to assume more responsibility to enlighten those within our families and communities about prejudice and quell any outright racism toward either Black, white, gay, Muslim, Jew, Latino, or any label that designates those different from you as "other."

The same Creator or force universally bestowed our spirits, our source. Ultimately, our *source-connection* is the key to every other individual. When we *source-connect* with one another, we are at one with the spirit of the other person and there are no labels, preconceived ideas, or feelings of suspicion or mistrust floating inside our heads. We believe in our hearts and souls that each individual is a fellow human being, an equal member of our U.S. American family, and an equal member of our extended global family. In this spirit, we interact respectfully with compassion and kindness. This belief advances inclusion and a sense of belonging as our arms spiritually reach around our planet. To embrace those who wish to do us harm will be challenging for most. Nevertheless, we can feel compassion toward those individuals whose hatred festers and who espouse evil and continue to believe in our hearts that somewhere, buried deep beneath all that hatred and distrust, is the human spirit that remains perpetually pure.

As I previously stated, even when laws are established, little will happen until our hearts and souls are willing to look within and monumentally reduce all injustices and pervasive inequality that we hold. I suggest that we set the service of the most esteemed police officers and chiefs as the standard by which we measure ourselves as a nation. We must uphold our Constitution and justly and equally provide the same benefits of access to clean air, food, water, shelter, education, health care, and safety. Then, each will finally enjoy their deserved rights and the dignity to live without fear, see the fruition of their and their loved ones' endowed potential, and obtain the same opportunities and pleasures that many people of other heritages consistently experience.

In the introduction of Bryan Stevenson's compelling book *Just Mercy: A Story of Justice and Redemption*, he relates about his first visit with a prisoner in Alabama. Stevenson began by profusely apologizing for his lack of experience in law. Even so, the prisoner was so elated that he grabbed Stevenson's hand. Stevenson revealed that a few moments later, the man "squeezed my hands tighter and tighter," saying, "You are the first person I've met in over two years after coming to death row who is not another death row prisoner or death row guard" (Stevenson 2014). The man who was imprisoned reached such comfort with Stevenson that he allowed his emotions to surface. Then, he and Stevenson conversed on a broad range of topics and even laughed together. What was supposed to be a one-hour visit stretched into three hours before the guard angrily dismissed him.

Stevenson focuses on the narrative of numerous individuals and their cases whose outcomes were unjustified, cruel, and merciless. He presents a lengthy, in-depth discussion that highlights legal rulings that significantly stand in the way of equal justice, especially against those of African heritage in Alabama. These rulings include the sentencing of mentally disabled people and minors, who are tried as adults, to lifetime sentences; deplorable conditions in the prison system; excessive sentencing for crimes that did not warrant the length of imprisonment; and judicial and jury misconduct that results in wrongful sentencing. At times, even when the evidence presented against them was dubious, individuals who strongly claimed innocence have spent many years of their lives behind bars. Sometime later, evidence provided by DNA testing proved that many were innocent.

Stevenson represented a prisoner of African heritage who was condemned to death row even though all the evidence indicated that this man was innocent. Although the man had established a reputable business, he was known for his philandering and an affair with a woman of European heritage. Although the courts had already overturned the "antimiscegenation" laws, culturally, they still existed in the minds of many people in the South. When another woman of European heritage was murdered, although persons testified of his presence with them at the time of the crime and other information clearly showed his innocence, the man was found guilty of murder and sentenced to the death penalty. In 1993, Stevenson appealed several times until finally, on the fifth appeal of *McMillian v. State*, the man was exonerated and set free.

Issues that obstructed justice in the first place included the fact that witnesses lied and prosecution did not disclose exculpatory evidence that would have indicated his innocence. Stevenson also suggests that perhaps those former laws regarding race mixing were on the judges' minds when they made their rulings (Stevenson 2014).

Although Stevenson was not directly involved in the 2005 U.S. Supreme Court *Roper v. Simmons* ruling that the death penalty for juveniles was unconstitutional, he was a strong vocal advocate for that principle. In 2012, Stevenson successfully argued before the U.S. Supreme Court in the *Miller v. Alabama* ruling that life without parole for juveniles was unconstitutional.

With the unjust principles and cases presented and further noted on social media and the news, we must question how society or the system can possibly pay restitution for the dehumanization of the human spirit and the suffering and loss of these individuals' loved ones. These individuals have endured bitter separation caused by unjustifiably harsh death sentences out of proportion to their loved ones' crimes, or worse, the wrongful execution of people later determined to have been innocent, or still worse, the death of a child or a mentally disabled person who lacked mental health care and the ability to understand their crime or its ramifications.

In a 2016 edition of *The New Yorker*, Jeffrey Toobin penned a compelling profile of Bryan Stevenson, the Founder and Executive Director of the Equal Justice Initiative (EJI). Stevenson is no newcomer to obtaining justice for people of African heritage. During his studies at Harvard Law School, he took a month's absence in 1983 because the courses there "seemed esoteric and disconnected from the race and poverty issues" (Toobin 2016). During that time, Stevenson discovered his "calling" while serving as an intern in Alabama at what was then named the Southern Prisoners Defense Committee. Since then, "he has spared a hundred and twenty-five offenders from execution" (Toobin 2016).

Stevenson lives in Montgomery, Alabama, the location of historical markers celebrating the Confederacy. When he initially petitioned to place markers where lynchings had taken place in Montgomery, his petition was denied. Eventually, permission was granted. Stevenson realized that "the markers will give you a little snapshot, but we need to tell the whole story." When he first addressed a diverse group of volunteers about his dream, he stated, "I continue to believe that we're not free in this country, that we're not free at birth [in] a history of racial injustice" (Toobin 2016). Stevenson feels that a shadow follows those of African heritage as they seek equality and justice.

At last, he began his latest major project, *Race and Poverty*, which includes the Lynching Markers Project. These bring to light a resurrected history of violence against those of African heritage. The *Race and Poverty* project also includes the Memorial for Peace and Justice, meant to create a rich, deep space as a comprehensive memorial for the thousands of lynching victims. The intention of the memorial is to highlight their stories and honor those individuals by displaying their names and the reasons they were lynched. At times, the fatal error might merely have been a Black person accidently bumping into a person of European heritage. Although I have mentioned lynchings in this book, lynching certainly is not a topic that often—or ever—comes up in mainstream media or in conversations within the homes of those of other cultural heritages.

On the August 22, 2016, edition of *CBS This Morning*, Stevenson pointed out that the United States never raised awareness about slavery in the South by displaying historical markers similar to the multitude of markers and flags commemorating the Confederacy. He also noted that the national holiday commemorating Dr. Martin King is jointly named and celebrated as Martin Luther King–Robert E. Lee Day in two Southern states. Stevenson further states that South Africa has an Apartheid Museum and Rwanda has a memorial that acknowledges the impact of genocide. Germany erected memorials to pay tribute to those who died in concentration camps and encourages that "visitors go to Auschwitz," the worst of all concentration camps. "Even in Berlin there are markers on stones to note the homes of Jewish families whom they abducted during the Holocaust" (King 2016b).

Stevenson recalled that the "old people of color" were the first to remind him that those who say that there was no domestic terrorism until 9/11 are incorrect, as lynchings qualify as racial terrorism. Stevenson was the first person that I heard to link the word *terrorism* with lynchings, pointing out that these and other murders were perpetrated with "complete impunity." The Memorial for Peace and Justice will honor the millions of African Americans whom slavery plagued and traumatized. Stevenson continues that while lynchings no longer occur outdoors in town squares, the practice continues inside prisons under the guise of the death penalty. He further claims that the millions of African Americans who fled the South to the North did so primarily as refugees from terror. Stevenson's gentle soul beacons softly as he passionately speaks from the heart to simply enlighten and seek justice. In an article in *The New Yorker*, Anthony Romero, the Executive Director of the American Civil Liberties Union, states, "Most of us who do this kind of work are good. He's head and shoulders above us all. He's a genius. He's our Moses" (Toobin 2016).

Since I never comprehended the depth of racism in the United States, especially against those of African heritage, I often wondered if there was another element besides experience or lack of enlightenment in those people who chose to watch and enjoy lynching decades ago. I often question if there is an unknown factor, or lack thereof, that was passed down to their descendants who still hold such fixed views of deep racial hatred.

Most significant during this national dialogue season was the inauguration in the fall of 2016 of the Smithsonian National Museum of African American History and Culture (NMAAHC), a museum of "a people's journey and a nation's story" (https://nmaahc. si.edu/). It serves as an affirmation of the awesome contributions that those of African heritage gave to enrich our national tapestry and our lives.

Founding Director Lonnie G. Bunch III's passion and tenacity steered a vision into a monumental testament. The visionary seed, planted one hundred years ago by Civil War veterans and supporters of African heritage, was carried forward for generations until congressman and activist John Lewis from Georgia tirelessly devoted his time for fifteen years to secure a commitment to build this century-old dream. In 2003, President George W. Bush designated the last five acres on the National Mall for its site. Funds were raised equally between those allotted by Congress and donated by institutions and corporations, along with support from the Smithsonian Institute and about one hundred thousand new members from a broad spectrum of humanity and multiple walks of life. Even more significant were the thousands of people who trustfully opened their hearts, shared their stories, and donated thirty-six thousand artifacts, all of which served as an impetus to inspire and propel the project forward.

The NMAAHC's stunning, innovative bronze edifice features a multitiered corona inspired by an African statue now displayed in the museum. Through stories, sayings, and memorabilia, the museum magnificently showcases the achievements and continuous breakthroughs of our sisters and brothers, those who left a known mark and those whose mark was only known to a few—until now. These highlight their spirit, struggle, faith, hope, resilience, and triumphs during slavery and the outstanding ways in which they contributed their cultural exceptionalism to make the United States democracy the greatest idea in the world. The monument stands to validate those of African heritage who never lost hope or gave up. Instead, they forged ahead to continue to break racial barriers and create broad shoulders for the next generation to stand upon and lead forward.

During the opening ceremony, Congressman Lewis passionately stated, "This museum is a testament to the dignity of the dispossessed in every corner of the globe who yearns for freedom. It is a song to the scholars and scribes, scientists and teachers, to the revolutionaries and voices of protest, to the ministers and the authors of peace. It is the story of life, the story of our lives" (C-SPAN 2016). For his passionate and tenacious efforts, the iconic John Lewis was honored as the Godfather of the National Museum of African American History and Culture.

Former First Lady Laura Bush served on the advisory council, and President Bush added profound support of the museum with his remarks. He forthrightly criticized Americans' "original sin" and cited John Adams, who called slavery "an evil of colossal magnitude." The president testified that the museum shows "our commitment to truth" as it tells of "a country founded on the promise of liberty [that] held millions in chains." He continued, "A great nation does not hide its history. It faces its flaws and corrects them" (C-SPAN 2016).

Chancellor of the Smithsonian Institution and Chief Justice John G. Roberts Jr. cited three historical cases that he described as "documents of shame and hope along the road to equal justice under the law." He cited *Scott v. Sanford*, which is the case of Dred Scott, a slave who, after his owner died, tried to purchase his and his family's freedom with money it took his entire life to save. When his owner's widow refused to allow his freedom, Scott turned to the courts, but they ruled that he and his family were not even persons under the law. Roberts stated, "The court made a mistake." The second case cited was *Plessy v. Ferguson*, which became a test case for the Jim Crow laws. Roberts stated, "The courts would fail." The story of Oliver and Linda Brown's faith and courage to enroll their eleven-year-old daughter in an all-white school became the triumphant case of *Brown v. Board of Education*, which "changed America forever." Roberts concluded that cases are there to read how the courts reacted, "but if you want to know what these people were about, you can do that in this new museum" (C-SPAN 2016).

After praising those of a multitude of backgrounds, including the "famous and the neighbor next door," for their support and contributions, Kenneth Chenault, Council Advisory member and American Express CEO, offered this heartfelt and profound comment: "I think my parents, ancestors, the Chenaults and the Quicks, are more at peace." He resonated what many voiced: "What brings us together is stronger than what keeps us apart" (C-SPAN 2016).

Linda Johnson Rice, Council Co Chair of NMAAHC, spoke proudly of her parents, John H. and Eunice W. Johnson of Chicago, creators of *Ebony* and *Jet* publications. These were the first magazines devoted to Black lives. The editors filled their pages with stories, ideas, and aspirations that "allowed us to see ourselves as we had never before, to make us proud of what we have done and can do." Engaging the brightest writers, "thinkers, trendsetters, activists, celebrities, and next-generation leaders," the successful magazines' message and appeal "ignited conversation and became a catalyst for progress and pride" (C-SPAN 2016).

When President Obama elaborated on the significance of the mostly untold stories housed within, he began by noting that until now, they did not teach our history in its full content, dismissing and leaving behind much of the story and context. An exhibit near the sign that declares the familiar words "All men are created equal" displays a historical marker from Hagerstown, Maryland, that reads, "General Andrew Jackson and Henry Clay spoke from this slave block during the year 1830."

Obama continued by asking us to consider what the marker fails to tell us:

> On a stone, where day after day, for years, men and women were torn from their spouse or their child, shackled, and bound, and bought, and sold, and bid like cattle, on a stone worn down by the tragedy of over one thousand feet. For a long time, the only thing we considered important, the singular thing we once chose to commemorate as history, with a plaque, were the unmemorable speeches of two powerful men. And that block, I think, explains why this museum is so necessary, because that same object reframed, put in context, tells us so much more. (C-SPAN 2016)

The president acknowledged the necessity for a people to know its history by knowing those who led in battle and debates and those who "created industries and erected cities." He added that when a culture cheats, it "ignores or forgets" to include the millions and millions who also toiled for liberty and equality. He expanded, "There were also those who fought in battles to save our Union, served as teachers, cooks, maids, and workers, who built this nation just as surely, whose humble eloquence, whose calloused hands, whose steady drive, helped to create cities, erect industries, build the arsenals of democracy" (C-SPAN).

Toward the end of President Obama's speech, he remarked that he hopes the experience at the museum helps all individuals talk with one another, whatever their experiences or background. But more importantly, he hopes that they will listen and "see how our stories are bound together." He urged each to fully realize that everyone can make a mark.

Through striking displays of artifacts, memorabilia, photographs, quotations, replicas, and sculptures, NMAAHC celebrates leaders' achievements in areas of civil rights, politics, sports, entertainment, science, magazines, newspapers, and the military. These and numerous topics are easily viewed on their website, https://nmaahc.si.edu. They depict the life of a slave, individuals in the Jim Crow era, and those more recently. They also include Harriet Tubman's hymnal, Nat Turner's Bible, a dress sewn by Rosa Parks, a portrait of Frederick Douglass, a Pinback button featuring Martin Luther King Jr., and Andrew Young Addressing Marchers, Selma to Montgomery March, a photograph by James H. Karales. The following are also included: a baseball signed by Jackie Robinson, Olympian Jesse Owens' cleats, Olympian Carl Lewis' nine gold medals, uneven bar grips used by Olympian Gabby Douglas, and a terry cloth robe worn by Muhammad Ali. The *Musical Crossroads Exhibit* displays Louis Armstrong's trumpet, Chuck Berry's bright red Cadillac Eldorado convertible, rapper Chuck D's boom box, and a poster of a James Brown concert.

The museum houses a plane and a jacket that used to belong to one Tuskegee airman who flew 149 missions, while "white" soldiers flew only 50. A pilot's daughter reflected on the bittersweet moment when her dad returned home and he was met with the painfully familiar segregating restroom signs indicating "white" and "colored" (Rose, King, and O'Donnell 2016b). A descendant of a slave donated her great-great-great-grandfather's heirloom, a handwritten and meticulously folded letter, preserved in a small square tin box, proving that he was no longer a slave but a freedman.

One of the most challenging decisions that Bunch had to make was whether to display Emmett Till's casket. Till lived in Chicago, and while visiting Mississippi, he whistled at a white woman and was killed. This event galvanized the civil rights movement. Bunch had met Emmett's mother, Mamie Till Mobley, before her death; she told Bunch of her courageous choice to keep her son's casket open at his funeral (Thompson 2016). She told Bunch, "'Emmett was martyred on the cross of racial injustice,' and she wanted the world to see what they did to her son." Bunch agreed "that the world should see."

The casket is displayed atop a pedestal across from a mural of the choir singing at his funeral services. This sacred memorial is located on a lower, darker level, along with a slave ship that sank off the coast of South Africa. Till's mother poignantly declared, "What this museum is going to do is make sure that America remembers that at one point we killed our children." Deputy Director Kinshasha Holman Conwill remarked that it's "one of our most sacred objects" (Thompson 2016).

Displayed nearby is a small wooden cabin from Edisto, South Carolina. Within the cabin where a slave family lived, there is a set of tiny shackles that could only fit a young child. What an ugly scar the memory of these exhibits leave on our nation's soul. Sadly, similar events and scenes continue in our country.

The inclusion of 477 sayings of "famous and regular—often struggling—folk of Black voices were a top priority for Director Bunch" (Rose, King, and O'Donnell 2016b). Most, if not all, public figures of African heritage that you are aware of will somehow be included at the NMAAHC.

"Making a way out of no way" is the underlying theme of the museum's experience. An abundance of quotes is displayed throughout the museum, but I include a few that especially spoke to me (Conwill 2016). These enduring quotes include the following:

> Either the United States will destroy ignorance or ignorance will destroy the United States.
>
> —W. E. B. Du Bois

> None of us got where we are solely by pulling ourselves up by our boot-straps. We got here because somebody—a parent, a teacher, an Ivy League crony or a few nuns—bent down and helped us pick up our boots.
>
> —Justice Thurgood Marshall
> U.S. Supreme Court

> The way to right wrongs is to turn the light of truth upon them.
>
> —Ida B. Wells-Barnett
> Civil rights activist and original member of NAACP

If you are always trying to be normal, you will never know how *amazing* you can be.

—Maya Angelou

For while the tale of how we suffer, and how we are delighted, and how we may triumph is never new, it always must be heard.

—James Baldwin

In addition, Oprah Winfrey cited one of her favorite quotes by Toni Morrison, Nobel Peace Prize laureate in literature: "If there is a book that you want to read but it hasn't been written yet, then you must be the one to write it." Ava DuVernay, the independent filmmaker, summed up her response to rejection: "It's not about knocking on closed doors, it's about building our own house and having our own door."

A grateful, jubilant Lonnie Bunch began with, "A dream deferred too long is a dream no longer." During the course of the project, a journalist asked him if he believed he could actually achieve this goal. He responded, "How could we not believe when we can dip into the reservoir that is the African-American history? We believe because the enslaved dreamed of a world of freedom that once seemed impossible." He recalled the names of civil rights leaders Malcolm, Martin, Ella Baker, and Fanny Lou Hamer, who believed in an America that did not believe in them "and because a senator from Chicago told us 'yes we can'" (C-SPAN 2016).

Bunch thanked the collaboration of a "dream team" of creators, architects, designers, builders, intellects, his family, countless others, and especially, "all the amazing workers who, in the process of construction, soon realized that this was their building. This was their history as well" (C-SPAN 2016).

Bunch shared his heartfelt connection with the museum: "When I look at the museum, I do not simply see steel, glass, and concrete. I feel the spirits, hopes, and strengths of those who went before and upon whose shoulders we stand. It is those memories that breathe life into this building." Bunch felt the clarion call to remember the well-known and those more reserved, known only to a few, who each shaped this nation. He also reminded us of the pain of slavery, segregation, and second-class citizenship. But he also uplifted as he encouraged us to find the faith, hope, joy, and resilience that are a dominant feature of the African American community.

"We remember not out of nostalgia, but out of needs for the contact—from the contextualization and clarity from an unvarnished history. That may be that understanding can help America find healing and reconciliation. We remember so all that encounter the museum will understand American history through an African American lens and understand how central African American history and culture is to America's sense of self" (C-SPAN 2016).

At the conclusion of the celebration, President Obama introduced the oldest member of the four-generation Bonner family, Ruth, now ninety-nine, whose father became a doctor after he was freed. She and her young great-granddaughter, with the helping hand of First Lady Michelle Obama, rang a bell from the oldest Baptist Black church (of 1776) in Virginia. This bell also rang in harmony with others across the nation, celebrating emancipation and the end of slavery more than 150 years ago.

Prior to the grand opening of the NMAAHC, *CBS This Morning* devoted almost its entire two-hour program to preview the museum and interviewed many noteworthy individuals who offered significant comments. Colin Powell, the first Black Chair of the Joint Chiefs of Staff, stated that those of African heritage "were always willing to serve the nation, before it was there to serve them." Attorney General Loretta Lynch of Greensboro, North Carolina, shared that her father was a minister who supported the four Black youths who defied a posted segregation sign and refused to leave their seats at a Woolworth's lunch counter. Her father allowed the youth to use the church's basement to organize their protest, which grew into a nationwide movement. A stool from that lunch counter in Lynch's hometown is exhibited in the museum. Simone Manuel, first Gold Medal Olympian swimmer of African heritage, conveyed that she once felt the social strain of not fitting in. She continued by saying that she would bridge a gap for the generation behind her.

When I saw the preview of the NMAAHC, especially after I watched the opening ceremony, I felt such deep joy and pride that we had reached such a monumental milestone toward ensuring equality. I am especially grateful for my sisters and brothers and all people who will experience this treasure trove, now seen through the eyes of an African American lens. I can anticipate the elated bonding, pride, laughter, tears, and raised consciousness of all who visit this miracle on the mall, as it remains an evolving experience with a continuum of new stories. May the NMAAHC always beam brightly as a symbol of how far we have come and serve to enlighten, inspire, and uplift, to further reconciliation and healing, and to find commonality. Then, as human beings in our shared core ideals, we unite soul to soul and arm in arm toward that "more perfect union."

If you see people in your neighborhood who are of differing age groups, minority cultures, or styles, find a natural way to engage with them as fellow human beings. If the connection feels right, continue to build a relationship as you would with any person whose company you enjoy. You may be surprised what delights you discover. I found one of my dearest friends that way.

Would any of us like to be judged solely based on artificial labeling or placed in a category created by another person's perspective? I don't think so. I adamantly do not believe these harmful, demeaning labels and preconceptions were generated by our Creator. We each are a miracle endowed with glorious gifts and bodily characteristics that evolve over time.

Following is some food for thought simply meant to make a point. Many functions aren't even engaged at birth. Some functions don't even develop in the first years of life; some lie dormant for more than a decade. If whatever pure force created us envisioned that we required a label that would be divisive or discriminatory, at some point, wouldn't that label pop up, similar to the way our sets of teeth erupt?

We gained an in-depth recognition of our *preconceived ideas* about people, circumstances, events, and our *external lenses*. Consequently, we now realize how these disruptive and destructive misconceptions and false judgments distort how we perceive, process, and then act toward others. We must be crystal clear that when we act upon those thoughts, specifically prejudice, we also deny far too many of our fellow citizens their basic human rights, civil rights, voting rights, and equal opportunities. They are blocked from legitimate access to avenues meant to be awarded to all free persons. By denying them the opportunity to breathe fresh air, drink clean water, attain healthy nutrition and adequate education and health care, or amass sufficient wealth and power due to lack of opportunity and fair pay for hard work, we demean and obliterate the core values and principles of our idea of democracy and ultimately demean ourselves.

This profound immorality is the monumental injustice and attempted dehumanization that any of our *external lenses* or prejudice creates. That dishonor in no way reflects the person's genuine character or how they live their lives. These false perceptions cannot be healthy for anyone's well-being. It tramples upon the essence of a human being and robs their deserved dignity and serenity, and at a systemic level, it damages our serenity as well. We now move to eliminate or reduce our *external lenses*.

Identify, Block, Move, Delete, Replace (IBMDR) Technique for External Lenses

Similar to the *IBMDR Technique for internal lenses*, we now engage the *IBMDR Technique* to help *erase* and *replace* your *external lenses*. Once we truly recognize how abusive and obsolete your *external lenses* are, we begin the process. After you have *identified* your *external lenses*, list those *lenses*. First, list the preconceptions, then the biases, prejudices, or racism toward others based on cultural heritage, religion, political leanings, or any other negative bias you carry.

Think through each *lens* and step. Take your time to gain a clear recognition of the event, situation, or experience that created those negative thoughts, your *external lenses*. Was that preconception, *external lens*, bias, prejudice, or racism a response to a personal experience relating to you or a parent, caregiver, relative, or friend? Or was it a response to a perception or an event in your home, primary village, hood, tribe, clan, or neighborhood? Or did you acquire it from peers, teachers, clergy, community leaders, social networks, or the media? To gain awareness, prioritize your *external lenses* by placing the *lens* that is most demeaning to others at the top of your list. Then, one by one, recall, reflect, and *identify* the situation, conversation, or event that initially created those preconceptions, *lenses*, biases, stereotypes, prejudices, or racism that led to that *external lens*.

When did you apply each *external lens* to a select group of people or similar situations? Reflect on whether you think those views are obsolete, invalid, or unjust. These ideas dishonor others, and they certainly do not reflect your best. And what do your nonverbal, voice-tone, verbal, and written communication convey? Do you want to create comfort and trust in which family members as well as individuals of any religion, gender, sexual orientation, age, political leaning, background, or situation feel ease in approaching or being receptive to you? Do you want to uplift rather than push down others? Do you now hold a more positive and inclusive worldview, and do you want to make that change permanent? Do you want to do the right thing, be on the right side of history, and update and exchange your preconceived ideas, biases, stereotypes, or racism? If so, please proceed.

Choose the first *external lens* to eliminate. Now, *block* each specific *external lens*, similar to *blocking* text in a document. Visualize placing the thought of that particular *external lens* at shoulder height behind you to indicate that this is a perception, idea, experience, bias, or prejudice from the past. Then, use your right or left arm to comfortably reach behind you as far as you can. Next, with your open hand, grab and bring forward the *blocked* distorted *external lens*, perception, bias, judgment, prejudice, or experience. Then, *move* the negative idea into the present moment, directly in front of your open or closed eyes, until you feel a deep sense of it. When you have a strong sense of the demeaning impact of your *external lens*, temporarily *move* to the side the memory of the past perception, bias, prejudice, judgment, thought, or experience.

Now, list and pull together a clear sense of how you want to *replace* your former biased, demeaning, or distorted perceptions and thoughts for ones that encourage truth and harmony. Following are suggestions for positive, inclusive views and ideas to embrace: oneness, respect, equality, acceptance, accord, compassion, fairness, kindness, understanding, and at the very least, tolerance.

Next, one by one, bring in front of you each of the former preconceptions and biased, prejudiced, racist *external lenses* and demeaning thoughts of others that you had temporarily set aside. Again, place each *external lens* in front of your open or closed eyes. Keep in mind that these *external lenses* block and rob us of our best—our purest, most genuine *source-connection*—by creating harmful, depleting energy within that also affects others, our planet, and the universe. Continue to *delete*, one by one, each former negative *external lens*. Visualize tapping the Delete key on a keyboard while focusing on *deleting* each harmful, demeaning *external lens* from your mind.

Now, one by one, *replace* each of your former *external lenses* with just, inclusive, uplifting, and *source-connected* feelings and thoughts about your fellow human beings. Since you now possess a heightened awareness of your preconceptions, biases, and *external lenses*, as those former negative *external lenses* occasionally pop into your head, continue to repeat the *IBMDR Technique* until your former *external lenses* no longer harbor any biased, prejudiced, or racist thoughts about or directed at others. Be patient; this takes time, but it works.

To make these new insights and ideas permanent, you first create a clear vision in your mind and sense in your heart and soul of your newly discovered and enlightened beliefs of others. Then, most compelling, you *download* to *save* and *feel*, not in your head, but *below in your heart and soul*. Only when the new belief is *downloaded* and *saved* in our hearts and souls do these new, undistorted, inclusive ideas, beliefs, feelings, and perceptions become our *new truth*. Again, this is similar to downloading a document that you received and want to save on a digital device. Reviewing the information is not enough. You must engage the *save* command to access the ideas and feelings in the future.

Once these *external lenses* are no longer a part of your mind-set, you will feel lighter and more peaceful. You also will be gratified to know that as a change agent, you made a commitment to help heal your fellow human beings and hasten the world's transition into a better place.

Awareness

Over the years, several service providers of African, Asian, and Latino heritage have shared that often, upon first approaching a client's home or place of work, they can immediately sense whether they will feel welcome or wish that they could turn around and leave.

A few years ago, I saw an article in one of the leading news magazines in which the depictions of prejudice and racism jumped out at those who were aware. The article focused on a range of vehicles offered by a ride-sharing company. The piece included an illustration that presented four passengers, three automobiles, and a van.

The four types of vehicles that appeared began with those that were the most expensive and offered the most services. Entering the high-tech, sleek, and lengthy sedan was a fashionable woman wearing stiletto heels and a perfectly tailored navy suit; her blond hair was meticulously pulled back into a ponytail. She was clearly of European heritage. Entering the next vehicle, a hatchback that displayed funky car art, was a hip dude covered with tattoos, donning a T-shirt, and wearing thick-rimmed black glasses. He had dark curly reddish hair, and his heritage was not easy to decipher. The next car was a van; the ad showed a woman whose cell phone was dead, so she was thrilled that the vehicle was new and provided a charging USB port. She was dressed as chic as the first woman, but her hair and complexion resembled a woman of Asian or Latino heritage. The last car was a highly dented taxi that resembled former New York City police car models. It bore a sign on the side stating, "Taxi Rules." The man approaching that taxi was slouching, wore a wrinkled suit, and had disheveled hair. He was of African heritage, and he decided to pass and just walk.

Every person of a minority culture to whom I showed the article immediately saw the bias. Those people included family and friends whose professions encompassed a wide range, including service providers, medical experts, authors, professional colleagues, and high-ranking educators. I also showed the illustration to many people of European heritage who, over decades, shared their experiences, political preferences, and inclusive views. Most of these people expressed views that were socially progressive; I never heard a prejudiced thought or idea uttered by any of them. Except for two people, none of them saw the bias. That was a huge wake-up call for me. These people are caring, loving, and generous of heart, mind, and spirit. Some socialize with people of several differing minorities but are just totally unaware.

I recall in the 2013 context of voting rights and racial discrimination in U.S. elections, Hillary Clinton stated, "Anyone that says that racial discrimination is no longer a problem in American elections must not be paying attention" (Clinton 2013). Since then, much has transpired. People all over the world have witnessed and peacefully demonstrated against the horrific death of George Floyd and sadly several others.

I offer my views and experiences and those of others not to judge, but to enlighten, inspire, and uplift. As I often state, "You have to be aware to care, and if you care you are aware."

If you continue to enslave yourself in chains and shackles because of any condition under which you suffer or anything that you strongly feel you lack—if you, your ancestors, or others were enslaved spiritually, physically, emotionally, and mentally—I plead from the deepest place in my heart, BREAK your chains and unshackle your spirit. Spiritually free yourself of any condition that you developed that was imposed on you by your ancestors or society, or which enslaved a person and framed you. At the same time, also acknowledge that you have enabled that bondage by allowing those ideas and thoughts—which you consume and continue to hold tight—to have remained sealed within until now.

I have sensed enslavement in your voices, I have heard it in your words, I have seen it in your eyes, I have read it in your stories, I have experienced it in my loved ones' expressions and halted responses, and I have felt your piercing pain in my heart. You, just like everyone else, are far, far greater than anyone horrific experience or history. You and I, and those not yet born, and every other human being on this earth, past and present, came from the same vast, rich, beautiful, historical ancestry. In the Rift Valley of that ancient, abundantly endowed continent named Africa, the cradle of civilization began. I plead with everything that I have within that you rip off any yoke that stifles you, and that you and every person who remain captured and bound by a condition with which they were born, developed, or that family or society thrust on them—please break free.

The previous two paragraphs were inspired by an epiphany with a recognized person. That piece was penned under the umbrella of President Barack Hussein Obama's era with the deepest trust and belief that we would continue as a nation to move forward in a similar vein, even if not always at the same pace. President Obama consistently appealed to the better angels within us. But with a new, uncharted U.S. American course and environment, how much of that self-proclaimed liberty, which is fervently supported by millions of people, will understandably be scrutinized by each situation, and ultimately acted upon by each individual.

Individuals who experience discrimination or racism are highly attuned to pick up the lingo and vibes. Whenever we interact with another person without attaching any preconceived label or history, we perceive and experience that human being soul to soul. In that purest *source-connection*, others sense that trusting and deep connection. In a spiritual realm that remains the only pure way to interact with one another.

Glance at the sky that encapsulates our planet, which at some instant most can view. As you breathe in the air whose molecules have circled the planet, wonder how many other human beings have and will inhale and exhale those exact molecules. Perhaps you, along with every other person who has breathed and will breathe those molecules, added an invisible and undetectable molecule to it, and every other person until eternity will repeat—adding their one-and-only minuscule "breathspeck" as well.

Often, well-meaning, inclusive-minded, and caring people simply aren't aware enough to fully comprehend the manifestations of discrimination. I refer again to my meeting with the dean who had moderated a panel after the screening of the movie *Waiting for Superman*. After also I had mentioned that I had first become aware of prejudice at the early age of seven, discussing my life in Nevis totally immersed in local culture, the dean asked me, "Ruth, how would you help my staff and students identify prejudice within themselves?" Similar to the *source-connection* and *hand-dome*, the initial idea flowed down through me, and I expressed that insight with him. Over time and reflection, that seed evolved into the following exercise.

Forman Approach to Identifying Prejudice Within Ourselves

Before we begin, please find a quiet spot where you will be undisturbed. Move deeply within to engage in a private and nonjudgmental experience to identify bias, stereotyping, prejudice, or racism within yourself, of which you may be totally unaware, or a suspicion or discomfort of which you are aware. Take some moments, close your eyes, center yourself and feel a strong and deep connection with your soul, your essence. Reflect and ask yourself, "Who am I, and what is meaningful to me?" Connect deeply within to your special characteristics: gifts and traits that you bring to the world. Also, connect with the passion that drives and motivates you to dream, reach, achieve, strive, and thrive. Now, reflect on your likes, dislikes, fears, challenges, limitations, and boundaries. Include your family, lifestyle, surroundings, neighborhood, socioeconomic and educational level, and appearance. Again, ponder on how you feel and think about yourself and your self-worth and how you think others perceive and react to you.

Once you have a clear sense of who you are, continue keeping your eyes closed, as there is going to be a transformation. Nothing changes about your essence, your basic nature; all the attributes and imperfections that you possess and the challenges that you face—they all remain intact.

Now, if you are of European heritage, picture that your outward appearance resembles that of a person of African heritage. Conversely, if you are of African heritage, picture that your outward appearance resembles that of a person of European heritage. If you are of Latino heritage, picture that your outward appearance resembles that of a person of Asian heritage. Conversely, if you are of Asian heritage, picture that your outward appearance resembles that of a person of Latino heritage.

Please keep your eyes closed and fully realize that nothing about your essence, basic nature, attributes, imperfections, challenges, family, surroundings, neighborhood, and educational or socioeconomic level has changed except your outward appearance. In any of these instances, would you feel differently about yourself? If so, how? Do you think your family members, neighbors, colleagues, staff, and society would perceive you and react differently toward you? If so, how?

Now, if you are of European heritage, picture that your outward appearance resembles that of a person of Latino heritage. Conversely, if you are of Latino heritage, picture that your outward appearance resembles that of a person of European heritage. And if you are of African heritage, picture that your outward appearance resembles that of a person of Asian heritage. Conversely, if you are of Asian heritage, picture that your outward appearance resembles that of a person of African heritage.

Again, please keep your eyes closed and fully realize that nothing about your essence, basic nature, attributes, imperfections, challenges, family, surroundings, neighborhood, and educational or socioeconomic level has changed except your outward appearance. In any of these instances, would you feel differently about yourself? If so, how? Do you think your family members, neighbors, colleagues, staff, and society would perceive you and react differently toward you? If so, how?

Next, if you are of European heritage, picture that your outward appearance resembles that of a person of Asian heritage. Conversely, if you are of Asian heritage, picture that your outward appearance resembles that of a person of European heritage. And if you are of African heritage, picture that your outward appearance resembles that of a person of Latino heritage. Conversely, if you are of Latino heritage, picture that your outward appearance resembles that of a person of African heritage. Again, please keep your eyes closed and fully realize that nothing about your essence, basic nature, attributes, imperfections, challenges, family, surroundings, neighborhood, and educational or socioeconomic level has changed except your outward appearance. In any of these instances, would you feel differently about yourself? If so, how? Do you think your family members, neighbors, colleagues, staff, and society would perceive you and react differently toward you? If so, how?

Continue this process with the appearance of a person of Pacific Islander, Native American, or First Nations heritage. Picture yourself with the same innate qualities, conditions, and situations while your outward appearance resembles a person of those cultures. Again, please keep your eyes closed and fully realize that nothing about your essence, basic nature, attributes, imperfections, challenges, family, surroundings, neighborhood, and educational or socioeconomic level has changed except your outward appearance. Again ask, In any of these instances, would you feel differently about yourself? If so, how? Do you think your family members, neighbors, colleagues, staff, and society would perceive you and react differently toward you? If so, how?

Next, continue this exercise, changing your outside appearance to include being *handi-abled*, anorexic, obese, and of a different sexual orientation. Continue to picture yourself from different religions, socioeconomic levels, states, or regions within your country, different countries within a continent, or different islands in your geographic region. Would you feel differently about yourself, and do you think your neighbors, society, or those from any other culture would perceive and react differently toward you?

I shared the *Forman Approach to Identify Prejudice Within Ourselves* with people of various professions and walks of life over the last couple of years. Some remained silent, but most expressed surprise after this exercise. One was a woman who is an emigrant from Eastern Europe and specializes in immigration law, primarily serving those of the Latino culture. After I led her through this exercise, she responded, "Wow!" Others responded, "My neighbors won't know me," or "I wouldn't feel different about myself, but I know society would feel that I was inferior."

Before we leave this section, let me firmly state that I strongly support meaningful reparations as the honorable and essential step for individuals of the African Diaspora. Equally, I support equitable and essential national land back acts for the Indigenous Peoples. I leave the details and implementation to the leaders of African heritage, to the chiefs and elders of the various Indigenous Peoples nations, and the three branches of our federal government.

Reaching Out to Make Positive Changes

Hopefully, this guide helps raise awareness of bias, prejudice, racism, discomfort, and suspicion that you truly feel. You were either unaware of this or, at some level, you recognized that these feelings existed but chose to do nothing. The next question you need to ask yourself is, *What am I going to do now?* There are steps that you can take in your awareness and care for our fellow human beings. But first, you make positive and inclusive changes within your hearts, souls, and minds. Then, you genuinely, mindfully, and in a *source-connected* manner deeply feel within your core that we are each fellow human beings. This new mind-set is rarely achieved overnight; the process requires time. If you are truly committed to change, then through your own means, such as self-talk, discussion, group participation, meditation, and prayer, you will achieve this essential and a lofty goal.

Then, you comfortably begin to reach out, converse, and interact with those whom you had not previously felt comfortable approaching. That is a beginning, but only a small piece of the broader scope. Next, set aside time daily, weekly, or however often you can to dedicate yourself to uplifting others. Even if you can only devote a few minutes to help those who have not been privileged to experience life fairly or justly or have access to opportunities, please do so. This effort and commitment allow those who were left behind to gain the ability to attain their rights by honorable means. If you hear a disparaging remark, one that you wouldn't want uttered about your loved ones, or witness something that jumps out at you or subtly smacks of discrimination, prejudice, or racism, muster the courage to speak up in a mindful, *source-connected*, enlightening, forgiving, and nonjudgmental way.

The words "If we each do our part," recently spoken by a person who services our home, prodded me to react genuinely and politely during a public event in a way that I previously had not. I would have commented to those I was with but wouldn't have taken the next and most meaningful step to enlighten others. I began to speak out even more forthrightly when my husband and I attended a concert in a progressive mountain community of a hopeful 2015 springtime. The concert gave tribute to the music and lyrics of Pete Seeger, a legendary protest singer of the past civil rights era. Decades ago, we had taken our children and a relative to Seeger's concert. Now, nestled under the grandeur of majestic oak trees, a diverse artistic group of local and international fame performed. They sang and spoke words about injustice, some mirroring their own experiences. Perhaps these renditions are more relevant now than ever before.

An artist channeled Dr. Martin Luther King Jr.'s speeches. As I listened with closed eyes, enraptured by the words, I felt King's spirit and voice a few feet away. From the depth of her soul, a woman passionately bellowed the feelings of a Black woman. As the artists gathered close together in a long line across the stage at the finale of the first act, it immediately struck me that the performer, who had orated Dr. King's righteous and just words, and the woman, who had moved me with her heartfelt painful words, were off to the side and behind the other artists. The incongruity of it all hit me sharply as I felt that there was definitely something very wrong with this picture. So I found my relative and asked him to draw the performers in line with him for the final bow.

During the intermission, I sought out the director of the venue and, from my *source-connected* heart, passionately pointed out what I had shared with my relative. I told her, "If here in this venue, we can't walk our talk or aren't even aware enough, you can see the deep trouble that this nation is in." She was responsive to my heartfelt message and voiced that she would pass it on to the artists.

After the concert, I walked over to the man who had orated Dr. King's speeches and was also the drummer. After the crowd had left, I expressed what I had seen. During that final song of the first act, as I sat directly in front of where he stood, I had motioned him to move forward, and he acknowledged that he had observed my gesture. I told this gentle fellow human being that he belonged side by side with the other artists, certainly not behind them. I suggested that in the future, if others do not include him in the lineup, he rightfully step forward and, from the heart, simply state, "Excuse me, I want to join you," or "I belong here with you," or whatever words are comfortable and genuine.

At the end of the concert, I noticed that our relative brought these artists forward, in line with the others. My husband and I later sought the female performer, and we told her that she reminded us of one of our dear and passionate Nevisian friends who carries the same name. I suggested to the passionate Black artist that instead of standing on the sidelines, she belongs in the front row, especially for the final bow. She hugged and thanked us. I also hugged our relative and asked him to be aware and carry the gesture forward.

My experience resonated with my Universe-inspired phrase, "You have to be aware to care, and if you care, you are aware." As I previously stated, I believe most of the people living in our United States are good people, but they are just unaware. I believe that during their lives, either these topics were not addressed in their homes, schools, or houses of worship, they did not personally experience prejudice, or they have not yet cared enough to think through it or do anything about it.

A year later, following the unpredicted results of the 2016 presidential election, and in response to the divisive rhetoric that the new president and some of his supporters espoused, many who had never witnessed these massive public rants in our lifetimes—especially during an election cycle—began to speak out.

Lin-Manuel Miranda is a genius and the creator of the undeniably brilliant, revolutionary phenomenon *Hamilton*. The musical portrays the complex life of Founding Father Alexander Hamilton's surly, dissatisfied, but dedicated nature. The production highlights Hamilton's vast sacrifices to the United States, abhorrence of slavery, service as a patriot during the Revolutionary War, major contribution to *The Federalist Papers*, passion in promoting the U.S. Constitution, and profound comprehension of economic policies. Hamilton established the first U.S. national banking system and helped structure federal funding to pay off the states' debt.

The production *Hamilton* debuted in 2015 and was a sensation even before performances began. The rapidly paced rhymed lyrics of the Broadway production include hip-hop, rap, R&B, soul, and other genres. The diverse, multicultural cast replaces our familiar and deeply etched images of the Founding Fathers as men of European heritage. The show radically and permanently altered the historic framing of our founding men and women.

Moreover, shortly after the expressed emotions during the 2016 election, Lin-Manuel Miranda, director Thomas Kail, and producer Jeffrey Sellers learned that vice president elect Mike Pence would attend the performance. They quickly crafted a succinct piece expressing their "alarm" and "anxiety" about the approaching administration while rightfully and passionately proclaiming their hope.

Brandon Victor Dixon, who had recently assumed the role of Aaron Burr, was chosen and accepted the honor of stating their deep concern. After a few modifications, the cast and crew were all aboard as Dixon spoke the following words:

> We, sir—we—are the diverse America who are alarmed and anxious that your new administration will not protect us, our planet, our children, our parents, or defend us and uphold our inalienable rights. We truly hope that this show has inspired you to uphold our American values and to work on behalf of all of us. (Taylor 2016)

A couple of days later, Dixon was a guest on *CBS This Morning* and stated that he feels the "global community demands that we make important statements" (King 2016). The *Hamilton* team wanted to stand up and continue the conversation to "express a message of love and of unity considering all the emotional outpour since the election…and that we're all in this together and no one stands alone." When asked if he heard the president's remarks requesting an apology to Pence, Dixon said, "I heard," and then continued, "There is nothing to apologize for" (Morgan 2016).

Let me pose a question. The military honors a moral code that *we leave no one behind*. Why can we not apply that same moral promise to all the individuals in the United States for whom our valiant soldiers have always fought, sacrificed, or perished while defending our Constitution? Now more than ever, we are aware. If we don't care, don't stand strong, if we give up, become apathetic, or feel we can't make a difference, how can we possibly uphold or advance the basic values of our democracy and the monumental civil rights gained prior to and under the Obama era? A time may approach when you feel a collective righteous indignation in response to words or acts that strike against every core principle for which you have stood and fought, for which our country has symbolized, and which has been defended by righteous people.

These thrusts require an urgent, ongoing, vigilant, diligent, cohesive, collaborative, and galvanized nonviolent coalition of all like-minded national adults and, when appropriate, our youth. We must uphold and broaden positive changes to create an encompassing safe, decent, civil twenty-first-century way to live and lift the heavy burden that affects millions of individuals.

There are individuals of every cultural or religious minority who daily carry the burden of multitasking by first having to factor in their basic safety and minority (or minorities) status before they respond to any comment or situation. There are also those of African heritage who worry each day if the male members of their families will return home with some part of their body dismembered, or even alive.

We remain aware that even when women's lives matter, LGBTQ lives matter, veterans' lives matter, Asian lives matter, European lives matter, Latino lives matter, and Native American lives matter, until all Black lives matter, all lives will not matter. Additionally, even when those of any socioeconomic level's lives matter, *handi-abled* lives matter, those with mental illness's lives matter, and those with addiction's lives matter, until all Black lives matter, all lives will not matter. Moreover, even when Buddhist lives matter, Christian lives matter, Hindu lives matter, Jewish lives matter, Muslim lives matter, nonbeliever lives matter, and Rastafarian lives matter, until all Black lives matter, all lives will not matter. We must stay vigilant, point out, rebuke, and hold accountable those people who dishonorably view women, those of differing sexual orientation, and even worse, abuse children and women or fail to protect them, especially from violence. We must also continue to point out, rebuke, and hold accountable the people who favor emerging congressional policies that reward billionaires over assisting those at poverty level and in the middle class.

We must also continue to point out, rebuke, and hold accountable large organizations and those in power or in Congress who lack the courage, decency, and humanity to act. Finally, we must also hold accountable those who fail to denounce dishonest, divisive, or vitriolic rhetoric or neglect to provide access to or funding for necessary mental health programs. Worse yet is the continued slaughter on our soil of any person who is in the wrong place at the wrong time by those who create carnage with military-style weapons or who lack access to necessary mental health care.

On Martin Luther King day in 2017, the exceptional heroic, humble, nonviolent, lifelong civil rights and voting rights activists Congressman John Lewis declared, "Stand up, speak up. When you see something that is not right, and not fair, and not just, you have a moral obligation to do something, to say something, and not be quiet" (Howard 2017). Lewis became known as the Conscience of Congress, who promoted "good trouble" since his youth. Only in a society where all lives truly matter can that union serve as a beacon of justice to the world, its people, and its stature. This exemplifies an *idea,* named democracy, that is humanly possible. I hope that my generation lives to experience those positive changes that will significantly impact our—and all other—children and grandchildren in our nation and our world.

The youth who usually lead these movements are adept, bold, and willing to create more positive and inclusive solutions than I could ever imagine. In the post-Obama era, a broad, national, and organic grassroots movement of fair-minded folks began to join the charge to champion our nation into a more decent, inclusive, transparent, and fair society. If "we, the people," sisters and brothers, in days, weeks, seasons, not lengthy decades, create hashtags, post on social media, tweet, or join to channel our disgust into righteous acts, we progress to truly realize that every human deserves safety, fairness, and equal access to all opportunities including closing the wealth gap. To truly succeed, the majority has to be on board. As we recall, laws may be in the books, but righteous values become a social norm only when the hearts and souls of the "collective consciousness" of the majority of individuals in the United States refuses to tolerate these national cancers in our midst, especially toward those who are marginalized, maligned, downtrodden, or forgotten.

We of inclusive hearts, souls, and minds must harness our power and continue to commit a daily effort to sign petitions, donate, peacefully and compassionately verbalize, mobilize, demonstrate, and engage in our communities to erase divisiveness and fearmongering. We also denounce the threatened deportations of those of Muslim faith, Latino heritage, or any honorable individual. In Judaism, sins of omission are as faulty as sins of commission; therefore, silence is consent. We must proclaim equality and respect for all. Foremost, we must champion, support and vote for candidates at every level in every election to advance our ideals.

Then, those spewing divisive hatred and violence through racism and xenophobia will either become enlightened and join or be relegated to the sidelines, where they belong. Instead, leaders of decency, integrity, and merit will hasten an inclusive democracy that fairly provides the basic necessities. These include safety, clean air and water, nutritional food, proper housing, quality education, and affordable health care. These basics provide efficient transportation, meaningful employment at fair, living wages, and safety nets for all.

Except for the well-being and safety of my loved ones, and reducing climate change, nothing is more paramount or urgent than the assurance that these basic, just, and inclusive principles are applied to all.

If you are a person who wants to do right and continue to propel and uplift a more righteous and inclusive version of United States for present and future generations, then roll up your sleeves, get involved, and do something productive that promotes equality and liberty for all. Continue to stand strong for the ideals that elevate your conscience and join others to convince our leaders to seek justice. Each positive and inclusive voice, signature, and vote matters. In the modern era, it is a heartwarming phenomenon to realize that masses of fellow individuals among our global community observed injustice and wrongdoings and began to peacefully unite to demonstrate their stance for universal equality.

If we could easily have eradicated prejudice in one fell swoop, it would have been miraculous and already accomplished. However, prejudice has not been eradicated, and we did not attain that goal. Millenniums ago, Rabbi Tarfon said, "Do not be daunted by the enormity of the world's grief. Do justly, now, love mercy, now, walk humbly, now. You are not obligated to complete the work, but neither are you free to abandon it" (Tarfon 2013).

In 2020, a man named George Floyd uttered the words, "I can't breathe" while he pleaded for breath and called out to his Mama with a knee on his neck, as his life slowly faded away. This vision of this inhumane murder went viral and sparked an instant Black Lives Matters peaceful protest that rapidly grew to millions of folks around the world joining in.

During George Floyd's love and inspirational-filled memorial services, his family and friends' words filled the world with hope and a vision. I fervently believe that George Floyd's life and death are catalysts to continue the analysis of underlying racism and hatred with the goal to enlighten, dismantle, and positively transform former divisive and brutal norms of deadly law enforcement policies.

A few months later, another horrific incident occurred in Kenosha, Wisconsin. Jacob Blake was helping with domestic violence and his three children were sitting in the backseat of his car. The police approached him and he moved on to his car to drive away as quickly as possible for the safety of his children. Instead, the police accused him of having a weapon, which he did not have in his possession. There is still some question of whether there was a knife in his car. Without warning, police shot Jacob Blake in the back seven times while his children cried in horror, as crowds were shouting his children are in the car.

That same evening, Kyle Rittenhouse a self-proclaimed vigilante walked down the middle of the streets in Kenosha with a long AR-15 assault weapon flung over his shoulder. Obviously, he was a youth of European heritage as he waved and gave a high five to police officers who offered him water and cheered him on. It wasn't until Rittenhouse walked down the street and killed two innocent people and shot another that the crowd started yelling get that man, he shot two people. Instead of apprehending him, Rittenhouse drove twenty miles to find refuge at home in the neighboring state Illinois, where he was finally apprehended.

The leader of the free world stated that it is sad for any parent to go though what Jacob Blake had endured. However, the leader failed to mention the victim's name. Yet, the leader commended the likes of Rittenhouse. The evidence clearly shows that we are a nation with two distinct justice systems. One system is for those of African heritage and the other system is for those of European heritage. The justice system for those of African heritage is unmistakably more punitive than the consequences for those of European heritage. If this doesn't become as clear as the nose on your face and you cannot see the double-edged sword of democracy in our nation that espouses liberty and justice for all, I encourage you to privately go deep within and look again.

In addition to rectifying the undisputable monumental gap between the two very distinct justice systems, it is imperative that an overhaul current policy and major reforms are established. The goal is not to defund policing, but rather to create a holistic approach and reforms that include transformation of best practices from a warrior role to a guardian and community-based approach, and the punishment fits the crime.

Hopefully in the near future, the George Floyd Justice in Policing Act will be enacted into law. Let us also hope that finally a comprehensive bill is enacted that broadens the former voting rights acts, especially to assist youth, urban minorities, rural and tribal areas, the elderly, those with disabilities, and with limited technology or skills. More than any other moment in history, this inflection point will spring forth a more just world to include all human beings regardless of gender, religion, or ZIP code.

Let me suggest that in any interview and training session, whether in the classroom, business, medical, religious, or law enforcement settings, the *Forman Approach to Identify Prejudice Within Ourselves* is engaged. This technique is private and nonjudgmental. It is a very useful tool, as subtle and nonverbal clues are revealed only to the person who is asking the questions.

If there was ever a time to tread slowly, take baby steps, make sacrifices, or take that leap of faith to become a change agent to eradicate all unjust metastasized cancers in our society, that time is now. Let's follow Anne Frank's lead when she wrote, "How wonderful it is that nobody need wait a single moment before starting to improve the world" (Frank 1952).

To discover those who share similar interests as you seek common ground, become more mindful, listen deeper, and observe better on your walks, during your hikes, at the gym, on your team, in your class, attending family members events, or in houses of gathering or worship. Seize the moment when you can naturally reach out, open your heart, and extend your arms to include a broader spectrum of humanity. Bring into the circle your neighbors, colleagues, staff, service providers, workers, and others, including those of differing, but not divisive deeds and beliefs. For those who are willing to try to connect from the heart without judgment and deeply listen to a person's reasons for their support of leaders or policies that promote divisive and racist attitudes and deeds, may the force be upon you. The goal is to gain understanding. However, if you feel there is an opening, you might also mindfully try to enlighten them.

Everyone's spirits will begin to feel lighter as we mindfully sow compassion, forgiveness, love, goodwill, and understanding to reap and further embrace trusted and treasured connections with others. In time, as people of differing cultures continue to marry and bear children, we will be so blended and better off that the artificial lines of division will fade. Hopefully, the new generation will retain and pass forward their cherished, decent, and uplifting values that others endured and sacrificed to pass on. Then, the visions promoting justice, well-being and inclusion will soar as beacons that shine from within. Perhaps then too, each of us will be solely judged by our hearts, words, and deeds.

As you gain insights by engaging the *Forman Approach to Identify Prejudice Within Ourselves,* be kind to yourself. During and after the transformation, reach out to open your hands, hearts, and homes to others. Offer compassion and understandings as you become and remain source-connected with yourself and every person. The feeling that you are a part of a critical, healing, global movement benefits all. Would any of you in this or any country desire anything less for your loved ones, especially your children, grandchildren, spouses, partners, parents, friends, or neighbors? These broader and trusting connections among all create an essential, decent, desirable, calming, comforting, and refreshing twenty-first century universal paradigm. These ideals bestow a more just, peaceful balance and bring greater civility and harmony to fellow human beings, our community, country, planet, universe, and ourselves.

Soul to Soul Communication

Communication Is Connection

Communication is connection. In connection, there is trust. In trust, learning takes place, problems are solved, and needs are met.

What Is Communication?

Communication is the artful dance and connection that bond us with one another and is the supreme essence of our humanity. It is a vital manifestation of—not separate from—who we each are. Communication is a two-way process of listening and speaking. It is the vehicle through which we perceive, process, reflect, and then affirm, argue, convey, persuade, present, recommend, teach, and state our ideas, thoughts, feelings, and desires.

When we truly respond in the purest, *source-connected, positive communication environment*, suspending all judgment, we learn to listen through our ears and engage our hearts and souls without hidden agendas, ego, tribe or turf affiliation, labels, bias, or prejudice. In this approach, we do our best to optimally perceive and respond.

The most productive human interaction occurs when we receive and deliver messages in a mindful, inclusive, and compassionate manner. Communication encompasses nonverbal communication, voice tone, and verbal communication. Our body language, facial expressions, voice tone, and words are each nuanced and must be consistent with one another to accurately convey our message in a way that speaks our truth.

Figure 2. Ten steps to create a *positive communication environment*.

Reflect on the past week. How often were you misunderstood or afraid to say what you wanted? How often did your words not come out right, or did happenings just not turn out the way you hoped or planned? Did a person misunderstand you, or did you misunderstand another person? Did another person hurt your feelings, or did you inadvertently or purposely hurt another person's feelings? Were your needs and goals met? Were tasks completed the way you had anticipated, or was the person disappointed? Even in the most personal, loving, and familiar relationships, communication breakdowns do occur and unintentional misunderstandings happen. In part, communication breakdowns occur because of how we perceived, processed, and presented the information or because we simply weren't true to ourselves.

No one else knows or experiences us from the inside as we know and experience our total selves, yet I wonder if we truly ever honestly know ourselves. Even Stephen Colbert, host of *The Late Show*, posed the question, "Who is me?" (Colbert 2015). During the show, he underwent a lie detector test and passed. He doesn't lie; he just doesn't always know who he is. Everyone else experiences "us" through their own *lensed* interpretation of our words, deeds, and demeanor. We may be the most sincere, empathetic, caring, helpful, capable, or knowledgeable person, but if our attributes and gifts are not positively, effectively, and appropriately conveyed, no one may ever know, except perhaps those few who know us best—our innermost circle. It not only matters what we feel or think, but more important is how clearly we convey our message through the consistent delivery of all the communication facets. Only in that precise manner do we reflect our truth and come across sincerely and genuinely.

Positive Communication Tapestry

The ideas and feelings woven into our *positive communication tapestry* are essential. Comfort, courage, conviction, and confidence are the four cornerstones, and the words woven within hold the keys that guide us to evoke the most positive responses. We have comfort in knowing who we are, courage to be ourselves, conviction that arises from deep within, and confidence in knowing we express ourselves in the most mindful, *source-connected*, positive, effective, and appropriate way possible. Care, civility, culture, concern, camaraderie, constructiveness, consideration, commonality, community, connection, cooperation, compassion, and compromise, along with the cornerstones, are the woven threads of our thoughts and feelings as we *source-connect* with others.

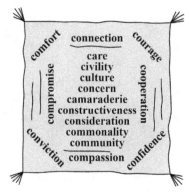

Figure 3. Positive communication tapestry.

Before moving on, we briefly pause to reflect on listening, which is the most essential facet of the two-way communication process. The art of deep and compassionate listening is one of the greatest gifts we offer and reveals how much we respect and care. "Too often we underestimate the power of a touch, a smile, a kind word, a listening ear, an honest compliment, or the smallest act of caring, all of which have the potential to turn a life around" (Buscaglia 1996). I was so touched by these words I saw in a diner decades ago that I scribbled them on a paper napkin. (A more in-depth presentation on listening follows in the next chapter, "You Hear Me, But Are You Listening?")

Difference Between Talk and Communication

There is a monumental difference between talk and communication. Talk is talk; *communication is connection.* To highlight the difference between the two, please place your hands in an upright separated position with fingers similar to the image marked talk. In the book *7 Habits of Highly Effective People,* Covey calls this "collective monologues" (Covey 1989). The further the hands are apart, the less chances for success.

Next, intertwine your fingers as the image marked communication to feel the connection. It is this sense of connection that makes the significant difference. Unless there is a sense of connection between you and the other person, communication doesn't happen. Neither person deeply listens, senses, nor gets what the other person is expressing. Therefore, little or anything significant ever gets accomplished or resolved.

My motto is: *"Communication is connection. In connection, there is trust. In trust, learning takes place, problems are solved, and needs are met.*

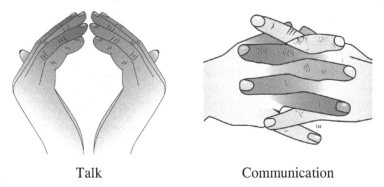

Talk   Communication

Figure 4. The difference between talk and communication.

Communication Between and Among People

Again, we stop to pause, reflect, and gather a sense of who we are, similar to the other pauses along our journey. By now, we know and hopefully fully recognize that we are all human beings, persons, or spiritual beings in human form before we fulfill any role or define ourselves or others by any previous label. Realistically, even before our gender is revealed, regardless of which culture or socioeconomic strata we arrive in, we enter the world as a human being, a member of the very same, one and only human race, and a global citizen on this planet named Mother Earth. As we learned in the first section, *Soul to Soul Connection*, the moment we take our first breath, each of us is already an awesome star who energizes and radiates softly or brightly our specialness and ability to gift others, although at that instant, we certainly are clueless to what roles or paths we will take as our lives unfold. One thing we now know for sure is that at each instant, we always have the choice to respond positively or negatively and sensitively or insensitively. Likewise, we choose to honor or dishonor ourselves and others.

As we gain an awareness of our individuality and begin to ponder who we are, first as youth and then as adults, we gaze into the night sky and marvel at the inspiring beauty of the illuminating stars, often without marveling at or even having a sense of our own beacons. Some people know or feel a stirring passion at an early age about what they want or definitely don't want to be when they "grow up." I came to believe that for many, that spark of passion ignites and shines brighter at some time during our lives. When we look around our planet today in the early decades of the twenty-first century, life often takes us on a most disheartening path that we would never in a million years have chosen for ourselves. The only choice available besides giving up is to pull ourselves together, pick ourselves up, cope, join, do what we can to survive, and carry on. Though others may comfort and support us, no individual can take those necessary first steps in our place; that challenge rests solely on our shoulders.

In life, we choose some roles, and life chooses other roles. When my Nevisian friends ask, "When are you returning to Nevis?" my response is, "I have a plan, but if God has a different plan, that's the one I'll follow." Whatever our life's history, when we feel or can even get a glimmer of ourselves first as a worthy and deserving person, hopefully we recognize and honor—even if others do not—our self-worth, inner beauty, and strength and recognize that we are relevant, do matter, and have a purpose. That deep sense of a glorious, unique individual, which we alone bring to the planet, shapes and defines our expectations and guides how we live and honor ourselves in our various roles.

Hopefully, by now we have a *source-connected* sense that every person on this planet is a fellow human being and we know and feel that we are interconnected with every other person. In this sphere, *there is commonality that binds us instead of a difference that divides us*. The *I* and *they* become *we*. Dhyani Ywahoo of the Etowah band Tsalagi (Cherokee) says it this way: "In reality, in the circle of right relations, there is no above and no below, no in or out, all are together in the sacred circle" (McFadden 1994).

Decades ago, as I became a mother, I lovingly looked at our newborn son as he lay in his crib. I felt in my heart and soul that he was first a deeply loved, special, and dearly cherished human being endowed with his own uniqueness. I recalled the lines from *The Prophet*, "You may house their bodies but not their souls, for their souls dwell in the house of tomorrow, which you cannot visit, not even in your dreams" (Gibran 1959). Reflecting back, I didn't always feel that person-to-person connection with other people.

When we converse soul to soul and person to person, devoid of labels, we no longer intimidate others and others no longer intimidate us. Another person may not feel or trust our intention immediately, and that mistrust often is based on their own experiences with you or with others. Hopefully, in time that new sense of equality that you advocate sinks in and the other person gains comfort and trust. Those people who once intimidated or controlled us no longer can, as we are now *source-connected* with them as a person, not as a figure holding power over us. It doesn't matter that other people continue to try to intimidate or control us by connecting with us from their role or by whatever means they feel superior. If you perceive yourself as worthy and deserving, and as an equal human being, then others can no longer browbeat you or hold that former debilitating force over you. You communicate with self-respect, knowing that in your heart, soul, and mind, you "leveled the playing field" by connecting person to person with them. Over the years, clients repeatedly shared that connecting and communicating person to person is one of the most valuable lessons they learned in feeling greater self-esteem and significantly reducing their sense of anxiety, inferiority, and vulnerability. That view also promoted greater equality for and inclusion of others.

In the first and second decades of the twenty-first century, strongly propelled by search engines, Facebook, and other social media, individuals around the globe also began to see others as fellow human beings, although they formerly seemed so distant and different. Therefore, when we remotely connect and chat with a tech support person from another culture oceans away, we comfortably connect and converse with them as a fellow human being.

An exercise that benefitted my clients is placing your hands side by side (palms down) in front of you. Choose which hand represents you and which hand represents the other person. Next, raise the hand that represents the other person above the hand that represents you. This gesture illustrates intimidation and control and represents any person who held that power over you. Now, lower that hand next to the hand that represents you so that it sits on the same plane next to your other hand. Close your eyes and visualize that you are now equal to that person and you no longer will allow that person to hold any power over you. If you are in a situation where you cannot change the environment, at least silently practice this visualization. Realize that in truth, that person is and has always been a fellow human of equal worth. It doesn't matter how they perceive and present themselves or how you allowed them to hold that power over you. In the end, we are the only ones who can change a perception and eventually a reality within ourselves. We have to accept or reject the intimidation. I know this, as I have been there.

Now, let's reverse the situation. You were the one who felt superior and tried through manipulation, intimidation, or control to overpower or taunt another person. Take your hand again, and this time place it below your other hand that represents the other person, so you feel inferior. Imagine they're doing to you what you intentionally or unintentionally have done to intimidate or control them. As a human being, do you feel it is right? And if others ever intimidated you, how did that feel?

Even experiencing living under another person's thumb, on occasion, I also intimidated family members. Now, I do everything possible to make sure that I no longer intimidate. Intentionally intimidating others often reflects your own insecurity or need to control. That demeans you and others, which is neither nice nor fair. Your intimidation also creates an unpleasant environment that others avoid.

There is a beauty to reaching one's eightieth birthday, as I gained the wisdom to attempt, and usually succeed in, immediately blocking and transcending the negative or toxic energy of others, which I cannot change. When a person feels respect and acceptance, they are more willing to seek and enter your personal space, where they sense your aura and know they can find ease and trust.

I always try to offer that inviting aura, but I am human, and I do miss my mark. Whenever I see a homeless person, I pause and look into that person's eyes and recognize that a pure and beautiful soul exists behind or underneath that wall of anguish or isolation. At the very least, I always offer a heartfelt smile. When time allows, I greet the person, offer a few dollars, buy groceries, or sit with the person while they eat their meal, in hopes that they feel and know that another person cares.

As mentioned before, Muhammad Ali was a global iconic hero. Shortly after Ali's death, George Foreman, two-time world heavyweight champion, declared, "[Ali] was the greatest man I ever met. To say he was a boxer, is a putdown." Foreman went on to share that no matter your profession, you became better just by being with Ali. When questioned about Ali's trademark skills, the rope-a-dope and his punch as a boxer, Foreman replied, "He didn't have the best power or the best anything…but his presence, this was something different…and you knew you couldn't beat it.…His greatest power was his greatest presence.…He had great compassion for others and children. He made you feel so important. He just listened" (King 2016).

How We Communicate, What We Say, and How We Act Civilly

Civility is a state of mind. At its core is a basic decency built on mindfulness, gratitude, concern, integrity, empathy, equality, and respect for others. Civility extends far beyond politely uttering "Good morning," "Good afternoon," "Hello," "Excuse me," "Pardon," "Please," and "Thank you." When we live in a state of civility, we take nothing for granted. We are grateful for the smallest gestures, realizing deeply that they are often more gratifying than the bigger things in life. Small annoyances, which may be irritants to others, are just not a part of our day. We just don't sweat the small stuff or take it on. Bearing an attitude of "Good enough," "Make do," "I'm okay," and "Strive to do my best" is a response that develops gratitude and encourages ingenuity and creativity to work with what we have to achieve what is possible and "making a way out of no way" (Conwill 2016).

When we are civil, we carry enough respect for others and *source-connect* with each person, child, spouse, partner, sibling, peer, patient, nurse, student, colleague, staff member, service provider, law enforcement officer, and others as unique individuals. In small and close professional and group settings, we offer our names and initially address each person by their name. If we do not know the person's name, we offer our name and then ask for theirs. In any workplace or professional setting, we also offer our name as part of our greeting when we answer the phone. We are mindful of how our words or deeds affect others. When civil, we do not blame, bicker, or shirk our responsibilities. Civility remains vital in every arena, especially within the home, classroom, physician's office, shops, restaurants, at work, on our commute, and in our neighborhood.

With each contact or interaction, especially as parents, spouses or partners, educators, neighbors, health-care providers, and law enforcement officers, we first *source-connect* with the essence of each person, not a label or stereotype, which would immediately distort their purity and dishonor everyone. The intent not only deeply touches and benefits each person but holistically benefits our family, community, country, planet, and well-being as well.

While at dinner, I asked a colleague in her thirties if she ever allows anyone to describe her; tears welled up in her eyes. She shared that she has very high professional standards and always reaches higher than expected. That also has been my experience with her. She shared that her director had recently told her she is a type A personality. Her remark stunned me because in our numerous conversations, I've noticed that she is one of the loveliest, most capable, and most soft-spoken individuals that I know. I shared that perhaps her supervisor misunderstood her ambition of trying to raise the bar of her already-high standards. I also recommended that the next time a similar comment is uttered, if she is comfortable, then, in her usual soft-spoken style, she reply, "You don't know who I am."

In Nevis, politeness is paramount. During my twenty-three years of experience there, it was the most important value, instilled in childhood by parents, caretakers, and teachers. *"Good morning," "Good afternoon," "Good evening,"* or *"Good night"* were the expected first words uttered when greeting or interacting with a person. Since then, with the advent of social media, "Hi," "Hello," and "Wassup?" are often the preferred lingo of the youth. As a newcomer to Nevis in the late 1990s, I paused to ask a man for directions, "Excuse me, what is the direction to…?" I was immediately cut off with his words, "Good morning…" I got the pivotal message that forever was imprinted into my head. In the mornings of those early years, as my husband and I stretched and exercised on our veranda, toddlers (who are now young men), accompanied by their mothers, passed our home while walking down the mountain village road to our local primary school; they called out each morning, "Good morning, Ruth. Good morning, Lee." If they didn't greet us, their mothers promptly stopped, called out their names, and firmly prompted, "I didn't hear…"

During the last twenty-five years, in more than a hundred flights we took to or from Nevis, there has not been a single time when, upon our arrival or departure, the St. Kitts-Nevis Federation welcoming team did not recognize us. First, they greeted us as tourists; later, as elderly; and even later, with our aging faces, they are happy to see us return. Baggage handlers immediately make certain that one of them, definitely not us, move every bit of our baggage. Even as we descend the stairs from the plane, there is always a person who takes our carry-on and lifts it up or down the stairs as needed. We never have to ask; it is the only place in all our travels that we have experienced this kindness.

Civility requires no explaining or complaining and removes any mention of personal challenges or conversation about intimacy or sexual conduct from public space; that is reserved for a later, private time with willing listeners. At any institution of learning, all should refrain from burdening students with matters that pertain to the workload, class size, materials, funding, policy, gossip, or administration; these are borne by teachers. These matters are best discussed with willing colleagues in areas specifically designated for teachers or staff. When explaining or correcting, the student's spirit must be honored. We mindfully enlighten them with compassionate constructive criticism of solely their attitude or behavior, never their individual being. Absolutely never demean, admonish, or humiliate a student, colleague, or staff member in any way or discuss any personal issue in front of their peers, siblings, or others.

In the health-care setting, when congregating in open rooms adjacent to patients, health-care providers should keep their voices down, refrain from complaining or discussing personal matters, patients' conditions, political preferences, or what lavish meals the pharmaceutical representative provided. This is especially annoying to patients who are waiting for a long time in their examining rooms while health-care providers indulge in personal matters.

Civility in all arenas also engages several characteristics and behaviors, such as compassion, consideration, fairness, nonjudgmental listening, punctuality, taking turns, washing hands after using the restroom, covering mouths when sneezing, and coughing into the crook of ones' arm. Also called for is replenishing or notifying someone when the last of an item was used, and cleaning up after ourselves—especially at home, in a common or shared space, in public places, and during our travels.

Furthermore, civility includes awareness while standing in line, driving a car, and parking within designated lines to give others ease of fitting in their fair-share space. It also includes being mindful of others' time constraints. Personal and cell phone conversation civility in the public space requires us to lower our voices or (even better) delay our call for a future private place, so that others' privacy is not invaded by our mundane, negative, or too often, personal and disturbing conversations. Consideration of others also includes keeping our commitments or giving notification within an adequate period of time when we can't and following through with what we stated or promised. In addition, we sincerely apologize when we know we've made an error or intentionally or unintentionally hurt another person's feelings. There are numerous examples of lack of civility in our culture, but those mentioned are most pertinent in my life's experience. Ponder and add some to your own annoyances that you want to enlighten others about or that you need to improve. After all, we are human, so no one is perfect.

When we embrace and sow heartfelt courtesies such as "Excuse me," "Please," and "Thank you," into all conversations, a tone is set that creates a *positive communication environment*. That energy radiates far beyond the moment or place. Setting examples that foster civility and inclusiveness asserts that we are ultimately all fellow and equal human beings; therefore, we treat all others in that spirit. It is another wonderful avenue where we can express, "Love thy neighbor as thyself." If we can't feel this type of concern, at the very least, we owe a sense of decency and civility to all, even to those whose personal beliefs and attitudes are distasteful to us.

Respect

A colleague recently asked me *how I define respect*? I decided that it doesn't matter how a dictionary or another person defines respect, it only matters how each of us define the word. After pondering this over with a niece, I came up with the following response: Respect for others as fellow human beings is significant. Equally important, we must have respect for ourselves. If we don't respect ourselves, others may not respect us either. Therefore, we must ask ourselves, "Do I have enough self-respect that I get from others what I feel I deserve?" Let me also note from my own experience that, in certain situations, we can respect others without having self-respect. Respect is one of the most sought-after values for any individual of any culture, even in cultures where respect is not equally awarded to men and women or those of various socioeconomic strata, religions, sects, differing abilities, cultures, or status. Respect is esteem desired by many that is not awarded outright but is mostly earned by our words and deeds. It is also the manner in which we communicate and interact with others. Do we listen, void of judgment, from our hearts and souls along with our ears and respect and acknowledge that another person's opinions and standards matter, even if they differ from ours? Or do we feel that only we or our culture establishes the norm?

The best for us is not always compatible with what is best for others. Though others know us by our words and deeds, our actions always speak far louder than our words. Do we practice what we preach? We may convey (or preach) a belief or value from our mouths, yet our footsteps practice something else. During the "Quotation of the Day" segment of the *Morning Inspiration Programme* on VON Radio in Nevis, I heard, "If your head and heart are going in the right direction, you won't have to worry about your feet" (Herbert 2010). When we advocate one belief yet our actions do not support that, what do you think others, especially our children, students, patients, colleagues, staff, clients, neighbors, or peers, pick up?

When Fareed Zakaria asked Susan Rice, the former U.S. ambassador to the United Nations, about the "tough" approach of a previous U.S. ambassador to the United Nations, Rice offered quite a succinct response. She stated, "I'm not sure that approach was altogether successful. You need a combination of toughness and diplomacy and a willingness to work with others in a constructive and collaborative way and be very plain about what we stand for and what we believe in....If America leads with respect for the institution fully cognizant of our flaws and tries to make it a better institution, we are most effective there" (Zakaria 2016a).

What better iconic symbol to immortalize respect than the queen of soul Aretha Franklin's passionate rendition, singing "R-E-S-P-E-C-T"? When nurses and physicians greet the patient in the operating room and each gives their name prior to surgery, that shows respect and adds comfort for the patient.

Integrity is one of the most valuable characteristics of a person, and it remains trusted unless we tarnish it. We must be more concerned with our character than our reputation, as our character reveals who we truly are; our reputation is simply what others think we are. This is especially relevant during most challenging times and major crises.

What message does a teacher give when they advocate health and proper diet yet eat candy bars and other fatty, processed, or preservative-rich foods for lunch? In court chambers, a judge teaches the unquestionable importance of ethics to his law clerk, yet when they go to lunch, the judge fails to inform the waitress of the ten-dollar error on the check in the judge's favor and he gloats to his clerk.

I can still remember my father telling me at a young age that reputation is similar to a linen handkerchief. Once you crush it so it is wrinkled, it is never quite the same. As a young child, I vividly recall walking hand in hand with my father on a snowy night with Christmas lights aglow in downtown Columbus, Ohio. We had just left the Lazarus department store. Within a block, my father reached into his pocket to find his parking stub and change. He immediately stopped and said, "Ruth, we have to go back to the store. The last clerk gave me too much money and her cash drawer will be short." The tingle of the cold, the fresh snow on my face, and the image of the lights forever framed the lesson on integrity that continues as my North Star.

Labels

Labels and categories are a necessity in our current culture for all sorts of reasons. Used positively and effectively, labels help us classify, give meaning to, and understand generations, demographics, education priorities, funding, health-care delivery, marketing, customer service, sales, and swaths of other topics; labels are ubiquitous. Unfortunately, as we learned in the chapter *"Personal Lenses,"* labels also have a powerful, harmful effect. When we label an individual, we combine an idea with that label and then attach that to the person. When we attach any label to our thoughts—whether based on role, culture, age, generation, gender, condition, ability, or creed—we unintentionally restrict and prejudice our thoughts as we impose barriers. When parents converse with their children as parent to child instead of person to person, and teachers address their students as teacher to student rather than person to person, there is a probability that, to some degree, comfort, learning, resolution, and trust are impeded. When physicians impersonally speak with nurses as they "give orders," especially in a facility setting, and do not perceive the nurse as an equal human being or equal partner of the team, how does the nurse feel? Because of expectations associated with a thought or label, the more labels we apply, the more barriers we erect, and the more we distort our message. Again, each label becomes a hoop of expectations and distortions. The more hoops we pass through, the more we pollute our perception, thoughts, and responses with fears and negative expectations. We denigrate our connection and minimize the positive impact we can have on others. Besides, we are each far more than the segmented sum of our parts.

When we *source-connect* and communicate person to person, heart to heart, soul to soul, we eliminate the barriers and bypass all the labels. We bypass the idea that the person is a woman, man, old, young, rich, poor, homeless, leader, terrorist, change agent, worker, staff, secretary, or CEO. It is also best to *source-connect* with every student, teacher, doctor, nurse, patient, *handi-abled*, healthy, ill, criminal, militant, officer, gay, straight, transgender, husband, wife, partner, child, teenager, parent, centennial, Greatest Generation, Silent Generation, Baby Boomers, Generation X, Generation Y, also known as the Millennials, Generation Z, and Generation Alpha, the first born entirely in the 21st century. Furthermore, it is best that we also *source-connect* with every person who is a Christian, Jew, Muslim, Hindu, Buddhist, Rastafarian, Sikh, nonbeliever, or agnostic, or of African, European, Latino, Asian, First Nation heritage, or any person of another religion or cultural heritage. Each person primarily is a fellow human being who shares our planet, Mother Earth. People sense that commonality.

Communication Is Complex and Challenging

No joke. When we realize that the human brain is the most complex organ on the planet, perhaps we can begin to appreciate the complexity of communication and why successful communication is one of the most challenging feats people accomplish. When human beings first evolved, they lived in a simple and homogeneous environment, and the earliest communication consisted of grunts and gestures. These primitive forms evolved into syllables, words, phrases, and sentences. As cultures evolved and people moved farther apart, drums and smoke signals became their method of connecting with those afar.

Today, communication is exceedingly more sophisticated and complex; that presents innumerable opportunities for error. When we need information, we access the internet, and within seconds, we can span our globe to access the material. We rely heavily on smartphones, texts, social media, computer networks, fax machines, voice mail, and augmented communication devices. We also rely on and relay using tools, apps, and voice recognition, and we will continue until others replace those with more complex functions that we cannot yet fathom. Still, with the use of all these remarkable, high-tech tools, our most effective, accurate, and holistic communication remains our ability to communicate face-to-face, from person to person.

The more commonalities we discover and the more familiar we are with another person, the fewer words we need to exchange to get the message. In close personal, professional, or vocational relationships, one uttered word or the slightest nuance of a facial expression or voice tone conveys a meaning that is quite limited, or perhaps no other person but the two people comprehend. Even within that intimacy, our thoughts and visualizations never exactly mirror each other. Situations in which we have less in common and a lower degree of understanding require more precise communication to accurately convey the *meaning* and *intention* of our feelings, thoughts, desires, and objectives.

Do you think communication is easy because you did not take lessons in it, the same way you never took lessons to walk? It undoubtedly is easy enough to open our mouths and speak without forethought, concern for others, or the consequences. But it is definitely not that simple or easy to communicate if we mindfully want to reach out to others, realize our desires, achieve our goals, convey our care and support, or fulfill our destinies.

Communication is far more demanding and challenging today because of the complexity of issues and the diversity of people. Those whose families were entrenched in U.S. culture for generations now mingle with recently arriving individuals from near and far-flung corners. Currently, this migration is substantially from Asia, Latin America, and the Middle East. Initially, anthropologists thought that the route of the earliest migration from Asia to the Americas crossed the Bering Straits between ten- and twenty-four thousand years ago, to initially populate Western North and Central America. The next wave of immigrants arrived from Europe beginning in the 1500s. Then, those of African heritage unwillingly arrived. Later, consenting folks arrived from Asia, Latin America, and other areas around the world. Eventually, this experiment evolved into an idea named democracy as people joined what would emerge as the greatest mosaic in human history.

Although our most recent immigrants may be those refugees displaced from the Middle East, there is currently a halt on their entry. At the halfway mark of the second decade of the twenty-first century, the United States had anticipated an influx of millions of people escaping ISIS terrorism and the catastrophic civil war in Syria. By 2016, 240,000 Syrian citizens were killed, and millions of other persons from Middle East and northern African crises have fled and live in the diaspora. These fellow human beings escaped with only their most precious and necessary possessions, with their young loved ones strapped on their backs, carried in their arms, or led by hand. They often bring customs and scents that are still unfamiliar, wear clothing that is not mainstream, and bear names that we previously have not heard of. Initially, these names may sound strange and be challenging to pronounce correctly. However, we mindfully remember to show compassion and express our desire to learn how to accurately pronounce a person's name. That is the very least we can do. This simple, sincere gesture in itself is a comforting welcome in a situation that unfortunately is also marked with hostility, pushback, and resentment.

In reflection, we recall that many of our ancestors from Irish, Italian, Jewish, and Polish cultures also faced harsh discrimination. If we express the tenets of most religions and practices to kindly and compassionately welcome our recently arrived newcomers, this will minimize their discomfort so they do not suffer as our loved ones did. Hopefully, persons will realize that each individual and their families provide a new adventure, as each new culture and subculture offers something special, interesting, and fascinating that we may one day eventually cherish and accept as mainstream.

As you will learn, what is appropriate in one culture is often not in another. At times, it is exactly opposite. Sometimes, the differences are significant; other times, they are slight. Realistic and managed solutions demand a profound understanding and monumental bridging of people's differing ideas, aspirations, hopes, and dreams. Desire and *source-connected* communication, not just talk, are key to developing the dialogue and happiness for each. It is also best to first observe or recall facts to converse meaningfully in context.

Communication among loved ones requires even more care as feelings are than in other situations. In addition, people desire more fulfilling and deeper personal relationships. Issues are sensitive to discuss because of the emotional web woven through the years and the inherent "bumpy road" of transformations in lifelong relationships. Twenty-five years ago, my son told me, "Mom, you were lucky. When you and Dad got married, your roles were clearly defined." Little does he know how much communication it took and how much continues to occur behind the scenes as my husband and I mature and age and at times struggle. I continue to rely on the *hand-dome* to help guide me as we reach yet another stage in our sixty years of marriage. A widespread difference exists in our perception of "wife" and "husband" (which in 1962 was primarily based on gender) and the reality of how we interact and live today. It is best to maintain an open mind as lives are fluid and circumstances and needs change. With my husband resigning from his major client and my needing help to finish this book, he supported my work and took on some roles that he had never performed in his life. As he approaches eighty years of life, I had to resume my former roles and assume new ones. I continue to declare that "the person who is able does."

We have passed through many stages, and if we continue to be blessed with more years, we will pass through more phases that require acceptance, adjustments, flexibility, and further role reversals. Fortunately, so far, each of our deficits is the other's strength. We also entered the stage where we begin to decline in many ways except in acceptance, tolerance, and wisdom. We continue to change as time unfolds, and I am often reminded of my father's wisdom that he uttered on the day he died, "Ruth, you learn till the day you die."

If you look into your personal lives, you will find that lack of positive communication is often fundamental to the greatest challenge between people and that successful communication leads to solutions and personal fulfillment. Decades ago, on a classroom bulletin board, I noticed a picture of a telephone with its handset and its elongated coiled cord dangling off the hook. The caption read, "A relationship is only as good as the lines of communication."

When you converse with another person, you sense if they respond positively or negatively. Sometimes, you leave a conversation knowing that you "blew it" but you are not sure why. The other person's reaction may be in response to the negative communication environment you created, or your perception of their response may have nothing to do with what you said or how you said it. Though love runs deep and values are similar, communication can still be the most challenging aspect of a long, deep, and love-filled relationship that requires that both parties are willing and engaged.

Everything Is Relative

If you recollect from the *Hand-Dome*, you learned why people feel, think, act, speak, and write as they do. Hopefully, you also recall that everything is relative. This becomes more apparent when you view the national and international situation, converse with people from other cultures, or broaden your perspective.

Unfortunately, there are people all over the world who are either homeless or live in impoverished conditions or substandard housing. Others who are more fortunate live in primitive, rural, and permanent huts. Yet even among them, there are those who are relatively well-off. These folks enjoy proximity to wells or possess land to grow crops and raise a few animals. They also are a short distance to shops, open markets, and schools. Some even have solar lighting.

Therefore, it is hard to understand when people in a privileged culture complain because their gourmet meal at an upscale restaurant was not up to snuff, while those who either are homeless, less fortunate, or fleeing their homeland with scant possessions on their backs would rejoice for a scrap of those gourmet bites. Even better for these fellow human beings would be to sit amid loved ones, eating a warm meal tasty to their palates, comforted by familiar faces and words in peaceful surroundings.

During an early Monday-morning ride on a busy freeway in Seattle, the driver remarked, "This traffic doesn't bother me much as it does the other drivers." I asked, "Why?" He replied, "I am from Los Angeles, and I know what heavy, stop-and-go Monday-morning commuter traffic can be like."

A businessman lives in Southern California and commutes more than two hours both directions every day, which in Los Angeles isn't that unusual. When he traveled to Nevis, which can be circumnavigated in forty-five minutes, he called his colleague's parents to invite them for dinner.

They asked, "Where are you staying?" When he replied, "I'm at the hotel, twenty minutes away," they declared, "That's so far." In a similar instance, physicians often have difficulty empathizing with patients' minor complaints when other patients are fighting for their lives.

When I approached seventy-five years old, I chatted with Blind Eileen as she mentally noted how many months remained until she reached one hundred years old. She delighted in remembering and announcing my birth date. I told her that I was going to be seventy-five, and she quickly and adamantly quipped, "Oh, you're a young one."

Find Commonality

Because of my rich, broad life's experience and interest in people, especially those of differing cultures, my profession, and my travels to unusual places, I mostly find commonality—although not necessarily agreement—with other people.

One can find an adversarial facet in any relationship if one chooses, but one can also seek the *source-connection* between people. During a meeting of inspectors and health-care providers, IRS auditors and businesspersons, supervisors and staff, or any such discussion, first focus on the person-to-person connection and then on the role that each fulfills. Often, we allow ourselves to be intimidated by a person whose job or role is more instrumental than ours or who challenges us or by possible outcomes in which we played a role. In every situation, relate from person to person and find a commonality so that connection and communication take place. This fosters a smoother flow, even during an adversarial interaction.

A cosmetic buyer at a specialty shop was often at odds with her supervisor, who criticized her in front of their patrons. She asked her supervisor, "Do you think the customers are comfortable when you put me down in front of them? I can't believe this is company policy." Nothing seemed to faze her. Finally, the employee moved the conversation from the professional to the personal arena. She began to peel away the differences until she found a common experience. The relationship rapidly shifted as they had lunch together and began to work more closely. If you cannot seem to connect with a person, continue exploring various avenues and attitudes to find similarities rather than focusing on the barriers and differences. Switch the topic and converse at a person-to-person, not a role-to-role, level. Unless a person is uninterested, stubborn, purposely defiant, or lacks courage, you will eventually find commonality.

Crossing political party lines to vote for a candidate in "that other party" is a perfect example of bypassing the label of the candidate's party and evaluating the person's basic principles, priorities, and platform. Do you ever hear a person say, "He's conservative for a Democrat," or "She's progressive for a Republican"? A less emotionally charged response is simply, "He's *conservative*" and "She's *progressive*."

A clerk at a trendy boutique had difficulty breaking the habit of labeling customers. As they entered her shop, she mentally thought "Skinny," "Fat," "Rich," "Poor," "Persian," "Japanese," "Christian," or "Jewish." To break the habit, she watched television while repeating the word *person* to herself as different people appeared on the screen. It took a while, but eventually the clerk connected person to person without the divisive labels that formerly popped into her head.

When a neighbor returned home after his freshman year, he and his mom made the "usual" adjustments and negotiations. He had been at college for nine months and had experienced a freedom that allowed him to determine when he arose, what he ate, how neat or messy his room was, and how he spent each day. During the same time, his mom had become accustomed to a quiet and tidy home without children. At the end of each teaching day, she returned home to find her house in the same shape as when she left. After her hectic day, if she didn't feel like cooking, conversing with anyone, or engaging in any other "mom duties," she didn't bother. When her almost-grown child returned home to spend the summer, both he and his mom had expectations about each other's roles. In the youth's mind, "Mom" was still expected to provide certain functions. And the mom anticipated a more mature child who had been on his own for the last nine months. She expected a more considerate and self-sufficient young man. Both were in for a surprise. In the roles they had anticipated, the young adult wanted his mom to be the same and yet different. He wanted her to provide the same cooking and cleaning functions, expressing "mom love," but also allow him as much freedom as he had enjoyed at college. When chatting with the son about his bumpy road, I suggested, "Think of your mom as a person who happens to be a mom. Do your expectations change a little? Do you look at her differently?" He later shared that he gained insight and understanding of the situation.

When teachers connect with a student of any age who has a mental or any other type of disability and only think of the child as "disabled," that attitude hampers the student from reaching his or her given potential and limits the child's life in many ways. If, from the get-go, the teacher mindfully and in a *source-connected* way communicates solely person to person at a level the student understands, the teacher gives the student an advantage to achieve their most cherished desires and sought-after goals. When we look at a person who is *handi-abled* and think they have little to offer, we lose, because each human being is endowed with an ability to gift others in numerous loving and special ways.

In their soulful compassion, neither Mother Teresa nor Princess Diana rejected an individual regardless of poverty, illness, sexual orientation, or whether they had contracted AIDS but especially championed them as human beings to be respected. When you connect person to person, soul to soul, you perceive and experience each person on their own merit. You consider neither their appearance nor how family, society, a group, a condition, or an event defines them. You also do not presume anything based on preconceived ideas, expectations, labels, or what you've heard. It is best not to hinder your perception of that individual but *source-connect* with the person as who they are.

In her book *No Human Involved*, Barbara Seranella states that in the 1970s, police informally used a radio code among themselves describing transients involved in crime. The code was "No human involved." Contrast that with a remark from a deputy chief of police who said, "When I arrive at a murder by a gang member some will use the term 'innocent bystander' if the deceased person is not a gang member. The implication is that if the deceased is a gang member, his life is not worthy, and he is guilty by association. Who are we to decide the value of a person's life? We are not the Creator." The compassionate deputy sheriff further added, "Every life is precious, a flame which is worth keeping alive. When a flame goes out, we all lose" (Seranella 1997).

Anticipating a problem, a physician's claims representative called to warn me, "Ruth, you're going to have difficulty with him. He's male, he's Muslim. You're female, you're Jewish." I responded, "I don't think so. We are both human beings," and we got along fine. People are far more similar than different. Bernie S. Siegel, MD, lectured, wrote books (*Peace, Love and Healing* and *Love, Medicine and Miracles*), and helped terminally ill patients cope with their challenges. He shared that he develops a rapport with his patients within ten minutes because he converses heart to heart and soul to soul with them.

People sense whether you *source-connect* and bond with them as a person or if you think of them as a label or thing. That soul to soul and person-to-person connection is the foundation of trust. Just pause for a second and reflect on a person with whom you are comfortable. Doesn't that person relate to you as a person, as just you and all that you are?

Following is another deeply stirring and poignant experience about the teachers Cedric Anderson and Sandy Osborne and the *turn-around* youth at Rosewood Community Education Center in Bellflower, California, which I mentioned in the chapter "*Hand-Dome.*" The students who formerly held metal guns now held metal spoons to feed children with severe disabilities. This innovative program helped the students form bonds while aiding wheelchair-bound children with serious impairments. At first, the *turn-around* students couldn't get past the deformities of the severely disabled children. In time, these youths transcended their outer shells and found the commonality to connect soul to soul with the other children. The bond brought joy to the children who were *handi-abled* and softened the hearts of the *turn-around* youths. These teens touched their own essence and felt a self-worth that was almost blocked. A fourteen-year-old with a substance abuse history said, "I like working with the disabled. They bring out all of my feelings. It makes me feel good about myself."

After a presentation I gave to her class, a tenth-grade student sent me a note. She wrote, "A girl called me a nasty name and tried to start a fight with me. All I did was pace around, shaking, trying to think. She's a human being just like me. I am sure deep down she's very nice. It was very hard, but I managed and everything is okay now."

When I was on the East Coast, one of the one hundred best physicians in the country, as rated by his peers, asked me, "What do you do to help a Black and a Korean physician get along better?" (Naifeh and Smith 1994). I said, "Get the Black and the Korean out of it, relate person to person, focus on the topic of conversation, not the color of their skin nor shape of their eyes." Each becomes sensitive to the discrimination and oppression that the other has felt, and each must be aware of different cultural communication and styles. Once awareness exists and communication styles are understood, conversations transcend to a person-to-person one. This practice laser-focuses on the issues by abandoning all former thoughts of heritage or other labels. Please, let me remind you, "You have to be aware to care, and if you care, you are aware."

Communication Comfort Levels

Individuals have different communication comfort zones. If you compare communication with an onion, the outer layers of the onion are similar to your most superficial communication level. The core of the onion is similar to your deepest core and represents our most intimate thoughts and communication. Assigning hypothetical numbers, 1 through 10, to the outer and inner layers of the onion represents our most shallow and deepest feelings, respectively. Number 10 represents the skin of the onion and our most superficial communication. Number 1 represents the core of the onion and our most intimate communication, which we only share with those whom we most trust. *We communicate at different levels, with different people, in different situations, and at different times.*

Individuals who are reserved and private tend to keep their innermost feelings and thoughts to themselves. This reflects a response to past experiences or simply a person's nature. They usually do not resolve issues by talking with others, but they keep their own counsel. They are comfortable communicating at levels 4 or higher. Usually, but not always, sharing their most personal feelings is difficult; they prefer to keep all communication at levels within their comfort zones. Although I would burn out if I constantly conversed at level 1, I am comfortable at that level when deeply touching soul to soul.

Trust is the key in the most personal communication that occurs between levels 1 and 3. Challenges arise in personal relationships when a wide gap exists in the comfort zones between the individuals. One person's comfort zones may be between levels 6 and 10, and the other person's comfort could be between levels 1 and 7.

The core of the onion also represents our most in-depth, intense, analytical, and complex communication level and requires the most focus and energy. For most people, it is exhausting to listen or converse at that in-depth level for any length of time. When you approach the point of near exhaustion, take a break and speak with less intensely. You can also change the topic, "lighten up," or when appropriate, add humor. You can always take a few mindful breaths or grab a quick break to gaze out a window to catch a cloud, view the sky, or reflect on a loved one or precious experience that put a smile in your heart and on your face.

Meaningful small talk is an art and a good example of chatting at level 8. Some folks who easily gab quickly find a commonality that puts the other person at ease. For others, small talk is more challenging and meaningless. When small talk is sincere, it comes across as friendly. People who find small talk difficult may avoid large groups or parties where conversations often shift from person to person and tend to be more trivial.

Communication levels at various comfort zones are also nonverbal. Communication levels 1 to 3 represent intimacy that takes place among friends, family, and lovers who are completely comfortable with each other. This nonverbal communication comes in the form of holding, hugging, and touching. The more intimate any type of communication, the more vulnerable we are.

We immediately sense the other person's trust in and respect toward us, our ideas, and feelings and their confidentiality. If an individual continuously mocks or ridicules our feelings or ideas, it is best that we not discuss any meaningful topics with them and expect a different attitude or response. If the person gossips about others, they most likely gossip about you. If we lack trust, especially with a family member or an individual with whom we are in a close relationship, we may be reticent, even when necessary, to express our feelings, thoughts, needs, disappointments, or violations.

Communication—that connection and bond with a loved one—often leads to a longing intimacy between the two. When that is lacking, at an appropriate time or when necessary, try to create an environment in which you can relate your lack of trust or comfort; use this opportunity to voice specific concerns and desires. This ambience helps couples get back on track to regain what they had and return to intimacy. For many, lovemaking is the most intimate form of communication, and ultimate lovemaking is experienced when all barriers are temporarily set aside and the synergy between the two flows into a sense of oneness.

Personal, Public, and Professional Facets

Before we leave this section of the chapter "Communication Is Connection," let us take a closer look at who we each are. Holistically, we are multifaceted beings capable of being known in totality only to ourselves, if that is even possible. Yet our interaction varies slightly with each individual. This is similar to how we portion each piece of a pie with the same ingredients but we add varying toppings to best suit the person's needs and taste.

We each possess personal, private, public, and vocational facets. In each role and situation, we respond slightly or significantly differently to each individual. When we connect with another person, *only* we know which "slice of our pie" connects with that person and *only* that other person experiences the nuance (or piece of pie) to which they connect. As the *hand-dome* illustrates, in varying degrees, each individual is different. Accordingly, we perceive and receive each person differently. Similarly, we interact differently with each. In this light, we fully comprehend that, to some degree, communication is fluid and fluctuates with each person, in each situation, and in each conversation. This certainly does not imply that we compromise ourselves; we are just making adjustments for a stronger connection. The core of your personal integrity and principles remain the same with each response; however, your nonverbal and verbal communication style, voice tone, and word choice slightly fluctuate to enhance the connection with the person or in response to the situation.

The degrees of our emotional investment and vulnerability are also significant factors in the way we communicate in our various roles. We may be loving and soft-spoken as we hold a newborn infant. Yet later in the day, we can be bold and charming as we court a new client, or reserved, pleasant, or nasty with a spouse. Or we may "dangle" as a "fish out of water" on a first date, first day on the job, or first day in a new setting or role. We may engage in an eloquent, positive communication style in our professional role yet choose not to apply those attributes into our personal life, or the opposite. We may be laid-back, cool, and comfortable in one environment but rigid and contrary in another.

Decades ago, a family member created the terms *in-house* personality and *out-house* personality, which I perceive as being on the same personal communication spectrum. It is the degree to which the advocacy and adversary roles are apart—that is problematic and challenging for those involved. My mother used the phrase "house angel, street devil," or sometimes just the opposite, "house devil, street angel." A health-care provider shared that many of his patients are challenged by living with a person who is extremely nice when they socialize in public but quite different while living under the same roof.

A consultant was mature and polite at her client's office but immature and brash at her own office—she was unable or unwilling to equally apply positive communication to all areas of her life. People at such a workplace, who only see the positive side of such a person, find it difficult to believe when others tell them about the person's other "dark or nasty" side.

When I was a speech therapist helping individuals recover from strokes or brain injuries, I often saw patients and their family members in hospital settings and rehabilitation facilities, and then later in their homes. There were only a few instances when family members gave the person the same respect, invited them to participate in major decisions, or showed the same concern at home that I observed at the previous facilities. We cannot presume that how a person acts with us in one role or situation indicates how they communicate in any other role, situation, with any other person, or behind closed doors. At times, we would be unpleasantly surprised or dismayed with the difference in their attitudes and behavior.

If you are a teacher, doctor, mother, father, or caregiver, you are quite aware that each role necessitates a different response. When a student falls and injures themselves, you respond as a caring and concerned professional. If your child falls and hurts themselves, you also respond emotionally—consoling, kissing, or hugging the child. The parent (or caregiver) response is not appropriate in the classroom, and the professional-teacher response is appropriately different from the emotional response of a parent. Many physicians often expressed their comfort "talking medicine" with patients but have difficulty conversing person to person on nonmedical topics. A physician must emphatically express care and concern to their patients, especially in the hospital. Will it be the same depth of empathy given by their loved ones? Probably not, but empathy still is required to convey comfort and build rapport. Similarly, a probation officer may be stricter with his own child than with a gang member because of his child's needs or the situation.

Have you ever observed a heated conversation interrupted by a phone call? A person who had just been shouting now answers the phone, greeting the caller in a pleasant voice. Are your body language and voice tone the same at work as at home? For those of you who swear at home, do you curse at work? Where do you offer more patience? Do you regularly divulge your true feelings? Do you treat your family with the same respect you accord your colleagues or patients? Do you treat your staff as well as your colleagues? Is your standard of pursuing tasks the same for your family as for your students, patients, or clients?

Years ago, each of my three children viewed my interaction with them as an indication of how I interacted with their siblings. I love each child equally and try to be fair in what I give of myself to each child. Each child was raised with similar basic values. However, since each child was unique and had differing perceived needs and each was born and raised during a different stage of my developing maturity levels and our evolving financial position, standards and expectations were different for each child. Some rules became more lax, others more strict, and at times expectations and standards were unintentionally and unfortunately unfair. The communication between us now has matured and continues to evolve as it grows deeper and more positive, trusting, and loving.

My Rabbi Stan Levy, shared, "When you meet someone, there are actually six people present: who you think you are, who the other person thinks you are, who you actually are, who the other person thinks she or he is, who you think the other person is, and who the other person actually is." Consequently, we rarely truly know another person.

We know about another person based on our experiences with them, our interpretations and feelings about what they say, what they do, and how they live their lives, and perhaps by what others say about them. Because of our *personal lenses*, we are always at least one step away from the other person's reality. When we think about it, it is truly amazing that we do as well as we do. It is understandable why so many monumental personal, national, and global issues and (often polarizing) priorities challenge us. Similarly, views and conversations on values, economics, equality, justice, climate change, geopolitical shifts, and terrorism are challenging as they affect our loved ones, communities, and global citizens. These struggles are compounded with ego, greed, posturing, power, tribalism, and turf. All these require an overwhelmingly honest, mindful, *source-connected* intricacy and delicacy in accomplishing collaborative resolutions. And to that, we add, "Men are from Mars, women are from Venus" (Gray 1992).

Private Feelings

What we privately feel about ourselves and others isn't always honestly conveyed. Picture yourself as you shave, apply deodorant, lotion, or makeup, style your hair, brush your teeth, and choose appropriate attire for the day's events. Aren't there days when you would rather lounge in your nightwear? Wouldn't you prefer occasionally going to work in your grungy old jeans, with no makeup, unstyled hair, or unshaven? Doesn't your communication change slightly to conform with some perceived "expected standard"?

Presentational Self and Representational Self

At a Sabbath gathering, Noah ben Shea, author of *Jacob the Baker* (1993), compared a person with a tapestry whose front side is seen by the public and whose back side is hidden from the outside world. LaFrance and Mayo, in *Moving Bodies: Nonverbal Communication in Social Relationships* (1978), present the difference between the *representational self* and *presentational self*. These two ideas are combined in an analogy of the front and back of a tapestry to illustrate the public, private, personal, and vocational dimensions of people and their *representational selves* and *presentational selves*.

The following image offers an insight into ourselves, others, and varying communication forms. Picture the front and back of a tapestry. The front side is as close to perfection as possible in color, pattern, texture, and design, and this side is presented to the public. The back side has loose, dangling threads, knots, and erratic designs that are concealed. Sometimes, there is little difference between the front and the back of a tapestry; all the knots are neatly woven into the back, creating a design similar to the front. Other times, there is a monumental difference between the front and the back of the tapestry; the back is in total disarray, with threads hanging and crossing over one another and knots everywhere.

We are similar to the tapestry. The back of the tapestry represents our genuine feelings, aspirations, dislikes, fears, abuses, negative thoughts, and deceptions. Our physical scars, disabilities, and imperfections are visible to others, yet the emotional scars and impediments, which are often more excruciating, are invisible and only privately felt within ourselves. We are the only ones who know what we feel inside—what we value, love, and hold most dear, or what we fear, dislike, or abhor. This most authentic side is our *representational self.* The front of the tapestry represents what we reveal to others, our *presentational self.* Sometimes, as in a tapestry, there is a slight difference between these two *selves.* Most of the people whom you know socially and professionally present their pleasant, groomed, public side, their *presentational selves.*

The more confident and authentic we are, the less posturing exists between our *representational* and *presentational* selves. For some, the total *representational self* is held privately or only revealed amid closest friends, loved ones, staff, or colleagues. We connect with them as our most authentic, imperfect, and vulnerable selves. The more people with whom we are our true selves, expressing all our concerns and feelings, the more fortunate we are. The Bible states that we are blessed to have one true friend, a person with whom we can share our deepest and darkest thoughts and greatest joys, along with our concerns, dislikes, *lenses,* and exposed imperfections.

A niece remarked, "It seems as if everyone I know is together but me." I assured her that is far from the truth. People may appear together on the outside, but inside, they are often doubtful, frightened, insecure, lost, repressed, out of control, or in turmoil. They may even have similar concerns and fears to yours. "Will I be accepted?" "Will I be okay?" "What will others think?" "Will love last?" "Will I keep my job?" "Am I a good parent?" "What will my spouse or partner do?" These are concerns I repeatedly hear. A very professional and presentable woman made an excellent first impression. She was friendly, poised, dressed impeccably, and employed by a reputable company. Her *presentational self* was in order. Yet internally, she was a mess. Her *representational self* was in total chaos, so much so that she had contemplated suicide. If you had met her, you would never have guessed from her appearance the anguish, self-doubt, and isolation that lived within.

I observed a significant shift in U.S. culture in the past quarter century. Now, people more readily express their feelings. Social media, texts, internet, and television all expose more brutal and raw honesty. Usually, people who are more private, especially my generation, feel there is too much personal and intimate information on the airwaves.

Often, it is not in our best interests to express our frustration and what we really feel. We may not communicate our frustration or annoyance with a certain employee who rarely completes a task on time because their specific expertise is difficult to replace. Our frustration or anger would further upset the employee, which would add to the negative feelings that already exist between us. If we are upset with a client because of a substantial unpaid bill yet do not want to lose that client, we are reticent to express our concern. We may be quite aggravated that our supervisor often piles a load on us at the last minute, but we probably would not say, "This is unfair. You have known about this project for a long time. Why did you delay until the last minute to hand it to me?" In this case, the objective is to keep our job, not to get fired, so we accept the task and silently grin and bear it. There are times we all have to suck it up, and the more gracefully we can truly accept the burdensome reality that "it is what it is," the better off we are.

Physicians, politicians, psychiatrists, lawyers, and other professionals occasionally modify their communication style with patients, constituents, and clients who are considerably different than they are. Physicians, together with family, first evaluate when it is or when it isn't beneficial to reveal the truth, especially if an elderly person or child cannot comprehend an explanation. When physicians use a serious or negative voice tone and facial expression throughout their message, the sustained impact on the patient may be harmful, as they may become more anxious or depressed, and they may even give up any hope. Each situation requires a sensitive evaluation of and balance for the patient—an honest approach in the most positive, caring way. This manner best serves the patient and fosters the patient's acceptance of the outcome or the inevitable as comfortably as possible.

At home, we may repress our feelings because we fear confrontation, consequences, or abandonment. We communicate in a *presentational* manner because it is necessary and helps us achieve our desired goal to remain in the relationship. At times, we refrain from saying what we truly feel and respond with what we feel we "should" say. We alter our *representational selves*—what we really feel—to modify our *presentational selves* to what we feel is conducive for the situation; that widens the gap between our *representational selves* and *presentational selves*. This is difficult for many people. It is especially challenging for persons of high integrity or those who are especially sensitive. Those who bear the sole responsibility of raising children, paying the mortgage, or making ends meet may feel there are no other opportunities, especially when jobs are scarce. In those situations, a person may feel there is little choice but to conform to insensitivities, deception, shoddy work, or competition. It also is difficult for people who are afraid to change jobs for other reasons or for those who want to remain in a relationship. The fact that the further anyone strays from their *representational selves*, the more alienated they become, is reflected in their disingenuous response. Since they can't change policy or determine events, often their only conceivable survival plan is to become *source-disconnected*, which leads to further withdrawal from their true selves. Unfortunately, at times posturing and conformity are the only means people know to reconcile their high standards and a sense of necessity.

The wider the gap between our *representational selves* and *presentational selves*, the more uncomfortable we are with our deception; our communication reflects that. When we are dishonest with ourselves, we are more hesitant, negative, controlled, and impersonal and often come across as rude, abrupt, condescending, patronizing, or demeaning. We may also simply raise our voice or speak too quickly or haltingly or in a hysterical manner. What's worse, we may not even be fully aware of what's happening.

Yet, during global crises, people of all ages and backgrounds often let go of their roles and let their hair down as they become more real. They feel the need to open up to express their anxieties, fears, and gratitude as they seek comfort and commonality with others.

There Is a Solution

On *60 Minutes*, Anderson Cooper (2014) interviewed Jon Kabat-Zinn, who demonstrated the art of meditation and how three breaths restore us to the present. Cooper highlighted that major organizations, such as Google and Facebook, now begin each meeting with this technique to restore oneself and connect with one's core. This improves performance and focus.

In the interview, Kabat-Zinn also stresses the importance of living in the "present" and being mindful of each moment. He invites people to try to void their lives of daily distractions. Being mindful is being aware—that is, being aware of even the simplest things, especially your breathing. He states that being aware is the key. "Get out of bed with awareness, brush your teeth with awareness." It's not as simple as it seems, and since your mind tends to wander, you'll have to gently rein it back in. He tells us to "simply rest in awareness." He reminds us that "mindfulness is not a 'doing.' It's a 'being,' and being doesn't take any time" (Cooper 2014).

In the grips of any confrontational situation, we can change if we engage our Mona Lisa smile and *instant mindful breath-boosters* to restore our *source-connection* and touch our true core, our *representational self*. We instantly feel lighter and more positive. Our voices and body language positively reflect our shift, and that inviting and inclusive energy flows from us to others. In that "calm and civil aura," we connect soul to soul with every other person. Our preconceived thoughts, fear, suspicions, and formerly held labels, biases, or prejudices are set aside as we are enveloped in a pure connection. In mindful comfort, we receive and convey the *intention* and *meaning* of our message. In a respectful manner, we acknowledge the other person's right to their viewpoint and respect those aspects that are positive, though they may be different from ours. We must never attack or demean another person's idea but instead offer positive, realistic suggestions that elevate the objective and best practices of what we hope to achieve in a win-win for everyone.

At this point, you may be asking yourself, "Is this a pipe dream or a reality?" If you hone and adopt these skills, you create a more inviting, civil, and enduring environment. It requires time and practice, and there will be times when it just doesn't work, but most of the time it will.

Let me close by highlighting that comfort, trust, and respect are among the highest honors that we grant and receive. Treasure them, as they are valuable. And as I kindly remind you, civility is experienced through all our words and deeds and is expressed through our heartfelt, *source-connected* nonverbal communication, voice tone, and word choice. These factors remain consistent with one another. A truly remarkable person treats each person individually with compassion, decency, and dignity, and helps to uplift others along life's way.

You Hear Me, but Are You Listening?

I believe the greatest gift I can conceive of having from anyone, is to be seen by them, heard by them, to be understood and touched by them. The greatest gift I can give is to see, hear, understand and to touch another person. When this is done I feel contact has been made.

—Virginia Satir

Listening

When my youngest daughter was growing up, she often said, "You hear me, Mom, but are you really listening?" Yes, I heard the words, but I didn't always pay attention to what she said. We can hear without listening. Just think of all the background sounds in your life—at home, the workplace, or on your commute. Which sounds fade into the background, and which noises remain an annoyance, if you let them? Are they loud voices, crying, bickering, shouting, barking, alarms, rumbles, printers, traffic, rodents, sirens, gunshots, or unceasing digital beeps? There are some sounds that you prefer not to hear and other sounds to which you definitely do not want to listen. It behooves all of us to separate substance from noise.

Listening is a significant feature of conveying respect and care. Information in our culture is often "in your face." We see huge billboards and hear TV advertisements (which at times are louder than the programs). Many communicate directly, without subtlety. If a person doesn't speak loudly enough, we often say that we don't understand instead of trying to listen more attentively. Because of these factors, many people in the U.S. culture are conditioned to focus less intently on received auditory information.

In my personal and professional experience, people in mainstream U.S. culture do not value listening as much as people of other cultures do. While schools offer us classes on becoming a better speaker, how many classes are offered on improving listening? If listening had more value, wouldn't schools introduce the art of true listening in early childhood education, or wouldn't they offer us Listening 101, 102, and 103 in high school or college? In Judaism, the Shema prayer begins with Hear Israel. This is a most holy and significant prayer that is recited at every service and at night before sleep. The Shema also offers an immediate response, often with the very next breath after a most urgent event. In my adult experiences, although the word Shema means "to hear," now I always hear the words more deeply as the command to listen more carefully and intently from my heart. In some cultures, they revere listening more than speaking. Many people from Asian and indigenous cultures appreciate listening to delicate and subtle changes. Listening to the shift of the wind, the flow in the course of a stream, or the song of a bird is a pleasant and pivotal feature in daily life. In the book *Seven Hands, Seven Hearts*, Elizabeth Woody, a Native

American, says, "The skill of telling and listening was 'handed down,' a legacy from a very ancient art form of imparting and storing knowledge and wisdom. It requires patience to listen to hours of 'testimony.' We must also learn to listen without judgment, overruling, interjection, or suppression" (Woody 1994).

Two days after the terrorist strikes at the Charlie Hebdo Newspaper in Paris, Lester Holt, anchor for NBC's *Inside Nightly News*, stated, "There are times when words can't capture a moment, so you stand back, take it all in, just listen, and let the story speak for itself" (Holt 2015).

A nurse works in an assisted-living residence for seniors as a member of the team that admits new residents and as an advocate for patients in hospice care. She shared that she learned to listen until the patient, resident, family member, or caregiver "gets everything off their chest," even if it takes almost an hour before she begins to respond. A colleague named this "verbal vomiting." Since I am the mentoring type and have a tendency to want to jump in and offer ideas, I am fully aware that I haven't always been as patient as necessary. In my eightieth year, I continually strive to improve.

Is there a person in your life who truly listens to you? When that person listens to you, you probably feel that you are the most important person in their life while their entire attention is focused just on you. They not only pick up your words but also sense your feelings of joy and worries. In those moments, *nothing else really matters in the world but you*. They do not advise, ignore, interrupt, judge, placate, or rush you. They are not distracted by anything else that is happening; they just listen to you. Doesn't it feel wonderful? My brother-in-law is such a person. His lean-in body language reflects that he is fully engaged. He is more interested in others' lives than speaking about himself. When I am with him, he always makes me feel good. Philosophically, we don't always agree, but I deeply appreciate his receptiveness, his attentiveness, and when needed, his concern.

In a past study on solutions to school violence, student participants perceived that active listening and other counseling skills were the most important training for teachers preparing to address school violence (Dear 1995b). Twenty years later, in 2015, on NPR's *TED Radio Hour*, Reverend Jeffrey Brown again highlighted the importance of listening, especially in reducing gang violence. His presentation "How Can Listening Transform an Entire Community?" highlights how *listening is the first step and most important part of the communication process* (Brown 2015). If you don't listen, how are you possibly going to understand another's needs, follow instructions, sense urgency, respond accurately, resolve issues, or offer compassion? When we listen with both ears along with our heart, things begin to change.

Listening is an act of empathy. By deeply listening to individuals, we form relationships and bring people together. Actively listening allows us to experience and view people and situations in their own light. Thus, we permit serious change to take place, perhaps even saving lives. Reverend Brown proved this was true with his decade-long mission known as the Boston Miracle, which began in the mid-1980s. His church, the Union Baptist Church, was solely responsible for a significant decline in the homicide rate—a reduction of 79 percent—simply because they listened to at-risk youths in the Boston area. He tells us, "By listening, you find yourselves drawn into this greater presence where you can find answers that may not be audible answers, but it's something that you feel in your spirit" (Brown 2015). He further states, "In the dialogue that occurs, you find that there is a magnetism, where you come together in a way that is greater than the sum of its parts."

If your mind starts to wander while listening, gently bring it back to the conversation. Listen to the voice tone as well as the words to gain the full impact of the message. Along with listening, remember to observe nonverbal communication to sense what the other person is feeling. In time, with desire, motivation, and the skills that you will learn in this chapter, you become a better communicator. Be patient with yourself.

Good Listening Skills

Good listening isn't a passive skill; it is a mindful activity requiring complete focus and an open attitude. When we focus and gain a sense of the other person's nonverbal communication, voice tone, and word choice, we gain additional clues that also help us fully understand the nuances of their message.

Becoming a good listener requires diligent practice—similar to any other skill. You most likely participate in an activity that requires practice: exercising, organizing, cooking, navigating, playing sports or an instrument, or learning new technical or digital skills. These skills require time to master and perfect; and so does listening. To be a mindful and effective listener, the following steps are recommended:

1. Stop thinking, assume receptive body language, and shift into *source-connected* listening with a "what's up" attitude.
2. Focus all your attention on the person speaking or what you are listening to.
3. Do not anticipate or assume what the other person is going to say.
4. Eliminate any bias or preconceived ideas and suspend any judgment.
5. Be aware of your *internal* and *external lenses* and their impact on what you hear.
6. Do not interrupt the other person. Let the other person complete their thought before you respond.
7. Do not begin to formulate your response until the other person has finished speaking.
8. If you cannot listen, kindly inform the other person and offer a time when you are available.
9. Do not filter the information to process only what you want to hear.
10. Remember to listen compassionately from your heart along with your ears.

The instant you begin to listen, immediately slide into a *source-connected* listening mind-set, stop thinking, and start deep listening. Then, direct your complete focus on listening to what the other person says. An open mind, appropriate attitude, body language, and eye contact are essential for good listening. It is not an easy task to listen without preconceived ideas or prejudices, but it is possible. To be an effective listener, we also set aside our emotional "baggage." If those or other thoughts or our *personal lenses* or prejudices begin to invade or interfere with listening, quickly become aware of them. Block them or imagine pouring the thoughts into a paper bag and dumping them in the trash.

If we fidget, doodle, gaze around, or are engaged in something else while listening, it sends the message that all our attention is not focused on the individual, signaling that perhaps we are bored, uninterested, or don't care. We certainly do not want to come across as indifferent.

In deep listening, we cannot think about anything else, formulate our response, glance away, turn our back, work at the computer, perform other tasks, or engage in other activities and listen simultaneously. If your mind whirls in anticipation, busyness, chaos, concern, or rumination, take a minute or two and practice your three mindful breaths to calm yourself until you feel at ease and can return to the present moment. By performing this exercise, you increase your ability to gain focus. If you don't think that you are capable of tuning out irrelevant stimuli or do not have the ability to remain focused, just reflect on an activity in which you are fully engaged and able to block other thoughts to remain fully focused. If you are a sports fan, nature lover, religious person, creative artist, or avid reader, you most likely block out irrelevant information when fully engaged in those activities.

In a heartfelt manner, we also observe nonverbal communication, sense the feeling and voice tone, and listen to the word choice. When engaged in that type of deep listening, we pay attention and are as receptive to information as a blank document screen awaiting text. When we pull up a blank screen in a word processing program, defaults can be programmed, such as page size, margins, and fonts, but not the words that we anticipate will appear on the screen after the message is created. In the same way, when we engage with a person in a personal, social, professional, or any other type of conversation, we may have an inkling of what is going to be said because of the context, but we can't be certain. If we don't know the person or are unaware of the topic, we have fewer, if any, cues. Unless the person is responding to a specific situation or question, we can't even predict the topic. Even then, the other person may avoid answering or pivot to another point.

There will be certain situations where listening continues to be a challenge, but persevere to diligently work through to improve that skill. Be patient; it requires time, but it works. One thing I know for certain—when I am *source-connected* with another person, there is no question about listening because I am so deeply connected. It is as though the other person and I are one. Our connection is all that matters, and the synergy of the moment is the only thing in my world.

If a person's manner, voice tone, or word choice is abusive, we absolutely do not have to listen. Politely ask the person to change their tone, manner, or topic. If they don't, switch to another topic, simply turn and politely walk away or end the call.

Listen in Comfort

During the years I consulted with physicians from other cultures, many expressed that at times they were emotionally exhausted while listening to their patients. When I asked what they do when they listen, they often responded, "I listen deeply and absorb the patient's words and feelings." I suggested that they *go for a visit* instead and offered the following approach and image to help them understand and adopt the concept.

Imagine that you are talking on the phone with a person. Instead of holding the receiver at your ear, you engage the speaker mode and *go for a visit*. When you *go for a visit*, envision placing the phone facing the person a foot in front of you. You receive the information, but it is not as close to your heart and soul as if you were holding the receiver at your ear. When the person has finished speaking, return the receiver or phone closer to you so you can respond. Whenever necessary, engage the plastic or plexiglass shield.

When you need to *go for a visit*, the concept is similar. Rather than bring the patient's painful, distraught, or negative energy into your personal space, you move into their personal space. After you have engaged the *go for a visit* skill to listen, bring your personal energy back to respond. Using this approach, you are empathetic without taking on energy of the emotional burdens and pain of others as intensely. Perfecting *going for a visit* takes time, but the approach benefits your well-being by allowing you to listen and respond with compassion and empathy while protecting yourself and preventing the depletion of your emotional well-being. Another person cannot measure how open your heart and soul are to their message and energy. Practice the concept of bringing the other person's feelings into your space and *go for a visit* in their space.

On the other hand, if a person you trust and are comfortable with is expressing loving, joyful, uplifting, or humorous thoughts, "let the sunshine in." Feel the smile in your heart and on your face as you sense that positive energy flow into you. A friend suggested that when a very special event happens, you grasp one wrist tightly with your other hand, close your eyes, then focus that joyful energy from your hand to your wrist to penetrate deeply, allowing you to further absorb and imprint those good vibes. Later, when you need that reserve, you can place your hand over the same spot on your wrist to retrieve that positive energy.

Every person performs different tasks with varying degrees of ease. It's not always easy to observe or recognize a task's degree of easiness or challenge. Some people easily multitask in a situation in which another person has to singularly focus. If a task or situation is more challenging, a person is unable to listen, process, or absorb new or additional information. They become overloaded with the conversation and feel they are caught in a verbal labyrinth. This is especially significant for those who are not auditory by nature. (The Neurolinguistic Programming is presented later in this section, in the chapter "Touch, Sight, or Sound," which explains how we learn best.)

If there are situations or circumstances in which you cannot listen, I recommend you say, "Excuse me. I can't listen right now." Then add one of the following:

1. "I can only do one thing at a time."
2. "Please state the most important information first."
3. "Please state only the most important information."
4. "Please write it down."

5. "Please tell me later."
6. "Please say it another way."
7. "Please simplify the information."
8. "Please break down the information by pausing as you would between reciting the digits in a phone number."

If you are unable to focus on lengthy conversations or the voice or words are too intense, one option is to reduce how intensely you listen. Do not turn off your listening process but adjust how much energy you receive. This is similar to turning down the volume on an electronic device or narrowing the *lens* on a camera. Become keenly aware of persons or situations where you partially "close down" to a more comfortable zone. Engage the same "closing down" when listening to people who speak too loudly, too rapidly, too intensely, or just too much. Do not disconnect from the other person; just reduce how much energy you use to listen or tell them to please speak slower or softer.

There are times when other people want to share feelings, events, or stories and you don't want to listen. This is especially relevant if the issue does not pertain directly to you or a person you know or if you are uncomfortable with the topic. Perhaps the person repeated the same or a similar story several times. Negative attitudes, racial slurs, intricate minutia of sexual activities, or detailed complexities of illness, surgery, hardships, or accidents are topics you may not want to hear, or the person may be sharing too much information. The discussion may be too painful to process, or you may not like gossip. You have the right and the option not to listen. If you are comfortable and don't think you will offend the other person, you can offer how they can modify the information so that you can listen. In a polite way, you can also change the topic, set time constraints, or excuse yourself.

No one enjoys listening to a grumpy, ornery, or nagging person. When folks get upset, even when what they utter is accurate, they often use harsh language or a nasty voice. When a person shouts or calls names, firmly yet politely tell them to stop and modify the way they are talking. I suggest stating, "I will be glad to listen when you are calmer and can speak in a pleasant tone." The only time you disconnect is when an individual is verbally abusive or the language is vitriolic. You determine that boundary. Mary Ylvisaker Nilsen (1990) says, "Thoughts from others are observations, not prescriptions. You choose whether to accept, ignore, or reject their ideas."

When loved ones offer constructive suggestions or attempt to enlighten my awareness of their needs, I try to honor that. But there are times when it may take several attempts because of their tone, or at times my busyness. I try to be receptive even when the information is something that I am not ready to hear. It is much easier when the information is presented in a *source-connected*, civil, conversational tone rather than in frustration, confrontation, or from a perception that is 180 degrees from my reality or my truth. My boundary is that I won't allow others to call me names or speak rudely. There are some things I simply refuse to hear. I do not tolerate prejudice or racial slurs, usually do not engage in negative gossip, and rarely listen to unnecessary negative information or statements that do not add positive energy to the universe.

If you are not in the mood to listen, I suggest some options:

- Politely inform the other person, "I'm not interested in listening to that," "I don't want to hear it," or "I can't listen now."
- Quickly get yourself into a listening mood.
- Offer another time that you are available.

When a person is trying to tell you something that they find difficult about you, it's best not to say, "I don't want to hear it," "I can't listen," or "I'm busy now" (unless you are), especially if they communicate in a constructive, civil, *source-connected* manner. If you tune out the other person because you do not want to hear something about yourself that is unpleasant or unfavorable, you discount the other person's reality and dismiss them. This creates a chasm in the relationship. If it isn't "small stuff" to them, unresolved issues remain a thorn in their side. At some point, it has to be resolved if you are to return to the close bond that you had and still desire. Sometimes, this takes a long time to resolve, and the emotional tear remains between the two of you.

Do not tune out or let the information "go in one ear and out the other" with matters that must be resolved. Rarely do two people place the same value, priority, or time commitment on resolving every issue. Some people think that if they avoid dealing with an issue, eventually it disappears. Generally, resolution on major issues does not happen that easily. Find a time and place that are mutually acceptable to discuss and resolve each issue and challenge. Understand that compromise of behavior and attitude—not principle—is a key factor in the solution.

If a person is tired or has said that they had a rough day at work, at home, or on their commute, or if they appear preoccupied, respect that. Unless there is an emergency, that moment is definitely not the time for a discussion. If a person has not directly stated that they do not want to listen, it is best to observe their body language before you begin an important dialogue. When a person is not in a receptive mood to listen, their body language is tense; their arms may be crossed in a tight, rigid, and closed position across their chest. If when you begin the dialogue the person appears tired, becomes defensive, knows all the answers, or has a "my way or the highway" attitude, it is definitely not the time to continue. Wait until the person is more receptive or has a better attitude, or lean into a nonthreatening familiar activity, behavior, or attitude that will create a more receptive environment.

When children are young, they often interrupt their parents or caregivers when they are busy, on a computer or other electronic device, or on the phone. I observed that not only children but spouses or partners as well often do the same. Naturally, you cannot effectively listen to two conversations simultaneously. Excuse yourself from the phone conversation for a moment and remind the children or adult in the room, "I'm on the phone and can't possibly listen to you and the other person. I will talk with you when I am finished." If a young child nudges you, try to redirect them, provide an alternative, hold them on your lap to comfort them, or return the call at a more suitable time.

There are some issues that are critical and must be discussed or resolved immediately. If there is an emergency or urgency within the family or at work, even if you are not ready or do not want to face the issue, it needs to be addressed. When a supervisor asks to speak to you, it is best that you listen or give a good reason explaining why you can't talk at that time. You may be involved in another project, not have the time or the necessary information, or not know how to perform the task. However, all these require a response.

A relative required a painful but necessary oral surgery. It was the only permanent beneficial resolution for her situation. When she shared the procedure with her neighbor, her friend said that her dentist had recommended the same course but she didn't like what she heard, so she switched to another dentist. In many critical medical challenges, it is wise to seek a second or third opinion, but occasionally we look elsewhere when we can't face reality and there is no plausible solution other than to do nothing.

Sometimes a person who is listening simultaneously begins to stare into space. It is difficult for others to decipher exactly what that means. The person who is staring may be contemplating something relevant to the subject, or they may comprehend more accurately without visual cues. Some people even close their eyes to concentrate so they can improve their processing of the information, allowing them to be the best listener that they can be.

Never fake that you are listening. It is rude, insensitive, and often hurts others' feelings; this does not encourage productive dialogue. Furthermore, others expect that you are paying attention, so they exchange ideas, affirm their beliefs, express concerns, vent feelings, and suggest solutions but do not necessarily offer advice. In the future, you may also need the information that you purposely missed and that the other person thought you heard.

Become a Better Listener

Now that you know what it takes to be a good listener, how can you improve? If you do not understand the information, it is essential to inform the other person, especially in the United States. In other cultures, "face-saving" is the custom. There, asking questions is often inappropriate or impolite. People from other linguistic and cultural backgrounds may not want to appear ignorant. They may be embarrassed when they do not know something. Often, they may pretend they understand, falsely nod yes or shake their heads no, or give an irrelevant response.

If you do not understand, asking a person to repeat once is okay. But chances are that if you ask the person to repeat something, they will repeat it in the same way they initially stated it. Unless you think that you did not comprehend because you were not paying attention, I suggest that you tell the other person why you did not understand the information.

Say, "Excuse me. I don't understand." Then add one of the following that will help you:

- "Please repeat it louder."
- "Please repeat it slowly."

- "Please spell the word."
- "Please break down or simplify the information."
- "Please say it another way."

Two brothers had disagreed over the care of their elderly parents. The younger brother, who lived near his parents, had the major responsibility of overseeing their care. The older brother, who lived three thousand miles away, was unable to assume the same load. Several times over the years of caregiving, the older brother apologized that he hadn't helped. Although the younger brother understood that the older brother couldn't help, he resented the situation.

Years after the parents had passed away, the younger brother became quite ill. During his illness, he and his older brother reminisced about the past. Again, the older brother apologized. This time, his younger brother said, "Thank you. Now I can let go of my resentment." The older brother replied, "I apologized several times over the years," to which the younger brother responded, "Maybe so, but this is actually the very first time I heard you." Recognize that often in life an issue or topic may be considerably important to you but for unknown reasons the other person is just not willing or receptive at that time. Until a person is ready to own and deal with an issue, no matter how compassionately, positively, effectively, and appropriately you give your message, that person is simply not going to hear what you said or process the information.

Listen to Your Source-Voice

Keep listening to your *source-voice* in mind. Whenever you are in any situation or about to make a comment to a person and begin to feel a sense that pulls you back, a knot in your chest, a grab at your stomach, or any feeling in the place in your body where your *source-voice* signals, acknowledge and respond immediately, even if only mentally to yourself. Check the source of that disease, and when you become aware of that signal, silently acknowledge it. When necessary, or if another person is the catalyst of your feelings, either hold the thought or, in a *source-connected* manner, express your concerns or questions to them. Sometimes you need to address the discomfort by disengaging, handling the situation on your own, or letting it go. Whatever you do, do not discount that negative or uneasy signal from your *source-voice*.

Too often, we ignore that signal and let it slide. We then suppress our feelings, which is rarely in our best interest. It may be moments, days, years, or decades later when we finally acknowledge that inner *source-voice*'s plea. The longer we wait, the less we honor ourselves and others because we have been disingenuous. Unless circumstances change, that issue remains lodged in that particular situation, wedged between you and the other person, creating a kink in the lines of communication and your relationship.

Spiritual Listening

At times, we are angels to one another, giving messages that perhaps are divinely or universally inspired to help one another gain ease or solutions that we cannot find ourselves. Not only do I listen to *what* another person says, but I also try to understand *why* they are saying it. Often, the comment is in response to an important decision I need to make, a challenge that I face, or a pertinent issue of which I am not yet aware.

Suddenly, "out of nowhere," a person brings up a pertinent topic or I "inadvertently" meet a person who has the knowledge to help resolve an issue or give me additional insight. Albert Einstein stated, "Coincidence is God's way of remaining anonymous" (2000). In his book *Celestine Prophecy*, James Redfield (1993) alludes to these "coincidences." He feels, as many believers do, that these coincidences are not coincidences but events meant to happen. When they occur, do not fear them or negate them. Embrace them and allow them to guide and contribute to your well-being.

For those of you who are interested in developing the spiritual side of yourself, listening has another dimension. When we quiet our mind, we are more open. Messages from the universe, ancestors, angels, or a deeper or higher source become more readily accessible and easier to receive and flow into us. When we stop thinking, fighting ourselves, or vacillating between what we want to do and what we feel we "should do," these spiritual feelings and insights are free to flow through our *Spiritual Internet* into our *source-voice*. These spiritual messages are universally inspired acts that lift our sense of well-being. At its ultimate, we feel enveloped in the moment and a spiritual interconnectedness with the Universe.

A friend traveled to Egypt, and for years he had dreamed of climbing to the top of Mount Sinai to experience a sunrise at this holy site. At dawn of the ascent, because he lingered below to chat with some friends, he had to hasten his pace to reach the top to witness the birth of a new day. His strenuous climb up the mountain became more challenging and took more time than he had planned. As sunrise approached, he realized that he wasn't even close to the top. The faster he tried to walk, the more painful, difficult, and encumbered his journey became. Suddenly, he stopped and reflected. Here he was on Mount Sinai, a place with anticipated bliss he had dreamed of for years. Instead, he was distraught and quite disappointed as he realized that he was not going to summit Mount Sinai to experience the sunrise. As he took fewer steps at a time and agonized for an hour, he decided to stop and see if there was anything positive that he could embrace to overcome his disappointment. He asked himself, "What can I learn from this experience?" He realized that he didn't actually have to climb to the top of Mount Sinai for the sunrise to spiritually enjoy the experience. He learned that the "top" of Mount Sinai could be anywhere he wanted it to be.

Active and engaged listening is pivotal in building more meaningful, respectful, and loving *source-connections* with others, and it purifies our *positive communication environment*. You gained numerous insights into the stumbling blocks of and solutions to deep listening, which are significant gems in your "communication jewel box." You are aware of *source-connected*, compassionate listening in comfort from the heart and soul, eliminating assumptions and bias from unfiltered information, politely telling a person when you cannot listen, and becoming a more spiritual listener.

Following is a *Communication Enhancement Guide* to further achieve mindful, positive, effective, and appropriate listening skills.

Features of listening that I want to improve:

- Do I listen with my heart and ears?
- Do I suspend all judgment?
- Am I acutely aware of preconceived ideas and biases?
- Do I eliminate the impact of my *internal* and *external lenses*?
- Do I filter information?
- Do I interrupt others to get my point across?
- Do I politely express "I can't listen"?
- Do I listen in comfort?
- How focused am I? Can I bring my mind back when it begins to wander?
- Do I honor my *source-voice*?
- Do I believe in spiritual listening? If so, am I clearing my mind to allow messages from the *Spiritual Internet*?

Mindful listening is one of the most important features in gaining an understanding of the needs and wants of another person, and it enriches relationships and connections. Maintain the awareness that when you do not listen, you "turn off" the very people you want to connect with at home, work, and play. With patience, kindness, and diligence, you improve listening to everyone. Listening is an art void of all judgment and negative or biased thoughts. Mindful listening encompasses compassion, heart, and soul. Like any type of art, listening also requires time to master. Embrace the journey.

When you are in the present moment and connected with life, you will be amazed at the beautiful sounds in your life and in nature at the dawn of and during each new day. In gratitude, I marvel at my husband's and my breath, a loved one's patter or footsteps, a baby's coo, a child's laughter, a teenager's bounce, a senior's shuffle, a kitten's purr, a dog's collar, the wind's whisper, a brook's flow, a hummingbird's flitter, a bird's song, and finally, at the end of the day, the night's stillness. What delights you? If you let it happen, you can also create a more joyous and serene journey by listening to the thankful sounds around you.

Mental Processes for Communication

Perceive positively, process realistically, and respond accurately.

Effective Communication Is a Two-Way Process and Feedback Loop

Conversation is a two-way process—a feedback loop—between the speaker and the listener. One person transmits or speaks while the other person perceives and listens, and then the functions are reversed. We listen and respond from the heart to create a connection that must exist among all those present to achieve effective communication. Similar to learning to share our food, room, clothes, or toys when we were children, we also share the dialogue by listening and speaking.

Let's compare two people conversing with two people playing tennis. One person hits the ball down the court while the other awaits, ready to receive the ball. Then, the second person hits it back. If you observed a tennis game, the person receiving the ball has their arm fully extended and posed a little to the back. If they positioned their arm directly to the side, they would not have as much control or strength to return the ball with the necessary speed and accuracy to play a winning shot. Communication is similar. If we do not focus on listening to the person, then we cannot possibly pick up all the information or fine nuances.

Communication continues to mirror the tennis game. The first player hits the ball down the court, representing the role of the speaker. The second player—on the other side of the net—initially receives the ball, representing the role of a listener. Then, they instantly shift to become the hitter and return the ball, assuming the role of the speaker. In the next play, the roles reverse. Whether you play singles or doubles, the communication pattern is similar. And if more than two people are conversing, only one person can respond effectively while the others listen attentively. This communication cycle continues until the conversation is finished.

Basic Concepts of Mental Processes

For the purpose of this book, I present how we process information at the most basic level so that readers without a scientific background can easily grasp the information. There are primarily three mental processes that occur during communication. The first step includes *perception and listening*. We continue to listen to the voice tone and words with our hearts and ears while we observe body language and facial expressions. We cannot allow our preconceived ideas, biases, or *internal* or *external lenses* to enter this process.

The second step includes *recall* and is followed by *comparison* of past information and previous experiences. The brain is quite complex, but it is an organized and expedient system that *integrates* the information that you heard, saw, or sensed from long-term or short-term memory. Then, in milliseconds, the brain *synthesizes* and *formulates* the response and delivers that information to all our senses and external messengers. They are our eyes, mouth, lips, tongue, muscles, joints, limbs, hands, fingers, feet, and toes, which optimally join in a systemized and coordinated effort to deliver our response. These internal processes take place in our brains and are invisible to ourselves and others.

The final step is *response* and is visible. This step includes body language, voice tone, and spoken words. As you will learn in the chapters "Take a Look" and "It's Not What You Say, but How You Say It," our body language, facial expressions, and voice tone reflect our *intention*. We remain aware that nonverbal communication, voice tone, and verbal communication are consistent with one another to relay our exact thoughts and purpose.

These different processes or functions occur in separate areas of our brains, and the transmission relies on a highly tuned neurological and muscular network. If you compare the three primary mental functions—perception, process, and response—to simultaneously watching several different screens on a computer, digital device, or television, you realize that you cannot successfully watch more than one screen or focal point at the same time. Yes, we can step back and view the entire screen at one time, but we lack the ability to fine-tune the information unless one eye is focused on a specific spot.

In the same way, we cannot effectively listen, process, and respond at the same time. To gain the best results in the first step of *perceiving* and *listening*, our entire attention exclusively focuses and remains in that process for the necessary milliseconds until we are finished. When we shift to *integrate and formulate* information, we continue to exclusively focus and remain in that process until all our thoughts are together. When we *express our response*, we monitor the consistency of the communication factors to accurately convey our message. When we pause and reflect how rapidly, seamlessly, effectively, and accurately our mind synthesizes and processes so much in seconds, it is indeed a miracle.

To be thoughtful and successful communicators, we remain in each process as long as necessary. No one but ourselves can estimate or determine how much time that requires. There are various reasons why people do not communicate as positively, effectively, and successfully as they could. The following is an abbreviated list:

Listening Errors
1. From the start, we are uncomfortable with the person, situation, or topic.
2. A person signals a nonverbal or verbal cue, or an event, sound, or noise knocks us off our *source-connected* center. The annoyance may be a distracting sound or an inappropriate glance, impatient sigh, flung hands, arched eyebrow, puckered lip, or any other nonverbal gesture or vocal inflection that sends a negative signal.
3. Our *internal* or *external lenses*, which take a split second to affect our initial perception—at that very first instant—distort and contaminate everything down the line.

4. Our minds wander in the first step, so immediately there is an information gap as we already missed something.
5. We listen, but at some point, we tune out the information and focus on our own thoughts, another person, or something else. Again, we lost information.
6. Our minds do not return to attentive listening during the remaining conversation.

Processing Errors

1. We prematurely move to process the information before the person is finished speaking because we anticipate what the other person is going to say or we think that we know the answer.
2. We do not take the necessary time because we feel unworthy, intimidated, rushed, or just want to move on.
3. Unless we go back and ask the person to repeat what they said, we do not attain all the information.
4. We do not include or take the time to think about the consistency of our nonverbal communication, voice tone, and verbal communication to accurately and genuinely reflect our *meaning* and *intention*.

Responding Errors

1. Our responses may be totally irrelevant.
2. We may give incorrect responses for the topic of conversation or the question that was asked.
3. At some point, we realize that we missed something, want to correct a thought or response, or are distracted. We then insert fillers, such as "Um," "Well," "Okay," or "You know," or there are pauses of silence in our responses.
4. With the addition of fillers, pauses, gaps, or silence, we do not come across as comfortable, personable, knowledgeable, professional, or confident as we otherwise would.
5. We begin our responses, but sometime during that process, we go off on a tangent and do not complete our original response.
6. We present ideas and skip to subtopics before completing our main ideas. This is a sequencing issue. Instead of going from A to B to C to D, we skip from A to D, to B to C. When we speak in this pattern, it is more difficult for the other person to follow our train of thought. This potentially presents a gap in the listener's ability to understand the information.

In summary, at all times, only you know how much time you need to process and develop your thoughts and respond mindfully, positively, effectively, and appropriately. Remain in each process as long as required. Try not to allow anyone or anything to intimidate or rush you and knock you off your center. This off-kilter status robs us of the time we need to think through our thoughts and formulate our most accurate response, reflecting our truth at the moment, as only we know it. When we remain *source-connected*, we have the best chance to be as successful as possible and come across as compassionate, comfortable, competent, and compelling speakers.

Touch, Sight, or Sound

I just don't get it!

Neurolinguistic Programming (NLP)

The appreciation for and implications of Neurolinguistic Programming (NLP) are extremely important, but too often we overlook its value. It is an imperative tool that reveals how each person optimally understands and processes information.

The term *Neurolinguistic Programming* in an article in the *American Journal of Nursing* (Knowles 1983) piqued my interest. In my experience, knowledge and use of NLP significantly enhances effective communication in any personal, vocational, or professional setting. Neurolinguistic Programming refers to the way we best make sense of things or learn material, and it affects how we perceive, store, interpret, and formulate information. There are three NLP modalities—also named channels—that are located in different areas of the brain. The three NLP channels are kinesthetic, visual, and auditory, or touch, sight, and sound. A person usually has one preferred channel, though the secondary channel is also significant. We engage all three in different situations. If you sense best through your kinesthetic NLP channel (by touch), you perceive, interpret, formulate, store, and learn information best by manipulating or tinkering with objects. If you sense best through your visual NLP channel (by sight), you perceive, interpret, formulate, store, and learn information best by seeing it. If you sense best through your auditory NLP channel (by sound), you perceive, interpret, formulate, store, and learn information best by hearing it. Your optimal learning takes place when you engage your strongest NLP channels, though we cannot often choose the channel in which information is presented to us.

Whenever feasible, make sure that you receive information in the way you can best understand, interpret, and memorize it. It also is necessary to become aware of the preferred NLP channels of your family members, students, patients, colleagues, staff, associates, service providers, and other significant people in your life so that you connect and communicate most effectively with them. This is most significant for children, the elderly, or those requiring special attention. Recognize that there are also situations, especially in the classroom, where you or your child may be unable to receive the information in their most fitting channel. This may significantly hinder their learning ability.

Kinesthetic learners or communicators need to touch, feel, or manipulate their environment to make sense of and best comprehend messages. They are hands-on learners who learn by trial and error. Visual learners or communicators need "to see," read the information, watch a demonstration, or observe another person doing what they want to learn. Auditory learners or communicators need "to hear" the information. They learn best by listening to others, lectures, audio recordings, or repeating silently or aloud the information and instructions. They may also require another person to explain the material, project, or task.

People remember where they parked their car by relying on their preferred NLP channel. Kinesthetic people usually recall the route walking to their car. Visual people also recall significant landmarks or visualize and memorize posted letter and numeral markers. Auditory people usually tell themselves where they parked their car or silently verbalize significant landmarks or posted letters and numbers.

To further help you understand the implications of NLP, let us compare the three channels—kinesthetic, visual, and auditory—to three television channels, 2, 4, and 6, respectively. Let us say the reception on channel 2 is very strong, but the reception on channels 4 and 6 are weak. If you watch channel 2, which has good reception, you are going to grasp, retain, and enjoy what you watched more easily than if you watch channels 4 or 6. If you watch channels 4 or 6, the picture may have weaker reception, duller color, and more distortion and static. Therefore, it is more challenging for you to appreciate, understand, or retain what you viewed. In the same way, when you have the choice, make certain that you receive or learn information in a way that is most compatible with your preferred NLP channel.

In *Communication Briefings* (1994), Marcia Yudkin presents different styles of learning and areas of interests of the different NLP channels. Kinesthetic learners and communicators are very active and often have difficulty sitting still. In the classroom, especially at an early age, they fidget a lot. As adults, they tend to play sports, tinker, garden, dance, and participate in activities that require physical activity. When they speak, they tend to include hand gestures, shoulder shrugs, or widen their eyes. Kinesthetic learners are also affected by a heightened awareness of their physical discomfort or comfort. When a client who is a kinesthetic learner was under stress, he felt every wrinkle in the sheets on his bed. A family friend's son was a kinesthetic learner and quite tall. Teachers allowed him to sit with his feet in an unusual position so that he was comfortable enough to absorb the information. Individuals whose kinesthetic channel is strong may not prefer to remain still to relax. They might rather engage in an activity or enjoy the feel and sense of nature.

Visual NLP learners and communicators learn best by reading or viewing visual information. They like to read, shop, and spend time in front of digital screens. They also enjoy observing art, nature, sports, and other activities. Too much clutter usually affects them more than it does kinesthetic or auditory learners.

Auditory NLP learners and communicators learn best by hearing information. They prefer to listen to music and chat. They are often more sensitive to excessive noise. Trial lawyers, debaters, writers, and lecturers have strong auditory NLP channels.

Each person tries to engage their preferred channel. Many people whom I know or with whom I consulted are competent in two modalities. In my experience, very few people in my personal and professional experiences are competent in all three NLP channels. If they are, they tend to be exceptional in retaining information, perhaps because they can easily absorb, process, integrate, and learn information in all three NLP modalities.

Among those who are strong in both kinesthetic and visual modalities are artists, painters, carpenters, designers, engineers, mechanics, handymen, surgeons, hairstylists, and athletes. They visualize a goal or scene and possess the fine-motor eye-hand coordination to artistically create on paper or digital device the visions or concepts in their minds, achieve precise sport plays, or duplicate hairstyles. They also visualize, create, or repair intricate pieces of jewelry, repair or exchange mechanical parts, or surgically remove specifically diseased or potentially menacing body parts.

One NLP channel is not better than the others, though some make it easier to gain and absorb information. If you are a kinesthetic learner, it is easier to manipulate objects that are in front of you because they do not independently move or disappear, unless they are controlled remotely. Visual learners also have the ability to review written information on a page or digital screen that they control. This information also does not independently shift or disappear. Therefore, visual learners are also at an advantage.

Verbal information is the most difficult to absorb because immediately after the information is uttered, the words pass and do not return unless you can request that the person repeat or play back the information. This remains challenging in many situations, especially in a classroom, where most of the information is presented in a verbal form. A person often does not have the choice of requesting that information be repeated or asking a question every time they do not understand. In this situation, visual aids are especially helpful. Challenges arise when information is presented in your weaker channel or you explain something to a person who engages their weaker channel. When that happens, information and instructions are not going to be as easily or successfully understood or recalled. To some degree, this hinders the ability to comprehend, achieve objectives, or complete tasks. If you have not initially understood the instructions, the request, or the required task, how are you going to accurately complete the task, solve the issue, or accomplish the goal? The more channels that you combine, the more effectively you comprehend, integrate, memorize, and learn.

Before understanding NLP, one of my teacher clients thought she was stupid. She regularly had to jot down things to retain them. Without making notes, her husband could recall information by hearing it just once. After gaining an awareness of NLP, she no longer felt frustrated or inadequate, because she understood that he was an auditory learner and she was a visual learner. Before I was aware of the implications of NLP, I had an associate who rarely completed her time report accurately. Although I explained the five steps to her each month, her time sheet was usually slightly off. Once I understood the significance of NLP and realized that I was an auditory learner and she was a visual learner, I wrote down the five steps for her. After that, her time reports were exact. When my husband runs errands, he only retains what he is supposed to do if I write down the information and instructions. On the other hand, since I am an auditory learner but a poor reader, I can usually remember a few items without writing them as I repeat them silently to myself. When I was in my forties, before my medical procedures, I could run all my errands without a list. I had memorized what I needed. While attending graduate school, I could retain almost 100 percent of the information presented in a lecture, along with a few notes. On the other hand, if I had to learn the identical highly technical information from a book or visual material, comprehension often required ten reads. Even then, my husband occasionally still had to break down the information and verbally explain it.

When our family took up skiing, my husband, who is a kinesthetic learner, learned by trial and error. Watching others or listening to the instructor's directions was not useful; the only way he learned was by practicing. One of our children, who is a visual learner, learned by watching the instructor demonstrate the moves. As an auditory learner, I learned by silently repeating the information and then hoping that I was coordinated enough to follow the instructions. We each learned the same skills in a different way, reflecting our NLP preference. When you fail to communicate to a person in their best NLP channel, it is almost as if you are speaking in a different dialect. It makes communication more challenging.

In my professional experience, more people are kinesthetic or visual learners than auditory learners. If you are an auditory person, you may wonder why most of your colleagues just don't get it when you tell them something or ask them to do something, especially if the task is more complex or technical. However, you are now aware of NLP and its significance. Therefore, I suggest that besides telling a person what they need to do, ask them if it would help if they also had printed instructions or material. Everyone's job performance and tasks will improve, and you will save everyone a lot of time, frustration, cost, and energy.

If you do not already know your best NLP channel and that of your colleagues, staff, family members, partners, students, clients, or patients, how do you discover which NLP channel is most effective? There are several subtle ways to find out. The first way is to observe eye movement. Information about where memory is stored in the brain continues to unfold as older theories are replaced with new ones. So while I mention where most of the consensuses had been, be aware that the information is shifting rapidly and, in the future, conclusions may differ.

Our eye movements connect with the different areas of the cerebral cortex. These areas of the brain are divided into four locations, named lobes. Specific types of information are stored in the different lobes. This is similar to a computer, where information is stored in different areas of the hard drive.

- If a person glances downward while thinking, that person is a kinesthetic NLP learner and communicator. They are trying to get a sense or feel of muscle memory that is stored in the frontal lobe, toward the front and top of the brain.
- If a person's eyes trend upward while processing or recalling information, that person is a visual NLP learner and communicator. They are trying to picture and recall visual information that is stored in the occipital lobe, at the rear of the brain.

- If a person's eyes fixate in a stare straight ahead, or glances from side to side at the level of their ears, that person is an auditory NLP learner and communicator. They are trying to recall sounds or meaningful verbal information that is stored in the temporal lobe, behind the temples.

Another clue to your NLP channel is word choice. We subconsciously sprinkle our speech with words or expressions that reflect our preferred NLP channel. By listening for verbal clues in other people's comments, we gain additional tips about which NLP channel is most suited for them. They infuse their speech with words or expressions that reflect their NLP channel to help them understand and communicate. Following is a list of words, phrases, and expressions that reflect and offer clues to a person's strongest NLP channel. This list was modified from the original chart by Dorothy Young Brockopp in her 1993 article, "What Is NLP?"

Kinesthetic	Visual	Auditory
feel	see	hear
think	look	listen
sense	observe	sounds good
a sore spot	notice	nice ring
in touch	perceive	tune in
dance to a different tune	point of view	tell it like it is
beat around the bush	bottom line	hear what you say
lay your cards on the table	see what you mean	overheard them
if you want to know the truth	catch sight	speak highly
gives me the creeps	seeing is believing	hang on every word
there you go	did you see that	it's a hoot

In helping an attorney prepare a client for trial, our mutual client looked down as he tried to recall information. This implied that he was a kinesthetic learner. The attorney looked up to recollect information, so I gained a clue that his best NLP channel was visual. Therefore, I added "visual" phrases along with "kinesthetic" phrases in my conversation to improve their comprehension.

Individuals whose primary NLP channel is kinesthetic usually use their hands and gesture when speaking. A friend's husband is kinesthetic. When he drives, he often fidgets with the knobs on the radio. She also shared that when he watches TV, he accidently switches the channels because he constantly plays with the remote control.

When I reviewed one of my first videotaped presentations, I noticed that I was constantly gesturing. Because this was very distracting to some in the audience, I became more aware. When I noticed participants paying attention to my hands, I realized that my gestures were a distraction. I then held my hands together in front of me or behind me or placed them in my lap or below the lectern. If people focus more attention on your hands than on your face when you are speaking, monitor your gestures.

Because my visual channel is the weakest, I had failed to see that my handwritten poster boards were sorely inadequate. After one of my first presentations, long before Microsoft PowerPoint was developed, a participant called me aside and shared that while my presentation and handout were excellent, my visual aids were certainly not commensurate with the other aspects.

A friend's considerably bright son disrupted other students. He annoyed other students when he fidgeted and made things at his desk with his paper, pencil, or supplies. When he was tested, the results revealed that his strongest channel was kinesthetic. Counselors recommended that teachers provide the youth with as many interactive learning activities as possible, including manipulative math. If he quietly sat at his desk, listened, and did not disturb the other students, he could simultaneously build bridges with paper clips or do any other hands-on activities. By teachers respecting his specialness and implementing these new learning routines, he also learned to respect others. He was no longer disruptive, and his grades improved.

A psychologist recorded a relaxation tape for a woman whose preferred NLP channel was auditory. The client was unable to fully benefit from the tape because the psychologist used visual imagery, such as "See the fall colors of the trees" or "Picture the sun." When the psychologist switched to auditory imagery "Hear the cascading brook" and "Listen to birds' call," the client benefitted. The psychologist also modified to "Feel the cool wind on your face" and "Feel the warmth of the sun" for her kinesthetic clients.

One client, who was vice president of an accounting firm, is a visual and kinesthetic communicator—a bottom-line communicator who easily gets lost in verbal detail. Now, he informs his colleagues and clients, "I will grasp the information better if you give me the conclusion and then the reason as precisely as possible." Since he is quite kinesthetic, his gestures and facial expressions become more energetic when he is frustrated or upset. He realized that too much verbal information is overwhelming. He became aware that his excessive gestures and subtle facial grimaces may also make others uncomfortable.

A urologist's strongest modalities were visual and kinesthetic. When he began practicing medicine, he was very successful. He performed surgeries and procedures that were compatible with his best channels. With the changing nature of medical practice in the 1990s, his responsibilities became more diagnostic than surgical, and this required more communication. The shift was quite problematic, and he resented feeling like "a fish out of water." Since he was not a verbal person and his auditory channel was his weakest channel, he was not comfortable communicating with his patients and colleagues. His bedside manner was poor. When he learned about NLP, he realized that diagnostic practice is primarily a verbal practice. Relying heavily on his weakest NLP channel was far more difficult than the former hands-on practice he used in surgeries and procedures that utilized his visual and kinesthetic strengths. Once he understood the issue, his resentment faded and he learned to communicate far more personably and pleasantly with his colleagues, staff, and patients.

A physician had passed the written portion of his diplomate boards eight years before he sought my services. After four failed attempts, he still lacked the ability to pass similar information in the oral portion of his exam. After learning that he had very poor "sound" or spoken word retention, he learned to strengthen his weaker auditory NLP channel. He practiced silently saying words while he took notes. Then, he recorded the information and listened to the recording. He linked his weaker auditory NLP channel with his stronger visual and kinesthetic NLP channels and successfully passed his boards.

Whenever you give important information in the classroom, in therapy, in the doctor's office, at work, or any place, if feasible, offer demonstrations and written instructions along with the verbal instruction. It is important to not only tell *what* but explain *why* and show *how.* When possible, include *how* to provide hands-on practice. When feasible, give the person who is learning the opportunity to experience the information in as many NLP channels as possible to increase their ability to comprehend, retain, and call forth the material. Although it takes more time, make the time for a "communication investment." If a person does not comprehend a task after you repeatedly explained and demonstrated it, recommend that the person actually practice by performing the task for you. That way, you will see where the breakdown occurs.

When a friend who is a kinesthetic learner took physical therapy, she couldn't get the gist of the therapist's instructions until she felt tension and movement in the muscles on which she was working. In occupational, physical, or speech therapy, or whenever you are teaching skills requiring the precise placement and movement of a body part (arms, legs, hands, fingers, tongue, lips, and jaw), *show* and *tell* the person how to move. Explain the correct position of their body part in relation to the skill and allow the patient to get the feel by also sensing tension in the body or body part. Also, include a tapping pattern of their hands against an object to help them get the feel and rhythm—long or short, or soft or strong. A music teacher encourages his students to feel the vibrations of the guitar as it resonates through their bodies. A woman who is deaf feels the vibrations of the music through her feet.

Part of the training for the sales personnel of a blue-jean chain required memorizing the styles and colors of the jeans. In addition, supervisors recommended that the salespersons pick out all six styles in their size and try them on so they could see how each feels and fits.

If your child is preparing for a test, using a computer (or other digital device) will definitely help. However, it is best if the child practice *giving the answers* in the same form they will use to take the test. If the test requires a written response, it is best if students actually write the answers after they learned to give them in another form. Also, until you become an expert, when you prepare for a presentation, the task requires more than just writing the speech. Initially, it is best to practice giving the speech aloud without anyone present. Record or video yourself and review if necessary. Make certain that you, or the person learning, always practices in the identical way they will actually present the material.

The next time that you cannot remember a phone number, try to sense your fingers as they touch the number pads to let your "fingers do the walking," and repeat the number to yourself. This may help you recall the number without having to look it up and improves memory, which helps as you age.

Before moving on, note your best NLP channel and those of the people with whom you most frequently interact at home or at work, among family, colleagues, or staff. Once you gather the information, when possible, begin to communicate with them and encourage them to learn in their preferred NLP channel. Recall the comparison of each NLP channel to the TV channels. If you had a choice, wouldn't you rather watch the station with the best reception? In the same way, make certain that you use your best channel for learning the most essential information. If you are kinesthetic, get hands-on experience or take notes. If you are visual, read the information or watch demonstrations or videos. When suitable, adding PowerPoint is quite valuable. If you are auditory, listen to the information or request that another person explain it or talk you through it.

It is also important not to overload a person in their weakest channel. If there is excessive verbal information, it is best to add charts and demonstrations to facilitate learning. A person who is not visual has challenges performing tasks that require a lot of visual detail, such as sorting or filing. An individual who is not auditory will have difficulty with tasks that require listening to a lot of detail, such as taking messages and noting a long string of numbers. A person who is not kinesthetic has difficulty with tasks requiring fine motor skills. People who have poor eye-hand coordination have either weak kinesthetic or visual channels or both. For the utmost ease and success, tasks are best when compatible with a person's most effective NLP channel.

Anthony Robbins, author of *Awaken the Giant Within* (1991), gives a synopsis of how NLP influences a person's choice of the type of presents they give. The gifts you wish from others often do not come in your desired form but in the way they give them. People like to receive gifts that reflect their preferred NLP channel. They often give gifts that also reflect their best NLP channel rather than giving the gift that mostly is compatible with the *recipient's* NLP channel. A kinesthetic person may express affection through touch, such as holding hands, stroking, and hugging, but have difficulty sitting still. The person may be particularly sensitive to other people's moods. A visual person may enjoy sending (and receiving) cards and gifts. An auditory person may note affection with words and may be sensitive to noise. Auditory people enjoy conversation and music and may be comfortable hearing and saying "I love you." For the person who is not auditory, verbal endearments may be too repetitive. I know some people who are kinesthetic do not respond if a person expresses why they are upset and describe the act or words. Yet when the person expresses their feelings associated with those actions, words, or attitude, they may be more receptive and willing to modify their annoying ways. This also may reflect individuals of all modalities.

Improve Your Weaker Neurolinguistic Programming Channel

Now that you've gained a greater awareness of your stronger and weaker NLP channels, what can you do to improve your weaker channels? When you have to learn something presented in your weaker NLP channel, link your weaker channel to your stronger channel. Recall the example of the physician who had difficulty passing his oral boards although he had passed the written part of his exam. He learned to link his weakest auditory channels (recalling the words) with his stronger visual and kinesthetic channels. He repeated the information aloud and recorded it while he was taking notes. This included visual and kinesthetic input. He then listened to the recording.

Please allow me to review. If your best channel is auditory and your weaker channel is visual, you may have trouble understanding written information. Read the information aloud or talk yourself through the difficult parts of a written text. Read the information, then stop and take the time to verbalize or summarize silently or aloud to yourself. If that still does not help, ask yourself what you need. Continue to talk to yourself until you recognize what you need. If your strongest channel is kinesthetic, it is often difficult to have a hands-on experience. Try to sense the feeling until you can actually get the tactile experience.

If you were previously unfamiliar with Neurolinguistic Programming and think that since you have gone through life without using this, why busy your head with it now? then think again. Understanding and engaging the NLP channels of family, friends, colleagues, staff, workers, students, patients, or clients continues to significantly strengthen one's connection and help create bridges where gaps may otherwise occur. Ponder about both your and the other person's communication needs for a more solid bond. Personalize the NLP skills so they feel right. You and others will benefit as you broaden and apply these insights and skills to include more people.

Take a Look

If you do not understand my silence, you will not understand my words.

—Anonymous

Nonverbal Communication

By now, we have gathered that communication is complex and there is far more to communication than just talking. Mehrabian (1981) states that we perceive face-to-face communication 55 percent through nonverbal communication. When a person gives a smile, winks their eye, checks us out, or gives a glaring scowl, their nonverbal impact is greater than 55 percent. During my years of consulting with a broad range of individuals from many cultural backgrounds, I decided to include many other facets under nonverbal communication: facial expression, eye contact, body language, body space, touch, gestures, attire, colors, and scent.

How We Perceive Face-to-Face Communication

Often, the first impression we present is a lasting one, and if it is not our best, that is unfortunate. Initial perceptions create a baseline of feelings and observations that others form about us. Much of that everlasting first impression is based on our nonverbal communication and voice tone. It is definitely in our best interest to present a genuine and positive presence from the start.

In the previous chapters, I stressed the steps to accurately convey the *meaning* and *intention* of our message. When our voice tone conveys one message and our words send a different message, we discredit our point. Our inconsistency may unintentionally offend and turn people away. Shortly after birth, a mother felt unduly disturbed when a nurse delivered concerning news about her infant son with a smile and condescending voice. Do you think that was the nurse's intention?

When we are distraught about a situation or upset about an issue, a smile along with a joyous voice conveys inconsistencies and minimizes our concern and frustration; therefore, others may not take us seriously. A smile may also give the impression that a person is making fun or light of the situation. A client had this inconsistent pattern and couldn't figure out why others didn't take him seriously about meeting deadlines.

First Impression

Years ago, when lecturing on this topic, I asked participants to recall their first impression of me. I then asked what opinion they would have formed if during my introduction my clothes were stained and wrinkled, my hair was unkempt, or I slouched and looked at the floor. They responded that my appearance would detract from my professional presentation, I would be less credible, and they might question my expertise. Leaving aside my attire and posture, I was still the same person with the same knowledge.

However, when we form an opinion solely on a person's nonverbal communication or appearance, we distort reality. We also risk valuing "form" over "substance," and substance is the "real deal" and most valid. We have to be aware and scratch below the surface or form to gain an honest assessment and understanding of the substance. The body is an outer shell that houses the person's soul. In much of the United States and many other cultures, we are far too focused on appearance and not the inner depth or inner beauty of a person. A *source-connection* remains essential and valuable in helping move inward to sense the person's true essence.

Fashion is fun, and I certainly enjoy it, but what the media dictates rarely intimidates me. Though much of my apparel is fifteen to thirty years old, I continue to enjoy and wear those styles even when I lecture or attend gala events. It is sad when people of all ages feel embarrassed or "too poor" to afford the luxury of current fashion. Sadly, they refrain from going to functions, events, and even religious services, all of which they would really like to attend. Others go into great debt and max out credit cards to "fit in." We also have to look past another's baldness, paunch, or *handi-abled* or drool on a young adult, acne on a teen, or wrinkles on a senior. When a grandchild asked her Nana, "What are those line on your face called?" the grandmother replied, "Wrinkles. But they don't stop me from loving you just as much as I always have."

When people are terminally ill, others are often so aghast by their appearance or frightened of their own mortality that they stop visiting the person who is fading. Shortly before my childhood friend died of cancer in her midforties, she said, "Visitors are dropping like flies. They don't come to see me anymore." She was hurt. Although her rosy complexion paled and her limbs withered, her beautiful soul, courage, and optimistic attitude remained with her until the moment she died.

In our culture, we pay a lot of attention to how we look, dress, and act. It is just as important, if not more so, to notice how we feel, again moving inward from the outer shell of our bodies to the inner connection with our souls. With that in mind, let's now take a look at nonverbal communication.

When we mindfully and *source-connectedly* engage in positive, effective, and appropriate facial expressions, eye contact, body language, body space, touch, gesture, attire, and pleasant natural scent, our nonverbal communication provides a genuine and strong advantage. That is a positive factor in creating connections and building communication bridges with others.

Look back at Princess Diana. At the age of nineteen, she was shy and dressed as a schoolgirl. With maturity and reaching out to help others, she created her own fashionable style. She became and remains a beloved world icon. She was always a deeply devoted, loving, and fun mother. Diana significantly raised awareness and advanced understanding of AIDS as she shook the hand of a person who carried the dreaded disease. That simple and spontaneous barehanded touch demonstrated to the world that AIDS could not be transmitted by that type of physical contact.

This gesture forever changed our perception about AIDS, as it fostered a willingness to reach out to help those with AIDS.

To use nonverbal communication to our advantage, we first become aware of our feelings, the authentic impression we want to convey, and the goal we seek to achieve. Do we feel genuine, compassionate, empathetic, confident, persuasive, concerned, scared, insecure, angry, or that we do not belong or do not matter? Which feeling do we want to convey? Look into a mirror to check if you convey your true feelings. We can't change what we feel. However, when necessary, we can compartmentalize that negativity and engage the Mona Lisa smile to help us genuinely shift our focus to feel and convey a positive message. One way is to get in touch with our *source-connection* or reflect on an experience where we felt good. After mindfully breathing on a positive memory of a person or an event, hold on to that feeling in the present. Then, glance in the mirror, observe the positive reflection, or shift to a positive stance—especially your facial expressions and body language. Humming, singing, or self-talk of uplifting thoughts aid to alter our feelings.

At some point, we apply this shift to personal, vocational, or professional settings when we are not in the mood to attend a required meeting or desired event. We are usually able to park our negativity somewhere inside our heads and only allow the presence of positive feelings, but there are times, such as during tragedy, deep depression, dire challenges, violent events, prolonged illness, physical pain, or heartbreaking arguments, when we cannot escape the deep despair or attempt to shift or mask our feelings. When those occur, do not beat yourself up but accept the circumstances and show kindness and compassion toward yourself. If no one else is around and there are no pets to give you a lick or a snuggle, give yourself a loving hug. Nothing remains the same forever; eventually, circumstances change, a new day dawns, and life does not feel as dark.

It would be wonderful if we could each be authentic all the time and express how we truly feel in a positive way. If authenticity were ubiquitous, or if we could read one another's minds, our true feelings would not be an issue, as everyone would be on the same plane. Marlo Morgan's book *Mutant Message, Down Under* (1994) offers a spiritual vision about her walkabout in the Australian Outback among the Aborigines. They engage in telepathic communication, so all feelings and thoughts are common knowledge.

When I had an extremely stressful day facing too many deadlines, a 5 star driver of a ride-sharing company was also having an off day. The street leading to the on ramp was blocked and the alternative route was out-of-the-way. Since I'm very familiar with the other route, I suggested that route and directed him. When it was time to merge into the lane for the on ramp, he was busy talking to his wife in his native language, and therefore was not focused on merging. We barely made it. The rest of the ride was smooth.

When I arrived at my destination, reflecting on the day so far, I felt such profound gratitude that I had actually made it. So, naturally, there was a huge smile on my face. As I walked into the lobby approaching from the opposite side, I saw a young man with a small frame and brown skin who had one of the most beautiful smiles I had ever seen. When I told him, "You have a beautiful smile," he replied, "Your smile inspired me," and proceeded to get on the elevator. As other passengers joined him and before the door closed, we simultaneously said, "God bless you." In a persuasive voice, I also declared, "Make sure you stay in touch with that part of you all the time because that reflects who you truly are. Don't let anybody or any situation rob that from you!"

When I arrived at my destination, reflecting on the day so far, I felt such profound gratitude that I had actually made it. So, naturally, there was a big smile on my face. As I walked into the lobby approaching from the opposite side, I saw a young man with a small frame and brown skin who had one of the most beautiful smiles I had ever seen. When I told him, "You have a beautiful smile," he said, "Your smile inspired me," and proceeded to get on the elevator. As other passengers joined him and before the door closed, in a persuasive voice, I declared, "Make sure you stay in touch with that part of you all the time because that reflects who you truly are. Don't let anybody or any situation rob that from you!"

In *Successful Nonverbal Communication*, Dale Leathers states, "The face has long been a primary source of information in interpersonal communication, in the transmission of meaning" (Leathers 1992). Ekman and Friesen conducted studies that indicate some facial expressions and emotions are universally recognized. They are anger, disgust, fear, happiness, sadness, and surprise. The duo's work significantly contributed to the literature on facial expression. They state, "The kind of emotion you are experiencing shows in your face; the intensity shows in your eyes."

Facial expressions comprise three areas: the forehead, eyes, and mouth. A furrowed brow across the forehead reflects anger, stress, worry, or concentration. You can observe these expressions, but often you are unaware of the cause. Some people use various or intense facial expressions to reveal their feelings; others are more private and expose less. This type of expression is named the "poker face," which serves folks well in many situations.

A continued pleasure is walking on the campus of my alma mater, CSUN. There, almost everyone's facial expression and body language are positive, and their gait has a purpose. The students, faculty, and support team rarely bear frowns on their faces, and the folks are usually engaged in conversation, especially as they walk across campus.

A physician was unaware of the furrowed lines etched across his forehead that gave the impression that he was constantly upset. He certainly did not want to convey those feelings to his patients. Actually, he was burdened with the responsibility of his patients' ability to recover. Another client walked around in deep thought and gave the impression that she was always angry. Upon reviewing a video and recognizing the lines of concentration etched on her forehead, she understood why her colleagues and staff had that impression. One client usually smiled, presenting an image that she was happy. Her colleagues were shocked when they learned that she was severely depressed. Without knowing what a person feels, we have no way of knowing whether that person is angry, stressed, concerned, or concentrating, unless they expressed that or, when appropriate, we ask.

A neighbor observed a famous UCLA basketball player eating lunch alone. She said, "He looked like a real loner." While the observation was made that he sat alone, we cannot know the exact reason. People often incorrectly interpret others' nonverbal communication. When they make assumptions, it is often a projection of their own feelings or experiences with similar situations and may have nothing to do with what the person experiences.

Eyes

In the book *A Time for Peace*, Nilsen states, "You can tell happiness by a smile or a laugh. But real joy, is something else, something that only the eyes reveal" (Nilsen 1990). S. W. Janik states the saying "evil eye" conveys something bad and eyes are the "gateway to the soul." During the COVID-19 pandemic, this became quite apparent when many wore masks, especially while also wearing a hat. Then, our eyes clearly revealed that they are all we need to visit with another's soul.

Think of the positive ways we describe eyes and the messages we receive from looking into others' eyes: kind, warm, sincere, compassionate, friendly, soft, harsh, strong, fun, captivating, alluring, and sexy. Janik also states that during conversation, 43 percent of attention is focused on the eyes (Janik 1978). It is no wonder that women in many cultures spend much time, money, and effort enhancing their eyes with kohl, cosmetics, creams, treatments, plastic surgery, contact lenses, or fashionable eyewear.

Eye contact in everyday conversation is, at best, a positive gaze, not a glare or stare—and certainly not an exaggerated "holding pattern," which is uncomfortable, threatening, or hostile. Maintaining constant eye contact has a persuasive effect on the listener and gives the speaker control. If you are engaged in any situation such as litigation, or when a person or an opposing attorney attempts to intimidate by locking eyes, do not look away. To disengage that lock, look directly above or below, focusing at the person's forehead, nose, or mouth. That lock "throws off" the other person and gives *you* the power.

Maintaining eye contact in our culture implies that you are interested, confident, honest, sensitive, sincere, understanding, and concerned. These are important features in any relationship or interaction. If you are unable to maintain eye contact because you are absorbing information or taking notes, at least face the person part of the time. If possible, keep the note-taking to a minimum. But if you have to note or document, after you have paused to make these, engage eye contact as quickly as possible with the other person. This is especially pertinent if you are a physician conversing with a patient.

When you converse with a small group, make eye contact with everyone. It is insensitive and rude to exclude a person by not acknowledging or making eye contact with everyone. While giving a presentation to a large audience, glance around in all directions.

Lack of eye contact usually conveys lack of interest, dishonesty, embarrassment, insecurity, guilt, or shame. It is necessary to realize that just as it is appropriate to maintain eye contact in the U.S. culture, it is as inappropriate in many other cultures. This topic is further presented in the chapter "Embracing Diversity" in the next section *Soul to Soul Intercultural Communication*.

We often conclude that when a person does not maintain eye contact, frequently looks down, or blinks, those deviations suggest that a person may be shy or lack confidence or that they are dishonest. If a person appears shy, accept the lack of eye contact as part of their personality or a condition of interacting with them. If they are outgoing *USAans* and cannot maintain eye contact, I question their credibility. Frequent blinking also occurs during stress and often suggests nervousness or deceit, although it may also be due to allergies.

It is appropriate and may be necessary to look away when recalling information. That pattern was presented in the chapter "Neurolinguistic Programming." However, when you begin conversing, you return to making eye contact. While facing a person, it is not cool to check them out or size them up. This type of nonverbal communication remains acceptable in some other cultures but is not appropriate in mainstream U.S. culture.

If a person's glance breaks away for a split second during a conversation, that person is usually either uncomfortable about something or dishonest. It may be the topic of conversation or uncertainty, or they may be contemplating a dishonest response. Again, you cannot accurately guess the reason another person does not maintain eye contact. Remain cautious of a person who cannot maintain eye contact for long periods, especially if the person was born in the United States. An important exception, and a time to offer compassion and understanding, is if a person is *handi-abled* or appears mentally ill.

When I observed an interview with a tobacco grower whose family had owned the plantation for one hundred years, as he gave the reasons that he was going to lose the plantation, he maintained eye contact with the commentator. Yet when they questioned the tobacco grower if he thought tobacco was harmful, the grower shifted his eyes downward while stating he did not think it was.

Mouth

Janik states that attention is focused on our mouth 12 percent of the time during communication (Janik 1978). Similar to eyes, it is no small wonder that women in many cultures continue to spend time and money on cosmetics, treatments, or plastic surgery to shape or augment their lips to allure. Many individuals in the United States invest vast sums of money on orthodontia not only to correct dental and jaw alignment but also to enhance physical appearance.

When an individual appears upset, I give them a genuine smile to try to help lighten their negative feelings into positive ones. When I hiked with a group, two disgruntled cyclists waited for us to pass so they could continue up the hill on which we were walking down. One cyclist was frowning, so as he passed, I spontaneously smiled, and he smiled back.

Covering one's mouth—even slightly—when talking often conveys discomfort or dishonesty. When observing trials, I am wary of witnesses who cover their mouths while answering questions. A teacher noted that students who aren't prepared often cover their mouths when they answer questions. Yet a probation officer shared that before she had orthodontia, she had covered her mouth when she spoke because she didn't like the appearance of her "fang tooth."

A smile sends a friendly, inviting message, and a frown turns people away. A smile also makes us feel better and relaxes our facial muscles. In some cultures, a wide smile with exposed teeth is an inappropriate response in public or professional life. We often incorrectly draw the conclusion that a person who does not smile is unfriendly. Their repose expression may just reflect their basic nature or how they were raised, especially if they are from another culture. They may express their friendliness in different forms, such as by offering to help or do something special for you. If a person from another culture seems unfriendly because of their blank facial expression, give the person a chance. Try to get to know them better, as you may discover a pleasant hidden trait.

Individuals smile (or giggle) when they are uncomfortable in a situation or embarrassed when they do not know the answer. Unfortunately, in a serious matter, critical situation, or when a person is upset, others may interpret their smile as insensitive, snickering, demeaning, or rude. Smiling (and giggling), which is an inappropriate response in certain situations in the U.S. culture but appropriate in other cultures in similar or the same situation, is presented in the chapter "Embracing Diversity" in the following section, *Soul to Soul Intercultural Communication*.

Body Language

Body language communicates a powerful message to others; it invites them to engage or discourages them from engaging with us. Ease, confidence, stress, or anger are feelings felt or observed by "reading" body language. Open body language reflects a receptive person who appears approachable. The person's arms are either dangling loosely at their side, resting, held gently in their lap, or laced behind their head. Their legs rest in front of them, crossed either at the ankle or with their feet flat on the floor. It is inappropriate to sit with legs spread far apart, though some people tease in that "come on" pose.

Closed body language typically indicates that the person is not that receptive to what you say and probably will not listen to you. Their hands are usually crossed tightly in front of their chest, and they appear tense. This person, who is going to be challenging to engage, sends a nonverbal message, "*Not now*" or "*Don't mess with me*." A person whose hands rest lightly on their hips with their body perpendicular to the floor or slightly leaning back usually reflects a relaxed position. A person who stands leaning forward, with shoulders tense and hands firmly on the hips, reveals an assertive or aggressive stance.

According to Mehrabian, "When two people meet, the more relaxed person is probably accepted as the person of higher status" (Mehrabian 1981). Again, I firmly believe that roles may be ranked, but in their humanity, all people are equal. The president of the United States has greater access and influence on world affairs than the janitor at the White House, but as people, they are equal. In most regions and cultures, this is not yet mainstream thinking, but hopefully, it eventually will be. In my observation, the person who perceives themselves as inferior usually defers to the other person or attempts to mirror the other person's body language.

During interviews, watching the body language of the moderator and the person being interviewed is fascinating. It was especially interesting during Barack Obama's presidency. During interviews, he usually leaned in to the other person, indicating his ease and desire to fully engage. When he became uncomfortable with harsh, "gotcha" questions, he pulled back. This pattern is similar to most interviews, but few persons leaned in as far and consistently as did President Obama. The president's style and walking stride were often very firm, straight, and wide, indicating his sense of purpose.

Good posture wasn't my strong suit until my unusually visually perceptive and youngest four-year-old grand softly stated, "Nana, you walk low." "Oh," I responded as I was closing my suitcase, rushing to catch the approaching shuttle. A year later, when she visited in California, as she walked behind me into the house, she again commented, "Nana, you walk low." This time I stopped and asked, "What do you mean?" She demonstrated as she leaned over at her waist and commented, "This is low." And so I asked, "How should I walk?" She straightened her shoulders and stood erect in her usual perfect posture and said, "High, like this." I asked a massage therapist how I should practice standing erect as I was throwing my shoulders back and not finding success. My friend suggested that I picture an invisible string centered right above my sternum up that is pulling me. I practiced that technique for three months until my posture had improved.

When we returned to Nevis later that year, several people commented that I looked much younger. So I quickly engaged my former stooped shoulder posture, paused, then stood up tall, and asked, "Is this the difference?" Everyone echoed a resounding "Yes!"

People in Nevis of all walks of life have a unique gait and stance. As a culture, the people have outstanding posture. I do not recall seeing anyone slouch; even senior citizens stand upright. There is a purpose to their gait, as they are assured of themselves and proud of their heritage. An island grand shared that at her young age, her teachers instructed and constantly reminded students to stand tall. Even Blind Eileen always stood and sat straight and tall like a queen.

Standing up, breaking eye contact, shifting body position, or offering a handshake usually denotes that the person wants to end a meeting, leave an event, or has had enough.

Although you may not feel confident, there are situations in which you want to convey confidence. Sitting or standing tall—naturally erect but not rigid—keeping your shoulders back and your head parallel to the floor, and maintaining eye contact all project confidence. You may also let your arms hang, keep your hands loosely behind your back, or hold them together in front of you while you are talking.

When our housekeeper and friend visited from Nevis, we went grocery shopping. I was amazed how many people paused to glance at her. She is attractive and has rich dark-brown skin, but I don't think that was it. I think it was her stance, grace, dignity, and the ease that she softly radiates that attracted the looks.

In *Responsible Assertive Behavior*, Lange, Jakubowski, and McGovern (1976) state, "When you convey lack of confidence, you slouch, drop your shoulders, smile out of context, wring your hands, and lick your lips." Fidgeting with objects, shuffling your feet, cracking knuckles, or tapping also conveys lack of confidence, restlessness, nervousness, or hyperactivity.

Body Space

Comfort in the amount of your body space, touch, and gestures is determined primarily by you but strongly influenced by your native culture. In the book *The Silent Language* (1959), Edward T. Hall states that spatial memory is exceedingly persistent. Recent studies reveal that the dimension of your body space, the amount of space that is comfortable between you and another person, is established early in life and remains fixed throughout life. However, if you experience significant psychological changes, your definition of acceptable body space may also change.

Although space has no finite boundaries, there is a comfort zone (distance) in which you are at ease in relation to the other person. Hall describes four types of informal distance between people: intimate, personal, social-consultative, and public. An intimate space of zero to eighteen inches is reserved for people with whom you are in a very close relationship, personal space is between one and a half to four feet, social-consultative distance is between four feet and twelve feet, and public space is twelve feet or more. These are considered appropriate comfort zones for those of European heritage.

The more familiar and comfortable you are with another person, the nearer you stand or sit with them. You usually sit and stand closer to someone in a personal setting than in vocational or professional settings. In Latino cultures, people stand between one and a half to two and a half feet apart. They may stand closer than most of European or Asian cultures would with familiar people. In Asian cultures, people generally stand at least two feet apart in professional settings. In my experience, people of African culture stand close to me, and I am comfortable with that.

It is important to remain aware of another person's body space in relation to you. If a person subtly moves back, that person may be uncomfortable with the lack of space between you. Their uneasiness may reflect the topic, your voice, or how you express yourself. Conversely, if a person moves toward you, that reflects ease and interest. If you are comfortable, accommodate the other person and remain. If not, soften your voice and genuinely smile as a substitute positive gesture to bridge the space gap.

In certain cities, notions of personal space differ. A friend observed that although New York is crowded, people learned to respect one another's personal space. In Los Angeles, where people are usually more laid-back and do not use public transportation as readily, individuals tend to stand closer together in public places. Therefore, they are less aware and, at times, less respectful of others' personal space.

Body space may also be affected by gender. When traveling down a hall, women often defer to men by stepping aside. This action is so ingrained and subconscious that it comes to be expected, even to the point that occasionally men crash into women who do not step aside.

At a national conference on diversity, I gave two presentations. At each, I asked two people to simultaneously come and stand on either side of me. In both cases, men who were of African or Latino heritage stood closer than women of European heritage.

Touch

Helen Keller shared, "I am sure that if a fairy made me choose between the sense of sight and that of touch, I would not part with the warmth, endearing contact of human hands or the wealth of form, the mobility and fullness that press into my palms" (Wepman 1987). Helen Keller could neither see nor hear, yet through her touch, smell, and taste, she experienced and treasured life with a profound depth and appreciation. Most of us have our senses of sight and sound and rely heavily on both of them. "Touch is probably the most basic component of human communication" (Lustig and Koester 2013). Just think of all the positive and negative ways that we use touch: hug, kiss, slap, hit, punch, beat, trip, kick, and hold hands. In *Successful Nonverbal Communication* (1992), Dale Leathers quotes a study by Nguyen where Heslin and Nguyen identify four different types of touch: a squeeze, brush, pat, and stroke. The meaning of the squeeze and brush vary with the situation. A pat is usually more playful, and a stroke signals affection or sexual desire. Recognizing the fine nuances of touch is especially difficult for people from different cultures.

Touching another person during conversation is a very personal form of expression. Touching has to be comfortable for everyone involved. In a vocational or professional environment, "the person perceived as the more important figure initiates the touching," states Henley (1977). Since I try to live by the rule that we are all equal and that no person is more important than another, I prefer a touch to be spontaneous and sincere and initiated by whoever feels like it. Because this concept is not mainstream, I do not recommend initiating, unless you are certain that it is appropriate in a specific situation or acceptable with the person. In the U.S. mainstream professional environment, one touches on the shoulder or taps on the back. Touching with a pat on the hand or the shoulder to console also is appropriate in a physician-patient interaction. Touching a friend, holding hands, or hugging in a friendly way is appropriate and often desired. Touching a person's head—that typical pat on the head—is offensive to some people, especially in some sectors of Asia, and particularly if the person is of African, Vietnamese, Korean, Laotian, or Thai culture. Touching others in any way when you know they do not want to be touched is a form of physical abuse or sexual harassment.

We have to be very careful that others do not misinterpret our touch as sexual harassment or abuse. A young man on staff at a day-care facility with young children made certain another adult was always present. When a child wanted to sit on his lap, he was cautious. The youngsters could hold on to him, but he did not touch them except to help them maintain their balance.

When my husband and I traveled to Europe, we often saw women holding hands as they strolled. Occasionally, friends who are *Born-abroad* or are *USAans* walked in our neighborhood holding hands or with interlocked arms.

Blind Eileen thoroughly enjoys stroking hair and has rare opportunities to do that. When four of our grands jointly visited Eileen in 2014, she very much enjoyed touching their hair. She especially got a kick out of stroking the hair of one grand because she had thick long silky hair. Almost every conversation since then, Eileen comments about how much she enjoyed that experience. It reminds her of former times when, even though she was blind, she took care of young children.

An elderly person living alone or with family far away, a person in the military, or any person in rehabilitation recovering from a stroke, trauma, or an accident, or a person in their own home receiving hospice care may or may not appreciate a touch of kindness from a health-care provider or a friend. If you are comfortable and sense the person would enjoy that gesture, you can always ask, "Would you like a gentle hug?" Or in the more intimate setting of their home, we may sense that touching or holding their hand may be beneficial. We have to be especially mindful of those in a hospital or rehabilitation setting, as they are most vulnerable, and we especially remain mindful that we never take advantage of that vulnerability.

Holding oneself is a form of self-nurturing. When we hold our hands or arms or rest our jaw or chin between our thumb and forefinger, we nurture ourselves. If we hold or touch ourselves when we are stressed, tired, not feeling well, or uncomfortable in a situation or with the topic of conversation, we subconsciously self-nurture. During the first two years of President Bill Clinton's television appearances, he often rested his chin between his thumb and forefinger. During television interviews, many people express discomfort when they cup one side of their face in their hand with their thumb under their jaw and the side of the face resting in the palm of their hand.

Even the most experienced news anchors' eyes may moisten while they tightly clutch and hold their face as they also rest their chin on the bottom of their hand if the topic is excruciatingly painful to report.

Gesture

A modest use of gesture adds animation and interest to speech and conversation. Gestures are used more frequently by women than by men. The amount and intensity of gestures we use are expressions of our personality. People who are kinesthetic tend to use more gestures. One's native culture and basic nature also influences their use of gestures. People of Middle Eastern, Jewish, Italian, and Greek cultures often use more gestures when they speak than people of other heritages. When you give a lecture, you are often limited to standing in one place. Gestures generally add interest to your presentation. However, including lighting and temperature, there is a fine line in those areas between an individual's comfort and distraction. Monitor the audience; if you observe that participants focus on your hands instead of your presentation, make necessary adjustments.

In *Managing Diversity* (1993), Gardenswartz and Rowe state that in the United States, a head nod—the up-and-down movement of your head—signals that you understand and probably agree with the speaker. Many people who speak English as their second language nod yes when they have not understood but are too embarrassed to ask again or acknowledge their confusion. An occasional nod is appropriate when listening and shows interest in the conversation. In Asian cultures, a nod may mean "*I heard you*," but it does not necessarily mean agreement. Many misunderstandings occur because of this misconception.

Pointing to an object with your index finger is not considered rude in the United States, yet pointing to or beckoning a person with your finger is disrespectful. A client of Filipino culture felt humiliated because her supervisor often motioned her with that gesture. She questioned, "Does she think I'm an animal?" If you have to use a gesture to indicate direction, use an open hand with fingers together, not spread apart, and engage in a sideways waving motion toward the direction that you are indicating. The "okay sign" made with the thumb and forefinger is obscene in Greece and areas of South America.

If you are conversing with a person from a different linguistic and cultural background who uses gestures that are offensive, try to be tolerant. Perhaps you are unfamiliar with the meaning of a specific gesture in their native culture or the other person has not mastered the nuance of that gesture in the mainstream U.S. culture. If you are familiar with the person, privately connect with them and inquire what the gesture indicates in their native culture. Then, mindfully explain what it means in U.S. culture.

Attire

Attire remains an integral aspect of how we express ourselves. Many individuals are influenced by what society markets and dictates, and as children, what parents permit. Much of the attire in the Western world follows the styles of those in the entertainment industry, though many individuals create and honor their own style. Clothing and fashion are personal choices that reflect who we are, what we can afford, how we want to present ourselves, and what is appropriate for the situation or occasion. In the United States, there are many styles of clothing in a wide price range from which to choose. Our sense of modesty is expressed in our apparel. Cleanliness is valued in the United States, so clothing is usually clean and pressed. Unless uniforms are required or your workplace has a dress code, you are free to choose what you wear.

There are all kinds of levels of appropriateness in clothing: age-appropriate, place-appropriate, occasion-appropriate, in-style, and out-of-style. In the end, our choices create our individual style.

There are many types of traditional dresses worn by women around the world and embraced in the United States. The cheongsam or qipao is a tasteful, classic dress originating in China. The differing names reflect the Cantonese and Mandarin dialects; both describe a long banner dress created in the seventeenth century as the epitome of elegance. Both are one-piece, body-hugging dresses reaching to the ankle or below the knee and are sleeveless or cap sleeve. The sari of India is a colorful, simple length of fabric that may be up to nine meters long, and it is most versatile, as it can be draped in several styles. The Japanese kimono, which was created as a means of expression for individual wear, is often seen in Japanese restaurants. African dress is as varied as the continent is huge, comprising fifty-five countries, all with diverse cultures, ranging from the Masai people to the South Afrikaners. The fashion fabrics range from gauze to cotton and are worn loose, draped, or formfitting. However, the geometric and jungle prints, the vibrant palette, and their unusual combinations and adornments stand out as novel features of African fashion.

In my lifetime, women's fashion vacillated between suits and dresses. As a young woman, I recall when dresses were far more stylish, until the suit became popular again. In the 1960s, the pantsuit for women also became stylish. During the "Camelot years" of the Kennedy presidency, the suit that was created by Chanel in France for First Lady Jacqueline Kennedy became the style. Each first lady in recent times left a new imprint. Former First Lady Pat Nixon was the first to wear pantsuits in public. Hillary Clinton was the first to wear a pantsuit for her official first lady portrait. Michelle Obama had a different style and was the first to wear a sleeveless dress for her official first lady portrait. She led women's fashion away from the predominant business suit to again wear dresses of many flattering styles. These later included lace, patterns, and an interesting mix of colors of a broad stylish gamut. During Michelle's era as first lady, dresses became fancier for day wear. Several female news broadcasters wore very colorful, stylish, sometimes lavish dresses, including lace and bling, during daytime reporting. Jeans are always in style for any age group.

Menswear also has its own national fashion. In Africa, the boubou and dashiki are robes or tunics with flowing wide sleeves. The djellaba is a traditional Egyptian garment and differs from the Arabian thawb, which is wider and has no collar. The Nehru jacket and its type of collar still appear, and the kilt is worn on ceremonial occasions.

Religious habits comprise a distinctive set of garments worn by members of a religious order. The beanie-type hat that the pope wears is named a zucchetto, and in the Vatican, the color white is reserved for the pope. Red is set aside for cardinals, and purple for bishops. The biretta is another type of headpiece worn by clergy. The skullcap named a kippah or yarmulke is always worn by observant Jewish men and, at times, by both men and women in Conservative and Reform synagogues. Turbans are worn by those of the Hindu faith for ceremonial events. Some Sikh men and women wear turbans all day, though some Sikhs only wear them when they enter a temple. As with all other religions, these headdresses are worn in respect and reverence for God or a higher power.

In the United States, people of the Amish religion and culture, and, to a lesser degree, the Mennonite people, wear plain and simple clothing and ban color and belts from their wardrobes. To some small degree, these restrictions vary from community to community. A nun's outfit is called a habit, and their headpiece is called a veil or cornette, referred to as a wimple. Burqa, niqab, hijab, chador, khimar, and the veil to cover one's head are prominent among women of Muslim faith. For some, these are worn to promote cultural identity, while for others, it is a religious choice. Some women view these headpieces as symbols of female suppression.

There are several types of headdresses worn around the world and in the United States. First Nations people wear feathered headdresses, which is a badge of honor and power that they earn as a sign of respect. Each feather had to be earned, and various bird feathers were chosen by the tribe for the specific occasion. In the past, headdresses were sometimes worn into battle, but today, the headdress is worn primarily for ceremonial moments. Later, the feathered headdress became a stereotypical image of all Native Americans. With the influx of global citizens from around the world, we see Hindu turbans, Jewish yarmulkes, Latino sombreros, French berets, Bolivian bowler hats, Vietnamese conical hats, Panama hats, Australian Tilley and Kaminski hats, and the mortarboard, which is symbolic at graduations, designed by the British centuries ago. The fez has a history in the Middle East, North Africa, and Eastern Europe and is worn by Shriners. The United States created its own baseball cap, Stetson, and cowboy hat.

There are various types of neckerchiefs, scarves, headbands, hoods, do-rags and scrunches worn to express one's own taste. The hoodie was worn by Mark Zuckerberg, founder of Facebook, but it also became a symbol of the youth of African heritage in the United States in the early twenty-first century.

In the early 1980s, an acquaintance entered a small private Quaker college in the suburbs of Philadelphia, Pennsylvania. Soon after he arrived, his freshman class was invited to a Sunday open house hosted by the president of the college. The invitation read "casual attire." The student was raised in the very casual Los Angeles environment. He thought that "casual attire" at the progressive college on a Sunday afternoon was the same as "casual attire" in the San Fernando Valley on a Sunday afternoon. He arrived at the event wearing khaki shorts and a polo shirt; he soon realized that he was inappropriately dressed for the occasion. Fifteen years later, a neighbor moved to Atlanta, Georgia. She was invited to the home of her husband's boss on a Saturday night. The attire was also casual. She wore a stylish pair of slacks and bodysuit; some people wore jeans and others wore dresses.

Many companies implement a daily or weekly casual day, when wearing jeans is acceptable; in some organizations, jeans are the daily attire. Until certain ground rules are established within each company, an employee may not understand the dress codes or casual standards. Usually, the standards in the professional environment are more meticulous than casual wear worn at home or on the weekend. Unpressed or torn jeans or T-shirts are usually not appropriate casual wear at the office, unless the dress code is quite relaxed.

In the 1990s, a college student from Korea was invited to a casual barbecue on a Thursday night to celebrate a fellow student's birthday. He asked me if a suit and tie would be appropriate, as that would be the required attire in his native Korean culture. Dress codes remain fairly strict in Korea, and shorts at certain events are still frowned upon. There are numerous times when I questioned my husband about what was appropriate to wear to his clients' functions, as I don't travel in those circles. Occasionally, I wasn't dressed appropriately; I was either underdressed or overdressed. If you are uncertain of what is appropriate to wear, ask a person who can best advise you. Husbands or significant others aren't necessarily the best people to ask, though. They may be wonderful in telling you what they think looks good or what they prefer to see you wear, but they may not be the best at knowing what is appropriate for an occasion. In the end, it is your choice to decide what you want to wear and how "appropriate" you want to be.

Scent

Years ago, our pediatrician told me, "Ruth, most people have some body odor." We each emit our own scent. Have you ever handled a family member's clothing and picked up their personal scent? When family members traveled overseas, we dog-sat their pooch. They had asked me to take some clothing to the dry cleaner, so I piled them on a chair. After their departure, their dog immediately jumped on the clothing and snuggled for comfort. When you enter a person's home, there is often a specific aroma associated with that family. A nine-year-old neighborhood friend stopped at our home, and she said, "I like the smell in here. It smells like wisdom."

However, smelly clothing and strong body odors are offensive in mainstream U.S. culture. Many *USAans* frequently shower or bathe and often rinse or wash their hair. Brushing teeth twice daily and visiting the dentist twice a year are considered important aspects of personal hygiene and health. If you belch a lot, pass a lot of gas, or are concerned about personal body odor—including in your genital area—speak with your health-care provider and ask for recommendations to eliminate those concerns. The pharmacist at your drugstore can also offer suggestions.

You would be amazed at the number of products, fragrances, lotions, balms, and powders that mask our natural body odors, ranging from our head to our feet. There are overwhelming choices of toothpaste, mouthwash, deodorant, perfume, body lotions, and aftershave. Sometimes, there are almost tenfold more than were available when I was younger. Even so, people are becoming more mindful of others' allergies, as perfume or aftershave can be harmful. Sometimes nothing is done to mask normal body odors, as they are appreciated and natural.

Understanding the numerous facets of nonverbal communication is an essential skill to help you enhance your *positive communication environment* and significantly influences how you are received. You gained valuable insights of these fundamental features and a realization of the challenges that unintentional and inappropriate use creates. You learned how to use facial expression, eyes, body language, body space, touch, gesture, attire, color, and scent to your advantage. Maintaining eye contact, leaning in toward the person, genuinely smiling at the appropriate time, maintaining open body language, using touch and gesture, directly facing a person, keeping an appropriate and comfortable space between you and the other person, and nodding in agreement and understanding, along with deep listening, are examples of using these nonverbal skills to complement your communication.

Personalize these to suit who you are, what brings you comfort, and the message you want to deliver. In some ways, you may want to remain just as you are; in other ways, you may want to change. Most significant is the adage expressed four hundred years ago by William Shakespeare: "Above all, to thine own self be true." These words remain relevant and ring true today. In the end, as long as you respect others, it is up to you to decide how genuine and appropriate you want to be and what feels right for you.

Try to banish (and replace) negative thoughts that you do not want others to perceive. If you don't, they will pop into your mind at some unexpected or inopportune moment and your eyes or facial expressions will betray you. If you feel a negative thought pop into your head, do not even process it. If you hold the thought, even though you don't verbally express it, sometimes the negative feeling manifests itself in your facial expression or body language, and others detect that. By not further processing the negative thought, or not *"taking it on,"* you maintain your genuine positive demeanor.

Positive *nonverbal communication* usually advances solutions. But there are times when we are *source-connected* and engage all the tools and insights yet reconciliation or solutions are unattainable. In these instances, we are unable to influence or modify a major aspect of a person's behavior or attitude through conversation. What life and listening to others' experiences taught me is that communication is akin to a song and dance. You may recall my previous analogy of one person singing a song while, in response, the other person dances to the tune. But if the singer changes the tune, the dancer eventually changes the step. And if the dancer alters the step, the singer usually changes the song.

Two nonverbal events had a significant impact on me. The first incident occurred in 1984, when Lee and I traveled to the country then named Yugoslavia. There, I purchased and then wore the unusual, simple, two-piece olive-green cotton dress with brass buttons. For local standards, the outfit was pricey. While we waited at a corner for the light to turn green to cross the boulevard, a younger woman on the other side glanced our way and gave me a dirty look. An organic and natural response was to simply smile back. In that instant, she changed. As we crossed paths crossing the boulevard, she returned the smile.

The second incident occurred in Nevis as I visited a friend on a Saturday afternoon. In Nevis, unless you are of a faith that celebrates the Sabbath on that day, it is custom to houseclean in the morning and into the day. It also is traditional for those who love cricket to reward themselves by "limin'" (a term that means relaxing and having fun), which often includes a cricket match in the late afternoon. On this day, my friend had asked family members to pitch in with Saturday chores, but to no avail. They were busy puttering around the house or watching televised sports. As was custom on cricket days, after the chores were completed, everyone bathed and dressed for town. My friend was the only driver in the family, and she knew what to expect. She had parked herself on the front porch in her rocking chair. While sitting next to her, chatting, the others readied for town. When they were all spruced up, they reminded her it was time for her to drive them into town. She didn't respond. She just sat with a neutral expression on her face and silently continued to rock.

After a few moments, the family members got the message and they walked into town. In Nevis, that type of nonverbal, nonargumentative communication is called "not making noise." It got the point across. In the future, especially on cricket days, everyone helped. The incident brought to mind an expression that my mother had often stated, "Show them, don't tell them."

This powerful type of nonverbal communication makes a positive point in a neutral manner and avoids a heated argument. Wasn't this type of nonverbal communication the foundation of the principles of peaceful, nonviolent sit-in protests against injustice espoused by Mahatma Gandhi, by Dr. Martin Luther King Jr., and more recently, by the Black Lives Matter movement? Another way to positively express ourselves is to let our feet do the walking rather than our mouths do the talking. When we are upset, rather than remain and argue, poised in grace and silence, turn around and simply walk away. That also avoids further confrontation. This response requires a long-lasting commitment to do just that.

I hope that you have gathered a greater understanding of nonverbal communication, including those highlighting individuals from differing linguistic and cultural backgrounds. Embracing and applying these facets contribute to more pleasurable, productive, and comfortable conversations and relations with others.

Let me remind you that a broader exploration into intercultural communication, especially for those *Born-abroad* or who speak English as a Second Language, is presented in the following section, *Soul to Soul Intercultural Communication*.

It's Not What You Say, but How You Say It

My voice tone is the ultimate barometer that signals that I am off-balance and that I just need to lighten up.

Voice Tone

Mehrabian (1981) states that voice tone represents 38 percent of how we perceive face-to-face communication. When we hear a person's voice over the phone, media, or public-address system (PA), the voice takes on greater significance.

On January 15, 2009, US Airways Flight 1549 experienced engine failure as multiple bird strikes crippled both engines. In an icy, calm voice, Captain Chesley B. "Sully" Sullenberger announced to his passengers and crew, "Brace yourself for impact," as he miraculously piloted his stricken plane to safety. What if his voice had expressed panic? Would passengers have remained calm, and would they have reacted differently?

Voices can sound and feel like soothing rhapsodies, healing touch, blissful melodies, or light-hearted inspirations. They can also be frightening or as irritating as fingernails screeching across a chalkboard. Our voices are similar to our fingerprints. Each pattern is recognizable as belonging to us throughout most of our lives. People can usually recognize our voices, even if we have not spoken with them for years. Many people do not like the way they sound when they hear themselves on their greeting or voice mail, but that is the voice that others hear. People are curious why their voice sounds so different to them when they speak than when they hear it recorded. Sound is heard through two media—air transmission and bone conduction. The eardrum converts the air-transmitted waves to vibrations and transmits them to our inner ear, our cochlea. When we speak, the sound is conducted through the bones and fluid in our skull. That is called bone conduction.

My voice tone serves as another barometer to reflect my mood. When I hear myself sound abrupt, I have usually been interrupted in the middle of a project, am pressed for time, have dealt with the same computer-related issue several times without resolution, or have (formerly) repeatedly received relentless robo-calls or a sales pitch from telemarketers. When I notice frustration in my voice, I immediately attempt to chill. It is unfair for the person who is calling to receive a part of my negative energy, even if their call is unsolicited.

When a child shares a feeling or concern with a parent or caregiver, a person with their spouse or partner, a student with a teacher or counselor, or a patient with a nurse or physician, each wants to feel safe and at ease expressing their feelings or concerns. As a society, we suggest that the youth seek their parents, teachers, counselors, law enforcement officers, physicians, clergy, partners, and supervisors to discuss their concerns and challenges. Yet often, the person seeking advice or comfort feels rebuffed, rejected, or disregarded, not necessarily by what the other person said, but by the tone in which they deliver the message. The optimal type of voice tone in this situation expresses willingness, compassion, and concern. If our voices carry an angry, impatient, frustrated, condescending, or patronizing tone, the person who sought comfort or advice may not as readily approach us again. We may unintentionally turn away those who we most want to seek our guidance. Even though people may be good-hearted, they may come across as uninterested, distasteful, or lacking confidence because their voice tone reflects these feelings. In all these examples, it is often *not how they respond but how they say it.*

On the flip side, when a child seeks help from a parent or teacher and communicates in an upbeat voice, or a patient who is ill sounds as cheerful and animated as usual, or a spouse or partner confronts a serious issue with their loved one but uses a voice that reflects everything is okay, how can anyone ever detect what the person really feels or needs? When a doctor yells at his staff, claiming it is in the patients' best interest, what do the patients in the waiting and examining rooms really perceive?

In many situations, voice impacts our conversation more significantly than 38 percent. Our voice tone reflects the truth in our hearts and minds in a way that not only conveys our message but also what we feel. If our goal is to create calm, care, comfort, empathy, interest, understanding, or urgency, our voice must reflect that. If we want to express frustration, persuasion, or strength, our voice must also resonate that.

In my experience, unless an individual is cruel, is disingenuous, or has a pattern of ridiculing others, people are often "right on" with their message. However, it often is their voice tone that offends, turns folks off, and betrays their true feelings. Voice tone is a pivotal factor of our *positive communication environment*. It conveys the full gamut of our feelings and emotions: joy, surprise, serenity, acceptance, doubt, frustration, indifference, anger, boredom, doubt, lack of confidence, or sense of superiority and all the other feelings we experience if we are honest with ourselves. Reflect a moment about people in your life whose voices provide comfort, trust, or other positive feelings, or those whose voices cast doubt, fear, frustration, intimidation, or other negative feelings. One type of voice attracts, one type questions, and another type repels.

Six Factors of Voice Tone

The six factors of voice include *projection, pitch, rate, volume, intonation,* and *phrasing* and serve as the foundation of good voice tone. In addition, correct *word syllable stress patterns* are necessary, as they place accurate stress on syllables within a word to ensure its meaning. We modulate each factor to accurately convey our truth.

Projection

Projection is the first factor in the foundation of voice tone and rhythm. Projection is critical when speaking U.S. English. To project is to broadcast our speech outside our mouth rather than hold the sound within the mouth. The accurate amount of projection conveys confidence, interest, and honesty. When we do not project, people think we mumble. In mainstream U.S. culture, when we mumble, we give the impression that we are not interested or lack confidence or send other negative messages. When a person improves their projection, they automatically enhance their communication.

Resonance creates our voice quality and determines our one and only voice. The quality and sound are formed by our vocal cords vibrating within the chambers of our mouth, pharynx, and nasal passages. Since the shape and size of these chambers are formed slightly differently within each of us, we sound different from others, though sometimes relatives sound quite similar.

The following discussion of projection is beneficial for both the *USAan* and the person who speaks English as their second language (often referred to as ESL) or who speaks U.S. English as a foreign language (often referred to as FL). The person who is an ESL speaker is acquiring English to become fluent, while a person who speaks U.S. English as an FL uses English not as a second language but as a foreign language. To clarify, this includes individuals such as an exchange student, a businessperson, a physician, or a family member who only uses U.S. English for temporary trips to the United States.

In David Alan Stern's audio tapes from Dialect Accent Specialists (1982, 1992, 2003) he states, "When speaking any language, the energy of your voice is concentrated in a specific area of the mouth." Compare the flow of your breath to the flow of a river. In most every other language except U.S. English, the sound is focused somewhere inside the mouth—akin to eddies in a pool of water. When one speaks French, the energy is concentrated in the upper back portion of the mouth to create the nasal quality of the French language. In Spanish, the sound is concentrated behind the top lips. In the Vietnamese, Thai, and Korean languages, the sound is concentrated in the lower part of the mouth. The different locations where sounds are concentrated are a factor in its resonance, and that gives each language its own unique sound.

In nonregional U.S. English, you *project the sound* or energy outside in front of the mouth, "*open up and project*," which has a megaphone effect. Morton Cooper, in *Change Your Voice, Change Your Life* (1984), states, "The megaphone effect is in *direction* not in *loudness* or *volume*." Imagine an acrylic board six inches in front of your mouth. Project all your speech, even whispers, to at least that distance in front of your mouth. While you are learning to improve your projection, place your hand six inches in front of your mouth to target a spot and sense of where to project.

When teaching projection, I recommended that my clients open their mouths wide enough to easily slide in their little finger sideways. If you mumble or are an ESL speaker, slightly opening your mouth to about three-eighths of an inch between your top and bottom front teeth provides ample space for the varied and more extensive tongue movements of U.S. English. The speech sounds *p*, *b*, and *m* are said with the lips closed. While it is considered rude in many cultures to expose one's teeth or open one's mouth when speaking, it is necessary to maintain that space of three-eighths of an inch when speaking U.S. English. Learning projection in U.S. English does not affect the way a person speaks their native language.

If you compare the various movements of the tongue used for speech to the movements of a skilled acrobat, you realize they both require adequate space. It would be difficult for an acrobat to confine their feats to the limited space under a table. In the same way, it is difficult to pronounce U.S. English speech sounds with mouths and lips almost closed. Therefore, it is very important to maintain that opening and project. Listen to various news anchors and observe who projects their words and is easily understood. Years ago, Walter Cronkite's voice was the gold standard. Which newscaster's voice do you prefer, and why?

There are several sounds in U.S. English that are more complex and require room for their positioning and successful production. The sound "r" is produced by lifting the tongue and then rolling the tip slightly backward toward the back of the mouth. The "th" sound is produced by placing the tongue between the upper and lower front teeth so they are slightly ajar. The sound is accompanied by soft-blowing air.

In the Asian, Indian, and Pakistani cultures, it is considered rude to open your mouth and project. People from these cultures were taught not to expose their teeth while talking or smiling. People from these linguistic and cultural backgrounds are often perceived in the U.S. culture as mumbling. They do not mumble intentionally, and unless they are aware, they do not realize that it is necessary to slightly open their mouths. They speak in a manner that reflects politeness and appropriateness in their native culture. They may also be unaware of the negative impression they give when they speak U.S. English in this manner.

Pitch

Pitch is the second factor in voice tone. Pitch is relative to age and gender. Using a natural pitch suited to the size and shape of our vocal cords imparts authenticity and helps maintain healthy vocal cords. Sometimes, women use a *little-girl "voice-costume"* to sound helpless, sexy, or alluring. Sometimes, men use a lower pitch to sound more masculine or sexy. When you artificially raise your pitch to sound more feminine or lower your pitch to sound sexy or more masculine, you do not come across as genuine.

Continued misuse of your vocal cords may temporarily or permanently cause hoarseness and result in muscle tension or vocal cord lesions. These dysfunctions take time to overcome, if the vocal misuse patterns can even be reversed. There are people in public office, leading roles, and many fields who cultivated a voice and style to portray a desired image but you can sense their voice is somewhat disingenuous.

Morton Cooper suggests that you can find your natural and optimal pitch by closing your lips and saying "umm-hmmm" using rising inflection, your pitch rising. He teaches how to apply that technique to all your speech (Cooper 1984).

There are four pitch levels in U.S. English. Most speech takes place between pitch levels 1/2 to 1 and 3 to 3 1/2. You usually begin to speak at pitch level 1 or 1 1/2, rise to 3 to 3 1/2, then lower to pitch level 1 1/2 at the end of a phrase, and then drop to pitch level 1 at the end. However, a question ends with a rising pitch.

- Pitch level 1 has no intonation and is used on structural words, such as conjunctions and articles.
- Pitch level 2 is the lowest pitch and signals that a person is finished speaking and indicates it's others' turn to speak.
- Pitch level 3 indicates the more important words.
- Pitch level 4 is the highest pitch and denotes passion, excitement, or alarm. Strong intonation is used on the most important words.

In addition, pitch rises slightly on words that convey a positive meaning and falls slightly on words that convey a negative or serious meaning. If you combine a rising, positive pitch with a negative message or serious situation, or a falling, negative pitch with a pleasant message, the other person will not understand the inconsistency; pitch and words must be consistent. Usually, voice tone takes precedence over the words to relate the *meaning* and *intention* of your message.

In my professional experience, individuals who convey negative impressions due to their voice tone fall into four categories: they are unaware of the feeling or meaning their voice conveys, they are *source-disconnected*, they engage a *voice-costume*, or they are people who tend to be negative. Several clients felt that they had to severely modify their personality, their *representational self*, and only present their posturing, *presentational self*, to keep their jobs. In choosing what they felt were appropriate voices, they were actually causing more harm than good. The *voice-costume* that they chose was false. They often sounded affected, impersonal, or demeaning. Changing your voice without changing the negative feelings behind the voice is not enough. In a way, you are changing your *voice-costume*, but it remains a costume. Your *voice-costume* eventually reveals your true feelings. My clients learned to replace their fear and negative attitudes with pleasant thoughts and feelings and engage their *source-connection*.

An accountant in securities who worked with a large prestigious firm discovered that her strengths of checks and balances, research, and concern for her staff were totally worthless to her employer. Her supervisor was more focused on how long it took to complete the task than doing it right. The supervisor forced her to work quickly, cutting corners if necessary. She felt that she had to assume a *voice-costume*. To cope, she became disconnected from her *source-connection*. When she could no longer feel her *source-connection*, she felt a deep void, so she worked hard to regain her *source-connection*. When her authentic voice returned, she realized that her genuine voice proved more productive. The voice tone and demeanor that she had chosen reflected her *presentational self* but totally disregarded her true personality—her *representational self*. The *voice-costume* conveyed a largely affected, flat, and monotone style that several colleagues perceived as condescending.

A physician whose colleagues told him that he was quite animated when he chatted with them felt that he was unable to express concern when communicating with his patients. Using role-playing and videotaping, he tapped into the positive voice tone he used with people other than his patients. After a few role-playing situations, he said, "You want me to talk like a person." I responded, "Precisely."

Patients and colleagues misinterpreted another physician and thought he was rude because he used a falling pitch when a rising pitch was appropriate. When he greeted a patient either in person or on the phone, he said, "Hi, Mrs. Jones," in a falling pitch. The patients thought he was upset, angry, or curt. It certainly wasn't the message or feeling he wanted to convey.

Think of a person asking you to join them for dinner; you respond, "Okay." Say "Okay" with rising pitch. It sounds as if you genuinely want to go. Now, say "Okay" with falling pitch. Doesn't it sound as if you would rather decline the invitation?

A man from Honduras was unable to convince his badgering coworkers that he was no longer going to complete their tasks. When he listened to his recorded message communicating with his colleagues and staff, he heard that his pitch rose on the word *not* in the phrase "I'm not going to do it." After listening to his voice, he quipped, "I sound as if I'm joking. No wonder nobody takes me seriously." He changed his *not* to a falling pitch while continually using a pleasant tone. His colleagues no longer hassled him.

Compliments, pleasantries, and well-wishes are voiced with higher pitch. Otherwise, the message comes across as insincere or sarcastic. Serious and negative matters are accompanied by lowering pitch. Otherwise, people do not get the urgency of your message. If others do not perceive you the way you want, monitor your voice. Listen to make certain that you are using the appropriate rising or falling pitch. An honest example of your voice in various situations can be revealed if someone records your conversations without your knowledge. You can then play back the recording to listen to what you sound like. Do you sound like a person whose company you would seek?

Some people who come across as quite negative use a downward pitch on many of their words instead of just the key words. When a physician uses a negative, downward pitch on the entire sentence "Your lab tests came back and confirmed the cancer has spread," he conveys far more pessimism than necessary. The only words that require additional noting are *cancer* and *spread*, and this can be conveyed simply by prolonging the vowels in those words. In addition, the word *spread* is the last word in the sentence. Say the sentence two ways and compare the difference. First, say the entire sentence in a lower pitch. Next, say the sentence with the lower pitch on the words *cancer* and *spread*. Although the message is not what anyone wants to hear, which way would you rather hear it? Think of an individual you know who appears happy. That person usually has a pleasant voice tone that appropriately rises in pitch.

When you want to be firm to get your point across, you do not have to sound mean or angry. Just use a convincing voice that leaves no doubt that you are serious and use intonation that has a lower pitch on the word or words you want to emphasize. In the statement "I really don't want to do it," the words *don't want* are the words that require a lower pitch.

A further presentation on intonation is presented later in this chapter.

Rate

Rate also highlights the importance of words, and it is the third factor in voice tone and rhythm. Rate is the speed at which you speak. In *Successful Nonverbal Communication*, Leathers (1992) states, "A conversational style is 125–160 words per minute in American English." When one speaks too fast, people often find it difficult to follow. Speaking too rapidly or haltingly indicates dishonesty and nervousness. Speaking too slowly gives the impression that you are dull, are disinterested, or lack initiative. Morton Cooper says, "Conversation speech is 125 words per minute" (Cooper 1984). Often, people who process information rapidly also speak faster. With ever-increasing demands in most of our lives, it is important to maintain a rate that is pleasant, even when we are hassled or rushed.

We slow down our speech by elongating or "holding out" the vowels in each word. We do not reduce the rate by saying one syllable or word at a time. The rhythm remains the same; only the process moves slower—similar to slowing down from a driving speed of sixty-five miles per hour (mph) to fifty miles per hour. People who are hard of hearing, speak English as a second language, or are mentally challenged have more difficulty understanding you when you speak too rapidly. If you speak too slowly, it is difficult for the listener to remain focused.

Volume

Volume is the fourth factor in voice tone and is the loudness of speech. If your voice is too soft, people have difficulty or have to exert greater effort to hear and understand you. It is your responsibility to speak loudly enough or inform others that you are unable to do so.

too soft_____TOO LOUD

When your voice is too soft, others may perceive you as lacking confidence. Volume is a decisive factor when conversing with a person who is hard of hearing. You also facilitate their ability to understand you by directly facing them when you speak. When possible, position yourself with light on your face. If they lip-read, it will be easier for them to view your mouth and read your words.

Many people who are hard of hearing are reticent to tell others about their situation. This may be because people do not like to admit their imperfections or because they may have difficulty in responding to discrimination against those with disabilities, or because they are elderly. It is the responsibility of the person who is hard of hearing to inform others of their disability. Often, people who do not wear hearing aids are unaware that the device amplifies not only speech sounds but also all sounds, including background noise. At present, there is a hearing aid that cancels noise, but it is not very user-friendly. The user has to know how it works and alter their listening habits for it to function well. Therefore, it is best for the person who is hard of hearing to distance themselves from as much interfering background noise as possible.

The lovely mother of a professional colleague shared that she doesn't like to tell others about her hearing impairment because she doesn't like people to talk with her as if she is stupid or talk in a louder tone. In that process, they move into her personal space and make "exaggerated, scrunched-up facial expressions." These are natural responses when people raise their voices, especially if they are unfamiliar with the best way to communicate with people who are hearing impaired.

There are additional factors that may be more challenging for a person to hear and ultimately comprehend, especially if the auditory NLP channel is their least preferred channel. The challenges occur especially when the individual is on a call at a location that is not their home or is surrounded by more than usual or loud background noise. If you have hearing loss, I suggest that you help block this noise by gently placing your little finger in the ear with the greatest loss and holding the phone's earpiece close to your other ear.

In these situations, it is far more demanding to concentrate. I recommend keeping the conversation shorter and letting the person with hearing loss set the tone and time. When I called a friend whom I had seen weekly for years but had since moved, our phone calls were quite lengthy. While writing this book, I had not chatted with her for quite a while, so I was unaware that her hearing loss had significantly progressed. When I called her, she asked how much time I had available. Since we hadn't spoken for a while, I offered her up to forty minutes. During our conversation, there were many folks chatting in the background. After a while, she said that she had to go because it was exhausting to focus on a lengthy conversation with severe hearing loss. In hindsight, I should have requested that she set the time limit. When you are in a crowded room or restaurant with a person who is hard of hearing, ask that person about their seating preference. If you are aware of which ear is their best, direct your conversation to that ear and always maintain eye contact. If they still are unable to hear you, it is their responsibility to remain focused, lean into you, wear a hearing aid, bring extra batteries, or learn to lip-read. It is not your responsibility to strain your voice, talk so loudly that you are uncomfortable, or lean into that person and speak to their good ear just so the other person hears you. However, some situations occur that require you to do just that. If they fail to inform you of their hearing loss, do not wear hearing aids, often ask you to repeat, or respond inappropriately, show compassion and make necessary adjustments to help them when you can.

If you invariably speak a lot louder than most people, others may perceive you as angry, rude, aggressive, or obnoxious. Those who traveled abroad or are immigrants know that U.S. English is one of the louder languages spoken. There are regions in the United States where people speak louder than other regions. The communication styles of the primary family and native cultures also influence loudness. The loud and demanding voices of some *USAans* are often annoying or frightening to people from "softer-spoken" cultures. A loud voice can frighten anyone who is unaccustomed to being spoken to in that manner, whatever age, gender, or culture.

In many cultures, women use softer voices than men, so a loud voice may be even more intimidating to them. Most people perceive others, especially men, as frustrated or angry when they raise their voice. In some cultures, even the slightest increase in loudness implies anger. If you are a *USAan* whose family integrated decades ago and you use appropriate projection and volume, you may be overbearing to an individual who recently emigrated from an Asian culture. If a person looks at you with raised eyebrows or a frown when you speak louder than is necessary, take that as a cue to lower your voice.

When I visited the Netherlands, a person reminded me that I was not in California and what is appropriate there is inappropriate in Northern Europe. On one of my husband's and my trips to Europe, we were at an outdoor café at a town square in a popular Italian resort town. The joyous and lively voices of the people sipping espresso certainly would not have been well-suited in the more reserved Netherlands. It is important to become aware of how loudly or softly we speak. Monitor your voice to make certain that the volume is suitable for the surroundings and situation, especially when traveling abroad or in any common space, such as an elevator, a waiting room, reception area, or checkout line.

Intonation

Intonation is the fifth factor of voice tone and encompasses the rise and fall of our voice to highlight and give meaning. To highlight *key written words*, we bold, underline, italicize, or note with a bullet, check, or asterisk. To highlight *key spoken words*, we modulate pitch, rate, and volume. Along with giving additional meaning to words, intonation conveys the impression that you are caring, confident, persuasive, interested in the topic, or frustrated, upset, or angry. Intonation is similar to adding color to gray. Some people incorrectly slow their speech by pausing between each word or syllable.

To *intone* or highlight words in a positive way:

- Say it *slower*, prolonging the vowels;
- Say it *louder*; and/or
- Slightly *raise* the pitch.

Next, say the first of the following two sentences with your pitch rising on the word *like*. Then say the second sentence with your pitch falling on *like*.

- I *like* the new manager. (Rising pitch.)
- I *like* the new manager. (Falling pitch.)

Which sentence sounds more convincing? The first sentence is correct, with rising pitch reflecting the positive meaning of the word *like*.

To *intone* or highlight words to express negative, serious, or urgent meaning, say the words *slower* and *louder* and slightly *lower* the pitch.

In the first of the following two sentences, pronounce *upset* using falling pitch. Then say the second sentence with rising pitch on *upset*.

- I am *upset* with this report. (Falling pitch.)
- I am *upset* with this report. (Rising pitch.)

Which sentence sounds more credible? The first sentence's falling pitch is correct because it reflects the negative meaning of the word *upset*.

In the first of the following two sentences, pronounce *worried* using rising pitch. Then repeat the second sentence with falling pitch on *worried*.

- I am *worried* about your health. (Rising pitch.)
- I am *worried* about your health. (Falling pitch.)

In the first sentence, using rising pitch sends the message that you are concerned. In the second sentence, using falling pitch shows a more urgent concern. If the person does not want to hear about their health, your falling pitch may turn them off.

Repeat the following Shakespeare saying using a monotone voice, then repeat it using proper intonation, and listen for the difference: "To be, or not to be, that is the question." Which best reflects the meaning?

The following is a list of positive or negative impressions that we impart and that are influenced by the pitch, volume, and intonation of our voice.

Positive Impression	Negative Impression
• Caring	• Aggressive
• Compassionate	• Arrogant
• Confident	• Condescending
• Convincing	• Confrontational
• Empathetic	
• Enthusiastic	
• Persuasive	
• Pleasant	

Phrasing

Phrasing is the sixth and final factor in the foundation of voice tone and rhythm, and it is expressed in the flow of our speech. Many experts, including Deborah Tannen (1986), include "pausing" as a part of intonation. I separated pausing from intonation and named it *phrasing*. Phrasing *consists of necessary pauses at the appropriate places*. Without these pauses, the *intention* of your message is more challenging to understand.

In U.S. English, words within a phrase are grouped and flow as one unit. In other languages, especially those of Indian or Pakistani cultures, they pronounce words individually, sounding more staccato or chopped than the flow of U.S. English. In the Chinese language, each syllable is uttered separately. French is an example of one of the most flowing and melodic languages. In U.S. English, *words within a phrase flow as one. There is no pause between the words in a phrase* within dependent clauses.

Pauses are not similar to a red light, but they reflect the yellow light of a traffic signal. Speech pauses while you maintain voice tone. If you have to take a breath, the pause is a perfect time to take it. Pauses usually occur between groups of words, such as nouns or pronouns and their adjectives, verbs and their adverbs, noun phrases, verb phrases, prepositional phrases, and dependent clauses.

An Asian-born teacher had a considerably serious and harsh tone along with a phrasing pattern typical of many Asian languages; he turned off his students and their parents as well as his colleagues and staff. When he learned of the negative impression his vocal patterns created, he modified, recorded, and practiced. Then, others perceived him as a caring and empathetic teacher.

Beneficial examples and practices for phrasing used in U.S. English, which are targeted especially for the English as a second language speaker, are presented in the voice tone section in the chapter "Embracing Diversity" in the following section, *Soul to Soul Intercultural Communication*.

In face-to-face communication, nonverbal communication comprises 55 percent and voice tone comprises 38 percent of how you are perceived. If your voice or rhythm patterns and nonverbal communication are negative, 93 percent of how you communicate is unfavorable. Although it may not be your intention, that is how you are perceived.

I consulted with people whose family, colleagues, or staff feared them or tuned them out simply because of their "nasty" voice. These clients were basically caring people and knowledgeable in their professions but had learned inappropriate negative voice tone patterns, harbored negative feelings, or became *source-disconnected*. Because their voice tone and rhythm patterns were negative, they were not respected or as readily sought out by their peers, colleagues, students, clients, or patients. After working diligently, those who turned to a more positive style expanded their circle to include others who then felt more comfortable with them.

You have gained significant insights into the many facets of voice tone and rhythm, an understanding of the challenges and issues that may arise, and their solutions. If family members or colleagues imply that you are unpleasant to be around, I suggest that you begin to pay attention to the negative features of your voice. Listen to your voice and focus on the tightness in your throat and neck area when you are upset. Let these sensations act as a barometer to monitor and check in to see what you are *really feeling*. Then, express your negative feelings and thoughts in a more positive way.

Tonal

Tonal is not a feature of U.S. English, but many Asian languages have a tonal component at the end of the word to give different meanings to the identical speech sounds. When people from

Asian and other cultural backgrounds sound "singsong," it is because they still apply the tonal features of their native language. A broader discussion of this feature also is presented in the following section, *Soul to Soul Intercultural Connection and Communication*.

When conversing with people from other language and cultural backgrounds, remember that their primary family's and native culture's communication style may still affect how they speak U.S. English. What may appear as lacking confidence, monotone, mumbling, or rude may just be a lack of understanding. It may also be that the person has not learned to eliminate tonal components, lacks the ability to discriminate the finer nuances of voice tone and rhythm in U.S. English, or lacks the will to change.

You have gained a greater awareness of your own voice tone and rhythm and that of people from differing linguistic and cultural backgrounds and have acquired numerous insights and tools. Please remember to include your *source-connection* and these voice tone and rhythm facets to favorably reflect the *intention* and *meaning* of your message. Embracing and applying these will contribute to more comfortable, fulfilling, and productive conversations and relations with others.

Honor Yourself and Choose Your Words Wisely

What brings about the most conflict is that you do not say what you mean and you do not do what you say.

—Martin Buber

Verbal Communication

If you recall, Mehrabian (1981) states that verbal communication represents only 7 percent of how we perceive face-to-face communication. No matter how small a percentage is dedicated to verbal communication, words give meaning and are significant. At times, the impact is far greater. Rabbi Zelig Pliskin penned the following eloquent words in *Love Your Neighbor* (1977): "Like darkness and light, wet and dry, cold and warm words also have opposite strengths—to heal and to hurt." The phrase "*Sticks and stones may break my bones but names will never hurt me*" was and remains a response to others' taunts. Nevertheless, *names do hurt* at any age. Can you recall words that deeply hurt you? Does the memory of those words remain deeply etched inside? Hopefully, you can also recall with similar intensity the words that consoled, brought joy, or led you out of dark misery.

There are numerous features included in mindful, positive, effective, and appropriate verbal communication. They are *source-connection*, mindfulness, proactive and reactive, acknowledgment, direct or indirect communication, positive vocabulary, emotionally charged words, evasiveness, I mode, focus, questions, responses, precision, appropriate levels, assumptions, use of "No," small talk, fillers, *communication investments*, and appreciation.

Source-Connected Communication

As you recall, I believe that *source-connection* is at the heart of ultimate goodness and the foundation of a genuine, compassionate, and holistic view, as presented in the first chapter, "*Source-Connection.*" Lack of *source-connection* is the root of many communication challenges, and it is most significant in your personal mind-set and in how you perceive and respond to others. Before we continue, I would like to expand on a few more insights into *source-connected* communication.

You probably heard the expression "She marches to her own tune." Folks who "march to their own tune" tend to create their own paths through life and are true to themselves. They dedicate themselves to live life, select careers, and participate in activities that feel right. For the most part, they also choose with whom to bond for desired relationships and friendships, reflecting what they feel in their hearts and souls and believe is in their best interest. Is their choice always perfect? Of course not, but they do not let perfection stand in the way of good. Given a choice, *source-connected* individuals usually do not remain involved at any significant level with people who, or situations that, are abusive, disagreeable, or disrespectful. When genuine, they express what they feel is the right response, not thoughts or opinions that others want or expect. *Source-connected* people hold secure feelings of self-worth and try not to allow abuses to continue. They often live in consideration of others, but not because of them. When you are *source-connected*, you do not speak from negativity or fear, nor do you respond with what *should* be said; rather, you speak mindfully from your heart and soul. You communicate your best because you are your *source-connected* best. Having said that, I seriously doubt that any individual is *source-connected* every moment of their lives.

Proactive and Reactive Communication

In *Prayers for the Jewish High Holidays*, Rabbi Stan Levy cites a 150-years-old quotation by Miniatum Mendel of Kotzk, Poland. He quotes, "If I am I because I am I, and you are you because you are you, then I am I and you are you. But if I am I because you are you, and you are you because I am I, then I am not I and you are not you." I interpret that the first sentence describes people who are *source-connected*, believe in themselves, and are proactive. They live their lives the way they feel is best and are most satisfied. The second sentence describes people who are reactive, live their lives trying to please others by doing what they believe is expected or desired, or by trying to obey the "shoulds" they hear from others or often echoing in their own heads.

Proactive communication better prepares us to intervene in or control unexpected situations, especially those that are most challenging. Years ago, my husband and I visited a small community in Oregon. Some "Caucasian" boys had beaten up a youth who was Latino. The small community responded with a demonstration of one hundred citizens to express their disgust with the bigotry. When I spoke to a spiritual leader in the community and expressed my support of the demonstration, he said, "It was good, but we have to become more proactive in our response. Currently, our point of reference is reactive. The 'collective consciousness' is negative. By demonstrating, we are reacting positively to a negative situation. If we can find a way to reach out, include the Latino community, and embrace diversity, we will establish a new point of reference. By embracing pluralism and finding commonality in our lives, we will positively alter the 'collective consciousness.'" In light of the 2016 presidential election, awareness and positive actions are more critical than ever; resignation was and remains the worst possible response. A proactive man spoke up when his colleagues made discriminating comments, and a *source-connected* woman mindfully rebuked the chatter of divisive political policies at her workplace.

When individuals communicte harshly or act unkindly and we are reactive and respond in the same manner, we allow their negative feelings to permeate and fuel our response. We become what is so distasteful or abhorrent to us. When we are reactive, start playing to the lowest common denominator, and begin mudslinging, the mud may comeback and hit us at some unexpected point. In the process, we demean, disappoint, and dishonor ourselves, our loved ones, and others. We would not automatically turn over our car keys for another individual to drive away with our car, so why would we automatically turn over the control of our integrity or our power to others?

When we expect or anticipate challenges at home or work and address them before they occur, we are proactive. Unfortunately, many individuals, organizations, and governments are reactive. They constantly respond to situations and issues to "put out fires" instead of taking the lead and the time to anticipate, analyze, prevent, or discuss the issues to seek positive and lasting solutions. People are afraid to take risks in their personal lives for fear of rejection or failure. In their vocational and professional lives, they fear losing their jobs. They hold back, and so they avoid speaking up when decision makers do not reflect what they think is best. They may accept the idea that the most relevant factor in completing a project is meeting the deadline, coming in within budget, or coming up short in any area instead of expressing their belief that it is paramount to do it right. If more people who wish to be proactive pooled together and expressed themselves, that would benefit everyone. In the end, every team member pays a price for the obvious neglect or wishful, unrealistic, or harmful goals.

Over the years, I often reflected on the tragic *Challenger* space shuttle that blew apart in the air seventy-three seconds after liftoff in January 1986. Later, they discovered that a faulty O-ring was the problem. A special commission established by then President Ronald Reagan determined the cause of the accident and noted that NASA's decision to launch the shuttle was flawed. Top-level decision makers were informed of problems with the joints and O-rings and of the possible damaging effects of cold weather. I often wondered if there was one individual who was fully aware of the issue but was afraid to stand up and speak out because of deadlines or budget constraints. If so, this is a dreadful, sorrowful example of a lack of proactive communication.

When we are afraid to follow our own instincts because we fear failure, rejection, or criticism from family members, we again dishonor ourselves and everyone around us. Resentment and anger build up within. If we do not have a positive outlet, that anger and energy remain suppressed, and it will eventually seep out or we will explode. Then, we and others suffer the physical, mental, emotional, and spiritual disease and the consequences.

A friend who firmly believed in acupuncture and observed its benefits in many of her friends was afraid to explore the treatments herself because she did not want to be ridiculed or criticized by family members. A high-level executive wanted to change jobs to one less demanding, less financially rewarding, and less time-consuming. He was offered a job where the rewards were more in line with his spirit than in his wallet. His family was not supportive with the idea, and they were concerned that current "expected excesses" would become "extras." Buckling under family pressures, he declined the position. Years later, his decision still gnawed within. His decision not only nagged him but also created powerful resentment that reflected in his subtly negative, passive-aggressive communication. It also affected his word choice with his family, especially his spouse. He eventually divorced and created a harmonious lifestyle.

When we become frightened and reactive, it is best to take time and think through what we fear and the choices and opportunities that are available. One of the most paramount commitments that we keep is to remain *source-connected* and true to ourselves. Our *source-connection* gives us the strength and courage to make the hard choices and decisions that are both best for us and, when feasible, considerate of others.

Acknowledge Others

People must be heard, and acknowledgment affirms that. Acknowledgment also expresses respect. These confirm that needs matter and promote positive feelings and connections. Most of us know how it feels when we are not acknowledged. A person "sloughs us off," discounts us with a condescending voice or a nonverbal flick of a hand, rolling eyes, curling lips, or makes comments such as "C'mon," "Oh sure," or "You must be joking." If we allow that, those actions detract from the ambience of our *positive communication environment.* As differences occur, we first *source-connect* with the person and acknowledge their feelings and thoughts. Then, at the appropriate time, when they appear receptive, we offer our responses, ideas, or solutions. The difference between talking, arguing, or acknowledgment is the *trusted connection.*

Recall Figure 4 in the chapter "Communication Is Connection" that illustrates the difference between talk (separated hands) and communication (intertwined hands). Now, visualize the separated hands as you slowly move each hand back and forth. This represents speaking, while rapidly moving the hands denotes arguing. The further you move the hands apart, the less chance there is for the connection and ultimately resolution or success.

Next, visualize your intertwined hands to represent communication and turn your hands to face the other person. Void of judgment, preconceived ideas, bias, or negative *lenses,* try to sense what the other person feels. Observe their nonverbal communication and deeply listen from your heart to what they say and how they express that. Then, *connect* with them regardless of whether you agree with them or not. That is acknowledgment. Without that connection and acknowledgment, the possibility of a win-win resolution is hampered. The other person may be less receptive to what you say and may even become more entrenched in their opinion.

Finally, slightly pull back your intertwined hands while they still face the other person. This visualization illustrates how to best offer your comments. In your connection and acknowledgment, try to find common ground or compromise so that all can reach an amicable solution. *In that connected trust, learning takes place, problems are solved, and needs are met.*

When colleagues are resistant to anything we suggest, especially at a university (which is an environment where we expect conflicting ideas and dialogue to flourish), it is paramount that our comments reflect their ideas and not them personally. Remain positive and focused on the students. Naysayers do not belong. First, get your ego, tribe, or turf out of the way. Then, with a laser focus, find a solution that best serves the students. After all, isn't the intent of educators to initiate, collaborate, and serve the students, who are the foundation and leaders of the next generation?

When students and faculty from very liberal or archconservative campuses boycott, boo, or protest speakers who espouse strongly held opposing views, void of malice, they need to examine and question their motives. Again, I ask, Isn't the purpose and value of an educational institution also to provide a forum where dialogue, including those of opposing views, flows so that greater understanding evolves? We must recognize the difference between "hate speech," which is protected as free speech under the First Amendment of the Constitution, and "vitriolic rhetoric" that incites violence, which is against the law. During these trying times, we must set aside our passion and engage reason.

When patients are worried or show frustration in their inability to find answers, acknowledge their concerns. Acknowledging concerns is far more beneficial in building rapport than ignoring, minimizing, or denying them. Simply say, "We'll keep trying and work together until we find an answer." Even if the answer is "There is no answer," compassionately acknowledge the patient's concern, disappointment, or frustration and explain the options, which may be positive. It is also demeaning to tell patients that there are other patients who are worse off than they are. Do not compare. The only valid comparison is the patient's present condition and acceptance of or hope for the future. If a patient is worried about an illness, surgery, or procedure, the worst thing you can say is, "Don't worry." Acknowledge their concerns with "I understand your concern, but I have performed this procedure hundreds of times." Then point out all the factors in the patient's favor. When I underwent cataract surgery, whose outcome has one of the highest rates of success without complications, I had complications. I was less concerned than my highly rated physician because I knew I was in good hands and that eventually I would be okay and my sight would be fine.

I also know that before anyone is a physician, they are first a human being, and we all have "off days" and make mistakes. When preparing doctors for malpractice inquiries, I asked them how they felt when their attorneys told them *not to worry*. They said they did not like it and that response usually did not alleviate their anxiety.

When your spouse, partner, child, or parent utters that they had a horrible day, acknowledge them by saying, "I can see [or hear or feel] that. I am sorry it was so difficult." If they are the type of person who accepts help and you are willing, you may add, "Is there anything that I can do to help you or make you feel better?" Your concern makes it easier and helps maintain the desired positive bond. When you do not acknowledge others' frustration or anger, or you do not validate their feelings, you send a message that either you do not care or it is not important. When you respond with "My day was even worse than yours," that adds nothing to uplift their spirit.

Some people just desire an acknowledgment, an "Okay" or "I am sorry," but keep their own counsel and do not appreciate further remarks. In any case, not affirming or validating another person's feelings, thoughts, or concerns often contributes to frustration, resentment, anger, and withdrawal.

A husband whose father had harshly criticized him since early childhood was anxious when his father came for a monthlong visit. After the "honeymoon" was over, the father began to indirectly criticize, and the son became more distraught each day. The remarks were not as harsh as before, but there was a cumulative effect from the previous forty-five years. His wife could not comprehend why her husband was so upset; his father's remarks sounded benign. The husband continued to seek comfort from his wife, but to no avail. Eventually, he became solemn, stayed late at the office, and went to bed early. He had emotionally disconnected from his wife because she had not acknowledged his prolonged anguished feelings or provided the ease he sought. When his wife became upset with the distance between them, she never understood that she had helped create that chasm. I would guess that at times this pattern of disconnecting happens to all people, despite their age. A physical or emotional withdrawal is one of the most monumental and painful challenges and disappointments between spouses or partners, children and their parents, and parents and their children.

After you listen to another person air their grievances and "get it off their chest," aim to connect and acknowledge them, although you may not agree. If after a *source-connected* dialogue you still disagree, at least agree to disagree agreeably. Sometimes timing is the key. They do not want to hear it then, or perhaps ever.

Direct and Indirect Communication

Communication is either direct, indirect, or evasive. In direct communication, all the information is stated. In indirect communication, only a part of the message is expressed while other parts are only alluded to, and there is an assumption that the other person understands the implied message, which was not stated. Sometimes, individuals use indirect communication because they do not want to hear "No," they want to avoid confrontation, they are more reserved, or it is just their style.

Often, misunderstandings occur because one person prefers direct communication and the other prefers indirect communication. Using indirect communication becomes frustrating when the other person does not pick up the implied message. Yet to some, direct communication is too blunt or too "in your face."

Some people are quite concrete, while others can imply, intuit, or read between the lines. People who are concrete need to receive the information as precisely and completely as possible. Direct and indirect communication isn't an either-or but lies on a spectrum. The following is an analogy to help explain the difference between direct and indirect communication. Picture me handing you a card. It is quite clear that I want you to take the card. That is similar to direct communication. Now, picture me laying a card on the table with the expectation that you will pick it up. Unless both parties recognize what is implied—that the card is to be picked up—the card remains on the table, which potentially creates a void. In the same way, in the use of indirect communication, the *implied* message of what has to be conveyed to the other person is not communicated. If the other person does not comprehend the implied message, a misunderstanding or a communication gap occurs.

In homogeneous societies, such as many Asian cultures, people usually have more similar experiences and more in common than those in heterogeneous societies, such as in the US. Therefore, in homogeneous cultures, communication nuances and indirect style are easier to understand, although it still depends on the individual's ability to comprehend the differences. Traditional Asian cultures prefer indirect communication, as members feel it is more harmonious and less embarrassing. To understand indirect communication, everyone must comprehend the implied meanings.

In the heterogeneous U.S. society, even the actual meaning of indirect communication is often difficult to grasp. Even some *USAans* have difficulty understanding and knowing when to use indirect or direct communication. This difference is especially important to recognize if your colleague is from an Asian or another culture or is a *USAan* who prefers indirect communication.

If you prefer an indirect communication style in your vocational or professional life and the tasks that you request are accomplished and accurate, then continue to use indirect communication. If you use indirect communication and tasks are not completed timely or correctly, then switch to direct communication. When giving your direct statement, remember to engage mindful, positive voice tone and nonverbal communication style in most instances so that you do not come across as bossy.

The following sentences illustrate indirect and direct styles of expressing similar thoughts for personal interactions and professional, educational, business, and medical conversations, or other situations.

Indirect and Direct Communication

Personal Examples

Indirect: The trash bin is full
Direct: Please take out the trash.

Indirect: Your favorite actor is in a movie.
Direct: Do you want to go to a movie?

Indirect: Have you ever thought of doing it this way?
Direct: I prefer that it is done this way.

Indirect: You were busy traveling.
Direct: I miss you when you're away.

Indirect: I am tired of getting up with the baby.
Direct: Please get up with the baby.

Teaching Examples

Indirect: The books that I ordered didn't arrive.
Direct: Please check where the books are.

Indirect: I know you don't like teaching that class.
Direct: Would you like to switch classes?

Indirect: Are you aware that we have limited time?
Direct: The project is due in three days.

Indirect: The students are having a difficult time understanding you.
Direct: Your presentation is too difficult for the students to understand.

Indirect: I am tired of chairing the math committee.
Direct: Please find another person to chair the committee.

Business Examples

Indirect: We are out of toner.
Direct: Please order more toner.

Indirect: We specialize in resolving the issues you face.
Direct: We would like your business.

Indirect: Is there a chance that you could finish the project by Thursday?
Direct: The deadline is Thursday. I need it by then.

Indirect: It would be helpful if you get back to me by Monday.
Direct: I need an answer by Monday.

Indirect: Another company could service you better.
Direct: I don't think that we should continue our business relationship.

Unquestionably, in an emergency, you need to be direct. When talking with a patient or their family about a serious, negative, or grave matter, I recommend that a physician give an indirect statement followed by a direct statement. This style is more compassionate, not as abrupt, and gives time for the patient to process and prepare for the information that is coming yet still presents the necessary information.

Medical Examples

Indirect: It could be an unpleasant situation.
Direct: The patient could die.

Indirect: I have some sad news for you.
Direct: Carol passed away.

Indirect: It would be nice if you put the cap on the needle.
Direct: Please put the cap on the needle.

Indirect: What do you think of trying this procedure?
Direct: I recommend that you use this procedure.

Indirect: I could use assistance.
Direct: Please help me.

Indirect: The infant is in distress.
Direct: We have to perform a caesarean section.

It also helps to observe whether your spouse, partner, or child prefers indirect or direct communication. Some of my family members prefer direct communication, and others prefer indirect communication. A friend's husband is far more willing to help if she uses indirect communication. If while he is reading, surfing the net, or watching TV she comments, "I still have to go to the store this afternoon," he usually responds, "Would you like me to go for you?" If she asks him directly under the same circumstances, "Would you go to the store for me?" his usual response is, "Not now." A person may use direct communication on the job and prefer indirect communication at home, especially from their spouse or partner. It often varies with the situation and with whom you are conversing.

For those individuals who have difficulty taking any type of directions or instructions, I suggest three more approaches. First, wait until the person reaches out or brings up the subject. Then, plant the "idea seed" in the other person's mind. This is especially beneficial with people who are resistant to listening to you or others.

The second suggestion occurs in situations in which you deeply love the other person. Their parent, spouse, or child may voice a strong concern about them to you. At times, you just need to listen, but at other times, you feel compelled to make suggestions, although it is best that you not approach the subject matter. Have a response ready and place it "on hold." When the person brings up the subject, you sense the timing is right, and they appear receptive, take your chance and state the recommendation.

The third suggestion is to find the right time and place and, in a mindful, *source-connected manner*, inquire why they are unable to take any instructions, directions, or recommendations from you or why they are so invested in being right. Be prepared, because they may not respond, but they may change their ways. But also recognize that the previous behavior remains their default approach.

Give a Negative Message in a Positive Way

Focusing on the negative is key to our personal survival, but at times, that negative focus isn't required. Often, our media is preoccupied with seeking and then describing situations or public figures' attributes in a more negative way than is necessary. That was exemplified during the 2013 New York Marathon. I heard an announcer comment about one runner's style, "She has an ugly stride." If the announcer felt he had to remark, why couldn't he have simply said that she had an unusual or different stride? Hurray for the runner, as she won a medal.

As a young child, one of my granddaughters was very selective of the persons to whom she would go. When I occasionally asked, "Isn't that nice," or "Isn't she nice?" she never replied, "No," but in her soft, sweet voice always used to say, "Not so much." When another granddaughter did not like the taste of certain foods, she said, "It's not so tasty." These are examples of giving a negative response in a pleasant way.

I firmly recommend that whenever you have a choice, use positive instead of negative words. Many of my clients did not comprehend why they were perceived negatively, as they used a preponderance of negative words such as *don't, can't, won't, never, couldn't, shouldn't,* or *wouldn't* instead of using positive words to express themselves. When you combine the *I mode* with a more positive style, you communicate and are perceived more favorably; thus, others are more receptive. The following sentences express similar thoughts in a positive or negative style. State what you need, what you prefer, or what is possible. Do not use negative words. Be as specific as possible.

The Difference Between Positive and Negative Communication

> *Positive*: I'll do it later.
> *Negative*: I can't do it now.
>
> *Positive*: We disagree.
> *Negative*: We don't agree.
>
> *Positive*: I will contribute this amount.
> *Negative*: I will not contribute that much.

Positive: Please speak nicely.
Negative: Don't yell at me.

Positive: I can see her Monday. Schedule the meeting in the afternoon.
Negative: I can't see her Tuesday. Don't schedule the meeting next week.

Positive: I will take responsibility the first two weeks.
Negative: I will not take responsibility for a month.

Positive: He is always late.
Negative: He is never on time.

Positive: How are you feeling? Pretty good.
Negative: How are you feeling? Not bad.

A physician who might diagnose a patient's lumps as malignant without first having reviewed the lab results may give the patient a more severe diagnosis, which may not be accurate. When a patient asks, "What do you think the results will be?" I strongly recommend stating, "Let's wait until the test results are back." I know too many people who spent days waiting in anguish and suspecting the worst because their physicians said, "It's probably malignant," when it wasn't. If the physicians had waited for the test results before giving an incorrect diagnosis, these people could have been spared days of apprehension and worry. When offering treatment options to a patient, I recommend that physicians start with the least severe protocol and move to the most severe.

For example: Anticipating her patient's usual immediate complaints, upon greeting the patient, an astute physical therapist jumps in and states, "Hi, tell me something that feels good today." When instead the patient complains about their discomfort, the therapist immediately responds by gesturing to the opposite or a different part of the body and asking how that feels. The patient will usually say, "Oh, that's okay," or "That feels good." Then, the physical therapist quickly states something akin to, "Okay, let's move some of that good energy to…," as she names the challenging body part.

Emotionally Charged Words

A woman apologized that she could not return my call because there was "mayhem" in her comfortable beach-side home. There were no calamities, emergencies, or injuries in her family, in her extended family, or among her friends. With an approaching storm, she was concerned that if the electricity failed, she would not be able to charge a dead cell phone so that her one-year-old daughter could fall asleep listening to soothing sounds. One reason that life is so stressful in the United States is our overuse of emotionally charged words, such as *Armageddon*, *mayhem*, or the ubiquitous *urgent* in the subject line of our e-mails.

Guns are rightfully valued in many sectors of the U.S. culture, yet gun violence is a major problem that grows exponentially more dangerous. In a way, we cannot be surprised or shocked as terms referring to guns are subtly woven into our songs, movies, theater, entertainment, and daily news. Just think of how often we hear or use the following: *gun* shy, *shoot* me an email, *triggered* a response, she is a *pistol*, he went *ballistic*, he is *half-cocke*d, she is a *straight shooter*. When we hear these terms, at some level, we respond favorably, unfavorably, or not at all.

Evasive

When you are evasive, you do not answer the question asked. In social, personal, political, and all situations, evasion is a way of avoiding a response, idea, commitment, flaw within yourself, or hurting another human being's feelings. Being evasive may be appropriate in some situations, but it certainly is not in others. When you are evasive in an educational, business, medical, or professional arena, you may appear unknowledgeable or ambiguous, or you may give the impression that you are disingenuous, you do not mean what you say, or you are not interested. Some smooth-talkers or politicians have turned evasion into an art form.

If you are in litigation, discuss with your attorney whether and when to use indirect or direct communication during the deposition or testimony. In these environments, you must directly and precisely answer the question. An evasive response gives the impression that you are hiding something, which may cause you to appear guilty when you are innocent.

It is important to realize the difference between evasive, indirect, and direct communication and when to use each. Analyze each situation and decide which form is suitable and appropriate. If either indirect or direct communication would be appropriate, then choose the style you prefer.

I Mode

In what potentially leads to a counterproductive response, it is best that you not begin your thoughts with an accusatory "you." In that type of interaction, people often become cautious and defensive as "you" infers blame and immediately puts the other person on guard. Therefore, they are not going to be as receptive to your comments. By changing the word *you* to *I* or *my*, you own and take full responsibility for your thought. This often leads to a more receptive attitude. The following sentences give examples of using *I* or *you*. Which way do you prefer being spoken to?

> *I*: I think there is a better way to do that.
> *You*: Your way is wrong.
>
> *I*: I would like to suggest another way.
> *You*: You are not analyzing the project accurately.
>
> *I*: I am tied up right now. Can we talk later?
> *You*: You caught me at a bad time. Can we talk later?
>
> *I*: I need you to work on the Henderson case.
> *You*: You are working on the wrong case.
>
> *I*: I am upset with your attitude.
> *You*: Your attitude sucks.
>
> I: I have to leave by six o'clock today.
> *You*: You're wasting my time.
>
> *I*: I want to make sure that I gave the message so it was understood.
>   Please repeat what I said.
> *You*: Did you understand what I said?

I: I need you to listen closely. This is important.
You: You're not listening to what I am saying. This is important.

I: I know this is difficult. How can I help you?
You: What's the matter with you? Why don't you get it?

Focus

Focus is an integral feature in most aspects of our lives, and communication is no exception. We communicate our best when we engage, focus, remain on topic, follow up with mindful and thoughtful responses, and remain in the present moment. When our minds wander, we ruminate on the past, are lost in something irrelevant to the topic, anticipate, plan, or experience fear about the unknown future. When we are completely focused, all our attention perceives what is present. We listen to and observe the other person, or we are focused on a situation or event. We take as much time as *we need* to perceive, absorb, and process the information and then frame and formulate our response. While we plan our response, we are not concerned about the other person's reaction, opinion, reply, or any other matters. In significant situations, it is imperative to remain focused.

Sharp focus is required for deep listening without judgment to family members and friends. Accompanied with unbiased listening, this allows us to respond kindly and accurately to students, patients, clients, colleagues, staff, workers, servicepeople, and others. This is especially imperative when discussing crucial, detailed, or technical information, as experienced by first responders, physicians and nurses, those involved in litigation, and those in any other critical situation.

When we are on overload with too many thoughts colliding in our heads, have too many distractions, or are preoccupied with personal, family, or business issues, health matters, looming deadlines, or other challenges, the mind tends to wander off or ruminate. It is often difficult to remain focused. Prioritize what must be achieved and then focus on the most pressing issue or task. My father had a succinct saying framed in his office that read, "*First Things First.*"

Do not start another thought or project until the first is complete. When you are tired or have personal, health, financial, or any other major challenges and you are discussing a significant matter or engaging in a demanding task, inform those close to you that your focus is not up to par. Then, they can be aware that you may not grasp all the information and that you may not be as sharp as they are accustomed to. If you are asked, definitely do not deny the circumstances. My clients used many different tools to help reduce stress and remain focused. Many, especially senior citizens, consciously narrowed their focus, especially when driving, measuring, dealing with financial issues, or planning or responding to complex issues or projects. At any age, there occurs a point or period when the ability to accurately multitask temporarily or permanently ceases. Prioritize and concentrate on one thought or task at a time. Take breaks and engage in mindful breaths to return to the present. I also highly recommend to neither contemplate nor make any major decision when you are already overburdened with too much on your plate, not in the best frame of mind, or recovering from a recent, drastic, life-changing event. In simple matters, the "three mindful breaths" practice is a valuable tool to heighten focus.

The concept of the here and now was profoundly seared into my brain while watching the *Hubble* 3D film at the IMAX theater at the California Science Center. Our grands sat at the edge of their seats, as did my husband and I—we were all blown away! We remained totally captivated and enthralled viewing what was then the Hubble telescope's twenty-year journey (1990–2010) in outer space. We felt we were "voyaging through the cosmos," whizzing by familiar constellations, such as Orion's Belt, then on to the nebulas and beyond, to the farthest reaches of the universe, ending at the beginning of time billions of light-years away.

Watching the film through a bird's-eye view gave a feeling of "intimacy and immediacy," especially as spacewalkers Andrew J. Feustel, known as Drew, and John Grunsfeld removed two bolts and then a cover to replace a razor-sharp circuit board and add a new wide-angle field camera. After four other space shuttle missions to repair the Hubble telescope (that included thirty-two astronauts), this was the fifth and final mission. The crew of seven astronauts on the *Atlantis* spaceship was the last hope to correct the malfunction before the telescope continued exploring farther into outer space. The task on one of the two spacewalks by Feustel and Grunsfeld was to remove a cover and replace a faulty optical circuit board. That delicate task had to be completed in a limited time while they were wearing thick, padded space gloves; they were fully aware that if the skin of the glove punctured, they would die. Feustel later remarked, "Imagine a brain surgeon wearing oven gloves." There was no room for error; precision and perfection were required.

Once back in the spaceship, spacewalker Drew reflected that he had to take a very Zen approach, completely focused on the meticulous and daunting task of removing the thirty-two screws, one screw at a time, to reach the damaged optics. He said, "There's no point thinking about how many screws I have ahead of me or how many I have completed. It will just be one screw. Eventually, I will get to the last screw and then I'll be done" (Warner Bros. 2011).

I was so awestruck by his Zen moments that finally, at age seventy-five, whenever I begin to feel angst about too much on my plate, an approaching deadline, or completing a specific task in a very limited time, I bring to mind Drew's image and reflect on his spacewalker approach as he and his partner, Grunsfeld, along with their tools, were tethered to the spaceship, dangling in space as darkness set in. Drew was laser-focused, totally immersed, engulfed in the task one step at a time, wholly in the "*I am here*" moment, in harmony with himself and the universe.

Questions

Asking relevant questions is a necessary component of conversations in many arenas and situations within the family, at work, in the situation room, and in any critical environment, especially regarding health care, which requires informed decisions. Questions are also fundamental in the classroom to elevate best practices so students can best learn or when people need additional information to move forward. A significant portion of learning occurs when those present pay close attention, listen to the dialogue to find and build a consensus, and then offer suggestions or recommendations. Solutions and resolutions require an open forum, where everyone feels safe posing inquiries. Do not put down any individual, even when sincere questions may not make sense to you or others. Can you imagine a group dynamic in which members, especially children with parents, students in a classroom, or patients with their health-care provider, do not feel safe and at ease asking questions? In these situations, where else should the person go? Just imagine the missed opportunities to provide comfort, learning, and guidance.

At work, if you have tried in earnest to find an answer to a question and explored all your possibilities and still cannot find it, it is appropriate and necessary to first seek "in-house" resources. Mindfully, choose the right time, right place, and right person. Ask the person at the lowest level who you think has the knowledge to respond correctly. Do not go to a person at a higher level than required. It is annoying when you ask a question that was previously answered or pose a question that is irrelevant to the topic being discussed. It is also bothersome to others to ask a question about information that you could easily research on your own.

People are frequently unwilling to ask questions because they don't want to appear ignorant, don't want to put a person on the spot, or don't really want to know the answer. Pertinent questions are a form of direct communication. People who are from cultures that engage in indirect communication are less apt to ask questions, which may become a challenge when conversing with those who speak directly. Even university students who are from underserved neighborhoods, on scholarships, the first generation in their families to enroll in higher learning, or exchange students are somewhat reticent or embarrassed to ask questions; however, they may have a greater need to do so. In certain situations, especially classrooms or professional or health-care settings, you must ask questions when you do not understand the information or consequences or you do not know how to proceed or complete a task. When you don't ask necessary questions, the other person assumes that you understand when you don't.

If I hadn't paid close attention and asked multiple questions during my numerous hospital stays, on rare occasions, the nurse would have given me the wrong dosage or medication. If I had not had training as a speech pathologist specializing in stroke rehabilitation, or if I could not read and comprehend CT scan reports, I probably would not be alive. Immediately after my first angiogram, the cardiologist and my husband bounded into my room and announced that they had scheduled me for angioplasty two days later. When I instinctively suspected something was grossly amiss, I read the report and sought the advice of one of the top cardiologists in Los Angeles. After my examination and a review of the CAT scan records, he declared that the other doctor's recommendation could have been a "disaster." Subsequently, I underwent my first (quadruple) coronary bypass.

When medical personnel told a family member that her blood pressure was good, she asked, "What was it?" The nurse questioned why she needed to know, and she simply said, "I want to know about my health." I can't think of any field in which asking pertinent questions is not a beneficial step in the process to gain comprehension and comfort, accurately complete a project, or make an informed decision.

Many people who are unfamiliar with varying cultural norms are not aware that it can be inappropriate to ask questions in some people's native cultures. When communicating with ESL speakers, others who recently immigrated, or anyone who you think does not understand you, confirm that the information is clear by using a *source-connected* voice. Monitor yourself to make certain that you are not condescending in any way. I usually say, "I want to make sure that I clearly gave you the information, instructions, or directions. Please repeat what I said." After their response, I say, "Thank you."

Decades ago, a former colleague, and now dear friend, would consistently ask anyone on the phone for their name if they didn't offer it after the initial greeting. Since so many names are now of differing cultures, if I can't understand the name, I politely ask them to repeat it. Then, I can converse more personally with them and note their name for future reference if needed.

Asking too many questions is annoying. Observe the other person's body language and voice tone in response to your questions. If you are getting negative feedback, limit your questions to the most pertinent. Because I have a natural curiosity about life, I ask relevant questions to expand my knowledge, not to judge. Some of my family members, friends, colleagues, or others are considerably private. Since I want to respect and not offend them, I learned to limit questions, monitor the subject, and try hard not to cross their boundaries. I observe their nonverbal communication and listen to their voice tone for any signs of discomfort or annoyance.

Ask the Questions that Require Answers; Make Certain You Get the Necessary Response

When giving presentations, after I and everyone else introduced themselves, I always inquired if anyone had to leave early. Once, when I asked the question, a physician responded that he had to leave to go to the hospital later in the afternoon. I asked what time he was leaving. He told me, "I have to be at the hospital at four o'clock." I knew that the hospital was five minutes away, so I planned a worthy, interactive segment for 3:30 p.m. This would allow more than enough time for fifteen minutes of role-playing with him. When he began to leave at 3:25 p.m., I asked him where he was going. He said, "I have to stop at my office and make some phone calls before I go to the hospital." Had I taken the time to make certain that I got the answer to my original question, "What time are you leaving?" I would have planned the role-playing earlier.

When a teacher asks a student, "Is your project going to be finished by next Thursday?" and the reply is, "My mom or dad couldn't take me to buy what I needed," the teacher didn't get the answer to her question. When a roommate who is looking to catch a ride asks, "What time are you leaving for class tomorrow?" and the reply is, "I have to be in class at 9:00 a.m.," the question was not answered. Many misunderstandings occur because we do not ask the precise question that we need to or get exact answer to the question we ask. If the other person does not answer your question or goes off on a tangent, repeat your question until you get the required answer. *It is your responsibility to ask until you get the information you need.* If necessary, tell the person why you are asking.

Sometimes It Is Better to Ask, Even if the Answer Is No

My mother taught me this valuable lesson. If you want something, it doesn't hurt to ask, even if the answer is no. She said that if you want something and don't ask for it, no one will ever know that you want it. If you make ten requests and only one is granted, you are still better off than if you hadn't asked at all. My mom also warned me not to be disappointed if I don't get what I had asked for.

In 1977, our family traveled to the northern border between Israel and Lebanon to experience the Good Fence. Barely within the Israeli border, a trailer was set up as a clinic. It was staffed by Israeli doctors, and Lebanese families traveled by foot to bring their ailing family members to this remote clinic. The Lebanese people entrusted their loved ones to the Israeli staff, knowing their cherished ones would receive outstanding and free medical care. I wanted to go to the border and witness the sharing and trust between the people of these two cultures.

We drove to the nearest town and learned that we couldn't go to the Good Fence without military permission, so we returned to the town where the military headquarters was located. When I asked who was in charge of the operation at the Good Fence, I was informed that it was a captain in the Israeli Army, who happened to be at the same outdoor café where we had stopped. I approached and informed him that I was from the United States and I was very interested in going to the Good Fence. I asked him if there was an opportunity for my family to go. He said, "Yes," and so we went. It was one of the highlights of the trip. If I hadn't asked, we would never have experienced that oasis of trust in an otherwise-hostile area.

Another time, when my husband celebrated his birthday, his sister and her husband unexpectedly dropped in just before dinner while on their way to visit their daughter's family, who lived nearby. I asked if they could stay for dinner, as I knew that their daughter was busy with a repairman. My sister-in-heart hesitated because she had promised her daughter that she would bring in dinner. I suggested that she call to inquire if there was a problem if she stayed with us for dinner. When she called, her daughter replied, "Not at all. We're kind of busy with all the repairs." It turned out best for everyone. Sometimes we don't want to ask because we don't want to disappoint or offend. But if the question is sincere, comes from the heart, and isn't meant to hurt another person, I strongly believe in asking the question. You may think that you know what's going on or what another person needs, but sometimes you don't. At times, the person's response totally surprises others. *If you don't ask, you don't get.*

Permission by Question

Many men and women I know personally and professionally often question their spouses or partners regarding personal decisions. Their sole objective is to obtain approval, avoiding confrontation or disapproval if the decision is not to the other's liking. By questioning prior to making a decision, they knew what the other person approved. Often, they followed those directives just to keep peace, even though it was not what they desired. Eventually, their attitude and communication became resentful and negative. When my clients became *source-connected*, this permission-by-question type of conversation stopped, communication became more positive and constructive, and their well-being took a forward leap.

You Don't Have to Answer the Question

I have a philosophy that *if you don't want to know the answer, don't ask the question.* My children and friends know that when they ask me a question, I offer what I feel. It may not be the answer they want to hear, but they know it comes from my heart. Sometimes I answer indirectly, "It may not be the way that you would do it, but this is what I would do."

If you feel it is in the other person's best interest not to know, don't answer the question, despite how hard they persist. When I held an extended family get-together, several relatives asked me a question, but I knew the answer would embarrass them. My response was, "You don't want to know." One posed her question several times during the evening, and again the next day. I started kidding with them but remained firm with "You really don't want to know," and then I stopped responding.

If you ask a question, have the courtesy to patiently listen to the answer. When you don't, you give the message that you don't respect the other person or think they can't answer correctly. In the past, I sometimes asked questions and didn't wait to listen to the complete answer. I had the tendency to "cut off" people when I realized they didn't have the information that I needed or if I wanted to offer help. There were times that I posed a question without thinking it through and I immediately realized that I did not particularly want to hear the response just then.

How to Convey Your Message So It Is Understood
With a rapidly increasing and diverse population, introduction of new terms and ideas, exponentially expanding information, digital technology, and increased use of texts and voice mail, it becomes even more imperative to communicate succinctly and slowly enough so that the other person comprehends.

When people do not understand your question or information, repeat yourself once, then rephrase it or find another way to say it. If the other person still does not understand, inquire how you can help them comprehend. If you express frustration, the other person may feel intimidated, tune you out, or walk away. If that happens, it's most certain that neither you nor the other person will obtain the necessary information. Try to realize that the other person is not being difficult but simply does not understand. What is clear and simple to you may be "rocket science" to the other person. There are many strategies that you can use to increase understanding in face-to-face, video, or phone communication; these methods are effective.

Frequently, phone numbers or any long sequences of numbers or information are given so rapidly that they require repeating. Often, several repetitions are required until the person gathers the details. When you leave a message on any device that goes to voice mail, speak more slowly, enunciate more clearly, and *pause longer* between thoughts, groups of numbers, or bits of information. This facilitates the listener's ability to absorb the information and details at a pace that ensures they will be comfortable and confident in correctly noting or responding, with perhaps only a quick review.

Some people are quite concrete and have difficulty comprehending pronouns—*it, she, he,* or *they*—in remarks immediately following naming the person, object, or event. They are unable to draw the information from the pronoun but require the noun to comprehend the meaning. When I replace pronouns with the noun, the person immediately understands.

In addition, if the person still does not comprehend, slow the pace or simplify your comments. Use simple rather than complex or compound sentences, shorter phrases, or one or two words when that is all the other person can grasp. You may have to pause longer or more frequently between thoughts or give more time to allow the person to absorb and process the information. It is best to let the other person set the pace and request additional information as needed. Note that since you brought up the topic, you are already familiar with the subject, which the other person has to absorb before they respond. Continue to monitor their body language, nods, eye contact, or the time it takes them to respond and when to proceed. For additional approaches to bridge a gap, monitor your conversation partner's preferred NLP channel and try to include words relevant to their channel. If you can't understand, never use a condescending voice or show frustration. Be mindful and show compassion, even when the situation is frustrating.

Why Ideas Stick

In my life's experiences, messages stick either because they had monumental impact the first time we heard them or the sound bite was so repetitive that we began to believe it. When one of our granddaughters was almost three years old, she and my daughter-in-law visited us in Nevis. As we drove up our then deeply potholed road to our home and got stuck in the mud, she exclaimed in her very unusual, succinct style, "We're *S-T-UUU-CK*."

Closely following the political arena of 2016 and recalling previous presidential election cycles, I wondered why certain negative messages stuck to one candidate and yet the same standard did not apply to another candidate. After a while, I realized that if a "seed" is planted about a person and that seed is repeated and spread often enough, even if it isn't the truth, people begin to believe it is fact.

Sometimes a "honeymoon period" is offered to those candidates who are newcomers to the arena. Others who have been around for some time are primarily identified by the image with which they "got stuck," even if there is only a hint of truth in it.

The same happens in the rest of our prejudiced world. I have observed far too often that people of minorities are described or framed worldwide in terms quite different from those of more upscale backgrounds or higher socioeconomic levels. This practice occurred even when they were engaged in the exact same illegal activity. At times, even when statistics within the same group or similar groups are identical, the outcome or penalties have been quite different and significantly harsher.

In her authentic, brilliant, and eloquent style, Rachel Maddow tried to get "a truth to stick." She nailed Michigan governor Rick Snyder's response to the poisonous lead contamination of the water in Flint, Michigan. At the end of her report, she dramatically added the word *still* to each violation.

When Governor Snyder appeared before the judiciary committee of the House of Representatives and was questioned by Elijah Cummings, the leading congressman of South Carolina, Snyder acknowledged his obvious disregard for Flint's citizens, who were primarily minorities. When Cummings questioned whether taxpayers were aware that Snyder had asked the citizens of Michigan to pay more than $1 million of taxpayer funds for his criminal defense fees, the governor replied, "Yes." Cummings, who was quite irritated, further declared, "You found a way to have the people of Michigan pay over $1 million for your legal and defense fees, but you thought so little of the people of Flint [that you] could not be bothered to ask the legislature for money to switch them over to clean water" (Maddow 2016).

While looking straight into the camera, into viewers' eyes, Maddow emphasized that this is not "normal politics." She went on, "But for all the politics that have been brought to bear on this issue now, think about what it says about the state response that *still* there is no clean water being delivered in Flint. Even today, today, *still* they haven't replaced the ruined pipes. *Still*, houses are testing at over [twice of what] is hazardous waste. *Still, still,* you're not getting clean water brought to your house in Flint, *still,* and that's regardless of who resigns or gets indicted. *Still.*"

I said to myself, perhaps now the message will stick with those who haven't yet listened, as if they never heard. On May 4, 2016, Maddow handed over the programming to the next host, Lawrence McDonnell. He publicly acknowledged that she alone brought the Flint water crisis to the forefront, so much so that it became a pivotal piece of conversation during the 2016 primary cycle (O'Donnell 2016). The ongoing reporting drew President Obama to visit Flint and drink the water. In a way, his gesture was more of a photo op, as six months later, people still did not have clean drinking water piped into their homes, and they *still* don't as I write this book.

Say Precisely What You Mean—Be Specific

To avoid misunderstandings and disappointments, be as specific or precise as possible. Many misunderstandings occur because the information offered is vague or misleading. Abstract terms are interpreted personally, and the conclusion may be far different from what you expected.

When a friend's daughter returned home after studying abroad for a year, the daughter announced, "I want my independence." After some frustrating days, the mother finally asked, "How do you define *independence*?" The daughter replied, "I want to do what I want to, when I want. You and Dad seem to be able to do that all the time."

When you use abstract terms, others may have difficulty comprehending what is expected. Along with using abstract terms, e.g., *better*, *more*, or *poor*, give concrete examples of what you want. When a teacher tells a student, "I want a better report," the request is vague. *Better* may indicate more research, neater presentation, graphs, or visual aids to illustrate the point. When a supervisor utters to a colleague, "Be a team player," she is vague. When she gives precise examples, "Be a team player, collaborate with your colleagues, attend the Monday weekly meetings, facilitate the implementation, when necessary, work as long as your colleagues," she is precise. When a mother tells her child, "You're difficult," what does she mean? The words may pertain to something specific, but the child may interpret the message altogether differently.

When a supervisor tells his employee, "I need the report this afternoon," he is too vague, as *afternoon* usually extends from noon to 5:30 p.m. "I need the report by 3:00 p.m." is more precise. When a person says, "I will call you back shortly," what does that mean? To some, it means within fifteen minutes, to others it implies sometime the same day, yet to others it may mean never. Since I want to be available, I ask, "Approximately how long will that be?" A more specific response is, "I will call you back in five minutes," "I will call you back in half an hour," or "I will call you this afternoon."

An effective response requires precise answers so that you do not waste time playing "telephone tag" or chasing e-mails or text messages. Do not add to the confusion because you do not reply accurately. You may answer a question with a "Yes" or a "No" or another short response without a detailed explanation, such as "I don't know," "I don't remember," "Let me research that and I will get back to you tomorrow," or "I'd rather not say." A physician who is an ESL speaker had a difficult time answering questions during her deposition. She didn't want to appear stupid. Instead of referring to her chart notes when she couldn't recall the information, she guessed the answer. She frequently guessed wrong. I tried several different ways to point out the necessity of answering precisely and answering only the questions asked. I suggested that she decide if the question required a "Yes" or "No," "I don't know," or "I can't remember" response or a brief explanation. *The important point was to respond precisely to the question asked.* She still didn't comprehend and continued to give answers that were irrelevant to the question. Then I asked the doctor to name some instruments and supplies that she used during surgery. She replied that she used "sutures," "clamps," "retractors," and "pads." I asked her how well she could perform surgery if she asked the surgical nurse for sutures and she gave her clamps instead. She replied that it would be difficult. I then asked, "What if you asked for sutures and the surgical nurse gave you pads?" Again, she replied, "It would be difficult." I further questioned, "What if you asked for sutures and the surgical nurse gave you retractors, or if you asked for retractors and she gave you forceps?" The doctor said that it would be challenging to perform the surgery and detrimental to the patient's outcome. Finally, she understood the reason to give the precise answer to the question asked. Always listen carefully to the question so that you can give the correct and appropriate response.

When a friend had knee surgery, the surgeon informed him, "Your leg will be back to normal in three months." He thought *normal* meant that he would be as fit to perform as he had prior to knee injury. What the surgeon had meant was that his knee would be healed enough to *begin* exercising again. After three months, my friend was disappointed because he hadn't recovered as anticipated, to the level he was at prior to his injury.

The term *arthroscopic surgery* often misleads patients to believe that this type of surgery is significantly less painful, traumatic, or severe than other surgery. They misinterpret a "small scar" to mean a minor operation. Even when the physician discusses the procedure with their patient, they often do not comprehend that there may be severe trauma to the surgical area and that recovery and rehabilitation may still take a long time.

A patient who was anticipating major surgery asked his doctor, "When will I be okay?" The doctor replied, "You will be okay tomorrow." The patient definitely didn't feel "okay" the day after surgery. He was considerably upset and perceived the situation as a "setback." A more appropriate response from the surgeon would have been, "You should feel better each day, but don't be concerned if there are slight setbacks." Physicians often, perhaps unintentionally, predict a shorter recovery time or don't inform the patient about how uncomfortable a procedure will be. Although each patient recovers differently, I suggest that the physician's responsibility also include discussing what the "probable results" are. It is unfair to the patient for the physician to paint a rosier picture without also disclosing other minor possibilities.

A person underwent an outpatient surgery from which doctors usually discharge the patient the same day. Following the procedure, non-life-threatening but excruciating pain developed. The next day, when discharge plans were awaiting a return phone call from the specialist to the internist, discharged orders were delayed. When the initial phone call was made, the receptionist posed to the internist, "The doctor is in with a patient. Should I interrupt him?" The internist replied, "No." So the specialist followed his usual routine and planned to return the phone call after he had completed all his morning appointments. In hindsight, the internist would have been better off requesting that the specialist call him after he had finished with the patient that he was currently seeing.

When giving the patient their prescription for blood work, it is also best for the physician's administrative assistant to refer the patient to the most convenient and best-equipped lab that can perform the tests, especially if the tests are complex.

A friend's speech was slurred, and his vision was blurred. Comprehensive testing confirmed the presence of a brain tumor requiring surgery. The surgeon told him that he would go home four days after the surgery and that the symptoms prior to surgery would begin to disappear. The surgeon didn't say, "The earliest that you can go home is four days after surgery." When surgery was far more extensive and complicated than had been anticipated, four days stretched into a longer hospitalization and rehabilitation stay. The family recalled being told prior to surgery that there was a risk of bleeding or infection. It wasn't until symptoms developed after the surgery that the family and patient became concerned and upset that the doctor hadn't informed them that due to the complexity and lengthy duration of the surgery, the situation might get worse before it got better. It would have been best for the patient and his family if the physician had communicated precisely so that they were better prepared for the outcome. To convey the most effective information, be as specific as you can and remember to note that each patient responds differently. In any situation, the more precise you are, the more successful you are in getting what you want. There is less chance of misunderstanding, frustration, and disappointment.

Communicate at the Appropriate Level for the Individual
When a photographer taught her son how to take pictures, the subjects were on the floor. Kneeling, she said, "You must be on the same level as your subjects." Communication is similar.

Even if the conversation level is more elementary than you usually use, choose vocabulary that the other person can easily grasp. Mindfully communicate in a kind, respectful manner. It is best not to communicate in a demeaning or condescending manner. If you are an educator, a lecturer, an attorney, a philosopher, or a brainy person with a scholarly vocabulary, use your highbrow vocabulary with your intellectual peers, who easily comprehend and appreciate your style. If you are a physician speaking with patients, use lay terms along with the medical terms so that patients can gather the information and gain comfort in understanding enough to make an informed decision. When a physician tells a patient, "This is the mandated protocol," what the doctor really means is, "This is the usual procedure [or practice]." Often, the patient does not have a clue what the doctor is saying. The first example intimidates the patient and perhaps makes them feel inferior or reticent to further inquire about their health. The second example makes more sense. Physicians who solely rely on medical terms often frighten their patients. They are talking physician to patient, not *source-connected* person to person. Most people are uncomfortable or concerned when they don't understand. It is even more frightening when the topic pertains to health, well-being, loved ones, safety, employment, or finances. While it is appropriate to use medical terminology when conferring with other medical professionals, it is seldom appropriate to use the same language when speaking with patients unless they work in the health-care field and are familiar and comfortable with medical terminology. Few people grasp the jargon of automobile mechanics, such as "Your camshaft has seized" or "Your carburetor is flooding." Similarly, few patients comprehend the implications of "The results of your lab work were positive" or the technical lingo "Your CBC test denotes too many polys" (which notes that your blood test revealed that you have an infection). In most medical situations, the word *negative* notes there is no problem, that everything is okay.

When you converse with children, speak positively and at a level they easily understand and with which they are at ease so they can connect with you. Refrain from using terms or words that are "over their heads" or "beneath them." Do not belittle anyone, especially children, peers, or people who speak English as their second language. This insult turns children and adults away and may cause them to further question their self-esteem. Sometimes, it is best to sit at their level, even if it is on the ground.

A youngster in the neighborhood was chatting with our preteen daughter and showed her a condom. My husband saw the incident, quickly called him aside, and then sat beside him on the grass in the privacy of our backyard. He told him, "I want to talk to you about what you're doing." The child had a very strict and abusive father and was naturally scared. My husband told him that what he was doing was inappropriate but he wouldn't tell his father. He also told him, "If you ever do it again, I'll beat the crap out of you." The youngster was relieved, continued to visit, and chatted about more appropriate topics.

A young man in his late-teen years e-mailed a request to a group inquiring if they wanted to pitch in and buy a gift for a friend. Several people responded. Yet in his follow-up e-mail instructing them to send the money via Facebook Messenger, no one responded. He didn't understand that the folks were mostly seniors and unfamiliar with that process.

Sometimes people will use erudite communication to try to intimidate you; try not to let them. Since English is my second language, there are areas in which I don't have as extensive a vocabulary as my family members, friends, or professional peers. When I don't understand, I ask for an explanation. I am not apologetic or embarrassed, since I know that I am doing the best that I can. Oftentimes, I note the word I didn't understand, try to learn it, and later use it when appropriate. At the very least, I will comprehend the word or term. As I previously mentioned, "You can only do with what you have at the moment." Also, refrain from idioms and jokes with people of other linguistic and cultural backgrounds, as they may not yet grasp the finer nuances of your culture.

On the other hand, if you converse with a person whose is commensurate with you, go ahead and "strut your stuff" at a conversation level you each enjoy. If you don't have as extensive a vocabulary as the other person, try not to feel intimidated or embarrassed. Even the most learned individuals may not be knowledgeable or competent enough to perform certain tasks that are familiar to and easy for you. If you relate to the other person as a fellow human being instead of relating to their role, you avoid feelings of inadequacy.

When giving presentations, always observe your audience for their nonverbal communication—especially facial expressions or hand and arm positions—to monitor if they understand you. If you are a teacher, while you are presenting information, observe if your students are gazing out of the window, texting, resting their heads down on their desks, doing other homework, doodling, or talking with other students. These nonverbal communication cues imply that your students probably aren't comfortable, listening, or paying attention. Make the necessary adjustments to pique their interest. Naturally engage them so they are attentive and receptive to the material or message. Then, include them in the dialogue, perhaps by asking their opinion. Students may need a break, a quick stretch, some fresh air in the room, some TLC (tender loving care), or a simplified presentation. When they aren't paying attention, always refrain from purposely asking them a question to embarrass them in front of their peers—that is cruel!

Assumptions

Do not assume that any other person knows what you want or feel. When a friend returned home after surgery, she was upset that her family did not step up to the plate as she had anticipated. She hadn't informed the family specifically what she would need; she assumed they would know.

It is best not to assume that anyone is aware of every specific detail that is familiar to you and is required to complete a task. Think through the process and make note of as much as possible—although we can never anticipate every detail in many situations, especially those that are less routine. Mindfully, and *source-connected*, positively and effectively communicate your needs and desires.

Many challenges occur because one person has a different understanding of the other person's responsibility. By specifically clarifying each person's role in a process, you significantly reduce misunderstandings and issues. A partner in an accounting firm thought that his role was to bring in new clients and review reports before they were sent out to the clients. He felt his responsibility was the last 10 percent of the job. His support staff misunderstood and perceived the partner's responsibility as the final 20 percent of the job. There was a gap in their perceptions of their respective responsibilities. Consequently, work was rarely completed on time, and everyone was frustrated or upset.

Another annoying situation occurs when a person continually does not follow through on directions or instructions and replies, "But I thought…" The best response is to kindly remind the person what you noted or jotted down. If they continue the pattern and do not follow the request, the results continue to be inadequate or incorrect. When appropriate, mindfully inquire why they deviated from the instructions or did not take your words literally.

No matter what culture, field, or industry, certain individuals assume that they can get away with abhorrent behavior that has been tolerated since the beginning of time. Stellar reputations of persons who are pillars in the entertainment, medical, sport, and other fields are immediately destroyed when one person has the courage to speak out against their wrongdoings. Then a few more individuals have the guts to speak up, and then the floodgates open as more speak out against that abuse. Within a short period, at times almost instantaneously, simple hashtags are created that span the globe. Consequently, old "norms" and "cultures" begin to break down, gain traction, and significantly disrupt or even shatter former behaviors.

Comfort in Saying "No"

When you are unable or do not want to do something, especially between family and friends, politely replying "No" is appropriate in mainstream U.S. culture. Regardless of culture, saying "No" is difficult for many. Persons may not want to disappoint, or they may anticipate that the other person does not want to accept that they cannot do something. But when you know that you can't, won't, or don't want to do something, positively convey "No, I can't" or "I don't want to." Even when the other person persists, if you know that you can't fulfill their request, remain mindful and firmly say "No." If there is an option, in a *source-connected* way, state what you can and will do. Whenever anyone asks me, "Can you do me a favor?" I used to say, "Sure." Over the years, I learned to reply, "I will try," or "If I can," which takes me off the hook if I can't.

In the chapter *"Hand-Dome"*, you identified your boundaries. Sometimes, you have to say "No" to honor yourself. At home and work, others often prod you to do more than you want to do. They also request or demand what is physically and emotionally uncomfortable or what you no longer can accomplish. You decline to respect your principles, health, or well-being, especially if the request spans a prolonged period. Understandably, we get upset when people continue to pile on the work or make demands all within the same time frame. If you are an employee who will not receive additional compensation, especially if your boss or the owner of the company is living luxuriously at your expense, you certainly deserve to be miffed. When you have a valid option, it is *your responsibility* to honor yourself and communicate to those who are making demands and crossing your boundaries about what you will do and how you want to be treated. If you have no other choice, try to find gratitude in the people or the simple joys in your life.

In life, there are times when we have exhausted all options. Therefore, we just have to pull it together, "suck it up," do our best, and accept that it is what it is. Even taking three mindful breaths, gazing at a special memento, or glancing out of the window to catch some of nature's beauty can be uplifting. Bringing you back to the present moment brings joy, as you are in control of—and in—that "now moment." Whenever possible, promise yourself that even when others don't comply, *trust* that you will honor your boundaries and halt the demands if and when you can.

A kind and helpful owner of the print shop that I have frequented for decades often comments that customers frequently walk in at the last minute and insist that he immediately take a job that he knows he can't do or doesn't have the time to do. No matter how firm and polite he is, they remain insistent that he do the job. In a polite and firm way, he repeats until they finally comprehend, "I'm sorry, I can't do the job." He *doesn't feel good* that some people have such disrespect for others.

Occasionally, friends, colleagues, and family members have a special way of trying to manipulate you to do something that you do not want to do; they can be quite persistent. Their manipulation is not perpetually negative. Sometimes they engage sweet talk to charm you or use indirect communication to try to persuade you to change your mind with phrases such as the following: "Are you sure you don't want to go?" "I know you will have lots of fun," or "Can I please have it?" When your gut or *source-voice* signals that you do not want to or cannot do what they request, first use a firm but lighthearted reply, like, "No, thank you," or "Not now." Then, if necessary, try positive and stronger intonation patterns and, finally, firmly and simply say, "No, I can't," or "No, I won't."

People from many other cultures have difficulty saying "No" because, until recently, it may not have been appropriate to say "No" in their native culture. Many Asian cultures value harmony and don't want to disappoint; they choose to please. Years ago, a Japanese client thought that many *USAans* meant "Yes" when they said "Yes" and "No" when they said "No." He soon gathered that just as at home, actions speak louder than words. We give a confusing, frustrating, and sometimes disappointing message when we say "Yes" and our actions reveal "No." This incongruence is further highlighted in the next chapter, "Embracing Diversity."

Small Talk

Small talk is speech that is desirable in many situations, offers moments of lightness and laughter during serious matters, and is a significant feature in much of US mainstream culture. Filipino, Caribbean, Central and South American, Southern European, Middle Eastern, and Indian subcontinent cultures also find small talk pleasant. Small talk is especially meaningful in the South, the Midwest, and smaller cities. It also is useful when you do not know the other person's interests; it serves to fill the silence that many find uncomfortable and gives the impression that you are interested, which you hopefully are. To others, small talk provides no real solutions and is inconsequential chatter.

Following are some examples of small talk. After meeting a new client with whom you previously noted the meeting time, location, directions, information, fees, and necessary materials required, you begin the conversation by giving a pleasant greeting. An example is "Good morning (add their name) and continue with "It's nice meeting you," instead of going directly into the conversation pertaining to their appointment.

In Nevis, upon entering an office, school, facility, or waiting room, or being outdoors, it is customary for those in their forties or older to first utter "Good morning," "Good afternoon," or "Good evening." Younger folks may also use these greetings or slang such as "Hello," "Hi,"

"Hey," or "Whass up?" before they begin their conversation. This tradition provides a positive foundation for each encounter.

I always try to find something sincere and pleasant to say to each person. Sometimes, I comment that I am delighted to see them or that they look good, or I inquire about their family, work, an activity, the weather, a pleasant current event, or a common interest. If there is something specific going on in the person's life, I take the time to comment or inquire about it. Small talk may also include sharing an appropriate joke. I think people feel special when we take the extra time to include sincere, personal, and especially uplifting comments. It shows we care and certainly adds positive energy to the universe. The personal interaction makes life more rewarding and enjoyable and helps balance whatever else is going on in their lives.

To me—and many others—the greeting, "Hi, how are ya?" is insincere. People who use this greeting in passing generally do not really care to know how you are. Often, they have passed by the time it would be your turn to respond. If saying "Hi" isn't enough, try including the person's name along with the greeting. If that doesn't work, greet with "Good morning," "Good afternoon," or "Good evening." The day after our dog died, I walked around the neighborhood. A young man walking toward me said, "Hi, how are ya?" As he passed, the tears filled my eyes. Often, people in similar circumstances respond, "Fine," when they are really in pain or upset. And if you ask sincerely, be willing to pause and patiently listen to the answer.

For some people, small talk is integral to being social and polite, yet you would be surprised how many people are uncomfortable with small talk, causing them to omit the pleasantry of small talk in their conversations. With the lack of desire or inability to engage in this type of conversation, they may begin a conversation that is inappropriate or hurtful. Similar to other skills previously mentioned, the use of sincere small talk is another skill to help communicate more positively and build connections.

Fillers

Fillers are words or sounds such as "Ah," "Um," "Okay," "Wella," "Like," or "You know." They are different from small talk. We use fillers when we haven't pulled together our thoughts, are uncomfortable, or are not well versed in the subject matter. Fillers also provide time to pause and formulate the remainder of our conversation. They are used when we are uncomfortable with the person, situation, or topic or when we have to pause, observe, and factor in someone's reaction to what we said. Using fillers in our speech presents an unfavorable impression, such as a lack of confidence, and sometimes creates discomfort for others.

When I first went into business, I gave a presentation to a malpractice insurance company. I was promoting additional communication programs for insured physicians. Then, marketing was quite challenging. I had also broken my personal rule not to engage in marketing on our Sabbath (which I have not repeated). After my forty-five-minute presentation, a physician shared that he had counted more than thirty "You knows" during my talk. Based on my poor presentation, it didn't surprise me that I didn't get that specific additional work, although I continued to consult with the company for several years. When I feel passionate about a subject, I have little difficulty expressing myself.

A good way to monitor our use of fillers is to record our presentations, conversations, phone calls, or face-to-face communication. If you record in the presence of others, you must inform them. Play back the conversations or presentations and monitor for fillers. Once you are aware that you overuse fillers, focus on eliminating them.

Don't Complain and Don't Explain

I do not know who is credited with the phrase "Don't complain and don't explain." Throughout this country, there are those who broadcast their complaints and explanations on talk shows or via social media, phone, and face-to-face conversations. It is especially annoying at houses of worship or in elevators, waiting rooms, checkout lines, restaurants, and most arenas. Since we moved to Nevis, I've tried to hold complaints and explanations to a minimum.

In Nevis, I rarely hear any friends complain about life's burdens or explain "why" or "what." They do complain about the weather and politics. Some shared their innermost feelings about the present and past challenges they faced. But I never heard complaints or explanations. "It is what it is" is how they handle life. When there are multiple incidences of the same types of errors or tragedies, when feasible, they begin to question the cause and make adjustments. But they don't complain or explain. Since I have only spent a brief time in Nevis in the last few years, the younger generation may more readily complain.

This attitude of gratitude is a beneficial gift from living among the Nevisian people for many years. Whenever I return to Nevis, the transition into the culture is seamless. On my return to the US, the constant complaining about minutia and inconsequential or personal matters, expressed quite audible in so many common spaces, create a hesitancy to fully engage. Consequently, I experience a temporary culture shock in many situations. There are a few treasured havens where I feel "at home."

I certainly recognize and respect complaining when loss, illness, pain, tragedy, or death cling to the heart. But I have a difficult time understanding privileged whining about a chipped fingernail, a broken treadmill at the gym, or when a person who has many (often expensive) physical comforts grumbles that they are "barely getting by" or complains about the age-appropriate behavior of infants, toddlers, and well-mannered children.

Some complain because they seek comfort, others complain just to get it off their chest, and the response that they each desire is altogether different. Many, especially parents, offer comfort or add insights in response to those who share their deepest concerns. But often, people who complain—especially children, young or old—just want a person to listen and a safe place to vent. When children unburden themselves, their parents may still fret days later. When they finally ask their children how things turned out, they often reply, "Oh, that was nothing," or, "I forgot about it."

Communication Investment

We invest in all sorts of activities and endeavors during our lives, such as health, education, pleasure, retirement, leisure, fun, and insurance. How about *communication investments*? These investments are beneficial and require making the necessary time to ensure that our communication is understood and framed to reflect our exact thoughts and requests.

We must remain alert and immediately respond when our *source-voice* cheers a resounding "Yes" or signals a halting or gripping "No." We communicate our needs and what matters to us so that issues do not escalate and create greater disharmony. When we don't communicate, people often have no clue as to the cause of our discomfort or silence, so they often draw the wrong conclusions. When we withhold conversing with family and team members, especially in critical situations, we create a void. Others in frustration, resentment, or uncertainty may project their feelings into that space, creating fake facts that potentially lead to false rumors.

When children, spouses, partners, or others continually leave messes in common areas that were tidy and areas where they are expected to pick up after themselves, or they don't complete homework or chores after school or work, it is best to make them aware of your realistic and managed expectations to avoid disharmony. Making that *communication investment* saves energy, time, and money and promotes harmony for everyone.

One of our dear island grands shared that when she was younger, her mom held two jobs to ensure that all three children had what they needed, including a private education one child needed to achieve her peak potential. Each morning, after she had shared quality time and wisdom with her children, ironed their clothes, and prepared a warm breakfast, she announced loud and clear what she expected from them when she returned home after a long day's work. She demanded that all chores and homework be complete and done well. There were no "ifs," "buts," or "maybes"; excuses were unacceptable. She was a loving but strict mother. As adults, all three of her children are either gainfully employed by outstanding companies, seeking higher education abroad, or continually broadening their and their children's horizons. They each give their mother much credit for their success, speak extremely highly of her, and deeply appreciate her. Whenever I unexpectedly dropped in during their younger years while their mother was at work, they carried on with their duties as if she were present, as though she were a fly on the wall.

One challenge presented to me over the years by workers or professionals in business or industry is the considerable time wasted each day due to the lack of communication. These persons estimated that 10 to 50 percent of their time was lost by not taking the necessary steps to precisely convey issues and expected objectives. They said they had to "reinvent the wheel" or continue to put out the same old "miscommunication fires." A salesman on the road called his office and told the receptionist to take care of an emergency for an important client. He didn't take time to follow through with complete instructions in another call, text, or fax. Three thousand dollars and twenty hours later, he had a very unhappy client and an angry supervisor, and he was frustrated because the issue was still unresolved. When I questioned how much longer it would initially have required to follow up and made certain everyone understood, he replied, "Twenty minutes at the most."

It is not always the best decision to set an arbitrary date on a calendar by which we hope that a project or task will be accurately completed. We first need to complete the project or task before we make any promises to others about setting a date. By not following the recommended procedure, we often disappoint others or fail to meet unrealistic expectations. Consequently, our project is often fraught with omissions and errors.

Focus on challenges and issues that frequently occur. When a staff or team member doesn't understand the task or goal and you are frustrated over the same recurring mistakes or issues, I suggest that you make *communication investments.* Break down the process to identify the misunderstanding so that you can *"connect to correct"* and resolve the issue. Initially, *communication investments* require additional time as you gather the necessary information to isolate the issue. Eventually, the work flows more smoothly, efforts are more productive, and everyone is relieved that the former constant frustration is gone. You cannot expect a different outcome if the same unsuccessful procedures continue.

Communication investments are essential when developing or modifying a procedure. By initially asking for the input of those who will implement the modifications and explaining your anticipated outcomes or why you are making the changes, you save yourself and others involved potential headaches. The more people who are invested in the decision, the more productive the outcome. Since every person is invested, when hurdles occur, each is more willing to take the responsibility to fix it. When the administrator of a long-term health-care center wanted to transform the impersonal environment of a three-hundred-bed facility into five separate sixty-bed units, he conferred with the staff for six months before they implemented the changes, reviewing the pros and cons of each step. The administrator had anticipated numerous challenges to develop during the transition; surprisingly, there were only a few.

A person who underwent surgery following an accident used the treadmill for the first time. When he first got on, he asked another patient, "How fast are you going?" He then adjusted his speed to match the other person's pace. At the end of his exercise, he got off the treadmill without slowly decelerating the speed, and he felt light-headed. No one had explained to him that at the start of his treadmill workout, he should gradually increase his speed and before he got off he should gradually decrease his speed to prevent dizziness. A *communication investment* by his physical therapist would have benefitted him.

On April 14, the day before the annual U.S. tax deadline, a partner in an accounting firm gave his colleague verbal instructions for completing a complex tax return. Instead of taking five minutes to have his exhausted and frazzled associate note the six issues to review, he said, "When you get back to the office, make sure you write down what has to be done." A few interruptions later, the associate was back in his office and realized that much of the information was lost or transposed in his mind. The following morning, it took one hour to correct the errors that they could have avoided with a five-minute *communication investment.*

What type of silent *communication investment* do we carry? Do we tend to look for shortcuts that leave us short, or do we follow the lead that the task requires?

There can only be one priority at any time—that single task or goal that demands your utmost attention and effort. As I previously mentioned, too often the priority is to complete a task within a certain time instead of taking the time to do it right. I suggest that you take the time to accurately complete the task at hand; when necessary, communicate every step of the way. I have noticed that within the last five years, far more items that my husband or I ordered by phone or online arrive faulty because they were improperly packed, a part was missing, or they substituted a similar item. The return and replacement of the item at the expense of the company rob them of time, resources, and profits and harm the planet by increasing carbon footprint.

People can increase productivity if they take the time to make a *communication investment* to accurately review the order and double-check the process (of any function) before it is sent or executed. If we save the time and energy we waste resolving emotionally and financially costly challenges, issues, and misunderstandings, our lives, profits, and the planet benefit.

Commitment

Most of us make promises and commitments during our lives, but do we always honor them? Even if we do, each individual defines to what extent they will carry out that commitment. The same word is also interpreted slightly differently by each person. When a person offers that they will be available as needed during extenuating circumstances and then their phones and devices are mostly turned off, what did their commitment mean? For others, availability means 24-7 until everything is back on course and that type of commitment is no longer required. For most, it is somewhere between.

When I asked a teenager how she feels when a person makes promises and for no apparent reason rarely keeps them, she stated that she didn't like it. When I asked how she feels when people keep their word, she said that it felt like standing on solid ground. I believe at times we express a desire to get together or offer to do a task because that's what we feel at the moment, yet the ability to follow through is unrealized due to time, health, strength, or monetary parameters. I have been guilty of this to some degree, but now I hold my thoughts until I know the path is clear and I will have the ability, energy, means, and time to keep my word.

Appreciation

In this culture, and perhaps in most others, we desire appreciation for who we are and what we do. "Please" and "Thank you" are expressed in many ways. We can hold the most cherished feelings about others or tremendous appreciation for their acts of kindness, accomplishments, or for just being themselves. If we do not express our gratitude, they will never know about our feelings. I suggest that while we mostly express our appreciation in our preferred NLP channel, it also is fitting to express our feelings in the recipient's best channel for a heartfelt connection.

A client mentioned that her husband complained that she didn't appreciate him. I questioned, "Does he appreciate you?" She replied, "I don't think so. how would I know?" Some show gratitude with a glance, a wink, a hug, a kiss, a bow, or special, private treats. Others send loving texts, notes, flowers, or gifts; others simply smile and say "Thanks." Still, others engage in special gestures, such as holding a hand, giving a massage, preparing a romantic dinner, participating in an activity the other person enjoys, or sharing a walk, the rain, a sunrise, or a sunset, admiring beauty in a child's eyes, giving thanks together to the Universe for life, or simply taking the time to be together for the simple or the sublime. Others assume another's responsibilities and give them "time off" to spend as they wish. The time can span from five minutes to five days, to however long is feasible. It turned out my client and her husband hadn't built appreciation into their thirty-five-year relationship. Ultimately, we realize that *being with* a person surpasses *doing for* a person. The greatest gift is to honor the person for whom they are and then express our appreciation with words or deeds.

We are often quick to criticize certain attitudes or behaviors that we perceive as excessive or deficient, yet we fail to acknowledge or appreciate the care and effort it takes when the change that we requested is achieved. The lack of encouragement or compliments may discourage the other person's willingness to make further amends in the future. A balance between criticism and appreciation and acknowledgment is the very least we can do. However, it is always best to tip the balance toward appreciation. Gratitude or recognition is profound in building and strengthening the bonds we desire with our loved ones at home and our colleagues at work.

Source-connected, mindful, positive, effective, and appropriate verbal communication is an important facet of our *positive communication environment*. But similar to the other communication factors, when either positive or negative words emit powerful vibrations, their impact is far more profound. Honest, precise, positive language and the *I mode* unite; deceitful, evasive, negative language and the *you mode* divide. Be mindful of what you say. Once the words are released, you cannot control the consequences, and they live on forever. So at each moment, we choose to respond positively or negatively and sensitively or insensitively. Likewise, we choose to honor or dishonor ourselves and others. These are our choices, and they are a formative facet of our character and aura.

One Word Can Make a Significant Difference

The December 2015 United Nations Climate Change Summit conference was held in Le Bourget, a suburb of Paris, France, and representatives from nearly two hundred countries attended. There, a glitch over one word nearly torpedoed an agreement. The text of the agreement contained the word *shall*, which indicates a legally bound obligation. President Barack Obama and the U.S. negotiators at the summit realized that the use of the word *shall* would require congressional approval. There was serious doubt that approval in the current political environment could be achieved. After much negotiating, it was agreed that the word *shall* would be changed to *should* to eliminate the agreement's challenge of a binding obligation. Therefore, U.S. congressional approval was not required.

When a similar type of wrongdoing is exposed about two individuals, one responds, "I am embarrassed," while the other states, "I am ashamed." The singular word choice shines light on an aspect of each person's character.

Soul to Soul Intercultural Communication

Embracing Diversity

*The first day or so we all pointed to our countries. The third or fourth day
we were pointing to our continents. By the fifth day we were aware of only
one Earth.*

—Sultan Bin Salman al-Saud,
Astronaut,
Kingdom of Saudi Arabia
Kevin W. Kelley

Deeply Touched by the Rich Tapestry of Diversity

I have been incredibly blessed and gratified from the bountiful experiences I've gained from working with hundreds of individuals from a host of cultures, living among the Nevisian people for more than fifteen years, interacting with family members, dear friends and colleagues from a variety of cultures, and touring on my world travels. This rich tapestry of diversity has deeply touched and enlightened me to celebrate with others' ideas, traditions, resolutions, and well-being, especially their values of cohesion, family, friends, and community. Collectively, these relationships broadened and uplifted my outlook and guide how I live each day in deep gratitude. This chapter on "Embracing Diversity" is dedicated to all the people of differing cultures whom I met along my life's journey. I have laughed with them in play, smiled with them in joy, consoled and cried with them in sorrow, and felt their pain in my heart.

In this chapter, I continue to share my life's experiences with those from differing cultural backgrounds and minority groups and the deeply appreciated, enriching insights and wealth of knowledge on intercultural communication that I have gained. I gathered these during the past thirty-five years while consulting, lecturing, traveling, and living amid the Nevisian people.

The purpose of the information in this chapter is twofold. The first objective is for *USAans* to gain an understanding of the values and communication style of individuals *Born-abroad*. This leads to an ease and willingness to reach out and connect as we discover and embrace our similarities and delight as human beings. In a sense, we share life in our local, national, and global communities during our earthly sojourn.

The second objective is devoted to people who are *Born-abroad* and their second-generation children. The objective is to offer an understanding of core values and the broader and finer nuances of mainstream and regional U.S. society. A thoughtful presentation also provides insights and skills to learn a positive, effective, and appropriate communication style. These jewels and tools provide understanding and comfort to gain a greater sense of belonging in their neighborhood and the larger community.

At the same time, the *Born-abroad* individual is encouraged to remain confident and *source-connected* enough to hold dear the most positive, revered, stalwart, and treasured values of their original cultural heritage that were passed down to them, and then pass these forward to the next generation. In this way, they continue to enrich their families and themselves. And just as important, they also enrich those lives and spirits whom they touch in their new homeland. This can happen at work or play, in their houses of worship, during meditative gatherings or lively discussions, or in classrooms, sporting events, or any other facet of their new surroundings.

With greater comfort, confidence, familiarity, and knowledge, each person then chooses to what extent they modify their approach and communication to gain their desired sense of belonging and integrate as much as they choose.

Between the time I first entered the discipline of speech and hearing therapy in 1959 and then specialized in personal and intercultural communication in 1985, social norms and values significantly shifted. The values of equality and inclusion made tremendous gains. In the new political global era of early 2017, many global societies reverted to embrace a more insular approach. How powerful this insular movement, in its infancy, evolves is yet unknown. But the youth led a revitalization of all generations' passionate desire for equality and justice for all. Hopefully, in time, these values will emerge as the prevailing universal policy.

A few decades ago, when a dear friend was a librarian and weekly hiking buddy, she and I reminisced about our experiences growing up in the late 1950s. We vividly recalled the opening lines of the "Ballad of East and West": "East is east and west is west and never the twain shall meet" (Kipling 1889). We recently reviewed the final lines of the ballad, which expressed equality, and found the words most relevant for these times. Almost fifty years later, when I wrote *Communication Is Connection*, the chapter on intercultural communication was named "When Yes Means No and No Means Yes." Now, twenty years later, this chapter highlights embracing diversity. Thankfully, it seems that many positive features of each culture are slowly meshing into our mosaic culture.

When I spoke at the Society of Human Resource Management's Seventh Annual Workplace Diversity Conference in Washington, DC, in 1997, a woman in the audience asked, "If we're trying to embrace diversity, how can we ask other people to change?" I responded, "Our primary goal is to embrace the person's individuality both personally and professionally. However, it is best if the person who is *Born-aboard* assesses their challenges when communicating in U.S. English from two aspects: how well they comprehend U.S. English and how well others understand them. Then, they can decide how much change is necessary and determine their willingness and commitment to make the effort to modify, apply, and adapt. Their decision also depends on their needs, goals, and understanding of the disadvantages of their current inability to best comprehend and communicate. It is best that they also gain an awareness of their lack of familiarity with the finer nuances of U.S. communication styles, social mores, and norms. With this foundation, they evaluate the effect their communication deficit has on colleagues, staff, patients, students, clients, or those with whom they interact in their new homeland. It doesn't matter whether you are born in the United States or in another country; if your communication and style 'turns off' the very people you want to 'turn on,' you create a communication gap."

Each person and situation is different, requiring a different set of solutions. Every person in such a situation deserves respect for trying. You certainly don't want to offend anyone. The examples in this chapter demonstrate how people learned to appreciate and understand one another, how some people wanted to modify and adapt while others did not, and the solutions they found together. Please let me remind you that in a mindful, *source-connected* manner, we perceive and interact with each person as the unique individual that person is. No one person or group speaks for all people who fall into that category, whether we are discussing family, culture, condition, religion, regional, organizational, political, or any other group.

Diversity

Diversity is the richness and strength that built this country and continues to flourish. The United States is based on the visions, ideals, sweat, and tears of human beings from every corner of our planet. There are few urban or rural communities in this vast land that haven't been touched and honored by being among people of differing heritages. Folks *Born-abroad* continue to live in our communities, sharing similar joys, sorrows, freedoms, limitations, burdens, achievements, satisfaction, disappointments, calm, stress, inclusion, or dreaded rejection or expulsion.

The United States truly is a fascinating mosaic of cultures and languages. It is a country where you can arrive as a peasant and your children can be elected president. Personal and religious freedoms, potential for individual success, financial security, safety, and asylum are only some of the reasons that multitudes have flocked to the United States. They continue to immigrate to become a part of the incredible fabric that makes this nation a unique, special, and bountiful home for many. Our monumental national feats are due in large measure to their contributions.

According to the 1990 census, "Ethnic and racial minorities grew much faster than the U.S. population as a whole. Over the next half century, more than half the growth in the U.S. population will consist of young Asians and Latinos" (Plate 1996). In 2015, twenty-five years later, an NPR Twitter feed by Bill Chappell stated that "by 2020, the minority will be the majority." Many new citizens carry the Old World values of commitment to family and community, concern for others, dedication to hard work, and diligence in learning. Children of these immigrant families often are tenacious and rank first in their classes, which raises the bar of excellence for everyone; this is significantly valuable for our nation. Just look at faces of recent immigrants; they are dynamic entrepreneurs, spelling bee winners, leading scientists, academic leaders, and Nobel Prize, Grammy, Emmy, and Oscar winners, excelling in every field.

We don't have to look far to discover leading innovators of diverse backgrounds. Sergey Brin, who was born in Moscow, Russia, joined fellow Stanford University student Larry Page, who was born in Lansing, Michigan, to cofound Google, the masterful global search engine.

The word *Google* began as a noun, but following its debut, the term quickly gained verb status: "Google it."

We all know Apple's significant impact on digital technology: personal computers and the brilliant genius of iPhones, iPads, FaceTime, and what is yet to come under Tim Cook and in the future. Steve Wozniak and Steve Jobs cofounded Apple. Wozniak was born in the U.S. and is of Ukrainian and German backgrounds. Jobs was born in the U.S. and of Syrian heritage.

Jeff Bezos is a *USAan* entrepreneurial billionaire who was raised by his mother and her second husband, Miguel Bezos, who emigrated from Cuba and later adopted Jeff. Bezos is a genius who founded and remains CEO of Amazon, and he played a pivotal role in the development and growth of e-commerce. Amazon is the largest online retailer, a model for online shopping, and is so innovative that in some cities, they deliver fresh produce to your door within hours. Amazon Fulfillment Centers are now prevalent in many locales.

Former California Governor Arnold Schwarzenegger and Congressman Brad Sherman are usually on opposing sides of political issues, but they were on the same side, smiling side by side, when they cut the ceremonial blue ribbon for the hallmark completion of the sixty-seven-mile Backbone Trail in the Santa Monica Mountains. The dream of a continuous trail was realized by combining old ranches and public lands. This effort created the milestone that serves as the spine for a five-hundred-mile network through the urban metropolis of Los Angeles, California. The persistent and collective fifty-year endeavor of many people stitched this monumental endeavor together. This magnificent gift is now available to ten million residents and countless national and international visitors.

After all the acquisitions and every parcel was in place except the last stretch, which was missing two pieces of land, Governor Schwarzenegger donated a forty-acre area valued at more than $500,000. His generosity represents the single largest private donation to the Backbone Trail. After his donation, Schwarzenegger convinced fitness entrepreneur Betty Wieder to donate the last piece. The trail was the culmination of a collaborative effort of elected officials, parks agencies, volunteers, and philanthropists and is now managed by a group of federal, state, and local agencies (Sawiki 2016).

Schwarzenegger, who emigrated from Austria, was a former professional bodybuilder and was named Mr. Universe in 1967. He became an actor, businessman, and activist. In his speech at the blue-ribbon event, he expressed that he gave the land in deep gratitude to this nation for allowing an immigrant like him to come to America and fulfill his dreams to achieve what he had accomplished.

Dr. Ernest Moniz, a US nuclear physicist, was born to parents Georgina (Pavão) and Ernest Perry Moniz, of Portugal heritage. Moniz served as U.S. Secretary of Energy in the Obama administration. He was tasked with implementing the goals of "growing the economy, enhancing security, and protecting the environment. This encompasses advancing the President's all-of-the-above energy strategy, maintaining the nuclear deterrent and reducing the nuclear danger, promoting American leadership in science and clean energy technology innovation, cleaning up the legacy of the cold war, and strengthening management and performance" (http://energy.gov/contributors/dr-ernest-moniz). Moniz played a critical role in negotiating the complex ten-year nuclear nonbinding framework accepted by President Obama and the P5+1 members of the United Nations National Security Council: China, France, Russia, the United Kingdom, the United States, and Germany. The framework enticed Iran to halt the development of their nuclear weapons programs in exchange for lifted economic sanctions, which would allow them to reap billions of dollars.

During the 2016 heightened xenophobic era, the hundreds of people of Mexican and Central American heritage who crossed our borders in great numbers were met with inhumane responses. It was especially heartbreaking for women and children, who were unduly "warehoused" in disgusting conditions. In that light, I offer a few of my positive experiences with those of Mexican and Central American heritages.

A woman I knew had a spirit that felt like a breath of fresh air as she entered the building. When we gathered with a handful of educators and clinicians sitting around the table and getting to know one another, she soon shared how grateful she was that her elderly father was fitted with a hearing aid, which broke him out of his shell. He returned to the warm, friendly person she had always known and loved. She added, "We [of Mexican heritage] define who we are by how we treat our families." Her comments instantly captured my heart, as her words deeply moved me. A nurse, also of Mexican heritage, shared that her father was an orphan. Even so, he taught and lived by his profound values and commitments: "God first, family second, then serve the community." For years, I observed that my friends and service people of Mexican heritage make tremendous sacrifices for their families. They weren't so generous of spirit simply because it was traditional or expected but because it came from their hearts. When a former gardener was shot while working in a client's garden, each of his three brothers took up a rotation and, for three months, came from other states to assume their brother's responsibilities until he returned to work.

Another dear friend, whom we embrace as an extended family member, is now in her seventies. She became a U.S. citizen under President Reagan's amnesty program. In the 1980s, she watched over our children when my husband and I traveled to Europe. She also stayed in our California home for most of the years while we were in Nevis and still does when we travel. When we are in California, she comes weekly to help with the laundry, prep light meals, and assist with easy garden projects. She is loved and attends as a guest to celebrate life events, including my recent seventy-fifth birthday luncheon, where she sat next to me.

When she and her siblings bought a house, her mother, who had become a U.S. citizen, lived with them most of the time. The mother often returned to visit her brother, who lived in her former remote village in Mexico. During her last year of life, the mother was weak and in pain. She wanted to return to Mexico to see her brother, and she wished to be buried in her homeland. When she hurt herself at her children's house, she was admitted to the hospital. After a week in the hospital, during their routine visit, our friend and her brother discovered that medical personnel were ready to transfer their mother to a nearby convalescent home. The papers were all ready to be signed, and the social worker expected our friend and her brother to immediately comply. When our friend asked the social worker who had given her permission to make this decision, the social worker replied, "We thought that's what you wanted."

Out of respect for the social worker, our friend suggested that she and her brother at least visit the facility. When they arrived, my friend asked to see her mother's room. They showed her a room that her mother would share with another person. Then, my friend asked where she would spend her day. They showed her an area that was lined with people in wheelchairs, many leaning over or "looking completely out of it." My friend told her brother, "This looks like a waiting room to die." Her brother replied, "Let's get out of here. She's not coming here. Our mother is coming home with us."

My friend returned to the hospital and adamantly notified the social worker that they would take their mother home. For eight months, filled with deep love, devotion, gratitude, and reverence for their mother, and at tremendous sacrifice but without complaint, they took turns sleeping with her and making sure a warm, fresh lunch was ready for her each day. Family members, including a former daughter-in-law, took turns and flew from Mexico to assist. When their mother, aided by an oxygen tank, finally gained enough health and strength to travel, her son accompanied her.

In Mexico, their mother lived in a tiny remote village, where she was highly respected. A granddaughter and another person whom they hired took shifts so that their mother was never alone. That meant that the family also had the daily expense of feeding extra people. When my friend's mother died, she told her siblings that in respect to their mother, they would provide all the meals for three days for the almost one hundred people who had looked in on their mother. She further instructed that they not accept any food from anyone else; the family alone would provide. Her brother owned some cows, and they slaughtered one to feed everyone.

I often told the family, "You must have loved your mother very much, as you all gave from your hearts without ever complaining or feeling it was a burden." Family members consistently replied, "Of course. She was a great mother, who had lived a hard life. She always looked after us and gave us her best."

For the past twenty years, a reputable company regularly safety-trimmed the huge sycamore and eucalyptus trees in our backyard. Many of the original crew members are from El Salvador, and they remain part of the team. They now work in less strenuous and less dangerous jobs, as the younger guys now climb the high trees.

Upon arriving, one man knocked on the door to let me know that his seven-man crew was here. He also shared that he remembered coming many times and always felt welcome. One of the guys, who is now the crew's leader, and I began our usual chat.

He shared that his mother, wife, and children are the only things in life that really matter to him. He said that after his mother passed away, he has told his three children since they were very young, "No matter what happens to me, always protect your mother." On the day my father died, he told me, "Take care of your mother." I'm sure that this message is often implied, but I never heard it expressed as beautifully as the crew leader had stated.

Of the few people who possess keys to our home when we travel abroad or go to Nevis, several are from Mexico, El Salvador, and Costa Rica. A few arrived illegally decades ago, gained citizenship, and contributed significantly to their new homeland. So when you hear or read derogatory or slanderous remarks about people who crossed the border, recall these touching stories. Since individuals of the Latino/a heritage are a very diverse group, my friends associate themselves with various groups. These include Chicano, Hispanic, and most recently LatinX. This is a relatively new term that is primarily associated with younger folks. They often are more educated and prefer to be identified as genderneutral.

In 2016, there were an estimated eleven million people living in the United States who were undocumented, yet the majority contributed to society and paid taxes. Most of them had no felony convictions. They hoped to remain and find a permanent solution that paved a path to citizenship. The preceding immigrants, who entered with visas, work permits, under asylum, or illegally before becoming residents or citizens contributed to the heavy lifting and grunt work that laid and built the infrastructure to make the United States of America great. Both undocumented and legal immigrants, especially those of Mexican and Central American cultures and Muslim faith, continue to diligently serve the public in caring and compassionate roles, especially in health care, tourism, agriculture, and food services.

While immigration reform continues to be a hot political issue, make no mistake—there are strong prejudices, false sound bites, inaccurate news, and rumors that fuel that divide. In addition, all types of legal and undocumented immigrants from these countries and religions are often lumped together as "immigrants," and that term is applied to all *Born-abroad* individuals, whatever their status. We also take special notice of the difference between those of Latino heritage, who are now citizens, and those who live in the United States under the Deferred Action for Childhood Arrivals (DACA) program. This program "provides work permits and a reprieve from deportation to people who arrived in the United States as children, and who meet certain other requirements" (NCLR, n.d.). The Development, Relief and Education for Alien Minors Act, the DREAM Act, provides a conditional permanent residency to certain undocumented immigrant students. They are required to receive a college degree within six years or serve two years in the military to expedite a path to citizenship. The "Dreamers" are those of "good moral standing" between ages twelve and thirty-five who must have entered the United States before they were sixteen and who have lived at least five consecutive years in the United States (http://immigration.laws.com/dream-act).

I do not intend to demonize any group of immigrants. Nevertheless, I want to highlight the distinctions between them so that folks implement compassionate and informed decisions. Many people have not made that differentiation. When I recently conversed with a woman who lives in a state that borders Mexico, she noted that she favors deporting all immigrants. When I questioned her about splitting families with no convicted felons, she replied, "Of course not." I explained to her that she had lumped all groups into one category, "immigrants."

Especially in this time of increasing national terrorism and heightened xenophobia, it is vitally imperative to rethink the concept that U.S. citizens are primarily of European heritage. With the exception of those from African backgrounds who arrived in the early 1600s, later and recent citizens are more likely to be Asian, South Asian, Middle Eastern, or of Latino heritage. The diversity in the shapes of their eyes, textures of their hair, hues of their skin, varieties of their style, sounds of their speech, fluctuations of their voice, and delicacies and aromas of their spiced cuisines is in harmony with our nation's scenery. They are the oceans, rivers, streams, lakes, ponds, plains, meadows, forests, deserts, mountains, and glaciers that create our magnificent national landscape on our splendid planet.

The volume of hateful rhetoric espoused by some candidates during the 2016 presidential campaign deeply disturbed multitudes, including me. The lowest common denominator and the most divisive and demeaning attitudes were thrown at minorities and immigrants. Statements that preyed on fears and suspicions were hurled, while others highlighted the collective, cohesive, and collaborative strength of people from all cultural backgrounds. Historically, when individuals from all cultural backgrounds collectively joined forces to create, innovate, or pull us through as a nation, we have met every major national disaster, obstacle, or challenge. Each wave of immigrants brings its own strength and special attributes. They eventually join those who came before to enrich the expanding fabric of this exceptional experiment of an idea named democracy. None of us are indigenous to this continent. For years (although this theory is now under scrutiny), it was considered that even those of the First Nations Peoples and Native American cultures crossed the Bering Straits in significantly limited numbers. Their descendants eventually populated North America, Central America, South America, and the Caribbean islands.

Your forefathers and foremothers probably were perceived negatively and discriminated against, especially if they were Asian, German, Italian, Irish, Latino, Polish, Catholic, or Jewish. As they sat around the kitchen table, they most likely shared painful tales of the humiliation, ridicule, discrimination, abuse, and derogatory ethnic slurs that they encountered shortly upon their arrival in the United States. They also faced scrutiny during their acclimation and assimilation, as they were perceived as "too" Asian, "too" Black, "too" German, "too" Irish, "too" Italian, "too" Latino, or "too" Polish. "Too" Catholic, "too" Jewish, "low life," "snooty," "scoundrel," "thug," "uneducated," and other foul terms were thrown at them. These are the same labels that some folks still slap on them today. They also faced backlash from members of their ethnic families and communities as they were (and are) perceived as disloyal to their original heritage. They tried to find their balance between the values and manners of their former homeland and how to blend those with the values and manners of their new mosaic U.S. homeland. Fortunately, most *Born-abroad* individuals clutched close to their hearts the cherished, righteous, rich, inspiring, and uplifting values of family, hard work, education, honesty, and justice, which their ancestors had carried in their own hearts and souls and passed on to our formerly and recently arrived newcomers alike.

I believe that much of the current ugly, venomous, divisive, "rabble-rousing," xenophobic rhetoric voiced by some groups of *USAans* toward minorities, especially those of Mexican and Central American heritage, initially stemmed from economic fears—many people are concerned about losing their jobs.

Many also continue to be suspicious and terrified of those *Born-abroad* who recently arrived, specifically from the Middle East and Syria, and those of Muslim faith. With the potential of a humanitarian influx of displaced persons, refugees, and victims of the heart-wrenching crises in the Mideast, a heightened fear-based-mongering and unenlightened viciousness "sirened" a clarion call to "keep them out."

Those holding these misguided ideas also fear that their culture will be compromised, displaced, destroyed, or taken over by those who are "others" and are not "one of us." These decades-long deeply held beliefs underlie their unsubstantiated fear that immigrants' sole intent is to cause great harm. Also at stake is their dread of a broad-based terrorist plot to wipe out their way of life and possibly themselves and their loved ones.

That blind, hateful distaste does not only stem from job loss due to obsolescence, automation, and globalization but also arises from an unenlightened misunderstanding of folks who appear different, whose names sound different, and whose priorities and customs are also different. For many, it is insecurity, a lack of will or curiosity to investigate the facts, or outright bigotry. If they look beyond themselves and their own values, they might discover and appreciate that others may hold different values, beliefs, palates, and lifestyles and that there is profound worth in those as well.

As a presidential candidate, Donald Trump stirred up the existing fear, distrust, polarization, and hatred. He had proposed barring any individual who "somebody senses" is a Muslim from entering the United States. Radical jihadists may claim to be of a certain religious following, but their dastardly and cowardly perversions and hatred, ruthlessness, and cold-blooded mass murder certainly do not define the millions of law-abiding, inclusive, honorable, hospitable, productive, and harmonious Muslims. Centuries ago, those of Christian faith participated in pogroms annihilating Jews in Russia and the Rhineland massacre, those of Catholic faith joined to take the holy sites from Turkish hold, and Christians participated in the Crusades. They ruthlessly raped women and children and murdered Jews and Muslims. The people who participated in such atrocities certainly did not represent those who positively practiced Catholicism or any other form of Christianity.

Every individual, culture, and subculture bring differing values, languages, and communication styles along with greetings, meals, fashion, holidays, stories, art, and music. In time, many of these differences become integral parts of the vibrant fabric of our US culture. This adds to the charm and splendor of our society as we delight in a plethora of choices and diversity.

Before we dig in, let's begin with the pleasantries as we acknowledge the numerous cultural words and forms to greet one another. Many philosophies or greetings that are familiar to us and that we embrace originated in other cultures. "Shalom" is a Jewish and Israeli greeting, and "Salaam" is an Arabic greeting, both of which denote "peace." "As-salamu alaykum" is a Muslim greeting denoting "peace be upon you." "Namaste" is a Hindu greeting meaning "the divine in me meets the divine in you" and is conveyed with hands pressed together with thumbs directed toward themselves and fingers pointing upward, as they simultaneously slightly bow to one another. A client who was a physician from Taiwan shared a Confucian concept that evolved into a major tenet of Buddhism and other ways of life or religions. She gave me a symbol written in Taiwanese that represents more than destiny; the symbol represents "everything that you are, have been, and will be, everything that you do, have done, and will do." It isn't controlled by God or another energy. It just is; the energy is forever. She believed that from the beginning of time it was destined that our paths would cross at a certain time. I treasure this symbol and its meaning so much that it is found later in this book. A similar Jewish concept, "besheret," also coveys that life is meant to be as it is.

In the U.S. culture, a verbal "Hi," "Hello," "Good day," "What's up," "Hey, dude," or "High five," hopefully accompanied by a smile and often a firm handshake, is appropriate between people of any gender. Unless they are an observant Jew or Muslim, or simply choose not to, men and women generally offer their hand to the other person, whatever their gender. In Russia, a close-held and tight hug is appropriate, even among men. In Asia, people bow to express respect. In France, men and women kiss several times on the cheek. In some countries, people place their hands with palms touching each other and hold them in front of their hearts and bow slightly. People from Arab cultures often express great affection by grabbing each other and loosely holding hands while standing closely to each other and looking into each other's eyes. The intimacy among friends is expressed that way. A man of the Cherokee Nation demonstrated that when members of his tribe greet, they each place one of their hands over the other person's wrist so that their pad rests on the pulse below the thumb. The placement of the two free hands forms two continuous loops between the people, and they feel warm energy flow between them. He shared that this symbolizes two things. Feeling the pulse expresses life in both people: positive energy that emanates from each, then flows to a higher power that created life.

The fist bump, which became more popular in the United States in certain circles due to its occasional use by President Obama and First Lady Michelle Obama, is the greeting of choice among the locals in Nevis. At times, the fist bump is called "dap." Either way, the sequence and movements vary. The most familiar begins with gripping and closing fingers with thumbs free, then each sliding their hand toward themselves, closing their fist then tapping their heart. At times, they continue by opening their hand with the palm upward and motioning the love from their heart to the other person's heart. Since I mostly use the dap in Nevis and am most socially comfortable with that form, I increasingly and spontaneously engage the simple fist bump in California, except in professional settings.

Think of the many types of breads you relish: tortillas, pita bread, croissants, and bagels; the variety of entrées you order in the oodles of international restaurants such as sushi, egg rolls, dim sum, tandoori chicken, curry, pizza, hummus, burritos, omelets, black-eyed peas, gumbo, beans and rice, ham hocks and lima beans, stroganoff, and hot dogs. All came from other cultures and are now tasty to many of our palates. Exotic fruits, vegetables, herbs, and spices are now on shopping lists, in grocery shelves, and in our kitchens.

Broomstick skirts, kimonos, sarongs, berets, Nehru jackets, and kilts represent fashion from other cultures. *Mantra, guru, klutz, schlepp, angst, haute couture, glitch, gesundheit, gourmet, mañana, yin* and *yang,* and *karaoke* are words or expressions from other cultures that are now integrated into and enrich our language and our experiences. Many of us, our children, or others we know participate in yoga, karate, jiujitsu, tae kwon do, tai chi, qigong, or other martial arts and meditative motion practices, which all came from Asian or Asian Indian cultures. Where would we be without country, Celtic, and folk music, operas, symphonies, and the soulful music of gospel, jazz, blues, rhythm and blues, and the melodies, lyrics, and beat of rock 'n' roll, hip-hop, and rap? How empty would our lives be without printed or digital versions of tales, poems, dramas, philosophies, mysteries, history, autobiographies, biographies, and cartoons created by individuals from every culture around the world?

Homeopathic medicine, Chinese herbs, acupuncture, and other forms of alternative or complementary medicines are more broadly accepted into the healing protocol of mainstream U.S. culture. Study of their healing properties began decades ago by the Office of Alternative Medicine at the National Institutes of Health. The results were positive (Hall and Greene 1997). I share with many of my diverse medical team that "Western medicine keeps me alive; eastern medicine keeps me well."

Stress-reduction therapy in the forms of tai chi, yoga, and meditation is extremely beneficial. As I mentioned in the previous section, *Soul to Soul Communication*, Google, Facebook, and Instagram began offering free meditation classes to fifty-two thousand employees in the belief that the three mindful breaths improve focus. I think engaging in "three mindful breaths" practice would be a significant, beneficial practice at the beginning of every meeting, class, and meal in the United States and throughout the world.

Traditionally, many cultures value and respect the community elders far more than does the mainstream *USAan* culture. A social worker who consults with patients in convalescent homes observed that families of African, Asian, and Latino heritages in many inner-city neighborhoods spend more time with their elders than those of other cultures. For centuries, tribal members of Native American heritage revered their elders. With assimilation and the rise of modern technology, often to their own detriment, youth abandoned the rich traditional wisdom and knowledge of their elders. Instead, they once favored the more popular, enticing technology and lifestyle of their mainstream peers.

Over the years, an increasing number of those of Native American heritage are returning "home" to their roots, spiritual core virtues, and traditions of their forefathers and foremothers. They began to appreciate and embrace their elders' love and deep respect for Mother Earth, the environment, and sacred animals, which had been the foundation of their ancestors' values, knowledge, and wisdom. They are finding paths to live harmoniously, balancing modern-era technology and reverence for the spiritual practices of their elders. When I was a Girl Scout sixty-five years ago, I recall the saying "Make new friends, but keep the old; one is silver and the other gold." When I was a regular on the *Youth on the Go* program on VON Radio in Nevis, I often offered that wisdom to the youth and continued to do so when appropriate.

While other cultures valued conformity and group harmony, U.S. culture traditionally valued individuality and personal achievements. Some *USAans* cling to the independent, stoic nature of their ancestors, while others treasure the importance and necessity of communally joining for the common good.

Susan Rice, senior national security adviser under the Obama administration, appeared on the program *GPS* (*Global Positioning System*), moderated by Fareed Zakaria. She spoke at length on the topic of diversity. She recently gave a commencement speech at the Florida International University (FIU), one of the most diverse national universities, with a 60 percent minority student population.

Rice commented about the lack yet importance of diversity in the national security workforce. She included the following areas of that workforce: civil and foreign service, security, defense, development agencies, and the military senior leadership and rank and file. She further expressed that "one of our greatest strengths as a nation—in addition to our innovation and our fearlessness when we look at our people—is our extraordinary diversity" (Zakaria 2016).

She added that people who come from a broad spectrum of cultural backgrounds, ethnicities and races, religious groups, age groups, genders, and sexual orientations bring a broader perspective of ideas and resolutions that avoid groupthink. This wide-ranging and inclusive approach "offers creative and acceptable solutions, and solutions that are likely to be acceptable in the environments in which they need to stick" (Zakaria 2016).

Rice positively noted that an increasing number of people of minority backgrounds are receiving higher education and training from outstanding institutions and "ought to be encouraged to come into national security and foreign policy" (Zakaria 2016). Although her comments pertained to the narrow field of national security, the message is relevant and can be applied to every sector of the U.S. culture.

Before we continue, please take to heart the eloquent excerpt that President Ronald Reagan stated in his last statement as president on January 19, 1989:

> "You can go and live in France, but you cannot become a Frenchman. You can
> go and live in Germany, Turkey, or Japan, but you cannot become a German,
> Turk, or Japanese. But anyone from any corner of the earth can come to live
> in America and become an American." (Reagan 1989; Scarborough 2018)

We have come to the conclusion of highlighting the basic values and the broad and significant contributions that persons of various cultures have made for centuries and continue to make today. Next, we turn to the presentation of intercultural communication. This information is beneficial for persons who are *USAans*—mainstream or minority—born in the United States but raised in a home in which a foreign language was the dominant language. These individuals are commonly referred to as English as a second language speakers (ESL). The material also is valuable for those persons who are *Born-abroad* and immersed in the U.S. culture, for those who have yet to assimilate, or for those who have chosen to cling to their original culture.

This knowledge offers the ESL speaker an understanding of the appropriate use of nonverbal communication, voice tone and rhythm, and verbal communication in *mainstream USAan* culture. The information also provides the *USAan* with greater understanding and tolerance of the communication styles of people from other linguistic and cultural backgrounds. These new insights and tools reduce misunderstandings as you gain comfort and confidence speaking with your family, neighbors, colleagues, staff, professionals, workers, and service providers of diverse cultural backgrounds.

My initial goal is to further others' willingness to converse with individuals of various backgrounds. My ultimate intention is to provide a plethora of approaches, insights, and skills to create a mindful, *source-connected*, and *positive communication environment* in which any willing person looks forward to entering and joining an enjoyable and enriching conversation and experience. These break down walls and help build a more cohesive and harmonious society and twenty-first-century communication paradigm.

Intercultural Communication
Four A's (AAAA) for Successful Intercultural Communication

The four As (*AAAA*) for successful intercultural communication are *awareness*, *appropriateness*, *acknowledgment*, and *acceptance*. As you acknowledge and embrace cultural differences, you reach acceptance and then feel free to enter a more mindful, meaningful, and comfortable intercultural conversation. Tolerance is a good start; acceptance is the next step, and inclusion is the goal.

Labels serve an important role in society. Please let me remind you that when used positively, labels help to classify and give meaning and understanding to benefit our lives. When used negatively, they imprison our thinking and distort and dishonor the integrity of others. When we attach a label to something, we combine ideas with that label. Negative and divisive labels immediately erect barriers that cage us. When we apply the label—the name of a culture, region, or religion—to our thoughts, we unintentionally restrict and prejudice our thoughts. Corrosive and repugnant attitudes and behaviors and dishonest statements must never be normalized; instead, we must immediately recognize, scrutinize, marginalize, point out, and deal with these anomalies.

Intercultural communication takes place between people of different linguistic, cultural, and regional backgrounds. At the very crux is the belief that we are foremost *source-connected* with every fellow global citizen on our planet and they with us, and we are all interconnected at some level with every other person, including the very best and very worst of humanity. We are usually far more similar to another person than we are different from them. In a *source-connected communication paradigm*, we enter in commonality as a member of the human race. This inclusive mind-set is fundamental, and that foundation immediately creates a bridge of understanding that furthers trust to create mindful and productive dialogue between and among us.

One of my first clients, who had recently moved to the United States, was vice president of a Japanese car-manufacturing company. It was of utmost importance that along with being liked and accepted he use appropriate words at the right time. I recall thinking that I had similar concerns. No matter from which culture a person arrived, or their role in life, each has held similar hopes and aspirations, concerns, and fears for their own and their family's well-being, safety, and security.

The more familiar we are with a person, the more we get the fine nuances of their facial expressions, body language, gestures, and voice tone. Recollect a familiar person, family member, close friend, or associate. We often grasp the slightest change and signal by the look on their face, the arch of an eyebrow, the shrug of a shoulder, a shift in their voice, or a sigh. In part, our familiarity also reflects our understanding of the communication style of the person's native culture. As we learned in the previous section of the book, even in the most familiar and loving relationships, communication is not easy and far too many misunderstandings occur. Add to this the layer of interculturalism and you quickly realize the complexity of an already-challenging conversation arena.

Each culture brings different styles to appropriately express nonverbal communication, voice tone, and verbal communication. Even within the United States, people from various industrial, professional, and regional subcultures dress and communicate differently. A successful car dealer, a Wall Street businessman or businesswoman, a nurse, an artist, a techie, a broadcaster, or a cowboy may communicate effectively while being considerably different. People from the inner city often use lingo and communicate in styles that those on the other side of town wouldn't grasp. Those in the inner city don't always dig or trust the ways of those who are different.

Individuals may speak African American Vernacular English (AAVE), once named Black English. This is a recognized dialect with set patterns and grammatical rules. In 1996, David Shipley stated, "There is a whole set of attitudes that many whites have that if a Black person speaks Black dialect, he [or she] is automatically inferior in some ways, i.e., less intelligent, potentially violent, threatening in some way that is difficult to define" (Shipley 1996). This is unfortunate, as none of the above conclusions may be true. Although the term Black English evolved to Ebonics and is currently called African American Vernacular English, the attitudes toward it have not changed much among certain groups of people. As always, the arts—and now social media—are rapidly and positively uplifting that attitude beyond the youth. Initially, the youth and those of African heritage embraced rap music and hip-hop. Now, the youth and adults of many cultures embrace these art forms. An overwhelming multitude of individuals of all ages traveled and swarmed to buy extremely expensive tickets to experience the brilliant, innovative, and record-breaking Broadway musical *Hamilton*.

Each communication style is appropriate for the subculture in which the person lives. The confusion, mistrust, and misunderstandings occur when we are unfamiliar or we assess a differing communication style as inferior based on what we think is the only correct manner to communicate. Our standard usually is based on our family, peer, and cultural styles. We are often unaware of what communication style is appropriate in other cultures. This became quite evident during the trial of George Zimmerman when they called a witness to testify for Trayvon Martin. Her response represented an appropriate communication style of the hood in which she lived, where her peers would not question her appearance, ability, or response.

Increasing polarization occurred during the 2016 U.S. presidential election cycle, which demonstrates that we also must continue to reach out further to a broader group of individuals in regions within our nation who've had different experiences and hold opposing views. We must actively listen from the heart so that we engage in productive dialogue to seek mutually acceptable solutions.

People from other linguistic, regional, community, or cultural backgrounds have not only accents that interfere with their ability to communicate effectively but also different communication styles. Rather than assume our communication style is the only proper way to converse and to express capability, intelligence, and mastery, compassionately recognize that there are differences.

Invariably, people are rude in every culture. However, rudeness is not intentional when it reflects a trait that is appropriate in the person's native culture. The person most likely has not learned or mastered the subtleties of the *mainstream USAan* communication style. That person may also be unaware of the nuances of that person's native culture's communication style. If you visited another country, you probably did not understand the appropriate nuances of everything that you saw, said, or did. Therefore, unbeknownst to you, and certainly unintentionally, the way you acted or spoke may have been perceived as inappropriate, offensive, or crass.

Why Is It Challenging to Understand People from Other Cultures?

I have been in the field of speech and communication for fifty years and have specialized in intercultural communication for more than thirty years. In my professional experience, the two factors of intercultural communication that create the most obstacles and misunderstandings are heavy accents and differing, and at times opposing, verbal, nonverbal, and voice-tone communication factors.

Which specific factors cause an ESL speaker to sound different? You hear and correctly perceive pronunciation, grammatical rules, voice inflections, and rhythms that are different from what you are accustomed to. At times, voice tone or cadence are almost the total opposites of what are pleasant, practiced, and appropriate in mainstream U.S. English.

When ESL speakers learned to speak their native languages, they learned the projection, intonation, phrasing, word-syllable stress patterns, vowels, consonants, grammar, and syntax of their native language. When they learned U.S. English, they transferred some of those patterns to English. That is why they speak with an accent and sound different. This recognition helps to clarify why communication can be challenging. If you are a *USAan* speaker and converse in another language, you probably don't sound exactly like a native speaker of that language either. Just as some speech sounds in U.S. English are difficult for people of other linguistic and cultural backgrounds to pronounce, some speech sounds and patterns of other languages are difficult for *USAans* to pronounce.

The different pronunciation of speech sounds, consonants or vowels, between U.S. English and a person's native language is one factor of an accent. When a person attempts to say *three* and says *tree*, or tries to say *mother* and instead says *modder*, the substitution is because the "th" sound isn't present in their native language. Therefore, they haven't learned to pronounce "th" in U.S. English. Other sounds that aren't common in other languages are the "f" and "v" sounds, and "r" and "l." "R" and "l" often are confusing for Asian speakers. They may either substitute "r" for all words containing "l," or "l" for all words containing "r." Or they may inconsistently substitute the "r" for "l" or the opposite. When a patient says, "I cut my rip," instead of "I cut my lip," the doctor may not comprehend. When a new minister announces, "Let's play," instead of "Let's pray," his congregation is confused or amused. An insurance agent didn't understand when a client explained, "My pants fell down in the storm." He intended to say, "My fence fell down in the storm." When my daughter lived in the Netherlands, she substituted the Dutch word for *vegetables* when she meant *greetings*. The two words were similar, except for the initial sound.

In addition, spoken U.S. English not only has one consonant that stands and is uttered alone but often has two or more consonants blended at the beginning or end of words. Examples of initial blends are *bl*ue, *tr*ack, and *str*eet. Examples of final blends are ca*t*, ca*ts*; pa*nt*, pa*nts*; bri*dge*, bri*dges*; bouleva*rd*, bouleva*rds*; appointme*nt*, appointme*nts*; and joi*n*, joi*nt*, and joi*ned*. Many Asian languages do not have any final consonants, let alone several combined consonants. In many Asian languages, the word pattern is consonant/vowel, consonant/vowel. Therefore, multiple sounds at the end of words in U.S. English are often difficult to learn, are hard to retain, and tend to be challenging to pronounce.

Final sounds, pronunciation of past tense and plurals, and *correct use of pronouns* are challenging to people of differing linguistic backgrounds. When I refer to "final sounds" and "word endings," I refer to the consonants or group of consonants at the end of a word or the sounds that denote past tense and plurals. Note the italicized final consonants or sounds at the end of the following words: jo*b*, ca*t*, ca*n*, can'*t*, accountan*t*. Also, note the plural word endings: cat*s* (s is pronounced "s"), job*s* (s is pronounced "z"), and house*s* (es is pronounced "ez"). Further, note the following verbs ending in silent sounds: si*pped*, cha*tted*, che*cked* (the final sounds are pronounced "t"). Also, the verbs ending in voiced sounds: ga*bbed*, a*dded*, ga*ged* (the final sounds are pronounced "d").

In U.S. English, letters (sounds) are added at the end of words to signify plurals or past tense, such as "one dog," "two dogs" (z), "I pass," "I pass*ed*" (t). The Chinese languages do not have gender pronouns. That is why people from Chinese or Mandarin language and cultural background don't often use "she," "he," "her," "him," "hers," or "his" in their speech. If they do, they may get the genders mixed up, substituting "he" for "she" or "she" for "he."

People who are ESL speakers may desire to improve, but similar to any skill, some individuals catch on quickly, some more slowly, and some are unable to grasp the concepts at all. Either they diligently try, they don't try, they try but aren't very invested in the outcome, or they just can't succeed to the level they desire. In the same way, some people easily learn a new skill or sport, while others, even after applying their best effort, still are unable to achieve their goals.

Bridging the Communication Gap

As you know, the difference between talk and communication is the *connection*. The remainder of this chapter offers insights and skills to help you create a stronger, more positive, and more comfortable connection with people from other cultures. If each person desires and is willing, productive and pleasant communication is possible with any person, regardless of regional or cultural background.

If you perceive a difference in communication style, your purpose is to thoughtfully enlighten, never to criticize or ridicule. It is best to begin to bridge the communication gap by first acknowledging the appropriate style of the other person. Connecting with the other person is illustrated in Figure 4 in the chapter "Communication Is Connection." When I sense that connection, no matter how long it takes to achieve, I then ask in a mindful, *source-connected* way, "What is the meaning of that gesture, voice tone, or word in your native culture?" After the person explains the meaning of a nonverbal communication style, voice-tone feature, or verbal communication factor of their native culture, I highlight and explain what that feature denotes in mainstream U.S. English or U.S. culture.

When speaking with people from other cultures, I discovered that there is a progression from the most effective to the least effective communication:

- *Two people from the same linguistic and cultural background speaking face-to-face*
- *Two people from the same linguistic and cultural background speaking on a landline*
- *Two people from different linguistic and cultural backgrounds speaking face-to-face*
- *Two people from different linguistic and cultural backgrounds speaking on a landline*
- *Two people from different linguistic and cultural backgrounds speaking on a cell, cordless, or speaker phone*

What can you do to help reduce the potential misunderstandings and close a gap to improve communication? There are many strategies that can be very effective in helping you engage and increase comprehension during face-to-face or telephone communication.

The strategies are:

- *Break down information or thoughts into smaller phrases.* When giving a telephone number, group and pause between the area code, prefix, and the remaining four numbers, such as "**888**," pause, "**555**," pause, "1212." When giving any series of numbers, such as confirmation, case, ID, social security, credit card, or any other lengthy set, pause the same way so that people will understand. When giving information with two or more ideas or specific details, such as "I would like to set up a meeting for lunch next Tuesday in Chicago," note that the keywords are *meeting, Tuesday* and *Chicago.* Pronounce those words slightly slower and slightly louder and use appropriate rising or falling pitch.
- When giving instructions or directions, *pause long enough for the person to write down or get a sense of the information.* For example: "Go to the first street and turn left," pause, "go four blocks up the hill until you see the school," pause, "make a right turn at the school and go to the end of the cul-de-sac," pause. "The house is the third one on the left," pause, "23089 Clark Street."
- *Reduce how much information you give.* Speak in shorter sentences or phrases or, if necessary, one or two words at a time. If that does not work, slowly spell out the key words. Since comprehending important information is essential, if the person still does not understand, use gestures if both of you are present or kindly ask to speak to another person (or supervisor) who will understand.
- *Pause longer and more frequently* for those persons of differing linguistic backgrounds and cultures who have difficulty understanding you. These pauses allow more time between ideas and groups of information to help process the information. They may first have to mentally translate the words into their native language to comprehend and then translate their response back to English. This additional pause time allows them time to effectively process that information. *When beneficial or necessary, write down pertinent information* or have a prepared memo or handout on the topic for the person. Also, encourage students, clients, patients, nurses, workers, and associates to ask meaningful questions or call you. These strategies can also be applied to the elderly, for individuals with speech and language disorders, or for any other seemingly fit reason.

Two Steps from the Norm

The U.S. English spoken by most national radio or television broadcasters is considered non-regional U.S. English. In my professional experience, when two people from different linguistic backgrounds converse, comprehension is more challenging than when both are from the same background. The person who speaks their second language is one step away from the norm, the native language of that culture, or the dialect of that region. Misunderstandings occur more frequently when two people from two differing linguistic cultures—such as Russian and Taiwanese, or Mexican and Iranian—both speak English as their second language. They are two steps from the norm, their native language, and their present culture. Challenges occur due to their dialect or accent, their use of nonverbal communication, voice tone, word choice, grammar, syntax, pronunciation, other linguistic features, or a combination of these factors. The following graphic illustrates two steps from the norm.

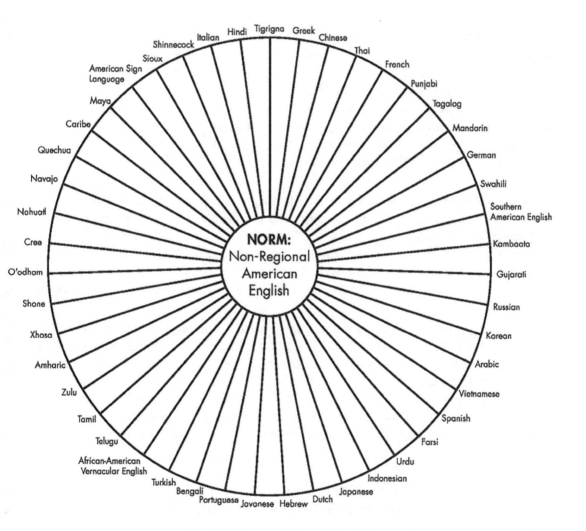

Figure 5. Two-steps from the norm.

Four Roles in an Intercultural Communication Conversation

There are four roles between two people in an intercultural conversation. The four roles are the *USAan* speaker, the *Born-abroad* listener, and the reversed roles of the *Born-abroad* speaker and the *USAan* listener.

Any intercultural dialogue is most effective when each person enters the conversation with a positive, *source-connected* attitude and assumes as much responsibility as they can. But first, it is best to remove any doubts of success from the process, such as "I can't" or "They won't." These distracting ideas minimize both participants' comfort, confidence, and focus in achieving a pleasant and productive conversation. Each person assumes responsibility. This shared effort does not necessarily indicate equally; instead, they listen or speak to the best of their abilities. Then, they can begin to engage and enjoy their *source-connected* conversation with greater ease.

When a *USAan* person speaks with a *Born-abroad* listener who indicates that they are having trouble understanding, the *USAan* speaker assists them by pausing longer between thoughts, using effective intonation on key words, and shortening sentences to phrases, or phrases to words, when necessary. If they still do not understand, repeat and then state it another way. Be patient and remain positive and *source-connected*. When the other person just doesn't get the basics, as a last resort, draw or use universal gestures to portray your exact meaning. A few of the rare universal gestures include the one for sleep, which is placing your head sideways on your hands and closing your eyes, or the gestures for eating or drinking.

When conversing with people in the Middle East, be careful not to point to or glance at your watch. That indicates that you are in a hurry and is considered rude. Folks from these regions feel that once a conversation begins, it must run its course. Also, be aware that in the U.S. culture and most English-speaking and other European cultures, the "okay" hand sign signifies that everything is good, perfect, or on course. But in Brazil and other countries, that gesture insults gay people. Also, some gestures that are acceptable in one culture may be lewd in other cultures.

Before expanding your use of hand signals, realize that many gestures that send a positive message in the U.S. culture often have different meanings in other cultures. I recommend that before traveling abroad, you check the internet to confirm which gestures are inappropriate, rude, or lewd so that you show respect and don't insult the people in that culture. I know that it is considered rude to expose the soles of your shoes in many cultures. In some cultures—especially in the Eastern cultures—shoes are often left outside or taken off upon entering a home. (More people in the United States now request that "outdoor shoes" be left at a designated spot as you enter their homes.)

A *Born-abroad* speaker conversing with a *USAan* listener must speak with an "attitude for success," no matter the competence level that the person speaks. It is essential to slightly open your mouth and project your words, as these are essential in helping others understand you. See the chapter "It's Not What You Say, but How You Say It."

The *USAan* listener speaking with the *Born-abroad* must also observe body language. Although many gestural signals are considerably different in other cultures, as noted in the chapter "Take a Look," some facial expressions are universal. They are anger, disgust, fear, happiness, sadness, and surprise (Ekman and Friesen 1975). Gestures and body language that convey an emergency are easily recognized by the urgency or fear expressed in the eyes. Listen more attentively than usual; be patient and tolerant. The objective for everyone is to bridge the communication gap for a comfortable, enjoyable, productive, and rewarding interaction.

As a *USAan* speaker, if an interaction becomes frustrating, reflect on a family member or an ancestor whom you may or may not have known. Most likely, they encountered the pain of discrimination and intolerance as a recently arrived immigrant. Try to make it right this time for the person in a similar situation. With such a current heightened level of animosity toward those who are different in our country and many other nations around the world, it is imperative to put forth more effort to infuse compassion and kindness into all conversations. In this way, we facilitate a more pleasant experience each time. By being more aware and showing we care, we each add a sprinkle of support to counter the significant amount of negativity that currently permeates our world. We also add positive energy to our community, our planet, the universe, and ourselves.

Patience, flexibility, and acceptance are essential. All our ancestors came from other places. Besides the struggle to acclimate and integrate into a new culture and lifestyle, people struggled to learn a new language and be understood. The transition was rarely easy. Most who made the journey and became entrenched in their new homeland did not make it easy for the next wave of newcomers. Multitudes want to protect their turf and minimize the perceived potential competition; some want to close the gates behind them.

But the times, they are a-changin' and, hopefully, will continue to do so. In these xenophobic times, it deeply warms the heart to witness a growing revitalization of folks of all cultural, religious, political, and generational backgrounds who coalesce. As a broad, collaborative, and cohesive force, they express an open-arms welcome to those who were forced to escape unbearable and insurmountable situations and environments. Many have fled their homeland, especially those refugees of Muslim faith or Syrian backgrounds. Sadly, this inclusive view is often in opposition to ruling government policy. Along with everything immigrants or refugees have to endure, they now also bear the brunt of collective, unenlightened, and uncalled-for, divisive, hateful rhetoric and, worse, blocked entries to safe havens and the U.S.A. Even more disheartening are those left to perish, often as young children washed up on distant shores.

To balance that opposition, it also is profoundly heartening that individuals whose homelands are not on peaceful terms with one another still empathetically support one another in a person-to-person connection. This becomes especially apparent in global responses to sacrilegious and heinous acts, as individuals prove that despite such atrocities, resounding good will truly exist among human beings of diverse cultural and religious communities.

We thoughtfully recall that most of our ancestors encountered discrimination and injustice as they began a similar journey, adjusting to a new life in a new land. Though resistance, rejection, or hatred were hurled at them, those forces were definitely not as virulent, tenacious, robust, or global in that former predigital world. How much more pleasant would it have been then, and would be now, if we, the established folk, support those who recently arrived and mindfully reach out to make every effort to further an inclusive transition, advocate for greater acceptance, and be less judgmental? Not surprisingly, many faith-based conservative groups are reaching out to accept those of Syrian heritage into their communities.

In 2015, it was heartening to learn that in Dallas, Texas, the Reverend David Houk, rector of St. John's Episcopal Church, led his parish to open their hearts and doors to Syrian refugees to enjoy a Thanksgiving feast. The rector said, "I'm thinking of a verse in the book of Romans that says, 'Welcome one another as Christ has welcomed you.' We who are Christians believe that our job is to open our doors and our arms wide to others." This was the third year that the congregation joined with the organization Gateway of Grace to provide Thanksgiving dinner to the refugees. The organization specializes in helping refugees from war-torn countries who have suffered severely (Hawkins 2015).

I was most deeply heartened when the current wave of Islamophobia was strongly rejected by San Bernardino County Supervisor Janet Rutherford—and others—as she eloquently conveyed her genuine, heartfelt, and inclusive message at a gathering following the dastardly terrorist attack in San Bernardino, California, in 2015. Rutherford began, "The purpose of terrorism is to make ordinary people afraid to do the ordinary things that make up their lives." She shared that on that December day, ordinary people had gathered to celebrate their accomplishments and receive training to serve the community even better. "They were soldiers, who became the front line against terrorism when they were attacked." She reminded everyone that "we cannot be afraid, but we must honor them by being ordinary as we continue to live our lives and not be fearful of our neighbors, our coworkers, or the people in our community." She commended the staff and the workers, who are ordinary people acting in an extraordinary manner, as they return to work to continue "to provide the dedicated service that they give throughout the community... and we have to fight to remain the 'ordinary.'" She warned the terrorists, "You may not have our fear, you may not have our liberty, and you may not have our love. Those are the things that make us distinct and it is that love for each other that gives us the hope, the strength, and the resilience to embrace the ordinary again" (Rutherford 2015).

Supervisor Robert Lovingood spoke next, and Supervisor James Ramos introduced the doctors of uniquely diverse cultural backgrounds. As members of the Arrowhead Regional Medical Center (ARMC) Trauma Team, they feverishly worked together to save lives. What struck me was the broad diversity of this outstanding team: Dr. Dev GnanaDev, Dr. Michael Neeki, Dr. Kona Seng, and Dr. Rodney Borger. Dr. GnanaDev, who emigrated from India, is Chief of the Trauma Surgical Team. He shared that "every patient, whom they evacuated and took to either Loma Linda University Medical Center or the ARMC trauma center survived." He further expressed, "It isn't easy because, after all, we are human beings." Another physician stated that in order to solely focus on saving the patient, whoever it was, he had to immediately set aside any emotional feelings for a later time. Dr. Michael Neeki, from Iran, is an osteopathic surgeon who takes a holistic approach toward the patient. He also serves as Chief Medical Officer of the San Bernardino County Probation Department. Neeki had served in the Iran-Iraq War, which gave him medical and tactical training. This additional expertise allowed him to become a member of the Special Weapon and Tactics (SWAT) team. Consequently, they swiftly took him to the site of the tragedy. He declared, "We have to protect each other and be prepared to take a bullet ourselves....We must remain strong and show ISIS what we are about" (Rutherford 2015). In a conversation with Dr. Neeki, he confirmed his previous sentiments, "When I left Iran, I never thought that I would experience the terrorism here."

Public Health Director Trudye Raymundo and Assistant Public Health Director Corwin Porter pleaded to the community to hold one another, protect one another, and be grateful as we prevail and heal together. The fact that San Bernardino is primarily a conservative community proves again that compassionate and generous-hearted human beings are found in all corners of our world, sometimes where you would least expect.

Until I spoke with Dr. GnanaDev, I was unaware that Dr. Sanjay Gupta had joined the surgical team the day after the terrorist incident. Dr. Gupta had asked Dr. GnanaDev, "How do you know which patient to save?" Dr. GnanaDev shared his response with me, "As members of a trauma team, especially when you have multiple patients arriving at the same time, you are trained that you have to concentrate your resources on the patient who has the greatest hope and chance to survive. Otherwise, you lose even more patients. This is the most difficult choice we make, and it really should not be left up to human beings." He also added that he has a strong belief in God and implied that this is what guides him.

Dr. Gupta is a neurosurgeon, associate professor of neurosurgery at Emory University, associate chief of neurosurgery, and a multiple Emmy award winner. He serves as the chief medical correspondent for CNN.

Fortunately, the anti-Muslim wave continues to be strongly rejected by former president George W. Bush, former President Obama, and the majority of the U.S. citizens, those *USAan* or *Born-abroad*, with the full spectrum of cultural diversity. This response was voiced in the majority popular vote for Hillary Clinton for president in 2016. Democratic, practical, realistic, and complex issues facing our nation require a profound, mindful, and monumental collaborative bridging of people's ideas, hopes, and dreams. Acceptance, desire, cohesion, and communication—not rejection, rejection, rejection, or talk, talk, talk—are keys to developing that inclusive dialogue that honors the essence of US ideals and its very foundation.

Intercultural Communication Style

As you recall from the *hand-dome*, we respond by meshing our basic personality, our emotions, our past experiences, and the values and communication style of our primary family and native culture. Furthermore, the person with whom we interact mirrors the process. Each *hand-dome* factor plays a key role in our communication style, and we interact with one another in varying degrees at different times. In each situation, one factor is dominant and determines your response.

With the impact of social media and its instant global reach, lines in the sand between cultures and communication styles are eroding. Strict conformity to former traditions and communication rules depends on many factors. Several features in communication, especially verbal communication, are changing. When I was conversing with a woman who worked for a leading Japanese business organization, she confirmed that the ability and ease of younger people to say "No" depends on the situation but certainly is not as strictly adhered to as their elders did. A former surgeon in China who became an alternative health-care provider and educator in the United States shared that though he prefers indirect communication, he still says "No." He added that "anything goes" with the younger generation. Because of the monumental significance of the U.S.-China relationship in the twenty-first century, I include a very short piece about the communication style within business and other areas of conversations.

China is the second largest economy in the world, and California is the eighth-largest economy in the world. A positive strategic relationship between them is extremely relevant as the West Coast is the gateway to U.S. trade with China and other Far East countries. So it makes perfect sense to meet and highlight the benefits of a relationship of mutual respect that fosters prosperity for each. The California–China Business Summit, also known as CHINAWEEK, is an annual event held in Los Angeles, California.

In 2016, a premier event provided a unique opportunity for several California business executives and political leaders from the seven most economically advanced Chinese provinces to gather "for the first time under California's strategic Memorandum of Understanding (MOU) with China's Ministry of Commerce." California Governor Edmund G. Brown Jr. and President Xi Jinping forged this agreement not only to advance a foundation that boosts economic growth but also "to enhance communication between China and California" (http://chinaweek.la).

At the event, Governor Brown noted that the many languages, customs, and differing views of China and the U.S. create the need to "build connective tissue to slowly bring the world together." A gathering of people and ideas such as CHINAWEEK helps to "make sure the China relationship works to minimize the dangers of today's world." Governor Brown further noted that people of both countries will be positively or negatively affected, depending on how the relationship between the two nations unfolds. It behooves both countries and the entire world to see that China is prosperous and advances technology to reduce harmful greenhouse emissions and find ways "to protect our natural environment" (http://usa.chinadaily.com).

"In a very profound way, human beings are inclusively tied together by their mutual impact based on what they do.… That's a big problem, because we have so many languages and differences" (http://usa.chinadaily.com). It is understandable that the leaders view the world through different eyes. If both countries respect each other and work together, the outcome is mutually beneficial on many levels—promoting prosperity for each, minimizing danger, and significantly benefitting the well-being and health of each other.

China Foundation is a top firm helping to bridge communication gaps between the local Chinese businesses and visitors who come from different cultures. The organization is recognized for "building trust and a safe environment to accelerate excellence" (http://www.chinafoundations.com). In e-mails, a consultant shared that a singular set of communication rules is very difficult to apply to a country as vast as China, for many reasons. China is segmented regionally and within industries. There are foreign private entities, local private entities, foreign private and local private joint ventures, foreign private and local state-owned enterprise joint ventures, and local state-owned enterprise joint ventures. For example, the type of industry culture, such as fuel (oil or gas), differs from the technology culture.

Overall, people's values, customs, and habits have developed from school, family, and society. These institutions often taught individuals to listen and follow rather than question and offer. Of course, when each individual and area are factored in, responses will be different.

Fundamental Chinese philosophical teachings require harmony and acquiescence. However, like most societies, China is socially layered. The first layer pertains to formality, doing what others see as proper and harmonious. But when you get to the core of an interaction where strong trust and safety exist, those who are insiders can feel free to be honest. If there is a group setting, even among close friends, any variable can send them back to the beginning, where formality rules and truths are disguised.

Traditionally, most companies emulate U.S. military leadership with directives given from the top down. The Chinese society also reflects Confucian hierarchical teachings. From afar, the hierarchy may seem rigid, but within safe groups and in more modern industries with younger employees, a slow but definite shift toward more consensus-building is developing.

In the traditional Chinese culture and business environment, people always preferred indirect or implied communication style. If you ask a handful of Chinese people if their parents told them, "I love you," many will say they have never heard those words but they know it to be true. Young parents may say that even though they never heard it, they do like to verbally express those feelings to their children.

Business environments, and most other environments in a culture, are a reflection of the people and society. People who are accustomed to hinting don't necessarily prefer it; they are just used to it. Those who are more involved in Chinese traditional society are familiar and okay with indirect communication, while those in international work environments see the value in being more direct and "telling it like it is."

The tables presented in this chapter highlight traditional nonverbal and verbal features, which are certainly not as rigid as they once were. Unless the communication factors used are noteworthy, where adjustments have to be made, each conversation will require initial observation, monitoring, and perhaps some modification for positive, effective, and appropriate responses. The shift depends on the person and situation. If a person is sixty years or older, they will usually be more entrenched with the former, more familiar rules; therefore, they are more reluctant to change.

On the following pages, you learn the different traditional communication styles of the several major cultures: mainstream U.S. American, Latino, Asian, Indian, and Middle Eastern. These are presented to help you gain a greater appreciation for and understanding of other cultures' styles. These insights and skills foster your ability to mindfully communicate more positively, effectively, and appropriately with your neighbor, student, classmate, client, patient, colleague, employee, worker, service provider, physician, supervisor, family, friend, or acquaintance.

In the United States, a verbal "Thanks" expresses appreciation. In Asian cultures, a bow conveys appreciation. In Turkey, India, and some Middle Eastern countries, a loud burp following a meal is a nonverbal way of offering a thank-you. The louder the burp, the better the meal. In the *USAan* culture, a loud burp is usually considered rude.

A female doctor from Taiwan was preparing for a trial. During her deposition, they questioned her about her colleague, "Is the doctor your friend?" She froze and didn't respond. She later explained that in her native culture, a married woman cannot be friends with another man. She was comfortable substituting *colleague* for *friend*. After weeks of preparing, she still was not sufficiently projecting her voice to convey confidence. Her attorney remarked, "Her inability to project is probably cultural." When I discussed this with my client, she explained, "No, I'm an introvert." In one instance, this physician's culture was the basis for her response; in another, it was her personality. It is best not to presume that culture solely explains an individual's specific communication style, as there are many factors, as highlighted by the *hand-dome*.

A nurse from the Philippines called quite early one morning to notify the doctor of an emergency. By accident, she reached the doctor who was on call. The *USAan* doctor snapped at the nurse for waking him instead of calling his partner. The Filipino-born nurse hung up without relaying the emergency. The doctor later stated that he thought the reason the nurse hung up and didn't tell him about the emergency was because she was Filipino. My response was, "Why do you assume that it was her culture? Perhaps she didn't like getting yelled at or, as a nurse, she felt inferior to you."

Please recall that it is best not to perceive a person's ideas or behavior as exactly aligned with any type of group or label. Their thoughts or deeds may be strongly influenced by their background or association with a group or organization, but mostly they adhere differently because of each person's unique response to life. Also, keep in mind that individuals may not always use the specific communication style of their native culture. The person's basic personality, present emotions, and past experiences, along with influences from their primary family, native culture, and childhood neighborhood are all factors.

This hit home when I traveled in Europe, as a tourist on a shuttle questioned, "What are the folks in your neighborhood like?" One of my island grands later asked me the same question.

Having more time, I responded, "Deep down, we share a few similar values—family and education. The original design of our moderate-size, single-story, midcentury, ranch-style homes consist mostly of three or four bedrooms, all close to one another. The master bedroom is not a suite but a tad larger than the other bedrooms. But whom we each love, how we prioritize time, give to others, spend money, vote, and live life is considerably varied."

As I previously mentioned, body language, facial expressions, and attire are distinct among various professions, companies, industries, and regions of the country. In more homogeneous cultures or subcultures such as industries, communication styles don't alter as much. When in Nevis, we occasionally enjoy lunch at the Four Seasons Resort, which offers group packages, especially to business and professional groups. They are mostly similar, but after observing one group, I told my husband, "These people look like they are from the technology world," and they were.

Communication style among people in the same profession is challenging for individuals from other linguistic and cultural backgrounds. The different dress codes and communication styles among members of an accounting firm confused a Japanese accountant who wanted to be appropriate. In his native homogeneous Japanese society, differences in communication norms within an industry were almost nonexistent, and they invariably accorded respect to a supervisor.

Because each person is unique, the values and communication style of a person's native culture influence each person differently. To illustrate my point, picture the sky. What color do you think of? Although the sky is usually blue, at times it is also pink, fuchsia, orange, peach, mauve, gray, brown, dotted, or adorned with white clouds. At times, the sky is the background for an approaching destructive—at times a deadly—swirling gray-funneled tornado, ominously dark when preceding a hurricane, or illuminated by a stunning, though potentially destructive or deadly, lightning bolt. Have you ever seen two sunsets that look alike? Similarly, the comparison of the various cultures in tables 1, 2 and 3 in this chapter are presented as broad tendencies; not everyone in each culture adheres to a specific rule or to the same degree.

Intercultural Nonverbal Communication

A comprehensive discussion of insights, tools, and usage of the facets of nonverbal communication was presented in the chapter "Take a Look." Nonverbal communication is the most significant factor and comprises 55 percent of how you are perceived in a face-to-face conversation in the U.S. culture (Mehrabian 1981).

Except for time usage and priorities, that chapter also covers the essentials to comprehend the following pertinent intercultural nonverbal communication material. If you have not yet read the chapter "Take a Look," I recommend that you first read that chapter to best grasp and apply the following information.

Table 1. *Comparison of Traditional Nonverbal Communication Styles of Mainstream U.S. American, Latino, Far East Asian, and Middle Eastern Cultures*

Mainstream U.S. American	Latino	Far East Asian	Middle Eastern
Facial Expression Display rules. Controlled or different facial expression.	Minimal display rules. Often show much facial expression.	Strong display rules. May show little or different facial expression.	Minimal display rules. Arabs show strong facial expression. Persians may vary in expressing.
Eye Contact Necessary to maintain when speaking. Those of African heritage may look down while listening.	Usually maintain eye contact. May stare, which may be offensive to others.	May not look directly in the eye; may appear to lack interest, confidence, or honesty.	Eye contact is necessary, especially between men. May even stop and face each other when walking and talking.
Body Space Usually between 1.5 and 4.0 feet.	Stand close together, 1.5–2.5 feet.	Stand 2 feet or more apart.	Stand quite close to each other. Arabs may need to feel the other's breath.
Body Contact/Touch Minimal touching except persons of the same gender in the African heritage.	Much touching when talking, especially with same gender.	Usually no touching in public.	Much touching when talking with persons of the same gender.
Gestures Gestures vary. Women use more than men.	May use many and broad gestures.	Usually no gestures; if used, they are quite limited.	May use many and very broad gestures.
Emotions Somewhat controlled in public.	Usually display more than in US.	Very controlled in public.	Men and women may be emotional in public.

Monochronic/ Polychronic Time Medicine is polychronic, many tasks at a time. Business is monochronic. Task often more important than person.	Business is polychronic. Many tasks at one time. Person may be more important than task. Often late.	Business is monochronic. One task, event at a time. Person as important as task. Quite punctual.	Business is polychronic. Many tasks at one time. Person as important as the task. Often late.

Facial Expression

Because the people of the U.S. culture and most other cultures engage both *representational selves*, who they genuinely are and what they truly feel, and *presentational selves*, what they express in public, facial expressions portray their two selves. Because of this, *display rules* are necessary. *Display rules* are *facial masks* that are unwritten rules of each culture, which determine what type of and how much facial expression is appropriate in various personal and professional settings. Many cultures have *display rules*. Carley H. Dodd, in *Dynamics of Intercultural Communication*, states that Ekman and Freisen first noted that the Japanese hid their negative emotions with a smile. Northern Europeans and most *USAans* control their facial expressions or change them to convey what they feel is appropriate. The expressions may not represent their true feelings (Dodd 1991).

In most professional or vocational environments, you don't let your true feelings "hang out." A computer programmer from a major insurance company found this deception most difficult to accept when she began her career in California. In her former Soviet Union homeland, she knew that to survive, she had to lie about her political views. She didn't think that she would have to be deceptive to survive in the U.S. workforce. To her deep disappointment and frustration, she soon learned that she couldn't express the truth about the facts that she discovered while working on her projects; she had to keep much to herself. She had to display a *presentational-self* facial expression contrary to what she felt.

Latino cultures typically show fewer display rules. Individuals from Latino cultures often exhibit facial expressions that more closely reflect what they feel. Far East Asian cultures engage *display rules*. Individuals from those cultures have the same emotions of joy, pain, anger as other human beings, but traditionally, they don't display their facial expressions in public. If they do, they slightly reveal the facial expression. Instead of a broad smile, persons may slightly smile and often smile through their eyes, not their mouths. In traditional Japanese culture, it was inappropriate to publicly express anger or frustration. Traditionally, smiles to mask anger or negative feelings are appropriate. If a person of an Asian culture or any culture smiles in response to a *USAan* who is upset, a misunderstanding may occur because others do not understand the person's response. This and the different types of *giggle responses* presented later in this chapter are often a source of confusion.

In the Middle East, although facial expression is often more animated, the number of facial expression varies. Again, the individual's personality influences differences, along with the style of their primary family and native culture.

A personable and caring internist from Taiwan, involved in litigation, showed no facial expression. Yet he was quite concerned about his patients. He stated that in his native culture, being involved in litigation was a very serious matter that requires a serious attitude; smiling did not reflect that. Therefore, he felt it was inappropriate to smile during testimony. I explained that to help him present himself in a way that more accurately portrayed his caring nature, a smile at the appropriate times is beneficial. Similarly, it was challenging for an otolaryngologist of Korean heritage to learn to smile to convey his care to patients.

Eye Contact

Eye contact, looking into the other person's eyes while conversing with them, is extremely important in the U.S. culture. Eye contact conveys honesty, interest, concern, and confidence. When a person does not make or maintain eye contact, others often perceive that they are dishonest, are disinterested, don't care, or lack confidence. This creates mistrust, confusion, or frustration, especially in a health-care environment. Most *USAans*, and especially those of Latino heritage, prefer that their physicians display warmth, empathy, or concern. Eye contact and a smile validate these feelings. I repeatedly heard, "Why is it so difficult for my doctor to look into my eyes when we are talking?" It is also difficult for some people of other cultures or religions to make eye contact with individuals of the opposite sex. This is especially significant for those who are of observant Jewish or Muslim faiths. Eye contact is essential in all professions but especially paramount in the health care, education, and business fields and the judicial system.

Historically, in the African heritage and Native American communities, it was, and often remains, appropriate and polite to look away while listening. Occasionally, as a sign of respect and attentiveness, individuals from these backgrounds only make eye contact when they begin to speak. Those of Native American heritage may look sideways instead of directly at the person. If a person of these backgrounds avoids direct eye contact when they are spoken to, their conversation partner will often perceive them as rude because they are unaware of these customs. Occasionally, others also avoid direct eye contact for the same reasons. Sustained eye contact is often interpreted as a challenge to authority (Taylor 1989). In some subcultures in the United States and many cultures abroad, people, especially boys or men, "check each other out." They also "size each other up" to determine if the other person is friendly, receptive, or harmful or carries a displayed or concealed weapon.

In the Arab culture, maintaining eye contact is appropriate and essential even with members of the same sex. Eye contact is so relevant that when simultaneously walking and talking, people often stop walking and face the person with whom they are conversing. In this instance, eye contact is never broken during conversation.

If you are a *USAan* conversing with an individual from another culture and they don't look at you, don't use your U.S. norm to interpret and give meaning to their lack of eye contact. Try to realize that just because a person from a different culture or religion doesn't make eye contact does not imply that they are not concerned, don't care, or lack interest, honesty, or confidence. It may be extremely difficult for them to change a pattern that has been deeply ingrained since their earliest childhood as a "don't do."

Although I do not equate the acts as equally important, I would like to point out that similarly to the same way children raised in the United States are taught not to pick their noses in public, traditionally, individuals of Asian culture were taught not to make eye contact in many situations.

Body Space

In *Silent Language*, Edward T. Hall states that one reason people think of one another as "pushy" is their use of body space (1959). Comfortable body space is established early in life and usually remains set with an individual their entire life. When interacting, *USAans* usually prefer one and a half to three and a half feet between them. Latinos are usually comfortable with less space and stand between one and a half and two and a half feet apart. Far East Asians like more space and usually stand two feet or more apart. In the Middle East, both Israeli and Arabic men stand quite close to other males of their own culture. In the Arab culture, it is considered appropriate and necessary to feel the heat of the other person's breath when talking. Studies indicate that of all cultures, Arab men stand the closest to each other and Japanese men stand the farthest apart from each other when talking or walking.

When a high school student was offended by how near some of her male classmates of Mexican heritage stood next to her, she remarked, "They are invading my space." I explained that in the Mexican culture, people stand closer to each other than they do in the U.S. culture. It wasn't until she grew up and traveled abroad that she began to comprehend that trait. Understanding something doesn't necessarily make us more comfortable, but hopefully, it promotes greater tolerance and acceptance for others' norms.

To respect the comfort of a person's private space, it is important to monitor their movements in relation to you. If they pull back, they may personally prefer more space, or they may be uncomfortable with what you are saying or how you are expressing it. If a person moves closer to you, they prefer less space between you or are indicating an interest in what you say. If you are okay, remain at your comfort zone; if you are uncomfortable, step back. To help bridge the gap that you sense, you can soften your voice or add a sincere smile. During the years when I presented to physicians, I asked them to stand next to me. In my experience, a Vietnamese male doctor stood the farthest apart and a Jewish male doctor from New York stood the nearest. Your personal comfort is the most decisive factor in deciding how close or apart you stand or sit to another person.

Touch

Touch is primal and basic in human beings. Touch is also an important aspect of conversation for those of African, Mediterranean, and some Latino (especially Mexican) cultures (Smith, Willis, and Gier 1980). Gesture-expressions such as "High five," "Give me five," or "Slap me some skin" began in the African culture community and are now mainstream. They are greetings or signs of agreement. My granddaughter began using the "high five" gesture when she was two years old. A general contractor of African heritage showed me numerous hand-touch forms and movements that convey individualism and camaraderie during greetings.

An extended family member of African heritage shared that she grew up in a home where there wasn't much touching or display of affection among her nuclear family. She is a very warm, witty, and capable woman, and although she hugs our family members, she isn't usually a touchy-feely person. Her primary family's culture and basic nature played a greater role in her discomfort than did her "Black heritage."

Those "acceptable" and familiar pats on a child's head in the United States (which the child may or may not appreciate) are usually offensive to people of African, Thai, or Vietnamese cultures. People from Vietnam consider their heads to be their holy spiritual center and do not want others to touch them. Some people of African heritage are offended when others touch their hair.

Touching is not an acceptable way of communicating with strangers or business associates in many Asian cultures. A merchant of Korean heritage in Los Angeles placed change on the counter instead of handing it to patrons; this practice deeply offended a patron of African heritage. If an individual from an Asian culture doesn't place your change directly in your hand but instead lays it on the counter, it may not reflect prejudice or mean anything against you. Similarly, if a salesperson hangs a clothing article on a hook instead of helping you into it, it may not be due to discrimination or a personal slight. It is often a customary response of their native culture. This is even more puzzling or challenging to accept when the other person is of a culture that engages in touch or holding hands and you are not.

Lack of touching often remains a real challenge when doctors or nurses from nontouching cultures serve patients of African or Mexican cultures. Many patients or parents from Mexico expect their pediatricians to touch or hug their children during an office visit. A pediatrician of Asian heritage had a considerably difficult time when her patient's parents encouraged their child to "kiss the doctor goodbye." The doctor learned to extend her arms so the child could hug her to bridge a cultural gap. The parents felt good about the physical contact, and the pediatrician was relieved that she didn't have to kiss the child.

The opposite also causes misunderstandings. When physicians, nurses, nurses' aides, or teachers of African or Latino cultures—or any touching culture—use touch to express their care and concern, some patients, residents, or students who are not from a touching culture dislike the gesture. This is particularly challenging in skilled nursing facilities for geriatric residents. The residents who come from Asian cultures are often offended when nursing aides touch them to show they care. If a person is uncomfortable, respect them, support their comfort, and don't touch them unless it is necessary to perform your duties.

During my lectures with physicians, some from differing cultures were uneasy in responding to friendly hugs from a patient or parent, which is paramount to people in many cultures. Comfort in hugging was exceptionally pertinent in Southern California, where many residents are of Mexican heritage. They are distrustful of individuals who seem distant, especially when treating their children. During the role-playing, as I hugged a physician from an Asian culture, he patted me on the behind. I stood back, smiled, and inquired where he learned that. He said that he watched football and when the team goes into a huddle, before they break to play, they sometimes pat one another on the rear.

A physician from the Philippines specializing in obstetrics and gynecology shared that he had two patients who were sisters from India. Even after he had delivered her child, one sister remained quite uncomfortable with any touching or examination by the doctor, yet her sister was okay. Each sister's personality, experience, or beliefs, and not necessarily their culture, were the factors in their opposing comfort levels during examinations. At times, patients of any culture can be uncomfortable with disrobing or having physicians check their pulse by touching their wrist, neck, or ankle. The examination of the genital area may feel intrusive or invasive and may be more challenging for a woman if the physician is of another culture or male. This type of examination is necessary for further diagnoses or to rule out the presence of any unusual or life-threatening lump or other signs of disease.

I observed that individuals who are perceived as the most important often initiate touching. It is sad that a friendly touch on the hand, arm, or shoulder, given in genuine friendship to a person who enjoys the touch, depends on rank or status. This is my personal belief and certainly not mainstream U.S. culture.

Touch is offensive for any individual who does not like to be touched or touched in a place or manner that is not welcome or professional. It is abusive and considered sexual harassment. In your personal life, the amount and placement of touch is always your choice.

An endearing gesture named "mano po" expresses the utmost respect that Filipinos have for their grandparents. When a child greets a grandparent, they typically reach out and place the front of their grandparents' hand on their forehead to receive their blessings. This gesture is not restricted to grandparents or elderly relatives but is often offered to other elderly folks.

Some elderly people are comforted by a soft touch, but others don't enjoy or appreciate it. When I used to serve seniors as a speech pathologist, they often shared how much they appreciated a kind, gentle touch. So if you work with the elderly, the *handi-abled*, those in rehabilitation, or other patients, or if you are in any situation where the person is more vulnerable, be aware so that you express extra care. If you and the person are comfortable with touching or stroking, they probably would appreciate an occasional loving touch.

Gesture

Gestures are used more frequently by women than by men in mainstream U.S. culture and are often used by people from Mediterranean cultures, especially Italian, Greek, and some Latino cultures. Jewish people often use many gestures. I consulted with an obstetrician of Mexican heritage, and she was quite emotional, as expressed in her broad sweeping gestures. Her attorneys felt she did not portray a good professional image for her upcoming deposition. After I had suggested that we focus on toning down her gestures and voice and encouraged her to engage those new communication skills during the deposition, she was more comfortable. She was pleased to find that her case was dropped. Use of gestures and display of emotions are strongly influenced by native cultures, but they must be appropriate for the culture and the situation in which a person finds themselves.

It was surprising to see a warm, caring gynecologist from Russia use his index finger in a strong, downward pecking gesture while telling a patient that she had cancer. In his native culture, the gesture meant this is urgent and to take care of it immediately—in the same way an exclamation mark in written communication serves to inform. In the United States and many other cultures, that sharp downward gesture clearly sends a degrading message to a patient. When I explained the meaning of the gesture to the physician, he was appalled. Urgency, not degradation, was his intention. This is another example of opposing meanings among differing cultures that lead to misunderstandings.

Attire

An integral part of the distinctive beauty of people from other cultures is their wardrobe and fashion. Many mainstream U.S. styles now include looks from other cultures. These clean, sleek, muted, bold, or floral prints made their way into U.S. fashion. Dressing appropriately, especially for those who are *Born-abroad*, is occasionally challenging. What is considered modest in one family, region, or culture may not be reasonable or acceptable or may even be completely inappropriate in another. People from other cultural backgrounds may be totally unaware what attire would be appropriate for a given function or may misinterpret terms such as *business attire, sporty, beachwear, funky, casual, dressy casual, cocktail, semi-formal,* or *formal*. If a person's apparel is completely inappropriate and you attend similar social events or you are both in the same professional settings, you could inform them. In a kind, *source-connected* way, first connect and ask what attire is appropriate for different venues in their culture, then inform them as to what is appropriate for the occasion in the U.S.A. Ultimately, what they wear is their choice, but with the additional information, they can make an informed choice.

When attending religious services or government functions of Middle Eastern or Asian cultures, conservative attire is best. To be safe, revealing cleavage, wearing miniskirts, or exposing shoulders, arms, and knees may be inappropriate. If you are uncertain, inquire before attending. Pants and pantsuits are appropriate in most situations in the United States.

Scent

People from other cultures often derive pleasure from natural scents of the human body. They choose not to mask the scent with deodorants or artificial or natural fragrances, so they do not realize the importance of masking body odors in the U.S. culture. Oral hygiene, including brushing teeth twice daily and periodically visiting the dentist for cleaning, is not as common in all other cultures. Various cultures have different personal hygiene standards. If a person's body odor is offensive, first mindfully *source-connect* and inquire how odors are perceived in their native culture. Then, explain how body odors are perceived in the United States. If you have the time and desire, offer to go to the drugstore with the person and show them the multitude of fragrances used in the U.S culture to mask unpleasant odors. If not, inform them of the numerous fragrances and deodorants available. The Chumash Indians of Southern California rubbed sage leaves under their arms to improve body odors.

People from different cultures add different spices to their food. Sometimes, these spices' odors linger in clothing that the person wears to work or school. If the food smells unpleasant, in a nice way, show the person or their caretaker how to use airtight containers so the odors don't escape. In North Hills, a suburb of Los Angeles, California, an international potluck served as an innovative high school fund-raiser. Additionally, the potluck meal served various ethnic foods and is a positive example of sharing a pleasant experience to break down cultural barriers.

Emotions

Not too long ago, in the United States, you rarely revealed your true feelings in professional settings and crying usually wasn't appropriate nor considered an "acceptable professional image" unless a death, emergency, or other tragedy recently occurred. In other cultures, specific feelings are not expressed in public. As stated earlier, in the Japanese culture, a person smiles in public to hide anger or frustration. Thanks to social media, these social norms regarding feeling and publicly expressing our true emotions are gaining tolerance, acceptance, and support. Teenagers feel they can readily express their emotions in all forms of social media, though many choose not to.

Military personnel used to represent one group in the US culture in which a person kept a "stiff upper lip." On a visit to Ohio in the early 1990s, I stopped to visit a family whose children I once babysat. The father, who had been in the Navy and the Navy Reserve for several years, was now in his seventies. He had devoted decades of personal time to his community coaching and refereeing basketball, serving as mayor and on the city council. He was one of the most liked and respected people I have ever met. While visiting him and his wife, I observed that during personal interactions, he often smiled and was quite friendly with everyone. Yet in most of the pictures commemorating his service or pictures with his family, he usually bore a serious facial expression. When I spoke with him about this, he shared that during World War II, when he was twenty-one years old, he was a skipper for a ship of thirty-five soldiers. During that past wartime, U.S. leaders usually publicly portrayed a stoic and stern image. Decades later, his military experiences still affected how he presented himself.

That rigid control has changed. The 1995 photo of Captain Scott F. O'Grady, who was miraculously rescued from Bosnia, showed his tearful embrace when he was reunited with his friend. Now, in the second decade of the twenty-first century, it is common to see visions of our current soldiers' and veterans' homecoming. Upon their return, they immediately head off to surprise their families, often interrupting classrooms to hug and shower love on their children. Everyone is delighted to see the full spectrum of ecstatic shouts and joyful tears that erupt from loved ones who find that their husband, wife, partner, mother, father, son, daughter, or friend is home safe with them.

At the opposite end of the spectrum are the heart-wrenching views of the funerals in the Middle East of either Israeli or Palestinian fatalities, which are broadcast to many of our screens. Typically, the families and friends wail with heartbroken grief. Does their intense wailing suggest that death is more heart-wrenching to them than to those who are stoic and hold their feelings close to their heart? I don't know. I would guess that people feel deep pain in every culture. How much they allow themselves to feel or display their grief, how they power through, or how quickly they shift to feel gratitude for having had that person in their lives significantly differs.

In most Asian cultures, people of older generations keep their personal feelings to themselves more than younger folks. Again, the advent of social media furthers the blending of the Asian, U.S American, and other cultures as differences erode, indicating new trends in the global society.

Remember, you may observe another person's expression, behavior, and emotion without necessarily knowing the reason behind their expression or lack thereof. Does a person who doesn't express strong feelings through facial expression, gesture, or voice have strong feelings? I think so. In talking with my *Born-abroad* clients, they repeatedly shared that although they have strong and deep feelings, they do not publicly display them. We can measure emotions, yet we are in the infancy of measuring feelings (Damasio 2003).

Time

Time travels through space and is a gift that we cannot buy, and time waits for nobody. How an individual prioritizes or spends time is a personal preference. Culture plays a significant role in determining what does and doesn't have value. The importance of leisure, education, sports, family, travel, and career is culturally influenced. In the end, when given a choice, each person decides how to spend their time and prioritize what is meaningful to them. Whether they honor that commitment is another question.

Monochronic and Polychronic Time

In *Dynamics of Intercultural Communication*, Carley H. Dodd (1991) discusses monochronic and polychronic time orientation and how they are used. Monochronic time notes that people perform tasks one at a time and punctuality is paramount. Since those in the U.S. business world focus heavily on time constraints, individuals usually complete tasks in a systematic order, especially when deadlines are pressing. In that arena, time is spent with one client at a time and the organization does not interact with three different clients in different rooms as you alternate between them. In monochronic settings, being punctual and meeting deadlines are often more crucial than interpersonal interactions or getting the task completed accurately.

In some medical practices, physicians first consult with the patient, then examine the patient, then again consult with the same patient to relate on-site test results and examination findings. Once that patient's visit and documentation are complete, the physician moves on to the next patient. This represents the usual routine of regular and boutique practices, also referred as concierge, 360, or some other names. The physician focuses on one patient at a time and is only interrupted for emergencies.

In polychronic time, time is less rigid and more responsive to arising circumstances. So numerous tasks occur simultaneously and workers shift from one task to another as necessary. Some physicians practice in polychronic time. In that situation, a physician often shifts from patient to patient and activity to activity. They examine a patient, take phone calls, examine another patient, make notations, send a patient to the lab, examine another patient, and then consult face-to-face with an earlier patient.

In the business world, *USAans* and people from Far East Asia are usually punctual. Dodd states, "Latin American, African, Middle Eastern, and Southern European cultures tend to be polychronic, though individuals clearly tend to be one way or another" (Dodd 1991). In these cultures, especially in Central America, you may tend to several things at once, meet with different people, and move from office to office or task to task. People from the Philippines (Filipinos) are often less punctual, which is similar to the more relaxed Latino attitudes than neighboring Far East Asians' punctual norms. There is another substantial difference. People conforming to cultures of polychronic time place as much priority, if not more, on the personal relationship rather than the task. When the interaction with the client is complete, they may chat for couple moments rather than leave to be "on time" for their next appointment.

People in monochronic cultures prioritize the task more than the person, so the commitment to the person is not as strong. Challenges arise when people from monochronic cultures work with individuals from polychronic cultures, creating asynchrony. These differences often lead to misunderstandings in personal or professional situations.

Different Ways to Prioritize Time

People of other cultures and some of U.S culture prioritize their use of time differently; some value family more than monetary gains. They take time off from work that *USAans* would not. A husband may think nothing of taking the afternoon to sit in the doctor's office while his wife undergoes a routine examination. Whenever an illness or extreme challenge occurs within the extended family, they take necessary time from their jobs to lend support.

Many folks, regardless of cultural background, choose not to work overtime at greater pay. They also reject promotions that demand more responsibility, longer hours, or require travel that necessitates time away from family. A person who refuses such opportunities may appear lazy, ungrateful, or unambitious to others. None of these may be true; their values are simply different. At times, *USAans* judge these "family first" decisions as irresponsible.

Many individuals from other cultures are ambitious and hold more than one job. They might also work sixteen hours a day to make ends meet, get ahead, help their extended family, or save money for a lofty goal. Often, those individuals are recent immigrants, living paycheck to paycheck at a measly or minimum wage, not a living wage.

In my experience, people of Mexican heritage significantly value time with their primary and extended family members, including their siblings, parents, grandparents, and great-grandparents. They cherish and feel a strong responsibility to assist, perform their duties, and help their elders as necessary. A woman of Mexican heritage who became one of my closest friends and referred to me as a "soul mate" grabbed my attention at a professional event when she expressed the importance of family. Although she is a leader at a polytechnic university, she continues to carve out time to equally share responsibility to provide aid and comfort to her and her husband's aging and ailing parents.

Regardless of culture, some people value personal and leisure time and time with family more than they value career advancement. It is a different set of values—again not right or wrong, but possibly different from yours.

Different Paces and Concepts of Time

Traveling between New York City, Nevis, West Indies, and laid-back San Fernando Valley in California, I noticed a difference in pace. Naturally, Nevis's tempo was the most relaxed. Even younger people walk slower than me. New Yorkers generally have a lot to do, and so they usually move more rapidly. I live in Southern California, which is more casual and slower paced. Not having traveled to Asia, I am unfamiliar with their tempo.

Native Americans and people from other cultures also view time differently. In the Hopi culture, there is no word for *time*, e.g., seconds, minutes, or hours; nevertheless, Hopi Indians live by time. "They perceive time in organic or natural phenomena, such as a sunrise, position of the stars or moon" (Restak 1988). The friend who took care of our children when we traveled in the 1980s and who now stays in our home when we travel or are in Nevis told me, "It is amazing that I grew up in a small mountainous village by a river in Mexico. There were no clocks in the entire village. We just knew when to come home and when to eat meals."

In some cultures, members also do not conform to an external clock. Their internal clock or instinct signals when to move from activity to activity, when to rise, eat meals, and go to bed. Some Native Americans believe that the time to do something is when they feel like it; they eat when they are hungry and sleep when they are tired. Elizabeth Woody (1994) recalls visiting relatives; some slept on the floor, while others ate together.

A supervisor from a rehabilitation facility called me for advice on how to teach patients from Native American cultures to keep their appointments. I suggested that she first acknowledge that they often keep time by the position of the moon and the stars in the sky. They sow, reap, hold ceremonies, and travel guided by the celestial navigators. In a mindful and *source-connected* tone, inform the patient that at the rehabilitation facility, a clock tells time. That is as important in keeping appointments and order at the facility as the stars and moon were when the patient was home planting and harvesting crops.

My husband and I were invited to a wedding in which the bride and groom were of Persian heritage; the invitation called for the ceremony to begin at 8:30 p.m. When we arrived shortly before that time, neither the wedding party nor the guests had arrived. We later learned that the other Iranian guests understood that the wedding wouldn't begin until later in the evening. We also experienced this when attending concerts and when we were invited to our first New Year's Eve party in Nevis. We arrived at the family's home around 10:00 p.m., to find only the lights, tables, and chairs. Except for the bartender, who continued to set up, no other person was present. When we inquired where everybody was, he told us that they were in church and they would be home later.

As a *USAan*, you have attained a broader understanding of how individuals of other cultures are usually guided by different norms and preferences in their use of body language, eye contact, personal space, touch, gesture, appearance, and time. As a *Born-abroad* individual, you have gained insights and tools that are essential. Along with mindfulness and *source-connection*, these facets further comfortable, productive, and fulfilling conversations with folks of differing cultural backgrounds.

Intercultural Voice Tone and Rhythm

A comprehensive discussion of insights, tools, and usage of the facets of voice tone and rhythm was presented in the chapter "It's Not What You Say, but How You Say It." Voice tone and rhythm are significant factors that comprise 38 percent of how you are perceived in a face-to-face conversation in the U.S. culture (Mehrabian 1981).

Except for tonal, that chapter covers the essentials to comprehend the following pertinent intercultural voice tone and rhythm information. If you have not yet read the chapter "It's Not What You Say, but How You Say It," I recommend that you first read that chapter to best grasp and apply the following information.

Table 2. *Comparison of Traditional Vocal Features and Rhythm of Mainstream U.S. American, Latino, Far East Asian, Middle Eastern, Indian, and Pakistani Languages*

Mainstream U.S. American	Latino	Far East Asian	Middle Eastern	Indian and Pakistani
Projection Project in front of the mouth to speak U.S. English well.	Project except when they do not feel comfortable or competent.	Do not project, making it challenging to understand. May appear as mumbling.	Do not project, making it challenging to understand. May appear as mumbling.	Do not project, making it challenging to understand. May appear as mumbling.
Rate 125–160 words per minute. Too fast or too slow may have negative impact.	Not available.	Not available.	Not available.	Often quite rapid.
Volume *USAans* speak louder than those of most cultures. Appropriate volume reflects confidence.	Not quite as loud as *USAans*. If not loud enough, may not be perceived as confident.	Much softer-spoken, especially women. May sound uncertain or incorrectly perceive a *USAan* as angry when using a loud voice.	Volume varies. If not loud enough, may be perceived as lacking confidence.	Softer-spoken than *USAans*, especially women. If not loud enough, may be perceived as lacking confidence.
Tonal Not used in U.S. English.	Not applicable.	Vary tones to give meaning.	Not applicable.	Not applicable.
Intonation/ Pitch Levels Necessary to intone key words; shows interest, competence, and confidence.	Good intonation patterns.	Minimal intonation, making it challenging to understand the intention. May be perceived as uninterested or lacking confidence.	Minimal intonation, making it challenging to understand the intention. May be perceived as not interested or lacking confidence.	Almost no intonation patterns, making it hard to understand pronunciation and intention. May be seen as uninterested or unsure.

Phrasing Necessary pauses at the appropriate places. Important in the rhythm and for comprehension.	Good phrasing patterns.	Different phrasing patterns; pauses after each syllable, not phrase. May be challenging to understand or perceived as abrupt.	May have different phrasing patterns, making it challenging to understand. May be perceived as abrupt.	May have different phrasing patterns, making it challenging to understand. May be perceived as abrupt.

Projection

Projection is the first feature in the foundation of voice tone and rhythm when speaking U.S. English. In my professional experience, no other language projects as much as U.S. English. When an individual speaks U.S. English, projection is required to be understood and convey confidence. Projection has nothing to do with volume but refers to direction. Many *USAan*s misinterpret lack of projection as mumbling.

In a previous section of this chapter, you learned that everyone has a responsibility in an intercultural conversation. However, *USAans* typically do not make the additional effort to understand the *Born-abroad* individual or those with a heavy accent. When a *USAan* listens to a person who does not project and sounds as if they mumble, the message is challenging to comprehend. In addition, a *USAan* often perceives that the person lacks confidence, is not interested, does not care, or is hiding something. Lack of projection by ESL speakers reflects a communication pattern adapted from the person's native language, not necessarily lack of confidence, disinterest, or dishonesty.

In many cultures, including the Far East Asian, and especially Indian and Pakistani languages, use of projection is very different from U.S. English. When speaking those languages, it is considered rude and appears crass to speak with one's mouth open so much that a person's teeth are exposed. However, when speaking U.S. English, a person has to open their mouth wide enough to project so that they don't mumble.

I often had a challenging time convincing clients that projecting in U.S. English is necessary and appropriate and that it would not change the way they speak their native language. Projection is not a difficult skill to learn. Resistance comes from changing an *attitude* about what is appropriate in their native culture to what is acceptable in the U.S. culture, which is often the exact opposite. The acceptance of different standards often takes a far longer time than actually learning to project. A woman from India was quite soft-spoken with slight projection. With her as an insurance agent, it was necessary to project more and speak louder to service an older clientele. Many complained that they couldn't understand her. When a manager offered her classes to improve her projection so that clients could better understand, she declined and returned to her computer data-entry position.

Pitch

Pitch is the second fundamental feature in the foundation of voice tone. There are four pitch levels in U.S. English. In the Chinese languages, there are several pitch levels to convey meaning, often of the same word. In some Chinese and Filipino dialects, speech is spoken at a higher pitch than in most other languages. In U.S. English, appropriately raising and lowering pitch to influence intonation is an essential feature for clarifying meaning. Pitch levels and intonation were presented in the chapter "It's Not What You Say, but How You Say It."

Rate

Rate is the third fundamental feature in the foundation of voice tone and rhythm. Some people naturally speak rapidly, as they also process information quickly. Even when these individuals master U.S. English, they continue to speak their acquired language quite fast. A person's basic nature also affects how rapidly or slowly they speak. Usually, the Indian and Pakistani languages are spoken rapidly. Therefore, the pronunciation of the words from these regions often remains challenging to grasp due the differing projection and intonation patterns.

People from the Southern states often speak more slowly than people from other sections of the country. I consulted with professionals from the South who perceived their slower speech as sounding "dumb." I assured them that if the other features of their communication are good, a slower rate is not going to be detrimental. Former President Jimmy Carter is a slower speaker, yet he is quite articulate. In the South, if a person speaks too fast, others in that region may request that they slow down.

Volume

Volume is the fourth fundamental feature in the foundation of voice tone and rhythm. Volume is the loudness of a language. Those of you who have traveled abroad or are *Born-abroad* know that U.S. English is one of the louder languages spoken. Just sit in any airport and listen to which language is among the loudest. There are regions in the United States where people speak louder than other regions. The communication style of one's primary family and native culture also influences volume. The loud and demanding voices of some *USAan*s are often annoying or frightening to people from "softer voice tone" cultures. Whatever the age, gender, or culture, a loud voice can frighten anyone who is not accustomed to being spoken to in that manner. It is important to become aware of how loudly or softly you speak. Monitor your voice to assure that it is not offensive to others and is appropriate for the situation and place.

Women in many cultures are more soft-spoken than men. A loud or harsh voice may be even more intimidating to them. Often, people, especially men, are perceived as angry when they raise their voice or talk loudly, although they are actually just expressing their passion. In other cultures, even the slightest increase in volume implies anger. If you are a *USAan* and use normal volume and projection, you may still be overbearing to an individual from an Asian culture or to a person from the United States.

I am constantly amazed that the manicurists I know, who are from Vietnam, speak in almost-inaudible tones yet their colleagues who are across the room pick up every nuance and word.

Intonation

Intonation is the fifth factor in the foundation of voice tone and rhythm. Intonation gives additional meaning to what you say and is an essential aspect of spoken U.S. English. In many other languages, intonation, as used in U.S. English, does not exist. The languages of Far East Asia, India, and Pakistan use very little modulation in their intonation patterns. David Alan Stern states, "There are no unstressed syllables in the Persian (Farsi), Arabic, or Turkish languages" (Stern 1982).

Who determines which words are highlighted or have more intonation? Established linguistic rules set the norm. But each speaker chooses how much stress and emphasis they want to use. They also intone the accurate word or words in response to specific questions asked. However, there are some basic rules for words that typically receive the most stress or the least stress on intonation. In U.S. English, the following words are stressed and listed in order of their decreasing degree of importance:

- *Nouns*—words for names of persons, places, abstract ideas, or things
- *Verbs*—words to describe action, states, or occurrences
- *Adjectives*—words to describe or modify a noun or pronoun
- *Adverbs*—words that qualify or modify an adjective, verb, or other adverb and often end with the letters *-ly* or *-ily*, such as *slowly, happily,* or *very happily*
- *Numbers and expressions of quantity*—one, twenty, many, some, quart, liter
- *Possessive pronouns*—mine, yours, ours, theirs, his, hers
- *Negatives*—no, not, never, none
- *Grammatical words*—which do not have specific meaning but are necessary for sentence structure, such as articles like *a, an, the* and conjunctions such as *and, but,* and *or*

Because of the different intonation patterns, even folks who are confident, fascinating, and interested often lack understanding of the necessity of these features. Again, they adapt appropriate communication traits from their native language and apply those traits, which are inappropriate, when they speak U.S. English.

If you are a *mainstream USAan* conversing with an individual who speaks another language or is from another cultural background, please understand that although you accurately observe their lack of intonation, you may have no clue as to the reason.

Stressing different words gives different *meaning* and *intention* to your thoughts. Listen for the difference in meaning of the sentences in the sets below. Say aloud the first sentence without stressing *this*. Next, say aloud the second sentence saying *this* slightly slower and louder while slightly raising the pitch. In the sentences below, capitalization and italics represent the words that require the most important and primary stress and receive the strongest intonation. Capitalization only represents secondary stress and still requires strong intonation, just not as much. Intonation fluctuations on different words respond correctly to the most pertinent statements or specific questions asked. Less important words require secondary stress. The unimportant words do not require stress and are pronounced without prolonging the vowel. Remember that primary stress is given to the most important word or words in a phrase. Primary stress is often at the end of the phrase.

Listen for the different meaning between these two sentences:

- I do *NOT* have a FAX MACHINE at this OFFICE.
- I do NOT have a FAX MACHINE at *THIS* OFFICE.

The first sentence implies that you do not have a fax machine. The second sentence implies that you do not have a fax machine at this specific office but have one somewhere else.

Listen for the different meaning between the two sentences:

- I am NOT sure that I am going to *ASK* RONALD to go.
- I am NOT sure that I am going to ASK *RONALD* to go.

The first sentence implies you are not sure that you're going to ask Ronald to go, indicating you may not be sure that you are going to ask anyone to go. The second sentence implies that you are not going to specifically ask Ronald but may ask another person to go.

Listen for examples of primary, secondary, and reduced stress:

- Your *APPOINTMENT* is at TWO O'CLOCK TODAY.
- Your APPOINTMENT is at *TWO O'CLOCK TODAY.*

The first sentence stresses what is taking place. The second sentence stresses the time and date.

Except for very strong emphasis, most of the pitch changes are minimal. In the following sentences, the same sentence is given three times, each a response to a different question.

- *MS. SMITH* BOUGHT a NEW CAR TODAY.
- Ms. SMITH BOUGHT a *NEW CAR* TODAY.
- Ms. SMITH BOUGHT a NEW CAR *TODAY.*

The first sentence answers the question "Who bought a new car today?" Ms. Smith bought the car, so *Ms. Smith* receives the strongest intonation. In the second sentence, the question would be, "What did Ms. Smith buy?" She bought a new car, so *new car* receives the strongest intonation. The third sentence responds to the question "When did she buy the car?" She bought it today, so the word *today* receives greater intonation.

Phrasing

Phrasing is the sixth and final factor in the foundation of voice tone and rhythm. The pauses in U.S. English follow phrases, not singular words or syllables. Phrasing is the necessary pause at the appropriate place. If the pauses are too frequent and there are more stops than pauses, the pauses have a staccato affect. The person sounds abrupt, unfriendly, or matter-of-fact, which may not be their intention. If they don't use necessary pauses, the person's message may be challenging to follow.

In other languages, the pauses follow syllables or are interjected whenever you have to take a breath. The pauses in the phrasing patterns of the Asian languages are after each syllable, so those languages sound choppier to the *USAan* and those who speak more melodic languages. An ESL speaker of Asian heritage may sound abrupt or unfriendly because they have not acquired or mastered the more melodic phrasing patterns of U.S. English. If an Asian speaker combines the less melodic phrasing pattern with a negative voice tone, they sound even more abrupt. In U.S. English, correct phrasing patterns and prolonged vowels add melody. A person who does not use melodic patterns is often perceived rude or matter-of-fact, though that certainly is not necessarily their objective, as stated in the chapter "It's Not What You Say, but How You Say It." Many believe that the French language is the most beautiful spoken language, and I believe its resonance and melodic pattern are the keys.

A physician from Germany largely used a staccato speech pattern, similar to the beat of a metronome. During malpractice litigation, his attorney was concerned that his speech pattern would negatively affect the jury, outcome, and settlement. By modifying his phrasing patterns and prolonging his vowels, he came across as more pleasant and won the case.

In this section, slash marks \ and / are used to denote pauses and stops. Spoken words within slash marks, such as "\let's get going/," indicate a phrase that flows continuously until the next pause or stop. Slash marks / going the same direction after each syllable or one-syllable words indicate stops, not pauses. The following slashes in "I/want/ed/to/leave/yes/ter/day" are examples of pauses after each syllable.

Again, let's use a traffic signal with a yellow and red light as an analogy to compare slowing down and pausing within a phrase marker \ /, which denotes the pauses between phrases. The halting pronunciation is indicated by this marker / and denotes that each syllable or one-syllable word is followed by a pause, similar to the blinking red light in a traffic signal indicating stop; do not pause or continue to move. We do not halt long, just linger. Using this type of pattern sounds choppy. When speaking U.S. English, you do not pause, stop, or take a breath *within* a phrase.

The following two sentences are correct examples of phrasing patterns.

- \On her way to the office/\she dropped off the package./
- \On her way/\to the office/\she dropped off/\the package./

The phrasing pattern in the first sentence is correct if you do not need to stop to take an additional breath or pause to get your thoughts together. The phrasing pattern in the second sentence is also correct but allows for more pauses. If you have to think about the meaning or pronunciation of a word, you may need to take extra pauses. Just make certain that you pause correctly within a phrase and do not drop your voice tone to the lowest pitch to indicate that you are finished until you actually are.

The following three sentences show incorrect phrasing patterns.

- \On her way/to the office/she dropped off/the package./
- \On/her/way/to/the/off/ice/she/dropped/off/the/pack/age./
- \On her way to/\the office she/\dropped/\off/\the/\package./

In the first sentence, the phrasing pattern is incorrect because they are *stops*, like red lights, *instead of pauses*, like yellow lights, so the sentence sounds choppy. In the second sentence, the phrasing pattern is incorrect because the pauses are *after each syllable* rather than *after the phrase*. This pattern is often common for ESL speakers from Far East Asian countries who are learning U.S. English. When they also apply a negative voice tone, the speaker may unintentionally sound abrupt, rude, or angry. In the third sentence, the phrasing pattern is incorrect because the pauses are at random—*within* the phrase itself, not *between* the phrases. This pattern is common for ESL speakers from Middle Eastern or Asian Indian linguistic and cultural backgrounds.

The following are examples of correct and incorrect phrasing patterns in different parts of speech. Remember, the *words within phrases usually flow continuously*, and the spaces between are pauses, not stops.

Example of a noun phrase and its adjective:
- Correct: *Her blue dress*/\has a spot on it./
- Incorrect: *Her blue*/*dress* has a/\spot on it./

Example of a verb phrase and its adverb:
- Correct: \His new car/*moved slowly*/\in the traffic./
- Incorrect: \His new/\car *moved*/*slowly* in /\the traffic./

Example of a phrase in a verb phrase:
- Correct: \Mary *is coming*/\to see us./
- Incorrect: \Mary is/*coming to*/\see us./

Example of a phrase in a prepositional phrase:
- Correct: \The family left/*on a trip*/\this afternoon./
- Incorrect: \The family left *on*/*a trip* this/\afternoon./

Example of a phrase in a dependent clause:
- Correct: \The book/\that she loaned me/\is due next week./
- Incorrect: \The/\ book *that/\she loaned/\me* is due next/\week./

Following are two sets of the same sentences. The first set has no phrasing marks. The second set has the correct phrasing marks. Without looking at the second set, try to place the correct pause marks (\ /) where you would pause in your speech in the first set.

- He played golf this afternoon.
- I am going on a business trip next week.
- How far is it to the freeway?
- Who is going to the baseball game tomorrow?
- Are you going to be finished with that report by five o'clock?
- What time do you want to leave this evening?
- I want to buy some walking shoes before I go on the trip.
- I talked to the head of marketing about transferring into her department.

After you place the pause marks in the above sentences, compare them to the following correct examples:

- \He played golf/\this afternoon./
- \I am going/\on a business trip/\next week./
- \How far is it/\to the freeway?/
- \Who is going/\to the baseball game tomorrow?/
- \Are you going to be finished/\with that report/\by five o'clock?/
- \What time do you want to leave/\this evening?/
- \I want to buy some walking shoes/\before I go on the trip./
- \I want to buy/\some walking shoes/\before I go/\on the trip./
- \I talked to the head of marketing/\about transferring into her department./
- \I talked/\to the head of marketing/\about transferring/\into her department./

The extra pauses are for people who require more time to process and respond or to take another breath.

If you desire to further improve your phrasing patterns, record yourself reading aloud and during spontaneous conversations. Listen to your voice. Does it sound pleasant or rude, abrupt, or choppy? If your voice sounds unpleasant or you feel you could or want to improve, copy an interesting article from one of your favorite magazines. Note the text with the phrase marks (\ /) and read aloud until you are satisfied with the way your speech sounds. Then record and listen to your voice again. Slowly begin to use your new phrasing pattern in spontaneous, everyday communication. Set aside a few minutes a couple times a day when you will concentrate on this skill. Use *Target on Communication* (TOC) to improve this skill.

Six voice tone and rhythm factors and their applications for people who speak English as their second language were presented. Positive or negative impressions that result from how you use components in your voice are noted in the following figures. You gain how to modify your voice to give a positive or negative impression. When you communicate mindfully, *source-connectedly*, positively, effectively, and appropriately, you speak in a pleasant, caring, compassionate, confident, enthusiastic, or persuasive manner, depending on the situation and what you want to impart. All these features are positive. When a person uses negative intonation with the falling pitch solely on the key words and not during the entire sentence, that person is also positively perceived as a strong and persuasive speaker.

Positive Feeling You Want to Convey	Projection	Rate	Volume	Pitch/Intonation	Phrasing
Pleasant and compassionate	Good	125–160 words per minute	Appropriate for the situation	Appropriate intonation, rising pitch for positive and pleasant message; falling pitch for serious or negative situations	Slower
Confident	Good	Not too fast	Slightly louder on keywords	Moderate to strong on keywords	Moderate
Enthusiastic and interested	Good	125–160 words per minute	Slightly louder on keywords	Moderate to strong, using mostly rising pitch on key words	Moderate
Strong, persuasive	Good	At the slower range	Slightly louder on keywords	Moderate to strong; rising pitch for positive and pleasant message, falling pitch for serious or negative message	Moderate

Figure 6. Factors of your voice tone and rhythm that project a positive message.

Negative Feeling Possibly Conveyed	Projection	Rate	Volume	Pitch/ Intonation	Phrasing
Abrupt, rude, or brusque	May be poor, fair, or good	May be faster, 160–200 words per minute	May be too loud	Too strong or too much use of falling or negative tone pitch	Rapid phrasing results in shortened annunciation of vowels. This reduces the melody in speech.
Angry or defensive	Good	May be too fast	Too loud	Too strong or too much use of negative or falling pitch	Harsher phrasing results in shortened annunciation of vowels. This reduces the melody in speech.
Aggressive	Good	Too fast, a rapid firing type of speech	Too loud	Too strong or too much use of negative or falling pitch	Harsher phrasing results in shortened annunciation of vowels. This reduces the melody in speech.
Deceitful	Poor or good	Too fast, 160 words or more	No change	Too high	Unnatural phrasing adds to dishonest perception.
Arrogant, sarcastic, patronizing, or condescending	Good	May be too slow.	No change	Too much use of rising and slurring	May prolong vowels too much while also slurring the words
Not interested	Poor, fair, or good	May be slow	May be quieter	Lack of intonation on key words may result monotone	Not necessarily affected
Lack of confidence or weak	Poor projection	May be too slow	May be too quiet	Poor intonation on keywords; may sound monotone	Not necessarily affected

Figure 7. Factors of your voice tone and rhythm that project a negative message.

Tonal

Many Asian languages have a tonal component that gives different meanings to the same word. In some Chinese dialects, tones signal past tense, plurals, or gender. Mandarin Chinese is the predominant language spoken in China. The language's four tones give different meanings to the same word. A friend shared that his last name is in the fourth tone. If his name is pronounced with the first tone, that signifies *aunt*, the second tone notes *wheel*, and the third tone indicates *drum*. At times, people from Asian and other linguistic and cultural backgrounds inadvertently apply the tonal features of their native language to their new language. This adds a "singsong" effect when they speak U.S. English.

As a *USAan*, you gained a broader understanding of the insights of voice tone and rhythm of individuals who are ESL speakers. Please keep in mind that their primary language likely had a considerably different set of linguistic principles. As a *Born-abroad* individual, you gained insights and tools that are basic to productive, effective, and fulfilling intercultural interactions and conversations with others.

Intercultural Verbal Communication

A comprehensive discussion about the insights, tools, and usage of verbal communication was presented in the chapter "Honor Yourself and Choose Your Words Wisely." Verbal communication is the least significant factor in face-to-face communication, comprising just 7 percent of how you are perceived in a face-to-face conversation in the U.S. culture (Mehrabian 1981).

The chapter referenced above covers the essentials to comprehend the following pertinent intercultural and verbal communication information, except for the comparison of low context and high context and the giggle response. If you have not yet read the chapter "Honor Yourself and Choose Your Words Wisely," I recommend that you first read that chapter to best grasp and apply the following information.

Table 3. *Comparison of Traditional Verbal Communication Styles of Mainstream U.S. American, Latino, Far East Asian, and Middle Eastern Cultures*

Mainstream U.S.	*Latino*	*Far East Asian*	*Middle East*
Low Context / High Context Low context. For resolving issues, strong reliance on verbal, sequential, and linear processing. Person and issue are separate. *Individualism trending toward group consensus.*	Middle context. For resolving issues, reliance on verbal and intuition processing. Person and issue are not separate.	High context. For resolving issues, strong reliance on nonverbal cues and intuition. Person and issue are not separate. *Group harmony trending to include individualism.*	Middle context. For resolving issues, reliance on both verbal and intuition. Person and issues are not separate.

Direct/Indirect Communication More direct than most other cultures. Need to be direct to accomplish task. With patients, combine direct and indirect.	Indirect and direct. More indirect than *USAan*.	Very indirect. May find *USAan* direct manner offensive. Are often indirect when must be direct to be understood. Do not want to offend.	Indirect and direct. May find *USAan* direct manner offensive.
Asking Questions Very important when information is not understood.	May be reluctant. Do not want to be embarrassed.	Reluctant; seeks to avoid embarrassment. Face-saving is key in Asian culture, especially in the Japanese culture.	Reluctant. Do not want to be embarrassed.
Ability to Say "No" Very important to say "No" when necessary.	Often difficult. Will often not state "No" when necessary.	Traditionally not appropriate. Will often not state "No" when necessary. Face-saving is quite important. *This is changing.*	Often challenging. May not state "No" when necessary.
Small Talk Some do not like silence. For others, small talk is an important feature of U.S. culture. Used in introduction, conversation, closure, and to fill silences.	Very social; therefore, small talk is very important because of social values.	Silence is appropriate. Small talk is not a major aspect of Asian cultures, especially in the Japanese culture. Zen philosophy values introspection and silence.	Extremely hospitable; therefore, small talk is a very important feature of cultural values.

Low Context and High Context

"A culture in which information about procedure is rarely communicated, but is reliant on social norms, values and beliefs is a high-context culture. A culture in which coded information is abundant is a low-context culture" (Hall 1977).

In high-context cultures, there is a strong reliance on nonverbal communication—inner sense and intuition—instead of verbal communication. People of high-context cultures also rely heavily on nonverbal communication to make decisions. Information is usually inferred from the situation without explanations. When persons of high-context cultures are negotiating a long-term contract, they are not as concerned with future modifications, commitments, meeting deadlines, or production costs as they are with the *feeling* that they sense of working together in a cooperative, successful, long-term relationship. If they feel they can work with you, then they know that they will resolve issues as they occur. Because high-context cultures are more comfortable with ambiguities, there is less need for small talk or micromanagement. Therefore, those of Asian or Native American culture, who already value silence, usually prefer that to small talk.

In low-context cultures, there is a reliance on mass verbal communication and written information that advise certain procedures and protocol to perform and complete tasks. To resolve issues, they strongly rely on verbal, sequential, linear processing, and analytical and logical thinking. Handbooks, memos, videos, specific instructions, and verbal explanations to complete tasks are abundant. There is also a focus on details. Since people of low-context societies are often uncomfortable with stillness, small talk is necessary. People from low-context cultures require more time to make decisions. If they are proactive, they anticipate the many challenges that may possibly occur and try to have solutions in place in advance.

The style and manner in which the news is presented by the media reflect the differences between a high-context or a low-context culture. In high-context cultures, the news supposedly is presented "objectively" without comments from the public. In the U.S. low-context culture, when a major news story breaks, they usually analyze the event from many angles. Not only are the experts interviewed but they also ask many lay people on the street to add their opinion. Reporting on cable networks is considerably biased. Some bend the truth or do not report the entire story, and some do not consistently fact-check the report prior to its release. Major networks tend to be more progressive.

There are several other differences between high-context and low-context cultures. In a high-context culture, the person and issues are not separate. Persons believe that when you criticize an idea, you also offend the individual. In a low-context culture, persons and issues are separate. If there is an issue, the person presumes that the issue can be addressed without offending the person or that demeaning a person doesn't always matter, although that is not the case.

Other contrasts between high-context and low-context cultures are the use of direct or indirect communication style and the value of individualism or group harmony. Low-context cultures tend to be more confrontational and engage in more direct communication. This pattern was significantly apparent during the 2016 U.S. presidential election cycle. High-context cultures are less confrontational. Face-saving and harmony reflect their preferred indirect communication style.

Individualism is a paramount value in low-context cultures. Group consensus and harmony are more important in high-context cultures. Gradually, some concepts of low-context and high-context cultures began and continued to meld into one another's national mind-set and practices. Youth and young adults in Asian countries are shifting toward more assurance of their benefits, seeking shorter hours, and demanding more time off from work for relaxation and personal goals. Mainstream U.S.A. business professionals are utilizing more group consensus and team decisions in resolving issues and finding solutions. They continue to become more collaborative by encouraging those who implement the decisions to give their input. Humility is a significant feature in the Asian cultures. People from these cultures are often uncomfortable or embarrassed when receiving compliments, especially in front of their peers or others. Consequently, they may be reluctant to offer praise.

Middle-context cultures combine features of both low-context and high-context cultures. North American and Northern and Western European cultures are inclined to be low-context cultures. Middle Eastern, African, and Latin American cultures are inclined to be middle-context cultures. For a far broader and more scholarly presentation including numerous studies and anecdotes in the area of intercultural communication, I recommend *Intercultural Competence: Interpersonal Communication Across Cultures* by Myron W. Lustig and Jolene Koester (2013).

When I first entered the field of personal and intercultural communication three decades ago, the general public more rigidly defined values within each context than they do today. In the United States, individuals focused on their best interests, and in Asia, the focus was predominantly on the groups', hospitals', or organizations' best interests. During that era, throughout the United States, businesses, hospitals, and organizations began moving from individual leadership to team management and consensus building.

A social worker at a large university medical center was excited after she attended a presentation relating to decisions that were built on consensus and assuming responsibility as a team instead of assigning it to just one individual. Individuals were no longer willing to take the risk of presenting, implementing, or being responsible for decisions. They feared failure, being blamed, or facing malpractice suits. In group or team decisions, everyone assumes responsibility for the decision and its results—success or failure.

Gradually, some concepts of low context and high context melded together. An anesthesiologist from Indonesia was chief of his department. Based on his native cultural values, he tried to instill his largely culturally diverse colleagues (what he named the United Nations department) to shift focus from their individual success to concern and effort for the success of their departments, hospitals, and patients. Organizations and companies followed the trend.

During the 1994 economic downsizing climate of reprioritizing, re-evaluating, and re-engineering, he tried to inculcate his colleagues with the "team philosophy." He stressed that if each made small sacrifices, the department, the medical center, and ultimately, the patients and each individual would benefit. Instead of laying the burden on few individuals, leaders distributed the load among the team. Initially, a typical response from his colleagues was, "The other departments aren't doing it, so why should we?" His colleagues eventually learned to make shared sacrifices that benefitted the departments, hospitals, patients, and themselves. During the 2008 Great Recession, there were also rare examples of companies in which everyone from the top down made sacrifices so that they would not lay off any workers, but that was not the norm.

In 2015, even at universities, individuals can no longer criticize others' ideas. They can only respond without offending the person who brought forth or disagrees with an idea or procedure. Persons must assume greater caution to ensure that productive dialogue continues. The ultimate goal is to engage a positive path for the best solutions that benefit the students and institution.

Challenges occur when a person from a low-context culture communicates with a person from a high-context culture. A woman from Turkey had difficulty communicating with her male supervisor from Asia. Her broad gestures, strong intonation, direct style, and focus on herself turned off her supervisor of Asian heritage. When talking with him, she frequently began with "I need…" She expressed a frustrating and ongoing inability to communicate with her supervisor because he didn't listen or acknowledge her views. She and I focused on modifying her communication to bridge the communication gap. She adopted a more professional and less emotional tone, used an indirect approach, and discussed benefits for the department rather than herself. Instead of her direct and personal style "I need…," she offered, "How do you think this idea would benefit our department?" After using her new communication approach with her supervisor, she was elated that her new style and focus on group harmony worked. "He [the supervisor] listened to me for the first time in two years and actually considered what I recommended."

Direct and Indirect Communication

The decision regarding when to use indirect or direct communication is a challenge not only for ESL speakers but also for many *USAan*s. In the highly diverse U.S. culture, the actual meaning of indirect communication is often difficult to grasp. Even *USAan*s have difficulty comprehending indirect statements and knowing when to use indirect or direct communication.

The issue is exacerbated for individuals who are from cultural backgrounds in which they primarily communicate indirectly. *USAan*s use both direct and indirect communication. In indirect communication, only some information is presented. There is an assumption that you understand the implied information that is not verbalized. In homogeneous societies, it is easier to grasp such nuances because people usually have more similar experiences and expressions than in heterogeneous societies. When a manager says to her secretary, "We are out of supplies," what the manager actually implies, in an indirect manner, is, "*We need more supplies, or please order more supplies.*"

In the U.S. business world, you often have to be direct to achieve objectives. If indirect communication, such as "I could use assistance," is not getting the task completed, switch to direct communication, along with a pleasant voice and effective intonation: "Please type this report for me." I recall when my children were young and living at home. If I asked, "Could you [please] do the dishes tonight?" they had the most ingenious excuses why they couldn't. Yet when I directly stated, "Please do the dishes," they usually washed the dishes without further discussion.

Communication in the medical field is especially sensitive, as conversation focuses patients or their families on topics that are usually more personal and often critical. Unquestionably, in an emergency, communication must be direct. When speaking with a patient or their family about a serious, negative, or grave situation, or an insistent question, I recommend leading with an indirect statement, followed by a direct statement. The indirect style is not as abrupt, as it provides the initial introduction, then, when needed, shifts to the pertinent information. I once spoke with an attorney whose physician-client was sued for a too direct and unfeeling remark he made when a patient died. The doctor had walked out of the operating room and flatly told the family, "Your husband is dead," and then he walked away.

As I evaluated a doctor who had difficulty communicating positively with his colleagues, I indirectly stated, "There is a communication challenge in your department." I didn't realize until a couple of sessions later that he was unaware that he was the person with the communication difficulty. After that, I was more direct and informed the persons of their challenge and the reasons their supervisors advised them to seek help. Although it isn't easy, it is important to understand and sense the fine line between indirect and direct communication and when to use each.

Not all indirect communication is verbal. Some is nonverbal. When a Japanese businessman came to the United States for a six-month internship, he felt that his *USAan* supervisor was rude. Remaining silent, the Japanese employee stood next to his supervisor and waited for his *USAan* colleague to break his focus. The Japanese associate did not realize that after a few minutes, he had to politely interrupt to gain his attention.

Power Distance

Although equality for all humanity is a primary concern among many of our fellow global citizens, the issue of inequality—to some lesser or greater degree—exists in most places, if not everywhere. Inequality certainly is and perpetually was a major issue in the United States and other democratic nations.

"Power distance refers to the degree to which the culture believes that institutional and organizational power should be distributed unequally and the decisions of the power holders should be challenged or accepted" (Lustig and Koester 2013). Cultures that prefer small power distance minimize the inequality of people based on status. These cultures adhere to an individual's right to question or challenge authority, which can only exercise power for just purposes. Those cultures that prefer large power distance believe that each person is designated a certain place in society and individuals of lower status should not question or challenge their unequal position. Only those deemed to be in a higher position and status control that right.

This becomes challenging in the areas of nonverbal and verbal communication for students, teachers, businesspeople, and medical professionals. It is also challenging for anyone who comes from a culture that embraces small distance power and then travels, studies, works, or later lives in a culture that conforms to greater distance power. During time of pandemic crises, social distancing of at least 6 feet from one another to prevent further transmission of the virus or disease takes precedence.

Evasive

Evasiveness often comes across as flippant. A doctor from India was involved in malpractice litigation. His attorney asked, "How many people do you employ in your office?" The doctor responded, "I have several." When the doctor and I discussed his vague response, he related that he had quite a large staff that reflected his affluent practice. If he had stated the size of his staff, which clearly implies his success, he would be boasting, which is an undesirable trait in his native culture.

Asking Questions

For several reasons, asking questions is difficult for many who are ESL speakers. In many cultures, especially the Japanese culture, asking questions is not appropriate because face-saving is a significant and integral cultural norm.

People who are ESL speakers may be comfortable asking questions in their native environment but reluctant to ask questions in the United States. They do not want to appear ignorant, or they fear their inquiry would be difficult to answer.

In the eighties, my clients of Japanese heritage shared that until recently, it had been inappropriate to ask any questions in classrooms in Japan. Few *USAans* can picture a classroom where students do not raise hands to ask questions. Norms in Asian societies such as China, and especially Japan, are no longer as rigid but are shifting to be more open. Based on an era of internationalization and the necessity for children to express their needs and ideas, youth are learning to be more direct and ask questions, and debate is becoming a teaching technique in many universities (Kang 1994). With the prevalence of social media, asking questions in these cultures is now more acceptable.

While introducing the Communication Enhancement Accent Reduction Program to a group of *Born-abroad* physicians, the medical group's training director and I gave a presentation focusing on the schedule for the course. We explained that there were two sign-up sheets that each doctor had to sign. The first sign-up sheet was for a one-time meeting of a one-hour-and-a-half evaluation of their speech and communication. The second sign-up sheet was for the actual course, the same hourly meeting for twenty-three weeks. Both the training director and I explained the schedule and asked in different ways, "Are there any questions?" None of the doctors raised their hands. The following week, half the doctors called the medical group training director and asked for further explanation.

When talking with people from other cultures, do not ask, "Do you have any questions?" Instead, pose questions that require a response that confirms that they understood the information. You are responsible for giving information so others easily understand it. It is also imperative that the message is presented so that it doesn't demean any person. When I require specific information and speak with a person with whom I haven't previously spoken, seems uncertain, or has a heavy accent, before the conversation ends, I take responsibility and ask the following: "I want to make sure that I gave the information [or request] so that it is easily understood. Please repeat what I said."

Face-Saving

Face-saving is the concept of protecting one's reputation and status. Some individuals and societies go to great lengths to maintain that prominence. Means such as not disclosing the entire truth or bending the truth are acceptable to guard one's dignity and prestige. To what extent and how a person enacts these techniques depends on each person and the situation. Individuals can even go as far as accepting blame to protect others or the circumstances.

Face-saving is an integral aspect of the Japanese culture. This was evidenced following the tragic 9.0-magnitude earthquake and tsunami in Japan when the Fukushima Daiichi Nuclear Power Plant was hit with a disaster on March 2011. Because it was difficult to admit the vast radiation leak, or perhaps because it would be an embarrassment to accept that the Japanese government required help from the United States, or some other reason, there was a twenty-four-hour delay before doctors from the United States treated the Japanese victims. The initial rationale given was that doctors from the United States weren't licensed to practice medicine in Japan.

Even in an emergency, do not criticize anyone in front of their colleagues or staff. It may boost your ego, but it demeans the other person; that is never appropriate or necessary. This is even more paramount with people from the Japanese culture, as face-saving is such a highly valued trait. Anything that causes a person to lose face with their colleagues or family is especially humiliating. People from any culture may feel their wrongdoings or mistakes are an embarrassment that places a stain on their character, but not every culture feels that stain also spreads to the reputation of their family, their community, and at times, their country.

Traditions in Asian cultures hold that family and unity are highly valued. When people give their names, they state the family name first and then their given name.

Generally, it remains challenging for a *USAan* to comprehend face-saving since the concept is nonexistent in the U.S. culture. Asking for help is an accepted norm. Some ask their family or friends for help. Others express themselves to inform or help find solutions. Many appear on television talk shows or post on social media and reveal their most intimate concerns, personal issues, and challenges.

Some folks are quite proud and don't ask for help. Years ago, while hiking in the High Sierra Mountains, a father had difficulty navigating a treacherous climb with his young son. A hiker in our group told the man, "I would be glad to assist, if you just ask."

Saying "No"

Using a pleasant and appropriate voice tone and intonation to say "No" is acceptable, appropriate, and necessary in the U.S. culture. If a person asks you to do something and you are unable to do it, do not understand how to do it, or lack the time, it is essential and appropriate to say "No." Nobuaki Hanaoka, a Japanese-born theologian at Berkeley, states, "We try to avoid saying 'no' preferring indirect communication as it creates less ill feeling" (Kang 1994). Another reason for avoiding the use of "No" is that it distracts from harmony and face-saving.

Thus, there are sixteen ways to avoid saying no in Japan:

1. Vague "No"
2. Vague and ambiguous "Yes" or "No"
3. Silence
4. Counterquestion
5. Tangential responses
6. Exiting (leaving)
7. Lying (making an excuse—sickness, previous obligation, etc.)
8. Criticizing the question itself
9. Refusing the question
10. Conditional "No"
11. "Yes, but..."
12. Delaying answers (e.g., "We will write you a letter.")
13. Internally "Yes," externally "No"
14. Internally "No," externally "Yes"
15. Apology
16. The equivalent of "No" (primarily used in filling out forms, but not in conversation)

(Graham and Sano 1984)

In 1994, a decade later, norms slightly shifted. Perhaps taking the advice of Shintaro Ishihara as stated in his book *The Japan That Can Say No* (1991), Prime Minister Morihiro Hosokawa said "No" when he rejected U.S. demands for measurable trade targets at a summit meeting with President Clinton in Washington. "There is no way I can agree with that" was Prime Minister Hosokawa's response to negotiations. In the second decade of the twenty-first century, the younger generation more readily says "No" if they are comfortable and the situation warrants it. The elders are more comfortable with the former norm.

The current president of China, Xi Jinping, has no difficulty in firmly disagreeing or stating "No" when he feels policies or actions are unfavorable to him, the People's Republic of China, or the region.

If you are an ESL speaker and are uncomfortable saying "No," it is important that you learn to say "No." When you are requested to perform a task that you know that you cannot do, it is best that you politely respond, "I can't do that," "I don't know how to do that," or "I don't have the time to do that." If you are responding to your supervisor, it is also in your best interest to relate the reason that you can't fulfill or accommodate their request. At times, you just have to power through.

In the U.S. culture, nodding your head up and down indicates "Yes" or "*I agree with you.*" In other cultures, the same nod implies "*I heard you.*" In my experience with *USAan* supervisors, a great source of frustration is the assumption that the person who nods yes understood the information and could complete the task, only to discover that it wasn't understood, and thus not started or finished. The misunderstanding occurred because the person of the other culture nodded yes, implying "*I heard you*" or "*I understood*," not meaning "*Yes*," or "*I can do it*," or "*I agree*."

If you are a *USAan*, observe the nonverbal communication of the other person when they say "Yes" or nod in agreement. You presume their nod indicates that they comprehend the message or they comply with your request. Verbally, they say "Yes"; nonverbally, they may say "No." Their facial expression and body language may express ambiguity. They probably realize that they won't or can't do it, but they may feel embarrassed or uncomfortable expressing that.

My friends and clients of Filipino heritage shared that dilemma in their culture. They often say "Yes" when they know that they can't or won't do something. It is culturally appropriate because they feel that they are offending less by saying "Yes" and not doing something than stating "No." A client asked me what to do. I recommended that in a mindful way, he state "No" when he knows that he can't or won't do something. I also suggested that when people say "Yes" to him and he doubts their intention, that he respond in a mindful, *source-connected* way, "I certainly don't want to offend you, but you often say yes and then you don't come through with what you've committed. It helps if I know when you are unable to complete what I requested, so that I can find another person or solution."

Saying "No," communicating indirectly, and asking questions generally are not aspects of Far East Asian cultures. However, in this instance, people in the Filipino culture do ask questions.

The editor of a prominent medical publication gave a tour to a group from her native Japanese culture. When they asked her the architectural style of some buildings in Downtown Los Angeles, the editor usually stated that she didn't know. One tourist said, "You don't know very much." The Japanese tourists found it strange that an editor, whom they perceived as an expert, would admit that she didn't know everything.

Small Talk

Although it is difficult for some *USAan*s to use small talk, it is a prominent feature in much of the U.S. culture. A secretary found a Japanese accountant rude when he requested that she make an airline reservation for him. He just handed her a memo with the information without saying anything. In the accountant's experience in the Japanese business world, small talk was considered a waste of time.

A *USAan* doctor attended a seminar presented by a gastroenterologist who was born in Japan. The *USAan* physician was quite impressed by the presenter's knowledge. During the break, the *USAan* physician tried to engage the lecturer in small talk. The Japanese-born doctor was unable to talk on a topic other than his field of expertise. For a moment, the *USAan* doctor questioned the speaker's credibility because of his inability to communicate on any other subject. Then, the *USAan* doctor recalled that Japanese individuals are often reticent to use small talk.

Many physicians from other linguistic and cultural backgrounds, and even some *USAan* physicians, shared similar experiences. They are comfortable talking with patients and colleagues about medicine but are often uncomfortable conversing on nonmedical topics. Therefore, they come across as impersonal when the real issue is lack of ease in using small talk.

People from middle-context cultures who highly value hospitality and friendliness, such as most Arabic, Caribbean, and many African cultures, comfortably engage in small talk. On some Caribbean islands, it is considered rude to ask for anything without greeting first. In Nevis, you would not begin any conversation without first greeting "Hello," "Good morning," "Good afternoon," or "Good evening," or recently, "Wassup."

Comfort in using small talk is not only a challenge for some ESL speakers, but it can also be a concern for some *USAans* and people of any cultural background. In the Southern United States and some small towns across the country, such as Angola, Indiana, small talk is quite meaningful and is a significant feature of their communication. If you get right to the point without first chatting on appreciated topics, you may be considered rude, snobbish, or downright unfriendly.

Giggle Response

In the U.S. culture, people laugh, chuckle, and giggle—without saying anything—when they are happy or find something amusing or comical. In many cultures, especially the Filipino, Japanese, Taiwanese, Chinese, and other South East Asian cultures, a *giggle response* also includes chuckling or laughing in an embarrassing situation without explanation or apology. This response is appropriate in many Asian cultures, where others grasp the circumstances and response. A soft giggle may accompany apologies or embarrassment. However, when you giggle or laugh *without also acknowledging* or *saying something* in response to a serious issue, your laughter further irritates *USAans* or people from other Western cultures. The message you unintentionally give to the person—who realizes that something is amiss—is that you are not taking the matter seriously or that you think the situation is funny. A giggle certainly isn't the response you want to give in that type of situation.

The *giggle response* might also occur in a critical or negative situation because the person is embarrassed, does not know the answer, has made a mistake, or has had a misunderstanding. These are challenging situations that require mindful, *source-connected* solutions. My clients who use this response explain that it is almost impossible to eliminate the giggle, as it is an ingrained response. If you are unable to eliminate the *giggle response*, at least acknowledge the situation while you inherently giggle. You can use phrases like "I'm sorry," "I apologize," "I didn't understand," "I don't have the answer," or "I will try again." For example, patients tend to become upset when a doctor does not have an answer for their questions and concerns. The doctor may chuckle while telling the patient, "I don't know," without adding something akin to "I'll check it out and get back to you." The patient then may assume the doctor is not taking the matter seriously or that the request is humorous.

There are also those in the U.S. culture, and perhaps other cultures, who react to adverse situations, such as the news of a loved one's death, with a spontaneous and inauthentic giggle.

This chuckling is a coping mechanism to lighten their load or situation and conceal their genuine feelings.

If you are the *USAan* person in an intercultural conversation and the other person giggles without saying anything in response to a situation or an issue, I suggest that you mindfully and *source-connectedly* respond with something akin to "I sense that you are embarrassed about this. That's okay, but let's try to move on and find a solution."

Hissing

Hissing to gain attention is acceptable in some Latino cultures. In Nevis, a tourist chatted with a Nevisian who couldn't understand why women from the United States and other countries were offended when he hissed to get their attention. She explained that hissing is not considered nice in *mainstream* U.S. culture.

Response to Prejudice

I cannot possibly leave this section on intercultural communication without sharing a few prejudiced interactions that clients and friends experienced. A builder from Nigeria was informed that a piece of property had been leased, but when he called the realtor to inquire, it was still available. A physician from Taiwan who was involved in litigation was deeply concerned that he would not receive a fair trial because of his Asian heritage. A U.S. citizen who was originally from Mexico was insulted with "You are stupid and lazy, just like the rest of your kind." She was anything but that; she worked sixty hours per week to build a home for her family in Mexico before she joined her siblings to purchase a home for themselves. When I introduced a guest from the Caribbean to a local California merchant, out of context the merchant said, "I like to be lazy too." She replied, "We aren't lazy, and work just as hard, but not as long as you do, because we value time with our families."

If you are a member of another culture and experience discrimination that you want to address, do not respond in anger or resentment. If you retaliate in anger or with sarcasm, you do not advocate for yourself or your culture, nor do you bring down barriers to build connections. Instead, you only feed more negativity into the situation, which does not solve anything. If you respond negatively in these or other similar situations, you again hand over to another person the power to determine how you respond. If you are comfortable and feel safe, from the deepest, most caring, mindful, *source-connected* human-to-human approach, notify the other person that you are a fellow human being and that their comment offends you. Simply enlighten the other person that they probably would not like to be treated in the same demeaning manner, especially when they travel.

There Are Other Ways

My life is continuously enriched with the views and values that people from differing back-grounds and cultures teach me. It has always been enlightening to learn how people from other cultures perform their tasks and achieve their goals in approaches that are different and often more efficient than mine. Besides the various communication styles, people from other cultures often value and differently approach life, birth, illness, death, marriage, divorce, and relationships. They also may differently prioritize work, leisure, pleasure, time, or money. Respect other people's beliefs, as long as they are not imposed upon you or hurtful to you or others. If you don't understand why a person is doing something that seems unusual, if and when it is appropriate, mindfully *source-connect* with the person to discover why or how tasks are accomplished in their native culture.

In time, innumerable new methods of accomplishing tasks, goals, habits, patterns, and lifestyles are integrated into mainstream U.S. culture. In all walks of life, communities, and neighborhoods, much can be gleaned from insights and recommendations of those individuals who were born or lived abroad and those who overcame challenges to experience success and comfort. Honoring, recognizing, and including others' mindful ideas, ideals, and attributes promote a broader, richer, more productive, civil, and cohesive society. This fosters a willingness to work and socialize together and creates a new, heightened sense of an inclusive and harmonious community.

When we don't comprehend, respect, or even listen to one another, trust deficits develop. An example would be a physician misunderstanding or even sneering at their patients of different cultures who trust in familiar healing and successful folk remedies to promote health and wellness. Not only do the physicians discourage such treatment, but worse, they often offend the patients or their families by implying that "they are off their rockers." With so many physicians from a broad group of diverse cultures now on staff at hospitals throughout the nation, I recommend that physicians who encounter these cultural differences confer with their *Born-abroad* colleagues from the same culture as the patients who use "strange" remedies. But also recognize that the remedies used are usually extracted from plants or animals indigenous in their native cultures or rural areas. They may not be found in urban communities where the *Born-abroad* physicians lived or trained.

A *Born-abroad* physician may be unfamiliar with the folklore but may have the ability to further shed light on whether the herbs or practices are harmful or toxic. In Nevis, many do not trust drugs or do not want to experience the side effects of Western "tablets." All my friends primarily rely on "bush tea" (plants) to heal. Many of these plants, shrubs, or trees provide basic elements for Western pharmaceuticals.

A deeply trusted and reliable Nevisian friend related the recovery of an elderly patient whose "imminent death" required the doctors to prepare the family. In desperation, the family and friends gathered to carefully pick the prickly leaves of a succulent named prickly pear. After they meticulously harvested the moist, thick meat of the plant, they covered the woman with the essential substance. It was no surprise to the locals when the patient recovered.

Lewiston, Maine, is a small cohesive community that wasn't always cohesive. In 1990, contrary to the locals' preference, immigrants from Somalia began to settle there. Roughly 25 percent of the community then was Eastern African refugees. "When the refugees began arriving fifteen years ago, many longtime residents were resentful, Lewiston's economy was tanking, businesses were closing, and jobs were scarce. The newcomers were seen as welfare freeloaders. Store owner Shukir Abasheikh recalled when they asked, 'Why did you come here? Go back where you came from'" (Dahler 2016).

Once the community realized how hard the people of Somalia were willing to work and that the budget for public assistance had not increased since their arrival, attitudes began to change. It wasn't easy, but in 2015, Lewiston was one big happy family. That year, the Lewiston High School's soccer team won its first state championship in its school history. The team consisted of twenty-one students of Somalian heritage and five Lewiston locals. Forty-five hundred people showed up to cheer on their kids that day. Following the event, members of the community accepted and trusted one another.

The Olympic Games occur every two years, alternating between summer and winter events. Billions of people around the world highly anticipate viewing the Olympians' flowing, electrifying, and often treacherous performances. Although the occasion is flawed on many levels, we gain a great deal from these outstanding events. Even if individuals face disappointment, defeat, or injury or never take home a prized medal, Olympians often begin dreaming at very young ages of participating and becoming a member of this prestigious global community in hopes of winning a medal to honor their country. Besides complete dedication and sacrifice for themselves and their families, they also endure years of an arduous and exhausting commitment. Some overcome Herculean hurdles of disease, injuries, injustice, and loss of loved ones. Others are burdened with not coming out and revealing their true nature as a member of the LGBTQ community. Yet they all power through their heartbreaking storms, and only a few receive the gold medal.

Some passionately root for their fellow Olympians, and others unite with their fiercest competitor. Others still support those of opposing political views or those whose leaders are considered enemies. Yes, each individual represents her or his country, but for their brief time together, most bond to become an Olympian. Let that Olympian spirit inspire people around the globe that universal inclusion is humanly possible.

Give It a Try

You gained a broad and inclusive understanding of the four As of intercultural communication: *awareness*, *appropriateness*, *acknowledgment*, and *acceptance*. Remember that each individual, to the best of their ability, assumes an equal role in the four roles of an intercultural conversation to create *source-connected*, thoughtful, and productive conversation. Compassion, patience, understanding, and flexibility are key. Just as each person is unique, interactions are fluid and never exactly duplicated. Therefore, there is no one specific formula for applying the communication insights and tools presented in this chapter. Each individual and situation requires a different approach and synthesis of insights and skills to create a *positive communication environment*. If everyone's heart is willing, a commonality between you and the other person is achieved. Then, you can continue and move the process forward as you gain comfort, joy, appreciation, and fulfillment interacting with people from other cultures and differing backgrounds. You are a change agent as you help to nullify the multitude of xenophobic and divisive attitudes that currently separate us. Instead, you promote well-being for yourself, others, and our nation as you continue or join to build bonds of friendship and community.

I fervently hope that you will now make it a point to take more time to reach out to your neighbors, students, patients, clients, colleagues, staff, supervisors, workers, service providers, tradespeople, or employees as fellow human beings. Broaden your experiences and revel in one another's glorious gifts. Discover how similar you are to one another and the life's joys and disappointments that you share.

In many ways, this country's previously cloaked divisiveness of pitting rich against poor, young against old, urban against rural, the disadvantaged in the hood against the disadvantaged on the farm, straight against gay, educated against street smart, abled against *handi-abled*, mainstream against minority, or *USAan* citizen against *Born-abroad* resident at last is exposed for all to see. In some way, nearly every community is touched by this destructive chasm. No family, community, or country can *unify* and *divide* its people at the same time; you can't productively build up and simultaneously tear down. In the end, either the building up or the tearing down prevails. To build bonds of community and friendship, we all need one another; no one individual can do it alone. We are at a crossroads in our democracy, where exceedingly disruptive ideas permeate much of the conversations. But hopefully, a period of enlightenment of similar needs and objectives will forge new paths to create, build, and bond inclusive and just solutions.

In the 2016 presidential election, Hillary Clinton, whose slogan was "Stronger together," received almost 2.9 million more popular votes than her opponent. This reflects that the majority of voters desired to move forward and continue to build a more inclusive society. They also voiced their wishes to hold together families whose children were born in the United States and whose parents are law-abiding undocumented immigrants. The voters also desired to continue to offer a haven for the "tired and poor huddled masses yearning to breathe free," and to maintain that opportunity for those who are of Muslim faith, or are Syrian, or are refugees fleeing from other tumultuous countries. Whatever their social status or socioeconomic or educational level, once they had undergone a vigorous vetting process, the majority of voters approved of these folks becoming residents of the United States. It is likely that they will become your neighbors, colleagues, friends, and employees, and perhaps even your loved ones, spouses, or partners.

Questions about the lack of inclusion in our country and the desire to remedy it have been raised regularly over the years, but never as outspokenly as at the current public level. In the *ASHA Leader*, the American Speech-Language-Hearing Association's magazine, I found the following: "Our clients are diverse: why aren't we?" asks Jacquelynne C. Rodriguez (Rodriguez 2016). According to ASHA, enrollment among minorities in the field was staggeringly low and not up to par with other fields at universities for the 2013–2014 academic year, with only 8 percent of ASHA members and affiliates identifying themselves as racial minorities (https://www. asha.org).

Rodriguez found it strange that what had attracted her to the field of communication sciences and disorders (CSD) was that "the opportunity to understand and celebrate diverse cultural and linguistic backgrounds were absent from the field itself" (Rodriguez 2016).

As a graduate student at Georgia State University, she experienced a lack of diversity and felt isolated. "Although it may not be what I initially expected, the field of speech-language pathology is one of the greatest. The opportunities across work settings, disorders addressed, and populations served are endless. The field of CSD has an immense need and a place for racial/ethnic minorities, like me, to help meet the needs of people with communication disorders" (Rodriguez 2016).

There is a demand for more diversity not only in schools but also in all arenas. Rodriguez urges her peers to "get involved" by joining certain CSD groups to bond with other minorities. She realizes that many people are totally unaware of this field and suggests that they "spread the word" by becoming CSD professionals. She warns of potential "awkward moments," especially around bilingual speakers, but these moments must be handled with grace. She suggests that they offer opportunities to educate and "encourage peers to consider biases that they have when treating linguistically diverse speakers." Rodriguez encourages her peers to "find a mentor." She was quite grateful for her mentor, who was pivotal, made all the difference, and immensely helped her. "A mentor with a personal understanding of the unique issues associated with being a person of color may help you negotiate the awkward moments and challenging situations, give you insight into finding a job, and brainstorm ways to make a difference in the field." (In addition, students of diverse cultural and linguistic backgrounds in that field also will serve patients and clients of differing backgrounds. Mentors also add that personal touch that offers guidance and comfort in these intercultural connections.) And finally, she tells them to "stick with it," informing them that it is the minorities who are essential to this particular field, as they will "serve as cultural brokers" (Rodriguez 2016). Education is the best way to attack the diversity problem and help these minorities feel less isolated and alone.

I am proud to add that in 2015, California State University, Northridge (CSUN) received the Eddy Award for Educational Leadership that the Los Angeles County Economic Development Corporation (LAEDC) bestows. CSUN is the fourth university to receive the honor and joins Caltech, USC, and UCLA. "The award honors those who have played leading roles in the development of the county's economy and the creation of well-paying jobs for its residents" (http://csunshinetoday.csun.edu/csun-receives-eddy-award).

For decades, CSUN has been recognized as one of the outstanding universities in the country promoting diversity and is among the leading institutions of higher learning in the country that promote inclusion. Incoming students achieve one of the highest income gains from the time they entered the university to the start of their first job after graduation. Yet a wide gap persists in attracting professionally established alumni of diverse backgrounds. That fact alone shines light on how much catching up is required as a nation to become more mindful. It is imperative that we especially strive harder to attract and include others of diverse backgrounds at all levels and in all areas of campus life.

If you feel a lack of diversity or spirit of inclusion in your department, at school, work, the medical center, house of worship, on the team, or in your community, in a thoughtful and *source-connected* way, share your heartfelt concerns with others and coalesce to advocate for and hasten inclusion.

As Dr. Martin Luther King Jr. stated more than thirty years ago, "I have a dream that my four little children will one day live in a nation where they will not be judged by the color of their skin but by the content of their character" (Jakoubek 1989).

Decades ago, when I shared Dr. King's vision with the classroom of *turn-around* students, I asked them about their own vision of a world that judges others by what kind of people they are, not by what they look like nor by their beliefs. One pupil said, "If I do, that's only a grain of sand." I quickly replied, "If you and I carry the dream, then there will be two grains of sand. If we tell others, soon there is a pile, then a mound, then a section, and then the entire area. That's how ideas change in the world."

Either we find commonality with people despite religion, creed, culture, or status and reach out to build bonds of trust and friendship, or we erect barriers. If we don't work toward connection, we may walk away in apathy or turn against one another, whether calmly or, worse yet, in violence. I fervently believe that nationally, most people of all ages will continue to peacefully express their desire to boost and build these inclusive connections. Collectively, they will create a more righteous and prosperous society for all.

Before leaving this chapter, I want to share a few experiences. The first is a joyous Thanksgiving experience in our California home. Some decades ago, the man who became our son by marriage, his friends from the Netherlands, a young client from Japan, our youngest daughter, my husband, and I celebrated this traditional festivity by sipping beer, wine, sake, or God's ale, better known as water. After we had given gratitude for our lives, feasting on Thanksgiving dinner, and toasting in several languages, one of the men from the Netherlands started to play "Let It Be" by the Beatles on the piano. Soon, everyone was singing along. I listened to a song written by a group in Great Britain sung by young and old and women and men from opposite sides of the planet. With the different accents and singing styles, each added a new tone to the song, adding joy to the moment. It was the highlight of the day. If it can happen in our home, it can happen in yours.

Decades later, my husband and I strolled along the Santa Monica pier, first passing the famous merry-go-round as the tune "The Entertainer" floated in the air. There, I saw a young father pushing fraternal twins in a stroller while chatting with his children's grandparents, each of whom was of a different heritage. Teenagers of various backgrounds, heights, hairstyles, and fashions grouped together, cajoling and slapping skin; they were having a groovy good time. A mother with her young daughter pushed her elderly mother in a wheelchair across the bumpy boardwalk as the multigenerational family then paused to buy cotton candy. A young couple of mixed heritage held hands and gently gazed into each other's eyes; they each wore a prosthetic leg and carried a military bearing. I saw people wearing turbans, yarmulkes, sombreros, saris, torn jeans, African prints, business suits, and a colorful collection of global fashion. I heard laughter, exhausted cries, and a litany of languages. The Greater Los Angeles metropolis is a multivaried community where 137 languages are spoken, and the Santa Monica pier is a top tourist destination attracting global citizens from around the world. It was a beautiful, sunny day in Santa Monica, California, United States of America, North America continent, planet Earth, Terran Solar System, Milky Way Galaxy, Universe.

Please recall and take to heart my story of taking a ride with an immigrant from Libya who turned out to be Jewish, refused any reimbursement, and told me "to pay it forward."

This chapter, "Embracing Diversity," offered a broad spectrum of insights and tools to bridge the gaps between those who appear and act differently but who commonly share similar concerns, values, and aspirations. I fervently hope that with a heartfelt and deeper recognition, the insights and tools of this chapter provide a path to greater comfort and success for the opportunity to build mutual respect and trust with people of different backgrounds and to treasure your newfound intercultural experiences.

Continue to deeply hold in your heart and soul that you and each fellow global citizen are the only ones who solely have the right and privilege to define who you are. Family members, colleagues, neighbors, leaders, groups, organizations, institutions, political parties, religions, regions, conditions, events, and numerous others, perhaps including yourself, will continually try to label you in a negative light. If you allow that, you and others suffer the consequences. Even if a person disrespected or wronged you, do not allow that to define or devalue you. Yes, we each are imperfect and most likely have engaged in activities or uttered words that demeaned others and dishonored ourselves. But do not allow any previous attitudes or acts that once described your deeds to determine who you now are. Embrace and celebrate your goodness and uniqueness.

I believe that with an unwavering *source-connection*, purely revealing your glorious, star-powered, endowed gifts remains the best guide to genuinely live life.

Appendix

Positive Solutions to Maintain Harmony

Life continually presents challenges—some simple, some complex, and some herculean, which seem impossible to overcome. Many facets of communication were presented that elevate the way we mindfully and *source-connectedly* interact with others. These encourage our and their well-being. I succinctly offer some gems that were not included or require a reminder to create harmony.

An ambitious, creative, intelligent, well-mannered person strived hard to become a millionaire. After reaching his goal, he discovered he had been embezzled. He fell on hard times, so much so that his family, a wife and six children, became homeless. He found soup kitchens, which provided warm meals. When his turn came to be served, he humbly and politely asked, "Could you kindly bless my children and wife with some nourishment?" As he pushed through and evolved from that painful period, he gained tremendous gratitude for even the tiniest gesture and blessing. He later discovered that although he had once possessed material wealth, he had now gained spiritual wealth, which was profoundly more valuable and gratifying. He shared, "Once I realized that my misfortune and missed opportunities had purpose, the stress was gone."

A friend who had been divorced for years recently married a very attractive, lovely, and stately woman. She demands politeness and a positive attitude. She waits at any door until he opens it for her. I suggested that he also change the term "I have to," which often suggests a burdensome task, and that he instead use the term "I get to." This positive term implies gratitude and the privilege that he has his health, a sharp mind, physical abilities, and the funds to enjoy an upscale lifestyle.

Even under severe duress, a seamstress of Mexican heritage is consistently positive. She shared, "We have to be positive. That is our happiness." In Nevis, positive and encouraging sayings are posted in businesses, agencies, and schools. Some of my Nevisian friends had crippling experiences. By remaining deeply devoted to their faith, they were able to pick themselves up, move on, remain in the present, and continually strive to do their best. Others may question our motives or priorities and offer advice, but in the end, we have to do what we have to do to enable us to do what we want to do.

A rabbi offered a valuable insight when he said, "A person lashes out against or most hurt those who they know will always be there for them. Others may fall by the wayside, but they will remain by your side."

For those who are deeply concerned or at times are overwhelmed by a continuing personal dilemma, a crisis, or a time of increased bomb threats, terrorist attacks, or national disarray, before the thought gets the best of you, immediately halt it. Please allow me to remind you to pause, reflect, and engage the three *instant mindful breath-boosters* and the *Mona Lisa smile* until you can recall, grab onto, and engage a peaceful, productive, and prompt solution. Often, it is simply looking at a photo of a loved one or a joyous experience on your smartphone. You can also jot down the thought, make a phone call, text, or go online to sign a petition. You also can send money to support the change you envision, support candidates, and then vote to advance the cause. Furthermore, you can text or post on social media the positive steps that you took to stand up for your beliefs and values. Others send positive energy to the universe or offer prayers. Just do something positive. In this type of divisive environment, it is imperative to dial back exposure of that information for younger children's tender spirits and receptive ears. That burden weighs far too heavily on young shoulders.

In most environments, there are individuals who strive to promote calm and peace, while others tend to agitate, exaggerate, gossip, and lie. In these situations, it is best not to respond in kind but to mindfully and positively state what you are willing and unwilling to do and keep your comments pertaining to the present situation using the "I mode."

Couples are typically in the same place when they court each other and eventually remain as a couple, whether living apart, living together, or married. Years ago, a therapist stated that long-term relationships pass through several different phases. She broke down the word *relationship* into three syllables and explained it pertaining to couples. She said, "'Re' denotes to come together, 'lation' notes to grow together, and the 'ship' signifies movement to become stronger than before."

I created a visualization of a young tree with two vine-like branches that began and grew at the same height on the small, thin, and immature trunk. Each vine represented one person in the couple and their varying growth at different times. During these growth and cycle changes, one vine separated and grew outward and apart from the tree. Then, at some point, the vine circled back to the tree to join the other vine. Then, the other person followed a similar path as they moved onward. These back-and-forth, sideways-and-upward, separated-and-joined trajectories between the two people continue and mirror life. Many times during these cycles, one or both endured in disharmony or one or both reveled in harmony.

Shortly after Lee and I celebrated our fifty-fifth wedding anniversary, Lee shared that event with a taxi driver in Nevis. The man quickly replied, "I am just behind you. I have been married for fifty-three years, and when things were bad, I made them good, and when things were good, I made them better."

While a friend earned her degree, and as she began her career, before she left for the day, her husband proclaimed, "Be good. If you can't be good, be great!"

One of our Nevisian neighbors, a woman from Guyana, is a positive, caring, and joyous person and a fabulous mother. She raised two very positive, upright, fun-loving, and well-rounded yet quite different sons. Since childhood, they respected and looked out for each other and continued to do so as young men. A couple of years ago, she and I have chatted often over the fence, in each other's homes, and while dining out.

A few years ago, she stunned me with the news that her husband, who is a soft-spoken, stay-at-home type of guy, had an affair and fathered a child. Understandably, she became extremely angry. In the process, she didn't like or recognize who she had become. She certainly did not want her sons to grow up in a nasty or gloomy environment. My neighbor and friend went into soul-searching and deep prayer and was guided to become the forgiving, caring, and joyous person she had always been.

Although my husband knew about the child, he was unaware of the conversations between my friend and me. On one of his visits to Nevis, he knocked on her door to say hello. When Lee saw a little girl sitting on her lap, he asked, "Who is that little girl?" She replied, "That is my granddaughter." Just then, the little girl looked at her and said, "Mama." My husband was surprised and told her, "There aren't many people in the world like you. May God continue to bless you."

At times, family members, friends, colleagues, staff, or others perceive an observation about themselves as a judgment. To me, an observation is expressing something that I noticed. When I ask a question without any further processing, comment, or implied opinion, that is to seek information, not to judge. When *but* and similar words or *why*, *were*, or *how come* follow the statement, when you don't need to know, then judgment is applied. There are folks who are quite sensitive to this issue, even when a simple observation is stated, a simple question is asked, or when the most *source-connected* constructive criticism is offered. They often feel that they are being judged. Perhaps they were frequently compared to others or they previously experienced harsh or unfair criticism—perhaps even from you. Either they perceived reality or falsely accused you. Therefore, they usually view an observation as judgment.

Teachers suggest, physicians recommend, families and friends prod; all are given from their hearts, mostly with the best intentions. Nothing changes until we each are willing to examine the issue, take it on, and alter our negative attitudes, behaviors, or actions. Until then, we just feel jabbed or nudged. The toxic, addictive attitudes and behaviors continue to be ingrained in our life's journey until we alone, each in our own time and place, decide to do something about it.

I know many people who are taking care of a parent—or parents—along with their other responsibilities. Many folks are sandwiched in between taking care of aging parents and raising children. The caretakers often become frustrated or stressed when their aging parent repeats or forgets or no longer lives in reality. Some elders repeat the same statements or questions over and over, or they view their world significantly differently than reality. To maintain harmony for herself, a business owner and manager who handled daily caregivers for her mother created a new approach to deal with her mother's dementia reality. As a former dancer, she created the "dementia dance."

In the dance, as in all communication, we have to let go and connect with others in their world, especially when there are differences. So she danced into her mother's reality. If, on a clear, sunny day, her mother utters, "It looks like it's going to rain," rather than trying to explain why it will not rain, the daughter simply replies, "It sure does." As my friend shared, "To truly get into a dance, we have to let go and let it happen."

A colleague who had formerly served as the Clinical Coordinator for the Language, Speech, and Hearing Center at California State University, Northridge received a significant award for creating an Early Intervention Program in the field of Communication Disorders and Sciences. In her acceptance speech, she declared, "I would be remiss if I didn't add that the chair of the department had encouraged, supported, and challenged me to try the things, create the things, follow up on the things or just plain write the things that I felt were important and vital to the mission." These succinct yet simple words serve as an excellent guide to any creative endeavor.

Studies indicate that empathy does not come naturally for some and the feeling is hard to teach. The three types of empathy are cognitive, emotional, and compassionate, and only the latter is hardwired. An individual who has cognitive empathy has an awareness of how the other person feels or thinks. An individual who has emotional empathy senses what the other person feels. And an individual who has compassionate empathy instinctively and immediately reaches out to help an individual in need (Goleman 2007). Therefore, an extra burden is placed on those individuals who instinctively and immediately reach out to help, especially when they themselves face acute personal, medical, or other challenges and are treated by those who lack empathy.

Understandably, a professional's response most likely won't mirror the depth of empathy that is given by a patient's loved ones, but a physician still has to express care and concern, especially in the hospital. There are some physicians who do not know how to express any type of empathy. When consulting with physicians who lack empathy, I suggest that they picture their child, spouse, parent, or best friend in that hospital bed, then ask themselves, "How do I want my loved one to be treated?" Then use their response as a guide when serving their patients. This insight can be easily modified to a specific situation and applied to any other personal or professional settings.

A practical and meticulous builder left his recently formed crew for a short while. When the builder returned, he noticed several obvious mistakes. Then, he realized that common sense is not so common.

An eighty-year-old serviceman who retained excellent eye-hand coordination repaired an appliance. Upon its perfect completion, I commented that he was lucky. He replied, "Yea, I am lucky with everything." Perhaps his grateful attitude fostered his well-being.

For those of you who are aging or are blessed to have elderly loved ones, let me remind you that as we or our loved ones age, many can only perform one task at a time. It is best that we or these folks slow down to focus more on the surroundings to prevent accidents, broken bones, bruises, and cuts. Compassion and patience are paramount during these elderly stages.

Throughout my life, I have observed people of all ages often prematurely venture out to return to their former routine while recovering from illness or surgery and shortly thereafter have a relapse or reinjured themselves, which sets back their recovery. So they have to return to bed rest, the hospital, or rehabilitation.

Decades ago, after my last such incident, I created an analogy: when I paint a room, I don't hang the pictures on the wall until the paint is dry. From then on, I questioned myself, Am I realistically ready to do this, and is the timing right?

Some people have difficulty accepting instructions or directions from those of the opposite sex. In these cases, it is best to frame your request so that the person thinks it is their idea. Sometimes I inquire, "What do you think about this idea?" Often, they think it is worthy and I do not have to go further to achieve my intention. Other times it is not quite so easy, and so I kindly and firmly convey, "This is what I would like to have done now." As best as you can, not through your own eyes, standards, encounters, or perspective, try to step into the other person's shoes. Our goal is no longer to seek agreement but instead shifts to a compassionate and thoughtful compromise that results in win-win solutions.

Resolution requires a two-way process of deep listening and mindful speaking to create a *positive communication environment*. We suspend all judgment as we listen with our ears and engage our hearts and souls without hidden agendas, ego, tribe, turf, labels, bias, or prejudice. Then, with laser focus, we seek a solution that benefits all. We most likely have to compromise some actions, but we never abandon our principles. In this approach, we do our best to optimally perceive and respond.

When my son attended a Quaker college, they taught him to refrain from flatly opposing any idea unless he also offered a positive and realistic alternative.

A friend learned that he carried a "worry folder" in his head. When he resolved one dilemma, another one popped into his "folder." It took decades until he realized that he had to replace the "worry folder" with a more positive one. He named his new folder "this will get resolved" and created a positive, silent, and spiritual approach that also reduced his blood pressure.

Over the years, I watched friends and dear ones grapple with making a decision when their mind indicated *yes* but their instincts signaled *no*. Added to the confusion were many professional and well-meaning voices who contradicted the gut's signals. The choices were either *yes* or *no* or *a* or *b*. The struggle seemed similar to the endless back-and-forth lobs of a lengthy tennis game. My sister-in-heart had a strong desire to see her only great-grandchild in his environment. With the arrival of spring weather, my niece struggled with the decision to undertake a six-hour trip with her eighty-three-year-old mother so that she once more could experience her great-grandson in his routine. Her mother lives in an assisted-living residence and has chronic obstructive pulmonary disease (COPD) and apathy dementia, unless in her loved ones' presence. Then, she becomes animated and quite fluent. The doctor stated that if she took her medication and an oxygen tank, he would be okay with granting her wish. After my niece spoke with a friend who provided a safe haven, she gained clarity, made her decision, and felt relief as everything fell into place. Afterward, she shared, "It's amazing what seemed so complex became so simple." Later, my husband added, "Don't make the simple complex."

An extremely positive and physically active medical professional shared that his wife, who never exercised or participated in yoga or similar activities, had undergone vital and vigorous treatments for her second bout with cancer, which had spread to a new site. After the treatments, she was diagnosed "clean," but physicians also warned her that this type of cancer may recur. He expressed that she often worried about the recurrence of the disease. I asked him if his wife was a positive person, and he said that she was not usually when regarding outcomes. He was quite concerned, as he knew that refraining from certain activities and maintaining a negative outlook are counterproductive to healing, harmony, and homeostasis. I suggested that every time she expresses her fear he pause, take her hand, stand or sit with her, and engage the following prac-tice. On each inhalation of breath, they draw positive healing energy from the powerful expanse of the universe and hold the image of a cancer-free body, and on each exhalation release her fear out to the vast universe. This also is an especially healing practice for those individuals or couples who make the time at dawn, sunset, or anytime to create togetherness or when facing any type of challenge.

I observed that people or groups who are activists often do not give worthy appreciation of any progress unless they completely attain their objective. Activists often help set an agenda, and leaders strive to meet the goals to implement the positive changes. Hopefully, both realize that change is a process that requires time to manifest—sometimes in fits and starts or two steps forward and one step backward. Both the activist's and the facilitator's roles have their places, for without the other, there would only be minimal change or progress, if any.

A friend who grew up overlooking a mountain in Armenia shared her mother's twilight ritual. Each evening, as the lights began to flicker in the homes on the mountainside, her mother called her children to the window. With her index finger, she pointed out and told her family, "See those houses? Every house has a problem. Some don't have food, some don't have a comforter, some don't have a parent, some have illness, but everyone has a problem." Then she reminded her chil-dren, "We have to be grateful for everything we have. And when you grow up, always remember never to judge others, have love in your heart, be compassionate, and help people." My friend continued, "That's why I love people." The sparkle in her eye radiated the feeling in her heart.

One of my editors shared the following compassionate idea: "Everyone you see may be fight-ing an internal battle that you know nothing about, so be kind." As Mark Twain wrote, "Kindness is the language which the deaf can hear and the blind can see." We can always express kindness with an acknowledging nod, a heartfelt smile, or a gentle touch.

What I offer next goes against our basic animal kingdom nature or instincts. As I sat on the beach, I noticed groups of birds scattered along the shore. I mostly saw that "birds of a feather flock together." But on the periphery of various species and flocks, there were often some from another flock who ventured to mingle with those outside their own comfort zone. In the animal kingdom, although members often squabble, the most prevalent behavior is that they are usually most comfortable or content with one another's company. However, occasionally, they become loving and protective buddies with those of different species. Our U.S. democracy is similar. As we continue to advance the "democracy" idea, although we may differ in our inherent values, spiritually and as human beings, we can, and more often will, be our best when we coalesce.

A meaningful lesson on forgiveness and redemption was expressed by two unlikely people in Benton Harbor, Michigan. It began in 2005 when Jameel McGee "was going about his day, when he was falsely arrested" by police officer Andrew Collins for illegally selling drugs. McGee was of African heritage; Collins was of European heritage (Golding 2016). The problem was that Officer Collins made up the entire incident—he framed McGee, thus sending an innocent person to spend four years in prison.

Later, Officer Collins admitted, "I falsified the report." He said, "Basically, at the start of that day, I was going to make sure I had another drug arrest." Unfortunately, it resulted in an innocent person going to prison. McGee said, "I lost everything. My only goal was to seek him when I got home and to hurt him" (Hartman 2016). McGee was eventually exonerated but still lost four years of his life. Meanwhile, it was also discovered that Officer Collins had falsified many police reports, planted drugs, and stole them; he eventually served eighteen months for his crimes.

What happened next was quite astonishing. In 2015, after both men had served time, Collins and McGee ran into each other at a faith-based employment agency in their small town. They ended up working together at a small café, and that was when Collins apologized to McGee. Collins said, "Honestly, I have no explanation. All I can do is say I'm sorry" (Hartman 2016). McGee forgave him and then said, "That was pretty much what I needed to hear." Since then, they have become very close friends—McGee has even expressed love for Collins that Collins doesn't believe he deserves. They now travel together, giving talks on the significance and power of forgiveness.

When Steve Hartman asked McGee why he forgave Collins, McGee said something akin to, "*I didn't forgive just for his sake, but for our sake, and everyone's sake.*" McGee continued to talk about his Christian faith "and his hope for a kinder mankind." He uses his experience along with Collins to give speeches about the importance of forgiveness and redemption. Hartman concluded, "And clearly, if these two guys from the coffee shop can set aside their bitter grounds, what's our excuse?" (Hartman 2016).

Although I am by no means an expert on teenagers, I feel compelled to address what my mother called those years between "fish and fowl," when hormones and occasionally acne explode. In today's world, teenagers must deal not only with these natural bodily changes but also with drugs and the scourge of opioid's disparaging deaths, catastrophes, erratic policies, diaspora, continuing school shootings, and being arrested for standing up for their beliefs. Previous generations never imagined having to deal with the constant barrage of these happenings that strip away innocence at an early age.

Social media is affecting teenagers from every direction, allowing them to be connected, creative, and worldly as never before. However, this platform also spreads falsehoods and bullying that takes aim at the human spirit and establishes very high expectations, many of which can never be met and often create a cynical outlook.

I wish that I had done things differently with my children during their teenage years. Supreme is my wish that I had immediately connected with their *source-connection* and felt their wondrous spirits. There were also a few things that particularly pertained to communication. I lacked the maturity to listen from the heart with an open mind and not take personally what they said. In that way, I could have better understood what they were going through to show the profound love that I felt for each child. I wish I had consistently led with and expressed realistic examples that promote optimism and hope.

Shortly before the production of this book, I spent time with an amazing human being who brings out the best in others and adds comfort to and support for them. With these gifts, they will be and perform their best. This safe environment also creates a space in which others are willing to take a first step. I shared these thoughts with the person, who responded, "I am doing my job." I tried to explain, "Your aura is so inviting, and it inspires others to be their best and take risks." The person understood my words but could not sense what I said. I later realized that we are never privy to our aura. Only others can sense it because we are the senders of our energy and others are the receivers.

During my high school and college days, a remarkable human being lived down the street in my suburban neighborhood. He was an only child, a wondrous, humble athlete on the OSU swim team, and spent a year in Norway as an exchange student. But his most remarkable trait was inclusivity. He had friends of diverse cultural backgrounds. On rare occasions, he drove me to campus. On a ride before winter break in December 1960, he shared his upcoming adventure. An attorney had invited three other OSU athletes (one of the individuals declined) to travel to New York to see a couple of Broadway productions. My friend remarked, "I don't ever want to get older." The next day on campus, I recall hearing about a midair crash; he was on one of the flights. Though I understand that, at times, people state that they don't want to get older, I plead that you not bemoan but be grateful for life.

Have you ever noticed that the darker the sky, the brighter the stars shine? Even during our doldrums or darkest hours, let us try to radiate our special soft or bright light.

I end on the note that we, and all others, are either alive or dead. There is no state of dying, although there are final life stages of the "*I am here*" moment.

Thank You

I believe as we arise each day, we each are given a daily gift of positive energy and well-being. Every negative, doubtful, or worrisome thought or deed drains our well-being reservoir and fills our internal toxic bin. While we can often muster additional energy to cope or meet challenges and deadlines, we gradually drain our physical, mental, emotional, and spiritual energy and our reserve. And so with the deepest gratitude for having reached more than three-quarters of a century and fully realizing that life passes as rapidly as flicking through the pages of a thick book in seconds, if there are a few gems I wish I had known all along, they are thus: default to gratitude as soon as possible when I get upset; hold that the yin-yang energies are in each whole; remember that at some time and to some degree every person has to live with a person or situation that is unpleasant, to say the least. Therefore, it is often best to accept "it is what it is" and move on to do our best under the circumstances; do not let perfect stand in the way of good. Be aware that you do not let simple things steal your joy; that is worse than having no joy at all. Also realize that when we are fully engaged, we are and become what we experience. If we are joyful, we are joy. If we are angry, we are anger. If we observe or engage in a positive thought or activity, we are positive, and if we spend our time in doubt, worry, self-loathing, or arguments, we are negative. If we are fully engaged in watching a dance, we are the dancer, and if we are fully engaged in watching killings, we are the killer. And worst of all, if we ruminate over an unpleasant situation or horrific experience, we holistically relive that moment and become locked in that pain, stress, isolation, or agony over and over. Looking back, I wish I had possessed these jewels to immediately discard or disallow further rehashing or relating that negative experience to others; I wish I had quickly pivoted to unite with my *source-connection*. Even the simple breath offers the path to return to our true home, and the gift of breath confirms that we are alive. Thây teaches words akin to "*Wherever you are, breathe in and breathe out on that and do no more. Stay in the moment. As you breathe in and breathe out, you will find joy in that moment that will help ease your concern.*"

Remember that *source-connection* and mindfulness are always at the heart of the ultimate connection and communication with all others. At each moment, we choose to respond positively or negatively and sensitively or insensitively. Likewise, we choose to honor or dishonor ourselves and others. These are our choices, and they are a formative facet of our character and aura.

My life's experiences taught me that the more *source-connected* we remain, the more calm, comfortable, confident, and courageous we are, and the more positive energy we exude, the greater we honor ourselves and others.

A gecko in Nevis confirmed that belief as I walked past it while it was lounging atop and blending into a low-lying rock. The longer I remained next to it, captivated by its presence, the greener and brighter it lit up to share its immense beauty. So the energy of our *source-connected* presence radiates comfort and infuses an energy that helps uplift others and ourselves to be their best.

Throughout this book, I have shared Thây's peaceful and wise teachings of interbeing and the profound gift of a single mindful breath to bring us home to the present moment; Blind Eileen's omnipresent faith in the Creator and her unwavering gratitude, wisdom, and wit; and my incredible experience of living amid the gratitude and "collective energy" of the Nevisian people. These continue to enhance my worldview and inspire and deepen my belief that I will have what I need and I will be okay. My deepest gratitude for the sustained support and belief of family, friends, colleagues, consultants, editors, and printers who buoyed me when I had no more strength. My faith in the Universe and love and energy from those loved ones in another realm who surrounded me, lightened my being, and carried me—ever so thankfully—so that I still had the ability and clarity to complete this labor of love, which you now read. I fervently hope that these teachings and stories have enriched and will continue to elevate your well-being and strengthen your belief and ability within to define yourself. Additionally, know that you truly matter; be who you are and are meant to be and invest in your destiny so that you can achieve what you once dreamed but thought was impossible. May you embrace your life's journey as you walk your path, be true to yourself, and connect with your *source-connection* and that within others. This basic belief bestows gratitude, fulfillment, self-actualization, and most of all, that amazing grace and precious peace of mind that we each yearn for and so deeply cherish.

It is not simply something that is destined. It has to do with everything that you are, have been, and will be, everything that you do, have done, and will do. *It is not controlled by God or someone else. It is forever.*

The above symbol and words were given to me by a former client and are deeply cherished.

Thank you for your time and trust during our *Soul to Soul Connection and Communication* journey. I hope our path together will continue to enlighten, inspire, and uplift you as you live a more fulfilling and harmonious life with yourself, others, and the Universe. Live each day fully present in your new "now" moments and continue to create, protect, and hold dear your most mindful, *source-connected*, compassionate, and inviting self-loving aura.

As your journey continues to unfold, I fervently hope that if a time comes when you receive a rare, astonishing, riveting, and sacred moment that resoundingly reverberates and shakes your deepest core and which offers you a never-before-even-vaguely-imagined choice, you embrace that moment. Heed its clarion call, have the courage, will, and belief in yourself and the Universe to take that giant leap of faith, and just go for it! In the meantime, do what you love with those you love.

Journey in peace, joy, health, and connections.

Ruth Lindeck Forman

A blessed and grateful Octogenarian!

Author's Journey

One of my earliest memories occurred when I was three years old. My mother, father, and I drove to New York from Columbus, Ohio, to visit Oma Johanna, my beloved elderly grandmother, who lived in a resident home for seniors in Kew Gardens, New York. On this visit, I recall seeing French doors at a restaurant in the Catskill Mountains. Someone seated me in my high chair with only a view of the wall. Already curious, I must have persistently tried to turn around to see what was going on. My Oma probably suggested that my mother place the high chair on the other side of the table where I could see everything, because I then recall noticing the forest-green trees beyond the French doors.

Shortly after my sister was born in the spring of 1945, our family visited the woman with whom my mother had shared a room in the maternity ward. We traveled to a rural area in Ohio and visited the woman's family. They lived in a very modest and tidy home where potatoes were stored under the wooden floor slats. My parents never spoke in front of me about the humble state of the home. I was already fascinated with different lifestyles, people's stories, and the aromas in their homes.

At the same time, I remember walking with my mother to the home of her seamstress, who was Japanese; she uttered the word *internment* to my mother. I could neither pronounce nor comprehend what it meant. On the walk home, I asked my mother to tell me what "that word" meant. She explained *internment*, but she did not include the fact that individuals of Japanese heritage, such as her seamstress, were rounded up and held against their will. She also did not mention that she had fled Germany because of Nazism and Hitler and that she lost her favorite cousin, three aunts, and three uncles to the ovens at Auschwitz. My mother also did not mention the harsh discrimination faced by minorities or the unjust history of people who came to the United States through the African slave trade, or the genocide of the Native Americans. It wasn't until some years later that I began to understand and weave those stories together.

During those early years, I also recall the frolic of shared backyard events with the children in our L-shaped row of flats, playing hopscotch, jumping rope, and engaging in a ball game called Oliver Twist. We also played hide-and-seek and put on summer shows, and one mother crafted Hawaiian hula skirts out of green crepe paper. There were cooling and fun-filled water fights with children and their dads. Mothers hung up and folded the laundry. Men returned from the war, and a few couples divorced. A nurse became a friend. I also recall babysitting, helping a mother take care of her newborn infant, and remaining with a woman at her bedside in the summer heat while waiting for her husband to come home to take her to the hospital to deliver their first son. In our childhood backyard group, there was also an eleven-year-old neighbor who died of heart failure; his dog, Queenie, was never the same. Another boy who lived down the street loved to receive a treat from the "yummy man." He had Down syndrome, and I recall his heartbroken wail when a car ran over his dog. A few of these people became lifelong friends, and two neighbors married and remained soul mates throughout their lives.

When I began elementary school, I soon discovered that I was the only Jewish student in my class and, perhaps except for one other student, the only Jewish child in my school. Looking back, my husband noted that I was "an American child raised in a German home." My classmates in our blue-collar neighborhood came from close-knit, two-parent families that honored their children and hard work.

In junior high school, I met a more diverse group of friends. Although I never felt that I belonged among them as much as they belonged with one another, my peers and their families always treated me fairly and included me in many activities. I loved attending a friend's Bible school graduation. My other Christian friend, who went to the same Wee Wisdom kindergarten as I did, was my first tent-mate at age seven at a rustic Girl Scout camp. At an early age, we enjoyed swimming lessons at the YWCA and shared in lighting Christmas trees in her home and Chanukah candles in my home. Later, we were counselors at the same Girl Scout camp where I was a lifeguard that paid for most of my college tuition and books. Though later in life we lived in different states, we visited and saw each other several times. During life, she and I shared tales about boyfriends, college, marriage, children, sickness, and health and the woes, joys, and challenges of each. She and her husband joined us for Passover during her final stage of ovarian cancer. She shared intimate details about the amazing and courageous battle she fought to stay alive until her son graduated high school. I last spoke with her in the hospital shortly before her mother arrived from out of state, the day before she died at the age of forty-two. The memories of her as a pioneer recipient of a bone marrow transplant and her fortitude in fighting cancer still inspire me, and the image of her gentle and loving mother still touches me. Later, her younger sister and her daughter remained in touch.

At quite an early age, I began to feel a strong connection with nature that sprang from sheer wonder and pleasure and that continues to be an integral part of my life. (I will share more in a few pages.) My interest in and curiosity about people of all ages from differing cultures and backgrounds, especially those experiencing hardships, facing prejudice, or surviving the Holocaust—all overcoming great odds—and a natural instinct led me to help others.

It was enjoyable visiting the elderly with my mother. Later, by myself, I also visited a meticulous and strict neighbor and her husband on Sundays. I continued spending time with the elderly, including neighbors in California, and then, several decades later, Blind Eileen in Nevis. They served as role models as I sat captivated, soaking in their wisdom and absorbing insights from their life's journeys, obstacles, and adventures. Their broad experiences highlighted the importance of making adjustments, overcoming hurdles, and remaining grateful and optimistic. Others became disappointed and despondent as their fortitude, memory, and ability variously declined. These individuals played a significant role in preparing me for life and my older age.

I recall a fond memory from when I was about ten years old and my family visited my father's barber and friend to celebrate Christmas. His home was no more than five blocks from where we lived in a flat with other blue-collar and middle-class families; however, he lived on the "other side" of Broad Street. When we arrived at my father's friend's two-story home, I was amazed by its elegance. As we entered the house, a gorgeous crystal chandelier hung in the entrance. A few moments later, Diane, his beautiful "angel," descended the staircase. He and his wife had recently adopted her. While enjoying a Christmas meal with them, I recollect my father and his friend conversing about law school. Apparently, he had received straight As in his undergraduate classes but was unable to get into law school because he was a Negro. I remember thinking how unfair it was, because he was a warm, soft-spoken, friendly gentleman and one person whom I always stopped to greet while running errands.

My father was not interested in the outdoors or sports, but my mother enjoyed walking and swimming. When we got a TV, the only sporting events that my mother watched on it were the tennis championship tournaments and the Summer and Winter Olympics. During the Summer Olympics, especially whenever they showcased track-and-field, my mother often mentioned that when she and my father lived in Berlin, they had attended the 1936 Olympics, when Jesse Owens won four gold medals and set world records. Despite his success, Adolf Hitler refused to shake his hand.

My mother shared that many people silently walked out of the stadium in support of Jesse Owens and in protest to Hitler's blatant snub. Owens was the most successful athlete at the games, and his outstanding achievements discredited Hitler's myth of Aryan supremacy. Owens attended The Ohio State University (OSU), and later, the university awarded him an honorary Doctorate of Athletic Arts. In 1960, Marlene Owens, the daughter of Jesse Owens and Minnie Ruth Solomon Owens, best known as Ruth, became OSU's first African American Homecoming Queen. At that time, I was elated for and proud of Marlene Owens and the students at my alma mater.

As a child and youth, I enjoyed attending Sunday School at my conservative Temple Tifereth Israel, and I continue to be in touch with the synagogue, a former religious school classmate, and Rabbi Emeritus Herman Berman. There, Rabbi Nathan Zelizer and a Sunday school teacher named Mrs. Shenker took me under their wings. They gave me the honor of presenting the "Floral Offering" at my confirmation. Our modest flat was down the street from the synagogue, where congregants parked during the High Holidays. I felt embarrassed to let them see where I lived, and I recall "dodging" into our flat as my peers were getting in their family cars, flocking to the suburbs. My involvement in the United Synagogue Youth (USY) group was fun. It was an honor to attend a conclave at the B'nai B'rith Perlman Camp in Starlight, Pennsylvania, where the most esteemed and civil rights activist Rabbi Abraham Joshua Heschel led the services.

When I was a sophomore in high school, my family moved to Bexley, one of the most upscale suburbs in Ohio, which had a large Jewish population. Fifty years later, the Bexley City School District remains among the most outstanding school systems in the country and ranks exceedingly high in the state. Although there were many of both the Christian and Jewish faith who reached out, there were a few who focused more on the labels of my less classy clothing than who I was as a person. The classmate who became homecoming queen was always sincere, friendly, and inviting. I also recall an incident in the restroom when a classmate pulled down the back of my sweater to check the label; another remarked that I would never fit in. I began to feel more like I was looking from the outside in.

During my high school years, I wrote for the *Torch*, our school newspaper, and was honored to become a member of the Quill and Scroll International Honor Society for High School Journalists. That experience probably was the first "official" step of my half-century of devotion to the love of writing. While on staff at the *Torch*, I met the editor, who became and remains a dear friend. Over the decades, we have shared the ups and downs of relationships, health, life's joys and challenges, and most passionate conversations of our similar progressive views. I also kept in touch with a close childhood friend whose parents were part of my parents' German Jewish social crowd. We continued to share the joys of life and volunteer projects that touched our hearts. Even with a background of childhood polio, she continues to travel, direct, and support many worthy organizations, including a local food bank.

I held great respect for Rabbi Nathan Zelizer, who used his pulpit to convey his voluminous progressive ideals. He often mentioned his visits to the prisoners at The Ohio State Penitentiary. I recall the chilling feeling and heavy banging doors when I went with a group that visited that maximum-security prison. As a teen and young woman, I often conferred with the rabbi in his home a couple of blocks from mine. He shared two meaningful concepts with me. The first was his answer to my question "What is God?" He replied, "God is man in his perfection, and man is God in the making." He also shared that "parents have the greater responsibility to the child as they brought the child into the world."

In my freshman year at Miami University in Oxford, Ohio, I majored in liberal arts. Lacking funds, I transferred to The Ohio State University (OSU), where I lived at home and held various jobs to pay for college. At OSU, I enrolled in the college of education and joined the International Students Association. During this time, I spent a lot of time with Lee, who had high standards, loved the outdoors, and was cool and always fun. He became my lifetime companion and husband. His family also valued education. Lee held several jobs and took out minor student loans to attend a small private school in Indiana, where he graduated with honors. He was in college during the same time as four of his siblings, and his father managed by securing loans to help pay for their college expenses on his middle-class income. When the bankers asked him for collateral, he responded, "My children."

During those early years at OSU, Lee's then girlfriend, his sister's boyfriend, and my boyfriend all lived out of town. So Lee, his sister, his best friend, and I spent most weekends going to movies and bowling. During a classroom presentation at OSU, four students who were receiving speech therapy at the OSU Speech and Hearing Clinic shared their experiences of overcoming their stuttering challenges. That was an "aha" moment, when I immediately knew I wanted to become a speech and hearing therapist—as the profession was then named. When I entered the department, I knew that I was home. I was extremely fortunate that OSU's Department of Speech and Hearing Therapy was one of the top ten in the country. I studied under professors who were among the pioneers in our field, then in its infancy. The discipline was established following

World War II. Shortly after I graduated with a Bachelor of Science degree in Education with a Speech and Hearing Therapy Certificate, I joined the staff at the OSU Speech and Hearing Clinic and married Lee. A year later, Lee, our infant son, and I moved to Southern California. There, I was on staff at the Community Speech and Hearing Center, primarily serving individuals who were recovering from strokes or head traumas.

In the late 1960s, I was again fortunate when I enrolled for my master of arts degree at California State University, Northridge (CSUN) in the then-named Department of Communicative Disorders. In its early stages, the department was housed in a converted groundskeeper house, double garage, and tack shack for horses, the smell of which permeated the building during rainy weather. Even then, it had, and has maintained, its high standard and status as one of the national top ten departments in our field. Outstanding and collaborative teachers and professors provided the context for an in-depth understanding of diagnoses, treatment, pragmatic insights, and tools. Learning took place during enlightening and often lighthearted dialogues in a warm and nurturing environment.

In 2012, Rebecca Mieliwonki was selected as the National Teacher of the Year; she is a graduate of the outstanding Michael D. Eisner College of Education at CSUN. The slogan *CSUN Rise* was created early in President Dianne F. Harrison's tenure. At the prestigious 2016 Annual Volunteer Service Award Luncheon, it was noted that *The Wall Street Journal* rated CSUN the third most diverse university in the country. In the fall edition of the *CSUN Magazine*, President Harrison noted that the journal *Nature* acclaimed "our university as a rising star and one of North America's top 25 institutions for science. CSUN held the highest percentage increase in publication rate at more than 190 percent in a year, followed by NASA, the US Geological Survey, Carnegie Mellon University, and Stanford University" (Harrison 2016). The article also pointed out that CSUN was the sole public institution in California that they recognized. Harrison highlighted a collaborative effort for piquing the interest and motivation of professors, students, and local and international projects and investing in infrastructure as keys to achieving this success.

In addition to CSUN's stellar achievements in academics, diversity, financial gains for students upon graduation, and several other areas, CSUN is the leader in sustainability among the twenty-three campuses within the California State University system. CSUN also earned LEED Certificates for Efficiency Design (Francis 2013). The appealing, multihued gardens and walkways display xeriscape landscaping that conserves water.

My marriage to Lee was founded on love, family, shared values, a mutual desire to spend time in the great outdoors and, as our rabbi, Stan Levy, declared, "the wonderment, miracle, and mystery of nature." After I had known Lee for seven years as my girlfriend's older brother, he asked if I would like to go with him to a water-filled quarry that had rings that spanned high above the water. We had a ball as we swung like monkeys from ring to ring before we plunged into the water. During those months when we dated and became engaged, he worked out of town. Unlike most of our peers, our weekends were spent walking in the woods, stargazing, and mostly enjoying nature. This pattern continued through the decades in Southern California with our children at local parks and beaches, spending summers in the High Sierras and other national parks. Years later, we traveled alone to the European Alps and have spent twenty-five years in Nevis.

I can still recall our family's first trip to Yosemite National Park. As we emerged from the Wawona Tunnel, the breathtaking scene of El Capitan captivated me; Yosemite Falls, the High Country, Half Dome, and the Yosemite Valley below unfolded in all their magnificence and grandeur.

Love of family, nature, swimming, hiking, stargazing, watching the journey of the planets and familiar constellations, photography, writing, and gardening continue to highlight my life. My California garden is a welcoming haven from my hectic lifestyle. Our Nevis garden abounds with a multitude of vibrant flora. There, the colorful flight of the yellow-and-black bananaquit birds, the stately elegance and patience of the slate-blue heron, and the piercing call and song of the locally named *perritata* continue to bring me delight and appreciation for the fact that they stopped to spend time with me.

During our early years in California, travels with our children began by camping in primitive tents and cooking over wood-burning firepits. I had waited on going to Israel for twenty-three years since the time my aunt and cousins from Israel had visited us in Ohio. So in 1977, fifteen years into our marriage, our family, which then included three children, aged seven, eleven, and fourteen, traveled there for three weeks. First, Lee, our youngest daughter, and I stayed with my aunt and uncle, and our two older children stayed nearby with my cousin whose children were about the same age. Our children felt perfectly safe in Israel. Within short time after we settled in, they went down to the courtyard to find some other children. Although some of the younger Israeli children didn't speak English, they invited our youngest daughter to play in their apartments. When I wanted to find her, I went down to the courtyard and asked in Hebrew, "Where is the American child?" One of the children immediately went and fetched her.

Later, our family went touring by ourselves. We rented a minicompact, and as we drove, the dashboard fell into my lap. The replacement vehicle didn't shift into reverse, so we had to push it out of parking spaces. Driving through the desert, we saw Bedouins camped in tents reminiscent of biblical times. We also picked up a small-framed Israeli soldier who carried an Israeli Uzi machine gun. One of our children who sat in the crowded back seat next to the soldier wasn't fazed by the gun but recalls feeling "squished." We visited Yamit, then part of the Israeli-occupied Egyptian Sinai Peninsula, and we also stayed at a youth hostel in Eilat. Our accommodation was a tiny round windowless concrete hut furnished with bunk beds and a fan that clanged so loudly it kept us up till midnight. At that magical hour, on a dreadfully hot night, we packed our small duffel bags and suitcases, and for ten minutes, we trekked across the dark desert to reach a resort, which fortunately had two rooms available. At the hotel, green plastic rings served as currency, and many youths strutted around to show off their multistranded ring necklaces.

Early one morning, we strolled through the Old City of Jerusalem as bakers were opening their stalls with aromas of fresh breads. The mosque bells' toll and the early-morning chants beckoned Muslims to prayer. While in the Holy Land, we stopped at the Wailing Wall, more commonly called the Western Wall. There, men, women, young, and old of various beliefs went to touch the holy site, offer prayers, and slip notes of prayers, thanks, or wishes between the stones. We were also fortunate that, although we were Jewish, we still were welcome to enter the Dome of the Rock. This sacred Muslim shrine is built on the same Temple Mount as the remnants of the second Jewish temple built by King Herod. (The Temple Mount also is known as Mount Moriah or Mount Zion.) We also walked the Via Dolorosa, the route that Jesus took between his condemnation, crucifixion, and burial. On the return from Jerusalem to Tel Aviv, our son commented, "Some people have hearts like stones, and some stones have hearts like people."

Before departing Israel, my aunt shared her experience of a terrorist attack. The bombing occurred decades ago, when she and my Uncle Zwi lived in Jerusalem. There, my aunt, with my infant cousin in tow, had shopped at a butcher shop. Shortly after they left, as she reached the other side of the street to run her next errand, she heard a loud explosion. When she turned around, she saw that a bomb had exploded in the shop that she had just left. My aunt and cousin narrowly escaping death had a profound lifelong impact that helped me frame life, death, and destiny.

Following Israel, we continued our trip on a flight to Bucharest, Romania. Shortly after takeoff, we had to return to the airport because the plane had lost power in an engine. When we arrived eight hours later in Romania, Rosie and Alexander, Lee's elderly relatives, awaited us clutching a bouquet of wilted flowers. There they lived in a very small two-room apartment that included a tiny kitchen and bathroom off to the side. Their bedroom served as their living room and contained twin beds and Rosie's half-filled wardrobe with five dresses. Yet by Romanian standards, they were well-off. They also were quite resourceful and worked out a system with close younger friends whose mother lived with them. The friends gave Rosie and Alexander enough money to purchase whatever limited food was available to the public for all four of them and the couple's mother. So every day, Rosie and Alexander shopped, prepared a meal, ate, and then left their apartment for the younger couple to enjoy a private dinner and evening. Rosie and Alexander also benefitted from cultural events, as their friends provided the funds for all four to enjoy the performances. Alexander received a retirement pension that provided a reasonably comfortable lifestyle exceeding that of their peers. Rosie enjoyed weekly manicures, and she and Alexander went to world-renowned baths and health spas on the Black Sea for a month every summer. Shortly before we arrived, Romania had just suffered an earthquake and was under communist rule.

I vividly recollect a family train ride and viewing women in a field with yokes on their backs, carrying buckets of cement at either end, while the men leisurely sat nearby and smoked their cigarettes. Each day after breakfast, one or another agency "secretly" followed us. We had to exercise caution as to the amount of goods brought from California we could take to our relatives each day. In Israel, Lee had purchased a small sculptured silver art piece that was placed on the front desk counter for "safekeeping" until we left. After Romania, we traveled on a train to Switzerland. Unknowingly, we had purchased second-class tickets that provided us with wooden bench seats similar to a wooden church pew. Either my husband or I had to stand up so the children could fall asleep while leaning on one another. A farmer who smelled "ripe" after working the field shared our small compartment. If our relatives hadn't packed lots of food, we would have had nothing to eat for a day and a half except the chocolate bars and Pepsi that they sold on the train.

Two years later, Lee and I returned to Israel and Romania without our children. While taking a shortcut during an outing to the Old City in Jerusalem, we unknowingly crossed a wadi.

My uncle admonished us for taking that route, as it was quite dangerous. When we returned to Romania, still during the Cold War era, we visited a remote resort high in the mountains where the cattle roamed freely on the front lawn. We walked up the mountain to a restaurant that served local game. Afterward, we went to a club, met a Russian couple, and exchanged partners to dance with each other. Before we left, we also exchanged gifts; I gave them chewing gum, and the man gave me a small set of Russian nesting dolls. We were the only English-speaking people present.

In the early 1980s, after Alexander retired, he and Rosie traveled from Romania to a family reunion on the East Coast and then to visit my family before going on to California. During their six-week visit, I learned an extremely valuable lesson. Compared with what their peers in the United States would enjoy, life and food choices were meager in Romania. So I suggested that Rosie and Alexander walk daily to the nearby local supermarket and buy anything they wanted. In return, they offered to prepare dinner.

Shortly before our relatives returned to Romania, Rosie leaned back at breakfast one morning after eating and, savoring as much of a plentiful variety of food as she could possibly eat, exclaimed, "All my life, I thought, if I had enough of all the food I wanted, I would be happy. But even with all that for six weeks, that didn't make me any happier." Her words taught me that we are slaves to an illusion that *if we only…life would be perfect.*

During the 1980s, my husband and I took several annual trips to Europe. After brief stops in the major cities to visit museums and historical and Jewish sites, we ventured and remained mostly in remote mountainous areas. In the quaint village of Beaufort, France, everyone in the bar curiously watched as we placed an overseas long-distance phone call to our children. We observed a bride and groom's matrimonial procession on the uneven old sidewalks around the small village. We asked a local person, "How old is the local church?" He replied, "Very old." As people of various customs, lifestyles, cuisines, scents, and cultures have always enthralled me, these unusual experiences were normal to me.

During the year that I developed the programs for my company, Communication Enhancement, I joined the Sierra Club and participated in a weekly Tuesday hike with a wonderful group of people. Many owned their own businesses, had just retired, or arranged their own professional schedule, some working four-day ten-hour shifts. We usually hiked at least eight miles along the beach or in the Santa Monica Mountains. As we hiked, we alternated with whom we strolled and chatted as we shared lighthearted conversations and deep discussions about life, relationships, and nature. During lunch, we laughed at many jokes and stories, especially those of the men who were childhood friends in Brooklyn. Loving and deep bonds among some grew into lifelong friendships. In 1984, I joined a Sierra Club outing, hiking ten days in the High Sierra Mountains between Mammoth Lakes and Tuolumne Meadows. Our hike was primarily spent on the Pacific Crest Trail in Yosemite National Park. As we began our ten-day trek, I recall the majestic green firs with the beautiful, pure blue sky as their background. Our primitive tent sites were adjacent to lakes or streams, and there was no electricity. Mules lugged our equipment and heavy packs, and I only had to carry a lighter backpack, water, and hiking stick. I trained for six months and dedicated my hike to my dear friend Nancy Phares Cornell, who had died of ovarian cancer two years earlier.

One day, we hiked from our campground to Thousand Island Lakes. There, the spectacular scenery made it one of the most superb hikes I had ever undertaken. My culminating feat of the approximately fifty-mile hike was reaching 12,300 feet at Parker Pass, 500 feet short of where the other hikers peaked. There were times that I couldn't take another step, but my fellow hikers stayed back and encouraged me to reach my goal. Then, they continued to the higher destination. I was getting tired, so I hiked down alone, surrounded by serenity and splendor, which gave me strength to walk back to the campground. That hike was my greatest physical accomplishment.

In the early 1980s, several people began to suggest that I develop a program to reduce the accents of *Born-abroad* professionals, especially physicians, businesspeople, and accountants. It was a natural transition to dedicate my work to helping people of diverse cultural backgrounds to overcome their communication obstacles and achieve a greater sense of belonging, fulfillment, success, and comfort in their newly adopted environment. After a year of research, audio-taping, and analyzing people's accents, I debuted the Communication Enhancement Accent Reduction Program, first to individuals and small businesses, and later to doctors and hospitals.

I recall how terrified I was when I presented my program to my first major corporate client on Wilshire Avenue. I had never presented in this type of setting, and there I was, dressed in a red jacket, facing a group of men sitting around the long table. I visualized clutching a shiny fireman pole to the heavens for help, and I began.

One man asked, Since they were spending all this money for this program, shouldn't the people speak English in their homes? I quickly replied, "No. Every person should have a place where they feel comfortable. And if their native language is more comfortable at this time, that's what I recommend that they speak."

Shortly after, I divided the program into medical and business editions. After the first group of individuals had completed the six-month program, both the participants and the personnel directors who had hired me implied that although the clients were pleased with the outcome and were far easier to understand, something about their communication style was still amiss. Then, I developed a one-day seminar that was initially named *Communication Skills and Protocol*, but within a few years, the title was changed to *Communication Is More Than Just Talking*. During those years, I authored fifty articles on intercultural communication, including a series for the Korean and Japanese newspapers in Los Angeles. I also wrote articles on intercultural communication pertinent to the medical and legal professions for *LACMA Physicians* and *Los Angeles Lawyer* and an article titled "I Say What" for *That Balance* magazine, on whose cover Dianne Feinstein appeared. She was the former and first female mayor of San Francisco and has served as U.S. senator from California since 1992. In her article, Feinstein shared how she attempts to remain balanced in her "overcommitted" state. She gardens, bird-watches, and strolls the beach to help maintain harmony. She stated, "One small lesson I've learned is to listen to my body and pace myself" (Feinstein 1990).

In 1987, I had to take the first of several health-related "time-outs" when I required a laminectomy, performed by a gifted and compassionate young surgeon. Two years later, I underwent a quadruple coronary bypass. Again, I was extremely fortunate that Dr. Taro Yokoyama, often referred as the King of Hearts, was local and served as my cardiac surgeon. Ten years later, I required a further coronary bypass to replace vessels that were too large (though no fault of my own). Afterward, Dr. Yokoyama thanked me for "being such a good patient." I shared that I had recently learned to meditate, and a week prior to surgery, I went into deep meditation, asked God to help guide his hand, and pictured myself jumping as high as a teenage cheerleader.

Then, in the mid-1990s, I was strongly urged to write a book that was called *Communication Is More Than Just Talking*. The book included an invaluable section on multicultural communication. Within a year, I added a more spiritual tone, so I edited the book and renamed it *Communication Is Connection: 10 Steps to Create Your Own Positive Communication Environment*. Twenty years later, in a broader, more spiritual, mindful, and inclusive tone, is the book that you are now reading.

Years ago, I had a profound cleansing experience during Yom Kippur, the Jewish Day of Atonement, led by Rabbi Stan Levy at B'nai Horin, Children of Freedom, our spiritual Jewish community in California. In his other role, Stanley Levy, JD, practices law and founded B'nai Horin fifty years ago. He passionately serves from his heart and gives time as rabbi and spiritual leader. Rabbi Stan Levy invites a wide range of individuals such as Palestinian artistic leaders and individuals who survived human trafficking to enlighten our community. As a humanistic and universal human being, he humbly offers deep, thought-provoking Jewish principles in a kind, healing, and inclusive manner that creates a protective umbrella. Engulfed within this safe surrounding, a person gains the ability to let go and feel vulnerable enough to deeply penetrate and soul-search within. After a profound, spiritual, and cleansing experience, I was wide open to forge a new and more positive path.

In his "spare time," Rabbi Levy, along with other Jewish attorneys, cofounded Bet Tzedek, the House of Justice. The nonprofit organization embraces the fundamental Jewish tenet "*Justice, justice, you shall pursue.*" Bet Tzedek serves a host of goals, including assisting individuals in poverty, those who experienced labor abuses, and those who have been discriminated against. In addition, Rabbi Levy was "the Executive Director of Public Counsel and the former Deputy Director of the Western Center on Law and Poverty. Furthermore, Rabbi Stan Levy is one of the founders of the Academy for Jewish Religion, California (a rabbinic and cantorial seminary in Los Angeles)." More information may be found at http://bnaihorin.com/about-us/meet-our-staff/. Rabbi Stan Levy also shared that he is the Founding National Director of Bet Tzedek's Holocaust Survivors Justice Network.

He met Laura Owens several years before he encouraged her to attend the academy to become a rabbi (http://www.ajrca.edu). She was formerly an actress, had spent years as an archeologist, and promoted healthy children, the environment, and wellness. In 2006, she was honored by the Wellness Community and received the Human Spirit Award (B'nai Horin 2016). Later, Rabbi Laura Owens became corabbi of B'nai Horin. She brings an inclusive, more traditional, and mostly lighthearted voice and shares stories and experiences related to Jewish tenets that easily connect with members of our community. In these times, their views are most welcome to uplift our spirits.

Another one of my greatest gifts during my transformation came from the profound enlightenment gleaned from a decade of experiencing and reading the teachings of the Buddhist monk and Zen master Thich Nhat Hanh. These tenets are collectively practiced during the weekly Malibu Sangha, when Rosemary Alden opens her heart and home.

In 2002, my husband and I joined our daughter and her husband during their worldwide travels. We met them in South Africa, beginning in Cape Town. There, we visited Robben Island, where Nelson Mandela was incarcerated for eighteen of his twenty-seven years spent in prison. While there, we toured and walked to the mines where the brutality of the reflecting, scorching sunlight robbed Mandela of his ability to tear up but could not tear down his spirit. During the tour, I remained behind to tightly grip the bars of his cell and tried to grasp a sense of Mandela's soul. It was one of the most moving spiritual experiences of my entire life, as I sensed the essence of his spirit of those past decades, spent in grace and dignity, defiant to every attempt to shatter his spirit. As I stood trembling and clinging to his cell, I knew and felt that I was standing on very hallowed ground. From there, the four of us took a local train to Johannesburg. Then, Lee and I went on a safari at Sabi Sands. Life in Nevis, West Indies, among our Nevisian family and community profoundly continue to affect my life. I expand on that in a few paragraphs.

Please pause as I share my and your prehistoric and more recent ancestors' journey. Currently, science supports that our journey began approximately 180,000 years ago, when all human beings sprang from the African Eve in the Rift Valley of Africa. With the information revealed by participating in National Geographic's Geographic Project, I discovered that somewhere in my genetic lineage, my clan was among the first to mutate and also the first to leave Africa. Through that lineage, my matriarchal ancestors' branch returned and remained in Africa until at least ten thousand years ago.

My aunt in Israel shared that our family on my maternal grandmother's line migrated directly to Germany following the Spanish Inquisition and the expulsion of Jews from Spain in 1492. I also discovered that the members of my paternal family from Frankfurt, Germany, had been political and progressive since the 1700s. My paternal grandfather, Gustav Levy, partnered with a company that manufactured wood molding for frames and trays. He was the first Jewish person to serve in some capacity at the Berlin Chamber of Commerce. From all stories, he and my paternal grandmother, Oma Johanna, were deeply devoted to each other, as each evening she walked to the train station to greet him. Unfortunately, my grandfather passed away before I was born. Although they were wealthy, my Oma Johanna wore winter coats that were lined with fur while the fabric appeared on the outside. Before she donated anything, if a part required fixing or changing, she had it repaired or replaced. In her profound wisdom, she commented, "If those receiving the gifts could afford something nice [or new], they would buy it themselves." Reluctant to leave Nazi Germany and also the grave sites of her beloved husband and fallen son, she finally left on one of the last ships in the fall of 1938 to immigrate to the U.S.A.

My maternal grandmother, Oma Selma, and my grandfather, Siegfried Richter, who also passed away long before I was born, established a twenty-one-windowed store named Richter, in Hamm, Westphalia, Germany. The store featured fine china, silver, and luggage. My grandmother had to leave most of that behind as she fled Nazi Germany and immigrated with her new husband to Brazil. I recall that when she immigrated to the United States in the early 1950s, although she had three maids and a summer and winter Mercedes in Germany, she donned a scarf around her head, got down on her knees, and helped my mother clean. There was no attitude; she just did what she had to do. Although she was hard of hearing and didn't speak a word of English, every Saturday after attending Sabbath services, while she remained dressed up, she rode a bus down-town by herself to shop. My Oma Selma and my mother were, and I continue to be, dedicated lifelong swimmers. Recently, my youngest daughter and her eldest daughter have joined the now five-generation female legacy.

Quite fortunately, I come from a line of strong, independent, progressive women. My moth-er's dream to become an interpreter was suddenly interrupted during her first year studying in col-lege in Lucerne, Switzerland. Her father had suddenly died of heart failure. She immediately left school to return home to comfort and support her mother in managing the store. When my very charming traveling salesman father, wearing white leather gloves, serviced my grandmother's store, he met my very attractive and sexy mother. He took one look at her legs and declared, "I came, I saw, I conquered."

Soon after my parents married, they moved to Berlin. When Nazism was on the rise, my par-ents took in a boarder who was a Turkish consul. This offered my parents the opportunity to hang a Turkish flag outside their apartment that provided a layer of protection. Following a dinner, their Turkish boarder let out a huge belch. My parents were stunned because they were unaccustomed to that. The Turkish guest enlightened my parents and explained that the large belch was a gesture of appreciation for the delicious meal. He gave my mother a beautiful silver cuff bracelet, etched in black with a camel, palm tree, and rose, which I continue to cherish and wear. Prior to the time my parents left Germany, my father and my uncle often slept on park benches at night to observe the movements of the Nazi soldiers. My mother had a first cousin who was half-Jewish. During World War II, her friend's Jewish husband was stationed with the Germans at the Russian front. Because he was circumcised, he concocted a tale that his father had worked in Egypt and this procedure maintained hygiene. In this deception, he could pass as a Christian. My cousin was quite clever, and she also passed as a Christian. She worked at Nazi headquarters, where she falsified documents and doctored reports to throw off the Nazis. She notified Jews when they were in danger. When she learned that her husband's troops were advancing, she pretended that she was his sister, forged some papers, and traveled the Russian front, where she rescued her husband with the story that "their" mother was dying. She also had forged papers so that she and her husband could escape and keep moving from place to place, disguised with the same modus operandi, until they reached the bor-der. She was quick on her feet and took charge whenever they were interrogated. They eventually reached Australia, where they lived happily and very much in love until old age.

Years later, when my parents immigrated to the United States, they arrived on a first-class ocean liner. In Germany, my mother had grown up with three maids, yet shortly after she arrived in New York, she went to work as a maid herself. Due to her absence of skills, the job didn't last a week. When my parents moved to Columbus, Ohio, when I was eight months old, my mother managed alone without hired help. Our neighbors came to her aid when necessary, as my father traveled for business. Her lifestyle and socioeconomic status had drastically changed, yet she never complained, was never jealous, and was continually grateful that the United States had taken in our family.

During my teenage years, after we had moved to the suburbs, she volunteered door-to-door collecting for various charities, visited the elderly, and even took in and cared for a friend following a colectomy so that her husband could continue to travel on business.

When the woman who had faithfully helped clean our home for years—first weekly, and then bimonthly—began to age, she could no longer complete all the tasks in one day. So my mother lovingly pitched in, got down on her knees, and cleaned the baseboards to help her finish so that she could keep her job and her dignity.

After my dad died when my mother was sixty-eight, she never lost her zest for life. In spite of fears brought on by her experiences with Hitler, she remained independent and traveled abroad. Three years before she died at the age of eighty, she entered the Senior Olympics at the Jewish Center and came in first place in swimming, beating those who were ten years younger. For that, she earned a plaque that read, "For demonstrating that age is no barrier in the pursuit of personal triumph and fitness." My mother never gave up on anything.

Although as a traveling salesman my dad was rarely home, I have loving memories of him, especially as a young child going to the central market, with him holding my hand. When in town, he attended some of my school and scouting events. My fun-loving, lighthearted father was foremost a cool gentleman and mostly quite humble. While in Germany, working at his father's tray- and frame-molding factory, he preferred to eat his lunch with the workers instead of the elites. Although only a few extended family members were present when he died, more than one hundred people attended his funeral. They included several clients, his friend the barber, and a skycap from the airport.

During the early years of Hitler's regime, against her mother's wishes, my maternal aunt joined a Zionist youth movement and left as a pioneer in her teens to immigrate to what was then named Palestine. In 1954, after not seeing her mother and sister for eighteen years, my aunt and my cousins visited the United States, first arriving in New York. There, they stayed with my paternal aunts until their papers were in order to travel within the country. Then, my father picked them up and brought them to Columbus, where all three stayed with us for nine months in our small, two-bedroom, one-bathroom flat. We had a blast. My aunt, whom I previously mentioned, remained a lifelong friend and mentor as we continued sharing life, first by mail, then later by phone. Years later, she and my uncle visited us a couple of times in California.

In their early twenties, my paternal aunts traveled unchaperoned by ship to visit Sweden, which was unusual for young women of upper-class Jewish circles. Both aunts became health-care professionals. One became a pediatric nurse. In 1940, after I was born in Manhattan, she spent six weeks with my mother. When my sister was born in Columbus, Ohio, my aunt traveled from New York and stayed for weeks with my mother while my dad traveled for business. While still in Germany, my other aunt began training for medical school and married. When she immigrated to the United States, she studied physical therapy and eventually became the director of physical therapy at the Hospital for Joint Diseases in Manhattan. She also volunteered offering the Lamaze method to women before childbirth; she was very, very cool. When I visited her in New York in my late teens, I loved to join her on her grocery-shopping jaunts because everybody was delighted to see her. One afternoon, we went to Greenwich Village to buy a "hippie" dress so we could blend in as we ventured through the village. As she aged, she apologized that she had to take a cab and could no longer ride the subway. When she moved into a senior citizen home, everybody called her by her first name, Anni, as she refused to be called Mrs. Biel. She had a hip surgery soon after she retired and shortly before her fiftieth wedding anniversary. She was in so much pain that her former teacher and mentor traveled from Switzerland to help rehabilitate her in time to dance at the celebration. Years later, when we attended my other paternal aunt's milestone eightieth birthday celebration in San Francisco, she still beamed with her glowing smile, radiant eyes, and vivacious personality. As all eyes were focused on my other aunt, I happened to glance around the room. In a moment of repose, when she thought no one was looking, I saw the physical pain etched on her face. My family roots and experiences led me into the health-care profession and fostered the risk-taking and adventuresome path I've taken. It all seems perfectly normal to me, as that is all I have ever known.

My eldest daughter serves a hospice nurse and is a third-generation health-care provider. She continues another female legacy.

As a speech therapist, I met the wife of one of my patients, who was recovering from a stroke. He became one of my dearest patients. At twenty-seven years old, I kindly requested—then firmly insisted—that his wife step outside her husband's room while I evaluated his speech and language. She didn't like that. Years later, she shared that she told her son, "I met a young whippersnapper who is going to give me trouble." Over the years, we became very close friends; she became a second mom, and I became the daughter she did not have. In my professional experience, she was one of the rare spouses or family members who continued to treat their spouse the same as they had treated him in the various facilities. Along with lighthearted humor between them, she always regarded her husband with respect and dignity. After he returned home from rehabilitation, his wife considered her husband an equal partner in making family and travel decisions. She also served as a terrific role model for being a devoted long-distance grandmother. For years, she not only opened her heart but also generously opened to our young family her family's remote, primitive mountain cabin (with an outdoor latrine) in Foresta, California, adjacent to Yosemite National Park. She was also quite courageous. After she became a widow, she lived alone in the wilderness cabin part of each year. Long before the computer age, she sent numerous typed letters, written by candlelight, often while whirling snowstorms caused power outages and coyotes howled outside. When I underwent my first heart procedure, for couple weeks, she sent daily get-well cards. She always supported me personally and professionally, lovingly declaring, "That's my girl."

For most of my young adult life, my children were my primary focus. I was fortunate that my husband and I had chosen that my role would be a stay-at-home mom, although I worked ten hours a week before our youngest daughter was born. My children were and always are deeply loved and cherished. They were among my first true teachers, and they continue to enlighten me. In their youth, they taught me to be more positive in more ways than most others combined had during my formative years. My six grandchildren are the icing on the cake, as they so delight and enlighten me by who they each are. Each of their spirits and how they approach and live their lives brings deep gratitude and joy to my husband and me.

One of my life's greatest treasures is nearly thirty years of traveling to and living in Nevis much of the time with my husband. Living in a local village, fully immersed in local life, amidst the "collective energy" of the Nevisian people gifted me with an immeasurable dimension of calm. There the deep connections of family, friendship, community, understanding, appreciation, mutuality, respect, love, and trust endure. With all my flaws and health-related needs, they accept me without reservation or expectation for whom I am. I am truly unconditionally loved. As a friend proclaimed when I had to cancel an event, "We're in it for the long haul not the short run." My husband and I take great pride as we are often referred to by the locals as "one of us."

Whenever I am not in Nevis, Nevis is always with me. Nevis is similar to a computer program that is always running in the background. Most mornings when I begin my morning yoga, pilates, qi gong, tai chi, and now physical therapy routine, I stand with eyes closed, as I go on a spiritual worldly journey to send blessings. I visit loved ones in their homes, on campus or travels, or those in special need. When I have the time, I linger over Nevis at each loved ones' or extended family's home. I also reflect on Nevis both when I open the front door to greet the morning or open the front door at night to give thanks for the day. I pause to observe what the heavenly pallette reflects.

During all our years in Nevis and now, there was never a time when any of my Nevisian friends or extended family members ever left their homes and had to be concerned that they would be pulled over, frisked, maimed, or killed by the police. Therefore, this freedom combined with many other wonderful experiences and blessings make Nevis the place on our precious planet where my spirit always soars and thrives.

My husband and I have been incredibly blessed by meeting Blind Eileen of Zion. More than anyone, she taught me peace of mind and to "accept life as it comes." She has been my sage for more than eighteen years and has been blind for eighty of her one hundred-plus years. I will share her story shortly.

Most of the women I know in Nevis are wise, deep, and lighthearted. They have enlightened me with their deep faith, gratitude, independence, resilience, commitment to family, and positive communication style. They are grounded and mostly "don't take it on," or make "no noise," which translates to "no argument." They exercise a strong, positive, nonverbal style of communication that gets the message across loud and clear and eliminates verbal discord. The Nevisian men are charming, wise, and hardworking, and they show great depth while they also have lots of fun.

In addition, Buddhist Zen master Thich Nhat Hanh, affectionately known as Thây, profoundly enlightens and uplifts me through his incredible, forthright, and easy-to-follow teachings, walking meditations, and multitude of books, but mostly by his humanity, humility, and the way he lives his life. Thây is originally from North Vietnam. During the Vietnam War, he left his monkshood to mingle with the people and inspire them to replace violence with accord. Later, Thây established Plum Village in France. Dr. Martin Luther King Jr. nominated Thây for the 1967 Nobel Peace Prize. King noted in his nomination, "I do not personally know of anyone more worthy of [this prize] than this gentle monk from Vietnam. His ideas for peace, if applied, would build a monument to ecumenism, to world brotherhood, to humanity" (King 1967).

My husband and I had the good fortune to be in Thây's presence several times, either in peaceful walking or totally immersed in the simple yet profound wisdom of his presentations. There I sat fully enveloped in the gentle, strong, centered energy that he exudes. In his late eighties, Thây had a stroke and lost the ability to communicate verbally. However, with sustained worldwide prayers and the support of his monastics and medical support teams, he continues to express his compassion, kindness, and Buddhist beliefs through gestures and his eyes.

All these life experiences have deeply affected and enhanced my life's journey. Please recall one of my all-time favorite sayings related to communication: When I pause to achieve loving speech, I try to remember this quite worthy Zen saying, "*Open mouth, already a big mistake* and frisk my planned utterance at three gates before I release it into the world. These three gates are questions: Is it true? Is it necessary? Will it do no harm?" (Johnson 2006). A simpler version to hold dear is, Is it honest, is it necessary, is it kind?

Our Nevisian friends, who now are mostly in their forties, fifties, and entering their sixties, grew up in spiritual wealth amid material poverty. Some were raised by aunties, a grandparent, or another individual than their natural parents in an era when it took a village to raise a child. As youngsters, before leaving for school, many of our friends walked to neighboring villages a few miles away to fetch daily water and tend to goats and returned to hand-scrub laundry. They lived without electricity or indoor plumbing. Lunch was often a sweet potato sunbaked on a rock. Many grew up in large single-parent families in limited, small two-bedroom homes. Some were abandoned by their fathers, although sometimes both parents were absentees due to circumstances beyond their control, as they were simply doing their best to earn a living for their families. Some absentee parents earned a living trekking miles to the other side of the island before the sun rose and returning long after it set, so their children rarely saw them. Others lived abroad on neighboring islands or other continents to support the family, and a few never returned. Each child was raised by a loving relative, and often it was a grandmother or aunt. Naturally, our friends grew up without TV, internet, or digital technology.

Even with the dearth of material goods in their youth, every one of our friends had one incredible gift that most of my U.S. peers and I did not experience. Our Nevisian and Caribbean friends in their early years already felt an abundance of embedded love and acceptance from God or Jesus. They cling to an unquestioning faith and unshakeable belief etched deep within that they will overcome, have enough, and achieve—all provided by the omnipotent God or Jesus. The elementary school songs often reflect, "I know I will have what I need."

Universally, there are children who do not receive the ideal amount of love, discipline, or nurturing and are abused; Nevis is no exception. However, during my years in Nevis, there were no hungry, homeless, or abandoned children. Stylish and various models of low-cost houses for ownership are offered by the government, and there are no dilapidated or run-down housing projects. Pride in home ownership and upkeep is paramount. Our friends in their forties and older who lacked emotional support and personal validation growing up now receive incredible, powerful, everlasting religious teachings that they pass on to their children. Whatever their circumstances, God or Jesus continues to look after them and provide the strength to overcome. Our local friends now own their own homes, drive cars, and have computers; most have acquired land for their children, and many travel overseas. Their children, many of whom I've known since kindergarten or younger, are now enrolled in technical classes, apprenticeships, colleges, or universities abroad, have graduated law school with honors, or are gainfully employed. Some of the older ones are now married and serve in the U.S. Navy. Others have received their PhDs, are married and have children, and are employed in high-level careers. Many of them continue to call us Nana Ruth and Papa Lee. We keep in touch from California, and some call us on special occasions.

I will forever hold dear the sound of the approaching melodic, happy voices, smiling faces, and the comforting and beckoning "Come, come" of the children of our village day care as they hold hands and walk up our road. I also pause, wave, or call out greetings as the elderly leisurely pace as they continue their stroll up the mountain.

While the young people strive to excel academically, true wisdom is found among the elderly in the villages and communities. In the Nevis that I have experienced, most children remain profoundly valued, deeply loved, disciplined, and nurtured. Politeness, family, and education were and remain the most highly prioritized values. Nevis continues to strive to maintain its high literacy rate, and everyone who wants electricity has it. Our local village primary school's slogan is "Learn today. Earn tomorrow." Although most of my friends have shared some of their most intimate feelings, people who are not as familiar are often very private about their personal challenges. When I inquire about their well-being, they respond with "Good enough," "Make do," or "Thank God for life." Phrases such as "Too blessed to be stressed" or "Believe and you will receive" are often prominently displayed on cars, walls, and highway signs or appear in schools, offices, and organizations. "Be yourself" is highly encouraged. Drive forty-five minutes around our island and you will not find any squalor, slums, homelessness, or beggars.

It is not only the "collective energy" of the Nevisian people that has drawn Lee and me for all these years, but the unpolluted air, shifting hues of the sky, and beckoning sea with its fluctuating hues of aqua, turquoise, or navy blue. At times, the inviting waves are almost flat; other times, they are crested with tiny lacy white tips. And Nevis Peak looms above from almost any spot on the island.

It also is exciting that each time we approach the island by ferry and view a few blocks of the bayfront of our historic capital, Charlestown, I know we are home. I also enjoy strolling along the five blocks of Main Street, where I admire some buildings that have been maintained since their construction three centuries ago. Along that road and in close proximity are the preserved African Cemetery, Slave Walk and Slave Marketplace, Jewish Cemetery and Jew's Walk, Charlestown Methodist Church, and Alexander Hamilton's birthplace. A short distance farther down the road is the more-than-two-hundred-year-old former Bath Hotel, a few steps from the Bath Stream. Lee and I often sit in the hot baths or warm stream, which are quite healing.

Years ago, after we had purchased our land in Nevis, but before we built our home, a neighboring couple, who have since become extended family, celebrated their twentieth wedding anniversary. Along with their children and the wife's mother, Lee and I were invited to celebrate with them and share their delicious anniversary dinner of local delicacies under star-studded sky, with Nevis Peak looming farther up the mountain. The woman's mother declared, "If you live among us, respect us, and don't try to change our ways, we will respect and protect you." We have all held on to those words in our hearts ever since, and that bond is now steeped in lasting love for them and their family. When I need local advice, I continue to turn to them.

In the late 1990s, as we were searching for a builder, a then-young man, who is now a lifelong dear friend, introduced us to a person who served as the foreman of the most prominent builder on the island. Our prospective builder possessed the rare combination of skill and integrity. When we chose him, the agreement was confirmed with a handshake as our builder stood poised with one foot on a rock. Others suggested that we seek a legal document, which we did. Our relationship was built on mutual trust and respect. In January 1999, when we broke ground, gave thanks, and toasted with a few friends, our builder remarked, "I hope we are also friends when the project is completed."

Shortly thereafter, I returned to California and soon discovered that I had to undergo the second coronary bypass. For months while I was recovering, the building process continued with a weekly two-hour phone session between the builder and me. Only one fax was required during the entire process. Lee returned in May for a short visit, we both went in July to make final decisions, and we moved in November 1999. Not one nail was missing, and a couple charming architectural designs awaited us.

Over the years, we have not only remained friends with our contractor, but the friendship also continues to grow deeper. There isn't a time when he comes to the house or we chat from California that we don't engage in lighthearted or deeper conversations about life, joy, and triumph. He continues to be one of the most admired, understated, grateful, trusted, and respected individuals we know and now is one of the leading builders on the island. When we recently spoke with him and congratulated him about his latest major project, he humbly commented, "If you do right things, right things come back to you."

The *Morning Inspiration Programme* on VON Radio with general manager and host Evered "Webbo" Herbert is among my favorite hour in Nevis. It may be heard at http://www.vonradio.com. The program begins with the national anthem, morning scripture readings—both Old and New Testament—gospel, and Black history. Also included are excellent weekly insights on "Parent Tips" introduced with "Good parenting for positive nation-building." One of my favorite moments of the program is the thought-provoking and uplifting quotation of the day. Each renders a positive and enlightening message to ponder with instructions from Webbo to "think through it—it's the quotation of the day." The message is so relevant that Webbo repeats it just before signing off as he adds, "If your journey is hard, and your vision not so clear, and life doesn't seem to go as it should, just remember that life isn't fair, but God is good." Then, he suggests offering a kind word or deed to "help lift somebody along the way."

My Nevisian friends have a profusion of flowers in their spiritual gardens and taught me the necessity of plucking and discarding the encroaching, destructive weeds—completely recognizing the disturbing nature of these negative thoughts.

Similar to all people throughout the world, the Nevisian people also have stress in their lives. In personal matters, the Nevisian people rarely complain and never explain; it's just not part of the culture. They simply and wisely accept that "it is what it is," do what they can, and move on. Years ago, a local friend shared his wisdom: "If it doesn't come your way, it wasn't meant to be." They consistently carry and continue to bear their burdens and tasks with hope, faith, dignity, and grace, even as worker layoffs occurred for the first time in decades. In addition, although import duty on most items is extremely high and there were (and are) taxes on properties, vehicle registration, hotels, and inns, there were no local or income taxes for the local people. Awhile ago, a 17 percent value-added tax (VAT) to create more revenue was temporarily thrust upon them.

The Nevisian people's deep belief and trust are embedded in their DNA. This faith continues to provide resilience, strength, and a will to push through, no matter the obstacle. I never heard the words "I quit" or "I can't." So asking "What if" or "How will I manage," saying "Oh my," whining, or focusing on the minutiae or small annoyances does not exist in the Nevis that I experienced. Instead, they rely on their faith to get them through. The Nevisians do not participate in analysis-paralysis or anticipate problems. Instead, they meet life's obstacles head-on as they appear. They begin hurricane preparedness months ahead of hurricane seasons. When people require expensive medical services overseas, community prayer meetings, bake sales, fund-raisers, and requests are announced on the radio. The community and island rally together and pool their resources for overseas travel and medical services, even flying a tiny infant and her caregivers to the United States for successful open-heart surgery.

You may recall Apollo 13 was crippled in space decades ago. With guidance and instruction from the NASA ground support team, the stranded-in-outer-space astronauts created the essentials with what they had. You may also recall your first glimpse of the horror of the devastating 2010 earthquake in Haiti and the Haitian people's resilience, faith, prayer, and music and their expressions of joy and gratitude to a higher power. The Nevisian people are similar; they are tenacious and improvise as necessary to get the job done.

The Nevisian people are strong, proud, and quite self-reliant. They carry the pride and knowledge that during colonial times, Nevis was and rightly remains the Queen of the Caribbean. As one of my friends shared, "During hard economic times or natural disasters, there are no food stamps, unemployment checks, bailouts, or government disaster loans, so we need to be strong and look out for one another. We rely on faith, family, and friends, and in that order." Others shared, "We have ourselves, our resilience, and know how to make do," all of which I witnessed during the twenty-five years that I have spent in Nevis. I never sensed that they felt victimized; rather, they are extremely proud of their esteemed Nevisian values and heritage. I witnessed daily their pride and often determination—expressed in their smile, gait, and carriage.

A wonderful memory is the day that Barack Hussein Obama became the forty-fourth president of the United States in 2009. For numerous reasons, I chose to remain in Nevis and did not join Lee, our daughter, and her husband for the inauguration in Washington, DC. Instead, I celebrated with twelve local and dear women friends and a friend from Michigan at a luncheon in our Nevisian home. In great joy, we all gathered to celebrate with a prayer circle on our front-covered veranda overlooking the Caribbean Sea. We held hands and each offered prayers from our own hearts and beliefs.

When the inauguration began and the "Star Spangled Banner" was sung, each Nevisian woman, along with my U.S. friend from Michigan, put their hands over her hearts and sang the words verbatim.

That evening, I was honored to be on a panel with General Manager Evered Webbo Herbert, of VON Radio and moderator of *Let's Talk*, the premier weekly talk show in Nevis. The other two panelists were the publisher of *The Observer*, one of the leading local newspapers, and a seasoned and respected businessman. The topic of our discussion focused on Barack Obama and "Can Nevisians change?" When Webbo introduced me, he reminded those listening that I had been an early supporter of Barack Obama when few thought he had a chance, and that I was white. I quickly interrupted Webbo and responded with words akin to, "*Webbo, I am no more white than you are Black. Yes, you are darker and I am lighter, but we are all on the same varied—hued—spectrum of the same human race.*" Even years later, when people saw me, they commented that they liked my message. I told them to "pass it forward."

I especially want to share the story of Blind Eileen, whose life story inspires all. Shortly after we moved into our home, my husband and I met Eileen in 2000, when she was eighty-three years old. She lives in Zion Village on the other side of the island from our home. Except for our downtown capital, Charlestown, street names are rarely posted in Nevis. Some expats name their property and display that name on a sign. To do that, we found a wood carver who, like his mother, is deaf and mute. As a youngster, he was sent abroad to receive woodcraft training so that he could support them both. We engaged him to carve a piece of local mahogany with the outline of Nevis Peak and flowers and the name of our home, *Nevisian Paradise*, which hangs on our fence.

As we were about to leave, Eileen, who lives next door, heard Lee, our granddaughter, and me conversing. She approached our car and asked if she could call me when the sign was finished; I told her she could. She told me she was blind, and my spontaneous response was, "But you are beautiful." In that fleeting moment, something in her soul had moved me. Our first and only grandchild, who was eight years old, was with us. She commented, "She is blind and he is deaf. Together they are one."

A couple weeks later, when Eileen called to inform us that the sign was completed, she asked if I could stop by her home after we picked up the sign. When I returned, she invited me into her then very small, traditional, old home with wooden floors and walls, without electricity or indoor plumbing. She led me to sit in a covered, open-sided vestibule that separated the house from her kitchen. As I sat on wooden crates covered with an old burlap potato sack, she got down on her hands and knees and, with her sightless eyes, looked up and said, "Help me ask her, Lord." I sat down with her as she shared two thoughts that she had held within for a long time. I can't possibly tell you how deeply moved I was by her trust; the moment was profound. After we chatted awhile, I asked her, "Did you know that I am Jewish?" She looked up, almost chuckling, as though speaking with God, and said, "Oh my, a Jewish lady in my quarters."

On our next visit, Eileen shared how two separate and bizarre sugarcane incidents blinded her first in one eye at eight and then in the other eye at nineteen. Yet she is one of the most sighted persons I know, as she sees from the heart instead of through her eyes. She remains curious, informed, witty, and inspiring. Back then, at eighty-three, she was still as spry and limber as a thirty-three-year-old, and her mind was every bit as sharp. When I told her that I was leaving some money, she immediately said that she was giving 10 percent to charity. I asked her why she confided in me, and she said it was because I had told her she was special; she later added that she had "heard God" in my voice. I told her that I teach and write about the Creator's presence within each of us and we are all connected to one another through the connection to that higher power within. This is what I call *source-connection*. It was truly a spiritual moment in the most meaningful sense. I was so caught up in our connection that I felt nothing else except the calm gratitude and peace of mind that enveloped this beautiful, special fellow human being in her humble home. That experience taught me that material things are not related to the priceless gift of serenity.

Over the years, Eileen, my husband, and I enjoyed an endearing, enduring, and trusting friendship with visits and frequent phone calls, whether on Nevis or in the United States. Her trust, peace of mind, gratitude, and profound wisdom on so many topics are the awesome gifts that continue to enlighten my husband, me, and numerous others. That experience continues with all my grandchildren, who visited with her on their last visit in 2014. Some of them chat with her from our home in California or when we visit them.

Eileen was given a piece of land next to her old home because she had taken care of an elderly man in her village. Every day she carried a pot of boiling water used to bathe and cook, balanced on a plank on top of her head. When she shared this story, she said, "See how God protected me, never letting me stumble as I walked barefoot on the stony path up the mountain." In 2002, members of a church in Canada came to Nevis to build her a beautiful, bright, airy, well-constructed, quality home with two bedrooms, a bathroom, and a living room that is pleasantly furnished. The spacious kitchen has plenty of counter space and an adjacent dining area. She moved in shortly before she had a mild stroke. She often commented on how fortunate she had been to move in and "familiarize" herself with her new surroundings before the stroke. It was the first time that she invoked the phrase "God had a plan all the time." For a very short time, following the stroke, she was unable to walk or talk. At that time, there were no speech or physical therapy treatments available on the island. So she continually massaged her palms with the fingers of the opposite hand and did the same with the toes on the soles of her opposite feet. With each new step, she asked for Jesus's help, and with each step achieved, she gave him thanks. Within a short period, her speech and ability to walk returned to their former levels.

Years later, as we sat in her living room with a sofa, four comfortable chairs, and the sounds of a chiming clock, this incredible, intelligent woman again shared her life's experiences with humor, appreciation, and wisdom. She lives by the rule that God helps those who help themselves and often quotes the Old Testament to further illustrate her beliefs. She shared that shortly before her mother died forty years ago, she asked her, "Mum, who gonna take care of a poor blind child like me?" Her mother replied, "I asked God to send people to take care of you." And Eileen's prayer was answered. When we last visited her, she always had enough food and clothing, and until she reached ninety-seven, she still did much of her own cleaning, laundry, and limited cooking. Then, folks from her church and in the village, or those she helped along life's way, stopped by to give her sustenance, care, love, and support and to soak up her spiritual blessings, insights, and humor. Whatever she has asked for, even what may seem impossible, always comes to fruition. But she continually adds, "If it is God's will."

When I spoke with her after she turned ninety and asked how she was, she responded, "A million times better than ever before." When she turned ninety-six, I reminded her of what she said when she reached ninety years, and she quickly and exuberantly added, "I am now six million times better off than before." She spoke of painful hardships that she had endured during her former years and how grateful she is for all she now has. She always has enough to eat and is "okay" with whatever she has.

She leads by example of how to gracefully age and adapt. A few years ago, she commented, "As we get older, we have to learn new ways to do things." That day, she remarked that she no longer felt safe walking outside on her uneven grounds to hang her laundry. So she placed the clothing between the louvers in her windows and then closed them so that the water dripped outdoors. Once the articles stopped dripping, she moved them to hang inside on the louvers until the cross-breeze dried them. As she continues to age, she increasingly uses the phrase "If my body tells me." After a while, I became curious, so I asked her, "Did you always only do what your body tells you?" She paused, chuckled, and then said, "Well, you know how it is. When you're young, you can do as you like." There has not been a time in our connection that I haven't gained an enlightening insight or laughed with her. When I call from California, I often sit with a pen in hand during our increasingly lengthy phone conversations as I learn the art of life, grace, and gratitude from a true sage.

On the morning of Halloween 2014, I called Eileen from California. Over the last few years, whenever I've called her, she always answers the phone with the greeting "Can I help you?" I begin our conversation with my usual "Good morning, Eileen. This is Ruthie. How are you?" After some delightful chuckles, she usually responds, "Praise the Lord, not too bad, and how are you? How is Lee?" She later added the names of two of our granddaughters, the first because when she was a very young child, she clearly exclaimed "Eileen" when she could barely speak, and as Eileen recalls, "She came into me." She also names the second grandchild because she has long silky hair. But the morning of Friday, October 31, her response was ominously different. This time I heard, "Not too good and not too bad." So I quickly but calmly asked, "What is different this morning, Eileen?" She responded, "I had a fall in the night and couldn't get back up." She quickly added, "I wasn't scared, but I called to the Lord to send help because I'm in trouble, and then I made myself comfortable." The next thing Eileen said was that she heard a man she knows, a well-respected Pastor, who is as devoted as a son. Eileen had helped raise him since he was nine years old, when his mother left for England to find work. Eileen knows that there is system in place so that a woman from St. Kitts calls her every morning, and if she doesn't answer, she calls the Pastor to check if the phones aren't working or if Eileen needs help.

I spoke with her or the Pastor every few days until the crisis was over, and then every week. When I later asked the Pastor who was staying with her, he quickly replied, "She has Jesus." Eileen continually shares what she is capable of doing and reminds me that she will not take one step more if she is not comfortable. She continues to gain strength, and just before my birthday in December 2016, with her main support off-island for almost a month, I asked her how she was managing. She simply said, "I make life what it has to be." While her support was off-island, Lee or I called more frequently, sometimes daily. She shared how very hard her life had been. But mostly, she shared her deep gratitude for all she now has—her clear mind, a comfortable home, always plenty to eat, and being well taken care of. I continue to remind her that I tell her inspirational story and deep belief often to family, friends, and neighbors, in my lectures, and in my book. She continues to chuckle and say, "Thank you."

Years ago, I asked, "Eileen, do you ever get scared?" She replied, "Fear grips me from time to time, but I immediately reach for the Lord." She never worries and continuously reminds me to look up to God and he will guide my path. In late 2015, she again expressed her deep faith, "I'm not going to have it hard tomorrow or look down the road, because I know God will provide. He always has, and I'm depending on that."

In her ninety-eighth year, she began to "labor" more, not in sorrow or pain, but in deep gratitude. As she continues to age, she never complains and is always steeped in profound gratitude. Without fanfare, she accepts that she can no longer do much of what she once could do. The neighbor who brings breakfast and dinner is deaf and mute, and the Pastor whom she helped raise now passes by twice a day. In the morning, he greets her with "Good morning" and brings her hot tea and a washcloth to wet her face and leaves lunch and drinks within reach on her bedside table. He returns at night to see how she passed the day, prepare dinner, help her get ready for bed, and pray. He and his wife look after all her other needs and concerns. She is grateful that she can still hear, speak, feel, taste, touch, and pray and has a good memory. Along with her loss of sight, she can no longer smell her food and requires help to "bathe her skin."

When I gave Eileen an approximate date my husband and I hoped to return to Nevis in late 2016, she responded, "It's a long way to Tipperary," which probably is a term she recalls from when the federation was under British rule. Eileen was somewhat in disbelief as she approached one hundred years. Then, she was amazed that she is still here and that she survived so many relatives and friends from school and in the village. She occasionally reminded me that her great-great-grandmother lived past a hundred, and if she reaches one hundred years, she will give thanks. She is grateful each moment that she still has "her right mind" and still remembers to say "Please" and "Thank you." She also shared that "we get older with every sunset and sunrise, and [she] gives thanks for each new day."

In early 2017, she began to lose her strength, and so my husband and I began to call her even more frequently. She reminded me that *she satisfies easily* and *she wants for nothing* and often states, "I am blessed, I am blessed, I am blessed." When my husband asked her, "What foods do you like?" she replied, "Whatever God provides." She also shares the condition of her fluctuating strength. After experiencing two falls in the last two years, she chooses to remain in bed, as she is tall and frail and fears if she falls again, she could break a bone or, worse, hit her head. As she regresses, she often quotes the Bible, "Once a man, twice a child." As her world diminishes, she reflects far more frequently on nature. She continues to listen to the radio and local and overseas news. What remains constant is her unwavering faith, wisdom, wit, and gratitude and the awe of our planet and wonderment at how far she has reached as she continues her life's journey.

I could not possibly leave without sharing a significant piece about Thich Nhat Hanh. People all over the globe, and now you, continue to be enriched by Thây's gentle, wise, and easy-to-implement teachings. In 2015, behind the scenes, Thây became the "Unsung Hero" as he helped Christiana Figueres, executive secretary of the United Nations Framework Convention on Climate Change, forge the International Climate Change Agreement that was backed by 196 nations. Figueres was going through some significantly challenging times but remained focused, supported by Thây and his teachings. These guided her to gain the "strength, wisdom, and compassion" she required to complete the monumental and demanding task. Thây's Buddhist teachings, nurtured by his deep love of nature, fostered the farthest-reaching accord to help save our planet yet (Confino 2016).

In the most profound gratitude and deep humility as an octogenarian, the Universe has blessed me with enough strength and clarity. That, combined with an inherited perseverance trait, helped me to reach the culmination of a more than twenty-five-year *Soul to Soul Connection and Communication* milestone journey. I didn't realize until late in life that this was always my destiny. My most endearing appreciation and thanks go to my husband Lee, who is eighty-five-years young. He encouraged me and supported this arduous process, and was always present to help with word choice and syntax. In the last few years, especially when Lee was in good health, he pitched in many ways so that I could complete this project.

As I look back, how else can I explain a seven-year-old girl of European and Jewish heritage riding a public bus in 1947 to the YWCA in Columbus, Ohio, and looking up to read a banner that said, "Ecidujerp-prejudice—either way, it makes no sense?" A few years later, without forethought or plan, I began to perceive prejudice, especially toward individuals of African heritage.

Both my husband and I attended schools whose student bodies included a fair number of classmates of African heritage. For a short period, I also attended the same high school from which Lee graduated. Since the student body had a substantial African heritage component, early in life we experienced the coolness, culture, and class of friends who imbued that spirit.

Amid all our world travels, what was the chance that one of my husband's clients owned a travel agency and owed my husband money but couldn't afford to pay and so instead offered us a complimentary week on a remote island named Nevis in the West Indies? On our first trip, our Nevisian guide drove us around and stopped at the Jew Cemetery. He conveyed those words with such heartfelt reverence that I can still recall and sense the goose bumps on my arm. After we had visited Nevis for five straight years, my husband insisted that I look at a piece of property, forty minutes before our launch would depart Nevis. So I drove with the realtor and the person who was our first guide into the rain forest and who remains a dear friend and extended family member. We drove for five minutes over potholes that were sometimes eighteen inches deep to a local village only a few minutes from the beach; we returned on fresh tire tracks through the field. Then, the land that would become our property was a brush-filled former pasture. Fields or a small road separated us from each of our neighbors, there were no streetlights, and Lee would be in California two months each season. I had also experienced two major surgeries.

The moment I put my foot on the land, an intense bolt of dense, warm energy sprang from the cauldron near the top of Nevis Peak behind me, shot through my very core from my head to my feet into the earth, and reverberated as powerfully as anything I had ever experienced. Seizing the moment of that December 1995 day, in April, when my husband received his first year-end bonus (which was the exact amount of the property), we purchased the land after his tax season. While we laid out plans to build, Lee stopped in Miami, called me, and said, "Some will think that we're crazy to do this. We know we're crazy if we don't." Shortly after we broke ground early in 1999 and we both returned to Los Angeles for short periods, I had a slight heart attack. My cardiac surgeon suggested that I remain in Los Angeles so that they could "monitor" me for the next eighteen months. I responded, "Then I might as well sit down and die right here." Shortly after, I required a second coronary surgery to replace the larger vessels that had previously replaced the originally occluded ones.

As you gleaned from our journey together, the Nevis that Lee and I experienced for nearly three decades profoundly enriched our lives. With gratitude for the continued profound blessings, Nevis will forever be my spiritual home. Now, let's return to the present in the United States and my 80 years marked on a calendar. I am extremely grateful to the Universe that for the most part, my spirit still feels *young at heart*.

The desire and passion that propelled this book were to help uplift a person's well-being as high as possible and to promote civility and inclusion in a heartfelt and civil manner to further each person to reach their endowed potential. I have included almost every kernel of wisdom pertinent to this book to create pages for the ages—a resource, guide, and friend that you will often turn to during your lives. Understandably, milestones will occur, events will change, scientific investigation will search for new theories, new discoveries and data will unfold, and situations and challenges on every level of life will continue to evolve as long as there is human civilization. Hopefully, the insights, tools, and stories in this book will remain as a reminder, especially of the essence of each human being, the *source-connection*, and the global web it creates with all humanity—the sacred and profane—and the *hand-dome* will serve as lifelong guides for better understanding ourselves and others. Both the *IBMDR Technique* and the *Forman Approach to Identifying Prejudice Within Ourselves* are nonjudgmental guides that privately guide us to look deep within ourselves.

A few summers ago, many students of diverse backgrounds who are close to my heart, as well as other acquaintances, graduated in the United States and in Nevis. As part of that celebratory and accomplished season, I attended a gathering of family, students, and adults to honor a special graduate whom I have known since birth. The joyous celebration took place in a lovely, upscale home in West LA. Shortly after we arrived, I chatted with the daughter of the hostess. She was quite understated and a beautiful nineteen-year-old woman majoring in neuroscience and psychology. She shared that before she was old enough to vote, her parents had signed her up to volunteer in a monthlong program of working with orphans in Cambodia. She discovered "the light behind their eyes and realized that happiness had nothing to do with material possessions." I asked her what she wanted to do when she graduated. She replied, "I want to help make the world a better place."

Other graduates joined nonprofit organizations; one planned to teach youth in Palestine how to play soccer. An honored graduate of my CSUN alma mater chose to give her talents within the public school system instead of working for a prestigious clinic or hospital. Another honored student, who is in my field, is gay. He collaborated with his clinical coordinator to develop a program for voice training for transgender people. Each individual indicates great promise as human beings. Later in the summer, as I lay on my yoga mat with clouds drifting and birds chirping, I reflected on the recent newborns of differing cultural heritages and my youngest great-niece, whose grounded, old-soul spirit and beauty of many heritages are reflected in her striking and serene little face.

As I look at the world, I see the gathering of a universal rising: cohesive, diverse collections of people, young and old, abled and *handi-abled*, and of every cultural heritage, sexual orientation, and religious and regional group joining as never before. This unified movement sustains and builds upon our collective gains and continues to elevate acceptance, love, respect, healing, equality, and inclusion for others and ourselves.

Our goals must ensure that we reverse the damage to our planet already caused by climate change. We must also preserve our planet to maintain its ability to nourish us, our descendants, and those within our global family. Without that, nothing else really matters. If you don't think that our precious Mother Earth is desperately shouting for help in her most compelling manner, just picture her fury of deadly tsunamis as they swallow the innocent; feel her huge tears as she pummels us with golfball- size ice pellets; hear her roaring howls as rapid tornadoes randomly strike; sense her deep pain as hurricanes blast destruction; witness her suffering with mega infernos that gut and ravage homes, structures, roads, communities, and forests, and suffocate; powerful destructive earthquakes as she bolts, shakes, and rocks humans. These are forever robbing us of security in our dwellings, work places, or locale. Sense her sadness as mega droughts parch our fertile fields into desert-like wasteland and then, pounds water that flood, thus devastating the fields and pastures that feed our seven billion fellow global citizens. Sense the sorrow of an iceberg as it calves from its home and is cast to wander an unknown path, and thus cause significant interruption, loss, and devastation as water levels rise. And the worst awakening message of all is that of Mother Earth's exponentially hurling her fury more powerful each season. If all her grief, horror, and suffering don't capture our collective attention, I wonder what realization will cause us to heed our planet's desperate plea before it's too late for all of us?

Nothing puts a bigger smile in my heart and on my face than the health and serenity of my loved ones, saving our planet, and the global, coalescing, nonviolent movement to collectively further well-being, civility, equality, justice, and inclusion for all. As I shared earlier, I believe in the blending of a mosaic humanity as long as we each carry forward those stalwart, just, loving, supportive, compassionate, respectful, and inclusive values that were preciously preserved and passed down to us.

In 2016, I began to hear the lack of veracity in the spoken word and in reported news and throughout social media. Until then, I could never have predicted the extent to which this permeated our respected institutions and presently threatens the very core of our democracy. I also heard the vitriolic rhetoric during the 2016 presidential election cycle. Still, I cannot help but believe that this millennium generation will get it better than any other previous one. They already show tremendous promise in their inclusive, nonviolent approach to furthering justice and equality for women, by living a simplified lifestyle and engaging in more community service than any previous generation and, most importantly, saving our planet. After all, their charge and efforts not only benefit them, but they also champion agendas that serve all our children, grandchildren, and loved ones around the world.

I am extremely grateful for the daily gift of heavy doses of a universal spiritual force and energy from my deceased loved ones that gently and firmly pushed and supported my back, especially this past year, to finally complete this arduous endeavor. I also want to profoundly thank my family, friends, and colleagues, but foremost my husband, who had to go at it alone on many occasions as he patiently waited, hearing my mantra: "Sorry, I have to work on the book."

Even though my book was not finished, I returned with Lee to see Eileen and connect with my community in Nevis. While there for a short visit, I realized that I had gained my Nevis voice and so began selected refinements at the very beginning of this book.

Now that the book is finished and my husband and I are older, individually and as a couple, we will have to forge new paths. Writing the book has taken its toll. I don't know where I will prevail once that burden is lifted and my physical and emotional energy are replenished. I plan to venture out to again enjoy life with family, friends, and colleagues, remain committed to my ideals, attend the arts, surround myself and hike amid nature, and hopefully continue to return to Nevis.

I am aware that family and friends my age either are facing their own declining health or have lost or will lose a loved one. When I asked Lee about how I will face my greatest challenges of life ahead, he replied, "It's all in your book." So my greatest challenge will be to walk my talk, even through my most difficult, darkest moments and days.

As I now have more wisdom to look back on my life, with all my trials and tribulations to which I alluded but purposely did not include, I realized there was always an energy and force protecting me and placing individuals and events in my path exactly when they were needed to help, guide, and mold me into who I am. I no longer question that positive, omnipotent force, because it is eternally present, even when I am not. Hopefully, as I face the challenges ahead, I will be able to believe and receive and look down the road that Blind Eileen has led. For her, that force has always been God or Jesus, whom she views as the same.

For me, that force is the Universe and my ancestors, unless loved ones or I face monumental life-threatening challenges. Then, I specifically reach out to the Creator. Although I didn't always feel that presence in my daily life, I always felt that presence during my surgeries. I hope that when my earthly journey comes to an end, I will follow Eileen's lead that she recently shared: "When the Lord comes to take my last breath, I will be *satisfied* and *serene* and will go in perfect peace."

A Time to Pause and Reflect

First Pause on Your *Soul to Soul Connection and Communication* Journey *Source-Connection*

1. Note good feelings about yourself. If you can't feel them, think of any situation in which you usually feel good. Then, think of which feelings you feel in those situations.
2. What does your soul feel like? Where do you feel it? Does it have color, intensity, or shape? What name would you give it? What are the positive feelings you have when you are *source-connected*?
3. Note one special feeling about each person who is important to you in your personal life. Can you feel their soul? Could you ever feel their soul? Try to feel their soul and specialness when you are with them.
4. Write down one special feeling about each person who is important to you at work. Can you feel their soul? Could you ever feel their soul? Try to feel their soul, their specialness, when you are with them.
5. Create an affirmation about yourself by listing five special qualities that you have.
6. List the activities that you enjoy, that make you feel good and complete, and that nurture your *source-connection*.
7. On your calendar, create a weekly guide to remind yourself to participate daily in those activities that nurture your *source-connection*. Begin each day with at least ten minutes in a quiet place where you evoke your feelings of *source-connection*.
8. Take the feeling of your *source-connection* with you. In fact, don't leave home without it.
9. Listen to your *source-voice*. When you don't, note what happens.
10. When you become disconnected, note what feelings and thoughts you can inhale to help you quickly regain your *source-connection*.

Second Pause on Your *Soul to Soul Connection and Communication* Journey
Hand-dome

1. What did you learn about your uniqueness from your *hand-dome*? Are you using those positive qualities every day? If not, how can you begin to include them in your life?
2. What limitations do you have? Write down how you honor them. If you don't, write down how you can.
3. Name a *twig boundary*, a *limb boundary*, a *branch boundary*, and a *trunk boundary*. How do you honor them? How can you begin to honor those boundaries that you previously have not honored?
4. What pleasant experiences are most often on your mind? What unpleasant experiences are most often on your mind? How do they affect your communication?
5. What positive emotions do you feel? Write down what you can do to have those feelings more often. How do they affect your communication?
6. Write down the *positive* ways your primary family communicated. Do you include those in your communication? If not, how can you begin?
7. Write down the *negative* ways your primary family communicated. Are those part of your communication style? With which positive communication patterns can you replace them? How does your *source-connection* help?
8. Write down the *positive* values and the ways the people of your native culture in your childhood neighborhood communicated. Do you include those in your communication? If not, how can you begin?
9. Note the *negative* values and the ways the people of your native culture in your childhood neighborhood communicated. Are those included in your communication? With which positive communication patterns can you replace them? How does your *source-connection* help?
10. What have you learned about other people's *hand-dome*? How will this help you have more tolerance and understanding? When differences occur, how can you now bridge those gaps?

> ### Third Pause on Your *Soul to Soul Connection and Communication* Journey
> #### *Personal Lenses*
>
> 1. What negative thoughts do you often have about yourself?
> 2. List all your *internal lenses*. Which is the most negative?
> 3. How powerful or debilitating are your *lenses*?
> 4. Recall the first time you felt the negative feeling of your most powerful *lens*. Note the incident as vividly as you can recall.
> 5. List all the achievements that you have accomplished and the skills that you have learned that you didn't have previously. How could they help you in a similar situation today?
> 6. Use the *Identify, Block, Move, Delete, Replace Technique* with each *lens* that you have.
> 7. When you feel your *source-connection*, what happens to the negative feelings from your *lenses*?
> 8. What are some of the *external lenses* that you perceive about the people with whom you work and live?
> 9. What are some of the biases and prejudices that you have toward other people? Write them down in big, bold letters so you are aware of these. Now, think of new, positive ways you can replace those perceptions and feelings. "Fellow human being" is a suggested beginning.
> 10. Who do you know has a chip on her or his shoulder and communicates with a bad attitude? Try to bypass that feeling and sense their essence. Find a commonality with that person on a personal or human level. Then connect soul to soul with them.

Fourth Pause on Your *Soul to Soul Connection and Communication* Journey
Communication Is Connection

---

1. Write down what you have learned about your own *communication needs.* Please review Figure 4. The difference between talk and communication. Then, gesture with your hands the separate hands for talk and say aloud *This is talk.* Next, clasp your hands as in the communication image and say aloud *This is communication.* Keep this image in your mind whenever there is a gap in communication, and focus on the tools that you previously gained to make that connection.

2. Think of people who are important in your personal life. What do you now know about their communication and their communication needs that you previously were unaware of?

3. Think of people who are important in your professional life. What do you now know about their communication and their communication needs that you previously didn't know?

4. The difference between talk and communication. Then, gesture with your hands the separate hands for talk and say aloud *This is talk. Next,* clasp your hands as in the communication image and say aloud *This is communication.* Keep this image in your mind whenever there is a gap in communication, and focus on the tools that you previously gained to make that connection.

5. Who intimidates you at work? Each time you interact with them, think of them as an equal human being. Reinforce the feeling by placing your hands in front of you on the same level and saying, "He [or she] is equal to me."

6. Do you use your "role" at home or work to make you feel more important than or to intimidate another person? Again, use the image of the hands on an equal plane to remind you that they are equal human beings.

7. Write down labels that you attach to people at home. What expectations do you give to the labels? How do those expectations negatively interfere with positive communication and connections? Write down labels that you attach to people at work. What expectations do you give to the labels? How do those expectations negatively interfere with positive communication and connections?

8. Name five values and concerns that you have in common with people whom you previously associated with a negative label. (Sharing the planet, breathing air, needing food and shelter, and wanting to belong are just a few.) Now add five of your own.

9. At which layer of the onion are you most comfortable communicating? What about the people with whom you live? When your differences create a challenge or issue, how can you communicate with them to build the best connections?

10. What can you do to move from the labels and outer shells of other people to connect person to person or soul to soul with them?

Fifth Pause on Your *Soul to Soul Connection and Communication* Journey
Listening: You Hear Me, But Are You Listening?

1. When you converse with others, picture the connected hands on the cover of this book and strive for that connection.
2. Besides conversation, in what listening activities do you participate?
3. Spend a couple minutes daily for the next month listening to sounds of nature. What sounds do you begin to hear that you never heard before?
4. On scraps of paper, write down preconceived ideas you have about the people with whom you live and work that interferes with a pure communication. Now throw the pieces of paper in the trash. Begin each conversation anew and fresh without preconceived ideas about what they are going to talk about.
5. Practice going for a visit with people who are having personal challenges or with people who are intense. Can you listen, affirming others, without giving advice?
6. When your mind wanders, mentally picture yourself gently bringing your mind back to the conversation. Mentally take your hand and bring your mind back so you connect with the person you are talking with.
7. Monitor how you inform others that you can't listen. If you haven't told them before or you used to say it negatively, how will you later tell them that you can't listen now in a positive way?
8. How do you honor yourself by not listening to things you don't want to hear or that are said in a negative or disagreeable manner?
9. Do you listen to your *source-voice*? Recall five instances where you didn't listen and wished that you had. Reward yourself with a hug or something special the next time you listen to your *source-voice*. Begin to pay attention to those coincidences. Listen to the messages others give you and the messages you receive out of nowhere on your spiritual internet.
10. What do you do to make other people comfortable so they will listen to what you say?

Sixth Pause on Your *Soul to Soul Connection and Communication* Journey How You Process Information

1. What *lens* do you think about many times a week? Recognize that it negatively interferes with your thoughts and communication.
2. How often does your mind briefly wander during a conversation?
3. How often do you pretend to be listening when you are on a digital device, watching television, or engaged in another activity?
4. How often do you stop listening to others and start thinking of something else?
5. How often do you stop listening and begin to plan your response before the other person is finished? How often is this an issue because you haven't heard everything that was said?
6. How often do you respond too soon—not taking as much time as you need—because you think the other person is rushing you or you feel they have more important things to do than listen to you? With which person and in which situations does this occur most frequently?
7. Do you ever give a response that you know doesn't answer the question? Why do you do it?
8. Do you give examples during your explanation, or do you wait until the end so others can best understand you?
9. Do you wander off from your response and begin to talk on another topic?
10. How can you plan your response to give the intention of your message for the best possible connection and positive results?

Seventh Pause on your *Soul to Soul Connection and Communication* Journey
Neurolinguistic Programming: Touch, Sight or Sound?

1. What is your strongest Neurolinguistic Programming channel (NLP)?
2. What is your weakest Neurolinguistic Programming channel (NLP)?
3. What is the preferred NLP of the people with whom you live?
4. What is the preferred NLP of the people with whom you work?
5. Who do you know who participates in many activities and helps you by doing things for you? Which NLP channel does this reflect? Which words can you use to communicate with them for a more solid connection? When recalling information, in which direction do their eyes move?
6. Who do you know who likes to receive gifts and expresses their affection with gifts or greeting cards? Which NLP channel does this reflect? What words can you use to communicate with them for a stronger connection? When recalling information, in which direction do their eyes move?
7. Who do you know who likes to talk about his or her concerns and needs and helps you by talking with you about your concerns and needs? Which NLP channel does this reflect? What words can you use to communicate with and support them for a better connection? When recalling information, what is the position of their eyes?
8. In what ways do people help you or offer support that you previously have not appreciated?
9. In what new ways can you express appreciation and communicate to best connect with others at home who learn best by touch, sight, or sound?
10. In what new ways can you express appreciation and communicate to best connect with others at work who learn best by touch, sight, or sound?

Eighth Pause on Your *Soul to Soul Connection and Communication* Journey
Nonverbal Communication: Take a Look

1. The next time you feel very positive, stand in front of a mirror and tell yourself why you feel so good. What facial expressions do you see? Think of ways to feel positive and stay *source-connected* so your expressions reflect a positive image.
2. The next time you feel negative, stand in front of a mirror and tell yourself what you feel. What facial expressions do you see? How do you think others feel seeing those negative expressions?
3. Begin to observe facial expressions in others and watch for inconsistencies in what they say and what they express through their nonverbal communication.
4. Do you have difficulty maintaining eye contact? If so, describe the times at which you do and note the people and the situations.
5. Note the body language of people at home. Listen to different ways they close doors, walk down the hall, or place things on a table. Learn to watch for the clues they give you about how they feel.
6. Note the body language of people at work. Listen to different ways they close doors, walk down the hall, or place things on their desk. Learn to watch for the clues they give you about how they feel.
7. Who stands close to you? Who stands farther away? When you converse with a person and they move away, think back on what you just said and how you said it. You may want to change your voice tone or the topic to add comfort to the conversation.
8. List the people with whom you live and note which of them enjoy touching, holding hands, kisses, or pats on the hand or shoulder. Note the people who don't like to be touched as a sign of affection. In which category are you?
9. At work, are you a person who shows care to others by touching them? How do others respond? Note those who appear uncomfortable with your touch. Monitor your touch to assure that you don't offend others. Do you use gestures when you speak? (Check videos of yourself.) If you use many gestures, pay attention to other people's responses to your movements.
10. Does your nonverbal communication reflect a person whose company you would seek? If not, what can you do to alter your nonverbal communication so that it is more acceptable?

Ninth Pause on *Soul to Soul Connection and Communication* Journey
Voice Tone: It's Not What You Say, But How You Say It

1. Listen to your voice on your answering machine. Is it the voice of a person whom you would like to be? If not, what doesn't sound pleasant to you? Note the positive and negative qualities you hear in your voice. How can you change the negative ones?

2. The next time you feel good, tape your voice. Record what you feel. Connect with the positive feeling inside of you. Try to nurture that feeling so that it becomes a greater part of you.

3. The next time you feel bad, tape your voice. Listen to what you hear. How do you think others feel when they hear your negative voice? Monitor to make certain that you aren't using a negative voice with others.

4. Listen to your voice and feel the tension in your body and throat when you are angry, rushed, or upset. Learn to monitor your voice and body tension for those feelings. Try to refrain from using that voice tone with others.

5. Listen to your voice when you are *source-connected*. How does it sound? How can you include that pleasant tone into your voice more often?

6. Do you speak too fast? If you do, begin to read the newspaper aloud, speaking at a slower pace. Tape your reading. Listen to and feel the differences. Practice speaking slower using the TOC method until your new, slower speech is a habit.

7. Make a list of people whose voices you find pleasant. What qualities in their voices appeal to you? What can you do to include some of those voice qualities in your voice so they become a genuine part of your voice?

8. Monitor other people's voice to discover what kind of mood they are in. If a person sounds rushed or angry, is that the time to ask them a question?

9. Listen to other people's voice tones as an indication of their moods.

10. Listen to your voice as an indication of how you feel and what message you send to others.

Tenth Pause on Your *Soul to Soul Connection and Communication* Journey
Verbal Communication: Honor Yourself and Choose Your Words Wisely

1. Note how you feel when your communication includes your *source-connection*. Where do you feel your *source-connection*? Begin to include that positive feeling in all conversations.
2. In which situations and with whom are you the most proactive?
3. In which situations and with whom are you the most reactive? What are you frightened of? What negative feelings do you feel, and where do you feel them? When you become *source-connected*, what happens to your fears?
4. The difference between talk and communication. Then, gesture with your hands the separate hands for talk and say aloud *This is talk*. Next, clasp your hands as in the communication image and say aloud *This is communication*. Keep this image in your mind whenever there is a gap in communication, and focus on the tools that you previously gained to make that connection.
5. When you differ with others, always acknowledge that difference by going for a visit and connecting with the other person. Review figure 4, where the separate hands represent "talk" and the connected hands represent "communication."
6. Which of the people with whom you live prefer indirect communication? Who prefers direct communication? Which style do you usually use at home?
7. Which of the people with whom you work prefer indirect communication? Who prefers direct communication? Which style do you prefer at work?
8. Are your questions being answered with information that you need? If not, check to see if your questions are stated so they give you the necessary information. Do you respond accurately to others' questions? If they ask you again, perhaps you didn't give the correct information the first time?
9. Write down five instances in which communication investments would have saved time, money, and frustration. Think about the issues at home and work that repeat themselves day after day. What communication investments can you make to eliminate those issues to save you time, money, and aggravation?
10. How do you express appreciation to people at home and work? Do you appreciate and honor them just for being who they are? How would you like others to show their appreciation of you? How will you inform them?

Final Pause on Your *Soul to Soul Connection and Communication* Journey
Intercultural Communication: Embracing Diversity

1. How do you perceive a person from a minority group or other culture? What will you do if a label pops into your mind? What term will replace that label?
2. List five new insights about intercultural communication that you learned in this chapter.
3. List foods from other cultures that you now enjoy that you didn't eat as a child.
4. List beliefs and activities of other cultures that you now embrace but didn't as a child.
5. List five positive insights about minorities and intercultural values and communication styles that you have gained that replace former negative perceptions.
6. Choose a person or family in your neighborhood from a minority group or different culture with whom you will connect by inviting them to your home or doing something with them.
7. Choose a person from a minority group or different culture at work that you will reach out to meet them for lunch or dinner or join them or invite them to join you in an activity.
8. If you immigrated to the United States, what will you do to connect with a person who was born in the United States or is from a different culture at work or in your neighborhood?
9. Note persistent feelings that prevent you from connecting with an individual from a minority group or different culture. What can you do to overcome those feelings? How can you ask a person to give you insight into something you don't understand?
10. List five ways that you can now best connect with people from minority groups and other cultures. What new visions do you have to broaden the outreach in the community in which you live and work?

Photos Reflecting Selective Narratives

Burst of sun rays.

Colorful sunset.

Cloud reaching beyond.

Sunset and yachts.

Sunset, crescent moon, and Saturn.

Sunset reflection and ferry.

Rainbow at Nevis Peak.

Full moon.

Approaching Robben Island by ferry.

Pelicans at sunset.

Burst of light from heaven sunset.

Gripping Nelson Mandela's cell
on hallowed ground.

Returning home by ferry to historical
bayfront of capital Charlestown, Nevis.

Plaque in Nevis in honor of
Alexander Hamilton.

The Jewish Cemetery sign in 2018.

Jewish child's tombstone inscribed in
Portuguese with stones from visitors to
remember the departed.

Learn Today Earn Tomorrow.

Hummingbird feeding.

Bananakeet enjoying rainwater in the gutter.

Nevis Peak from back veranda.

Pansies in springtime.

Gecko suns itself.

Mascarade dancers by the beach celebrating Nevisian culture.

Perritata on soursop tree calling to me.

Great blue heron walking by our home.

Bougainvalia reaching for light.

Autumn mums in vase from Margaret Hughes.

Gecko gets comfy.

Egrets waiting to kiss.

Baby doves in rafters above veranda.

Paradise Beach to ourselves.

Happy on my stretch band on the veranda.

Going to pick fruit in the orchard.

Gecko brightens as it senses me.

As long as www.positivecommunication is live,
these photos will be displayed in color for your pleasure.

Photos taken by Ruth Forman

Epilogue

Soul to Soul Connection and Communication serves as a guide with a detailed table of contents; its headings cover an extensive range of topics to which you can refer throughout your life's journey. The book is presented similar to an extensive and varied smorgasbord of fresh, favorite, unfamiliar, and previously tasted delicacies. Similar to a buffet, the book offers a wide variety of anecdotes, insights, and tools that you can revisit, much like a second helping of morsels on your plate. You will bypass some sections for now to read at a later time, yet others you will not read in the first place. Some pages will become familiar dear friends smudged by continued review and notes, while some pages will rarely will be revisited. All words were written from my heart to touch your heart.

Originally, the book's storyline ended when President Barack Hussein Obama left office on January 20, 2017. However, in 2018, significant abuses that were always prevalent, but previously had been hushed or brushed aside, were exposed. That year the Me Too movement began and quickly went viral as #MeToo, sparking a global response to sexual harassment and assault. These abuses were always prevalent, but also purposely silenced. Male leaders in many areas were exposed for their lengthy and previously secretive misconduct. Fortunately, many were immediately ousted from their positions. Their former admired reputations were shattered; then they were cast aside. The year 2018 was named the Year of the Woman, spurring a hastening rise of women's political advancement to elected positions. This way, women could put forth an agenda that would ensure every woman's right to make choices about her own body, protecting themselves as well as their sisters, daughters, and nieces. While these events and other abhorrent ones were not mentioned in the book, suggestions and adamant responses were sprinkled throughout specific and pertinent chapters. Since then, our nation and the world have also changed significantly, both for the better and the worse.

National political policies became more erratic, insular, and divisive. Attitudes such as "only for me" and "my kind," and use of the term "fake news became prevalent." The very core of our democratic principles, for which we have always stood and often died, were constantly tested and threatened. In the United States, children were purposely separated from their parents and remained in cages for months. Shortly thereafter, halfway around the world, a soccer team of twelve young boys and their coach were accidently trapped in a deepunderground, flooding cave for sixteen days.

As the world stayed tuned-in and prayed for the group, in a country where the belief and outlook were communal and optimistic, this bonded team was miraculously and timely rescued. Each survivor rapidly gained their health and strength and was reunited with their parents and loved ones. More than any time in my life, this singular event demonstrated the possibilities when our global citizens join to coalesce, sacrifice, and put aside their age, gender, political, cultural, and religious differences. Combined with deep faith and laser focus, a potential tragedy turned into a miraculous celebration. Hopefully, that unity, purpose, and precision will prevail and serve as a global paradigm when required.

Unfortunately, it did not hold in the U.S.A. and elsewhere in 2020, as the uninvited COVID-19 pandemic arrived early that year. By November and U.S. elections more than 225,000 souls had already been lost to the deadly COVID-19. However, this period also gave rise of a return to basics, family and community first. Individuals of all ages became more real. Gratitude, goodwill, acceptance, ingenuity, and virtuality took on new meaning amidst the prevalent, sorrowful pain, lingering virus effects, and death. Lack of stability, security, decency, normalcy, lost wages, and visits and hugs with dear ones were widespread. Institutions, organizations, religious, and youth groups kindly reached out to neighbors, the elderly, and strangers in need. Folks also began to examine, reprioritize, and restrategize what is important. During one of our frequent lengthy chats and laughs with a decades long hiking buddy and dear friend, I asked, "What's most new?" She replied, "I am now a Copi that rhythms with Hopi Indian and is short for coping." She had lost everything in the Woolsey fire, she kindly cares for her ailing spouse, they required several surgeries combined, and they rented three homes before they purchased their own. Many of our fellow global humanity also recognized that we are responsible for each other.

During that time several more brutal wrongful deaths of mostly males of African heritage by law officers occurred. First, Breonna Taylor and Ahmaud Arbery were killed. A few months later when George Floyd's dastardly murder occurred, the international Black Lives Matter (BLM) nonviolent phenomenon spontaneously sprang forth. Even during this growing pandemic, millions of the full spectrum of humanity risked their lives to join peaceful Black Lives Matter and other protests. Then, three more sorrowful deadly shootings of Rayshared Brooks, Elijah McClain, and Jacob Blake, Jr. occurred. Then another—as low as you can possibly get—killing occurred. It was revealed that months ago, Daniel I. Prude who was mentally ill was suffocated by police officers. In each instance BLM protests popped up. With a troubled heart, I know these individuals' tragedies are not the end of these events. Let me also state that I firmly oppose the misguided and totally unacceptable occurrences of agitators, looters, and vandals. At times, they pose under the guise of peaceful BLM protesters, as they deliberately turn a constitutional right into vicious and unlawful attacks.

As you gained from your reading, I am a kindred spirit with countless friends of African heritage in the U.S.A. and Nevis. During the latest slew of killings of human beings of African heritage in the U.S.A. I empathized with U.S. friends the deep pain we shared and my realization. I visualized a chain-link fence with a gate to safety that I can pass, but they are denied. I also realized that although I can feel with and for my dear ones, I cannot pass through the hovering and painful and gate to discrimination or possible death. I profoundly admire that my loved ones continue to persevere and deeply love our country, even though countless policies continue to significantly discriminate against them. The harm of this generational trauma on their well-being deeply concerns me.

In July 2020, the revered Honorable Congressman John. R. Lewis passed away. Fortunately, the Conscience of Congress John Lewis lived to see and took great pride as this new generation of global nonviolent activists carried forth his and others' of past generation the passion and dedication for justice and equality. He, as myriad others, was amazed that even during the costly COVID-19 pandemic, millions risked their lives to protest against systemic racism. To show his support for the BLM movement, Lewis visited the Black Lives Matter Plaza a month before his death.

Within a month of John Lewis's death, what a year ago was unthinkable occurred. Presidential candidate Joe Biden whose platform was *Restoring the Soul of America,* chose Kamala Harris as his Vice-presidential running mate for the United States of American. Harris was born in Oakland, California and became the first woman and woman of color to win elections in her numerous positions as she advanced her career. She is the first candidate from the Historically Black College University Howard University to be selected as vicepresident. Since Harris is from my home state, I became aware of her as attorney general, and strongly supported her goals to become US Senator. My support continued until Kamala Harris and Joe Biden were victorious.

Harris's mother was born in India and her father was born in Jamaica. She is the first woman of Jamaican, African, and Southeast Asian heritages to be selected by a major party. She is only the third woman to be selected as a vice-presidential candidate. She is married to Douglas Emhoff, a man of European heritage who is Jewish, and a graduate of my alma mater, California State University, Northridge. She stated that *Momala* to her two sons by marriage is her most important role.

Biden shared that his final decision for vice-president was based on the fact that the soul of his heart, his late son Beau Biden, simultaneously was Attorney General of Delaware on the east coast while Kamala Harris was Attorney General of California on the west coast. They spoke daily on the same pressing issues. Prior to his death, Beau had told his father that he respected Kamala.

I thought of our dearest Blind Eileen who always said, "God had a plan all the time." I reflected what is the chance that both Biden and Harris would work so closely as attorneys generals. In 2018, Lee and I had returned to Nevis for a brief visit to be with our community. At that time, Blind Eileen Smithen of Zion had reached one hundred and one year of life. She shared that a forty-year-long unfulfilled wish was granted. She commented, "It was meant from the beginning that I would have a large portion of life." Thankfully, for as long as she lived, she had no pain, lived by herself, and Jesus remained her constant companion. She continued to inspire with her wisdom, wit, and eloquent expressions. In Eileen's last six months of life, her memory began to fade as she often replied, "I don't remember." Slowly, her other senses began to diminish; eventually she could no longer hear nor speak. As long as she had her faculties, she was blessed with her "right mind." Prior to that time, she had frequently prepared us declaring, "One sad day Eileen will no longer be on this earth," and I immediately responded, "But you will always be in our hearts."

And she is.

References

Abagond, Julian. 2014. "White American Racism against Blacks: 1600s." *Abagond* (blog), February 6, 2014. https://abagond.wordpress.com/2014/02/06.

Abdul-Jabbar, Kareem. 2014. "Kareem Abdul-Jabbar: Welcome to the Finger-Wagging Olympics." *Time*, April 28, 2014. http://time2.com/79590/donald-sterling-kareem-abdul-jabbar-racism.

Academy for Jewish Religion, California. *Transforming the Jewish World*. http://www.ajrca.edu.

ACLU (American Civil Liberties Union). n.d. "Private Prisons." American Civil Liberties Union. http://www.aclu.org/issues/mass-incarceration/privatization-criminal-justice/private-prisons.

Ali-Khan, Sofia. 2015. "Open Letter: Dear Non-Muslim Allies." Facebook, December 7, 2015. https://www.facebook.com/sofia.alikhan.7/posts/10153301068060893?fref=nf.

———. 2016. "A Time for Discernment: A Muslim Woman Calls on Her Buddhist Cousins in Faith." *Tricycle*, December 12, 2016. https://tricycle.org/trikedaily/a-time-for-discernment.

Al-Khatahtbeh, Amani. 2016. *Muslim Girl: A Coming of Age*. New York: Simon & Schuster.

Allen, Samantha. 2016. "North Carolina May Never See a Celebrity Again." *The Daily Beast*, April 11, 2016. http://www.thedailybeast.com/articles/2016/04/12/north-carolina-may-never-see-a-celebrity-again.html.

Annan, Kofi. 2005. "Microfinance, Now Important Factor in Poverty Eradication, Should Be Expanded, Secretary-General Tells Geneva Symposium." Presentation at the United Nations Microfinance Symposium, Geneva, Switzerland, October 10, 2005. http://www.un.org/press/en/2005/sgsm10151.doc.htm.

Anne Frank House. n.d. "Anne Frank." Anne Frank Museum, Amsterdam. http://www.anne-frank.org/en.

Anti-Defamation League. n.d. Anti-Defamation League. http://www.adl.org.

AP (Associated Press). 2009. "Does Affirmative Action Punish Whites?" Race & Ethnicity on NBCNEWS, April 28, 2009. http://www.nbcnews.com/id/30462129/ns/us_news-life/t/does-affirmative-action-punish-whites/#.WMMn0fKBSSA.

Axelrod, Jim. 2016. "Female Players Demand Equal Pay and Treatment." *CBS This Morning*, April 1, 2016.

Baum, Gary. 2015. "Eva Longoria, Two 'Philanthropreneurs,' and the Dangers of Hollywood Charity: THR Investigates." *The Hollywood Reporter*, February 04, 2015. http://www.hollywoodreporter.com/features/eva-longoria-two-philanthropreneurs-dangers-769240.

BCU (Bethune-Cookman University). n.d. Bethune-Cookman University. Accessed 2016. http://www.cookman.edu/about_bcu/index.html.

BenShea, Noah. 1989. *Jacob the Baker*. New York: Ballantine Books.

Benson, Herbert, and Marg Stark. 1996. *Timeless Healing: The Power and Biology of Belief*. New York: Simon & Schuster.

Benson, Herbert, and William Proctor. 2010. *Relaxation Revolution: The Science and Genetics of Mind Body Healing*. New York: Simon & Schuster.

Bill & Melinda Gates Foundation. n.d. "Agricultural Development: Strategy Overview." https://www.gatesfoundation.org.

Biography. n.d. "Malala Yousafzai Biography." A&E Television Networks. https://www.biography.com/people/malala-yousafzai-21362253.

Blackmon, Douglas A. 2008. *Slavery by Another Name: The Re-Enslavement of Black People in America from the Civil War to World War II*. New York: Doubleday.

Blackstone, John, and Norah O'Donnell. 2016. "Raising Ryland: Parent's Journey as Child Makes Gender Transition." *CBS This Morning*, March 17, 2016. http://www.cbsnews.com/videos/raising-ryland-parents-open-up-on-childs-gender-transition.

B'nai Horin. 2016. "Meet Our Staff Stan Levy, Rabbi & Spiritual Leader," *Children of Freedom, Member of ALEPH, the Alliance of Jewish Renewal Communities*. http://bnaihorin.com/about-us/meet-our-staff.

Bosman, Julie, and Joseph Goldstein. 2014. "Timeline for a Body: 4 Hours in the Middle of a Ferguson Street." *The New York Times*, August 23, 2014. http://www.nytimes.com/2014/08/24/us/michael-brown-a-bodys-timeline-4-hours-on-a-ferguson-street.html.

Bouin, M. 1761. "Vous Dirai-Je, Mamam." ("Shall I tell you, Mother?"). *Les Amusements d'une Heure et Demy.* Paris, France.

Bowerman, Mary. 2015. "What You Need to Know about Indiana's 'Religious Freedom' Law." *USA Today Network*, March 30, 2015. http://www.usatoday.com/story/news/nation-now/2015/03/30/religious-freedom-law-indiana/70659788.

Brangham, William. 2016. "Despite Impending Deadline, Standing Rock Protesters Vow to Stay." *PBS NewsHour*, December 2, 2016. http://www.pbs.org/newshour/bb/despite-impending-deadline-standing-rock-protesters-vow-stay.

Bratton, Bill. 2016. "Exclusive: Ted Cruz Knows 'Absolutely Nothing' About Counterterrorism in NYC, NYPD Commissioner Bill Bratton Says." *New York Daily News*, March 26, 2016. http://www.nydailynews.com/new-york/ted-cruz-absolutely-war-terror-article-1.2578821.

Brockopp, Dorothy Young. 1983. "What Is NLP?" *American Journal of Nursing* 83, no. 7 (July 1983): 1,012–1,014.

Brown, Jeffrey. 2015. "How Can Listening Transform an Entire Community?" *TED Radio Hour*, National Public Radio, June 5, 2015. http://www.npr.org/2015/06/05/411731987/how-can-listening-change-an-entire-community.

Buber, Martin. 1970. *The Way of Man: According to the Teaching of Hasidism*. New York: Citadel Press.

Buscaglia, Leo F. 1996. *Love: What Life Is All About*. New York: Ballantine Books.

Bush, George W. 2016. "Full Transcript of Former President Bush's Speech at Memorial Service." WFAA, July 12, 2016. http://www.wfaa.com/news/local/dallas-ambush/read-full-transcript-of-former-president-bushs-speech-at-memorial-service/270770750.

Busiek, Julia. 2015. "Where They Cried." *National Parks Magazine* 89, no. 4 (Fall 2015). https://www.npca.org/articles/482-where-they-cried.

Calaprice, Alice, ed. 2000. *The Expanded Quotable Einstein*. Princeton, New Jersey: Princeton University Press.

Caniglia, John. 2014. "Cleveland Police Chase and Shooting Grand Jury: Patrolman and 5 Supervisors Are Indicted." *Plain Dealer*, May 30, 2014. http://www.cleveland.com/court-justice/index.ssf/2014/05/cleveland_police_chase_and_sho.html.

Carmon, Irin, and Shana Knizhnik. 2015. *Notorious RBG: The Life and Times of Ruth Bader Ginsburg*. New York: HarperCollins Publishers.

CASE (Council for Support and Advancement of Education). 2012. *Community College Advancement News* 1, no. 8 (February). http://www.case.org/Publications_and_Products/February2012.html.

Chamberlain, Andrew. 2015. "CEO to Worker Pay Ratios: Average CEO Earns 204 Times Median Worker Pay." Glassdoor Economic Research Blog, August 25, 2015. https://www.glassdoor.com/research/ceo-pay-ratio/.

Chassiakos, Yolanda Reid. 2016. "There You Are, Stephen Hawking." Huffington Post, November 30, 2016.

Chopra, Deepak. 1993. *Ageless Body, Timeless Mind*. New York: Random House.

———. 1996. "KCET Pledge Break." KCET-TV, March.

———. 2014. *The Future of God: A Practical Approach to Spirituality for Our Times*. New York: Harmony.

Clavin, Whitney. 2014. "NASA Technology Views Birth of the Universe." NASA/JPL California Institute of Technology, March 17, 2014. http://www.jpl.nasa.gov/news/news.php?feature=4079.

Clinton, Hillary. 2013. "Hillary Clinton Addresses Members of Bar Association." C-SPAN, August 12, 2013. http://www.c-span.org/video/?314513-2/hillary-clinton-addresses-members-bar-association.

Coates, Ta-Nehisi. 2015. *Between the World and Me*. New York: Spiegel & Grau.

Colbert, Stephen. 2015. "Who Is Me?" *The Late Show*, March 15, 2015.

———. 2016. "First Lady Michelle Obama." *The Late Show*, September 21, 2016.

Collins, Laura. 2015. "Exclusive: Jury That Cleared Darren Wilson over Ferguson Killing Was Directed to Follow Law on Deadly Force—a Statute Struck Down 38 Years Ago by US Supreme Court." *Daily Mail*, January 12, 2015. Last updated January 13, 2015. http://www.dailymail.co.uk/news/article-2906971/Jury-cleared-Darren-Wilson-Ferguson-killing-directed-follow-law-deadly-force-statute-struck-38-years-ago-Supreme-Court.html#ixzz3Or8qlcie.

CNN Wire Service. 2016. "Developing: Georgia Gov. Nathan Deal to Veto 'Religious Liberty' Bill." Fox 6 Now, March 28, 2016. http://fox6now.com/2016/03/28/developing-georgia-gov-nathan-deal-to-veto-religious-liberty-bill.

CN Traveler. 1995. "Readers' Choice Awards: The Top 100." *Condé Nast Traveler*, November 1995.

Confino, Jo. 2016. "This Buddhist Monk Is an Unsung Hero in the World's Climate Fight." Huffington Post, January 22, 2016. https://www.huffingtonpost.com/entry/thich-nhat-hanh-paris-climate-agreement_us_56a24b7ae4b076aadcc64321.

Conwill, Kinshasha Holman, ed. 2016. *Dream a World Anew: The African American Experience and the Shaping of America*. Washington, DC: Smithsonian Books.

Cook, Tim. 2015. "Tim Cook: Pro-Discrimination 'Religious Freedom' Laws Are Dangerous." *The Washington Post*, March 29, 2015. https://www.washingtonpost.com/opinions/pro-discrimination-religious-freedom-laws-are-dangerous-to-america/2015/03/29.

Cooper, Anderson. 2014. "Mindfulness Featuring Jon-Kabat-Zinn." *60 Minutes*. CBS, December 14, 2014. http://www.cbsnews.com/news/mindfulness-anderson-cooper-60-minutes/.

Cooper, Morton. 1984. *Change Your Voice, Change Your Life: A Quick, Simple Plan for Finding and Using Your Natural, Dynamic Voice*. New York: Macmillan.

Cordova, Teresa L., and Matthew D. Wilson. 2016. "Lost: The Crisis of Jobless and Out-of-School Teens and Young Adults in Chicago, Illinois, and the US." Great Cities Institute, University of Illinois at Chicago. February 1, 2016. https://greatcities.uic.edu/2016/02/01/lost-the-crisis-of-jobless-and-out-of-school-teens-and-young-adults-in-chicago-illinois-and-the-u-s/2016/.

Covey, Stephen R. 1989. *The Seven Habits of Highly Effective People*. New York: Simon & Schuster.

CRDL (Civil Rights Digital Library). n.d. "Martin Luther King Jr.'s Nobel Prize." Civil Rights Digital Library. http://crdl.usg.edu/events/mlk_nobel_prize/.

C-SPAN. 2016. "Smithsonian National Museum African American History and Culture Grand Opening." C-SPAN, Washington, DC, September 24, 2016. https://www.c-span.org/video/?415014-1/smithsonian-national-museum-african-american-history-culture-opens-dc&live.

Dahler, Don. 2016. "After Bumpy Start, Maine Town Embraces African Immigrants." *CBS Evening News*, April 28, 2016. http://www.cbsnews.com/news/after-bumpy-start-lewiston-maine-town-embraces-african-immigrants/.

Daly, Michael. 2014. "Guns Blazing: 49 Shots and The Cop Goes Free." Daily Beast, December 2, 2014. http://www.thedailybeast.com/articles/2014/12/02/the-cleveland-cops-who-fired-137-shots-and-cried-victim.html.

Damasio, Antonio. 2003. *Looking for Spinoza, Joy, Sorrow, and the Feeling Brain*. Orlando, Florida: Harcourt.

Dear, Joseph D. 1995a. "Creating Caring Relationships to Foster Academic Excellence: Recommendations for Reducing Violence in California Schools. Final Report." *ERIC*, October. http://eric.ed.gov/?id=ED391217.

———. 1995b. "Executive Summary of Final Report: Creating Caring Relationships to Foster Academic Excellence." Sacramento, CA.

Dodd, Carley H. 1991. *Dynamics of Intercultural Communication*. Dubuque, Iowa: W. C. Brown.

Dolan, Jack. 2016. "Times Investigation." *Los Angeles Times*, February 21, 2016.

Donadio, Rachel. 2013. "On Gay Priests, Pope Francis Asks, 'Who Am I to Judge?'" *The New York Times*, July 29, 2013. http://www.nytimes.com/2013/07/30/world/europe/pope-francis-gay-priests.html.

Ehrmann, Max. 1948. *Poems of Max Ehrmann*. Boston: Bruce Humphries Publishing Company.

Ekman, Paul. 1990. "Duchenne and Facial Expression of Emotion." In *The Mechanism of Human Facial Expression by G. B. Duchenne de Boulogna*, edited and translated by R. Andrew Cuthbertson. Cambridge [England]; New York; Paris: Cambridge University Press.

Ekman, Paul, and Wallace V. Friesen. 1975. *Unmasking the Face*. Englewood Cliffs, New Jersey: Prentice-Hall.

Ellison, Keith. 2016. "Ibtihaj Muhammad, Olympic Faithful." *Time*, The 100 Most Influential People, May 2/9, 2016.

Ensler, Eve. 2016. "Nadia Murad: A Witness for War's Victims." *Time*, The 100 Most Influential People, May 2/9, 2016.

Ezratty, Harry A. 2002. *500 Years in the Jewish Caribbean: The Spanish and Portuguese Jews in the West Indies*. Baltimore, Maryland: Omni Arts.

Feinstein, Dianne. 1990. "Professional Profiles." *That Balance Magazine*, Third Quarter, 1990: 4–6.

Fernandez, Manny, and Christine Hauser. 2015. "Handcuffed for Making Clock, Ahmed Mohamed, 14, Wins Time with Obama." *The New York Times*, September 16, 2015. http://www.nytimes.com/2015/09/17/us/texas-student-is-under-police-investigation-for-building-a-clock.html.

Forman, Ruth Lindeck. 1985. *Communication Enhancement: A Unique Program to Reduce Accents and Dialects*. Woodland Hills, California: Communication Enhancement Press.

———. 1988a. "Communicating More Effectively in the Diverse Environment of Southern California." Realtor Report, October 11, 1988.

———. 1988b. "Communicating with Patients Can Be Difficult—Even When You Speak the Same Language." *LACMA Physician* 118, no. 13 (August 1988): 37.

———. 1988c. "Understanding Communication Problems That May Arise in the Diverse Medical Environment." *LACMA Physician* 118, no. 13 (August 1988): 35.

———. 1989. "Communication Is the Key to Successful Patient Rapport." *LACMA Physician* 119, no. 9 (August 1989): 31 and 33.

———. 1990a. "Communicating Your Best." *Philippine Physician* 12, no. 1 (Summer 1990): 19 and 35.

———. 1990b. "I Say What?" *That Balance Magazine* 1, no. 3 (1990): 35.

———. 1991. "Preparing a Foreign-Born Client for Trial." *Los Angeles Lawyer*, March 1991.

———. 1994. "Can We Talk? Understanding the Communication Style of Other Cultures." *LACMA Physician* 124, no. 19 (November 21, 1994): 35–40.

———. 1996. *Communication Is More Than Just Talking: 10 Steps to Create Your Own Positive Communication Environment*. Woodland Hills, California: Communication Enhancement Press.

———. 1997a. "Enhancing Multicultural Communication." Presented at the Society of Human Resource Management's 7th Annual Workplace Diversity Conference. Washington, DC, October 1997.

———. 1997b. "What We Have Here Is a Failure to Communicate." *Los Angeles Business Journal* 19, no. 1 (January 1997).

———. 1998. *Communication Is Connection*. Woodland Hills, California: Communication Enhancement Press.

Foxhall, Emily. 2015. "A Literary Exploration at Los Angeles Times Festival of Books." *Los Angeles Times*, California Section, April 19, 2015. http://www.latimes.com/books/la-me-0419-latimes-bookfestival-20150419-story.html.

Francis. 2015. "Apostolic Journey of His Holiness Pope Francis to Cuba, the United States of America and Visit to the United Nations Organization Headquarters." *The Holy See*, September 19–28, 2015. http://w2.vatican.va/content/francesco/en/travels/2015/outside/documents/papa-francesco-cuba-usa-onu-2015.html.

Francis, Jimmy. 2013. "Leadership in Energy and Environmental Design (LEED) Gold Status Certification." CSUN. http://csun.edu/src/awards.

Frank, Anne. 1952. *The Diary of a Young Girl*. Translated by M. Mooyaart-Doubleday. New York: Modern Library.

Frazier, Herb. 2011. *Behind God's Back: Gullah Memories*. Charleston, South Carolina: Evening Post Books.

Free, Cathy. 2016. "How a Radio Show Saved This Ohio Woman's Life: 'I Probably Wouldn't Be Alive Today.'" *People*, October 10, 2016.

Friedman, Pavel. 1942. "The Butterfly." *International School for Holocaust Studies*, June 4, 1942. http://www.yadvashem.org/yv/en/education/lesson_plans/poems_paintings.asp.

Frost, Tony. 1997. "Corporate Responsibility and Social Change." Presented at the Global Human Resource Forum: 20th Annual Conference and Exposition of the Institute for International Human Resources. Los Angeles, CA, April 1997.

Fuentes, Carlos. 1997. "A Writer Looks at the 21st Century." Presented at the Global Human Resource Forum: 20th Annual Conference and Exposition of the Institute for International Human Resources. Los Angeles, CA, April 1997.

Gardenswartz, Lee, and Anita Rowe. 1993. *Managing Diversity: A Complete Desk Reference and Planning Guide*. Homewood, Illinois: Business One Irwin; San Diego: Pfeiffer & Co.

Garfield, Charles A. 1987. *Peak Performers: The New Heroes of American Business*. New York: Avon Books.

———. 1992. *Second to None: How Our Smartest Companies Put People First*. Homewood, Illinois: Business One Irwin.

Gates, Bill. 2013. "A Fairer Way to Evaluate Teachers." *Washington Post*, April 3, 2013. https://www.washingtonpost.com/opinions/bill-gates-a-fairer-way-to-evaluate-teachers/2013/04/03/c99fd1bc-98c2-11e2-814b-063623d80a60_story.html?utm_term=.0ad6e6880a32.

Gates, Melinda. n.d. "Makers Profile: Melinda Gates." *Makers: The Largest Video Collection of Women's Stories*. http://www.makers.com/melinda-gates.

George, Dan. n.d. "Chief Dan George." First People: Words of Wisdom Index. Accessed 2016. http://www.firstpeople.us/FP-Html-Wisdom/ChiefDanGeorge.html.

George, Dan, and Helmut Hirnschall. 2004. *The Best of Chief Dan George*. Surrey, British Columbia; Blaine, Washington: Hancock House.

Gibran, Kahlil. 1953. *The Prophet*. New York: Knopf.

Gindin, Matthew. 2017. "The Native American Genocide and Its Legacy of Oppression Today." All That Is Interesting, August 8, 2017. http://all-that-is-interesting.com/native-american-genocide.

Ginsburg, Ruth Bader, Mary Hartnett, and Wendy Williams. 2016. *My Own Words*: *Ruth Bader Ginsburg*: New York: Simon & Schuster. Kindle.

Golding, Shenequa. 2016. "Innocent Man Befriends Crooked Cop Who Sent Him to Prison." *Vibe*, April 17, 2016. www.vibe.com/2016/04/innocent-man-befriends-crooked-cop/.

Goldsmith, Marshall, and Mark Reiter. 2007. *What Got You Here Won't Get You There: How Successful People Become Even More Successful*. New York: Hyperion.

Goleman, Daniel. 1995. *Emotional Intelligence*. New York: Bantam Books.

———. 2007a. "Three Kinds of Empathy: Cognitive, Emotional, Compassionate." Daniel Goleman (blog). June 12, 2007. http://www.danielgoleman.info/three-kinds-of-empathy-cognitive-emotional-compassionate/.

———. 2007b. "Why Aren't We More Compassionate?" TED: Ideas Worth Spreading, March 2007. https://www.ted.com/talks/daniel_goleman_on_compassion.

Graham, David A. 2015. "The Mysterious Death of Freddie Gray." *The Atlantic*, April 22, 2015. http://www.theatlantic.com/politics/archive/2015/04/the-mysterious-death-of-freddie-gray/391119/.

Graham, John L., and Yoshihiro Sano. 1984. *Smart Bargaining: Doing Business with the Japanese*. Cambridge, Massachusetts: Ballinger Publishing Co.

Gray, John. 1992. *Men Are from Mars, Women Are from Venus*: *A Practical Guide for Improving Communication and Getting What You Want in Your Relationships*. New York: Harper Collins.

Green, Anne-Marie. 2016. "Epiphany Church." *CBS Morning News*, July 3, 2016.

Green, Eli R., and Luca Maurer, contribs. 2017. "Redefining Gender." In "Gender Revolution." Special issue, *National Geographic*, January 2017. http://www.nationalgeographic.com/magazine/2017/01/explore-gender-glossary-terminology/.

Gross, Natalie. 2016. "More Low-Income Hispanic Kids Are Getting Early Start to Education." *Latino Ed Beat* (blog). *EWA: Education Writers Association*, November 30, 2016. http://www.ewa.org/blog-latino-ed-beat/more-low-income-hispanic-kids-are-getting-early-start-education.

Guerrero, Diane. 2016. *In the Country We Love: My Family Divided*. With Michelle Burford. New York: Henry Holt and Company.

Guo, Jeff. 2016. "The Cunning Trick in North Carolina's Radical New Anti-LGBT Law." *The Washington Post*, April 1, 2016. https://www.washingtonpost.com/news/wonk/wp/2016/04/01/the-cunning-trick-in-north-carolinas-radical-new-anti-lgbt-law/?utm_term=.272b8613ba14.

Haley, Alex. n.d. "Quotable Quote." Goodreads. http://www.goodreads.com/quotes/25682-in-all-ofus-there-is-a-hunger-marrow-deep-to.

Hall, Bill, and Anita Greene. 1997. "NIH News Release." Bethesda, Maryland: National Institutes of Health, November 1997. https://consensus.nih.gov/1997/1997acupuncture107html.htm/.

Hall, Edward T. 1959. *The Silent Language*. Garden City, New York: Doubleday.

———. 1968. "Proxemics." *Current Anthropology* 9, no. 2/3 (1968): 83–108.

———. 1969. *The Hidden Dimension*. Garden City, New York: Doubleday.

———. 1977. *Beyond Culture*. Garden City, New York: Anchor.

Halpern, Howard M. 1976. *Cutting Loose*. New York: Simon & Schuster.

Harrison, Dianne F. 2016. "Fostering Research." *CSUN Magazine*, Fall 2016.

Harrison, Steve. 2016. "NC Gov. Pat McCrory Signs into Law Bill Restricting LGBT Protections." *Charlotte Observer*, March 23, 2016. http://www.charlotteobserver.com/news/local/article67845317.html.

Hartman, Steve. 2015. "Attitude More Important Than Altitude for High School Player." *CBS Nightly News*, September 25, 2015. http://www.cbsnews.com/news/attitude-more-important-than-altitude-for-high-school-football-player/.

Hattori, Yuichi. 1986. "Japanese Cultural Awareness Presentation." Los Angeles, CA.

Hawkins, Tim. 2015. "Dallas Church Serves First Thanksgiving to Area Refugees." *CW33 NewsFix*, November 26, 2015. http://cw33.com/2015/11/26/dallas-church-serves-first-thanksgiving-to-area-refugees/#.

Haworth, John. 2017. "Ofelia Zepeda: A Language for Praying." Language Matters. *National Museum of American Indian* 18, no. 2. Summer 2017.

Hayasaki, Erika. 2015. "Viola Davis' Personal Story Will Make You Love Her Even More." *Glamour*, March 11, 2015. http://www.glamour.com/inspired/blogs/the-conversation/2015/03/viola-davis-interview.

Heeb, Max A. 1988. "What I Learned about Patients the Hard Way." *Medical Economics*, April 4, 1988: 89–91.

Henley, Nancy. 1977. *Body Politics: Power, Sex, and Nonverbal Communication*. Englewood Cliffs, New Jersey: Prentice-Hall.

Henley, William Ernest. 1888. *A Book of Verses*. London: D. Nutt.

Herbert, Evered Webbo. n.d. "Morning Inspiration Program." *VON Radio*. Nevis, West Indies. http://vonradio.com/.

Holder, Eric. 2015. "Interview with Attorney General Eric Holder." Interview by Melissa Harris-Perry. *MSNBC*, February 8, 2015.

Holland, Jesse J. 2015. "Half of Blacks Say Police Have Treated Them Unfairly." *AP-NORC*, August 5, 2015. http://www.apnorc.org/news-media/Pages/News+Media/Half-of-blacks-say-police-have-treated-them-unfairly. aspx.

Holman, Bob. 2017. In "Ofelia Zepeda: A Language for Praying." Language Matters. *National Museum of American Indian* 18, no. 2. Summer 2017.

Holthaus, D. 1987. "Reduce Malpractice Risks through Better Communication." *Hospitals* 61, no. 22, (November 20, 1987): 50.

Howard, Adam. 2017. "John Lewis Urges More Love, Not Hate at MLK Day Breakfast." *NBC News*, January 16, 2017. http://www.nbcnews.com/news/us-news/john-lewis-urges-more-love-not-hate-mlk-day-breakfast-n707431.

Humes, Edward. 1996. *No Matter How Loud I Shout: A Year in the Life of Juvenile Court*. New York: Simon & Schuster.

———. 1997. "Rage Against the Machine." *Los Angeles Times Magazine*, November 23, 1997.

Hunger Is. n.d. Hunger Is. http://www.hungeris.org/.

Hunter, Gault, Charlayne. 2016. "As racial Hate Groups Rise, Strategies to Shut Them Down," *PBS NewsHour*, March 25, 2016. http://www.pbs.org/newshour/bb/as-racial-hate-groups-rise-strategies-to-shut-them-down/.

ICTMN (Indian Country Today Media Network). 2013. "Newark American Indian Mounds the Eighth Wonder of the World? You Decide." Indian Country Today Media Network, June 7, 2013. http://indiancountrytodaymedianetwork.com/2013/06/07/newark-american-indian-mounds-eighth-wonder-world-you-decide-149763.

Indianz. 2016. "Standing Rock Sioux Tribe Calls for Prayer Amid Additional Arrests." Indianz. com, October 11, 2016. http://www.indianz.com/News/2016/10/11/standing-rock-sioux-tribe-calls-for-pray.asp.

Invictus Games. n.d. "Invictus Competitors." Invictus Games. http://invictusgames2016.org/athletes/.

Jacobs, Louis. n.d. "Spinoza." *My Jewish Learning*. Accessed March 6, 2016. https://www.myjewishlearning.com/article/spinoza/.

Jakes, T. D. 2015. "In Good Faith." *CBS This Morning*, December 25, 2015.

Jakoubek, Robert E. 1989. *Martin Luther King Jr.* New York: Chelsea House.

Janes, Théoden. 2015. "Harriette Thompson, 92, Sets Marathon Record." *The Charlotte Observer*, May 31, 2015. http://www.charlotteobserver.com/news/local/article22753806.html.

Janik, S. W., A. R. Wellens, M. L. Goldberg, and L. F. Dell'Osso. 1978. "Eyes as the Center of Focus in the Visual Examination of Human Faces." *Perceptual and Motor Skills* 47, no. 3 (December 1978): 857–58. doi:10.2466/pms.1978.47.3.857.

Jarrett, Valerie Y., and Broderick Johnson. 2014. "My Brother's Keeper: A New White House Initiative to Empower Boys and Young Men of Color." *Home Room* (blog), February 27, 2014. https://blog.ed.gov/2014/02/my-brothers-keeper-a-new-white-house-initiative-to-empower-boys-and-young-men-of-color/.

Jennings, Tom. 1992. "International Medical Graduates: Striving for Equality." *LACMA Physician*, November 23, 1992.

John F. Kennedy Presidential Library and Museum. n.d. "John F. Kennedy and PT-109." John F. Kennedy Presidential Library and Museum Website. https://www.jfklibrary.org/JFK/JFK-in-History/John-F-Kennedy-and-PT109.aspx.

Johnson, Alex. 2016. "'Appalled': Minnesota Governor Says Philando Castile Would Be Alive If He Were White." *NBC News, US*, July 7, 2016. http://www.nbcnews.com/news/us-news/appalled-minnesota-governor-says-philando-castile-would-be-alive-if-n605496.

Johnson, Charles. 2006. "Dharma for a Dangerous Time." *Shambhala Sun*, September 2006. https://www.lionsroar.com/dharma-for-a-dangerous-time/.

Johnson, Jeh. 2016. Interview by Chuck Todd. *Meet the Press*, NBC, July 10, 2016.

Jones, Van. 2015. "Finally, a Movement to Roll Back the Prison Industry." *Sacramento Bee*, February 11, 2015. http://www.sacbee.com/opinion/op-ed/soapbox/article9757439.

Jones, Van, and Ariane Conrad. 2011. *Rebuild the Dream*. New York: Nation Books.

Jonsson, Patrik. 2016. "Why Georgia Governor Defied His Base Over Religious Liberty." *The Christian Science Monitor*, March 29, 2016. http://www.csmonitor.com/USA/Politics/2016/0329/Why-Georgia-governor-defied-his-base-over-religious-liberty.

Kakabadse, Andrew. 1997. "Global Teamwork: Building the International Organization through Human Resource Management." Los Angeles, CA.

Kang, Connie K. 1994. "When East Meets West Within the Same Person." *Los Angeles Times*, October 22, 1994.

Kelley, Blair L. Murphy. 2010. *Right to Ride: Streetcar Boycotts and African American Citizenship in the Era of Plessy v. Ferguson*. John Hope Franklin Series in African American History and Culture. Chapel Hill, North Carolina: University of North Carolina Press.

Kelley, Kevin W. 1988. *The Home Planet*. Reading, Massachusetts: Addison-Wesley.

King Encyclopedia. n.d. "Poor People's Campaign." King Institute Encyclopedia, Stanford. http://kingencyclopedia.stanford.edu/encyclopedia/encyclopedia/enc_poor_peoples_campaign/index.html.

King, Gayle. 2016a. "Celebrating the Champ, Inside the Ring, George Foreman on Life and Impact of Muhammad Ali." *CBS This Morning*, June 6, 2016.

———. 2016b. "Planned Memorial for Lynching Victims." *CBS This Morning*, July 11, 2016.

———. 2016c. "The Push for Peace, Stevenson on Race, Police and How to Move Forward." Interview with Bryan Stevenson, *CBS This Morning*, August 22, 2016.

———. 2016d. "Racist Poster." *CBS This Morning*, June 28, 2016.

King, Martin Luther, Jr. 1963. "I Have a Dream." Speech, Washington, DC, August 28, 1963. American Rhetoric. http://www.americanrhetoric.com/speeches/mlkihaveadream.htm.

———. 1967. "Letter to the Nobel Institute." January 25, 1967. Washington Mindfulness Community. https://www.mindfulnessdc.org/mlkletter.html.

————. 1968. "The Other America." Speech, Grosse Pointe Farms, Michigan, March 14, 1968. Grosse Point Historical Society. http://www.gphistorical.org/mlk/mlkspeech/.

Knowles, Ruth Daily. 1983. "Building Rapport through Neuro-Linguistic Programming." *The American Journal of Nursing* 83, no. 7 (July 1983): 1,011–1,014.

LaFrance, Marianne, and Clara Mayo. 1978. *Moving Bodies: Nonverbal Communication in Social Relationships*. Monterey, California: Brooks/Cole Pub. Co.

Lange, Arthur J., Patricia Jakubowski, and Thomas V. McGovern. 1976. *Responsible Assertive Behavior: Cognitive/Behavioral Procedures for Trainers*. Champaign, Illinois: Research Press.

Leathers, Dale G. 1992. *Successful Nonverbal Communication: Principles and Applications*. 2nd ed. New York: Macmillan.

Letterman, David. 2013. "Oprah Winfrey on David Letterman." *Late Show with David Letterman*, CBS, August 1, 2013.

Levy, Stan, ed. 1989. "Prayers for the High Holidays." Unpublished manuscript.

The Library of Congress. 2017. "Indian Removal Act." Primary Documents in American History, LOC, December 28, 2017. https://www.loc.gov/rr/program/bib/ourdocs/Indian.html.

Life After Hate. n.d. Life After Hate. https://www.lifeafterhate.org/.

Lim, Audrea. 2016. "Want to Know How to Build a Progressive Movement Under Trump? Look to Standing Rock." *The Nation*, December 20, 2016. https://www.thenation.com/article/want-to-know-how-to-build-a-progressive-movement-under-trump-look-to-standing-rock/.

Lipstadt, Deborah E. 1986. *Beyond Belief: The American Press and the Coming of the Holocaust, 1933–1945*. New York: Free Press.

Lloyd, Robert. 2015. "Ever a Fresh Voice." *Los Angeles Times*, May 17, 2015.

LoBianco, Tom. 2016. "Bernie Sanders: 'Nobody Has Ever Asked Me for My Birth Certificate.'" *CNN.com*, January 11, 2016. http://www.cnn.com/2016/01/11/politics/bernie-sanders-birth-certificate-obama-skin-color.

Loeb, Robert H. 1967. *Manners at Work: How They Help You Toward Career Success*. New York: Association Press.

Luibrand, Shannon. 2015. "How a Death in Ferguson Sparked a Movement in America." *CBS News*, August 7, 2015. http://www.cbsnews.com/news/how-the-black-lives-matter-movement-changed-america-one-year-later/.

Lustig, Myron W., and Jolene Koester. 2013. *Intercultural Competence: Interpersonal Communication Across Cultures*. 7th ed. Upper Saddle River, New Jersey: Pearson Prentice Hall.

Lynch, Loretta E. 2016. "Attorney General Loretta E. Lynch Delivers Statement on Dallas Shooting." Speech, Office of the Attorney General, Department of Justice, Washington, DC, July 8, 2016. https://www.justice.gov/opa/speech/attorney-general-loretta-e-lynch-delivers-statement-dallas-shooting.

Maddow, Rachel. 2016. *The Rachel Maddow Show*. MSNBC, March 17, 2016. http://www.msnbc.com/transcripts/rachel-maddow-show/2016-03-17.

Maher, Bill. 2016. "Earth Guardian, Xiuthezcatl Martinez." *Real Time*, HBO, June 24, 2016.

Mahesh, Maharishi. 1977. *Scientific Research on the Transcendental Meditation® Program*, volume 1. Livingston Manor, New York: Meru Press.

Malala Fund. n.d. "Malala's Story." Malala.org. https://www.malala.org/malalas-story.

Males, Mike. 2014. "Who Are Police Killing?" Center on Juvenile and Criminal Justice, August 26, 2014. http://www.cjcj.org/news/8113.

Mani, Tatanga. 1958. Quoted in "Teachings of the Great Circle." J. C. High Eagle, 2016. http://www.jchigheagle.com/1webgreatcircle.html.

Mann, Tanveer. 2016. "Woman Becomes Country's First Nursery School Teacher with Down Syndrome." *Metro*, October 24, 2016. http://metro.co.uk/2016/10/24/woman-becomes-countrys-first-nursery-school-teacher-with-downs-syndrome-6211370/.

Marech, Rona. 2015. "A First Lady." *National Parks* 89, no. 1 (Winter 2015): 58–59. https://www.questia.com/magazine/1P3-3558258331/a-first-lady.

Maresca, Rachel. 2013. "Eva Longoria Graduates, Earns Master's Degree in Chicano Studies from Cal State Northridge." *New York Daily News*, March 23, 2013.

Martin, Jorge. 2016. "All About Eva." *CSUN Magazine,* Spring 2016: 16–21.

Matthews, Chris. 2015a. Interview with James Clyburn. *Hardball with Chris Matthews*. MSNBC, April 8, 2015. http://www.msnbc.com/transcripts/hardball/2015-04-08.

———. 2015b. "Racism on Campus." *Hardball with Chris Matthews.* MSNBC, April 2, 2015. http://www.msnbc.com/transcripts/hardball/2015-04-02.

———. 2015c. "SC Officer Fired, Charged with Murder." *Hardball with Chris Matthews*. MSNBC, April 8, 2015. http://www.nbcnews.com/id/57220993/ns/msnbc-hardball_with_chris_matthews/t/hardball-chris-matthews-wednesday-april-th/#.WMSA9fKBSSA.

McFadden, Steven. 1994. *The Little Book of Native American Wisdom*. Shaftesbury, Dorset; Rockport, Massachusetts: Element.

McMaster, Gerald M., and Clifford E. Trafzer, eds. 2008. *Native Universe: Voices of Indian America.* Washington, DC: National Museum of the American Indian, Smithsonian Institution, in Association with National Geographic.

Mehrabian, Albert. 1981. *Silent Messages: Implicit Communication of Emotions and Attitudes.* 2nd ed. Belmont, California: Wadsworth Publishing Co.

Melendez, Macie. 2012. *Ellen DeGeneres: A Bibliography*. Hyperlink. San Francisco, CA.

Midgette, Anne. 2016. "'Justice at the Opera': Ginsburg Takes Center Stage at WNO and Brings Down the House." *The Washington Post*, March 10, 2016.

Migoya, David. 2016. "Super Racist: Red Cross Pool Safety Poster on Display in Colorado Targeted by Twitter Users." *Denver Post*, June 27, 2016. http://www.denverpost.com/2016/06/27/racist-red-cross-poster/.

Miller, Matt. 2016. "Here's Every Person and Business Boycotting North Carolina for Its LGBT Discrimination." *Esquire*, April 13, 2016.

Morgan, David. 2016. "'Hamilton' Star Responds to Trump: 'There's Nothing to Apologize For.'" *CBS News*, November 21, 2016. https://www.cbsnews.com/news/hamilton-brandon-victor-dixon-mike-pence-donald-trump-theres-nothing-to-apologize-for/.

Morgan, Marlo. 1994. *Mutant Message Down Under*. New York: Harper Collins.

Muir, David. 2016. "ABC News. The President and the People: A National Conversation." *ABC News Productions*. http://abcnews.go.com/US/video/president-people-race-america-40596406.

Murphy, Sean. 2015. "University of Oklahoma Unveils Racist Chant Probe Findings." *Seattle Times*, March 27, 2015.

Muslim Advocates. n.d. Muslim Advocates Promoting Freedom and Justice for All. https://www.muslimadvocates.org/.

NAACP (National Association for the Advancement of Colored People). 2015. "America's Journey for Justice." National Association for the Advancement of Colored People, August 2, 2015. http://www.naacp.org/campaigns/americas-journey-justice/.

———. n.d. "Oldest and Boldest." National Association for the Advancement of Colored People. http://www.naacp.org/oldest and boldest/.

Naifeh, Steven, Gregory White Smith, Lucy Potterfield Stec, Suzanne Flowers Arnold, and Christopher James Greame. 1994. *The Best Doctors in America, 1994–1995*. Aiken, South Carolina: Woodward/White.

National Museum of African American History and Culture. n.d. National Museum of African American History and Culture. Accessed October 24, 2016. https://nmaahc.si.edu/.

NCLR (National Council of La Raza). n.d. "Information on DACA: What You Need to Know." National Council of La Raza. http://www.nclr.org/issues/immigration/daca/.

New World Encyclopedia. 2015. "Trail of Tears." New World Encyclopedia, December 15, 2015. http://www.newworldencyclopedia.org/entry/Trail_of_Tears.

Nicolai, Meinie. 2015. "MSF and Woman's Health: Because Tomorrow Needs Her." *Alert (Medecins Sans Frontieres / Doctors Without Borders)* 16, no. 1 (Spring 2015): 3–9. http://cdn.doctorswithoutborders.org/sites/usa/files/attachments/spring_2015_alert_0.pdf.

Nicola, Linda. 2015. "Are Native Americans Treated Badly in the USA?" *Quora*, May 20, 2015. https://www.quora.com/Are-Native-Americans-treated-badly-in-the-USA.

Nilsen, Mary Ylvisaker. 1990. *A Time for Peace*. Iowa City, Iowa: Zion Pub.

Obama, Barack. 2015. "Remarks by the President at the 50th Anniversary of the Selma to Montgomery Marches." Presented at the Edmund Pettus Bridge, Selma, Alabama, March 7, 2015. https://www.whitehouse.gov/the-press-office/2015/03/07/remarks-president-50th-anniversary-selma-montgomery-marches.

———. 2016. "Remarks by the President at Memorial Service for Fallen Dallas Police Officers." Presented at the Morton H. Meyerson Symphony Center, Dallas, Texas, July 12, 2016. https://www.whitehouse.gov/the-press-office/2016/07/12/remarks-president-memorial-service-fallen-dallas-police-officers.

Obama, Barack, and Michelle Obama. 2014. "Remarks by the President and First Lady at College Opportunity Summit." Presented at the South Court Auditorium Eisenhower Executive Office Building, January 16, 2014. https://www.whitehouse.gov/the-press-office/2014/01/16/remarks-president-and-first-lady-college-opportunity-summit.

O'Donnell, Lawrence. 2016. "Last Word Campaign 2016." *Last Word with Lawrence O'Donnell*, MSNBC, May 4, 2016. http://www.msnbc.com/transcripts/the-last-word/2016-04-5.

———. *Last Word with Lawrence O'Donnell*, November 10, 2016. http://www.msnbc.com/transcripts/the-last-word/2016-11-10.

O'Donnell, Norah. 2015. "Norah O'Donnell's Report on Upcoming Interview with Ambassador Caroline Kennedy on 60 Minutes." *CBS This Morning*, March 9, 2015.

———. 2016. "Beyoncé Gets Political with Super Bowl Halftime Performance." *CBS This Morning*, February 8, 2016.

O'Donnell, Norah, Gayle King, and Charlie Rose. 2015. "Toya Graham." *CBS This Morning*, April 28, 2015.

Overbye, Dennis. 2016. "Gravitational Waves Detected, Confirming Einstein's Theory." *New York Times*, February 11, 2016.

OWN (The Oprah Winfrey Network). n.d. "Zainab Salbi on How to Give Fully Without Sacrificing Yourself." Oprah.com. http://www.oprah.com/steepyoursoul/zainab-salbi-on-how-to-give-fully-without-sacrificing-yourself#ixzz5LT64ibKh.

Pace, Julie. 2014. "Obama: Donald Sterling Comments 'Incredibly Offensive.'" Huffington Post, April 27, 2014. http://www.usatoday.com/story/sports/nba/2014/04/27/obama-donald-sterling/8264191/.

Parvini, Sarah. 2015. "Giving Thanks, with Mixed Feelings." *The Los Angeles Times*, November 26, 2015.

PBS (Public Broadcasting System). n.d. "Indian Removal 1814–1858." Africans in America, Judgment Day, PBS SOCAL. https://www.pbs.org/wgbh/aia/part4/4p2959.html.

Pearce, Matt. 2015. "John Legend's Oscar Remarks about Slavery, Incarceration Are True." *Los Angeles Times*, February 23, 2015. http://www.latimes.com/nation/la-na-john-legend-in-carceration-20150223-story.html.

Peterson, Jonathan. 1997. "Shades of Gray at 'Little Rock 9' Reunion." *Los Angeles Times*, September 25, 1997. http://articles.latimes.com/1997/sep/25/news/mn-35938.

Plate, Tom. 1996. "Education, the Wings of the Dream." *Los Angeles Times*, March 19, 1996. http://articles.latimes.com/1996-03-19/local/me-48550_1_public-education.

Pliskin, Zelig. 1977. *Love Your Neighbor*. Brooklyn, New York: Aish Ha Torah.

Powell, Colin, Loretta Lynch, and Simone Manuel. 2016. Interview by Gayle King. *CBS This Morning*, September 12, 2016.

President's Task Force on 21st Century Policing. 2015. "Final Report of the President's Task Force on 21st Century Policing." Washington, DC: Office of Community Oriented Policing Services, 2015. https://www.phillypolice.com/assets/forms-reports/TaskForce_FinalReport.pdf.

Providence. n.d. "Providence Mount St. Vincent." Providence Health & Services Washington. https://washington.providence.org/locations-directory/m/mount-st-vincent.

Reagan, Ronald. 1989. https://www.reaganlibrary.gov/january-1989.

Redfield, James. 1993. *The Celestine Prophecy*. New York: Warner Books.

Reilly, Mollie. 2016. "Paul LePage Makes Racist Claim About Drug Dealers Named D-Money Getting White Girls Pregnant." Huffington Post, January 7, 2016. http://www.huffington-post.com/entry/paul-lepage-heroin_us_568ef013e4b0cad15e643549.

Restak, Richard M. 1988. *The Mind*. Toronto; New York: Bantam Books.

Ricard, Matthieu, Antoine Lutz, and Richard J. Davidson. 2014. "Mind of the Meditator." *Scientific American* 311, no. 5 (November 2014): 38–45.

Robbins, Anthony. 1991. *Awaken the Giant Within*. New York: Summit Books.

Robertson, William O. 1985. *Medical Malpractice: A Preventive Approach*. Seattle: University of Washington Press.

Robles, Frances, and Julie Bosman. 2014. "Autopsy Shows Michael Brown Was Struck at Least 6 Times." *The New York Times*, August 17, 2014. http://www.nytimes.com/2014/08/18/us/michael-brown-autopsy-shows-he-was-shot-at-least-6-times.html.

Rodriguez, Jacquelynne C. 2016. "Our Clients Are Diverse: Why Aren't We?" *The ASHA Leader* 21, no.5 (May 2016): 40.

Rose, Charlie, Gayle King, and Norah O'Donnell. 2016a. "Hamilton's Declaration." *CBS This Morning*, November 21, 2016.

———. 2016b. "Tribute to the Smithsonian National Museum of African American History & Culture," *CBS This Morning*, September 12, 2016.

Rothschild, Henry. 1985. "The Role of Race in Medicine." *Internal Medicine* 6, no. 11 (November 1985): 111–23.

Ruhle, Stephanie. 2015. "No Ceiling Report: Women Not There Yet, We Have a Long Way to Go." Bloomberg Television, March 2015. http://www.bloomberg.com/news/videos.

Rutherford, Janice. 2015. "San Bernardino County Board of Supervisors Press Conference." San Bernardino County Website. December 15, 2015. http://www.sbcounty.gov/Rutherford/.

Sabia, Carmine. 2015. "Baltimore Mayor: 'If Three Black Women at Three Levels Can't Get Justice,' Where Will We Get It?" *Bizpac Review*, May 1, 2015. http://www.bizpacreview.com/2015/05/01/baltimore-mayor-if-three-black-women-at-three-levels-cant-get-justice-where-will-we-get-it-200445.

Sandberg, Sheryl. 2013. *Lean In: Women, Work, and the Will to Lead*. New York: Alfred A. Knopf.

———. 2014. *Lean In: For Graduates*. New York: Alfred A. Knopf.

Satir, Virginia. 2003. "Making Contact." In Teaching with Fire: Poetry That Sustains the Courage to Teach, edited by S. Intrator and M. Scribner. San Francisco: Jossey-Bass.

Sawiki, Emily. 2016. "Backbone Trail to Form One Continuous 67-Mile Stretch through Santa Monica Mountains." *The Malibu Times*, June 4, 2016.

Scarborough, Joe. 2018. *Morning Joe*. MSNBC, August 10, 2018.

Schieffer, Bob. 2015a. "Don't Overlook the Good Cops." *Face the Nation*. CBS, April 19, 2015. http://www.cbsnews.com/videos/bob-schieffer-dont-overlook-the-good-cops/.

———. 2015b. Interview with Congressman Elijah Cummings. *Face the Nation*. CBS, April 26, 2015. http://www.cbsnews.com/videos/open-this-is-face-the-nation-April-26/.

Schmidt, Michael S., and Matt Apuzzo. 2015. "South Carolina Officer Is Charged with Murder of Walter Scott." *The New York Times*, April 7, 2015. http://www.nytimes.com/2015/04/08/us/south-carolina-officer-is-charged-with-murder-in-black-mans-death.html.

Schroeder, Lauryn. 2015. "Indiana Faces Long Road to Restore Image after Religious Law." *AP News Archive*, April 5, 2015. http://www.apnewsarchive.com/2015/Indiana-public-relations-campaigns-may-not-quickly-restore-battered-image-after-religious-law/id-e46411e553164fdc8b66e189ef5 01b10.

Science Genius. n.d. Science Genius. https://genius.com/artists/science-genius.

Seelye, Katharine Q. 2016. "Gov. Paul LePage of Maine Says Racial Comment Was a 'Slip-Up.'" *The New York Times First Draft*, January 8, 2016. http://www.nytimes.com/politics/first-draft/2016/01/08/gov-paul-lepage-of-maine-denies-making-racist-remarks/.

Senghor, Shaka. 2014. *Why Your Worst Deeds Don't Define You*. TED Talks, June 23, 2014. https://www.ted.com/talks/shaka_senghor_why_your_worst_deeds_don_t_define_you?language=en.

Seranella, Barbara. 1997. *No Human Involved*. New York: St. Martin's Press.

Sheehy, Kelsey. 2013. "Graduation Rates Dropping Among Native American Students." *US News and World Report*, June 6, 2013. https://www.usnews.com/education/high-schools/articles/2013/06/06/graduation-rates-dropping-among-native-american-students.

Shipley, David. 1996. "Interview with Charlayne Hunter-Gault." *The NewsHour with Jim Lehrer*. KCET-TV, January 3, 1996.

Shyong, Frank, Hailey Branson-Potts, and Matt Stevens. 2015. "Where the Water Flows Like Money; In Well-to-Do Areas, Per-Capita Use Far Exceeds that of the Less Affluent." *Los Angeles Times*, April 5, 2015.

Siegel, Bernie S. 1986. *Love, Medicine, & Miracles: Lessons Learned about Self-Healing from a Surgeon's Experience with Exceptional Patients*. New York: Harper & Row.

———. 1989. *Peace, Love & Healing: Bodymind Communication and the Path to Self-Healing: An Exploration*. New York: Harper & Row.

Siegman, Aron Wolfe, and Stanley Feldstein. 1987. *Nonverbal Behavior and Communication*. Hillsdale, New Jersey: L. Erlbaum Associates.

Simons, Rae. 2016. *Ellen DeGeneres (LGBT Icons)*. New York: Village Earth Press.

SINA. 2005. "Annan Calls for Expansion of Microfinance." *SINA English*, October 10, 2005. http://english.sina.com/business/1/2005/1010/48761.html.

Singer, Michael A. 2007. *The Untethered Soul: The Journey Beyond Yourself*. Oakland, California: New Harbinger Publications.

Sit, Ryan. 2016. "Bratton Rips Cruz Again over Proposal to Monitor Muslims: 'You Cannot Police a Community Without Properly Working with Them.'" *New York Daily News*, March 28, 2016. http://www.nydailynews.com/new-york/bratton-rips-cruz-proposal-monitor-muslims-article-1.2579923.

Smiley, Tavis. 2016. *The Covenant with Black America: Ten Years Later*. Carlsbad, California: Smiley Books.

Smiley, Tavis, and David Ritz. 2015. *My Journey with Maya*. New York: Little, Brown and Company.

Smith, David E., Frank N. Willis, and Joseph A. Gier. 1980. "Success and Interpersonal Touch in a Competitive Setting." *Journal of Nonverbal Behavior* 5, no. 1 (September 1980): 26–34. doi:10.1007/BF00987052.

Snow, Kate. 2016. "Breaking News, Scott Family Lawyers Speak Out on Charlotte Shooting, Unrest." *MSNBC, A Place for Politics 2016*, September 22, 2016.

Sommer, Paul A. 1987. "Minimizing Malpractice Risk: A Patient Approach." *Group Practice Journal* 36, no. 5 (October 1987): 86–90.

Southwest Reservation Aid. n.d. Native Partnership. http://www.nativepartnership.org/site/PageServer?pagename=cin_index.

Spinoza, Baruch, Samuel Shirley, and Seymour Feldman. 1992. *The Ethics, Treatise on the Emendation of the Intellect, Selected Letters*. Indianapolis: Hackett Pub. Co.

Spinoza, Benedictus De. 2015. *Ethics*. Kindle. Munich: BookRix.

SPLC. 2015. "SPLC Reaches Settlement with Mississippi School District to Stop Anti-LGBT Bullying." *Southern Poverty Law Center*, February 24, 2015. https://www.splcenter.org/news/2015/02/25/splc-reaches-settlement-mississippi-school-district-stop-anti-lgbt-bullying.

Stand with Standing Rock. 2016. "Standing Rock Sioux Tribe Responds to Today's Law Enforcement Escalation." Press Release. Stand with Standing Rock, October 27, 2016. http://standwithstandingrock.net/press-release-standing-rock-sioux-tribe-responds-todays-law-enforcement-escalation/.

Stern, David Allen. 1982. *Speaking Without an Accent: Training in Non-Regional American Dialect*. Los Angeles: Dialect Accent Specialists.

————. 1992. *The Sound & Style of American English a Course in Accent Reduction for All Speakers of English as a Second Language*. Los Angeles: Dialect Accent Specialists.

————. 2003. *Acting with an Accent*. Lyndonville, Vermont: Dialect Accent Specialists.

Stevenson, Bryan. 2014. *Just Mercy: A Story of Justice and Redemption*. New York: Spiegel & Grau.

Stewart, Jon. 2014. "April 29, 2014: William D. Cohan." *Daily Show with Jon Stewart*. Comedy Central, April 29, 2014. http://www.cc.com/episodes/rb8qda/the-daily-show-with-jon-stewart-April-29-2014-william-d-cohan-season-19-ep-1996.

Strand, Ginger. 2016. "Carbon Cache." *Nature Conservancy* (October–November 2016): 40–48. http://www.nature.org/magazine/archives/carbon-cache.xml.

Symonds, Richard W. 2007. Words as Weapons (blog), July 1, 2007. http://wordsasweapons.blogspot.com/2007_07_01_archive.html?m=0.

Tani, Maxwell. 2015. "Democrats and Republicans in Congress Actually Found Something to Agree On." Huffington Post, March 30, 2015. http://www.huffingtonpost.com/2015/03/30/bipartisan-summit-criminal-justice_n_6971242.html.

Tannen, Deborah. 1986. *That's Not What I Meant!: How Conversational Style Makes or Breaks Your Relations with Others*. New York: Ballantine.

Tarfon, Rabbi. 2013. "Kindness quote by Rabbi Tarfon." June 2013. https://symphonylove.wordpress.com/2013/06/06/kindness-quote-by-rabbi-tarfon/.

Tavani, Andrew. 2015. "Toya Graham, Mom Seen on Video Dragging Teenage Son Out of Baltimore Riots, Speaks Out." *New York Times*, April 29, 2015. http://nytlive.nytimes.com/womenintheworld/2015/04/29/toya-graham-mom-seen-on-video-dragging-teenage-son-out-of-baltimore-riots-speaks-out/.

Taylor, Jane. 1806. "The Star." Darton and Harvey, London, England. All Poetry. https://allpoetry.com/classics.

Taylor, Jessica. 2016. "'Hamilton' To Pence: 'We Are the Diverse America Who Are Alarmed.'" NPR, November 19, 2016. http://www.npr.org/2016/11/19/502687591/hamilton-to-pence-we-are-the-diverse-america-who-are-alarmed.

Taylor, O. L. 1989. "Clinical Practice as a Social Occasion." In *Communication Disorders in Multicultural Populations*, edited by L. Cole and V. R. Deal. Rockville, Maryland: American Speech/Language and Hearing Association.

Thich Nhat Hanh. 1987. *Being Peace*. Edited by Arnold Kotler. Berkeley, California: Parallax Press.

————. 1990. *The Heart of the Buddha's Teaching:* Transforming Suffering into Peace, Joy, and Liberation. Berkeley, California: Parallax Press.

————. 1991. *Peace Is Every Step: The Path of Mindfulness in Everyday Life*. New York: Bantam Books.

————. 2001. *Thich Nhat Hanh: Essential Writings*. Edited by Robert Ellsberg. Maryknoll, New York: Orbis Books.

————. 2005. *Zen Keys*. Introduction by Philip Kapleau. New York: Three Leaves Press.

————. 2009. *Happiness: Essential Mindfulness Practices*. Berkeley, California: Parallax Press.

————. 2010. *Together We Are One: Honoring Our Diversity, Celebrating Our Connection*. Berkeley, California: Parallax Press.

Thompson, Krissah. 2016. "Painful but Crucial: Why You'll See Emmett Till's Casket at the African American Museum." *Washington Post*, August 18, 2016. https://www.washingtonpost.com/

lifestyle/style/painful-but-crucial-why-youll-see-emmett-tills-casket-at-the-african-ameri-can-museum/2016/08/18/66d1dc2e-484b-11e6-acbc-4d4870a079da_story.html.

Thompson, Krissah, and Zachary A. Goldfarb. 2014. "Michelle Obama Uses Life Story to Promote Education Initiative." *The Washington Post*, January 17, 2014. https://www.washingtonpost.com/politics/michelle-obama-uses-life-story-to-promote-education-initia-tive/2014/01/17/bb4f27f6-7eb4-11e3-93c1-0e888170b723_story.html.

Todd, Chuck. 2016. *Meet the Press*, MSNBC, July 10, 2016.

Toobin, Jeffrey. 2016. "Profiles: The Legacy of Lynching, on Death Row." *The New Yorker*, August 22, 2016. http://www.newyorker.com/magazine/2016/08/22/bryan-stevenson-and-the-legacy-of-lynching.

USCB (United States Census Bureau). 2012. "2010 Census Shows Nearly Half of American Indians and Alaska Native Report Multiple Races." United States Census Bureau. Census.gov Newsroom Archive, January 25, 2012. https://www.census.gov/newsroom/releases/archives/2010_census/cb12-cn06.html.

USDJ (United States Department of Justice). 2016. "Justice Department Files Complaint against the State of North Carolina to Stop Discrimination against Transgender Individuals." United States Department of Justice. Justice News, May 9, 2016. https://www.justice.gov/opa/pr/justice-department-files-complaint-against-state-north-carolina-stop-discrimina-tion-against.

USDL (United States Department of Labor). n.d. Bureau of Labor Statistics, United States Department of Labor. Accessed December 11, 2016. https://www.bls.gov/.

USDT (United States Department of the Treasury). n.d. Modern Money, United States Department of the Treasury. https://modernmoney.treasury.gov/.

Ushistory.org. n.d. "Japanese-American Internment." US History Online Textbook. http://www.ushistory.org/us/51e.asp.

Vance, J. D. 2016. *Hillbilly Elegy: A Memoir of Family and Culture in Crisis*. New York: Harper.

Vick, Karl, and Olivia B. Waxman. 2014. "Life After War: Veterans of Iraq and Afghanistan Are Battling Lasting Wounds—Both Visible and Invisible." *Time* 184, no. 19 (November 17, 2014): 46–55.

Walsh, Michael. 2016. "North Carolina Attorney General Won't Defend Transgender Law; It's a 'National Embarrassment.'" Yahoo! Politics, March 29, 2016. https://www.yahoo.com/news/ny-gov-cuomo-bans-travel-to-north-carolina-in-184327168.html.

Warner Bros. 2011. *Hubble 3D*. Produced and Directed by Toni Myers; Narrated by Leonardo DiCaprio. Burbank, California: Warner Bros. Pictures and Imax Film Entertainment, in cooperation with the National Aeronautics and Space Administration; Distributed by Warner Home Video.

WebMD. 2017. "Children's Health: Lead Poisoning-Topic Overview." WebMD, reviewed January 11, 2017. http://www.webmd.com/children/tc/lead-poisoning-topic-overview.

Wepman, Dennis. 1987. *Helen Keller*. American Women of Achievement. New York: Chelsea House.

Werner, Anna. 2016. "Church Unity, Two Religions Share Same House of Worship." *CBS News*, July 3, 2016.

West, Cornel. 1994. *Race Matters*. New York: Vintage Books.

———. 2015. "Why Malcolm X Still Speaks Truth to Power." *Smithsonian* 46, no. February 10, 2015: 54–55.

Wikipedia Contributors. 2013. "Salazar v. Ramah Navajo Chapter." Wikipedia, January 29, 2013. https://en.wikipedia.org/wiki/Salazar_v._Ramah_Navajo_Chapter.

———. 2014a. "Death of Eric Garner." Wikipedia. Last modified July 17, 2014. https://en.wikipedia.org/w/index.php?title=Death_of_Eric_Garner&oldid=850018235.

———. 2014b. "Invictus Games." Wikipedia, March 2014. https://en.wikipedia.org/wiki/Invictus_Games.

———. 2015. "Zainab Salbi." Wikipedia. Last modified December 6, 2015. https://en.wikipedia.org/w/index.php?title=Zainab_Salbi&oldid=847243842.

———. 2016. "Gender Neutrality." Wikipedia. Last modified December 2016. https://en.wikipedia.org/w/index.php?title=Gender_neutrality&oldid=850265035.

———. 2017. "Epaminondas Stassinopoulos." Wikipedia. Last modified December 4, 2017. https://en.wikipedia.org/wiki/Epaminondas_Stassinopoulos.

Williams, Timothy, and Mitch Smith. 2015. "Cleveland Officer Will Not Face Charges in Tamir Rice Shooting Death." *New York Times*, December 28, 2015. https://www.nytimes.com/2015/12/29/us/tamir-rice-police-shootiing-cleveland.html.

Winfrey, Oprah. 2016. *First Lady, Michelle Obama, Says Farewell to the White House*. CBS, December 19, 2016.

Wu, Preston Quo. 2016. "Solutions: General Societal Rules and Formalities." *Personal Communication*, June 24, 2016.

Yudkin, Marcia. 1994. "Communication Briefings." *Communication Briefings Newsletter*, October 1994. http://www.communicationbriefings.com/newsletter.

Zaimov, Stoyan. 2016. "Episcopal Church's Largest Congregation Is 300 Muslims Who Meet for Friday Prayers." *Christian Post*, July 21, 2016. http://www.christianpost.com/news/episcopal-churchs-largest-congregation-is-300-muslims-who-meet-for-friday-prayers-165924/.

Zakaria, Fareed. 2016a. "Rice on Lack of Diversity in US National Security Team." *GPS (Global Positioning System)*. CNN, May 15, 2016.

———. 2016b. "Understanding Trump's Working-Class Support." *GPS (Global Positioning System)*. CNN, August 14, 2016. http://www.cnn.com/videos/tv/2016/08/12/exp-gps-0814-vance-clip-poverty.cnn.

Zamata, Sasheer. 2016. "Yes, I'm Privileged." *STAND* (Summer 2016): 36.

Zeboski, Walt. 2009. "Does Affirmative Action Punish Whites?" *MSNBC*, April 28, 2009. http://www.nbcnews.com/id/30462129/ns/us_news-life/t/does-affirmative-action-punish-whites/.

Zonkel, Phillip. 2016. "CSU Chancellor Timothy White Evokes Moon Race in Charting the Future." *Long Beach Press-Telegram*, January 26, 2016. http://www.presstelegram.com/social-affairs/20160126/csu-chancellor-timothy-white-evokes-moon-race-in-charting-the-future.

CPSIA information can be obtained
at www.ICGtesting.com
Printed in the USA
LVHW050228170223
739429LV00001B/1

9 781646 288618